||||| |||| ||| ||||| ||||| ||||| |||||| || |||
☑ **W9-BUJ-613**

IMPORTANT

HERE IS YOUR REGISTRATION CODE TO ACCESS MCGRAW-HILL PREMIUM CONTENT AND MCGRAW-HILL ONLINE RESOURCES

For key premium online resources you need THIS CODE to gain access. Once the code is entered, you will be able to use the web resources for the length of your course.

Access is provided only if you have purchased a new book.

If the registration code is missing from this book, the registration screen on our website, and within your WebCT or Blackboard course will tell you how to obtain your new code. Your registration code can be used only once to establish access. It is not transferable.

To gain access to these online resources

1. USE your web browser to go to: **www.mhhe.com/coakley9e**
2. CLICK on "First Time User"
3. ENTER the Registration Code printed on the tear-off bookmark on the right
4. After you have entered your registration code, click on "Register"
5. FOLLOW the instructions to setup your personal UserID and Password
6. WRITE your UserID and Password down for future reference. Keep it in a safe place.

If your course is using WebCT or Blackboard, you'll be able to use this code to access the McGraw-Hill content within your instructor's online course.

To gain access to the McGraw-Hill content in your instructor's WebCT or Blackboard course simply log into the course with the user ID and Password provided by your instructor. Enter the registration code exactly as it appears to the right when prompted by the system. You will only need to use this code the first time you click on McGraw-Hill content.

These instructions are specifically for student access. Instructors are not required to register via the above instructions.

The McGraw-Hill Companies

Higher Education

Thank you, and welcome to your McGraw-Hill Online Resources.

ISBN-13: 978-0-07-304730-0
ISBN-10: 0-07-304730-9 t/a
Coakley: Sports in Society:
Issues and Controversies, 9/e

REGISTRATION CODE

FYAU-WHDY-4GJE-98YB-YEYV

REGISTRATION CODE

The McGraw-Hill Companies

McGraw Hill **Higher Education**

SPORTS IN SOCIETY

SPORTS IN SOCIETY

Issues & Controversies

NINTH EDITION

Jay Coakley, Ph.D.
University of Colorado
Colorado Springs

Boston   Burr Ridge, IL   Dubuque, IA   Madison, WI   New York   San Francisco   St. Louis
Bangkok   Bogotá   Caracas   Kuala Lumpur   Lisbon   London   Madrid   Mexico City
Milan   Montreal   New Delhi   Santiago   Seoul   Singapore   Sydney   Taipei   Toronto

Higher Education

SPORTS IN SOCIETY: ISSUES AND CONTROVERSIES, NINTH EDITION

Published by McGraw-Hill, a business unit of The McGraw-Hill Companies, Inc., 1221 Avenue of the Americas, New York, NY 10020. Copyright © 2007, 2004 , 2001, 1998, 1994, 1990, 1986, 1982, 1978 by The McGraw-Hill Companies, Inc. All rights reserved. No part of this publication may be reproduced or distributed in any form or by any means, or stored in a database or retrieval system, without the prior written consent of The McGraw-Hill Companies, Inc., including, but not limited to, in any network or other electronic storage or transmission, or broadcast for distance learning.

Some ancillaries, including electronic and print components, may not be available to customers outside the United States.

This book is printed on acid-free paper.

1 2 3 4 5 6 7 8 9 0 DOC/DOC 0 9 8 7 6

ISBN-13: 978-0-07-304727-0
ISBN-10: 0-07-304727-9

Editor-in-chief: *Emily Barrosse*
Publisher: *William Glass*
Senior sponsoring editor: *Christopher Johnson*
Developmental editor: *Lynda Huenenfeld*
Senior marketing manager: *Pamela S. Cooper*
Project manager: *Aaron Downey, Matrix Productions Inc.*
Senior production supervisor: *Tandra Jorgensen*
Developmental editor for technology: *Julia A. Ersery*
Media producer: *Michele Borrelli*
Media supplement producer: *Kate Boylan*
Interior design: *Adriane Bosworth*
Cover design: *Preston Thomas*
Cover art: *Ernie Barnes*
Art editor: *Aaron Downey, Matrix Productions Inc.*

This text was set in 10/12 Janson by Interactive Composition Corporation, India, and printed on 45# New Era Matte by R.R. Donnelley, Crawfordsville, Indiana.

Library of Congress Cataloging-in-Publication Data

Coakley, Jay J.
  Sports in society : issues and controversies / Jay Coakley.
    p. cm.
  Includes index.
  ISBN 0-07-304727-9 (alk. paper)
  1. Sports—Social aspects. 2. Sports—Psychological aspects. I. Title.

GV706.5.C63 2007
306.4'83—dc21   2005057980

This text was based on the most up-to-date research and suggestions made by individuals knowledgeable in the field of athletic training. The authors and publisher disclaim any responsibility for any adverse effects or consequences from the misapplication or injudicious use of information contained within this text. It is also accepted as judicious that the coach and/or athletic trainer performing his or her duties is, at all times, working under the guidance of a licensed physician.

www.mhhe.com

To Maddie, Ally, and Cassidy
—each with her own way of doing sports

The cover image, *Rising Expectations*, is a painting by Ernie Barnes, an internationally known artist who played professional football with the Denver Broncos and San Diego Chargers from 1960 to 1965. After his appointment as the Official Artist for the 1984 Los Angeles Olympic Games, Mr. Barnes's talent was recognized around the world. His commissions include a painting that hangs permanently in the Carolina Panthers football stadium and a painting to commemorate the 50th Anniversary of the National Basketball Association that is displayed at the Naismith Memorial Basketball Hall of Fame. His images frequently capture people expressing spirit and determination in the face of challenges and scarce resources.

Mr. Barnes has also used *Rising Expectations* as one of six images in a motivational sports poster series; it represents the Teamwork poster. Images from the poster series have appeared as covers on the seventh and eighth editions of *Sports in Society*. The image, *Night Games*, which appears on the sixth edition, is also a painting by Ernie Barnes. The posters and many paintings by Ernie Barnes may be seen (and purchased) at www.erniebarnesart.com. Mr. Barnes's work is represented by The Company of Art, 8613 Sherwood, West Hollywood, CA 90069 (phone 800-858-2941).

My thanks to Ernie Barnes for his willingness to share his images and ideas for this and past editions of *Sports in Society*. For me, his images capture the kinesthetic soul of in sports.

CONTENTS

PREFACE

PURPOSE OF THE TEXT

The ninth edition of *Sports in Society: Issues and Controversies* has a threefold purpose. First, it is designed to show students the ways that sociology can be used to study sports in society. Second, it is written to evoke critical questions from students as they think about sports in their lives and the world around them. Third, it is organized to facilitate the use of research, theory, and everyday experiences to learn about sports in society.

The chapters, organized around controversial and curiosity-arousing issues, present current research and theory in the sociology of sport so that readers may discuss and analyze those issues. Although popular sources are used in addition to sociological materials, the content of the book is grounded in sociological research and theoretical approaches. Therefore, the emphasis is clearly on sports and sport-related actions as they influence and are influenced by the social and cultural contexts in which they are created and played.

FOR WHOM IS IT WRITTEN?

Sports in Society is written for those taking their first look at the relationships between sports, culture, and society. Each chapter is written to be accessible to college students who have not taken courses in sociology or sport science. Discussions of issues do not presume in-depth experiences in sports or a detailed knowledge of sport jargon and statistics. The primary goal is to assist students identify and explore critical issues related to sports in their lives, families, schools, communities, societies, and the world as a whole. To achieve this goal, I use concepts, theories, and research as tools that enable us to visualize sports as activities that are inseparable from everyday life at the same time that they are more than mere reflections of the world in which we live.

The emphasis on issues and controversies makes the content of all chapters useful for people who are concerned with sport-related policies and program administration. My purpose is to assist those who wish to make sports more democratic and sport participation more accessible, especially to those who continue to be excluded or marginalized.

CHANGES IN THE NINTH EDITION

This edition was rewritten from start to finish so that it is easier to read and understand. Information, including the content of tables and figures, was updated. New substantive materials and examples have been added to maximize the timeliness of the text. Integrating this edition with the website (www.mhhe.com/coakley9e) enabled me to shorten all but one of the chapters. In the process, the Online Learning Center contains additional substantive materials related to each chapter topic.

Each chapter has been rewritten to be more concise and take into account new research and theoretical developments in the field. There are more than 400 *new* references cited in this edition, about 1200 references in all. Most of the new references identify materials published since the eighth edition went to press.

The most important addition to this edition is a series of sixteen Breaking Barriers boxes—one in each chapter. These boxes present issues and controversies associated with sports for people with disabilities. Their purpose is to provide the vocabulary and examples needed to think critically about the exclusion of people with disabilities from sports and to creatively consider the ways that inclusion might occur now and in the future. Being able-bodied is a temporary condition for most of us; if we continue to play sports through our lives, nearly all of us will eventually participate with some form of (dis)ability.

A major challenge faced when rewriting this edition was to identify topics and references that I would *not* include. The sociology of sport has expanded so much over the past decade that *Sports in Society* is now an introduction to the field more than an overview. To access materials from previous editions, including chapters on competition and on coaching (fifth edition), and timely substantive sections from the sixth through eighth editions, see www.mhhe.com/coakley9e and click on the link for Additional Readings.

Revision Themes and New Materials

This edition continues to emphasize the cultural, interactional, and structural dimensions of sports and sport experiences. Chapter 1 is reorganized so that readers are introduced to definitions of sports as they begin thinking about the ways that sports are connected with their lives and the social worlds in which they live. The chapter on theories (chapter 2) is shortened and revised to explain more clearly the usefulness of theory and differences between the theories widely used by those of us who study sports in society. The chapter on history (chapter 3) covers additional material on recent history to illustrate more clearly the ways that changes in sports are connected with changes in culture and society.

The chapters on socialization and youth sports (chapters 4 and 5) are revised to include discussions of health and obesity in connection with sports in society and to explain why parents have become so concerned about the sport involvement of their children. Chapter 6, on deviance in sports, includes a new section that compares an absolutist approach with a constructionist approach to deviance. This section emphasizes that theories influence popular definitions of deviance and the policies that people use to control deviance in sports. The chapter also contains an updated analysis of performance-enhancing substances and technologies in sports. The chapter on violence (chapter 7) has new material on player–fan violence, celebratory violence, and sexual misconduct by coaches.

The chapter on gender and gender relations (chapter 8) has an updated discussion of gender equity, the status and enforcement of Title IX, and gender relations in alternative and informal sports. The chapter now highlights the ways that gender ideology influences the culture and organization of sports. Similarly, the chapter on race and ethnicity (chapter 9) is revised to clarify the concepts of race and racial ideology. There is new material on genetic issues and athletic performance and an updated analysis of the use of Native American mascots, names, and logos in sports. Additionally, there is expanded coverage of sports and sport participation in North America among people with Latino and Asian backgrounds.

The chapter on social class and class relations (chapter 10) contains updated material on the ways that social class and life chances have become increasingly apparent and influential in sports and sport participation at all levels of competition and involvement. The chapter on economics (chapter 11) contains an expanded discussion of corporate influence in sports and updated materials on stadium funding. All data on salaries in professional sports are updated, and labor relations are discussed in connection with the full-season (2004–2005) lockout in the National Hockey League.

The media chapter (chapter 12) includes new material on selling and buying media rights as this process is related to the interdependence of commercial sports and privately owned media. There is updated coverage of the Internet and sport video games and the ways that ideologies influence media coverage of sports. The chapter on government, global processes, and politics in sports (chapter 13) is revised to highlight connections between sports, capitalist expansion, and global relations.

The chapter on education and sports (chapter 14) summarizes new issues and recent research on interscholastic and intercollegiate sports. The research is used to discuss current problems at both the high school and college levels. Additionally, new NCAA rules about academic progress rates (APRs) are explained. There is new material on world religions in the chapter on religions and sports (chapter 15), and the chapter on the future (chapter 16) has been shortened and revised to emphasize the role of human agency in creating the future of sports.

Suggested Readings and New Website Resources

Each chapter is followed by updated references to websites that are useful sources of information about the topics raised in the chapters. The Suggested Readings have been expanded for each chapter and included in the Online Learning Center (OLC); a link to the OLC ensures easy access to the annotated readings.

New Photographs

There are 135 photos and over 40 cartoons in this edition. About 60 of the photos are new. These images combined with diagrams, figures, and tables are used to illustrate important substantive points, visually enhance the text, and make reading more interesting.

Online Learning Center

The website www.mhhe.com/coakley9e is an important feature associated with the ninth edition of *Sports in Society*. The site contains general information about this edition, along with links to supplemental materials associated with each chapter. Those materials include

- Annotated Suggested Readings
- A downloadable PowerPoint® presentation
- Updated URLs for website resources
- Discussion issues and questions
- Group projects
- Materials from past editions that add depth and background to current chapter topics
- True/false self-tests for each chapter
- Learning objectives for each chapter
- A cumulative 2260-item bibliography from this and the last four editions of *Sports in Society*
- Additional readings and current news articles
- A link to PageOut to help you create your own website

ANCILLARIES

Instructor's Manual and Test Bank

An instructor's manual and test bank is available to assist those using *Sports in Society* in college courses. It includes the following:

- *Chapter outlines.* These provide quick overviews of topics covered in each chapter. They are useful for organizing lectures and may be reproduced and given to students as study guides.
- *Test questions (multiple choice).* These questions are designed to test students' awareness of the central concepts and ideas in each chapter. For the instructor with large classes, these questions are useful for chapter quizzes, midterm tests, and final examinations.
- *Discussion/essay questions.* These questions can be used for tests or to generate classroom discussions. They are designed

to encourage students to synthesize and apply materials in one or more of the sections in each chapter. None of the questions asks the students simply to list points or give definitions.

Computerized Test Bank

A computerized version of the test bank for the instructor's manual is available for both IBM and Macintosh to qualified adopters. This software provides a unique combination of user-friendly aids and enables the instructor to select, edit, delete, or add questions and to construct and print tests and answer keys.

ACKNOWLEDGMENTS

This book draws on ideas from many sources. Thanks go to students in my sociology of sport courses and others who have provided constructive criticisms over the years. Students regularly open my eyes to new ways of viewing and analyzing sports as social phenomena. Special thanks go to friends and colleagues who influence my thinking, provide valuable source materials, and willingly discuss ideas and information with me. Nancy Coakley, Laurel Davis, Bob Hughes, Rebecca Bauder, and Peter Donnelly deserve thanks for their assistance. Thanks also go to all those who so generously shared ideas, experiences, stories, and references related to the new essays on sports and people with disabilities. They are Diane Alford, Mike Frogley, Howard Nixon, John Register, Jen Ruddell, Bob Syzman, and Andrea Woodson; and a very special thanks to Camille O'Bryant and Eli Wolfe for their proofreading and critiques in addition to ideas and facts. Beverly Millson, photographer David Biene, and Ossur (www.ossur.com)—a company that designs and manufactures prosthetics and orthotics—graciously provided many of the new photos used in this edition.

My appreciation goes to the publisher's reviewers, whose suggestions were crucial in the planning and writing of this edition. They include the following:

Danny Essary
East Texas Baptist University
Wendy Frappier
Minnesota State University—Moorhead
Kathleen Kinkema
Western State University
Nancy Malcolm
Georgia Southern University

As with the last edition, thanks go to Lynda Huenefeld for her expertise and professionalism as an editor and to Aaron Downey who kept everything organized. Thanks also go to Rhona Robbin and Elaine Silverstein for teaching me to write more clearly and concisely.

Jay Coakley
Fort Collins, CO

SPORTS IN SOCIETY

(Steve Nesius, AP/Wide World Photos)

THE SOCIOLOGY OF SPORT

What Is It and Why Study It?

SPORT HAS BECOME . . . a major social institution in American society, and indeed, the modern world. Yet our understanding of this major social phenomenon remains limited.

—**Center for Research on Sport in Society, University of Miami (1999)**

 Online Learning Center Resources

Visit *Sports in Society*'s Online Learning Center (OLC) at **www.mhhe.com/coakley9e** for additional information and study material for this chapter, including

- Self-grading quizzes
- Learning objectives
- Related websites
- Additional readings

chapter outline

A complete outline is available online at www.mhhe.com/coakley9e.

Now that the sports business is a massive arm of the international entertainment industry . . . there's no way we can escape its economic, social and environmental footprints. . . . [T]he growing involvement of big business, of the media and of advertisers has helped reshape the rules of many games—and, in the process, fuelled new forms of exclusion.

—John Elkington, Environmentalist, president of SustainAbility (2004)

3

ABOUT THIS BOOK

Most of you reading this book have experienced sports personally, as athletes or spectators or both. You probably are familiar with the physical and emotional experiences of playing sports, and you may know the rules and strategies used in certain sports. You may even follow the lives of high-profile athletes in your school or on the national sports scene. Most of you have watched sports, read about them, and participated in discussions about them.

This book assumes that you are interested in some facet of sports, but it is written to take you beyond the scores, statistics, and personalities in sports. The goal is to focus on the "deeper game" associated with sports, the game through which sports become part of the social and cultural worlds in which we live.

Fortunately, we can draw on our emotions and experiences as we consider this deeper game. Let's use our experiences with high school sports in the United States as an example. When students play on a high school basketball team, we know that it may affect their status in the treatment they receive from teachers and fellow students. We know it may have implications for their prestige in the community, their self-images and self-esteem. We know it may affect their future relationships, opportunities in education and the workforce, and overall enjoyment of life.

Building on this knowledge enables us to move further into the deeper game associated with sports. For example, we might ask why people in the United States place such importance on sports and top athletes in schools, and what this says about American values? We might study how high school sports are organized and connected with ideas and beliefs about masculinity and femininity, achievement and competition, pleasure and pain, winning and fair play, and other important aspects of our culture. We might ask how school sports influence the status structure that exists among high school students and

how athletes fit into that structure. We also might ask if the organization of high school sports is influenced by corporate sponsorships and examine student ideas about the corporations whose names and logos are on their uniforms, gym walls, and scoreboards.

The assumption underlying these questions is that, sports are more than just games, meets, and matches. They are also important parts of our social lives that have meanings and influence that go beyond scores and performance statistics. Sports are integral parts of the social and cultural contexts in which we live. They provide the stories and images that many of us use to explain and evaluate these contexts, our experiences, and our connections to the world around us.

People who study sports in society are concerned with the deeper meanings and stories associated with sports. They do research to understand (1) the cultures and societies in which sports exist, (2) the social worlds created around sports, and (3) the experiences of individuals and groups associated with sports.

Sociology is helpful when it comes to studying sports as social phenomena. This is because **sociology**[1] *is the study of social life, including all forms of social interaction and relationships.* The concepts, theories, and research methods that have been developed by sociologists enable us to study and understand sports as they exist in our lives and as they are connected with history, culture, and society. Sociology helps us examine social life *in context* and see connections between our lives and the larger social world. In this book, we use sociology to see sports as part of social and cultural life and understand social issues as we study sports.

---

[1]Important concepts used in each chapter are identified in **boldface.** Unless they are accompanied by a footnote that contains a definition, the definition will be given in the text itself. This puts the definition in context rather than separating it in a glossary. Definitions are also provided in the index (p. 640).

ABOUT THIS CHAPTER

This chapter focuses on five questions:

1. What are culture and society?
2. What are sports and how might we distinguish them from other activities?
3. What is the sociology of sport?
4. Why study sports in society?
5. Who studies sports in society, and what are their goals?

The answers to these questions will be our guides for understanding the material in the rest of the book.

DEFINING CULTURE AND SOCIETY

As we use sociology to study sports, it is important to know the definitions of *culture* and *society*. **Culture** *consists of the ways of life that people create as they participate in a group or society*. These ways of life are complex. They are created and changed as people struggle over what is important in their lives, how to do things, and how to make sense of their experiences. Culture encompasses all the socially invented ways of thinking, feeling, and acting that emerge as people try to survive, meet their needs, and achieve a sense of meaning and significance in the process. Of course, some people have more power and resources than others in the culture-creation process, and sociologists study how people use power and resources in the social world.

As parts of cultures, sports have forms and meanings, which vary from one group and society to the next and vary over time as groups and societies change. For example, traditional martial arts and Sumo wrestling in Asia are organized differently and have different meanings and purposes than combat sports such as boxing and wrestling in North America. The meaning, organization, and purpose of basketball has changed considerably since 1891 when it was developed at a YMCA in Massachusetts as an indoor exercise activity for men who did not want to play football outside during the winter. Canadian James Naismith, who invented basketball as part of an assignment in a physical education course, would not recognize his game if he were to see Yao Ming slam dunk during the Olympics while a billion people watch on television and thousands of others pay up to hundreds of dollars per ticket to see the game in person. It is important to know about these cultural and historical differences when we study sports as parts of social life.

The term **society** refers to *a collection of people living in a defined geographic territory and united by a political system and a shared sense of self-identification that distinguishes them from other people*. The United States, China, Nigeria, and the Netherlands are societies. Each has a different culture and different forms of social, political, and economic organization. It is important to know about these characteristics of society as we study the meaning and social significance of sports from one social context to another.

DEFINING SPORTS

Most of us have a good enough grasp of the meaning of sports to talk about them with others. However, when we study sports, it helps to define what we're talking about. For example, can we say that two groups of children playing a sandlot game of baseball in a Kansas town and a pickup game of soccer on a Mexican beach are engaged in sports? Their activities are quite different from what occurs in connection with Major League Baseball games and World Cup soccer matches. These differences become significant when parents ask if playing sports is good for their children, when community leaders ask if they should use tax money to pay for sports, or when school officials ask if sports contribute to the educational missions of their schools.

Students ask me if jogging and jump roping are sports. How about weight lifting? Hunting?

Scuba diving? Darts? Automobile racing? Ballroom dancing? Chess? Professional wrestling? Skateboarding? The X Games? Paintball? A piano competition? Should any or all of these activities be called sports? In the face of such a question, some scholars use a precise definition of sports so that they can distinguish them from other types of social activities.

A Traditional Definition of *Sports*

Although definitions of *sports* vary, many scholars agree that **sports** *are institutionalized competitive activities that involve rigorous physical exertion or the use of relatively complex physical skills by participants motivated by internal and external rewards.* Parts of this definition are clear, but other parts need explanations.

First, sports are *physical activities*. Therefore, according to the definition, chess probably is not a sport because playing chess is more cognitive than physical. Are billiards and pool physical enough to qualify as sports under this definition? Making this determination is arbitrary because there are no objective rules for how physical an activity must be to qualify as a sport. Pairs ice dancing is considered a sport in the Winter Olympics, so why not add ballroom dancing to the Summer Games? Members of the International Olympic Committee (IOC) asked this question, and ballroom dancing was included in the 2000 Sydney Olympic Games as a demonstration sport.

Second, sports are *competitive activities*, according to this definition. Sociologists realize that competitive activities have different social dynamics from cooperative or individualistic activities. They know that, when two girls kick a soccer ball to each other on the grass outside their home, it is sociologically different from what happens when the U.S. women's soccer team plays China's national team in the World Cup Tournament, so it makes sense to separate them for research purposes.

Third, sports are institutionalized activities. **Institutionalization** is a sociological term referring

to *the process through which actions, relationships, and social arrangements become patterned or standardized over time and from one situation to another.* Institutionalized activities have formal rules and organizational structures that guide people's actions from one situation to another. When we say that sports are institutionalized activities, we distinguish what happens when two skateboarders compare tricks at a local skateboard park from what happens when skateboarders compete against one another during the X Games where their tricks are evaluated and scored by officials who represent ESPN and determine who wins medals. In specific terms, institutionalization involves the following:

1. *The rules of the activity become standardized:* Sports have official rules applied whenever and wherever they are played.
2. *Official regulatory agencies take over rule enforcement:* Representatives of recognized "governing bodies"—such as a local rules committee for a children's softball league, a state high school activities association, the National Collegiate Athletic Association (NCAA), and the International Olympic Committee (IOC)—enforce the rules.
3. *The organizational and technical aspects of the activity become important:* Sports occur under controlled conditions in which there are specific expectations for athletes, coaches, and officials so that results can be documented, certified, and recorded. Furthermore, equipment, technologies, and training methods are developed to improve performance.
4. *The learning of game skills becomes formalized:* Participants must know the rules of the game, and coaches become important as teachers; participants may also consult others—such as trainers, dietitians, sport scientists, managers, and team physicians—as they learn skills.

The fourth point in the definition of *sports* is that sports are *activities played by people for internal and external rewards*. This means that participation in sports involves a combination of two sets of motivations. One is based in the internal satisfactions associated with expression, spontaneity, and the pure joy of participation. The other motivation is based in external satisfactions associated with displaying physical skills in public and receiving approval, status, or material rewards in the process.

When we use a precise definition, we can distinguish sports from both play and dramatic spectacle. **Play** *is an expressive activity done for its own sake*. It may be spontaneous or guided by informal norms. An example of play is three four-year-olds who, during a recess period at preschool, spontaneously run around a playground, yelling joyfully while throwing playground balls in whatever directions they feel like throwing them. Of course, it makes sociological sense to distinguish this physical activity, motivated almost exclusively by personal enjoyment and expression, from what happens in sports.

Dramatic spectacle, on the other hand, is *a performance that is intended to entertain an audience.* It is guided by explicit expectations among the performers. An example of dramatic spectacle is four professional wrestlers paid to entertain spectators by staging a skilled and cleverly choreographed tag-team match in which outcomes are prearranged for audience entertainment. It also makes sociological sense to distinguish this physical activity, motivated almost exclusively by a desire to perform for the entertainment of others, from what happens in sports. Sports are distinguished from play and spectacle in that they involve combinations of *both* intrinsic enjoyment and extrinsic rewards for performance. This means that all sports contain elements of play and spectacle. The challenge faced in some sports is to preserve a relatively even balance between these two elements.

This is a practical approach to defining sports, but it has potentially serious problems associated with it. For example, when we focus our attention only on institutionalized competitive activities, we may overlook physical activities in the lives of many people who have neither the resources to formally organize those activities nor the desire to make their activities competitive. In other words, we may spend all our time considering the physical activities of relatively select groups in society because those groups have the power to formally organize physical activities and the desire to make them competitive. If this happens, we privilege the activities of these select groups and treat them as more important parts of culture than the activities of other groups. This in turn can marginalize people who have neither the resources nor the time to play organized sports or who are not attracted to competitive activities.

Most people in the sociology of sport are aware of this possibility, so they use this definition of sports cautiously. However, some scholars reject the idea that sports can be defined once and for all time and decide to use an alternative approach to identifying and studying sports in society.

An Alternative Approach to Defining *Sports*

Instead of using a single definition of *sports*, some scholars study sports in connection with answers to the following two questions:

1. What activities do people in a particular group or society identify as sports?
2. Whose sports count the most in a group or society when it comes to obtaining support and resources?

Asking these questions does not limit the analysis of sports in ways that might happen when a precise definition is used. In fact, asking these questions leads researchers to dig into the social and cultural contexts in which people form ideas and beliefs about physical activities. The researchers must explain how and why some physical activities are defined as sports and become important activities in the social and cultural life of a particular society.

Many sociologists define *sports* in precise terms so that they can distinguish sports from other activities such as informal play and dramatic spectacle. High school and college wrestling are sociologically different from wrestling that might occur in a backyard or in the televised spectacle *Raw Is War*. I used action figures to represent dramatic spectacle, partly because pro wrestling organizations exercise restrictive control over the images of their events and dramatic personalities. (*Source:* Jay Coakley)

Those who use this alternative approach do not describe sports with a single definition. When they are asked, "What is sport?" they say, "Well, that depends on whom you ask, when you ask, and where you ask." They explain that not everyone has the same way of looking at and defining *sports* and that ideas about sports vary over time and from one place to another. For example, they would note that people in England who raced horses and went fox hunting during the 1870s would be horrified, confused, or astonished by what Americans today consider to be sports. Similarly, the people who watch NFL football games today would look at many activities that were considered sports in nineteenth-century England and say they were not "real" sports because participants did not train, compete according to schedules, play in leagues, or

What is a sport? This question cannot be answered without considering cultural values and power in a society. In the Olympics, rhythmic gymnastics is a sport although people in some societies believe that "real" sports must reflect "manly" attributes. (*Source: Colorado Springs Gazette*)

reflect on SPORTS   Sports as Contested Activities

When sociologists say that sports are contested activities, they mean that, through history, people have regularly disagreed about what sports could and should be. These disagreements have led to struggles over three major questions about sports and a number of related questions.

As you read the following questions, remember that there are many possible answers to each. Sociologists study how and why people in different places and times answer these questions in particular ways.

1. WHAT ARE THE MEANING, PURPOSE, AND ORGANIZATION OF SPORTS?

The struggles related to this question have raised other questions such as the following:

- What activities are defined as "official" sports?
- How are sports connected with social values and people's ideas about one another, social relationships, and the social worlds in which they live?
- What physical skills are valued in sports—are strength, size, and speed, for example, more important than flexibility, balance, and endurance?
- How are sports experiences evaluated—is emotional enjoyment more important than competitive success?

- What types of performance outcomes are important, and how is success defined, measured, and rewarded?
- How is *excellence* defined—in terms of one's abilities to dominate others, all-around athletic abilities, or one's abilities to maximize everyone's enjoyment in sports?

2. WHO WILL PARTICIPATE IN SPORTS, AND UNDER WHAT CONDITIONS WILL THIS PARTICIPATION OCCUR?

The struggles related to this question have raised other questions such as the following:

- Will females and males play the same sports, at the same time, on the same teams? On what basis will people make such decisions? Should rewards for achievement be the same for females and males?
- Will sports be open to people regardless of social class and wealth? Will wealthy and poor play and watch sports together or separately?
- Will people from different racial and ethnic backgrounds play together or in segregated settings? Will the meanings given to skin color or ethnicity influence participation patterns or access to participation?

....

strive to set records and win championships. Maybe ninety years from now people will play virtual sports in virtual environments and see our sports today as backward, overorganized, and funless activities that don't allow participants to combine movement with fantasies in ever-changing environments.

Those who use this alternative approach to defining *sports* understand that there are cultural differences in how people identify sports and include them in their lives. For instance, in cultures that emphasize cooperative relationships, the idea that people should compete with one another for

rewards are defined as disruptive, if not immoral. At the same time, people in cultures that emphasize competition may see physical activities and games that have no winners as pointless. These cultural differences suggest that we should not let a definition of *sports* shape what is studied. Those who use this alternative approach do research based on what the people in particular cultural settings think is important in their own lives (see Bale and Christensen, 2004; Newbery, 2004; Rail, 1998; Rinehart and Syndor, 2003).

The assumption underlying this approach is that sports are **contested activities**—that is,

- Will age influence eligibility to play sports, and should sports be age integrated or segregated? Will people of different ages have the same access to participation opportunities?
- Will able-bodied people and people with disabilities have the same opportunities to play sports, and will they play together or separately?
- What meanings will be given to the accomplishments of athletes with disabilities compared to the accomplishments of able-bodied athletes?
- Will gay men and lesbians play alongside heterosexuals?
- Will athletes control the conditions under which they play sports and have the power to change those conditions to meet their own needs and interests? Will athletes be rewarded for playing, and how will rewards be determined?

3. HOW WILL SPORTS BE SPONSORED, AND WHAT WILL BE THE REASONS FOR SPONSORSHIP?

The struggles related to this question have raised other questions such as the following:

- Will sports be sponsored by public agencies for the sake of the "public good"? If so, who will determine what the public good is?

- Will sports be sponsored by nonprofit organizations? If so, how will organizational philosophies influence the types of sports that are sponsored?
- Will sports be sponsored by commercial organizations? If so, how will the need for profits influence the types of sports that are sponsored?
- To what extent will sponsors control sports and athletes? What are the legal rights of the sponsors relative to those of the athletes and others involved in sports?

As you can see, many aspects of sports are contested! Sports change depending on how people answer these questions. Furthermore, answers to these questions are never permanent. New answers replace old ones as interests change; as power shifts; as the meanings associated with age, skin color, ethnicity, gender, and disability change; and as economic, political, and legal forces take new and different forms.

This means that the definition of *sports* always reflects the organization of a society at a particular time. A precise definition of sports is helpful, but it should always be used with caution because truths about sports rest in people's lives, not sociological definitions. *What do you think?*

....

activities for which there are no universal agreements about meaning, purpose, and organization. This means that in the case of sports there are varying ideas about who will participate, the circumstances under which participation will occur, and who will sponsor sports for what reasons. The most important sociological issue to recognize when we use this approach is that people in particular places at particular times struggle over *whose* ideas about sports will count as *the* ideas in a group or society. A guide for thinking about these issues is in the box titled "Sports as Contested Activities."

Struggles over whose ideas count when it comes to the meaning, organization, and purpose of sports are much more common than you might think. To illustrate this, consider the different ways that *sports* might be defined as people make decisions related to the following questions:

- Should children younger than six years old be allowed to play sports? If so, how should those sports be organized, and what will be their meaning and purpose?
- Should money from a local youth sports budget be given to a program in which

young girls are taught to jump rope or to a program in which boys and a few girls compete in a roller hockey league at a local skating rink?

- Should the state high school activities associations in the United States include cheerleading as an official high school sport?
- Should skateboarding and hacky sack be funded by a university intramural sport program?
- Should tenpin bowling, darts, and men's synchronized swimming be recognized as Olympic sports in 2012?
- Should a permit to use a sport field in a public park be given to an informal group of Frisbee players or to an organized softball team that plays in an official community league?
- Should synchronized swimming events be covered in the sports section of a city newspaper or in the lifestyle section?
- Should wrestler Stone Cold Steve Austin be nominated for a "sports" person of the year award?

How these questions are answered depends on what activities are counted as sports in a society at a given time. These questions also remind us to be cautious in how we use a single definition of *sports*. For example, if sports are institutionalized competitive physical activities played to achieve internal and external rewards, then why aren't competitive dancing, aerobics, jump roping, and cheerleading counted as sports? They fit the definition. The fact that they are not considered sports when it comes to important issues such as sponsorships, funding, and formal recognition raises two questions: (1) What activities are defined as sports in a society, and (2) whose ideas and interests are represented most in those definitions?

Answering these questions requires a careful analysis of the social and cultural context in which decisions are made in everyday life. Asking what activities are identified as sports raises critical issues. These issues force us to look at the cultures in which people live, work, and play together and struggle over what is important and how they will set collective priorities in their lives.

WHAT IS THE SOCIOLOGY OF SPORT?

This question is best answered at the end of the book instead of the beginning. However, you should have a clear preview of what you will be reading for the next fifteen chapters.

Most people who do the sociology of sport agree that the field is a subdiscipline of sociology that studies sports as parts of social and cultural life. Much research and writing in this field focuses on "organized, competitive sports" although people also study other physical activities that involve goals and challenges (Martin and Miller, 1999; Rinehart, 2000; Rinehart and Syndor, 2003).

The people who do this work use sociological concepts, theories, and research to answer questions such as the following:

1. Why have some activities rather than others been selected and designated as sports in particular societies?
2. Why have sports in particular societies been created and organized in certain ways?
3. How do people include sports and sport participation in their lives, and does participation affect who we are and our relationships with others?
4. How do sports and sport participation affect our ideas about bodies, masculinity and femininity, social class, race and ethnicity, work, fun, ability and disability, achievement and competition, pleasure and pain, deviance and conformity, and aggression and violence?
5. How are the meaning, purpose, and organization of sports connected with culture, organization, and resources in societies?
6. How are sports related to important spheres of social life such as family, education, politics, the economy, the media, and religion?

7. How do people use knowledge about sports as they go about their everyday lives?
8. How can people use sociological knowledge about sports to understand and participate in society as agents of progressive change?

Understanding the sociology of sport is easier if you learn to think of sports as **social constructions**—that is, as *aspects of the social world that are created by people as they interact with one another under the social, political, and economic conditions that exist in their society.* To stress this point, I generally use the term *sports* rather than *sport.* I do this to emphasize that the forms and meanings of sports vary from place to place and time to time. I want to avoid the inference that "sport" has an essential and timeless quality apart from the contexts in which people create, play, and change sports in society. Figure 1.1 illustrates that this approach may make some people

uncomfortable because they have vested interests in sports as they are currently organized and played. They are not anxious for people to see sports as social constructions that are subject to change if people wish to organize and play them differently.

Differences Between the Sociology of Sport and the Psychology of Sport

An additional way to understand the sociology of sport is to contrast it with the psychology of sport. Psychologists study behavior in terms of attributes and processes that exist *inside* individuals. They focus on motivation, perception, cognition, self-esteem, self-confidence, attitudes, and personality. They also deal with interpersonal dynamics, including communication, leadership, and social influence, but they usually discuss these things in terms of how they affect attributes and

FIGURE 1.1 If sports are social constructions, it means that we create them and that we can change them. The sociology of sport helps people identify things about sports that could or should be changed; other people, including those associated with sports, may resist this notion because they benefit from sports as they are currently organized.

processes that exist inside individuals. Therefore, they would ask a research question such as "How is the motivation of athletes related to personality and the perception of their physical abilities?"

Sociologists study actions and relationships in terms of the social conditions and cultural contexts in which people live their lives. They focus on the reality *outside* and *around* individuals and deal with how people form relationships with one another and create social arrangements that enable them to control and give meaning to their lives. Sociologists ask questions about the ways that actions, relationships, and social life are related to characteristics defined as socially relevant by people in particular groups. This is why they often deal with the social meanings and dynamics associated with age, social class, gender, race, ethnicity, (dis)ability, sexuality, and nationality. A sociologist would ask a question such as "How do prevailing ideas about masculinity and femininity affect the organization of sport programs and who participates in sports?"

When applying their knowledge, psychologists focus on the personal experiences and problems of particular individuals, whereas sociologists focus on group experiences and social issues that have an impact on entire categories of people. For example, when studying burnout among adolescent athletes, psychologists look at factors that exist *inside* the athletes themselves. Because stress is a key "inside factor" in human beings, psychologists focus on stress experienced by individual athletes and how it affects motivation, performance, and burnout (Smith, 1986). When applying their knowledge, they help athletes manage stress through goal setting, personal skill development, and the use of relaxation and concentration techniques.

Sociologists, on the other hand, study burnout in connection with the social reality that surrounds adolescent athletes. They focus on the organization of sport programs and the relationships between athletes and other people, including family members, peers, and coaches. Because

athletes are influenced by the social context in which they play sports, the application of sociological knowledge emphasizes that to control burnout we must change the organization of youth sport programs and the dynamics of athletes' relationships so that athletes have more control over their lives and more opportunities to have experiences and relationships outside of sports.

Both approaches have value, but some people may see a sociological approach as too complex and disruptive. They feel that it is easier to change individual athletes and how they deal with stress than it is to change the social conditions in which athletes live their lives. This is why many people who control sport programs prefer psychological over sociological approaches. They don't want to change patterns of organization and control in their programs. Similarly, many parents and coaches also prefer a psychological approach that focuses on stress management rather than a sociological approach that focuses on changing their relationships with athletes and the organization of sport programs.

Using the Sociology of Sport

The insights developed through sociological research are not always used to make changes in favor of the people who lack power in society. Like any science, sociology can be used in various ways. For example, research findings can be used to assist powerful people as they try to control and enhance the efficiency of particular social arrangements and organizational structures. Or they can be used to assist people who lack power as they attempt to change social conditions and achieve greater opportunities to make choices about how they live their lives.

Science is not a pure and objective enterprise. Therefore, sociologists, like others who produce and distribute knowledge, must consider why they ask certain research questions and how their research findings may affect people's lives. Sociologists cannot escape the fact that social life is complex and characterized by conflicts of interests between different groups of people. Like the rest of us, sociologists must deal with the fact that some people have more power and resources than others. Therefore, using sociology is not a simple process that always leads to good and wonderful conclusions for all humankind. This is why we must think critically about the potential consequences of sociological knowledge when we study sports.

As a result of my own thinking about sports in society, I have written this book to help you use sociology to do the following:

1. Think critically about sports so that you can identify and understand social problems and social issues associated with sports in society.
2. Look beyond issues of physical performance and records to see sports as social constructions that influence how people feel, think, and live their lives.
3. Learn things about sports that you can use to make informed choices about your own sport participation and the place of sports in the communities and societies in which you live.
4. Think about the ways that sports in your schools and communities might be transformed so they don't systematically disadvantage some categories of people while privileging others.

> The rituals of sport engage more people in a shared experience than any other institution or cultural activity today.
>
> —Varda Burstyn, author, *The Rites of Men* (1999)

Controversies Created by the Sociology of Sport

Research in the sociology of sport sometimes creates controversy. This occurs when research findings suggest that there should be changes in the organization of sports and the structure of social relations in society as a whole. These recommendations may threaten some people, especially those who control sport organizations, benefit from the current organization of sports, or think the current organization of sports is "right and natural." These people have the most to lose if changes are made in the ways that sports and social life are organized. People in positions of power and control know that changes in society could jeopardize their positions and the privilege that comes with them. Therefore, they prefer approaches to sports that blame problems on the weaknesses and failures of individuals. When theories put the blame for problems on individuals, solutions generally call for better ways to control people and teach them how to adjust to society as it is, rather than calling for changes in how society is organized (Donnelly, 1999).

The potential for controversy that results from a sociological analysis of sports can be illustrated by reviewing research findings on sport participation among women around the world. Research shows that women, especially women in poor and working-class households, have lower rates of sport participation than do other categories of people. Research also shows that there are many reasons for this, including the following: (1) Women are less likely than men to have the time, freedom, and money needed to play sports regularly; (2) women have little or no control of the facilities where sports are played or the programs in those facilities; (3) women have less access to transportation and less overall freedom to move around at will and without fear; (4) women often are expected to take full-time responsibility for the social and emotional needs of family members—a job that is never completed or done perfectly; and (5) many sport programs around the world are organized around the values, interests, and experiences of men. As a result of these reasons, many women do not see

breaking BARRIERS

Cultural Barriers
Aren't We Athletes?

Randy Snow won his first international track medal in 1984. He is a ten-time U.S. Open Wheelchair Tennis Champion, an International Tennis Federation Champion, U.S. Tennis Association Player of the Year, and winner of many athletic awards. Today he is a film producer and social activist who has received national citizenship awards. Asked about the Paralympics for elite athletes with physical disabilities, he has this to say:

> Paralympians are better athletes than our able-bodied counterparts. We work just as hard, do it for a lot less money, carry education to our venue as well as competition, and have overcome [physical challenges to do our sports]. Our stories display . . . true resiliency . . . therefore better matching us with the way life really exists. (in Joukowsky and Rothstein, 2002b, p. 39)

Snow's comment plus the relative invisibility of sports for athletes with a disability raises a sociological question: Whose sports count in society? The answer is that ideas and decisions about sports are based on multiple interactions that occur under particular cultural, political, and economic conditions. For sociologists, this raises three additional questions: Who is involved in and excluded from these interactions? Whose interests are represented or disadvantaged by the decisions made? How can cultural, political, and economic conditions be changed so that decisions are more representative of all people in a social world?

Most readers of this book have never had friends whose physical or intellectual impairments made them "disabled" and never met an athlete from the Paralympic Games or the Special Olympics. This means that if I asked you to close your eyes and imagine five different sport scenes, few of you would picture a scene involving athletes with an amputated limb, in wheelchairs, blind, with cerebral palsy, or with intellectual or developmental disabilities. This imagination exercise is *not* meant to evoke guilt. Our views of the world, including my views, are based on personal experiences; and our experiences are influenced by the meanings that people give to age, gender, race, ethnicity, social class, sexuality, (dis)ability, and other characteristics that are defined as socially significant in our lives. Neither culture nor society forces us to think or do certain things, but the only way to mute their influence is to critically examine social worlds and understand the ways that cultural meanings and social organization create constraints and opportunities in people's lives, including people with disabilities.

In each of the following chapters, a "Breaking Barriers" box presents the voices and experiences of people with disabilities. If you are *currently* able-bodied, each box alerts you to social and cultural barriers that constrain the lives of people with disabilities. If you have a disability, each box acknowledges the barriers that you, Randy Snow, and millions of others face in the pursuit of sport participation.

These barriers, according to many people, are "just the way things are." Eliminating them is impossible or unrealistic because they require changes in the organization of relationships, schools, communities, and societies. However, we are not victims of culture and society. If we have informed and idealistic visions of what sports could and should be, it is possible to identify and eliminate barriers. Fung Ying Ki, a triple gold medal winner in the 2000 Sydney Paralympics, knew that it was possible to break barriers when she said, "I hope that, in the future, there will no longer be 'disabled athletes' in this world, only 'athletes'" (in Joukowsky and Rothstein, 2002b, p. 115).

sports as appropriate activities for them to take seriously.

It is easy to see the potential for controversy associated with such research findings. For example, sociologists might use them to suggest that opportunities and resources to play sports should be increased for women, that women and men should share control over

Are these athletes? Their times in the 100- and 200-meter sprints are better than all but a handful of sprinters worldwide. Why are some sports defined as more real or more important than others? Who determines the standards? These three sprinters run on Ossur's Cheetah Flex-Foot. Does this matter in terms of a definition of sport? (*Source:* David Biene; photo courtesy of Ossur)

sports, and that new sports organized around the values, interests, and experiences of women should be developed. Other suggestions would call for changes in gender relations, family structures and child-care responsibilities, the organization of work, the distribution of resources in society, and ideas about femininity and masculinity.

When sociologists say that increasing sport participation among women or achieving gender equity in sport programs requires such changes, they threaten those who benefit from sports and social life as they are currently organized. In response, these people see the sociology of sport as too critical and idealistic and often claim that these changes would upset the "natural" order of things. However, good research always helps people think critically about the social conditions that affect our lives. Studying sports with a critical eye is easier if we have informed visions of what sports and society could and should be in the future. Without such visions, often born of idealism, what would motivate and guide us as we participate in our communities, societies, and world? People who make a difference and change the world for the better have always been idealistic. This is illustrated in "Breaking Barriers" on pages 16–17.

Different Approaches in the Sociology of Sport *evolved largely in Germany*

Some scholars who study sports in society are more interested in learning about sports than

Sports are a part of everyday life in wealthy countries, when and where people have the time, energy, and resources to organize and play physical games. Every Saturday during the fall, thousands of people go to this park where young boys play football. It is a rich site for studying sports in society because social dynamics revolve around issues related to gender, social class, race and ethnicity, family, and community. (*Source:* Jay Coakley)

society. They focus on understanding the organization of sports and the experiences of athletes and spectators. Their goal, in most cases, is to improve sport experiences for current participants and make sport participation more attractive and accessible. They also may do research to improve athletic performance, coaching effectiveness, and the efficiency and profitability of sport organizations. These scholars often refer to themselves as **sport sociologists,** and see themselves as part of the larger field of **sport sciences.**

Scholars concerned primarily with social and cultural issues usually refer to themselves as sociologists who study sports or as cultural studies scholars. Their research on sports in society is often connected with more general interests in leisure, popular culture, social relations, and social life as a whole. They use sports as windows into culture, society, and social relationships, and they study sports as the stories that people tell themselves about themselves thereby revealing their values, ideas, and beliefs.

Differences between scholars are not unique to the sociology of sport. They occur in every discipline as researchers make decisions about the questions they will ask and the knowledge they seek to produce. Knowledge is a source of power, so our knowledge in the sociology of sport has practical and political implications. It influences the ways that people view sports, integrate them into their lives, and make decisions about the organization and place of sports in society.

WHY STUDY SPORTS IN SOCIETY?

This is a serious question for people in the sociology of sport. The answer that most of us give is that we study sports because they are given special meaning by particular people in societies, they are tied to important ideas and beliefs in many cultures, and they are connected with major spheres of social life such as the family, religion, education, the economy, politics, and the media.

Sports Are Given Special Meaning in People's Lives

We study sports in society because they are important parts of everyday social life around the world. As we look around us, we see that the Olympic Games, soccer's World Cup, the Tour de France, the tennis championships at Wimbledon, and American football's Super Bowl are now worldwide events capturing the interest of billions of people. As these and other sport events are viewed in person or through the electronic media by people in over two hundred countries, they produce vivid images and lively stories that entertain and inspire people and provide them with the words and ideas that they use to make sense of their experiences and the world around them. Even when people don't have an interest in sports, their family and friends may insist on taking them to games and talking with them about sports to the point that they are forced to make sports a part of their lives. Sport images are so pervasive today that many young people are more familiar with the tattoos and body piercings of their favorite sport celebrities than they are with political leaders who make policies that have a significant impact on their lives.

People worldwide increasingly talk about sports—at work, at home, in bars, on dates, at dinner tables, in school, with friends, and even with strangers at bus stops, in airports, and on the street. Sports provide nonthreatening conversation topics with strangers. Relationships often revolve around sports, especially among men, and increasingly among women. People identify with teams and athletes so closely that what happens in sports influences their moods, identities, and sense of well-being. People's identities as athletes and fans may be more important to them than their identities related to education, career, religion, or family.

Overall, sports and sport images and stories have become a pervasive part of our everyday lives, especially for those of us living in countries

The Body and the Sociology of Sport

Until recently, most people viewed the body as a fixed, unchanging fact of nature. They saw the body in biological rather than social and cultural terms. But many scholars and scientists now recognize that we cannot fully understand the body unless we consider it in social and cultural terms (Blake, 1996; Brownell, 1995; Butler, 2004; Cole, 2000; Shilling, 1994; Turner, 1997). For example, medical historians have shown that the body and body parts have been identified and defined in different ways through history and from one culture to another. This is important because it affects medical practice, government policies, social theories, and the everyday experiences of human beings (Fausto-Sterling, 2000; Laqueur, 1990; Lupton, 2000; Preves, 2005).

Changes in the ways bodies have been socially defined (or "constructed") over the years have had implications for how people think about sex, sex differences, sexuality, ideals of beauty, self-image, body image, fashion, hygiene, health, nutrition, eating, fitness, racial classification systems, disease, drugs and drug testing, violence and power, and many other things that affect our lives. In fact, body-related ideas influence how people view desire, pleasure, pain, and

quality of life. For example, nineteenth-century Europeans and North Americans used insensitivity to pain as a physiological indicator of general character defects in a person and saw muscular bodies as indicators of criminal tendencies and lower-class status (Hoberman, 1992). Today, however, partly in connection with how sports have been defined, people in Europe and North America see the ability to ignore pain as an indicator of strong character, instead of a sign of deviance and defective character. They now regard a muscular body as an indicator of self-control and discipline rather than criminality.

When it comes to sports, the physical body is social in many ways. Sociologist John Wilson explains this in the following way:

> [In sport] social identities are superimposed upon physical being. Sport, in giving value to certain physical attributes and accomplishments and denigrating others, affirms certain understandings of how mind and body are related, how the social and natural worlds are connected. The identity of the athlete is not, therefore, a natural outgrowth of physicality but a social construction. . . . Sport absorbs ideas about the respective physical potential of men versus women, whites versus blacks, and middle-class versus working-class

where resources are relatively plentiful and access to the media is widespread. For this reason, sports are logical topics for the attention of sociologists and anyone else concerned with social life today.

Sports Are Tied to Important Ideas and Beliefs in Many Cultures

We also study sports in society because they are closely linked with how people think about and see the world. Sociologists try to understand these links by studying connections between sports and cultural ideologies.

Ideologies *are webs of ideas and beliefs that people use to give meaning to the world and make sense of their experiences.* Ideologies are important aspects of culture because they embody the principles, perspectives, and viewpoints that underlie our feelings, thoughts, and actions. However, ideologies seldom come in neat packages, especially in highly diverse and rapidly changing societies. Different groups of people in society often develop their own ideas and beliefs for giving meaning to the world and making sense of their experiences, and they don't always agree. These groups may struggle over whose ideologies provide the most accurate, useful, or moral people. In doing so, sport serves to reaffirm these distinctions. (1994, pp. 37–38)

Due in part to sports science, many people now see bodies as complex machines with component parts that can be isolated and transformed to enhance specialized competitive performances. This, in turn, has led to an emphasis on monitoring and controlling athletic bodies in forms such as weigh-ins, tests for aerobic capacity, muscle biopsies and tissue analysis, the identification of responses to various stressors, hormone testing, the administration of drugs and other chemical substances, drug testing, blood boosting, blood testing, diet regulation and restriction, vitamin regulation, and the measurement of body-fat percentage, muscle size, anaerobic capacities, and on and on.

In the future, we are likely to see brain manipulations, hormonal regulation, DNA testing, body-part replacements, and genetic engineering. Therefore, the body is cultural in the sense that it is now studied and understood in terms of performance outcomes, rather than subjective experiences of bodily pleasure (Pronger, 2002). In many sports today, pain rather than pleasure is an indicator of the "disciplined body," and limiting the percentage of body fat is so important that some bodies are starved to be "in good shape."

Thinking about the body this way challenges traditional Western ideas about mind–body separation. It highlights the notion that culture is *embodied*, and raises critical research questions such as the following:

1. How do people form ideas about natural, ideal, and deviant bodies in sports and in culture generally?
2. What are the moral, cultural, and sociological implications of how bodies are protected, probed, monitored, tested, trained, disciplined, evaluated, manipulated, and rehabilitated in sports?
3. How are bodies in sports marked by gender, skin color, ethnicity, (dis)ability, and age, and what are the social consequences of such marking?
4. How are bodies in sports represented in the media and popular culture in general?

These questions make many people associated with sports uncomfortable because the answers often challenge taken-for-granted ideas about nature, beauty, health, and the organization and purpose of high-performance, competitive sports. But it is important to ask these questions. *What do you think?*

- -

ways of giving meaning to and explaining the world and their experiences in it.

As various groups use and promote their ideologies in society, sports become socially relevant. As social constructions, sports can be organized to reinforce or challenge important ideas and beliefs. People create and organize sports around their ideas and beliefs about bodies, relationships, abilities, character, gender, race, social class, and other attributes and characteristics that they define as important in their lives. Usually, the most popular forms of sports in a society reinforce and reproduce the ideologies favored and promoted by people with the most power

and influence in that society. In the process, those ideologies often become dominant in that most people learn to use them as they make sense of the world and their experiences in it. When this occurs, sports serve as cultural practices that support and solidify particular forms of social organization and power relations.

Gender Ideology   We can use gender ideology to illustrate these points. **Gender ideology** consists of *a web of ideas and beliefs about masculinity, femininity, and male-female relationships*. People use gender ideology to define what it means to be a man or a woman, evaluate and judge people and relationships, and determine what they consider to be natural and moral when it comes to gender. It also is used as people create, play, and give meaning to sports.

Dominant gender ideology in most societies has traditionally emphasized that men are naturally superior to women in activities that involve strength, physical skills, and emotional control. Through most of the twentieth century, this idea was used to establish a form of "common sense" and a vocabulary that defined female inferiority in sports as "natural." Therefore, when a person threw a ball correctly, people learned to say that he or she "threw like a boy" or "like a man." When a person threw a ball incorrectly, they learned to say that he or she "threw like a girl." The same was true when people were evaluated in terms of their abilities to run or do sports in general. If sports were done right, they were done the way a boy or man would do them. If they were done wrong, they were done the way a girl or woman would do them.

The belief that doing sports, especially sports that are physically demanding, would make boys into men has long been consistent with dominant gender ideology in many cultures. Consequently, when women excelled at these sports, many people claimed that they were "unnatural." Dominant gender ideology led them to assume that femininity and athletic excellence, especially in physically demanding or heavy-contact sports, could not go together. As they tried to make sense of strong, competent women athletes, they concluded that such women must be malelike or lesbians. When this conclusion was combined with related ideas and beliefs about nature, morality, and gender, many people restricted opportunities for girls and women to play sports.

This gender ideology was so widely accepted by people in sports that coaches of men's teams even used it to motivate players. They criticized men who made mistakes or did not play aggressively enough by "accusing" them of "playing like a bunch of girls." As they made sense of sports and gender, these coaches inferred that being female meant being a failure. This ideology clearly served to privilege males and disadvantage females in the provision of opportunities and the allocation of resources to play sports. Although it has been challenged and discredited in recent years, the legacy of this gender ideology continues to privilege some boys and men and disadvantage some girls and women.

Fortunately, ideology is always subject to change. People may question and struggle over it, and some people organize challenges that produce changes in deeply felt and widely accepted ideas and beliefs. In the case of gender ideology, sports have occasionally been sites or "social places" for challenging dominant ideas about what is natural and feminine. The history of struggles over the meaning and implications of gender in sports is complex, but recent challenges by both women and men who do not accept traditional ideas and beliefs have led to important changes in gender ideology.

Women athletes have illustrated clearly that females can be physically powerful and capable of noteworthy physical achievements surpassing those of the vast majority of men in the world. Furthermore, the accomplishments of women athletes have raised serious questions about what is "natural" when it comes to gender. We will discuss issues related to gender ideology in sports in nearly every chapter, but especially chapter 8. The box "The Body and the Sociology of Sport," presents issues related to another ideological issue in our lives: What do we consider to be natural when it comes to the body?

Racial Ideology   Sports are sites for important ideological struggles. For example, in the United States, they have been sites for either reproducing or challenging dominant ideas about race and the connections between skin color and abilities, both physical and intellectual. **Racial ideology** consists of *a web of ideas and beliefs that people use to give meaning to skin color and to evaluate people in terms of racial classifications.* Racial ideologies vary around the world, but they are powerful forces in the social lives of many people. They are used to place people into racial categories, and they influence important social practices and policies that affect people's lives.

The connections between sports and racial ideologies are complex. Racial ideology is often used as a basis for evaluating athletic potential or explaining athletic success. The notion that light-skinned people can't jump and that dark-skinned people are natural athletes are expressions of dominant racial ideology in certain cultures—an issue discussed in chapter 9.

Class Ideology **Class ideology** consists of *a web of ideas and beliefs that people use to understand economic inequalities and make sense of their own position in an economic hierarchy in society.* In the United States, for example, class ideology is organized around the idea of the "American Dream" of unrestricted economic opportunities and the belief that American society is a **meritocracy** *where deserving people become successful and success is achieved by those who deserve it.* Sports provide many stories and slogans emphasizing that people can achieve anything through discipline and hard work and that failure awaits those who are lazy and undisciplined. By extension, this ideology leads people to make positive conclusions about the character and qualifications of wealthy and powerful people and negative conclusions about the character and qualifications of those who are poor and powerless. Winners are assumed to have strong character, whereas losers

> [Sports] are why some people get out of bed. Sports define many of us. Some superstars command as much attention as heads of state and other leaders. Whether you weigh the good or bad of it—it's a fact.
>
> —Bob Davis, vice president,
> American Program Bureau (1999)

are assumed to have weak character. This way of thinking connects sports positively with capitalism and its competitive system of economic rewards in that it explains and legitimizes class inequality. This will be discussed in chapters 8–10.

Sports and Ideologies: Complex Connections
As we think about sports and ideologies, it is important to know that ideology is complex and sometimes inconsistent and that sports come in many forms and have many meanings associated with them. Therefore, sports are connected with ideologies in various and sometimes contradictory ways. We saw this in the example showing that sports are sites for simultaneously reproducing *and* challenging dominant gender ideology in society. Furthermore, sports can have many social meanings associated with them. For example, baseball is played by similar rules in Japan and the United States, but the meanings associated with baseball and with athletes' performances are different in the two cultures because of ideological differences. Team loyalty is highly prized in Japan, and emotional displays by players or coaches are frowned upon, whereas in the United States individualism is emphasized and emotional displays are accepted and defined as entertaining. Japanese baseball games may end in ties, but games in the United States must have clear winners and losers, even if it means playing extra innings and overtime or "sudden death" periods.

The complex connections between sports and ideologies make it difficult to generalize about the consequences of sports in society. Sports have the social potential to do many things. This is another reason for studying them as social constructions.

Sports Are Connected to Major Spheres of Social Life

Another reason to study sports in society is that they are clearly connected to major spheres of social life, including the family, the economy, the media, politics, education, and religion. We discuss these connections in various chapters in this book, but it is useful to highlight them at this point.

Sports and the Family   Sports are closely related to the family. In North America, for example, millions of children are involved in a variety of organized sport activities. It is primarily their parents who organize leagues, coach teams, attend games, and serve as "taxi drivers" for child athletes. Family schedules are altered to accommodate practices and games. These schedules also may be affected by sport participation by adult family members. The viewing of televised sport events sometimes disrupts family life and at other times provides a collective focus for family attention. In some cases, relationships between family members are nurtured and played out during sport activities or in conversations about these activities. Two of these situations are represented in figure 1.2. Family issues are discussed in chapters 4 and 5.

Sports and the Economy   The economies of most countries, especially wealthy postindustrial countries, are affected by the billions of dollars spent every year for game tickets, sports equipment, participation fees, athletic club membership dues, and bets placed on favorite teams and athletes. Sport teams affect the economies of many communities. Most countries use public monies (taxes) to subsidize teams and events. In fact, sports and commerce have fused together so that corporate logos are linked with sport teams and athletes and displayed prominently in school gyms, arenas, stadiums, and other places where sports are played and watched.

Some athletes make impressive sums of money from combinations of salaries, appearance fees, and endorsements. Corporations paid up to $4.8 million for a single minute of commercial time during the 2006 telecast of the Super Bowl.

"This won't take long will it?"

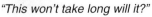

FIGURE 1.2   Families and family schedules often are influenced by sport involvement. Sometimes this involvement disrupts family life and interferes with family relationships (left); sometimes it brings family members together in enjoyable ways (right).

They have paid over $100 million to be international Olympic sponsors and have their brands associated with the Olympic name and symbol for four years. Sport stadiums, arenas, and teams are now named after corporations. Sponsorships and commercial associations with sports are so common that people now believe that, without Coca-Cola, McDonald's, Nike, General Motors, and other transnational corporations, sports could not exist. This indicates that sports are cultural practices deeply connected with the material and economic conditions in society. These issues are discussed in chapters 10 and 11.

Sports and the Media Television networks and cable stations pay billions of dollars for the rights to televise major games and events. NBC in the United States, owned by General Electric, paid the International Olympic Committee (IOC) $2.3 billion for the rights to the Summer Games of 2004 and 2008 and the Winter Games of 2006. People in sport organizations that depend on spectators are keenly aware that without the media their lives would be different.

The images and messages presented in media coverage of sports also emphasize particular ideological themes, and they influence how people see and think about sports and social life. The media have converted sports into a major form of entertainment witnessed by billions of people. Athletes are global celebrities, and the corporations that sponsor sports inscribe their logos in people's minds as they promote lifestyles based on consumption. These issues are discussed in chapter 12.

Sports and Politics People in many societies link sports to feelings of national pride and a sense of national identity. For example, in the aftermath of the terrorist attacks of 9/11(2001), many people in the United States used sport events as sites for reaffirming their collective sense of "we-ness" as Americans. Many events involved expressions of unity and patriotism, combined with memorials to commemorate those who died in the attacks. This allowed people at the games and watching on television to experience widely shared feelings and reaffirm their sense of national identity.

Most people around the globe have no second thoughts about displaying national flags and playing national anthems at sporting events, and some may quickly reject athletes and other spectators who don't think as they do about the flag and the anthem.

Political leaders at various levels of government promote themselves by associating with sports as participants and spectators. Former athletes, even professional wrestlers, have been elected to powerful political positions in the United States by using their name recognition and reputations from sports to attract votes.

International sports have become hotbeds of political controversy in recent years, and most countries around the world have used sports actively to enhance their reputations in global political relationships. Furthermore, sports involve political processes associated with issues such as who controls sports and sport events, the terms of eligibility and team selection, rules and rule changes, rule enforcement, and the allocation of rewards and punishments. Sports and sport organizations are political because they involve the exercise of power over people's lives. These issues are discussed in chapter 13.

Sports and Education Sports are integral parts of school life in many countries. They are taught and played in physical education classes, and schools in a few countries have interscholastic sport teams that attract widespread attention among students and community residents. Some U.S. universities even use intercollegiate teams for public relations purposes, making or losing large amounts of money in the process. School sport programs in the United States are unique.

The sports sponsored by schools in most other countries are low-profile, club-based teams that emphasize participation and student control—a model quite different than the one used in the United States. These issues are discussed in chapter 14.

Sports and Religion There is an emerging relationship between sports and religion in certain cultures. Local churches and church groups in the United States and Canada are active sponsors of athletic teams and leagues. Parishes and congregations sometimes revise Sunday worship schedules to accommodate members who don't want to miss an opening NFL kickoff. Athletes in the United States often express religious beliefs, and nondenominational religious organizations use sports to attract and convert people to Christian beliefs. Other U.S.-based religious organizations have used athletes as spokespersons for their belief systems, and some athletes now define their sport participation in religious terms. These issues are discussed in chapter 15.

WHAT IS THE CURRENT STATUS OF THE SOCIOLOGY OF SPORT?

Prior to 1980, very few people studied sports in society. Scholars were not concerned with physical activities and thought that sports were unrelated to important issues in society. However, a few sociologists and physical educators in North America and Europe began to think outside the box of their disciplines. They decided that sports should be studied because they were becoming increasingly important activities in many societies. During the last two decades of the twentieth century, the sociology of sport gradually came to be recognized as a legitimate subfield in sociology and physical education/ kinesiology/sport science.

Research and interest in the sociology of sport has increased significantly in recent years. For example, Amazon.com has nearly 900 books listed in the "Sociology of Sport" category. In 2000 only a third that number of books were listed. Recent growth has also been fueled by the formation of professional associations and academic journals devoted to the field. These associations and journals enable scholars studying sports in society to meet with one another and present and publish their ideas and research. The journals related to the field are listed in table 1.1. Sociology of sport organizations include the following:

1. *The International Sociology of Sport Association (ISSA).* This organization, formed in 1965, meets annually and attracts international scholars. Since 1965 it has sponsored publication of the *International Review for the Sociology of Sport.*
2. *The North American Society for the Sociology of Sport (NASSS).* This organization, formed in 1978, has held annual conferences every year since 1980, and it has sponsored publication of the *Sociology of Sport Journal* since 1984.
3. *The Sport Sociology Academy (SSA).* This loosely organized group is one of ten disciplinary academies in the National Association for Sport and Physical Education (NASPE), which is part of the American Alliance for Health, Physical Education, Recreation, and Dance (AAHPERD), headquartered in the United States. The academy does not sponsor a journal, but it does sponsor sociology of sport research sessions at the annual conferences of AAHPERD. There are similar organizations in many countries.

Growth in the sociology of sport will continue to occur if scholars in the field conduct and publish research that people find useful as they seek to understand social life and participate effectively as citizens in their communities and societies.

Table 1.1 Publication sources for sociology of sport research

Journals Devoted Primarily to Sociology of Sport Articles	Journals in Related Fields That Sometimes Include Articles on or Related to Sociology of Sport Topics
International Review for the Sociology of Sport (quarterly) *Journal of Sport and Social Issues* (quarterly) *Sociology of Sport Journal* (quarterly) **Sociology Journals That Sometimes Include Articles on or Related to Sports** *American Journal of Sociology* *American Sociological Review* *British Journal of Sociology* *Sociology of Education* *Theory, Culture, and Society* **Interdisciplinary, Sport Science, and Physical Education Journals That Sometimes Include Articles on or Related to Sociology of Sport Topics** *Avante* *Canadian Journal of Applied Sport Sciences* *Culture, Sport, Society* *Exercise and Sport Sciences Reviews* *Journal of Physical Education, Recreation, and Dance* *Journal of Sport Behavior* *Journal of Sport Management* *Journal of Sport Sciences* *Physical Education Review* *Quest* *Research Quarterly for Exercise and Sport* *Sport, Education, and Society* *Sport Science Review* *Women in Sport & Physical Activity Journal*	*Adolescence* *Aethlon: The Journal of Sport Literature* *The British Journal of Sport History* *Canadian Journal of the History of Sport* *European Sport Management Quarterly* *The European Sports History Review* *International Journal of the History of Sport* *International Journal of Sport Psychology* *Journal of Human Movement Studies* *Journal of Leisure Research* *Journal of the Philosophy of Sport* *Journal of Popular Culture* *Journal of Sport and Exercise Psychology* *Journal of Sport History* *Journal of Sport Media* *Journal of Sports and Economics* *Leisure Sciences* *Leisure Studies* *Olympika: The International Journal of Olympic Studies* *Soccer and Society* *Society and Leisure* *Sport History Review* *Sport Management Review* *The Sport Psychologist* *Sporting Traditions* *The Sports Historian* *Youth & Society*

summary

WHY STUDY THE SOCIOLOGY OF SPORT?

Sociology is the study of social life, including all forms of social interaction and relationships. Sociologists are concerned with social issues, social organization, and social change. Their goal is to enable people to understand, control, and change their lives so that human needs are met at both individual and group levels.

Sociologists study sports as parts of culture and society. They look at sports in terms of their importance in people's lives and their connections to ideology and major spheres of social life. Research in the sociology of sport helps us understand sports as social constructions created by people for particular purposes. As social constructions, sports are related to historical, political, and economic factors.

Some scholars in the field define *sports* as activities involving (1) the use of physical skill, prowess, or exertion; (2) institutionalized competition; and (3) the combination of intrinsic and extrinsic reasons for participation. Such a definition is problematic if it leads us to ignore or devalue the lives of people who do not have the resources and the desire to develop formally organized and competitive physical activities. For this reason, many scholars now recommend that, instead of using a single definition of *sports*, we should ask what activities are identified as sports in different groups and societies at different points in time. This question forces us to recognize that sports are contested activities. This focuses our attention on the relationship between sports and power and privilege in society and leads more directly to concerns for transforming social life so that more people have the resources they need to control their lives and make them meaningful.

When sociologists study sports in society, they often discover problems based in the structure and organization of either sports or society. When this happens, the recommendations that sociologists make may threaten those who want sports and sport programs to remain as they are now. Therefore, sociology sometimes creates controversies. Continued growth of the sociology of sport depends primarily on whether scholars in the field do research and produce knowledge that makes meaningful contributions to people's lives.

OLC See the OLC, www.mhhe.com/coakley9e for an annotated list of readings related to this chapter. The OLC also contains a key concepts list, a review test, and other helpful features.

WEBSITE RESOURCES

Note: Websites often change. The following URLs were current when this book was printed. Please check our website (www.mhhe.com/coakley9e) for updates and additions.

www.mhhe.com/coakley9e   Click on chapter 1; information on why sociologists tend to ask critical questions in their research; discussion of roller hockey and jump rope and what is counted as a sport in U.S. culture.

www.ucalgary.ca/library/ssportsite   A guide to online "Scholarly Sport Sites"; this is the most useful starting point I have found as I have looked for online information.

www.nasss.org   The official site for the North American Society for the Sociology of Sport; the Resource Center contains a list of experts in the field, along with graduate programs specializing in the sociology of sport.

http://u2.u-strasbg.fr/issa   The official site of ISSA, the International Sociology of Sport Association; this organization is a subcommittee of ICSSPE, the International Council of Sport Science and Physical Education, and is affiliated with UNESCO, the United Nations Educational, Scientific and Cultural Organization.

www.handilinks.com/Directory/Sports   This site provides numerous Internet links useful to sport scholars from many disciplines.

www.pscw.uva.nl/sociosite/TOPICS/Leisure.html Click on SPORT; this site, located in the Netherlands, provides excellent links to sites related to the sociology of sport, especially to international sites related to women in sports and to the Olympics.

www.sportinsociety.org   The site for the Center for the Study of Sport in Society that offers complete information on all the center's programs dedicated to promoting socially responsible changes in and through sports.

www.sportdiscus.com   A comprehensive international database of sports and fitness information, containing more than 500,000 references, which can be searched by using subject-related keywords; this site provides direct links to additional websites that contain articles.

http://physed.otago.ac.nz/sosol   The site for the Sociology of Sport Online: sosol is an international electronic forum that publishes articles and book reviews related to the sociological examination of sport, physical education, and coaching; it is hosted by the School of Physical Education at the University of Otago in New Zealand.

(*Source:* David Biene; photo courtesy of Ossur)

USING SOCIAL THEORIES

How Can They Help Us Study Sports in Society?

IN THIS FRAGMENTED AGE, it often seems that only sports can bind together the nation—across its divides of class, race, and gender—in common cause and celebration. [Sports are] a prism through which we view some of our most complex [social] issues.

—Mark Starr, *Newsweek* (1999)

 Online Learning Center Resources

Visit *Sports in Society*'s Online Learning Center (OLC) at **www.mhhe.com/coakley9e** for additional information and study material for this chapter, including

- Self-grading quizzes
- Learning objectives
- Related websites
- Additional readings

A complete outline is available online at www.mhhe.com/coakley9e.

SPORTS ARE A TREMENDOUS force for the status quo. . . . They do distract millions from more serious thoughts—as do . . . all other "escape" entertainments. As mass entertainment, they are definitely antirevolutionary.

—Leonard Koppett, sports reporter and columnist (1994)

Those of us who study sports in society want to understand four things: (1) the social and cultural contexts in which sports exist, (2) the connections between those contexts and sports, (3) the social worlds that people create as they participate in sports, and (4) the experiences of individuals and groups associated with those social worlds. We are motivated by combinations of curiosity, interests in sports, and concerns about social life and social issues. Most of us also want to use what we know about sports in society to promote social justice, expose and challenge the exploitive use of power, and empower people so that they might resist and transform oppressive social conditions.

As we study and apply knowledge about sports, we use social and cultural theories. Theories provide frameworks for asking research questions, interpreting information, and uncovering the deeper meanings and stories associated with sports. They also enable us to be more informed citizens as we apply what we learn in our research to the world in which we live. Because those of us who study sports in society come from diverse academic backgrounds and because social life is complex, we use multiple theories to guide our work. The three goals of this chapter are to

1. Identify and describe the theories used most widely to study sports in society.
2. Explain the ways that theories help us understand sports and the society in which we live.
3. Demonstrate how theories influence our view of sports and the practical actions we take in connection with sports.

WHAT ARE THEORIES AND WHY DO WE NEED THEM?

Whenever we ask why our social world is the way it is and then imagine how it might be changed, we are "theorizing" (hooks, 1992). **Theorizing** involves *a combination of description, analysis, reflection, and application.* When we theorize, we aren't required to use big words and complex sentences. In fact, the best theories are those we understand so clearly that they help us make sense of our experiences and the social world.

When we study sports in society, the best theories are those that describe and explain aspects of social life in logical terms that are consistent with systematic observations of the social world. Theories enable us to see things from new angles and perspectives, understand more fully the relationship between sports and social life, and make informed decisions about sports and sport participation in our lives, families, communities, and societies.

Many people think that theories don't have practical applications, but this is not true. Most of our decisions and actions are based on our predictions of their possible consequences, and those predictions are based on our "personal theories" about social life. Our theories may be incomplete, poorly developed, based on limited information, and biased to fit our needs, but we still use them to guide our behavior. When our theories are accurate, our predictions help us relate more effectively with others and control more directly what happens in our lives. When people make decisions about sports, formulate policies, or decide whether to fund or cut money from sport programs, they base decisions on their personal theories about sports and society.

The theories discussed in this chapter are different from our personal theories about social life. This is because they are based on a combination of systematic research and deductive logic. They have been presented in books and articles so that others may evaluate, test, use, and revise them. When logic or evidence contradicts them, theories are revised or abandoned.

People who study sports in society have used many theories to guide them as they ask research questions and interpret research findings. However, most scholarly work over the past half century has been based on one or a combination of five major theories:[1]

- Functionalist theory
- Conflict theory
- Critical theory
- Feminist theory
- Interactionist theory

Although there are important differences between these five theories, there are many points at which two or more of them converge and overlap. This is because people read and respond to the ideas of others as they do research and develop new explanations of society and social life. Therefore, theories are *emerging* explanations of what we know about social worlds at this time.

Each of the five theories discussed in this chapter provides a different perspective for understanding the relationship between sports and society. This will be highlighted through the following: (1) a brief overview of each theory, (2) examples of the ideas and research that have been inspired by the theory, (3) explanations of how the theory can be used as we take actions and make policies about sports in our everyday lives, and (4) an overview of the major weaknesses of the theory.

Table 2.1 provides a summary of each theory and how it helps us understand sports in society. The table contains a large amount of material. It may look confusing at first, but, as you read through the chapter, you will find it to be a useful reference guide to each theory. Most important, it will help you identify and understand similarities and differences between the theories.

FUNCTIONALIST THEORY: SPORTS PRESERVE THE STATUS QUO

Functionalist theory is based on the assumption that society is an organized system of interrelated parts held together by shared values and

---

[1]Figurational theory, widely used to guide research on sports in Europe, is explained and discussed in the Online Learning Center at www.mhhe.com/coakley9e.

established social arrangements that maintain the system in a state of balance or equilibrium. The most important social arrangements are social institutions such as the family, education, the economy, the media, politics, religion, leisure, and sport. If these social institutions are organized around a core set of values, functionalists assume that a society will operate smoothly and efficiently. When sociologists use functionalist theory to explain how a society, community, school, family, sport team, or other social system works, they study the ways that each part in the system contributes to the system's overall operation. For example, if Canadian society is the system being studied, a person using functionalist theory wants to know how the Canadian family, economy, government, educational system, media, religion, and sport are related to one another and how they work together in contributing to the smooth operation of the society as a whole. An analysis based on functionalism focuses on the ways that each of these social institutions helps the larger social system to operate efficiently.

According to functionalist theory, social systems operate efficiently when they are organized to do four things: (1) socialize people so that they learn and accept important cultural values, (2) promote social connections between people so that they can cooperate with one another, (3) motivate people to achieve socially approved goals through socially accepted means, and (4) protect the overall system from disruptive outside influences. Functionalists assume that, if these four "system needs" are satisfied, social order will be maintained and everyone will benefit. The first column in table 2.1 (pp. 34–35) summarizes functionalist theory.

Functionalist Theory and Research on Sport

Functionalist theory leads people to ask research questions about the ways that sport contributes to the organization and stability of organizations, communities, societies, and other social

Table 2.1   Using social theories to study sports in society: a summary and comparison

Functionalist Theory	Conflict Theory	Critical Theory	Feminist Theory	Interactionist Theory
I. ASSUMPTIONS ABOUT THE BASIS FOR SOCIAL ORDER IN SOCIETY				
Social order is based on consensus and shared values, which hold the interrelated parts of society together. All social systems operate efficiently when each part of the system stays in synch with other parts.	Social order is based on economic interests and the use of economic power to exploit labor. Social class shapes social structures and relationships.	Social order is negotiated through struggles over ideology, representation, and power. Social life is full of diversity, complexities, and contradictions.	Social order is based primarily on the values, experiences, and interests of men with power. Social life and social order is gendered and based on patriarchal ideas.	Social order is created by people as they interact with each other. Social life is grounded in social relationships and the meanings given to social reality.
II. MAJOR CONCERNS IN THE STUDY OF SOCIETY				
How do the parts of social systems contribute to the satisfaction of "system needs" and the efficient operation of the system?	How is economic power distributed and used in society? What are the dynamics of social class relations? Who is privileged and exploited in class relations?	How is cultural ideology produced, reproduced, and transformed? What are the conflicts and problems that affect the lives of those who lack power in society?	How is gender ideology produced, reproduced, and transformed? How do dominant forms of gender relations privilege men over women and some men over others?	How are meanings, identities, and culture created through social interaction? How do people define the reality of their own lives and the world around them?
III. MAJOR CONCERNS IN THE STUDY OF SPORT				
How does sport fit into social life and contribute to social stability and efficiency? How does sport participation teach people important norms in society?	How does sport reflect class relations? How is sport used to maintain the interests of those with power and wealth in society? How does the profit motive distort sport and sport experiences?	How are power relations reproduced and/or resisted in and through sports? Whose voices are/are not represented in the narratives and images that constitute sports?	How are sports gendered activities, and how do they reproduce dominant ideas about gender in society? What are the strategies for resisting and transforming sport forms that privilege men?	How do people become involved in sports, become defined as athletes, derive meaning from participation, and make transitions out of sports into the rest of their lives?

IV. MAJOR CONCLUSIONS ABOUT THE SPORT-SOCIETY RELATIONSHIP

Sport is a valuable social institution that benefits society as well as individuals in society. Sport is a source of inspiration on both personal and social levels.	Sport is a form of physical activity that is distorted by the needs of capital. Sport is an opiate that distracts attention away from the problems that affect those without economic power.	Sports are social constructions. Sports are sites at which culture is produced, reproduced, and transformed. Sports are cultural practices that repress and/or empower people.	Sports are grounded in the values and experiences of powerful men in society. Sports reproduce male power and distorted ideas about masculinity. Sports produce gendered ideas about physicality, sexuality, and the body.	Sports are forms of culture created through social interaction. Sport participation is grounded in the decisions made by people in connection with their identities and relationships.

V. SOCIAL ACTION AND POLICY IMPLICATIONS

Develop and expand sport programs that promote traditional values, build the type of character valued in society, and contribute to social order and stability.	Raise class consciousness and make people aware of their own alienation and powerlessness. Eliminate the profit motive in sports thereby allowing them to foster expression, creativity, and physical well-being.	Use sports as sites for challenging and transforming exploitative and oppressive forms of social relations. Increase the range and diversity of sport participation opportunities. Challenge the voices and perspectives of those with power.	Use sports as sites for challenging and transforming oppressive forms of gender relations. Expose and resist homophobia and misogyny in sports. Transform sports to emphasize partnership over competition and domination.	Allow individuals to shape sports to fit their definitions or reality. Make sport organizations more open and democratic. Focus on the culture and organization of sports when controlling deviance in sports.

VI. MAJOR WEAKNESSES

It does not acknowledge that sports are social constructions. It overstates the positive consequences of sport. It ignores that sport serves the needs of some people more than others.	It ignores that sport can be a site for creative and liberating experiences. It overstates the influence of economic forces in society. It assumes that people who have economic power always shape sports to meet their interests.	It doesn't provide guidelines to assess the effectiveness of particular forms of resistance as strategies for making progressive changes in social worlds. It often uses confusing vocabularies making it difficult to merge critical ideas and theories.	It doesn't provide guidelines to assess the effectiveness of particular forms of resistance as strategies for making progressive changes in social worlds. It sometimes uses confusing vocabularies making it difficult to merge critical ideas and theories.	It doesn't clearly explain how meaning, identity, and interaction are related to social structures and material conditions in society. It generally ignores issues of power and power relations in society.

Functionalist theory assumes that social order depends on maintaining social solidarity through established social institutions, including the institution of sport. (*Source:* USA Volleyball)

systems. Using functionalist theory, researchers have studied some of the questions and issues that are discussed in the following chapters. Examples include the following:

1. Do sports and sport participation influence social and personal development? This issue is discussed in chapters 4–7, 14, and 15.

2. Do sports and sport participation foster the development of social bonds and relationships in groups, communities, and societies? This issue is discussed in chapters 9, 10, 13, and 14.

3. Does playing sports have a positive impact on academic and occupational success, and does it teach people to follow the rules as they strive for success?

These issues are discussed in chapters 4, 6, 7, 10, and 14.

4. Do sports contribute to personal health and wellness and the overall strength and well being of society? These issues are discussed in chapters 4, 7, and 13.

Functionalist theory focuses on the ways that sports contribute to the smooth operation of societies, communities, organizations, and groups. This is why a functionalist approach is popular among people interested in preserving the status quo in society. They want sociologists to tell them how sport contributes to the smooth operation of the social systems in which they have been successful. Many people connected with organized competitive sports also prefer functionalist theory because it emphasizes the "functions" of sports and supports the conclusion that sports are a source of inspiration for individuals and societies.

Using Functionalist Theory in Everyday Life

Popularized forms of functionalist theory often are used when people in positions of power make decisions about sports and sport programs at national and local levels. For example, a functionalist analysis of sports in society would support the following actions: promoting the development and growth of organized youth sports (to build values), funding interscholastic sports programs in high schools and colleges (to promote organizational loyalty and attachments to schools), developing sport opportunities for girls and women (to increase achievement motivation among girls and women), including sports in military training (to increase military preparedness and the fitness of soldiers), and staging the Olympic Games (to build international goodwill and unity).

Functionalist theory generally leads to the conclusion that sports are popular in society because they maintain the values that preserve stability and order in social life. For example, in the United States it is assumed that sports are popular because they teach people to feel comfortable in tasks that involve competition, goal achievement, and teamwork under the supervision of an authority figure. Furthermore, because functionalist theory leads to the conclusion that sports build the kind of character valued in society, it supports policies that recommend the growth of competitive sport programs, the development of coaching education programs, the establishment of training centers for top-level athletes, and increased surveillance and drug testing to supervise and control the actions of athletes. In the case of youth sports, functionalist theory supports actions to expand developmental sport programs for children, establish criminal background checks and certification requirements for coaches, and build a sport system that trains young people to become elite athletes.

Overall, functionalist theory inspires research questions about the ways that sports contribute to the development of individuals and society as a whole.

Many people reading this book are attracted to functionalist theory because they like its emphasis on the positive aspects of sports in society. People in positions of power in society also favor functionalist theory because it is based on the assumption that society is organized for the equal benefit of all people and therefore should not be changed in any dramatic ways. The notion that the system operates effectively in its present form is comforting to people with power because it discourages changes that might jeopardize their privilege and influence. Because the functionalist approach is popular, it is important to know its weaknesses.

Weaknesses of Functionalist Theory

Functionalist theory has three major weaknesses. First, it does not acknowledge that sports are social constructions that take diverse forms as they are created and defined by people interacting with one another. Functionalists see sport as a relatively stable social institution that always serves specific functions in societies. Such an approach overlooks the diversity of sports, the extent to which sports promote the interests of powerful and wealthy people, and the possibility that sports may sometimes produce or reproduce social outcomes that actually disrupt the smooth functioning of society.

Second, functionalist theory leads to overstatements about the positive effects of sport in society and understatements about its negative effects. For example, it does not help us understand that women in society are disadvantaged when sports are organized in ways that legitimize the use of physical power to dominate others. Nor does it help us understand how sport teams in high schools and colleges can undermine social integration when status systems favor athletes and lead other students to feel marginalized.

"Ya know, I can't relate to these kids' music anymore, but at least I know we'll always have sports in common."
··········

FIGURE 2.1 Functionalists overlook the fact that sports can create divisions in society as well as unifying people.

Third, functionalist theory is based on the assumption that the needs of all groups within a society are the same. This overlooks the existence of real differences and conflicts of interest in society and cases when sports benefit some groups more than others (see figure 2.1). This limits our understanding of difference, conflict, and the dynamics of change in societies.

CONFLICT THEORY: SPORTS ARE TOOLS OF THE WEALTHY

Conflict theory focuses on the ways that sports are shaped by economic forces and used by economically powerful people to increase their wealth and influence. It is based on the ideas of Karl Marx and his assumption that every society is a system of relationships and social arrangements that are shaped by economic factors. In the case of capitalist societies, relationships and social arrangements are organized around money, wealth, and economic power.

Conflict theorists assume that all aspects of social life revolve around economic interests and that people who control the economy use their power to coerce and manipulate workers and their families to accept the existence of economic

inequality as a natural feature of social life. Conflict theorists often focus their research on **class relations**—that is, *social processes that revolve around who has economic power, how that power is used, and who is advantaged or disadvantaged by the economic organization of society.* Studies of class relations focus on the consequences of social inequality in all spheres of social life.

The primary goal of conflict theory is similar to the goal of functionalist theory: to develop a general theory that explains the organization and operation of all societies. Conflict theory emphasizes that economic power in capitalist societies is entrenched so deeply that progressive changes are possible only if workers become aware of the need for change and take action to make major changes in the organization of the economy. Sports, they argue, focus the attention and the emotions of the have-nots in society on escapist spectator events that distract them from the economic issues and policies that reproduce their own powerless in society. Therefore, sports, especially mass spectator sports, are organized and sponsored by wealthy people and large corporations because they perpetuate capitalist values and a lifestyle based on competition, production, and consumption. When people accept capitalist values without question, sport becomes an opiate in society—an aspect of culture that deadens their awareness of economic exploitation and perpetuates the privilege and positions of people who control wealth and the economy.

Conflict Theory and Research on Sport

Conflict theory is often used by people who ask questions and do research on the connection between sports and the dynamics of power and privilege in society. This research will be used in subsequent chapters as we discuss the following issues:

1. Why do athletes become so alienated from their bodies that they will risk injury and physical well-being to play sports? This issue is discussed in chapters 4–7.

2. How are sports related to socioeconomic inequality in society? This issue is discussed in many chapters—especially chapters 8–11.
3. What happens to sports when they become commercialized? This issue is discussed in chapters 10–13.
4. How do wealthy and economically powerful people use sports to further their interests? This issue is discussed in chapters 10–13.

Like functionalist theory, conflict theory is based on the assumption that society is a social system. However, it focuses on "needs of capital" rather than "general system needs." Therefore, conflict theorists explain that a capitalist society cannot survive and grow without exploiting workers for the sake of boosting financial profits. Conflict theorists also focus on the ways that sports perpetuate the unequal distribution of power and economic resources in societies. Therefore, they often identify the negative consequences of sports and conclude that radical changes are needed in sports and society if fairness and justice are to prevail. Only when those changes are made will sports become sources of expression, creative energy, and physical well-being.

Many people in countries with capitalist economies are not comfortable with the assumptions and conclusions of conflict theory. They say that the negative tone of conflict theory does not fit with their ideas about sports or society, and they are uneasy with conclusions that call for radical changes in the current structure and organization of sports and society. However, conflict theory calls attention to important economic issues in sports and to forms of inequality that create conflict and tensions in society as a whole.

Using Conflict Theory in Everyday Life

Conflict theory focuses on the need to change the organization of sports and society. The goal of these changes is to give workers, including athletes, control over the conditions of their work. Problems in society and sports are attributed to the lack of power possessed by workers. Therefore, conflict theorists support policies and programs that regulate or eliminate profit motives in sports and increase the control that athletes have over the conditions of their own sports participation. They also support policies that increase the element of *play* in sports and decrease the element of *spectacle* because it is designed to generate commercial profits. More play and less spectacle, they argue, would turn sport participation into a liberating and empowering experience for the masses of people in society.

In terms of specific issues, conflict theorists favor players' unions, organizations that represent the interests of people in communities where tax money is being used to subsidize wealthy pro-sport team owners, and radical changes in the overall organization of sports. Ideally, public resources would be used to sponsor sports designed to promote fun, fitness, and political awareness; spectator sports would exist for enjoyment in local communities rather than as tools for creating celebrity athletes and financial profits for a few wealthy people.

Weaknesses of Conflict Theory

Conflict theory has three major weaknesses. First, it ignores the possibility that sports in capitalist societies may involve experiences that empower individuals and groups. Conflict theorists talk about sports being organized to maximize the control that wealthy people have over everyone else in capitalist societies. They see sports as activities through which athletes learn to define their bodies as tools of production, becoming alienated from their bodies in the process. This approach does not acknowledge that sport can take forms that could serve the interests of the have-nots in society, and it denies that sport participation can be a personally creative and liberating experience that inspires people to make economic changes that promote equality and eliminate the vast income and power gaps that currently exist in capitalist societies.

Second, conflict theory assumes that all aspects of social life are economically determined—that is, shaped by the profit motive and the needs of capital in society. It focuses on the inherent conflict between the economic haves and have-nots, and assumes that the haves always use their power to control and exploit the have-nots who live in a state of powerlessness and alienation. These assumptions lead conflict theorists to focus exclusively on economic factors when they study sports. However, many sports, especially those emphasizing recreation and mass participation, are not completely shaped by economic factors or the interests of wealthy people in society.

Third, conflict theory underestimates the importance of gender, race, ethnicity, age, sexuality, disability, and other factors when it comes to explaining how people identify themselves, relate to others, and organize the social worlds in which they live. Therefore, it often leads people to overlook the possibility that power and inequalities in society are based on factors other than social class and economic differences.

> Today, sports has come to pit race against race, men against women, city against city, class against class, and coach against player.
>
> —Frank Deford, sportswriter (1998)

Beyond the Needs of Society

Functionalist theory and conflict theory both focus on societal needs and how sports are related to the satisfaction of those needs. They give us a view of sports in society from the top down, but they don't tell us about sports in everyday life or the ways that people are active agents who participate in the processes through which sports and society are organized and changed. They ignore a view of society from the bottom up—from the perspectives of people who "do" sports and give meaning to them in their everyday lives. They also ignore the complexities of everyday social life and that sports and society are social constructions that emerge as people struggle over what is important in their lives and determine

how their collective lives should be organized. The theories that focus attention on these issues are critical, feminist, and interactionist theories.

CRITICAL THEORY: SPORTS ARE SITES WHERE CULTURE AND SOCIAL RELATIONS ARE PRODUCED AND CHANGED

Critical theory comes in a variety of forms, and it offers a useful alternative to functionalist and conflict theories.[2] It is based on the following three assumptions: (1) Groups and societies are characterized by shared values *and* conflicts of interest, (2) social life involves continuous processes of negotiation, compromise, and coercion because agreements about values and social organization are never permanent, and (3) values and social organization change over time and from one situation to another as there are shifts in the power balance between groups of people in society. Forms of critical theory were developed as people realized that societies are too messy, complex, and fluid to be described as

---

[2]This chapter is a basic introduction to using theories, and the goal is to provide a general explanation and overview of the valuable work done by scholars using forms of critical theories to study sports in society. I attempt to pull together major ideas from the following theories and theoretical frameworks: *neo-Marxist theories, traditional critical theory* (combining ideas of Marx and Freud), *hegemony theory* (based on the ideas of Antonio Gramsci), *cultural studies* (as it focuses on cultural production, power relations, ideology, and identity), *poststructuralism* (based on cultural studies, semiotics, and forms of literary analysis dealing with language and the construction of power, meaning, representation, and consciousness under the unstable, fluid, fragmented, and often contradictory conditions of postmodern life), and *queer theory* (combining feminist cultural studies and poststructuralism). None of these frameworks is specifically identified, but I do highlight issues raised by people using these approaches.

"systems" and that it is not possible to develop a general explanation of social life that is applicable to all societies at all times in history.

Instead of focusing on society as a whole, critical theory focuses on the diversity, complexity, contradictions, and changes that characterize social life as it is lived and experienced by people who interact with one another and struggle over how to organize their lives together. Although critical theory comes in many forms, it focuses primarily on the following topics: (1) the processes through which culture is produced, reproduced, and changed, (2) the ways that power and social inequalities are involved in processes of cultural production, reproduction, and change, and (3) the ideologies that people use as they make sense of the world, form identities, interact with others, and transform the conditions of their lives.

People using functionalist and conflict theories often say that "sport is a reflection of society," but critical theorists explain that in addition to reflecting society, sports are sites where culture and social organization are produced, reproduced, and changed. This makes sports much more than mere reflections of society. This issue is discussed in the box "Sports Are More Than Reflections of Society."

Unlike functionalists or conflict theorists, critical theorists realize that there are many vantage points from which to study and understand social life and that the relationship between sports and society is always subject to change. Therefore, they study sports in connection with changes in (1) the organization of government, education, the media, religion, the family, and other spheres of social life, (2) cultural definitions of masculinity and femininity, race, ethnicity, age, sexuality, and physical (dis)ability, and (3) the visions that people have about what sports could and should be in society.

Critical theory also encourages action and political involvement. It has been developed by scholars dedicated to identifying issues and problems for the sake of eliminating oppression and seeking justice and equity in social life. Critical theory is a valuable tool when identifying and studying specific social problems. People who use it assume that social relationships are grounded in political struggles over how social life should be defined and organized. They study sports to see if they are organized to systematically privilege some people over others. Their goal is to explain how sports have come to be what they are and to inspire new ways to discuss, define, organize, and play sports.

Critical Theories and Research on Sports

Those who use critical theory to study sports generally focus on one or more of the following issues:

1. Whose ideas about the meaning and organization of sports are used to determine funding priorities for sports, who will participate in them, how they will be covered in the media, and how they will be used for social, political, and economic purposes?
2. How are sports and sport experiences influenced by the dynamics of power in social life, and how do sports reproduce patterns of privilege in society?
3. How are sports related to people's ideas about economic success or failure, work and fun, physical health and well-being, gender and sexuality, race and ethnicity, and physical ability and disability, and what is "natural" or "deviant" in society?
4. What are the ways that people struggle over the meaning, purpose, and organization of sports in their lives?
5. When do sports become sites where people challenge, resist, and change prevailing ideas and the organization of social life?
6. What are the narratives and images that people use to give meaning to sports and their sport experiences?
7. Whose voices and perspectives are represented in the media coverage of sports?

<table>
<tr><td>

reflect on
SPORTS
</td><td>

Sports Are More Than Reflections of Society
</td></tr>
</table>

When people study the social aspects of sports, they often say that "sports are reflections of society." This is true in that many aspects of society are represented in its sports. However, sports also are social constructions that have an impact on relationships and social organization in society as a whole. For example, sports in the United States are organized in ways that represent outdated ideas and beliefs about masculinity and gender relations. Therefore, they do not reflect the forms of masculinity and gender relations that are increasingly accepted by many people. At the same time, sports have been a social arena in which women athletes have displayed physical strength and skills that have long been defined as unacceptable in most spheres of life. As a result, new ideas about femininity and body image have become widely accepted in the rest of society.

The notion that sports are more than a reflection of society can be demonstrated by shifting our attention to another sphere of social life, such as the family. Like sports, families are reflections of society, but our personal experience tells us that everyday family life is more than that. Families are created by particular groups of people as they interact with one another in their own ways, depending on their abilities, resources, and definitions of family life. Of course, the opportunities and choices available to the members of any particular family are influenced by factors in the larger society, including laws, economic conditions, government policies, and cultural beliefs about the actions and interactions of husbands, wives, parents, and children.

This means that similarities will exist between families in the same society, but it does not mean that all families are destined to be the same or to be mere reflections of society. Society serves as a context in which individuals produce, define, and reproduce specific family practices. But real families are sets of relationships produced by people as they determine how they want to live with one another. This is why your family is different from many other families. At times, families even become sites (social locations) where people raise questions about the meaning and organization of family life.

These questions often force people to rethink larger issues related to cultural values and the organization of society as a whole. In this way, what we do in our families becomes part of a general process of cultural production, the impact of which goes far beyond family life. For example, between 1960 and 1980 some

8. What strategies can be used to empower people who are regularly excluded from the processes through which sports are organized and played?

One or more of these issues are discussed in each of the following chapters. Critical theories inspire interesting and provocative research on sports in society. This research is based on the assumptions that sports are complex and sometimes internally contradictory activities and that there are no simple or general rules for explaining them as social phenomena. The intent of research based on critical theories is to understand the structure, organization, and meaning of particular sports in connection with changing relationships in and between groups that possess different amounts of power and resources over time and from one place to another.

Critical theorists also study how sports affect the processes through which people develop and maintain **cultural ideologies**—that is, the webs of ideas and beliefs that they use to explain and give meaning to the social world and their experiences in it. They want to know how and when sports become sites for questioning and changing dominant ideologies related to social class, gender, sexuality, race and ethnicity, age, and (dis)ability. One of the mottos of critical theorists is a statement made by C. L. R. James, a native of Trinidad people in American families asked questions about the rights of women within the legal structures of marriage and family. These questions fostered discussions that ultimately led to changes in divorce laws. These changes encouraged people to rethink other ideas about intimate relationships, gender, gender equity, parent–child relationships, children's rights, and even the organization and delivery of community-based social services. In other words, families have always been much more than mere reflections of society. They are the creations of human beings and sites for producing and changing social worlds and the ways of life that constitute culture.

This means that human beings are active agents in the construction of social worlds—not just in their immediate family lives but also in the larger social settings in which they live. Through the things they do in their families, people reproduce and occasionally change the culture and society of which they are a part. So it is with sports and all the people associated with sports. People construct sports as they interact with each other. No voice comes out of the sky and says, "I am society, and sports shall reflect my image." Social conditions clearly influence the structure and dynamics of sports, but within the parameters set by

those conditions, people can change sports or keep them as they are. It is even possible for people to create and define sports in ways that differ from or even defy dominant ideas and norms and, in the process, to turn sports into activities that contradict the culture and society of which they are a part.

This way of thinking about sports in society recognizes that sports can have both positive and negative effects on participants, that people define and create sports in many different ways, and that sports are involved in reproducing and changing culture. This makes sports important in a sociological sense. Instead of being mirrors that simply reflect society, they are the actual "social and cultural stuff" out of which society and culture come to be what they are. When we understand this, we become aware of our capacity as agents of cultural production and social change. This helps us realize that we are not victims of society, nor are we destined to do sports as they are portrayed in the images promoted by Coca-Cola, Nike, or Budweiser. We can create new and different forms of sports, if we think critically about the contexts in which we live and learn how to work with others to change them. *What do you think?*

in the West Indies, who learned to play cricket after the British colonized his homeland. James said, "What do they know of cricket who only cricket know?" (James, 1984, preface). Critical theorists would answer this question by saying, "We know nothing about sports if sports is all we know." This means that if we want to know about and understand sports, we must also know about the social and cultural contexts in which sports are created, maintained, and changed.

Using Critical Theory in Everyday Life

Critical theory is based on a desire to understand, confront, and transform aspects of social life that

involve exploitation and oppression. Critical theorists emphasize that changes in sports depend on more than simply shifting the control of sports to the participants themselves, because many of those participants accept sports as they are and know little about sport forms that have different meanings, purposes, and organizational structures. Therefore, critical theorists emphasize the need for multiple and diverse forms of sport participation in society. This, they claim, would increase participation, diversify the stories told about sports, and add to the voices represented in those stories. As a result, sports would become more humane and democratic, and less subject to the exclusive control of any particular category

Rare air.

I love kids.
I love to see them running,
jumping and laughing.
But what hurts is to know
that the air they breathe
places them at risk.

That's why I'm involved with
Earthjustice Legal Defense Fund,
A group of lawyers who have
taken it to the courts to protect
our environment for over 25 years.

Recently, the Legal Defense Fund pushed
for regulations to protect the millions of
children who suffer from breathing polluted
air. In response, powerful industry groups
got together to fight these new standards,
turning their backs on public health.

Now the pressure is on and Earthjustice
Legal Defense Fund is back in the courts,
defending everyone's right to clean air.

You don't have to be a lawyer (or 6'5") to
get involved. Just call with your contribution
and help clear the air.

1-800-584-6460

E A R T H J U S T I C E
LEGAL DEFENSE FUND

The nonprofit law firm for the environment.
(Formerly the Sierra Club Legal Defense Fund)

Lisa Leslie photo by Jeff Katz

Critical theory calls attention to the possibility that sports can be sites for transforming social life. In a rare form of activism as an athlete, WNBA player Lisa Leslie supported cultural transformation when she endorsed EARTHJUSTICE Legal Defense Fund in the 1990s. However, the NBA told Leslie and EARTHJUSTICE to stop using this ad because it was "political." It is permissible to use sport images to sell products and promote corporate logos, but it is not permissible to promote ideas that might challenge the status quo. (*Source:* Provided by EARTHJUSTICE) of people. This is exciting or threatening, depending on one's willingness to view and experience sports in new and different ways.

Weaknesses of Critical Theory

There are two general weaknesses associated with most forms of critical theory.

First, most critical theory does not provide clear guidelines for determining when sports reproduce culture and social organization and when they become sites for resisting and transforming them. Although research has identified cases when sports were believed to be sites for resistance, critical theorists don't outline the criteria they use to determine when resistance occurs and the conditions under which it is most likely to create enduring changes in sports and the organization of social life. This is partly because most critical theorists focus on specific problems and don't think in terms of changing social systems as much as creating the processes through which previously underrepresented people can participate in social life. They explain that all knowledge is situation specific; therefore, there is no single way to explain or solve all social problems. This is a useful approach when dealing with a particular problem, but it does not provide guidelines for determining when oppositional actions are most effective and when they are most likely to produce changes that go beyond particular situations and problems.

Second, because critical theory emphasizes the need for actions that disrupt current forms of social organization, there is a tendency among those who use it to see value in all actions that violate prevailing norms or oppose prevailing ideas; this is especially true when critical theorists study the actions of marginalized or powerless people in society. However, prevailing norms are not always unfair or oppressive, and the interests of marginalized or powerless people are not always based on concerns about fairness and justice. It is important to respect the voices and creative potential of people who are marginalized or oppressed, but it is not politically wise to assume that the disruptive actions of all people and groups have equal value when it comes to making progressive changes in social life. Critical theorists do not provide the criteria needed to identify the characteristics of effective forms of resistance. Therefore, they cannot assess the value of change-producing strategies from one situation to the next.

Third, some critical theories use vocabularies that are confusing and make it difficult to merge different critical ideas into theoretical frameworks that expand our knowledge of the strategies that, under certain conditions, are most likely to produce progressive change.

FEMINIST THEORY: SPORTS ARE GENDERED ACTIVITIES

Feminist theory is based on the assumption that knowledge about social life requires an understanding of gender and gender relations. It has grown out of a general dissatisfaction with intellectual traditions that base knowledge on the values, experiences, and insights of men and do not take seriously the values, experiences, and insights of women. Feminist theory explains the ways that women have been systematically devalued and oppressed in many societies, and they emphasize that gender equity is a prerequisite for social development and progress.

Many scholars in the sociology of sport use critical feminist theory as they study issues of power and the dynamics of gender relations in social life.[3] Critical feminists focus on issues of power and seek to explain the origin and consequences of gender relations, especially those

---

[3]There are many forms of feminist theory, including liberal, radical, gynocentric, socialist, Marxist, black, and postmodern, among others. However, critical feminist theory focusing on issues of ideology, power, and change is most commonly used in the sociology of sport today.

"Feminists say that sports are organized around an ideology that emphasizes domination, conquest, and male superiority. Isn't that ridiculous?!"
....

FIGURE 2.2 Refusing to acknowledge the contributions of feminist theories leads people to overlook important and sometimes obvious aspects of sports.

that privilege men over women and some men over other men (see figure 2.2). They study the ways that gender ideology (that is, ideas and beliefs about masculinity and femininity) is produced, reproduced, resisted, and changed in and through the everyday experiences of men and women.

Critical feminist research has shown that sports are *gendered activities*, in that their meaning, purpose, and organization are grounded in the values and experiences of men and celebrate attributes associated with dominant forms of masculinity in society (Birrell, 2000; Burstyn, 1999). Therefore, in the world of sports, a person is defined as "qualified" as an athlete, a coach, or an administrator if he or she is tough, aggressive, and emotionally focused on competitive success. If a person is kind, caring, supportive, and emotionally responsive to others, he or she is qualified only to be a cheerleader, a volunteer worker for the booster club, or an assistant in marketing and public relations. These latter qualities, often associated with femininity and weakness, are not valued in most sport organizations.

Critical Feminist Theory and Research on Sports

Critical feminist theory emphasizes the need to critique and transform the culture and organization of sports, so that they represent the perspectives and experiences of women as well as men in society. Critical feminists argue that ideological and organizational changes are needed before there can be true gender equity in sports or society as a whole.

Studies based on critical feminist theory generally focus on one or more of the following research questions (see Birrell, 2000):

1. In what ways have girls and women been excluded from or discouraged from participating in sports, and how can gender equity be achieved without promoting sports that jeopardize the health and physical well-being of girls and women who play sports?
2. How are sports involved in producing and maintaining ideas about what it means to be a man in society and forms of gender relations that privilege tough and aggressive men over everyone else?
3. How are women and men represented in media coverage of sports, and how do those representations reproduce or resist dominant gender ideology?
4. What strategies effectively resist or challenge the male-centered gender ideology that is promoted and reproduced through most competitive sports?
5. How are sports and sport participation involved in the production of gendered ideas about physicality, sexuality, and the body?

When critical feminists do research, they often focus on whether sports are sites for challenging and transforming oppressive forms of gender relations, including expressions of sexism and homophobia. For many critical feminists, the goal is to change the meaning, purpose, and organization of sports so that caring for and competing *with* others is more important than dominating and competing *against* others (Duquin, 2000).

Using Critical Feminist Theory in Everyday Life

Critical feminist theory has had a major impact on the sociology of sport. It has increased our understanding of sports as a part of culture, and made us aware of gender-related issues in sports. For example, critical feminists focus on questions such as these: Why do many men around the world continue to resist efforts to promote gender equity in sports? Why do some women fear being called lesbians if they become strong and powerful athletes? Why are some men's locker rooms full of homophobia, gay-bashing jokes, and comments that demean women? Why aren't people more concerned about the 40,000 young men who incur serious knee injuries every year as they play football? Why do church-going mothers and fathers take their children to football games and cheer for young men charged and sometimes convicted of physical and sexual assault? Why do many people assume that men who play sports must be heterosexual? Why has there never been an openly gay, active male athlete featured on the cover of *Sports Illustrated*? Why are so many women's high school and college teams called "Lady this" and "Lady that"? These questions, inspired by critical feminist theory deal with issues that affect our lives every day. In fact, if we do not have thoughtful answers to these questions, we really don't know much about sports in society.

Weaknesses of Critical Feminist Theory

Critical feminist theory has some of the same weaknesses of critical theory. Although critical feminists have become increasingly aware of the connections between gender and other categories of experience related to age, race and ethnicity, social class, disability, religion, and nationality,

they have been slow to theorize these connections. Furthermore, there is an urgent need for more research on the sport-related experiences of women of different ages, abilities, religions (for example, Muslim women), and nationalities (Hargreaves, 2000; Walseth and Fasting. 2003).

INTERACTIONIST THEORY: SPORTS ARE GIVEN MEANING AS PEOPLE INTERACT WITH ONE ANOTHER

Interactionist theory focuses on issues related to meaning, identity, social relationships, and subcultures in sports. It is based on the idea that human beings, as they interact with one another, give meanings to themselves, others, and the world around them, and use those meanings as a basis for making decisions and taking action in their everyday lives.

According to interactionist theory, we humans do not passively respond to the world around us. Instead, we actively make decisions about our actions as we consider their potential consequences for us, the people around us, and the social world in which we live. Culture and society, according to interactionists, are produced as patterns emerge in our actions and relationships with others.

According to interactionist theory, our ability to reflect on our actions and relationships with others enables us to develop **identity**—that is, *a sense of who we are and how we are connected to the social world*. Identities are key factors as people interact with one another and construct their social worlds. They are the foundation for self-direction and self-control in our lives. Identities are never formed once and for all time; they change over time as our actions and relationships change, as we meet new people, and as we face new situations.

Research based on interactionist theory helps us understand how people define and give meaning to themselves, their actions, and the world around them. It also helps us understand human beings as choice makers and creators of identities and relationships. Interactionists generally do in-depth research that involves observations of and interviews with people who are members of particular groups or identifiable cultures. The goal of this research is to understand social worlds from the inside—through the perspectives of the people who create, maintain, and change them. Unlike functionalists and conflict theorists, interactionists view culture and society from the bottom up rather than the top down.

Interactionist Theory and Research on Sports

Interactionist theory is often used in research on the experiences of athletes and the ways that athletes define and make sense of their sport participation. A common goal of interactionist research is to reconstruct and describe the reality that exists in the minds of athletes, coaches, spectators, and others involved in sports.

The data collection methods used in this research is designed to gather information about the ways that people define and give meaning to their experiences as they form identities and interact with others. Those who use interactionist theory to study sports focus on the following issues:

1. What are the social processes through which people become involved in sports?
2. How do people come to define themselves and be identified by others as athletes?
3. How do people give meaning to and derive meaning from their sport experience?
4. What happens when athletes retire and make the transition into the rest of their lives?
5. What are the characteristics of sport cultures, how are they created, and how do they influence people's lives on and off the field?

One or more of these issues are discussed in all chapters. This is because interactionist research provides vivid descriptions of sports experiences and the social worlds in which they occur.

Using Interactionist Theory in Everyday Life

Interactionist theory focuses on the meanings and interaction associated with sports and sport participation. It emphasizes the complexity of human action and the need to understand action in terms of how people define situations and give meaning to their experiences as they interact with others. Interactionists generally recommend changes that represent the perspectives and identities of those who play sports. In many cases, this would involve restructuring sport organizations so that participants are given opportunities to raise questions and discuss issues related to the meaning, purpose and organization of the sports they play. Therefore, interactionists would support changes that make athletes more responsible for organizing and controlling their sports.

In the case of youth sports, for example, interactionists would support organizational changes that would give young people opportunities to create games and physical challenges that would more closely reflect their needs and interests, rather than the needs and interests of adults. Interactionists would caution parents and coaches about problems that occur when young people develop sport-related identities and relationships to the exclusion of other identities and relationships and to the point that burnout is likely.

In the case of elite sports, interactionists would support changes that discourage athletes from defining pain and injury as normal parts of the sport experience. Because the use of performance-enhancing substances is connected with issues of identity and the norms that exist in sport cultures, interactionists would argue that the use of these substances can be controlled only if there are changes in the norms and culture of sports; identifying substance users as "bad apples" and punishing them as individuals will not change the culture in which athletes learn to sacrifice their bodies for the sake of the team and their sport.

Weaknesses of Interactionist Theory

Interactionist theory has inspired many informative studies of meaning, identity, interaction, and cultures in sports. However, it has two primary weaknesses. First, it focuses our attention almost

Interactionists study meanings associated with sports and sport participation. Meanings vary from one culture to another. Players in Japanese youth sports give meanings to sports that differ from meanings given to youth sports in other cultures. (*Source:* Jay Coakley)

Social life is complex and is best understood when viewed from multiple perspectives. Each theory in this chapter can be used to ask sociological questions about this scene. Afghan boys (no girls) are playing Little League baseball organized by U.S. ground troops after the U.S. military had heavily bombed Afghanistan as it sought out terrorists. Adult male refugees watch as the soldiers teach the rules and the skills involved in the game. (*Source:* Wally Santana, AP/Wide World Photo)

breaking BARRIERS

Language Barriers
We're Not Handicapped; We Just Can't Hear

Len Gonzales is deaf. But more important, he is head football coach at the California School for the Deaf at Riverside (CSDR). When his team capped its 9–1 season by winning the 2004 championship of the San Joaquin High School League, a reporter asked Gonzales what other teams thought when they lost to CSDR. Gonzales explained that "teams hate to lose to us because they think we're a handicapped team. But we're not handicapped. We just can't hear" (in Reilly, 2004, p. 144).

Coach Gonzales is sensitive to the barriers created when people use the word *handicapped* to refer to physical and mental impairments and disabilities. Clear definitions of these words are necessary to understand and evaluate theories of disability.

An **impairment** *exists when a person has a physical, sensory, or intellectual condition that potentially limits full participation in social and/or physical environments.* Many people have impairments and, as we get older, impairments generally increase in number and severity. This is part of normal, everyday life. None of us is physically or mentally perfect, and we regularly make personal adjustments to limit the impact of impairments

on our lives. If we are lucky, we have access to technologies that make adjustments more effective. For example, I wear eyeglasses that "correct" my impaired vision. If I were a world-class archer I could be a member of the U.S. Archery Team, despite my impairment. I would face no barriers as long as I was allowed to wear eyeglasses; therefore, I would not have a disability.

An impairment becomes a **disability** only *when accommodations in social or physical contexts are not or cannot be made to allow the full participation of people with functional limitations.* This means that disabilities are created when relationships, spaces, and activities present barriers that limit the opportunities and experiences of people with particular impairments. For example, prior to the late-1990s, if my leg was amputated below the knee and I wore a prosthetic leg and foot, I could not have been a member of the U.S. Powerlifting Team because the International Powerlifting Federation rules stated that "Lifters without two real feet cannot compete in regular contests." This rule created a barrier making me disabled. However, after the rule was changed, the barrier was eliminated and my prosthetic

....

exclusively on relationships and definitions of reality without explaining the ways that interaction and the construction of meaning in sports are influenced by social organization, power, and material conditions in society. Therefore, interactionist research often ignores power dynamics and inequality in connection with sports and sport experiences.

Second, interactionist theory does not provide critical visions of the ways that sports and society could and should be organized. However, many people who use interactionist theory now combine them with critical and critical feminist theories to provide a basis for developing such visions (Coakley and Donnelly, 1999).

IS THERE A BEST THEORETICAL APPROACH TO USE WHEN STUDYING SPORTS?

Each theory discussed in this chapter has made me aware of questions and issues that are important to me, to the people with whom I work and play, and in the social worlds in which I live. In most of my research, I've used combinations of *interactionist, critical,* and *feminist theories* because I've wanted to view sports from the inside, from the perspectives of those who make decisions to play or not to play and who integrate sport participation into their lives in various ways. As I view sports from the inside, I also want to be leg and foot no longer made me disabled as a power-lifter. This shows that disability often has less to do with impairment and ability than with social, environmental, attitudinal, and legal factors (Brittain, 2004; Hargreaves, 2000; Higgins, 1992; Morris, 1996; Oliver, 1996). Therefore, a person may be (dis)abled in one context but not in another (Friedman et al., 2004). Only when there are barriers that exclude or limit people with impairments do disabilities exist.

People become **handicapped** *when others define them as inferior and "unable" due to perceived impairments.* For example, when opposing players defined the football team from CSDR as handicapped, they hated losing to them because it meant that they lost to players who they defined as inferior and unable.

These three definitions are based on critical and interactionist theories. They locate handicaps and disabilities in the social processes through which (a) environments are organized to meet the needs of temporarily able-bodied people, (b) norms (rules) are created that disadvantage people with impairments, and (c) people learn to equate particular impairments with inferiority and inability.

Other definitions, based on medical and psychological theory, explain disability as a characteristic of individuals. Medical–psychological theories locate disability in the physical and cognitive "abnormalities" of individuals and they lead to interventions emphasizing personal coping strategies and assistive technologies. Critical interactionist theories, on the other hand, locate disability in social and cultural barriers that limit participation; they lead to interventions emphasizing the elimination of cultural, organizational, legal, and environmental barriers.

Both approaches are needed, but people too often overlook the need to eliminate barriers. Coping strategies and assistive technologies are crucial for individuals, but eliminating barriers makes disability less relevant for entire categories of people (DePauw, 1997). Leslie Little, a sailor with muscular dystrophy, helps us understand what this means when she says, "Every day is a new adventure when I'm sailing . . . Plus, I'm not disabled when I'm on the water" (www.mdausa.org/publications/Quest/q82water.cfm). The goal therefore is to create social and physical worlds that are like being on the water for Leslie Little.

aware of the social, economic, political, and historical factors that influence access to sport participation and the decisions that people make about sport participation. Critical and critical feminist theories have also helped me think about very practical issues, such as how to vote on proposals to fund new parks or a new stadium for a professional football team. They've helped me assess policies related to sport programs for at-risk youth and to evaluate candidates for coaching jobs at my university. More recently this combination of theories has guided much of my thinking about sports for people with disabilities, as is shown in the box "Breaking Barriers" on pp. 50–51.

Although I have not used *functionalist theory* and *conflict theory* in my research, I have used them to inform my general understanding of sports in society. For example, functionalist theory helps me understand how other people think about sports in society, even though it does not help me identify the social issues and controversies connected with sports in my community and in the sport organizations in which I work with coaches and administrators. Conflict theory alerts me to issues related to social class and economic exploitation as I use *critical theories* to help me understand the dynamics of power in sports and society; the ways that power is related to gender, race, ethnicity, disability, and sexuality;

and the ways that people use ideologies as they explain and give meaning to the world and their experiences.

Overall, my preference for a combination of interactionist, critical, and critical feminist theories is based on my interest in making sport participation more accessible to a wider range of people in society. I am much more interested in increasing choices and alternatives for people in sports than I am in making sports a more efficient means of maintaining the status quo in society (a goal of functionalist theory) or in dismantling sports altogether (a goal of conflict theory). I think that many aspects of the status quo in the United States and other societies are in need of change and that sports are sites at which we can learn strategies for effectively making creative and progressive changes.

Creating alternative ways of doing sports requires an awareness of contemporary sports culture as well as a vocabulary for thinking critically about the future. A combination of interactionist, critical and critical feminist theories provides a guide for developing that awareness and vocabulary and creating new sport forms that offer human beings additional possibilities for physical and social experiences.

My theoretical preferences often conflict with the preferences expressed by some students and people who work for sport organizations. Students who want to work in sport organizations know that most people in those organizations see sports in functionalist terms, so they sometimes prefer functionalist theory. However, I remind them that it is important to understand issues related to power and culture so that they can critically assess organizational policies in terms of their impact on people in the organization and the surrounding community. When I work with coaches and sports administrators, they often tell me that my critical approach has helped them see things in their lives in new and helpful ways.

Finally, I've learned that true empowerment involves enabling people to be critically informed actors so that they can effectively "challenge and

change unequal power relationships" (Mahiri, 1998). As I participate in social worlds, I find that critical, feminist, and interactionist theories can be combined in ways that are especially helpful.

summary

HOW CAN SOCIAL THEORIES HELP US STUDY SPORTS IN SOCIETY?

Theories are tools that enable us to ask questions, identify problems, gather information, explain social life, prioritize strategies to deal with problems, and anticipate the consequences of our actions and interventions. Different theories help us understand sports from different angles and perspectives. In this chapter, we discussed functionalist, conflict, critical, feminist, and interactionist theories.

The purpose of the chapter is to show that each theory provides a framework that we can use as we think about sports in society and make decisions in our own lives. For example, functionalist theory offers an explanation for positive consequences associated with sports and sport involvement. Conflict theory identifies factors related to class relations and economic exploitation in sports. Critical theory shows that sports are connected with culture and social relations in complex ways and that sports change as power and resources shift in social, political, and economic relations in society. Critical feminist theory emphasizes that gender is a primary category of experience and that sports are sites for producing, reproducing, and transforming gender ideology and power relations in society. Interactionist theory helps us understand the meanings, identities, and social relationships associated with sport involvement.

As we use these theories it is important to know their weaknesses. Functionalist theory exaggerates the positive consequences of sports and sport participation because it is based on the assumption that there are no conflicts of interest between groups within society. Conflict theory overstates the importance of social class and economic factors in society, and it focuses most of its attention on top-level spectator sports, which make up only a part of sports in any society. Critical theory provides no explicit guidelines for determining when sports are sites at which resistance leads to progressive transformations in society. Critical feminist theory has not sufficiently explained connections between gender and other categories of experience, including age, race, religion, nationality, and disability. Interactionist theory does a poor job of relating issues of meaning, identity, and experience in sports to general social conditions and patterns of social inequality in society as a whole.

Despite their weaknesses, social theories are helpful as we explore issues and controversies in sports and assess research and ideas about sports in society. We don't have to be theorists to use theory as we organize our thoughts and become more informed citizens in our social worlds.

> See the OLC, www.mhhe.com/coakley9e for an annotated list of readings related to this chapter. The OLC also contains a key concepts list, a review test, and other helpful features.

WEBSITE RESOURCES

Note: Websites often change. The following URLs were current when this book was printed. Please check our website (www.mhhe.com/coakley9e) for updates and additions.

www.mhhe.com/coakley9e Click on chapter 2 for summaries of studies based on some of the theories discussed in this chapter.

www.socsci.mcmaster.ca/w3virtsoclib/theorie.html This site is a research source for information on sociological theory and theorists; it is not sports related, but it provides numerous links to sites around the world.

www.socqrl.niu.edu/FYI/theory.htm This site has valuable links to helpful sites on social theory.

www.tryoung.com/archives/108sports.html This site contains a clear statement of how sports are viewed and analyzed when using a Marxist-based conflict theory as a guiding framework.

www.sussex.ac.uk/Units/CST This is an advanced critical theory site.

www.feminist.org/research/sports2.html This site has special coverage of "Empowering Women in Sports"; this site not only is a good example of applied feminist theories but also highlights the issues that are most important in a feminist analysis of sports.

chapter

3

(Jay Coakley)

STUDYING THE PAST

Does It Help Us Understand Sports Today?

Online Learning Center Resources

Visit *Sports in Society*'s Online Learning Center (OLC) at **www.mhhe.com/coakley9e** for additional information and study material for this chapter, including

- Self-grading quizzes
- Learning objectives
- Related websites
- Additional readings

OF THE THOUSANDS of evils . . . in Greece there is no greater evil than the race of athletes. . . . Since they have not formed good habits, they face problems with difficulty.

—**Euripides, Greek dramatist (fifth century B.C.)**

A complete outline is available online at www.mhhe.com/coakley9e.

THEY WHO LAID the intellectual foundations of the Western world were the most fanatical players and organizers of games that the world has ever known.

—C. L. R. James, Sociologist and West Indian cricket player (1984)

To understand sports today, we need a sense of what physical games and sport activities were like in past times. This chapter presents brief overviews of sport activities in different cultural and historical settings. My intent is *not* to provide an integrated overall history of sports. Such a history would look at the development and organization of physical games and sports across all continents from one cultural group to another over time. This is an ambitious and worthy project, but it is far beyond the scope of this chapter.

This chapter focuses on (1) the ancient Greeks, (2) the Roman Empire, (3) the Middle Ages in parts of Europe, (4) the Renaissance through the Enlightenment in parts of Europe, and (5) the Industrial Revolution through recent times, with special emphasis on the United States. These times and places, often covered in history courses, are familiar to many of us, and they illustrate the ways that sports are connected with the social and cultural contexts in which they exist.

The goal of this chapter is to show that our understanding of sports depends on what we know about the social lives of the people who created, defined, played, and integrated them into their everyday experiences. As critical theory suggests, it is important to study the ways that people use their power and resources as they create and participate in physical activities.

When we view sports history in this way, dates and names are less important than what we can learn about social life by studying sports and physical activities at particular times and places.

UNDERSTANDING HISTORY WHILE STUDYING SPORTS IN SOCIETY

Many people think about history as a chronological sequence of events that gradually leads to a better and more "modern" society. Many historical accounts are full of references to societies that are traditional or modern, primitive or civilized, underdeveloped or developed, preindustrial or industrial. This terminology implies that history is always moving forward so that societies are improving and becoming more developed.

This approach to history enables some people to feel superior as they assume that they are the most modern, civilized, and developed people in the world. However, this conclusion is not historically accurate. In the case of sports, there are literally thousands of "histories" of physical activities among thousands of human populations in different places around the world. These histories sometimes involve patterns of changes that do not provide evidence of becoming more civilized or highly developed.

Research shows that physical activities and games have existed in all cultures. The specific forms of these activities and games, along with the meanings that people gave to them, were shaped through struggles over the meaning, purpose, and organization of the activities; over who should play them; and over the ways that they were to be integrated into people's lives. To say that physical activities and games over the years have evolved to fit a pattern of progress, or modernization, is to distort the life experiences of people all over the world (Gruneau, 1988). There may be fewer contrasts among the sports and games that different people play today, but this does not mean that sports are evolving to fit a grand scheme for how physical activities *should* be organized or what they *should* mean in people's lives (Maguire, 1999). Instead, it means that certain nations and corporations now have the power to define, organize, and present through the media particular sport forms for the entire world to see. Therefore, when beach volleyball was included as a new sport in the 1996 Summer Olympics in Atlanta it was an example of wealthy countries and corporations using their power to promote a sport through international travel, social connections, and access to resources. When beach volleyball became commercially attractive to the International Olympic Committee, it was not part of a general pattern of progress in the history of sports.

Therefore, this chapter is not a story of progress. Instead, it is a sample of stories about people at different times and places struggling over and coming to terms with what they want their physical activities to be and how they wish to include them in their lives. There is historical continuity in these processes and struggles, but continuity does not mean that history follows some grand plan of progress. Progressive changes do occur, but they are the result of actions taken by collections of people with the power to make them happen and then keep them from returning to what they were in the past.

SPORTS VARY BY TIME AND PLACE

People in all cultures, past and present, have used human movement in their ritual life. As we study history, we see that few cultures have had physical games that resemble the highly organized, rule-governed competitive games that we describe as sports today.

In prehistoric times, for example, there were no sports as we know them today. Physical activities were tied to the challenge of survival and religious beliefs (see figure 3.1). People hunted for food and sometimes used their physical abilities to defend themselves, establish social control and power over others, and appease their gods. These activities involved acting out events that had important meaning in their lives, and even though they were organized games, they were inseparable from sacred rituals and ceremonies. They often were performed as religious worship, and their outcomes were determined by religious necessity as much as the physical abilities of the people involved (Guttmann, 1978).

The first forms of organized games among humans probably emerged from this combination of physical challenges and religious rituals. From what we can tell, these games were connected

SIDELINES

"You weren't playing soccer last night—it won't be invented for another million years!"

FIGURE 3.1 In early human history, there were no sports as we define them. Physical activities occasionally were included in community and religious rituals, but their purpose probably was to appease the gods, rather than to entertain or build character.

closely with the power structures and belief systems of the societies in which they existed, and they usually re-created and reaffirmed dominant cultural practices in those societies. On rare occasions, they served as sources of protest or opposition to the status quo in particular groups or societies.

Historical and cultural variations in physical activities remind us that all cultural practices, even sports, serve a variety of social purposes. This raises the question of how the definition and organization of sports in any society promote the interests of various groups within that society. People create sport activities within the constraints of the social worlds in which they live. Therefore, everyone does not have an equal say in how those activities are defined and organized. People with the most power generally have the greatest impact on how sports are defined, organized, and played in a group or society. Sport activities do not totally reflect their desires, but sports represent the interests of the powerful more than they represent the interests of others.

This approach to studying sports in history is based on critical theory. It calls attention to the existence and consequences of social inequality in societies. Inequalities related to wealth, political power, social status, gender, age, (dis)ability, and race and ethnicity have always had a significant impact on how sport activities are organized and played in any situation. We will pay special attention to these in the following discussions of times and places.

CONTESTS AND GAMES IN ANCIENT GREECE: BEYOND THE MYTHS (1000 B.C. TO 100 B.C.)

The games played by early Greeks (circa 900 B.C.) were grounded in mythology and religious beliefs. They usually were held in conjunction with festivals that combined prayer, sacrifices, and religious services, along with music, dancing, and ritual feasts. Competitors in these games were from wealthy and respected Greek families. They were the only people who had the money to hire trainers and coaches and the time and resources to travel. Sport events were based on the interests of able-bodied young males. They usually consisted of warrior sports such as chariot racing, wrestling and boxing, javelin and discus throwing, foot racing, archery, and long jumping. Violence, serious injuries, and even death were commonplace in comparison with today's sports (Elias, 1986; Kidd, 1984, 1996b, Mendelsohn, 2004). Greek women, children, and older people occasionally played sports in these festivals, but they never played in the games held at Olympia.

The locations and dates of the Greek festivals also were linked to religious beliefs. For example, Olympia was chosen as one of the festival sites because it was associated with the achievements and activities of celebrated Greek gods and mythological characters. In fact, Olympia was dedicated as a shrine to the god Zeus about 1000 B.C. Although permanent buildings and playing fields were not constructed until 550 B.C., the games at Olympia were held every four years. Additional festivals involving athletic contests were also held at other locations throughout Greece, but the Olympic Games became the most prestigious of all athletic events.

Women were prohibited from participating as athletes or spectators at the Olympic Games. However, they held their own games at Olympia. These games, dedicated to the goddess Hera, the sister-wife of Zeus, grew out of Greek fertility rites. When women participated in sports, it was often to demonstrate their strength, sexually attract men, and eventually bear strong warrior children (Perrottet, 2004). In general, physical prowess was inconsistent with dominant definitions of femininity among the Greeks. Women were seen as inferior to men, they could neither vote nor be Greek citizens, wives were the property of their husbands and often isolated in their homes, and women did not participate in political or economic affairs.

The men's games at Olympia took on political significance as they grew in visibility and popularity. Winning became connected with the glory of city-states, and physically skilled slaves and young men from lower-status backgrounds were forced to become athletes, or wealthy patrons and government officials hired them to train for the Olympics and other games. Victories brought cash prizes and living expenses for many of these slaves and hired athletes. Contrary to widely believed myths about the amateur ideals held by the Greeks, many male athletes saw themselves as professionals. During the second century B.C., they even organized athletic guilds enabling them to bargain for rights, gain control over the conditions of their sport participation, and enjoy material security when they retired from competition (Baker, 1988).

Greek athletes were so specialized in their physical skills that they made poor soldiers. They engaged in warrior sports, but they lacked the generalized skills of warriors. Furthermore, they concentrated so much on athletic training that they ignored intellectual development. This evoked widespread criticism from Greek philosophers, who saw the games as brutal and dehumanizing and the athletes as useless and ignorant beings.

Representatives of the modern Olympics have romanticized and perpetuated myths about Greek games to connect the modern games to a positive legacy. However, the ancient games were not tributes to mind–body harmony. Athletes were maimed and killed in the pursuit of victories and the rewards that came with them (Mendelsohn, 2004; Perrottet, 2004); fairness was not as important as honor; and athletic contests were connected with a cultural emphasis on warfare.

Physical contests and games in Greek culture influenced art, philosophy, and the everyday lives of people wealthy enough to train, hire professionals, and travel to events. However, Greek contests and games were different from organized competitive sports of today (see the box "Dominant Sport Forms Today," pp. 60–61). First, they were grounded in religion; second, they lacked complex administrative structures; third, they did not involve measurements and record keeping from event to event. However, there is one major similarity: They often reproduced dominant patterns of social relations in the society as a whole. The power and advantages that went with being wealthy, male, young, and able-bodied in Greek society shaped the games and contests in ways that limited the participation of most people. The definitions of excellence used to evaluate performance even reflected the abilities of young males. This meant that the abilities of others were substandard by definition—if you could not do it as a young, able-bodied Greek man did it, then you could not do it the right way.

> Just as the dominant class writes history, so that same class writes the story of sport.
>
> —James Riordan, social historian and former soccer player (1996)

ROMAN CONTESTS AND GAMES: SPECTACLES AND GLADIATORS (100 B.C. TO A.D. 500)

Roman leaders used physical contests and games to train soldiers and provide mass entertainment spectacles. They borrowed events from Greek contests and games, but they focused athletic training on preparing obedient soldiers. They were critical of the Greek emphasis on individualism and specialized physical skills that were useless in battle. Because Roman leaders emphasized military training and entertainment, the contests and games during the first century A.D. increasingly took the form of circuses and gladiatorial combat. Chariot races were the most popular events during Roman spectacles.

Wealthy Romans recruited slaves as charioteers. Spectators bet heavily on the races, and when they became bored or unruly, the emperors passed around free food and tickets for prizes to prevent outbreaks of violence. This strategy pacified the crowds and allowed the emperors to use events to celebrate themselves and their power. Government officials throughout the Roman Empire used similar events to control people in their regions.

As the power and influence of the Roman Empire grew, spectacles consisting of contests and games became increasingly important as diversions for the masses. By A.D. 300, half the days on the Roman calendar were public holidays because slaves did most of the work. Many Romans held only part-time jobs, if they worked at all. Activities other than chariot races and boxing matches were needed to attract and distract people.

reflect on SPORTS   Dominant Sport Forms Today
What Makes Them Unique?

The organized competitive sports so popular today are very different from the physical activities and games played in the past. Allen Guttmann's study of sport activities through history shows that today's *dominant sport forms* (DSFs) have seven interrelated characteristics, which have never before appeared together in physical activities and games. These characteristics are the following:

1. *Secularism.* Today's DSFs are not directly linked to religious beliefs or rituals. They are sources of diversion and entertainment, not worship; they are played for personal gains, not the appeasement of gods; and they embody the immediacy of the material world, not the mysticism of the supernatural.

2. *Equality.* Today's DSFs are based on the ideas that participation should be open to everyone regardless of family or social background and that all contestants in a sport event should face the same competitive conditions.

3. *Specialization.* Today's DSFs involve athletes dedicated exclusively to participation in a single event or position within an event. Excellence is defined in terms of specialized skills, rather than all-around physical abilities.

4. *Rationalization.* Today's DSFs consist of rules that regulate the conditions of participation and rationally controlled strategies and training methods guided by "sport sciences."

Dominant sport forms today emphasize quantification. Performances are timed, measured and recorded. The clock is crucial, and digital scoreboards now show times in hundredths of seconds. (*Source:* David Biene; photo courtesy of Ossur)

5. *Bureaucratization.* Today's DSFs are governed by complex organizations and officials that control athletes, teams, and events; enforce rules; organize events; and certify records.
6. *Quantification.* Today's DSFs involve precise timing and measurements and statistics in the form of scores and performance data that are recorded and used as proof of achievements.
7. *Records.* Today's DSFs emphasize setting and breaking records. Performances are compared over time to determine personal, national, and world records.

One or some of these characteristics have been present in the physical activities and games of previous historical periods, but not until the nineteenth century did all seven appear together in *modern* sports (Dunning, 1999; Dunning and Sheard, 1979; Guttmann, 1978). This does not mean that today's organized competitive sports are superior to the games and activities of past times and other places. It means only that they are different in the ways they are organized and integrated into people's lives. Sociologists study these differences in terms of their connections with culture and society. Table 3.1 summarizes Guttmann's comparison of games, contests, and sport activities in each of the places and time periods discussed in this chapter. The table shows that the dominant sport forms that exist in many postindustrial societies today are different from the "sports" played by people in times past. However, it does not explain why the differences exist or the social implications of the differences.

The seven characteristics identified by Guttmann are not found in all sports today. Sports are social constructions. They change as social, economic, and political forces change and as people seek and develop alternatives to dominant sport forms. The DFFs played fifty years from now are likely to have characteristics that are different from these seven characteristics. *What do you think?*

Table 3.1 Historical comparison of organized games, contests, and sport activities*

Characteristic	Greek Contests and Games (1000 B.C. to 100 B.C.)	Roman Contests and Games (100 B.C. to A.D. 500)	Medieval Tournaments and Games (500 to 1300)	Renaissance, Reformation, and Enlightenment Games (1300 to 1800)	"Modern" Sports
Secularism	Yes and no**	Yes and no	Yes and no	Yes and no	Yes
Equality	Yes and no	Yes and no	No	Yes and no	Yes
Specialization	Yes	Yes	No	Yes and no	Yes
Rationalization	Yes	Yes	No	No	Yes
Bureaucratization	Yes and no	Yes	No	No	Yes
Quantification	No	Yes	No	Yes and no	Yes
Records	No	No	No	Yes and no	Yes

*Modified version table 2 in Guttmann (1978).
**This characteristic existed in some sports during this time, but not in others.

Bearbaiting, bullbaiting, and animal fights were added to capture spectator interest. Men and women were forced into the arena to engage in mortal combat with lions, tigers, and panthers. Condemned criminals were dressed in sheepskins to battle partially starved wild animals. Gladiators, armed with various weapons, were pitted against each other in gory fights to the death. These spectacles achieved two purposes for Roman rulers: They entertained an idle populace and disposed of socially "undesirable" people such as thieves, murderers, unruly slaves, and Christians (Baker, 1988).

Some Romans criticized these spectacles as tasteless activities, devoid of value. However, their criticisms were based not on concerns for human rights, but on their objections to events in which wealthy people and peasants mingled together. Other than some outspoken Christians, few people criticized spectacles on moral or humanitarian grounds. The spectacles continued until the Roman economy went into a depression and wealthy people moved from cities, taking their resources with them. As the Roman Empire deteriorated, there were not enough resources to support spectacles (Baker, 1988).

Women were seldom involved in Roman contests and games. They were allowed in the arenas to watch and cheer male athletes, but few had opportunities to develop athletic skills. Within Roman families, women were legally subservient to and rigidly controlled by men. As in ancient Greece, few women pursued interests outside the household.

Although local folk games and other physical activities existed in the Roman Empire, we know little about how they were organized and played and what they meant in people's lives. The gladiatorial spectacles did not capture everyone's interest, but they attracted considerable attention in major cities.

Roman contests and games differed from organized sports today because they sometimes were connected with religious rituals, and they seldom involved quantifying athletic achievements

or recording outstanding accomplishments (review the box "Dominant Sport Forms Today," pp. 60–61).

TOURNAMENTS AND GAMES IN MEDIEVAL EUROPE: SEPARATION OF THE MASTERS AND THE MASSES (500 TO 1300)

Sport activities in medieval Europe consisted of folk games played by local peasants, tournaments staged for knights and nobles, archery contests, and activities in which animals were brutalized (Dunning, 1999). The folk games, often violent and dangerous and sometimes organized to maim or kill animals, emerged in connection with local peasant customs. The tournaments and archery contests were linked with military training and the desire for entertainment among the feudal aristocracy and those who served them.

Some of the local games of this period have interesting histories. As Roman soldiers and government officials traveled around Europe during the fourth and fifth centuries, they built bathing facilities to use during their leisure time. To loosen up before their baths, they engaged in various forms of ball play. Local peasants during the early medieval period used the Roman activities as models and developed their own forms of ball games. They often integrated these games into local religious ceremonies and cultural events. For example, tossing a ball back and forth sometimes represented the conflict between good and evil, light and darkness, or life and death. As the influence of the Roman Catholic Church spread through Europe during the early years of the medieval period, these symbolic rituals were redefined in terms of Catholic beliefs. In these cases, sports and religion were closely connected with each other.

During most of the medieval period, the Roman Catholic Church accepted peasant ball games, even though they occasionally involved violence. Local priests encouraged games by

AT YOUR *fingertips* For more information on sports and religion, see Chapter 15.

opening church grounds on holidays and Sunday afternoons. As games became part of village life, people played them during festive community gatherings that also involved music and dancing. These local ball games contained the roots for many contemporary games such as soccer, field hockey, football, rugby, bowling, curling, baseball, and cricket. However, the games in peasant villages had little structure and few rules. Local traditions guided play, and traditions varied widely from one community to the next.

The upper classes in medieval Europe paid little attention to and seldom interfered in the leisure of peasants. They saw peasant games and festivities as safety valves defusing mass social discontent. The sport activities of the upper classes were distinctively different from those of the peasants. Access to specialized equipment and facilities allowed them to develop early versions of billiards, shuffleboard, tennis, handball, and jai alai. Ownership of horses allowed them to develop forms of horse racing, while their stable hands developed a version of horseshoes. On horseback, they also participated in hunting and hawking. Owning property and possessing money and servants clearly influenced their sports.

Through the medieval period, the most popular sporting events among upper-class males were tournaments consisting of war games to keep knights and nobles ready for battle. Some tournaments resembled actual battlefield confrontations. Deaths and serious injuries occurred, victors carried off opponents' possessions, and losers often were taken as prisoners and used as hostages to demand ransoms from opposing camps. Later versions of tournaments had lower stakes, but they also involved injuries and occasional deaths. Toward the end of the medieval period, colorful ceremonies and pageantry softened the warlike tournaments, and entertainment and chivalry

took priority over military preparation and the use of deadly violence.

Women during this time seldom participated in physical games and sport activities. Gender restrictions were grounded in a male-centered family structure and Catholic teachings that women were inferior to men. A woman's duty was to be obedient and submissive; however, peasant women were involved in some of the games and physical activities that occurred during village festivals.

Among the aristocracy, gender relations were patterned so that men's and women's activities were clearly differentiated. Aristocratic women did little outside the walls of their dwellings, and their activities seldom involved rigorous physical exertion for fun. They sometimes engaged in "ladylike" games, but, because women were subject to men's control and often viewed as sex objects and models of beauty, their involvement in active pursuits was limited. Feminine beauty during this time was defined in passive terms: The less active a woman, the more likely she was perceived as beautiful.

Even though some sports in Europe and North America today can trace their roots back to the medieval period, the contests and games of that time were not much like today's organized sports. They lacked specialization and organization, they never involved the measurement or recording of athletic achievements, and they were not based on a commitment to equal and open competition among athletes from diverse backgrounds (review the box "Dominant Sport Forms Today," pages 60–61). Historian Allen Guttmann has vividly described this last point:

> In medieval times, jousts and tournaments were limited to the nobility. Knights who sullied their honor by inferior marriages—to peasant girls, for instance—were disbarred. . . . Peasants reckless enough to emulate the sport of their masters were punished by death. (1978, p. 30)

Although some characteristics of medieval sport activities can be seen in the games and

SIDELINES

"Why don't we settle this in a civilized way? We'll charge admission to watch!"
············

FIGURE 3.2 Dominant sport forms in many societies have been organized to celebrate a particular form of masculinity, emphasizing aggression, conquest, and dominance.

contests of the Renaissance, Reformation, and Enlightenment, these later periods involved important social transformations, which shaped the forms and meanings of physical activities and games.

THE RENAISSANCE, REFORMATION, AND ENLIGHTENMENT: GAMES AS DIVERSIONS (1300 TO 1800)

The Renaissance

Wars throughout Europe during the fourteenth and fifteenth centuries encouraged some monarchs, government officials, and church authorities to increase their military strength and prohibit popular peasant pastimes. Those in authority felt that the peasants should spend less time playing games and more time learning to defend the lands and lives of their masters. But, despite the pronouncements of bishops and kings, the peasants did not readily give up their games. In fact, the games sometimes became rallying points for opposition to government and church authority.

At the time that peasants were subjected to increased control in many locations, the "scholar-athlete" became the ideal among the affluent. This "Renaissance man" was "socially adept, sensitive to aesthetic values, skilled in weaponry, strong of body, and learned in letters" (Baker, 1988, p. 59).

Throughout the Renaissance period, women had relatively few opportunities to be involved in tournaments and sport activities. Although peasant women sometimes played physical games, their lives were restricted by the demands of work in and out of the home. They often did hard physical labor, but they were not encouraged to engage in public games and sports that called attention to their physical abilities.

Upper-class women sometimes participated in bowling, croquet, archery, and tennis, but involvement was limited because women during this time were seen as "naturally" weak and passive. Some of these "Renaissance women" may have been pampered and put on figurative pedestals, but men maintained their power by tightly controlling the lives of women, partly by promoting the idea that women were too fragile to leave the home and do things on their own. The code of chivalry, popular during this time, had less to do with protecting women than with reproducing patriarchy and privileging men.

The Reformation

During the Protestant Reformation, growing negative attitudes about games and sport activities discouraged participation, especially where Calvinist or Puritan beliefs were popular. For example, between the early 1500s and the late 1600s, English Puritans tried to eliminate or control leisure activities, including physical contests and games. They were devoted to the work ethic and viewed sports in this way:

> [Sports] were thought to be profane and licentious—they were occasions of worldly indulgence that tempted men from a godly life; being rooted in pagan and popish practices, they

were rich in the sort of ceremony and ritual that poorly suited the Protestant conscience; they frequently involved a desecration of the Sabbath and an interference with the worship of the true believers; they disrupted the peaceable order of society, distracting men from their basic social duties—hard work, thrift, personal restraint, devotion to family, [and] a sober carriage (Malcolmson, 1984, p. 67).

The primary targets of the Puritans were the pastimes and games of the peasants. Peasants didn't own property, so their festivities occurred in public settings and attracted large crowds. This made them easy for the Puritans to condemn and control. The Puritans did their best to eliminate festivities, especially those scheduled on Sunday afternoons. They objected to the drinking and partying that accompanied the games and disapproved of physical pleasure on the Sabbath. The physical activities and games of the affluent were less subject to Puritan interference. Activities such as horse racing, hunting, tennis, and bowling took place on the private property of the wealthy, making it difficult for the Puritans to enforce their prohibitions. As in other times and places, power relations had much to do with who played what activities under what conditions. Despite Puritan influence and social changes affecting the economic structure and stability of English village life, many peasants maintained participation in games and sports.

During the early 1600s, King James I formally challenged Puritan influence in England by issuing *The King's Book of Sports*. This book, reissued in 1633 by Charles I, emphasized that Puritan ministers and officials should not discourage lawful recreational pursuits among English citizens. Charles I and his successors ushered in a new day for English sporting life. They revived traditional festivals and actively promoted and supported public games and sport activities. Consequently, cricket, horse racing, yachting, fencing, golf, and boxing became highly organized during the late 1600s and the 1700s, although participation patterns reflected and reproduced social class divisions in society.

In colonial America, Puritan influence was strong. Many colonists were not playful people; hard work was necessary for survival. However, as the lifestyles of the colonists became more routine and free time became available, Puritan beliefs became less important than the desire to include games from the past into everyday life. Towns gradually abandoned the Puritan "blue laws" that prohibited games and sports, and this made it possible for leisure activities, including sports, to grow in popularity.

During this time, the games of Native Peoples were not directly affected by Puritan beliefs and cultural practices. Native Peoples in the East and Northeast continued to play the games that had been part of their cultures for centuries. In fact, sports and sport participation have many histories across North America. This alerts us to the issue of whose voices and perspectives are represented in historical accounts of games, contests, and sports. The box "Lessons from History" emphasizes that most historical accounts do not represent the experiences and perspectives of those who lack the power to tell their stories and make them a part of dominant culture.

> **Sports may be among the most powerful human expressions in all history.**
> —Gerald Early, Distinguished Professor, Washington University, St. Louis (1998)

The Enlightenment

During the Enlightenment period (1700 to 1800), many games and sport activities in parts of Europe and North America began to resemble sport forms that we are familiar with today. With some exceptions, they were no longer grounded in religious ritual and ceremony; they involved a degree of specialization and organization; achievements sometimes were measured; and records

Lessons from History
Who Tells Us About the Past?

History is much more than a chronological series of events. Historical research should take us inside the lives of people who have lived before us. It should give us a sense of how people lived and gave meaning to their experiences and the events of their times. Therefore, when we study sports, it is important to be aware of whose voices and perspectives are used to construct historical accounts, as well as whose voices and perspectives are missing. This is the case when it comes to the physical activities, games, and sports of Native Peoples in North America.

Prior to the arrival of Columbus and other Europeans, the histories of Native Peoples were often kept in oral rather than written forms; they were local and personal histories. It was not until the late eighteenth century that accounts of the lives and cultures of Native Peoples were recorded in English. However, those accounts were written by Europeans with limited knowledge of the diverse languages, cultures, and complex social arrangements that made up the lives of nearly 500 unique cultural groups of Native Peoples in North America. This diversity was obscured by general accounts describing the lives and customs of "Indians," as if all native cultures were the same. These accounts provide limited information about the diverse games and sports played by Native Peoples. In many cases, accounts were written after the lives of Native People had been disrupted and influenced by European explorers and settlers. This history provides little information about the ways that traditional games and sports were played and integrated into the diverse cultures that existed in North America.

Europeans were seldom able to observe authentic expressions of traditional native cultures. When they did make observations, it was often under strained circumstances, and Native Peoples were unwilling to reveal their customs while being watched by outsiders who often viewed them as "oddities." The fact that the most important games in native cultures were connected with religious rites made it even less likely that Europeans would be allowed to observe them in authentic, traditional forms or understand the meanings associated with them. By the time Native Peoples provided their own historical accounts in English, their cultures had changed in appreciable ways, and few people were willing to listen to their stories and publish them in forms that were considered "real history." In the meantime, experiences and meanings were lost forever.

That we know so little about the many histories of games and sports among Native Peoples demonstrates that social, political, and economic forces influence our knowledge of sport history. For example, if we wish to understand the importance of an event, such as the establishment of the Iroquois National Lacrosse Team in 1983, we must know the following:

- The histories and cultures of specific native societies and the six nations of the Iroquois Confederation
- The formal and informal political relationships between native societies and the U.S. government
- The experiences of Native Peoples in North America as they struggled to maintain their cultures while others tried to strip them of their dignity, language, religion, and customs

Knowing these things enables us to begin an investigation of the significance of the Iroquois National Lacrosse Team in terms of those who formed it, participated on it, and followed its matches.

The scarcity of information based on the perspectives of those who lack power diminishes our awareness of sports history around the world. As social historian James Riordan (1996 p. vii) has said, "Just as the dominant class writes history, so that same class writes the story of sport." Therefore, when our knowledge of the past does not go beyond the experiences and perspectives of those with the power to tell their own stories, it is always incomplete. In the worst case, such stories reproduce stereotypes and justify discrimination against those with little power. This is why some people call for more cultural diversity in courses taught in high schools and universities. *What do you think?*

occasionally were kept. Furthermore, the idea that events should be open to all competitors, regardless of background, became increasingly popular. This commitment to equality and open participation gave rise to world-changing political revolutions in France and the United States.

However, sport activities during the Enlightenment period were different from the dominant sport forms of today in at least one important respect: they were defined strictly as diversions—as interesting and often challenging ways to pass free time. People did not see them as being useful for athletes in particular or society in general. No one thought that sports and sport participation could change how people developed or acted or how social life was organized. Therefore, there were no reasons for people to organize sport activities for others or create organizations to govern sports. A few people formed clubs, and they occasionally scheduled contests with other groups, but they did not form leagues or national and international associations. But things changed dramatically during the Industrial Revolution.

THE INDUSTRIAL REVOLUTION: THE EMERGENCE OF ORGANIZED COMPETITIVE SPORTS (1780 TO 1920)

It is an oversimplification to say that the organized competitive sports of today are simply a product of the Industrial Revolution. They clearly emerged during the process of industrialization, but they were actually social constructions of people themselves—people who played their games and sport activities while they coped with the realities of everyday life in rapidly changing families, communities, and societies. Of course, the realities of everyday life included economic, political, and social forces, which either enabled or constrained people, depending on their position in society.

The development of factories, the mass production of consumer goods, the growth of cities, and increased dependence on technology marked the Industrial Revolution. It involved changes in the organization and control of work and community life and was generally accompanied by an increase in the number of middle-class people in the societies where it occurred. The Industrial Revolution first began in England around 1780 and became a part of life after 1800 in other European countries, the United States, and Canada.

The Early Years: Limited Time and Space for Sports

During the early years of the Industrial Revolution, few people had regular opportunities to play games and sport activities. Farm and factory workers had little free time. The workdays, even for many child workers, were long and tiring. People in cities had few open spaces where they could play sports. Production took priority over play. Industrialists and politicians were not concerned with providing parks and public play spaces. Working people were discouraged from gathering in large groups outside the workplace. The authorities perceived such gatherings as dangerous because they wasted time that could be used for work. Additionally, they provided opportunities for workers to organize themselves and challenge the power of factory owners (Goodman, 1979; Mrozek, 1983).

In most industrializing countries, the clergy endorsed restrictions on popular games and gatherings. Ministers preached about the moral value of work and the immorality of play and idleness. Many even banned sports on Sundays and accused anyone who was not totally committed to work of being lazy. Work, they preached, was a sign of goodness. Not everyone agreed, but working people had few choices. For them, survival depended on working long hours, regardless of what they thought about work, and they had little power to change the conditions of their lives.

Early Americans had few play spaces. Playing in the streets was banned, but immigrant children were creative. Reformers who thought that introducing young boys to team sports would Americanize them and prepare them to be productive factory workers initiated the organized playground movement. When laws were passed to clear streets for commercial traffic, children like these would be chased home or arrested. (*Source:* McGraw-Hill)

In most countries, games and sport activities during this period existed *despite* the Industrial Revolution, *not* because of it. People in small towns and farm communities still had opportunities to play games and sport activities during their seasonal festivities, holidays, and public ceremonies. Most city people had few opportunities to organize their own games and sports, although the super wealthy lived highly publicized "lives of leisure" (Veblen, 1899). Among the working classes, sport involvement seldom went beyond being spectators at new forms of commercialized sport events. These events varied by nation, but urban workers in most European and North American cities watched a combination of cricket, horse racing, boxing and wrestling, footraces, rowing and yachting races, cockfighting, bullbaiting, and circus acts, among other things.

Rules prohibiting crowds were suspended when people participated in controlled commercialized spectator events. Local neighborhood events that attracted crowds were often defined as illegal, but organized commercial events were approved in most industrial societies, even when they attracted large crowds. These events were controlled and organized to benefit the interests of those with power and money in society.

Some sport participation did occur among urban workers, but it was relatively rare during the early days of the Industrial Revolution. In the United States, for example, it usually was limited to activities such as bowling and billiards, played mostly by men. The constraints of work and the lack of money and facilities made it difficult for working-class people to engage in anything but informal games and physical activities. Exceptions to this pattern were rare.

Similarly, African slaves, who made up 20 percent of the U.S. population during the early 1800s, had few opportunities to engage in any games or sports beyond what slaveholders permitted. The dancing and other physical activities that occurred in slave quarters emphasized cooperation and community spirit—qualities required for survival (Wiggins, 1994). These activities took forms based on African traditions and efforts to cope with the experience of slavery. According to former slave and noted abolitionist Frederick Douglass, the games and holidays that the slaveholders permitted "were among the most effective means . . . of keeping down the spirit of insurrection among the slaves" (in Ashe, 1993, p. 10).

Between 1800 and 1850, some people in Europe and North America became concerned about the physical health of workers. This concern was partly based on the awareness that workers were being exploited and partly on the recognition that weak and sickly workers could not be productive. Consequently, there were growing calls for new open spaces and funding of "healthy" leisure pursuits. Personal fitness was highly publicized, and there was an emphasis on calisthenics, gymnastics, and outdoor exercises. In the United States, these activities did not always include sports, but they definitely excluded hanging around pool halls, bowling alleys, and bars. Furthermore, the abolition of slavery made it possible for 4.5 million former slaves to participate in a range of sport activities. In the middle of the nineteenth century, there was an emphasis on exercise and fitness among some people. Exercises were often done by groups of men who worked together or had other community-based relationships with one another. There was no emphasis on organized competition or keeping records of achievements.

The emergence of formally organized competitive sports would require more than increased freedom and limited support for healthy leisure activities, but this was the time during which the foundations for organized sports were established. In discussing more recent issues related to sports in society, we focus on events in the United States.

The Later Years: Changing Interests, Values, and Opportunities

Over the past 150 years of U.S. history, there has been a growing emphasis on organizing all spheres of social life in a rational and systematic manner. For example, during the mid-1800s, newly formed clubs sponsored and controlled sport participation. Club membership usually was limited to wealthy people in urban areas and college students at exclusive eastern schools. However, the competitions attracted spectators from all social classes. The YMCA, founded in England in 1844 and in the United States in 1851, was a clublike organization that had a less exclusive membership policy. During the late 1800s it began to change the popular notion that physical conditioning through exercise and sports was anti-Christian.

The games and sport activities of working-class people did not usually occur under the sponsorship of clubs or organizations, and they seldom received publicity. An exception to this was baseball, a sport played by men from diverse social-class backgrounds. Working-class male participation in baseball was relatively widespread, and after the Civil War, games were organized, sponsored, and publicized in many eastern and midwestern towns and cities. Leagues were established at various levels of competition, and men's professional baseball became increasingly popular. Professional women's teams existed, but they seldom received the sponsorship needed to grow in popularity. African Americans developed teams and leagues around the country although racism prevented them from playing in many white-dominated towns in the South.

As sport activities became more organized, they generally reinforced existing class distinctions in society. Upper-class clubs emphasized achievement and "gentlemanly" involvement—an orientation that ultimately led to definitions of amateurism. The definition of *amateur*, which first appeared in England, became a tool for excluding working-class people from sports that were organized around the interests of upper-class people (Eitzen, 2003). The activities of the working classes, by contrast, involved local games and commercialized sports—a combination that ultimately led to professionalization. This dual development of amateurism and professionalization occurred in different ways in Europe and North America (Dunning, 1999).

The Seeds of New Meanings   Underlying the growing organization of sport activities in the decades after 1850 was a new emphasis on the seriousness of sports. Instead of defining sports simply as enjoyable diversions, people gradually came to see them as tools for achieving important goals such as economic productivity, national loyalty, and the development of admirable character traits, especially among males. This new way of viewing sports was fueled by changes in every segment of industrial society: the economy, politics, family life, religion, education, science, philosophy, and technology.

The Growth of Organized Sports in the United States: 1880 to 1920   The years between 1880 and 1920 were crucial for the development of organized sports in the United States (Cavallo, 1981; Mrozek, 1983). Wealthy people developed lives of leisure that often included sports, and they used participation in certain sports to prove that they were so successful that they could "waste" time by playing nonproductive games

(Veblen, 1899). Although the wealthy often used sports to reinforce status distinctions between themselves and other social classes, they also influenced how sports were played and organized by others, especially middle-class people whose status aspirations led them to emulate the rich and powerful.

In this way, the upper class influenced the norms for many players and spectators, the standards for facilities and equipment, and the way in which people throughout society defined and integrated sports into their lives. Specifically, wealthy people used their economic resources to encourage others to define sports as *consumer activities* to be played in *proper* attire, using the *proper* equipment in a *proper* facility, and preceded or followed by *proper* social occasions separated from employment and the workplace. Because many people followed these norms, sports became connected with and supportive of the economy. This connection was subtle because sports involved both consumption *and* worklike orientations while being popularly defined as "nonwork" activities, separate from the economy.

The emergence of these ideas about the ways that sports "should be" played was important. It enabled people with power to reproduce their privilege in society without overtly coercing workers to think and do certain things. Instead of maintaining their privilege by being nasty, people with economic power promoted forms of sports that were entertaining and supportive of the values and orientations that promoted capitalist business expansion. Critical theorists have noted that this is an example of how sports can be political and economic activities, even though most people see them as sources of excitement and enjoyment (Gramsci, 1971, 1988; Rigauer, 2000; Sage, 2000).

During the period of 1880 to 1920, middle- and working-class people, especially white males, had new opportunities to play sports. Labor unions, progressive government legislation, and economic expansion combined to improve working and living conditions. The exception to this pattern was African Americans, who faced new forms of racism and segregation beginning in the 1880s as whites sought to continue their oppression of blacks after slavery was abolished. The efforts of unions and social reformers gradually led to more free time and material resources among many white working-class people. As the middle class expanded, more people had resources for leisure and sport participation. The spirit of reform at the turn of the twentieth century also led to the development of parks, recreation programs, and organized playground activities for urban residents, especially boys and young men.

IDEAS ABOUT SPORT PARTICIPATION AND "CHARACTER DEVELOPMENT"   During the early 1900s, opportunities for sport involvement increased, but those opportunities were shaped by factors beyond the interests of the participants themselves. Important new ideas about human behavior, individual development, and social life led to an emphasis on organized competitive sports as "character-building" activities.

Through the 1880s most people believed that the actions and development of human beings were unrelated to social factors. They assumed that fate or supernatural forces dictated individual development and that social life was established by a combination of God's will, necessity, and coincidence. However, these ideas changed as people discovered that the social environment influenced people's actions and that it was possible to change patterns of individual growth and development by altering the organization of society.

This new way of thinking was a crucial catalyst for the growth of modern sports. It made sports into something more than enjoyable pastimes. Gradually, sports were defined as potential educational experiences—experiences with important consequences for individuals, communities, and society. This change, based on behaviorist and evolutionary theories, which were popular at the time, provided a new reason for organizing and promoting sport participation.

For the first time in history, people saw sports as tools for changing behavior, shaping character, creating national loyalty, and building unity in an ethnically diverse population.

People began to think about the meaning and purpose of sports in new and serious terms. For example, some religious groups, later referred to as "muscular Christians" (see chapter 15), suggested a link between physical strength and the ability to do good works; therefore, they promoted sport involvement as an avenue for spiritual growth. Others saw sports as tools for teaching immigrant children lessons that would turn them into contributing members of a corporate–bureaucratic–democratic society. These people also promoted organized playground programs that used team sports to suppress the traditional values of white ethnic groups (Italians, Irish, Germans, Jews, and others) and replace them with an Americanized view of the world. People interested in economic expansion saw organized sports as tools for generating profits by introducing untrained workers to tasks emphasizing teamwork, obedience to rules, planning, organization, and production. Sports, they thought, could create good workers who would tolerate stressful working conditions, obey supervisors, and meet production goals through teamwork on factory assembly lines.

In large part, organized sports became important because people with power and money believed that sport participation could be used to train loyal, efficient, and patriotic workers for the sake of capitalist expansion and the status of the United States as a world power. Sports were socially constructed and defined in ways that were believed to promote this type of character development. In the United States, this was done through new "Americanized" sports such as football, baseball, and basketball. Soccer, very popular among many central and southern European immigrants during the early 1900s, was believed to undermine patriotism by perpetuating potentially dangerous links with "foreign" cultures. Therefore, those who encouraged the development of American identities among new immigrants viewed soccer as dangerous and un-American. These views were so strong that it took nearly eighty years for soccer to overcome its stigmatized status and gain acceptance in the United States. (See the OLC for a discussion of this issue, www.mhhe.com/coakley9e.)

ORGANIZED SPORTS AND IDEAS ABOUT MASCULINITY AND FEMININITY   The new belief that sports built character was applied primarily to males. The people who organized and sponsored new programs thought they could use sports, especially team sports, to tame what they perceived as the savage, undisciplined character of young, lower-class males from Irish and southern European immigrant families. Their intent was to create obedient citizens and productive workers. At the same time, they used sports to counteract what they believed to be the negative influence of female-dominated home lives on the development of young males from middle- and upper-class backgrounds. Their goal was to turn "overfeminized" boys from affluent families into assertive, competitive, achievement-oriented young men who would become effective leaders in business, politics, and the military. In these ways, contemporary sports were heavily grounded in the desire of people with power and money to control the working classes, while preparing their own sons to inherit their positions of power and influence (Burstyn, 1999; Kidd, 1996b).

Although women's sport participation increased between 1880 and 1920, many sport programs ignored females. Organizers and sponsors did not see sport participation as important in the character development of girls and women. They sometimes included girls with boys in organized games at playgrounds, but they discouraged sex-integrated sports among children nearing the age of puberty. It was widely believed that if boys and girls played sports with one another, they would become good friends and lose their interest in being married, having children,

and maintaining beliefs in male superiority and female inferiority.

When boys were taught to play sports on playgrounds in the early 1900s, girls were told to sit in the shade and preserve their energy. Medical doctors during this time warned that playing sports would sap the energy that young women needed to conceive and bear healthy children. Luther Gulick, who shaped the recreational philosophy of the YMCA at that time, wrote, "It is clear that athletics have never been either a test or a large factor in the survival of women; athletics do not test womanliness as they test manliness" (1906, p. 158). Gulick also felt that strenuous activities were harmful to the minds and bodies of females. This was the gender ideology of the time.

Organized activities for girls often consisted of domestic science classes to make them good wives, homemakers, and mothers. When playground organizers provided opportunities for girls to play games and sports, they designed activities that would cultivate "ladylike" traits, such as poise and body control. This is why so many girls participated in gymnastics, figure skating, and other "grace and beauty" sports (Burstyn, 1999; Hart, 1981). Another goal of the activities was to make young women healthy for bearing children. Competition was eliminated or controlled so that physical activities emphasized personal health, the dignity of beauty, and good form. In some cases, the only reason games and sports were included in girls' lives was to give them the knowledge they would need to introduce sports to their future sons.

Limited opportunities and a lack of encouragement did not prevent women from participating in sports, but they certainly restricted their involvement (Vertinsky, 1994). Some middle- and upper-class women engaged in popular physical exercises and recreational sport activities, but apart from limited intercollegiate games and private tournaments, they had few opportunities to engage in formal competitive events. The participation of girls and women from lower-income

Leisure activities among wealthy people in the early twentieth century included sports. However, physical activities and sports for girls and women often stressed balance and coordination, which were defined as "ladylike" qualities. Girls and women were often trained to be graceful and coordinated so that they might become "ladies." (*Source:* McGraw-Hill)

groups was restricted to informal street games, a few supervised exercise classes, and annual "field days" in public schools when girls had an opportunity to run short races and compete in other events that would not be too physically taxing. Ideas about femininity changed between 1880 and 1920, but traditional gender ideology and many misconceptions about the physical and mental effects of strenuous activities on females prevented the "new woman" of the early twentieth century from enjoying the same participation opportunities and encouragement received by males (Lenskyj, 1986). Medical beliefs supported this ideology by providing "scientific evidence" showing that women's bodies could not tolerate vigorous activities. These faulty beliefs and studies damaged the health of women during these years (Vertinsky, 1987).

ORGANIZED SPORTS AND IDEAS ABOUT SKIN COLOR AND ETHNICITY   After the Civil War, some African Americans became involved in sports. Most participation occurred in segregated settings. This was especially true as whites established new forms of segregation and racism, designed to slow the changes that threatened long established social relationships organized around white privilege. Whites in both northern and southern states became increasingly uncomfortable with the prospect of more open forms of race relations.

This led them to draft "Jim Crow laws" that clearly divided people into categories of "white" and "black" and restricted the rights and opportunities of African Americans and all people who were not officially classified as "white." Definitions of who counted as white changed over time as courts made decisions on the ancestral origins of Italians, Greeks, Armenians, and others. Definitions of who was black varied by state but the general rules was that any black ancestor made a person black, no matter what they appeared to be. This has since come to be known as the "one-drop rule," meaning that only one drop of "black blood" made a person black (Davis, 2001).

Whites during this time (1890s to 1950s) increasingly believed that blacks were intellectually and physically inferior beings. During the early twentieth century, white scientists at Harvard and other prestigious universities published flawed studies "proving" white superiority and black inferiority. As this racist ideology became more deeply embedded in the dominant culture of the United States, many whites came to view black athletes as a curiosity. When some African Americans demonstrated skills in certain sports, whites quickly developed biological and genetic explanations for those skills. Therefore, many whites saw the achievements of blacks as "proof" that people with dark skin were less evolved than whites and had animal-like characteristics making them successful in sports that did not require intelligence. This racial ideology became so deeply ingrained in U.S. culture that it continues to influence sport participation choices and ideas about race and sport performance in the twenty-first century. (This and related issues are covered in chapters 9 and 10).

White ethnics during this time (1880–1920) also experienced discrimination limiting sport participation and forcing them to play their native games in ethnically segregated clubs. Public schools became the settings in which many young men from Irish, Scandinavian, German, Jewish, Italian, Greek, Armenian, Spanish, Chinese, and other ethnic groups came to learn, enjoy, and excel in "American sports" and drop their passion for soccer.

ORGANIZED SPORTS AND IDEAS ABOUT AGE AND DISABILITY   Aging involves biological changes, but the connection between aging and sport participation depends largely on the social meanings given to those changes. Developmental theory in the early 1900s emphasized that all growth and character formation occurred during childhood and adolescence. Therefore, it was important for young people to play sports, but older people were already "grown ups" and no longer needed the character-building experiences provided by sports.

Medical knowledge at the time also discouraged older people from engaging in sports. Strenuous activities were thought to put excessive demands on the heart and organs in aging bodies. This did not prevent some older people from playing certain sports, but it did prevent the establishment and funding of organized sport programs for older people. Furthermore, when older people were physically active, they participated by themselves or in age-segregated settings.

People with observable physical or mental impairments were denied opportunities to play sports and often told that strenuous physical activities were bad for their well-being. During this time, widely accepted definitions of mental and physical disability gave rise to fears and prejudices that led many people to think it was dangerous to allow people with disabilities to become physically active or excited. Therefore, programs to build their bodies were discouraged. This meant that people born with certain disabilities were isolated and destined to be physically inactive; obesity and problems caused by a lack of physical activity shortened their life expectancy. People with "acquired disabilities," usually those injured in war or accidents, were treated with physical therapy in the hope of some degree of rehabilitation. As explained in the "Breaking Barriers" box (p. 75), sports for most people with disabilities did not exist until after World War II.

"Other" Barriers
They Found It Hard to Be Around Me

Danny was twenty-one years old, a popular and able-bodied rugby player. Then came the accident, the amputation of his right arm just below the shoulder, the therapy, and eventually, getting back with friends. But reconnecting with friends after suddenly acquiring a disability isn't easy. Danny describes his experience with these words: "A lot of them found it very difficult . . . to come to terms with it . . . And they found it hard to be around me, friends that I'd had for years" (in Brittain, 2004, p. 437).

Chris, an athlete with cerebral palsy and one of Danny's teammates on the British Paralympic Team, explains why his friends felt uncomfortable: "They have very little knowledge of people with a disability and [they think that] if I leave it alone and don't touch them and don't get involved, then it's not my problem" (in Brittain, 2004, p. 437). Chris raises a recurring issue in the history of disability: What happens when people define physical or intellectual impairments as "differences" and use them to create "others" who are distinguished from "us normals" in social worlds?

Throughout history, people with disabilities have been described by words inferring revulsion, resentment, dread, shame, and a world of limitations. In Europe and North America, it took World War II and thousands of returning soldiers impaired by injuries before there were widespread concerns about the words used to describe people with disabilities. Language has changed so that people with intellectual disabilities now have opportunities to participate in the Special Olympics, and elite athletes with physical disabilities may qualify for the Paralympics ("para" meaning *parallel with*, not *paraplegic*). Words like *retard*, *spaz* (spastic), *cripple*, *freak*, *deaf and dumb*, *handicapped*, *gimp*, and *deformed* have largely been abandoned. However, they are not gone, and people with disabilities are still described as "others"—such as "she's a quad," "he's a CPer," "they're amputees," and "what a retard!"

Improvements have occurred, but when people with disabilities are defined as "others," encountering disability raises questions about personal vulnerability, aging, and mortality. It also highlights the faulty assumptions of normalcy around which we construct social worlds. Therefore, those identified as "normal" often ignore, avoid, or patronize people with disabilities, and this subverts the possibility of ever seeing the world through their eyes.

The fear of "otherness" is powerful, and people in many cultures traditionally restrict and manage their contact with "others" by enlisting the services of experts. These include doctors, mental health workers, psychiatrists, healers, shamans, witchdoctors, priests, exorcists, and all professionals whose assumed competence gives them the right to examine, test, classify, and prescribe "normalizing treatments" for "others." Therefore, the history of disability is also the history of giving meaning to difference, creating "others," and using current knowledge to treat "otherness" (Foucault, 1961/1967; Goffman, 1963).

As noted in Breaking Barriers in chapter 2, cultural traditions in the United States have long emphasized treatment-oriented approaches to fix impairments or help people adjust to living with disabilities. Only recently have these approaches been complemented by transformational approaches focused on creating barrier-free social spaces in which disabilities become irrelevant and "others" are no longer created. This is an idealistic project, and it requires actions that disrupt the "normal" order of social worlds. But Jean Driscoll, eight-time winner of the Women's Wheelchair Boston Marathon, has experienced such worlds, and she says that "when sports are integrated, the focus turns from the person with a disability to the guy with a great shot or the gal with a fast 800-meter time. Integration provides the perfect venue where 'actions speak louder than words'" (in Joukowsky and Rothstein, 2002b, p. 28). And I would add that interactionist theory helps us understand that words are the foundation for action.

SINCE 1920: STRUGGLES CONTINUE

By 1920 major connections between sports and American society had been firmly established. Sports were a growing part of people's everyday lives, and they were linked to major social institutions such as the family, religion, education, the economy, the government, and the media. Since 1920 the rate of change and the expansion of the visibility and importance of sports in people's lives have intensified. The past eight decades have been a time of many "firsts" in U.S. sports. They have also been a time for continuing struggles over the following:

1. The meaning, purpose, and organization of sports
2. Who plays sports under what conditions
3. How and why sports are sponsored

As explained in chapter 1, sports are social constructions *and* contested activities. Therefore, we can outline social trends and patterns in recent history by focusing on issues and events related to these three realms of struggle. They serve as useful reference points for discussing social history, and I use them to guide my choice of materials in the following chapters. They also provide a useful framework for understanding patterns and trends during the twentieth century.

Table 3.2 highlights events related to major struggles and changes in sports, providing a feel for the social side of what has happened in recent sports history. Of course, the timing, dynamics, and outcomes of these struggles and changes were related to larger historical events and trends such as wars, economic recessions, suburbanization, the growth of universities, the civil rights and women's movements, the development and expansion of the electronic media and other technologies, globalization, and the growing concentration of corporate power and influence around the world. (For a list of specific events and trends, see the OLC at www.mhhe.com/coakley9e).

AT YOUR *fingertips*   For more information on sports as contested activities and social constructions, see pages 10–11, 13.

Connections between the recent history of sports and these trends and events are too complex to discuss in this chapter. But it is possible to outline some of the major struggles that have occurred since 1920.

Struggles over Meaning: Is Soccer Subversive?

Sports have always had multiple meanings, and these meanings change over time. For example, national identity is a central realm of meaning connected with sports in the United States. Since 1920 certain sports and athletes have been associated with "Americanness." Through the 1960s, baseball was described as "America's pastime" and associated with apple pie and motherhood. Men and women played baseball through the 1930s, but after World War II, it became primarily a men's game and has remained that way ever since; and women turned to softball. This is one of many examples illustrating that the meaning of sports changes as ideas about gender change.

In the 1960s, football emerged as the classic American sport. It emphasized strength, power, confrontation, and strategy—all of which were consistent with dominant values and cultural orientations during the cold war between the United States and the Soviet Union. Men played football and defended turf, just as men in the military defended the United States from communist threats. College football became increasingly visible during the 1960s as baby boomers filled classrooms in record numbers, college administrators used football as a public relations tool, and many students used it as a ritualized occasion for escaping coursework.

During the twentieth century, sports clearly were linked to political and racial ideologies. At the 1936 Olympic Games in Berlin, Hitler and the Nazi Party used the games to promote their ideas about the superiority of the "Nordic race." This historic photo shows a German official giving the Nazi salute and Jesse Owens, the African American sprinter who won four gold medals during the games, giving the U.S. salute. Owens's success challenged Hitler's ideas about Nordic—that is, white—supremacy in sports. (*Source:* USOC Archives)

The sons of immigrants played both baseball and football as they sought to be assimilated into American society. Sports such as rugby and soccer, born in England and nurtured in Europe, were never associated with national identity in the United States in the same way that baseball and football were. Soccer teams and leagues came and went during much of the twentieth century, but the meaning of soccer was generally associated with ethnic communities, workers seeking to form labor unions, or wealthy people emulating European culture. It was not until the 1970s and 1980s that soccer gained popularity among boys and girls in white, middle-class families. But soccer remains more of an international game than an American game in the minds of most people, and it has never been tied to national identity among more than a small segment of the U.S. population. Soccer is no longer seen as subversive, but few people born in the United States line up to buy season tickets to men's or women's professional soccer games, even after the U.S. women's team won the World Cup in 1999. Additionally, Senator John Kerry, the Democrat Party presidential candidate in 2004 deliberately avoided talking about being a former varsity

Table 3.2   U.S. social history time line, 1920–1995

Since 1920 thousands of sports organizations have come and gone, hundreds of legal decisions have regulated and deregulated sports, and thousands of important struggles have occurred over (1) the meaning, purpose, and organization of sports, (2) who plays sports under what conditions, and (3) how and why sports are sponsored. This selective time line highlights events related to these struggles and the issues and controversies discussed in this book.

1920	The National Football League and a baseball league for black players are formed.
1921	The NCAA sponsors the first national college sport championship (in track and field).
1922	The U.S. Supreme Court rules that professional sports are not a form of "commerce" and exempts them from antitrust laws; the first Women's Olympic Games are held (in response to the exclusion of women in many Olympic events).
1923	The eastern Colored League for black men is founded (goes bankrupt in 1928).
1924	The first live radio coverage of the Olympics is broadcast (from Chamonix, France); the first Deaflympics (called The Silent Games) are held in Paris.
1926	Babe Ruth suffers from gonorrhea that is reported as "stomach cramps" in the media; the American Basketball League for men is formed (goes bankrupt in 1931).
1927	Socialists and communists form the Labor Sports Union of America and sponsor soccer and other sports.
1929	Carnegie Foundation for the Advancement of Teaching publishes a report critical of commercialization and professionalization in college athletics.
1932	The Summer Olympics are held in Los Angeles; Babe Didrikson sets two world records and wins two medals; the Labor Sports Union of America sponsors an alternative Olympics for working people.
1935	African American boxer Joe Louis defeats Italian champion Primo Carnera in a world heavyweight title bout before sixty thousand people in Yankee Stadium.
1936	The Olympic Games are held in Berlin; Jesse Owens wins four gold medals and challenges Hitler's ideas about race and white supremacy.
1939	Little League Baseball is founded; boxing becomes the first sport to receive regular TV coverage.
1943	All-American Girls' Professional Baseball League is founded (dissolved in 1954).
1946	The National Collegiate Athletic Association (NCAA) holds a major conference and drafts a "sanity code" to restore honesty and integrity to intercollegiate athletics; the American Football Conference is formed (goes bankrupt in 1950).
1947	Jackie Robinson signs with the Brooklyn Dodgers to become the first black since the nineteenth century to play Major League Baseball; the first Little League World Series tournament is held.
1948	The last baseball season is played by Negro National League; Stoke Mandeville Games for wheelchair athletes (mostly British war veterans) are held in England to coincide with the Olympic Games in London.
1949	The Ladies Professional Golf Association (LPGA) and the National Basketball Association (NBA) are formed; Mexican American Richard "Poncho" Gonzalez wins the U.S. Open Tennis Championship.
1951	An American Council on Education study reports that college sports are too commercialized and professionalized.
1952	The newly formed Soviet Union competes in the Olympic Games held in Helsinki, Finland; Sports Ambassadors, an evangelical Christian sport organization, is founded.
1953	The Little League World Series is televised for the first time.
1954	The first issue of *Sports Illustrated* is published; the Fellowship of Christian Athletes (FCA) is formed.
1957	Althea Gibson is the first black player to win a title at Wimbledon; ballplayers from Monterrey, Mexico, becomes the first non-U.S. team to win the Little League World Series (they win again in 1958).

Table 3.2 *(Continued)*

1960	Wilma Rudolph wins three gold medals at the Olympic Games in Rome, and Cassius Clay (Muhammad Ali) wins the gold medal in boxing; the American Football League (AFL) is formed; ABC is the first U.S. television company to pay for the rights to broadcast the Olympic Games in Rome ($4 million); the first Paralympic Games for athletes with physical disabilities are held following the Summer Olympic Games in Rome; Charlie Sifford is the first black to play in a professional golf tournament; the NFL Dallas Cowboys are bought for $500,000; the Negro American League ceases operation.
1964	The Olympic Games in Tokyo are the first to be televised; Cassius Clay (Muhammad Ali) wins the world heavyweight boxing title; Billy Mills, an Oglala Sioux from the Pine Ridge reservation, wins Olympic gold medal in the 10,000-meter competition; *Sports Illustrated* publishes its first "swimsuit edition."
1965	The Houston Astrodome, the first fully domed major stadium in the world, opens.
1966	The Major League Baseball Players' Association is formed; Athletes in Action is formed as an extension of the Campus Crusade for Christ.
1967	The first Super Bowl is played; the International Olympic Committee (IOC) defines and bans doping; the average annual salary of Major League Baseball players is $19,000; Muhammad Ali is stripped of his boxing title for "conscientiously objecting" to the Vietnam War and refusing induction into the army; Katherine Switzer registers as "K. Switzer" and runs the all-male Boston Marathon, and men try to physically remove her from the course.
1968	Many black athletes boycott the Olympic Games in Mexico City in protest of racial discrimination; Tommy Smith and John Carlos support the boycott by raising gloved fists and standing barefooted on the victory podium at Olympics; Mexican students protest against using public money for the Olympic Games, and police kill over thirty protestors; Olympic drug testing begins; the first Special Olympics is held for athletes with intellectual disabilities; women athletes in the Olympics are forced to "prove" that they are females by "passing" a chromosome-based sex test; Arthur Ashe becomes the first African American man to win a U.S. Open Tennis title.
1969	The AFL and NFL merge to create one pro-football league; Arthur Ashe and others form the Association of Tennis Professionals to represent players; Poncho Gonzalez defeats Puerto Rican American Charlie Pasarell in the longest match in Wimbledon history.
1970	The first *Monday Night Football* game is played and televised on ABC.
1971	An estimated 294,000 girls play varsity high school sports (1 out of every 27 female students); the Association for Intercollegiate Athletics for Women (AIAW) is formed to organize and administer intercollegiate sports for women; women are officially allowed to run the Boston Marathon for first time.
1972	Title IX, making gender discrimination illegal in schools that receive federal funds, is signed into law by President Richard Nixon; NCAA officials attempt to subvert Title IX; Palestinian terrorists capture eleven Israeli team members at the Olympic Village during the Summer Games in Munich—they kill two and the nine others are killed during a failed rescue attempt.
1973	Billie Jean King defeats Bobby Riggs in a made-for-TV "Battle of the Sexes" tennis match; scholar-activist Harry Edwards publishes the first sociology of sport textbook; the NCAA establishes Divisions I, II, and III and defines all athletic scholarships in Divisions I and II as one-year renewable contracts; tests are developed to detect anabolic steroid use among athletes.
1974	The World Team Tennis is founded; the World Football League is founded (bankrupt in 1975); the NCAA lobbies the U.S. Congress to exclude intercollegiate sports from Title IX law; Little League Baseball forms a softball programs for girls; an American Council on Education report concludes that college sports are too commercialized and professionalized; Lee Elder is first black man to play in The Master's golf tournament.

(Continued)

Table 3.2   U.S. social history time line, 1920–1995 (*Continued*)

1975	President Gerald Ford amends Title IX to clarify that the law does apply to interscholastic and intercollegiate sports because they are educational activities.
1976	The U.S. Supreme Court rules that Major League Baseball players are not permanently owned by teams; the ABA and NBA merge into one pro-basketball league; twenty-nine nations, mostly from Africa and Asia, boycott the Olympic Games in Montreal to protest New Zealand's sporting ties with white supremacist South Africa; the NCAA passes Proposition 48 to expand academic requirements for athletes in Division I schools.
1977	Janet Guthrie is the first woman driver in the Indianapolis 500; the all-male IOC prohibits women from running the 3000-meter race (about 2 miles) to protect women from physical damage; six-time Mr. Olympia bodybuilder Arnold Schwarzenegger poses naked for numerous photos in *After Dark*, a gay magazine.
1978	U.S. Congress passes the Amateur Sports Act, establishing the United States Olympic Committee (USOC) as the central governing body of amateur sports; the North American Society for the Sociology of Sport (NASSS) is founded; three sociology of sport textbooks are published, including the first edition of *Sport in Society: Issues and Controversies*.
1979	The Office for Civil Rights of the U.S. Department of Education defines the legal meaning of Title IX and presents enforcement guidelines; ESPN, an all-sports cable television company goes on air; Stanford University changes its name from the "Indians" to "The Cardinal."
1980	U.S Men's Hockey team defeats the heavily favored Soviet Union team at the height of the cold war and then defeats Finland to win the gold medal at the Winter Olympic Games in Lake Placid, New York, in February; in July the United States and more than fifty other nations boycott the Summer Olympic Games in Moscow because the Soviet Union unilaterally (without United Nations approval) invaded Afghanistan in 1979.
1981	Major League Baseball players hold the first midseason strike (average annual salary for players was about $185,000).
1982	NFL players go on strike for nine weeks (average annual salary for players was about $90,000); the Association for Intercollegiate Athletics for Women (AIAW) dissolved as the NCAA takes over women's sports; the first Gay Games are held in San Francisco; testosterone is added to the IOC banned-substance list; the IOC allows amateur athletes to accept money from sponsors, which enables U.S. athletes to receive corporate money to compete with state-supported athletes in socialist nations.
1983	The United States Football League (USFL) plays it first game (goes bankrupt in 1986).
1984	The Soviet Union and thirteen other nations say they do not trust U.S. security for their teams and boycott the Olympic Games in Los Angeles; the Los Angeles Games were the first to create a profit for the host city, and this intensifies competition among cities bidding to host future games; the U.S. Supreme Court restricts Title IX by ruling that it applies *only* to those programs that directly receive federal money in a school; the Little League Baseball charter is rewritten to allow girls to play (after dozens of lawsuits brought by girls against Little League); the Texas State Legislature approves "no pass, no play" rules governing eligibility in Texas high school sports.
1985	In connection with Super Bowl XIX, ABC sells the first million-dollar minute of advertising in television history.
1986	Lynette Woodward is the first woman to play on a men's pro-basketball team, The Harlem Globetrotters.
1988	U.S. Congress passes the Civil Rights Restoration Act and reaffirms that Title IX applies to entire schools, not just individual programs; Carl Lewis wins the gold medal in the 100-meter dash after the medal is stripped from Canadian sprinter Ben Johnson, who set a world record but tested positive for steroids.

Table 3.2   *(Continued)*

1990	The NCAA passes Proposition 42 to strengthen academic standards in Proposition 48; Olympic sports begin to abolish distinctions between amateur and professional athletes; Congress approves Student Right-to-Know Act, which requires public disclosure of graduation rates for varsity athletes and the general student body; Jean Driscoll sets a world record as she wins the first of seven consecutive wheelchair Boston Marathons.
1991	The U.S. Soccer Team defeats Norway to win the first Women's World Cup; "Magic" Johnson announces that he tested positive for HIV and his NBA career ends; the Women's Final Four of college basketball is televised live for the first time.
1992	At the Olympic Games in Barcelona, USA Basketball team ("The Dream Team") consisting of NBA players wins the gold medal; seven Native Americans file a lawsuit against the NFL team in Washington, D.C., for using the demeaning term "redskins" in their name; girls, for the first time, win all three divisions in the All-American Soap Box Derby.
1993	Sherry Davis is first woman to be a public address announcer at a Major League Baseball game; an obsessive fan of Steffi Graf jumps from the stands during a tennis tournament in Germany and stabs Monica Seles, ranked number one in the world at the time.
1994	The all-female Colorado Silver Bullets plays men's baseball teams; Major League Baseball season is canceled with seven weeks remaining as players start a 232-day strike opposing the owners' proposed team salary cap; Tonya Harding is banned for life from official figure skating events for conspiring to injure Nancy Kerrigan, her chief opponent at the Winter Olympics in Lillehammer, Norway.
1995	Julie Croteau is the first female assistant coach in men's collegiate division I baseball; 8200 athletes participate in the fifth annual National Senior Games; 7000 athletes from 143 countries compete at ninth Special Olympics World Summer Games; Native Americans protest use of their names and images as the Atlanta "Braves" and Cleveland "Indians" play in the World Series.*

*Struggles and changes have continued since 1995. For example, there continue to be notable "firsts" in connection with race and ethnicity, gender, sexuality, and disability; corporate interests have become a greater part of sports; and the lives of celebrity athletes attract media attention as never before.

soccer player at Yale because it might turn off some voters.

The meanings given to sports often vary from one region of a country to another. For example, stock car racing and the National Association for Stock Car Auto Racing (NASCAR) initially represented values, traditions, and histories common to the South but has come to be seen as a national sport in recent years. Rodeo traditionally had special meaning in midwestern and western rural areas where livestock and horses were important to local economies and people's everyday lives. But today there are rodeo events held in New York City and other places where

people have never seen a horse up close (Haney and Pearson, 1999).

The meanings given to sports generally reaffirm the values and lifestyles of those who play and watch them, and this has certainly been true since 1920. As cities have grown, so has basketball, often described as the city game (Axthelm, 1970). As black men have excelled at the highest levels of basketball, the game has come to be defined by many people as a "black game." In the process, basketball has taken on special meaning in many black communities. At the same time, basketball has been given different meanings by whites growing up in Indiana where "Hoosier

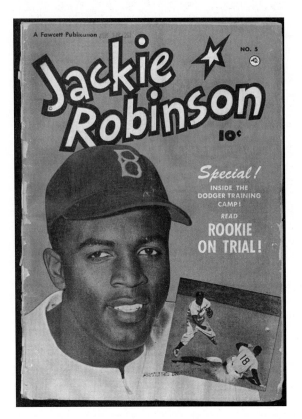

This is the cover of a Jackie Robinson comic book published in 1951. The headline, "Rookie on Trial," indicated that Robinson's performance in baseball was evaluated in connection with issues of racial desegregation in sports. Many others who have been "firsts" in their sport have felt the pressure that Robinson endured. (*Source:* American Memory Collection)

Hysteria" occurs every fall during the state high school basketball tournament. Basketball has had other meaning among girls who have played on high school teams in Iowa, where for many years girls' basketball was the major spectator event in the state. As we think about these changes, it is important to remember that understanding sports history depends on our knowledge of what sports have meant to those who have played, watched, and sponsored them.

Struggles over Purpose: Is Winning the Only Thing?

Meaning and purpose are closely aligned. On a general level, the central purpose of most sports between the 1920s and 1960s was to foster fitness and fair play. However, as occupational success and social mobility became increasingly important in a growing capitalist economy during the 1950s, there was a gradual turn toward an emphasis on competitive success and winning in sports. Competitive sports were seen to build the kind of character that many people felt was essential to American prosperity.

As sports teams and sports events were linked to schools, communities, and the nation, the primary purpose of sports continued to shift from participation and fair play to wins that brought prestige to sponsors. By the 1960s, many people felt that "winning is not the most important thing—it is the ONLY thing." With the 1970s and the dramatic growth of media coverage, entertainment became an increasingly important purpose of sports. As this occurred, the styles and personas of athletes took on new meanings, and teams built public relations profiles around values and identities that resonated with audience segments or large collections of spectators. This is when the Dallas Cowboys came to be known as "America's Team," while the Chicago Bears and the Detroit Lions were known as "blue-collar" teams that emphasized the fundamentals of traditional midwestern culture. Entertainment and winning were closely linked because winners filled stadiums and generated revenues for sponsors and owners.

There is never complete agreement on the purpose of sports. For example, physical educators emphasize fitness and health, whereas people associated with the commercial media emphasize entertainment. This and other disagreements occur today as people struggle to define the purpose of sports in their schools and community-based youth programs.

Struggles over Organization: Can We Play Without a Coach and Referees?

Since 1920 there has been a clear trend toward organizing sports in formal and "official" ways. Mainstream sports are increasingly organized around standardized rules enforced by official governing bodies. Some people have resisted increased organization and rationalization, but resistance has not slowed or reversed this trend. Even many alternative and recreational sports have become increasingly organized as people try to make them safer, more accessible, or more commercially profitable.

Hundreds of sport organizations have come and gone over recent years, but the emphasis on organization has become more prevalent. As this has occurred, classic and sometimes bitter struggles have taken place over who controls sports so that they will be organized consistently over time. In the process, governing bodies, coaches, and other officials have become key "players" in sports at all levels. In fact, many children today grow up thinking that sports cannot exist without coaches and referees.

The Conditions of Sport Participation: Can Everyone Play?

Some of the most contentious struggles in sports since the 1920s have revolved around who participates in formally organized, mainstream sport programs. Most sports were initially organized around various forms of exclusion and segregation based on race, ethnicity, gender, age, and (dis)ability. For example, men from relatively well-to-do white families have consistently had the greatest access to sport participation opportunities throughout their lives.

There have been constant struggles to expand participation opportunities for women, people from low-income families and neighborhoods, ethnic minorities, people with physical and intellectual disabilities, and people labeled as gay or lesbian. Complex histories are associated with

each of these struggles, but the general trend between 1920 and the early 1980s has been to open sport participation to more people, especially through sports funded by public money and played in public facilities. Private clubs and organizations have maintained exclusionary membership criteria over the years, and most continue to do so today. Increased privatization since the 1980s has made it more financially difficult for many people to initiate or maintain regular sport participation, and this trend suggests that sports will be characterized by increased socioeconomic segregation in the future.

Struggles over who participates under what conditions have been further complicated by the diversity of goals among the people involved. Some groups of people have fought to be integrated fully into organized, mainstream sports, whereas others have fought to have separate opportunities that meet their specific needs and interests. For instance, not everyone wishes to play sports developed and organized around the interests and experiences of young, able-bodied, white, heterosexual males.

Struggles over the conditions of sport participation have occurred when professional athletes have formed players' associations to bargain with team owners and leagues over issues related to the organization and rules of their sports. College students have struggled to obtain recognition and funding for club teams with the hope of eventually becoming official intercollegiate teams. Many struggles have occurred around issues of eligibility, the allocation of rewards, and the funding of new or alternative sport participation opportunities.

Sport Sponsors: Who Needs Them?

Struggles over sponsorship issues are difficult to detect in the time-line items listed in table 3.2. The Great Depression of the 1930s generally interfered with the funding and sponsorship of many sports. However, as government policies and programs were developed to cope with the

The suburbanization that occurred after World War II through the 1960s was accompanied by the growth of youth sports for boys and cheerleading for girls. Women who played sports during these years were frequently labeled as "dykes." Boys were "sluggers." (*Source:* McGraw-Hill)

consequences of the depression, there was an emphasis on the public sponsorship of sports, especially for children, adolescents, and young adults. After World War II, most American communities embraced the idea that tax money should be used to provide a range of sport participation opportunities, especially for boys and young men.

The growth of antigovernment sentiments, combined with the growth of corporate power and influence, led to a shift in sponsorship patterns in the 1980s and 1990s. After more than thirty years of increased sponsorship of sports by government organizations, public programs began to lose their funding. Some were replaced with programs funded by private money and corporate sponsors. This new form of sponsorship has had a major impact on the types of sports

that have become popular and who has had opportunities to participate in them.

Instead of being based on ideas about "the common good"—such as the reduction of obesity, for example—sports today often are sponsored in connection with the commercial interests of corporations. Struggles over sport sponsorships have recently involved corporations that sell tobacco, alcohol, fast foods, products made in sweatshops, and services defined by some people as immoral (related to gambling, strip clubs, and escort services). These struggles will continue as long as the sports that people want to play and watch require large amounts of capital and as long as people do not approve of their tax money being used to sponsor public sports and sport facilities. Eventually, this could raise the question of whether people want to play and watch sports that require external sponsors. If this happens, people may decide that it is possible to have fun playing and watching sports that they can organize and maintain by themselves, if there are accessible public spaces in which sports can be played.

USING HISTORY TO THINK ABOUT THE FUTURE

As we study the past, we learn that struggles over the meaning, purpose, and organization of sports always occur in particular social, political, and economic contexts. Sports history does not just happen; it always depends on the actions of people working with one another to construct sports to match their visions of what sports could and should be in their lives. Many people in recent history have ignored what others say is practical or realistic and pursued choices based on idealistic notions of what sports could be. These are the people who have inspired racial desegregation in sports, new opportunities for girls and women, new programs for people with disabilities, and the recognition and acceptance of gay and lesbian athletes. Table 3.2 does not do justice to those people and struggles they have waged to turn their idealistic visions into realities. Each of those struggles has its own history, and those of us who choose to be actively involved in creating future histories will shape them.

summary

CAN WE USE HISTORY TO UNDERSTAND SPORTS TODAY?

Our selective look at different times and places shows us that physical games and sports are integrally related to social contexts in which they exist. As social life changes and power shifts in any society, the meaning, purpose, and organization of games and sport activities also change.

In ancient Greece, games and contests were grounded in mythology and religious beliefs. They focused on the interests of able-bodied young men from wealthy segments of society. As the outcomes of organized games took on political and social implications beyond the events, athletes were recruited from the lower classes and paid to participate. The existence of professional athletes, violence, and an emphasis on victory shows us a side of sports in ancient Greece that contradicts many popular beliefs. It also demonstrates that sports may not represent the interests of everyone in a society.

Roman contests and games emphasized mass entertainment. They were designed to celebrate and preserve the power of political leaders and pacify masses of unemployed and underemployed workers in Roman cities and towns. Many athletes in Roman events were slaves or "troublemakers" coerced into jeopardizing their lives in battle with one another or wild animals. These spectacles faded with the demise of the Roman Empire. Critically assessing the contests and games of this period makes us more aware of the interests that powerful people may have in promoting large sport events.

Folk games and tournaments in medieval times clearly reflected and reproduced gender and social-class differences in European cultures. The peasants played local versions of folk games in connection with seasonal events in village life. The knights and nobles engaged in tournaments and jousts. Other members of the upper classes often used their resources to develop games and sport activities to occupy their leisure time. Studying the history of sports during this time period shows that gender and class issues should not be ignored as we analyze sports and sport experiences today.

Patterns from the medieval period continued through the Renaissance in parts of Europe although the Protestant Reformation generated negative attitudes about activities that interfered with work and religious worship. Peasants were affected most by these attitudes because they did not have the resources to resist the restrictive controls imposed by government officials inspired by Calvinist or Puritan orientations. The games and sports of the wealthy generally occurred in the safe confines of their private grounds, so they could avoid outside control. The Enlightenment was associated with increased political rights and freedom to engage in diversionary games and physical activities. Studying these historical periods shows us the importance of cultural ideology and government policies when it comes to who plays sports under what conditions.

During the early days of the Industrial Revolution, the influence of the Puritans faded in Europe and North America, but the demands of work and the absence of spaces for play generally limited sport involvement to the wealthy and rural residents. This pattern began to change in the United States from the late 1800s through the early 1900s when the combined influence of labor unions, progressive legislation, and economic expansion led to the creation of new ideas about the consequences of sport participation and new opportunities for involvement. However, opportunities for involvement were shaped primarily by gender ideology and the needs of an economy emphasizing mass production and consumption. It was in this context that people developed organized competitive sports. Studying this period shows us that the origins of today's sports are tied closely to complex social, political, and economic factors.

Sports history since 1920 has revolved around continuing struggles over (1) the meaning, purpose, and organization of sports, (b) who participates in sports under what conditions, and (c) who sponsors sports and why. These struggles have occurred in connection with major historical events, trends, and patterns. In most cases, powerful economic and political interests have prevailed in these struggles, but in a few cases, people motivated by idealistic visions of what sports could and should be like have prevailed. Every now and then, the visions of idealists have become reality,

but struggles never end. As we study current issues and controversies in sports, our awareness of past struggles is useful.

See the OLC, www.mhhe.com/coakley9e for an annotated list of readings related to this chapter. The OLC also contains a key concepts list, a review test, and other helpful features.

WEBSITE RESOURCES

Note: Websites often change. The following URLs were current when this book was printed. Please check our website (www.mhhe.com/coakley9e) for updates and additions.

www.studies.org   The Institute for Mediterranean Studies; site summarizes and sells audiotapes on the Olympic Games in ancient Greece and on sports in the Roman world.

http://depthome.brooklyn.cuny.edu/classics/gladiatr/index.htm   This site was developed by Roger Dunkle, an expert on Roman sports; excellent information and visuals related to the spectacles in which gladiators participated.

www.umist.ac.uk/sport/ishpes.html   International Society for the History of Physical Education and Sport provides links to many other sites for sports history.

www.nassh.org   North American Society for Sport History.

www.sover.net/~spectrum/index.html   The site of the American Soccer History Archives; excellent histories of both men's and women's soccer.

www.hickoksports.com/index.shtml   An easy-to-use site with many search options covering a wide range of history topics, events, athletes, and other sport personalities; tends toward the popular rather than academic, although there is an excellent bibliography of sport history books.

www.womenssportsfoundation.org/cgi-bin/iowa/
   issues/history/   A good site for obtaining
   information on the history of women in sports
   in the United States.
www.deaflympics.com/   Official site of the
   Deaflympics, established in 1924 as The
   Silent Games; this was the first international
   competitions for athletes with disabilities.
www.cureourchildren.org/sports.htm   A helpful site
   for anyone looking for information and creative

ideas about sports and recreation for people with
   disabilities; links to dozens of related sites.
www.gsml.org/field.html and
   www.ohiomiracleleague.org and
   www.mauldinrecreation.com/mauldinmiracle/
   index.html   These are three of the many sites
   related to local Miracle League programs
   and facilities; they provide everything from
   players' statements to photos of games
   and fields.

(Colorado Springs Gazette)

SPORTS AND SOCIALIZATION

Who Plays and What Happens to Them?

> SPORTS HAVE GIVEN me my foundation. . . . I'm an athlete inside and out. It's not something I try to be, it is who I am. I can't remember a time when I didn't play sports. It's truly all I know.
>
> —**Danielle Martin, multisport athlete, 2002**

 Online Learning Center Resources

Visit *Sports in Society*'s Online Learning Center (OLC) at **www.mhhe.com/coakley9e** for additional information and study material for this chapter, including

- Self-grading quizzes
- Learning objectives
- Related websites
- Additional readings

A complete outline is available online at
www.mhhe.com/coakley9e.

IT WAS THROUGH SKATEBOARDING that I received my education in life. . . . I had so little confidence and self-esteem. I just felt lucky to have found something . . . that I was good at. . . . I'm not sure where I'd be without skateboarding.

—**Stacy Peralta, former skateboarder, producer
of *Dogtown and Z-boys* (in Geffner, 2002)**

WHAT DO KIDS know about us? They only know that we play sports. They don't know who we are as people. You don't learn the important things about life by watching a person play football.

—**Emmitt Smith, NFL player, 1996**

Socialization is a popular topic in discussions about sports. We deal with socialization issues whenever we discuss the following questions:

- Why are some people fanatically interested in playing and watching sports, whereas others don't seem to care about sports?
- How and why do some people see themselves as athletes and dedicate themselves to playing sports?
- When and why do people stop playing competitive sports, and what happens to them when they do?
- What impact do sports and sport participation have on people's lives?

Many of us in the sociology of sport have done research to find answers to one or more of these questions. The search for answers has taken us in different directions, depending on the theories that we use to guide our thinking about sports and sport participation. The influence of theoretical perspectives is discussed in the first section of this chapter. Then we consider three topics that are central to most discussions of sports and socialization:

1. The process of becoming involved and staying involved in sports
2. The process of changing or ending sport participation
3. The impact of being involved in sports

As these topics are discussed, I provide tentative answers to the socialization questions that have been asked by researchers in the sociology of sport. As you read the chapter, you will see that most of the answers are incomplete and many others are so complex that discussions about them will carry over into other chapters.

The chapter closes with information about new approaches to socialization. These approaches are based on critical, feminist, and interactionist theories that emphasize socialization as a community and cultural process as well as an individual and personal process.

WHAT IS SOCIALIZATION?

Socialization *is a process of learning and social development, which occurs as we interact with one another and become acquainted with the social world in which we live.* It involves the formation of ideas about who we are and what is important in our lives. We are *not* simply passive learners in the socialization process. We actively participate in our own socialization as we form relationships and influence those who influence us. We actively interpret what we see and hear, and we accept, resist, and revise the messages that we receive about who we are, about the world, and about our connection with the world. Therefore, socialization is *not* a one-way process of social influence through which we are molded and shaped. Instead, it is an interactive process through which we actively connect with others, synthesize information, and *make decisions* that shape our own lives and the social world around us.

This definition of *socialization*, which I use to guide my research, is based on a combination of *critical* and *interactionist theories*. Therefore, not all sociologists would agree with it. Those using functionalist or conflict theory approaches, for example, would define *socialization* in slightly different terms. Like the definition I use, their definitions have an impact on the questions that they ask about sports and socialization, the research methods that they use to gather data, and the way that they make sense of their research data.

A Functionalist Approach to Socialization

Scholars using *functionalist theory* view socialization as a process through which we learn what we must know to fit into society and contribute to its operation. This approach to socialization is based on an *internalization model* (Coakley, 1993; 2006b). In other words, as we grow up in our families, attend school, interact with peers, and receive images and messages from the media, we learn the rules we should follow and the roles we should play in society.

When researchers use an internalization model to guide their studies, they focus on four things: (1) the characteristics of the people who are *being* socialized, (2) the people who *do* the socializing, (3) the *contexts* in which socialization occurs, and (4) the specific *outcomes*, or results, of socialization. In studies of sports and socialization, researchers focus on athletes as the people being socialized and on the **agents of socialization** *who exert influence on athletes.* Agents, or "socializers," generally include fathers, mothers, brothers, sisters, teachers, coaches, peers, and people used as role models. The most central and influential socializers are described as **significant others.** In some cases, contexts in which socialization occurs, such as the family, education, peer groups, and the media, are also studied in connection with sport participation. The socialization outcomes, or results, that are studied include personal attitudes, values, skills, and behavior patterns, especially those that are seen as contributing to the operation of society as a social system.

Those who use a functionalist approach also study what causes people to participate in sports and how participation influences them and the patterns of their lives. This research generally uses surveys to collect data. Researchers have done literally hundreds of studies by sending questionnaires to people, especially high school students. Their analyses compare those who do and don't play organized sports, and their goal is to discover the socialization experiences that lead to and result from sport participation (see figure 4.1).

Until recently, this research has provided us with inconsistent and contradictory findings about why people play sports and what happens to them when they do. However, more recent research, using large data sets collected through well-funded regional and national studies, have begun to provide more consistent and detailed analyses of the complex connections between sport participation and processes of socialization (Curtis et al., 2003; Guest and Schneider, 2003; Loveless, 2002; Marsh and Kleitman, 2003; Miller et al., 1999; President's Council on Physical Fitness and Sports, 1997;

"I know this is starting early, but I can't let him get too far behind the other kids if he's ever going to make a team in high school."

FIGURE 4.1 Research guided by functionalist theory has focused on who influences the sport participation patterns of children. Fathers and other family members have usually been identified as *significant others* who influence when, how, and where children play sports.

Sabo et al., 1998, 2005; Spreitzer, 1995; Tracy and Erkut, 2002; Videon, 2002). These studies provide us with many snapshots rather than videos of socialization as it occurs over the course of people's lives. But multiple snapshots can be used to identify general patterns and guide further research that is designed to study the specific details of socialization processes. These patterns will be discussed on pages 100–115 of this chapter.

A Conflict Theory Approach to Socialization

Scholars using conflict theory also view socialization in terms of an internalization model. However, they focus on the ways that economic factors influence sport participation and the consequences of sport participation on the economic organization of society. For example, studies based on conflict theory investigate questions such as these: (1) Does participation in organized competitive sports reproduce capitalist economies by creating conservative, militaristic, sexist, and racist orientations among players and spectators? (2) Are people from low-income and working-class backgrounds systematically denied opportunities to play sports on their own terms and in their own ways? (3) Are athletes, especially those from poor, minority backgrounds, victims of a profit-driven, win-at-all-cost sport system in which they have no rights? (4) Do people with money and power control the conditions of sport participation and exploit others to make money and maintain their own interests?

There are fewer studies based on conflict theory than functionalist theory. Some of these studies suggest that rigidly structured sport programs controlled by autocratic, military-style coaches attract and produce people who are politically conservative and supportive of the status quo. But the samples in these studies have been so small that research findings provide only fuzzy snapshots telling us little about the details of sport-related socialization. In general terms, these fuzzy snapshots do show us that economic resources are related to the organization of sports and the dynamics of sport participation, and that the people who control economic resources often use them to promote their own interests.

Unfortunately, the large data sets that enable scholars to examine questions based on functionalist approaches seldom include information about the ways that economic resources and power influence who does and does not play sports and what happens to them when they do play. Fortunately, new approaches to socialization help us understand some of these issues.

New Approaches to Socialization

Sociologists today are unlikely to view socialization as a process through which culture is passively internalized as it is transmitted from one generation to the next. Instead of using an internalization model of socialization they prefer an **interactionist model** *based on the idea that socialization involves participatory learning through which people are involved in larger processes of cultural production, reproduction, and change.* Researchers who use an interactionist model generally use qualitative rather than quantitative research methods. Instead of using questionnaires to obtain statistical data from large numbers of people, they use in-depth interviews and field observations. Their goal is to obtain detailed descriptions of sport experiences as they occur in people's lives. They seek information on the processes through which people make decisions about their sport participation and give meanings to their sport experiences. Finally, they seek to connect those decisions and meanings with the larger cultural context in which sports and sport participation exist. This approach, they argue, captures the complexity of processes related to becoming and staying involved in sports, changing or ending sport participation, and incorporating sports into people's lives. The rest of this chapter draws on old and new approaches to outline what we know about sports and socialization today.

BECOMING AND STAYING INVOLVED IN SPORTS

Research based on functionalist and conflict theories indicates that sport participation is related to three factors: (1) a person's abilities, characteristics, and resources, (2) the influence of significant others, including parents, siblings, teachers, peers, and role models, and (3) the availability of opportunities to play sports in ways that are personally satisfying. These are the snapshots that we have of *socialization into sports.* However, a fuller description of the ongoing process of becoming and staying involved in sports emerges when we obtain detailed stories from people about their sport participation. These stories are more like videos than snapshots.

Studies using in-depth interviews, fieldwork, participant observations, and strategic conversations indicate that sport participation is connected with multiple and diverse processes that make up people's lives, and it occurs as people make decisions about and give meaning to sports. Therefore, decisions and meanings associated with sports are not permanent. As social conditions change, so do sport-related decisions and meanings. Furthermore, as people stay involved in sports, their reasons for participating on one day may be different from reasons for participating on the next day. When there is no reason, they may discontinue or change their sport participation.

To understand how and why people become and stay involved in sports, it is helpful to review research on these issues. The following studies give us three sociological videos of the decision-making processes related to playing sports.

Example 1: The Process of Becoming an Elite Athlete

Chris Stevenson is a sport sociologist interested in how people become elite athletes. Using interactionist theory to guide his research, he interviewed and collected stories from elite athletes about how they were introduced to their sports and became committed to sport participation. As he analyzed the stories, he noticed that they sounded much like descriptions of careers. In other words, they had identifiable beginnings, followed by a process of development, and ultimately an end. Stevenson felt that he could understand these careers in terms of the decisions

Participation in sports is usually sponsored through important social relationships. This boy's participation in basketball is likely to be influenced by his father, an agent of socialization and a significant other in his life. However, continued participation also requires a combination of developing a commitment to the sport, receiving material and emotional support, and establishing social relationships and an identity related to the sport. (*Source:* McGraw-Hill)

that people made about sport participation and how those decisions were related to important issues and relationships in their lives over time.

In one of his studies, Stevenson (1999) interviewed twenty-nine international athletes from Canada and England. At first, he was struck by the diversity of the stories the athletes told him. But as he analyzed the data, he identified two processes that were common to nearly all the stories. First, there was a process of **introduction and involvement,** during which young people received support as they tried certain sports. His interviewees talked about being introduced to sports bit-by-bit over time through important relationships in their lives. Gradually, they chose to specialize in a particular sport based on an evaluation of their potential for success and their sense of being personally connected with the people associated with the sport. Second, there was a process of **developing a commitment** to sport participation. This process occurred as the athletes formed a web of personal relationships connected with their participation and gradually established personal reputations and identities as athletes in their sports. Their relationships and identities figured prominently in how they set priorities and made decisions about sport participation. Staying involved in their sport depended on active and thoughtful efforts to develop identities as athletes. This occurred as people who were important in their lives recognized and defined them as athletes. Over time, this social recognition led them to become more deeply committed to their sports and their lives as athletes.

Stevenson found that these processes did *not* occur automatically. The young people themselves helped them happen. Becoming and staying involved in sports was a complex process. The young people realized that they could not take for granted the social support that they received for playing sports or continued reaffirmation of their identities as athletes. They knew that the resources needed for participation could disappear and that changes in other parts of their lives could force them to alter the importance of sport participation.

Therefore, they made decisions to stay involved in sports day after day, and as they stayed involved, they impressed and influenced those who supported and influenced them.

Stevenson's research shows that the socialization process is *interactive* and that each of us participates in our own socialization as we make decisions and become committed to particular identities.

Example 2: The Process of Being Accepted as an Athlete

Peter Donnelly and Kevin Young are sociologists who have studied sports as social worlds, or subcultures in which people develop ways of doing things and relating to each other. In their research, they have paid special attention to how people become accepted members of those subcultures. Consequently, they have taken a closer look at some of the processes studied by Stevenson (Donnelly and Young, 1999).

On the basis of data that Donnelly collected from rock climbers and Young collected from rugby players, they concluded that playing sports occurs in connection with complex processes of identity formation. They explain that entering and becoming an athlete in a particular sport subculture occurs through a four-phase process:

1. Acquiring knowledge about the sport
2. Associating with people involved in the sport
3. Learning how those people think about their sport and what they do and expect from each other
4. Becoming recognized and fully accepted into the sport group as a fellow athlete

These details of sport socialization indicates that becoming involved in a sport depends on learning to "talk the talk and walk the walk" so that one is identified and accepted as an athlete by others who are athletes. This process of identification and acceptance does not happen once and for all time; it is continuous. When we lose touch and are no longer able to talk the talk and walk the walk, acceptance wanes, our identities become difficult to maintain, and overall support for our participation becomes weak. We are not athletes forever.

To understand what Donnelly and Young found in their study, just observe a sport group such as skateboarders, in-line skaters, snowboarders, beach volleyball players, or basketball players. Each group has its own vocabulary and its own way of referring to its members and what they do. The terms they use are not found in dictionaries. They also have unique ways of thinking about and doing their sports, and they have special understandings of what they can expect from others in their groups. New participants in these sports may be tested and "pushed" by the "veterans" before being accepted and defined as true skaters, riders, volleyball players, or ballers. Vocabularies may change over time, but this process of becoming accepted and gaining support for participation exists in all sports. Many people have discovered that, if they do not establish social connections and acceptance in a sport, their participation may be difficult to maintain over time. Becoming involved in sports clearly is part of a complex, *interactive* socialization and identity formation process.

Example 3: To Participate or Not to Participate

Anita White is a sport sociologist and former director of sport development at Sport England. Before she began working at Sport England, Anita and I did a study of sport participation among British adolescents in a working-class area east of London (Coakley and White, 1999). Our goal was to provide coaches and program organizers with information on why some young people participated in government-sponsored sport programs, whereas most did not.

Our in-depth interviews indicated that sport participation was the result of decisions based on a combination of factors, including the following:

1. Their ideas about the ways that sport participation was related to other interests and goals in their lives

2. Their desires to develop and display competence so they could gain recognition and respect from others
3. Social support for participation and access to the resources needed for participation (time, transportation, equipment, and money)
4. Memories of past experiences with physical activities and sports
5. Sport-related cultural images and messages that they had in their minds

We found that young people decided to play sports when it helped them extend control over their lives, achieve development and career goals, and present themselves to others as competent. We also found that young women were less likely than the young men to imagine that sport participation could do these things for them. Therefore, the young women participated in organized sports less often and less seriously.

The young people in our study did not simply respond to the world around them. Instead, they actively thought about how sports might be positively incorporated into their lives and then made decisions based on their conclusions. Their sport participation patterns shifted over time, depending on their access to opportunities, changes in their lives, and changes in their identities. Therefore, socialization into sports was a *continuous, interactive process* grounded in the social and cultural contexts in which the young people lived.

Our interviews also indicated that people make decisions to participate in sports for different reasons at different points in their lives. This fits with theories telling us that developmental tasks and challenges change as we move through childhood, adolescence, young adulthood, and adulthood. Therefore, the issues considered by seven-year-olds who make decisions about sport participation are different from the issues considered by fourteen-year-olds, forty-year-olds, or sixty-year-olds (Porterfield, 1999; C. L. Stevenson, 2002). Furthermore, when seven-year-olds make decisions about sport participation today, they do so in a different cultural context than the context in which seven-year-olds lived in 1970 or will live in 2020.

Sport participation decisions at all points during the life course and through history also are tied to the perceived cultural importance of sports and the links between playing sports, gaining social acceptance, and achieving personal goals. Therefore, studies of socialization into sports must take into account the ways in which sport participation is related to individual development, the organization of social life, and the ideologies that are prevalent in a culture (Ingham et al., 1999).

In summary, this study and the two previously discussed provide three videos about becoming and staying involved in sports. They show that sport participation is grounded in decision-making processes involving self-reflection, social support, social acceptance, and cultural factors. People do not make decisions about sport participation once and for all time. They make them day after day as they consider how sports are related to their lives. In fact, they sometimes make them moment by moment when coaches are making them run wind sprints and they are sucking air at the finish line! These decisions are mediated by the social and cultural contexts in which the people live. Therefore, social meanings attached to gender, class, skin color, ethnicity, age, and physical (dis)abilities influence sport participation decisions and these meanings are influenced by political, economic, social, and cultural forces.

CHANGING OR ENDING SPORT PARTICIPATION

Questions about becoming and staying involved in sports often are followed by questions about changing or ending involvement. Much of the research on this latter issue has been guided by "role theories" inspired by functionalist theory

> Athletics play an important role in shaping our character and values.
>
> —Bill Clinton, former president of the United States, 1999

or "alienation theories" inspired by conflict theory (see Coakley, 1993).

Researchers using *functionalist theory* have been concerned with identifying who drops out of sports and what can be done to keep them in sports so that they can learn the positive lessons taught through participation. This was a popular research topic when millions of baby boomers were flooding playgrounds and elementary schools, and parents wanted to know how to control and build character in their children. Research based on functionalist approaches also focuses on how to make sport programs more efficient in developing skills and preparing young people to move to higher levels of competition. This is currently a popular topic among people who have an interest in creating successful athletes and sport teams.

Researchers using *conflict theory* generally focus on the ways that rigidly organized, win-oriented programs turn children off to participation. They have hypothesized that these programs, along with autocratic, command-style coaches, alienate young athletes and cause them to drop out. Similarly, older athletes drop out because of injuries or alienation caused by years of being exploited. Their studies explore the ways that elite athletes are victims of exploitation and alienating experiences that damage their bodies and leave them unprepared for life after sport.

Studies grounded in functionalist and conflict theories tell us the following important things:

- When people drop out of particular sports, they don't drop out of all sports forever, nor do they cut all ties with sports; many people play different and less competitive sports as they become older, or they move into other sport roles such as coach, administrator, or sports businessperson.
- Dropping out of sports is usually connected with developmental changes and transitions in the rest of a person's life (changing

schools, graduating, getting a job, getting married, having children, and so on).

- Dropping out of sports is not always the result of victimization or exploitation although injuries and negative experiences can and do influence decisions to change or end participation.
- Problems may occur for those who end long careers in sports, especially those who have no identities apart from sports and lack social and material resources for making transitions into other careers and relationships.

Recent studies, especially those using qualitative research methods and based on critical theory and interactionist models of socialization, have built on these findings and extended our understanding. Following are three examples of these studies.

Example 1: Burnout Among Young Athletes

My work with coaches and my interest in identity issues led me to do a study of young people who, after being age-group champions in their sports, had decided to quit playing (Coakley, 1992). People described these young people as "burned out," so I decided to interview former elite athletes identified by themselves or others as cases of burnout; all were adolescents.

Data collected through in-depth interviews indicated that burnout during adolescence was grounded in the organization of the high-performance sports. It occurred when young athletes felt they no longer had control over their lives and could not explore, develop, and nurture identities apart from sports. This led to increased stress and decreased fun when doing sports. Burnout occurred when stress became so high and fun declined so much that athletes no longer felt that playing their sport was worth their effort.

The data also indicated that stress increased and fun decreased when sport programs were organized so that successful young athletes felt that

they could not accomplish important developmental tasks during adolescence. My conclusion was that burnout could be prevented only if sport programs were reorganized so that athletes had more control over their lives. Stress management strategies could be used to delay burnout, but they would not change the underlying organizational and development causes of burnout. Overall, the study indicated that ending sport participation during late adolescence sometimes occurs when young people feel that staying in sport prevents them from developing the autonomy and multiple identities that mark people as adults in U.S. culture.

Example 2: Getting Out of Sports and Getting On with Life

Konstantinos Koukouris (1994) is a physical educator from Greece who wanted to know why people who had been seriously committed to sports decided to end or reduce their sport participation. After analyzing questionnaire data from 157 former national athletes, Koukouris identified 34 who had ceased or reduced sport participation between the ages of eighteen and twenty-four. In-depth interviews with these people enabled him to construct case studies illustrating the process of disengaging from sports.

The data indicated that athletes voluntarily decided to end or change their participation. But this decision was part of a long-term process during which they stopped playing and then started again more than once. In other words, they hadn't gone "cold turkey" as they withdrew from sport. The decision to end or change their sport participation was usually associated with two practical factors: (1) the need to obtain a job and support themselves and (2) realistic judgments about their sport skills and the chances of moving to higher levels of competition. As they graduated from high school or college, the athletes faced the expectation that they should work and be responsible for their own lives. But jobs

Although people may drop out of sports at one point in the life course, they may return at a later point. This team of women, all over seventy years old, is playing an exhibition game against a group of younger women. The team is raising funds to travel to the national finals in the Senior Games. Most of these older women had not played competitive basketball for 30–50 years. (*Source:* Jay Coakley)

interfered with the time they needed to train and play sports at a serious level. Furthermore, as they spent money to establish adult lifestyles, they didn't have enough left to pay for serious training. At the same time, their sport-training programs were organized so rigidly that sport participation was difficult to fit into their new adult lives.

As serious training ended, many of these young adults sought other ways to be physically active or connected with sports. They sometimes experienced problems but, as they faced new challenges, most of them grew and developed in positive ways, much like people who had never been serious athletes. Disengaging from serious

sport training was perceived as part of inevitable, necessary, and usually beneficial developments in the lives of these young adults.

Example 3: Changing Personal Investments in Sport Careers

Garry Wheeler from the University of Alberta is concerned with the careers of athletes with disabilities and what happens when their playing careers end. Building on a previous study (Wheeler et al., 1996) of Paralympic athletes, Wheeler and his fellow researchers gathered data through interviews with forty athletes from Israel, the United Kingdom, Canada, and the

United States (Wheeler et al., 1999). Data indicated that athletes in each of the countries became deeply involved in playing sports and often achieved a high level of success in a relatively short time. Through sports they developed a sense of personal competence and established identities as elite athletes.

Withdrawing from active sport participation and making the transition into the rest of life often presented challenges for these athletes. Retirement often came suddenly and forced them to reinvest time and energy into other spheres of their lives. As they reconnected with family members and friends, returned to school, and resumed occupational careers, some individuals experienced emotional problems. However, most stayed connected with sports and sport organizations as coaches, administrators, or recreational athletes. Those few who hoped they might compete again often experienced serious difficulties during the retirement transition, whereas those who accepted the end of their competitive careers had fewer adjustment problems.

In summary, research shows that ending or changing sport participation often involves the same interactive and decision-making processes that occur during the process of becoming and staying involved in sports. Just as people are not simply socialized into sports, neither are they simply socialized out of sports. Changes in participation are grounded in decisions associated with other life events, social relationships, and cultural expectations related to development. This means that theories explaining why people play sports and change their participation over time must take into account identity issues and developmental processes that are part of the social and cultural contexts in which people make

Many factors influence the decisions to drop out of sports or shift participation from one sport to another. Identity changes, access to resources, and life course issues are involved. As our circumstances change, so do our ideas about ourselves and about sports and sport participation. (*Source:* McGraw-Hill)

decisions about sports in their lives (Dacyshyn, 1999; Drahota and Eitzen, 1998; Swain, 1999). Furthermore, the theories must consider the personal, social, and material resources that athletes have as they make transitions to other relationships, activities, and careers. Some people have problems when they retire from sports, but to understand those problems, we need information about the ways that sport participation has been incorporated into their lives and the resources that can be used as changes occur and challenges are faced. Research suggests that, if sport participation expands a person's identity, experiences, relationships, and resources, changes and retirement transitions will be smooth. Difficulties are most likely to occur when a person has never had the desire or the chance to live outside the culture of elite sports (Messner, 1992; Murphy et al., 1996).

BEING INVOLVED IN SPORTS: WHAT HAPPENS?

Beliefs about the consequences of sport participation vary from culture to culture, but the beliefs that playing sports builds character and improves health and well-being are widely accepted in many cultures. These beliefs are used as a basis for encouraging children to play sports, funding sports programs in school, building stadiums, promoting teams and leagues, and sponsoring international events such as the Olympic Games, the Paralympics, and the Special Olympics.

Do Sports Build Character?

For over a half century, researchers have examined the validity of the belief that "sport builds character." Many of the studies have involved comparisons of the traits, attitudes, and behaviors of people who play organized sports and people who don't play them. These comparisons have usually focused on differences between members of U.S. high school varsity teams and

AT YOUR *fingertips*   For more information, on postretirement adjustment issues, see pages 351–355.

students who have never played on varsity teams. These snapshot comparisons have produced inconsistent and confusing findings. This is because there are many different definitions of "character," and researchers have used inconsistent measures of *character* in their studies (Stoll and Beller, 1998). Furthermore, many researchers base their studies on two faulty assumptions (McCormack and Chalip, 1988). First, they mistakenly assume that *all* athletes have the same or similar experiences in *all* organized competitive sports. Second, they mistakenly assume that organized sports provide learning experiences that are not available to people in any other activities.

These faulty assumptions cause researchers to overlook the following important things when they study sports and socialization:

1. Sports offer many *different experiences*, both positive and negative, to participants because sport programs and teams are organized in vastly different ways. Therefore, we cannot make general statements about the consequences of sport participation. This point is explained in Reflect on Sports, pages 102–104.
2. People who choose or are selected to participate in sports may have different traits than those who do not choose or are not selected to participate. Therefore, sports may not *build* character as much as they are organized to *select* people who already have certain character traits that are valued by coaches and compatible with highly organized, competitive activities.
3. The meanings given to sport experiences vary from one athlete to the next, even when they play in the same programs and the same teams. Therefore, the lessons that athletes

learn and the ways they apply those lessons to their lives vary greatly.

4. The meanings that people give to their sport experiences change over time as they grow older and view themselves and the world in new ways. Therefore, people revise their evaluation of past sport experiences as they develop new ideas and values.

5. Socialization occurs through the social interaction that accompanies sport participation. Therefore, the meaning and importance of playing sports depend on a person's social relationships and the social and cultural contexts in which participation occurs.

6. The socialization that occurs in sports may also occur in other activities. Therefore, people who do not play sports can have the same developmental experiences that athletes have.

Due to these oversights, studies that compare "athletes" with "nonathletes" produce inconsistent and sometimes misleading evidence about sports and socialization. My review of these studies leads me to conclude that sport participation is most likely to have positive socialization consequences for people when it provides the following:

- Opportunities for exploring and developing identities apart from playing sports
- Knowledge-building experiences that go beyond the locker room and the playing field
- New relationships, especially with people who are not connected with sports and do not base their interaction on a person's status or identity as an athlete
- Explicit examples of how lessons learned in sports may be applied to specific situations apart from sports
- Opportunities to develop and display competence in nonsport activities that are observed by other people who can serve as mentors and advocates outside of sports

Alana Beard, an All American basketball player from Duke University, expressed some of these points when she said,

> I've developed a group of friends . . . and they know nothing about basketball. That's the best thing any athlete can do: get friends that don't know anything about your sport and accept you as just another friend and not because you're that basketball player. (Q and A, 2003, p. 28)

Research also suggests that when playing sports *constricts* a person's opportunities, experiences, relationships, and general competence apart from sports, it is likely to have negative consequences for overall development. Therefore, we cannot make a general statement that sports build *or* undermine character development. Neither positive nor negative character is automatically developed in sports. This is because sport experiences are defined and incorporated into people's lives in various ways depending on the social and cultural contexts in which they live.

This conclusion does *not* mean that sports and sport participation are irrelevant in people's lives. We know that discourses, images, and experiences related to sports are vivid and powerful in many cultures today. Sports do impact our lives and the world around us. However, we cannot separate that impact from the meanings that we give to sports and the ways that we integrate them into our lives. Therefore, if we want to know what happens in sports, we must study sport experiences in the social and cultural contexts in which they occur.

This type of research is exciting and provides insights into the complex connections between sports and socialization. Unfortunately, the uncritically accepted belief that "sports build character" has prevented this research from being taken seriously. Additionally, this belief has prevented people from recognizing that if we want sports to build character we must critically examine sports and determine the types of sport experiences that are sites where positive socialization outcomes are most likely to occur.

Power and Performance Versus Pleasure and Participation

Different Sports, Different Experiences,
Different Consequences

Sport experiences are diverse. It is a mistake to assume that all sports are defined in the same way, organized around the same goals and orientations, and played in the same spirit. In North America, for example, there are highly organized competitive sports, informal sports, adventure sports, recreational sports, extreme sports, alternative sports, cooperative sports, folk sports, contact sports, artistic sports, team sports, individual

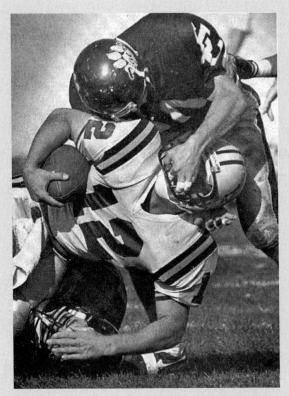

Power and performance sports involves the use of strength, speed, and power to dominate opponents in the quest for competitive victories. (*Source:* Bob Jackson, *Colorado Springs Gazette*)

sports, and so on. However, at this point in North American history, the dominant sport form is organized around a **power and performance model.**

Power and performance sports are highly organized and competitive. Generally, they emphasize the following:

- The use of strength, speed, and power to push human limits and dominate opponents in the quest for victories
- The idea that excellence is proved through competitive success and achieved through dedication, hard work, sacrifices, risking personal well-being, and playing in pain
- The importance of setting records and using technology to control and monitor the body
- Tryouts and selection systems based on physical skills and competitive success
- Hierarchical authority structures in which athletes are subordinate to coaches and coaches are subordinate to owners and administrators
- Defining opponents as enemies to be conquered, especially when they are confronted on "home turf"

These points exaggerate the characteristics of power and performance sports, but my purpose is to show that experiences in such sports are very different from experiences in sports with other characteristics.

Although the power and performance model has become the standard for defining "real" sports in U.S. culture, some people have maintained or developed other forms of sport. Some of these are revisions of dominant forms, whereas others represent alternative or even oppositional sport forms. The sports that are the most oppositional are organized around a **pleasure and participation model.** Pleasure and participation sports generally emphasize the following:

- Active participation revolving around connections between people, mind and body, and physical activity and the environment

Pleasure and participation sports may involve competition, but the primary emphasis is on connections between people and on personal expression through participation. (*Source:* Susanne Tregarthen/Educational Photo Stock)

- A spirit of personal expression, enjoyment, growth, good health, and mutual concern among teammates and opponents
- Personal empowerment created by experiencing the body in pleasurable ways
- Inclusive participation based on accommodating differences in physical skills among players
- Democratic decision-making structures characterized by cooperation and sharing power, even in coach–athlete relationships
- An emphasis on competing *with* others and defining opponents as partners who test skills

Again, these points exaggerate the characteristics of pleasure and participation sports, but they show that experiences in these sports would be very different from experiences in power and participation sports.

These two sport forms do *not* encompass all the ways that sports might be defined, organized, and played. Many people play sports that contain elements of both forms and reflect diverse ideas about what is important in physical activities. However, power and performance sports remain dominant today in the sense that they receive the most attention and support. When people play or watch these sports, their socialization experiences are likely to be different from their experiences when playing or watching pleasure and participation sports.

Why are power and performance sports dominant today? Critical theory tells us that sports are parts of culture and that people with the needed resources to sponsor sports usually want them to be organized and played in ways that promote their interests. They want sports to fit their view of the world and celebrate the relationships, orientations, and values that reproduce their privileged positions in society. Today, power and performance sports fit the interests of people with wealth and influence.

Wealthy and influential people in societies around the world use different strategies to maintain their privileged positions. Some use coercive strategies such as police or military force, but most use cultural strategies designed to create the belief that wealth and power are distributed in legitimate and acceptable ways in society. For example, in countries with monarchies, the privileged position of the royal family usually is explained in terms of its birthright. Kings and queens maintain their privileged positions as long as people in the society believe that birthrights represent legitimate claims to wealth and power. This is why the church and state are closely aligned in societies with monarchies—kings and queens use their association with divine external forces to legitimize their wealth and power. In democratic countries, most people use *merit* as a standard when judging whether wealth and power are legitimate. Therefore, status and privilege in democracies is maintained

Power and Performance Versus Pleasure and Participation (*Continued*)
Different Sports, Different Experiences, Different Consequences

only when most people believe that rewards go to those who have earned them. When there is widespread inequality in a democratic society, people with wealth and power must promote the idea that they have earned their privileged positions through hard work and intelligence and that poverty and powerlessness are the result of laziness and a lack of intelligence. An effective strategy to promote this idea is to emphasize that *competition* is a natural part of social life and a fair means of determining who gets what in the society. If people accept this idea, they will also believe that those with wealth and power deserve what they have.

This connection between wealth, power, and an emphasis on competition helps us understand why power and performance sports are so widely promoted and supported in many countries today. These sports are based on a class ideology that celebrates winners and idealizes the domination of some people over others. These sports also promote the idea that competition is the only fair and natural way to distribute rewards and that people with wealth and power deserve status and privilege because they have competed successfully—they are the winners.

Power and performance sports are most popular in democratic societies where there are widespread and highly visible economic inequalities between classes of people. These sports have also expanded globally as wealthy and powerful transnational corporations seek strategies to promote the idea that global economic competition is a good thing. Corporate executives collectively allocate billions of dollars annually to sponsor power and performance sports. They want people to agree that rewards should go to winners, that the winners deserve wealth and power, and that the ranking of people on the basis of wealth and power is not only fair but also natural. In other words, their sponsorships are based on concerns about ideology as well as financial profits that might be generated by sports.

Pleasure and participation sports and other sport forms that challenge this way of thinking may be popular among some people, but they generally do not receive sponsorships and support from people with money and power. For example, sponsorships and support are not given to alternative sports unless they are reorganized around the power and performance model. This is illustrated by ESPN's conversion of free-flowing, expressive alternative sports into the X Games organized around a power and performance model that fits the interests of wealthy corporate sponsors, *not* the interests of participants and spectators. *What do you think?*

Do Sports Improve Health and Physical Well-Being?

If something is said often enough, many people accept it as true. This has certainly been the case with the statement, "sports are healthy activities." Therefore, many people were surprised when a list of healthy physical activities identified in a report by the U.S Surgeon General (USDHHS, 1996) included only two competitive sports: fifteen to twenty minutes of playing basketball and forty-five minutes of playing volleyball. No other sports were on the list because the surgeon general reviewed research on sport participation and health and determined that the injury risks associated with nearly all competitive sports were so high that participation often created more health costs than benefits (White, 2004; Young, 2004a).

The Sport–Health Connection The relationship between sports, exercise, and health is complex.

However, people who list the health benefits of sports when they are really talking about the benefits of regular physical exercise often ignore this complexity. After reviewing dozens of studies on this topic, sociologist Ivan Waddington (2000a, 2000b, 2007) explains that the healthiest of all physical activities are rhythmic, noncompetitive exercises in which individuals control and regulate their own body movements. Health benefits decline when there is a shift from self-controlled exercise to competitive sports; in fact, the health costs of competitive sports are relatively high, due primarily to injuries. This benefit–cost ratio becomes even less favorable when there is a shift from noncontact to contact sports and from mass sports to elite sports in which players train intensely, put their bodies at risk, and play while injured. Overall, Waddington concludes the following:

> The health-related arguments in favor of regular and moderate physical activity are clear, but they are considerably less persuasive in relation to competitive, and especially contact, sport and very much less persuasive in relation to elite, or professional sport. (Waddington, in press)

Other scholars in the sociology of sport have made similar points. For example, Eric Dunning (1986) notes that many sports are mock battles during which aggressive and violent acts are common (see chapter 7, p. 194, for a discussion of violence in sports). Mike Messner (1992) explains that in heavy-contact sports, male athletes routinely turn their bodies into weapons and use them in ways that injure themselves and opponents. According to research by Kevin Young (1993), this orientation has made men's heavy-contact professional sport a hazardous workplace with a higher injury rate than construction sites, oil drilling rigs, or underground mines—the three most

dangerous workplaces apart from professional sports. Jennifer Waldron and Vikki Krane (2005) also explain that female athletes often participate in contexts where there are group pressures to engage in risky and unhealthy actions as they seek success and live up to the expectations of coaches and teammates.

Although risks are highest in elite sports, they also exist in mass sports where injury rates are regularly higher than in other everyday activities.

> Athletic participation at the elite level is an egoistic, self-centered activity, as athletes must continue to hone their bodies.
>
> —George J. Bryjak, sociologist, University of San Diego, 2002

In fact, researchers in England found that when they compared the health benefits and costs of exercise and sports, the health benefits outweighed costs for people forty-five years old and over. However, the costs outweighed benefits for people fifteen to forty-four years old. In financial terms, this meant that every young adult who regularly participated in exercise and sports "created" $45 per year of costs more than if they had not participated regularly (Nichol et al., 1993). In other words, the "disease prevention benefits" were lower than the medical fees for treating exercise and sport-related injuries in younger adults.

These findings about benefits and costs do not consider the difficult-to-measure social and psychological benefits of being active and having "good workouts" in competitive sports. But they clearly indicate that we cannot say that "sports improve health and physical well-being" without qualifying what we mean. In very practical terms, if you do not have health insurance, it would be wise to stay fit by doing aerobics, walking, swimming, and jumping rope; and if you play football, rugby, hockey, or other competitive contact sports, you need good health insurance. Even if you play golf, softball, and other sports that require sudden and forceful twisting motions or sprinting from a dead stop, it would be wise to be insured.

The Sport–Obesity Connection   Obesity is the most publicized health issue today, and nearly every discussion of this issue ends with the conclusion that eating right and exercising is the best way to avoid unhealthy weight gains. This is of course true, and research consistently supports the value of exercise in controlling body weight.

It would be nice if we could say that as sports become increasingly popular in society, obesity rates go down. But data suggest otherwise: Obesity rates have increased at the same time and in the same cultures that competitive sports, especially those organized around the power and performance model, have become increasingly popular. This does not mean that playing sports causes obesity, but it does mean that the popularity of sports in a society does not inspire more than a few people to embrace forms of exercise that enable them to avoid gaining weight.

Like the connection between sports and health, the connection between sports and weight is complex. Some sports emphasize extreme forms of weight control; wrestling and gymnastics are prime examples of this. Other sports emphasize weight gain for some or all the athletes involved. For example, many NFL players are encouraged to gain weight to the point that over half of the nearly 2200 players during the 2003–2004 season were classified as obese, and one-half of the obese players were in the severely obese range on the BMI–body mass index (Harp and Hecht, 2005). Although the BMI is probably not a good measure to use when studying the relationship between weight and health, the way that it is used in this study suggests that NFL players are not a good collection of athletes to use if one is arguing that playing sports is a good way to control weight. Expectations in football now demand excessive eating and/or taking nutritional supplements to gain size. In 1988 there were only 17 NFL players over 300 pounds, but in 2005 there were over 350, with some pushing 400 pounds, and they claim to have gained weight by overeating. This takes a serious toll on life expectancy as well as overall health (Briggs, 2002).

> *Neglecting . . . rules of health, [athletes] spend their lives like pigs— over-exercising, over- eating and over- sleeping. . . . Athletes rarely live to old age, and if they do, they are crippled by disease.*
>
> —Galen, Greek physician, A.D. 180

How Do Sports Affect Our Lives?

Sports and sport participation impact the lives of many people around the world. We are learning more about this impact through three types of studies based on a combination of critical, critical feminist, and interactionist theories:

1. Studies of sport experiences as explained through the voices of sport participants
2. Studies of social worlds, or subcultures, that are created and maintained in connection with particular sports
3. Studies of sports as sites, or "social locations" where dominant ideas and ideologies are expressed and sometimes challenged and changed

Taken together, these studies have helped many of us who are concerned with sports in society to rethink socialization issues. Now we view sports as *sites for socialization experiences*, rather than as *causes of specific socialization outcomes*. This is an important distinction. It highlights two things. First, sports are social locations rich in their potential for providing memorable and meaningful personal, social, and cultural experiences. Second, sports *by themselves* do not cause particular changes in the character traits, attitudes, and actions of athletes or spectators. Therefore, when positive or negative socialization outcomes occur in connection with sports, we don't simply say that they were caused by sports; instead, we view sports as sites for influential

Sports in many cultures are no longer seen as exclusively masculine activities. However, traditional gender definitions and associated clothing may still keep some girls out of the action. (*Source:* Jay Coakley)

experiences and then search for and explain the specific social processes through which particular socialization outcomes occur.

The following summaries of selected studies illustrates how this approach to socialization helps us understand what happens in sports and how sports are connected with social issues and forces in society.

Real-Life Experiences: Sport Stories from Athletes

The following examples provide three socialization videos. They illustrate what happens in sports from the perspectives of the participants themselves, and they show us how people give meaning to sport experiences and integrate them into their lives on their own terms.

Example 1: The Moral Lessons of Little League
Sociologist Gary Alan Fine (1987) spent three years studying boys in Little League baseball. Fine focused on the moral socialization that occurred as the boys interacted with each other, coaches, and parents. He found that the moral messages that coaches and parents presented to the boys were based on adult views of the world. But the boys heard and interpreted these

messages in terms of their views as eleven-year-old boys concerned with being accepted by peers and learning what it means to be a man in U.S. culture. Thus, socialization was an interactive process in which the boys played key roles in what and how they learned. What happened to the boys as they played baseball resulted from a combination of adult influence, the developmental issues associated with preadolescence, and the social reality of being eleven-year-old boys in U.S. culture during the late 1980s.

Among other things, the boys learned to define *masculinity* in terms of toughness and dominance and to express disdain for females and other boys labeled as weak or unwilling to take risks on or off the playing field. They learned other things as well, but their emerging ideas about manhood were influential in how they saw themselves and their connections to the world. Playing baseball did not *cause* the boys to define *masculinity* in a particular way, but their Little League teams were one of the sites where they considered various ideas about what it means to be men and how to act as men.

What made baseball significant was that these emerging ideas about being tough and aggressive were clearly endorsed by coaches, parents, and peers. Toughness and aggression were promoted in connection with team strategies, player evaluations, and peer acceptance. The impact of this social feedback was accentuated because it reinforced other cultural messages that the boys received in their relationships and through the media. Therefore, playing baseball was a heavily gendered experience for them—it involved a connection between their identities as males in U.S. culture and their identities as athletes. A more recent study by Ingham and Dewar (1999) reported very similar findings in the case of fourteen- to fifteen-year-old boys in an organized ice hockey league.

> [As a player, it was] what do I eat? What's going to be good for my tennis? When do I practice? It was me, me, me, and that gets very old and very empty.
>
> —Chris Evert, former professional tennis player, 2003

Example 2: Lessons in the Locker Room   Sociologist Nancy Theberge (1999, 2000b) spent two years studying an elite women's ice hockey team in Canada. As she observed and interviewed team members, she noted that their experiences and orientations were related to the fact that men controlled the team, the league, and the sport itself. Within this overall sport structure, the women developed a professional approach to participation. They focused on hockey and were serious about being successful on the ice. In the process, they developed close connections with each other. The team became a community with its own dynamics and internal organization. Within this constructed community, the athletes learned things about hockey, themselves, and teammates. The meanings that the players gave to their hockey experiences and the ways they integrated them into their lives emerged as they interacted on and off the ice.

The locker room was a key place for the interaction through which teammates bonded with each other and gave meanings to their sport experiences. The emotional climate of the locker room, especially *after* a practice or game, encouraged talk that focused on the athletes as people and their experiences apart from hockey. This talk gave shape and meaning to what they did on the ice. It also served as a means for expressing feelings and thoughts about men, sexuality (male partners and female partners), and families. The women talked and joked about men but didn't degrade or reduce them to body parts in their comments. They made references to sex and sexuality in their conversations, but the substance of these references inferred inclusiveness rather than hostility or stereotypes. This was very different from what has reportedly occurred in many men's locker rooms where women have been routinely derogated and objectified, and homosexuality has been vilified if it is discussed at all (Curry, 1993).

Theberge's study shows us that playing sports is a social as well as a physical experience. Hockey was a site for experiences, but it was *through social relationships* that those experiences were given meaning and incorporated into the women's lives. Theberge focused on relationships between the athletes, but also important were relationships with coaches, managers, trainers, friends, family members, sport reporters, and even fans. If we want to know what happens in sports, we must understand what happens in those relationships. It is through them that athletes are socialized.

Example 3: Stories of Gay Male Athletes The meanings given to sport experiences emerge in connection with social relationships. But those meanings vary from one person to another because social relationships are influenced by social definitions given to age, gender, socioeconomic status, ethnicity, skin color, (dis)abilities, and sexuality. This point is highlighted in Dan Woog's (1998) book about gay male athletes in the United States. Woog, a journalist, felt it was important to give voice to gay men in sports and hear what they had to say about themselves and their sport experiences. Using data collected in interviews, Woog tells twenty-eight stories about athletes, coaches, referees, administrators, and others in sports.

The stories indicate that gay men are especially cautious about coming out in sports. Successfully combining a gay identity with an athlete identity was a challenging process for nearly all the interviewees. Woog observed that the social contexts and relationships associated with individual sports, such as running and swimming, generally were more gay friendly than team sports although a cosmopolitan team sport, such as soccer, provided a more gay-friendly context than "a mechanized, play-by-rote game like football." Being out was liberating for most of the gay men, but it was also dangerous for some of them. They cared deeply about sports, and they feared that being open about who they were might lead others to exclude them from sports teams and programs. Positive experiences among openly gay athletes were most likely when there were organizations that supported them on and off the field, when family and friends provided overt support, and when someone in their sport, such as a teammate or coach, served as their advocate and showed others that sexuality should not undermine acceptance and friendship.

Despite similarities between the experiences of gay and straight men in sports, the meanings given to those experiences and how they are integrated into people's lives differ because of how *heterosexuality* and *homosexuality* are defined by many people. Those definitions influence the meaning and impact of sport experiences; as those definitions change, so will the meanings given to the experiences that people have in sports (see also Anderson, 2000, 2002, 2004).

Social Worlds: Living in Sports

Although sociologists study sports mostly as parts of the societies and cultures in which they are played and watched, some studies focus on sports as **social worlds,** a term used in interactionist theory to refer to *a way of life and an associated mind-set that revolve around a particular set of activities and encompass all the people and relationships connected with the activities.* These studies are based on the assumption that we can't understand who athletes are, what they do, and how sports influence their lives unless we view them in the context of the social world in which they give meaning to sport experiences. Unless we know about these contexts, we have difficulty making sense of sport experiences and their impact on socialization. This is especially true when we study people whose lives revolve completely around a particular sport—that is, when the social world of their sport is their entire world.

Studies of social worlds created in connection with specific sports provide useful information about socialization processes and experiences. Following are five examples.

Example 1: Learning to Be a Hero Sociologists Patti and Peter Adler spent nearly ten years studying the social world of a high-profile college basketball team. Much of their data, presented in the book *Backboards and Blackboards* (1991), focuses on how the self-conceptions of young men changed as they played big-time intercollegiate basketball. The Adlers found that the young men, about 70 percent of whom were African Americans, usually became deeply engulfed in their athlete roles. This influenced how they viewed themselves and allocated their time between basketball, social life, and academics. "Role engulfment" intensified as the young men became increasingly committed to identities based exclusively on playing basketball. Coaches, students, fans, community members, the media, and teammates all supported and reinforced their athlete identities. The social world of intercollegiate basketball became the context in which the young men identified themselves, set goals, and viewed the rest of the world.

The Adlers noted that the young men learned about setting goals, focusing attention on specific tasks, and making sacrifices to play basketball. However, they found no immediate evidence to suggest that the athletes applied these lessons to other aspects of their lives. The social world of basketball separated the men so much from the rest of life that the lessons they learned in that social world stayed there.

This lack of carryover between sports and the rest of life usually is more common among men than women because the social worlds that revolve around women's sports do not separate them as much from other spheres of life. However, there remains a need for further studies on how role engulfment influences the socialization experiences of athletes from different backgrounds, in different sports, and over the course of an athlete's time in college (Miller and Kerr, 2003).

Example 2: Realizing Image Isn't Everything
Anthropologist Alan Klein studied the social

> I don't know what life is like, I don't know how regular people live. I just can never understand it. My first job was the NBA.
> —Tracy McGrady, NBA player, 2005

world of competitive bodybuilding for seven years. In his book *Little Big Men* (1993), he explains that much of the lives of the bodybuilders revolved around issues of gender and sexuality.

The bodybuilders, both male and female, learned to project public images of power and strength although privately they experienced serious doubts about their identities and self-worth. The social world of bodybuilding seemed to foster a desperate need for attention and approval from others, especially other bodybuilders. Ideas about masculinity within the social world of bodybuilding were so narrow and one dimensional that the male bodybuilders developed homophobic attitudes and went to great lengths to assert their heterosexuality in public. Also, the focus on body size and hardness created such insecurities that the men learned to present and even define themselves in terms of exaggerated caricatures of masculinity—like comic-book depictions of manly men.

Overall, bodybuilding was a site for powerful socialization experiences in their lives. However, due to gender relations in the culture at large, these experiences took on different meanings for the female bodybuilders than they did for the men (see the box "Female Bodybuilders," in chapter 8, pp. 268–269).

Example 3: Living in the Shadow of a Man's World
Sociologist Todd Crosset (1995) spent fourteen months studying the social world of women's professional golf. He found that being on the LPGA tour created and in fact required a mind-set focused on using physical competence as a basis for evaluating self and the other golfers. He described this mind-set as "an ethic of prowess" and explained that it existed partly because the women wanted to neutralize the potentially negative effects that dominant ideas about gender could have if they entered the social world of women's professional golf. One golfer who he interviewed said that much of

what she did in her life was a response to the notion that "*athlete* is almost a masculine noun" in this society. The impact of being a pro golfer was summarized by one woman who said, "We are different than the typical married lady with a house full of kids in what we think and do." Crosset's study emphasized that we can understand the meaning of this statement only in the context of the social world of the LPGA and that we can understand the social world of the LPGA only in the context of gender relations in U.S. culture.

The cultural necessity of this mind-set has become less urgent over the last decade as female athletes have become increasingly visible and accepted in many societies. However, issues of sexuality continue to be discussed quietly, if they are discussed at all, and the LPGA has only recently sponsored day care for golfers who are mothers. In the meantime, Annika Sorenstam is the most accomplished golfer in the world, and she receives much less attention than the top male golfers, unless she plays with them.

Example 4: Surviving in a Ghetto   Sociologist Loïc Wacquant (1992) spent three years studying the social world of boxers in a gym located in a black neighborhood in Chicago. His observations, interviews, and experiences as a boxer helped him uncover the ideas and meanings that constitute the life and craft of boxing. He explains that the social world of the boxing gym is very complex: It is created in connection with the social forces in an ethnically segregated ghetto and its masculine street culture, but it also shelters black men from the full destructive impact of those forces. To learn the "social art" of boxing, the men at the gym engaged in an intense regime of body regulation focused on the physical, visual, and mental requirements of boxing. They had to "eat, drink, sleep and live boxing," and in the process, they developed what Wacquant described as a *socialized lived body*, which was at the very core of their identities and actions. The experience of living in the social world of the boxing gym separated the men from their peers and kept them alive as they navigated their lives in dangerous neighborhoods devoid of hope or opportunity. For these men, boxing was a powerful socialization experience, but it cannot be understood apart from the context of their everyday lives.

Example 5: Sport Worlds Portrayed in the Media
Joan Ryan (1995) and Christine Brennan (1996) are journalists who have studied and written about the social worlds of elite, competitive women's gymnastics and men's and women's figure skating. Their research methods and writing styles are different from those of academic scholars, but they contribute to what we know about socialization experiences in these two sports. For example, Ryan's descriptions of the social world of elite women's gymnastics provide a basis for understanding why girls and young women in that world frequently develop disordered-eating patterns. Although parents, coaches, and fellow athletes do not explicitly foster such actions, the young women often come to see them as part of their lives as gymnasts. As we know from a few highly publicized cases, when relationships and routines in sports foster eating disorders, they can be fatal. This is the *socialized lived body* in an extreme form.

Like the social worlds described in the previous four examples, gymnastics and figure skating are sites where influential socialization processes occur. Understanding those processes and the experiences involved in them requires knowledge of the particular social worlds in which they occur. Once we have a deep understanding of a social world associated with a sport, once we delve into it through good research, the things that athletes think and do become meaningful and understandable to us, regardless of how they appear to people who are not part of those worlds. This does not mean that we approve of everything that occurs in those worlds, but it enables us to understand why things occur and what might be done to make sports safer and more humane places for athletes to be.

Ideology: Sports as Sites for Struggling Over How We Think and What We Do

Socialization research has focused mostly on what occurs in the lives of individuals and small groups. However, as researchers have combined critical theories with cultural studies and post-structuralism,[1] they have done creative studies of *socialization as a community and cultural process.* Their research goes beyond looking at the experiences and characteristics of athletes. Instead, it focuses on sports as sites where people in society collectively create and learn "stories," which they use to give meaning to and make sense of the world and their lives. The stories that revolve around sports and athletes have their own vocabularies and images. The meanings in these stories shift, depending on who tells and hears them, and they often identify important cultural issues in everyday life. Researchers identify these stories and study how they fit into the culture and how people use them in connection with what they think and do.

Researchers also are concerned with whose stories about sports become dominant in the culture because so many stories *could* be told about sports. These stories are culturally important because they identify what is natural, normal, and legitimate and therefore give priority to ideas and orientations that privilege some people more

than others. For example, the vocabulary and stories that frequently are associated with sports revolve around heroic figures who are big, strong, aggressive, record-setting champions. Political scientist Varda Burstyn (1999, p. 23) says that these stories celebrate the notion of "higher, faster, stronger" that today serves the interests of capitalist expansion and traditional manly values associated with conquest. This is an important way in which comprehensive forms of socialization occur in connection with sports.

Researchers are also concerned with whose stories are not told and whose voices are silenced or "erased" from the stories that are told in the dominant culture. For example, the media coverage of sports might be studied to learn what is *not* contained in narratives and images as much as what is contained in them. This is because we can learn about culture by seeing what is *not* represented in narratives and images as well as seeing what is represented.

This type of research is difficult to do because it requires a knowledge of history and a deep understanding of the settings in which sports and sport stories come to be a part of people's lives. But it is important to do this research because it deals with the influence of sports in the culture as a whole, rather than in the lives of individuals and small groups.

The Politics of Socialization as a Community and Cultural Process Research on socialization as a community and cultural process is partly inspired by the ideas of Italian political theorist, Antonio Gramsci. When fascists in Italy imprisoned Gramsci for speaking out against their oppressive policies, he used his time in prison (1928–1935), to think about why people had not revolted against exploitive forms of capitalism in Western societies. Gramsci concluded that it was important to understand how people in society form their notions of common sense and ideas about how society ought to be organized socially, politically, and economically. He explained that powerful people could influence and win the support of the

---

[1]Poststructuralism is a theoretical and methodological perspective based on the assumption that culture today revolves around language and rapidly changing media representations. Functionalists and conflict theorists consider material production and empirical reality to be the foundation of culture and society; poststructuralists focus on language and media representations because they assume that social life in today's postmodern culture is constantly negotiated, constructed, challenged, and changed through language and images that represent people, ideas, and things. Research done by poststructuralists often deals with the media and focuses on how images, identities, symbols, and meanings are fabricated through media representations that constitute the contexts of our lives. Poststructuralists often do scholarly work that is intended to disrupt meanings and representations that oppress some people and privilege others.

people over whom they exercised power by providing them exciting and pleasurable experiences.

Gramsci suspected that most people use the cultural messages associated with the sources of excitement and pleasure in their lives to inform their notions of common sense and their ideas about the organization and operation of society as a whole. Therefore, existing forms of power relations in society could be maintained if people with power organized and sponsored exciting and pleasurable activities that promoted their perspectives and interests.

Gramsci's analysis helps us understand why large corporations spend billions of dollars every year to sponsor sports and present advertisements in connection with sports. For example, Coca-Cola, General Motors, and McDonald's have each spent hundreds of millions of dollars sponsoring and presenting advertising messages during the 1996, 2000, and 2004 Olympic Games. These expenditures were made to promote sales, but more important, they were made to use the Olympics as vehicles for delivering cultural messages that corporate executives wanted people in the world to hear. They wanted people watching the Olympics to agree that competition is the best way to allocate rewards and that wealthy and powerful people (and corporations) deserve what they have because they are the best at what they do.

The people who run Coca-Cola and General Motors want people to drink Coke and drive Chevy trucks, but they also want people to develop lifestyles in which excitement and pleasure are associated with consumption and in which social status is associated with corporate brands and logos. They want people to say, "These large companies are important to us because without them we would not have the sports we love so dearly." They want people to believe that their excitement and pleasure depends on large corporations and

> In his own way, [Michael] Jordan did spread an ideology. It was that sports are not just games but tools for advertisers. It was that basketball isn't a playground thing, but a corporate thing.
>
> —Jay Weiner, *BusinessWeek* (1999)

their products. They want to establish consumption as the foundation for measuring progress and defining prosperity. Their profits and power depend on it, and their marketing people use sports to promote an ideology of competition and consumption. To the extent that people in society accept this ideology, the power of corporations increases in society.

Many sociologists refer to this process of forming consent around a particular ideology as the process of establishing hegemony (heh·gem′ ōh·nee). In political science and sociology, **hegemony** is a *process of maintaining leadership and control by gaining the consent of other groups, including those who are being led or controlled*. For example, American hegemony in the world exists when people worldwide accept U.S. control as legitimate. Hegemony is never permanent, but it can be maintained in a society as long as most people feel that their lives are as good as can be expected and that there is no strong reason to change the way social worlds are currently organized. Similarly, corporate hegemony is maintained as long as most people accept a view of the world that is consistent with corporate interests. People in corporations know that their interests depend on establishing "ideological outposts" in people's heads. Sports, because they are exciting and pleasurable activities for so many people, are important tools for building such outposts. Once established, these outposts are useful to corporations because they serve as terminals through which many corporate messages can be delivered into people's minds. To paraphrase Gramsci's conclusion about hegemony, it is difficult to fight an enemy that has outposts in your head.

Research on Socialization as a Community and Cultural Process It is difficult to understand socialization as a community and cultural process unless we see it in action. The following examples

When corporations spend money to have their names, logos, and products associated with sports, they are looking for more than sales. In the long run, their executives hope that people will believe that their enjoyment of sports depends on the corporations. If this happens, people are more likely to support and less likely to interfere with corporate interests. Sport sponsorships were especially important after 2002 when accounting scandals and CEO excesses damaged corporate credibility. (*Source:* Jay Coakley)

of research highlight this informative approach to sports and socialization.

Anthropologist Doug Foley (1999a) studied the connection between sports and community socialization processes in a small Texas town. His findings indicate that high school football was important in the lives of many individuals in that small town. However, the stories created around football and the people who played, coached, watched, and cheered for it reaffirmed established ways of thinking and doing things in the town. In the process, sports became a means for maintaining the forms of social inequality that made life good for a few and difficult for many residents. For example, even though a young Mexicana could become popular as a cheerleader and a young Mexicano from a poor family could be a star on the team, this had no effect on the political and economic standing of women, Mexican Americans, or low-income people in the town. Experiences associated with football did not lead people to

challenge inequalities related to gender, ethnicity, and social class. Instead, those experiences reproduced ideas that supported those inequalities, even though individual lives sometimes were changed in connection with sports.

Mike Messner's (1992) interviews with former elite male athletes showed that sports were sites where these athletes created identities that influenced how they presented themselves in public, related to women, and evaluated themselves (go to the OLC for a summary of this study). These identities and the stories associated with them became part of popular culture in the United States and reproduced dominant ideas about manhood. Messner concluded that, as people struggle over issues related to gender, sports are important because they provide vocabularies and images that perpetuate actions and forms of social organization that privilege most men over most women and some men over others.

Susan Birrell and Diana Richter's (1994) observations of softball teams and in-depth interviews with players showed that feminist orientations can alter the way that women play sports. As the women organized their games around the pleasure and participation model, their experiences became sources of personal empowerment and a commitment to supporting each other. This made their sport experiences very different from the experiences of people who play power and performance sports. Additionally, it demonstrated that sports can be played in ways that challenge dominant ideas. When this happens, socialization in sports may involve changes in how entire groups of people think about what is important in life and how social relationships can and should be organized.

Other studies also have focused on the ways that popular images connected with sports become influential cultural symbols as they are represented in the media and everyday conversations. For example, David Andrews (1996b) used critical and poststructuralist theories to study the connection between racial ideology in the United States and the cultural stories created around Michael Jordan between 1982 and 1995. Andrews's analysis of commercials and other media coverage show how the "Jordan persona" was severed from African American experiences and culture so that white America, seeking evidence that it was colorblind and open to all, could comfortably identify with him and approve of their children hanging Jordan posters on their bedroom walls in their all-white neighborhoods. Andrews uses historical information about race and depictions of the Jordan persona in media commercials to argue that, even though race and skin color were erased from Jordan's public persona, we cannot understand Jordan's status and impact as a cultural icon without knowing how racism operates in the United States.

Andrews's research and similar studies done by others emphasize that *none of us lives outside the influence of ideology* (Andrews, 1996a, 1996b; Burstyn, 1999; Paraschak, 1997). This research is based on the premise that sports, because they are popular sources of excitement and pleasure in people's lives, are significant sites at which people learn and sometimes raise questions about ideology. This research holds the promise of showing us how sports influence widely held ideas in a culture and how people can disrupt that influence when it promotes stereotypes and exploitation (see Andrews and Jackson, 2001).

WHAT SOCIALIZATION RESEARCH DOESN'T TELL US

Existing research doesn't tell us all we want to know about sports and socialization. We have many research snapshots and a few videos to help us understand parts of socialization processes related to sports. But we lack information on how these processes operate in the lives of people from various ethnic groups and social classes. In North America, research on Asian Americans, Latinos, Native Americans, and French Canadians in sports is especially needed. We also need studies of sport participation in high-income

and low-income communities, as well as among wealthy and poor individuals and families.

We know that an eleven-year-old white girl from a wealthy Euro-American family playing tennis in an exclusive suburban club has different sport experiences than a Mexican boy playing in a pickup soccer game on a dusty road in the fields of lettuce where his parents are minimum-wage agricultural workers. Clearly, we need to know more about variations in sport experiences and how people from different social and cultural backgrounds give those experiences meaning and integrate them into their lives at various points in their life course. We cannot talk about the socialization consequences of sports without putting sport experiences into real-life contexts (see figure 4.2). That's why your sport participation has had a different impact on you than mine has had on me, and that's why it is senseless to argue about

"I don't think these guys agree about the meaning of boxing."

FIGURE 4.2 Meanings given to sports vary from one person to another. However, many power and performance sports are organized to encourage orientations that emphasize domination over others. Those who do not hold this orientation may not fit very well in these sports.

breaking BARRIERS

Socialization Barriers
Living in the Empire of the Normal

Popular images of bodies embedded in our culture, the media, and our minds are images of able bodies. Seldom do we see images of impaired bodies, except in notices for fund-raising events to "help the disabled." Images that represent disability as an embodied form that is valuable, beautiful, healthy, fit, or athletic are practically nonexistent (Seeley and Rail, 2004). This is because we live in an "Empire of the Normal" where productive, healthy, fit, beautiful, and ideal bodies are *able bodies* (Couser, 2000).

In the Empire of the Normal, the existence of a disabled body causes people to ask, "*What happened to you?*" People in the empire demand an explanation for a disabled body—a story that accounts for its difference from normal bodies. As people with disabilities are asked incessantly to tell their stories, their identities come to be organized around their accounts of "why my body is different from your body" (Thomson, 2000, p. 334).

This information helps us understand socialization and sports in more detail. For example, when people with disabilities make decisions to play sports, the *significant others* in their lives include physical therapists, physical educators, athletes with disabilities, sport scientists, and doctors as well as family members and peers (Schilling, 1997). In fact, the origin of today's Paralympics was in a British medical center for war

When people see a body with a disability, they often want to hear the story that accounts for its difference from "normal" bodies. Over time this may lead to the development of an identity organized around a person's account of "why my body is different from your body." (*Source:* David Biene; photo courtesy of Ossur)

whether all sports build character or whether all athletes are role models. Neither socialization nor sports are that simple, and research cannot give us unconditional yes or no answers about what sports do to us or to our communities and societies.

We also need research on sport participation careers among children and on how those careers are linked to overall social development, especially among girls, children with disabilities, and children from ethnic minority backgrounds. Similarly, we need research on older people, especially those considering or trying sports for the first

time or resuming participation after decades of not playing. We need research on how people make participation decisions about different types of sports. Sports come in many forms, and the socialization processes related to power and performance sports are different from experiences related to pleasure and participation sports.

If we knew more about each of these topics, we could provide sport participation opportunities that fit into the lives of a greater number of people. This would help us make sports more democratic and less subject to the commercial forces veterans with spinal cord injuries. Ludwig Guttmann, the neurosurgeon in charge of the center, was convinced that sports could be used as therapy for patients. His idea to schedule public games for people with disabilities at the same time as the 1948 Olympics in London was radical. People in the Empire of the Normal became uncomfortable when they were confronted with disabled bodies. "Out of sight, out of mind" has always been a norm in the empire.

After a person with a disability becomes involved in sports, decisions to stay involved are related to how other people define their bodies and treat them as athletes. Also important are participation opportunities, resources for transportation and adapted equipment, knowledgeable coaches, and programs that inspire achievement and success.

Changing or ending sport participation occurs in connection with many of the same factors that lead able-bodied athletes to disengage from sports. Injuries, a sense of reaching one's goals or hitting one's limits, responsibilities related to work and family, a lack of resources, and new opportunities to coach or work in sports influence decisions to alter or end sport participation.

The issue of what happens to people with disabilities when they play sports has seldom been studied. As with able-bodied athletes, socialization experiences among athletes with disabilities depend on their relationships, the general social and cultural context in which participation occurs, and the meanings given to participation.

In societies where power and performance sports predominate, people with disabilities seldom play with or alongside able-bodied athletes. Power and performance sports are exclusive: Only able bodies may try out. This forces athletes with disabilities to play in segregated or "special" programs or leads them to prefer those programs. This influences the meanings given to their sport participation.

Among many athletes with disabilities, sports are perceived as sites for challenging body images in the Empire of the Normal. Among a few, sports are sites for planning how to break through the empire's walls, open gates for others, and rebuild its foundation so that people no longer see disabled bodies as needing to be cured, fixed, regulated, or separated from other bodies (Thomson, 2002, p. 8).

Pam Fernandez, an eight-time U.S. National Champion in Road and Track cycling, speaks from experience when she says "if we could somehow bring the respect, dignity, and camaraderie of the Paralympic Village to the rest of the world, we could teach a lifetime of lessons in a single day" (in Joukowsky and Rothstein, 2002a, p. 93). These lessons just might hasten the fall of the Empire of the Normal.

that make them exclusive and elitist (Donnelly, 1993, 1996b). This is the focus of the "Breaking Barriers" box on pages 116–117.

We also need research on the emotional dimensions of socialization processes. Few sociologists have considered emotions in their research, but most of us know that decisions about sport participation are clearly connected with our feelings, fears, and anxieties. For example, some decisions may be linked with "psyching up," the emotional experience of forming expectations about what a person will encounter in sports.

These expectations are based on memories and the stories about sports that exist in the culture as a whole. Stories about the emotional side of sports have been collected by social psychologists who have studied "flow experiences" among athletes (Jackson and Csikszentmihalyi, 1999). Flow occurs when we face a challenge that requires us to use all of our skills and, in the process, lose track of time and get carried along by the activity itself. The "runner's high," "peak experiences," and "that game when everything just seems to click" are examples of flow in action. Even though flow is a personal experience, it is tied to sociological issues such as how activities are organized and the amount of control that participants have over their involvement in those activities.

Finally, we need more research on the ways that the vocabulary used in certain sports influences sport participation decisions and the meanings given to sport experiences. When words constantly refer to opposition, hostility, rivalries, confrontations, warriors, domination, and mastery over others, they set the stage for memories, fantasies, and identifications that serve as powerful sources of personal identity and social dynamics. This vocabulary tells us much about the organization and spirit of sports. For example, given the words that many people use when they talk about sports, it is not surprising that young women in U.S. high schools and universities are less likely than their male counterparts to be interested in or try out for and stay on varsity teams. If the language of sports is based on traditionally masculine images and orientations, many girls and women may not find certain sports very appealing. Furthermore, what types of boys and men are likely to be attracted to sports described as forms of "warfare," requiring aggression, toughness, and the desire to dominate others? Sociologists, especially those interested in gender equity and gender relations, would like to know answers to these questions.

In practical terms, when we learn more things about sports and socialization, we can become wiser parents, coaches, teachers, managers, and sport administrators. Then we can create sports that offer a wider array of challenging and satisfying experiences.

summary

WHO PLAYS AND WHAT HAPPENS?

Socialization is a complex, interactive process through which people learn about themselves and the social worlds in which they participate.

This process occurs in connection with sports and other activities and experiences in people's lives. Research indicates that playing sports is a social experience as well as a physical one.

Becoming involved and staying involved in sports occur in connection with general socialization processes in people's lives. Decisions to play sports are influenced by the availability of opportunities, the existence of social support, processes of identity formation, and the cultural context in which decisions are made.

Studies of socialization into sports show that sport participation decisions are related to processes of individual development, the organization of social life, and cultural ideology. People do not make decisions about sport participation once and for all time. They make them day after day, as they set and revise priorities in their lives. Research on sport-related decisions helps us understand the social dynamics of early experiences in sports and who influences those experiences. The reasons for staying in sports change over time as people's lives change, and it is important to study the complexities of these processes.

Changing or ending active sport participation also occurs in connection with general socialization processes. These processes are interactive and influenced by personal, social, and cultural factors. Changes in sport participation are usually tied to a combination of identity, developmental, and life course issues. Ending sport participation often involves a transition process, during which athletes disengage from sport, redefine their identities, reconnect with friends and family members, and use available resources to become involved in other activities and careers. Just as people are not socialized into sports, they are not simply socialized out of sports. Research shows that changing or ending a career as a competitive athlete occurs over time and is often tied to events and life course issues apart from sports. These connections are best studied by using research methods that enable us to identify and analyze long-term transition processes.

Socialization that occurs as people participate in sports has been widely studied, especially by people wanting to know if and how sports build character. Much of this research has produced inconsistent findings because it has been based on oversimplified ideas about sports, sport experiences, and socialization. Reviews of this research indicate that studies of sports and socialization must take into account variations in the ways that sports are organized, played, and integrated into people's lives. This is important because different sports involve different experiences and produce different socialization patterns. For example, the experience and meaning of playing power and performance sports is different from the experience and meaning of playing pleasure and participation sports. The visibility and popularity of power and performance sports are related to issues of status and ideology: these sports fit the interests of people who have the wealth and power to sponsor and promote sports.

We know that sports have an impact on people's lives. The most informative research on what happens in sports deals with (1) the everyday experiences of people who play sports, (2) the social worlds created around sports, and (3) community and cultural processes through which ideologies are created, reproduced, and changed. As we listen to the voices of those who participate in sports, study how they live their lives in connection with sports, and pay special attention to the ideological messages associated with sports, we learn more about sports and socialization.

Most scholars who study sports in society now see sports as sites for socialization experiences, rather than causes of specific socialization outcomes. This distinction recognizes that powerful and memorable experiences may occur in connection with sports, but it emphasizes that these experiences are given meaning through social relationships, and these meanings are influenced by the social and cultural contexts in which sports are played. Therefore, the most useful research in the sociology of sport focuses on the importance of social relationships and the contexts in which sport experiences are given meaning by a wide and diverse range of people who play or watch sports in some form or another.

See the OLC, www.mhhe.com/coakley9e, for an annotated list of readings related to this chapter. The OLC also contains a key concept list, a review test, and other helpful features.

WEBSITE RESOURCES

Note: Websites often change. The following URLs were current when this book was printed. Please check our website (www.mhhe.com/coakley9e) for updates and additions.

www.mhhe.com/coakley9e   Click on chapter 4; see information on the concept of competition, the relationship between competition and culture, and the persistent belief that sports build character.

www.charactercounts.org/sports/sports.htm   This site is a loosely organized coalition of individuals and organizations committed to the idea that sports should build positive character; the goal of the coalition is to change how sports are played, coached, and watched by individuals.

www.sportsmanship.org   This site is a loosely organized coalition of organizations with the goal of fostering changes so that sports will build positive character traits; the focus is on changing individuals rather than organizations.

www.sportsethicsinstitute.org   This site has Go to Youth Sports and other topics on the Sports Ethics issues page; this site highlights ethical issues at all levels of sports.

chapter

5

(Jay Coakley)

SPORTS AND CHILDREN

Are Organized Programs Worth the Effort?

SPORTS ARE A GREAT way to teach kids to be successful, to teach them life lessons, and they can apply that to every level of their life.

—**Glen Kozlowski, youth sport coach, parent, and former NFL player, 2000**

Online Learning Center Resources

Visit *Sports in Society*'s Online Learning Center (OLC) at **www.mhhe.com/coakley9e** for additional information and study material for this chapter, including

- Self-grading quizzes
- Learning objectives
- Related websites
- Additional readings

A complete outline is available online at www.mhhe.com/coakley9e.

KIDS DON'T GO to the playground anymore. When they practice there's a coach telling them what to do and how to do it. What happens to the kids' passion and heart in all this?

—**Ken Ravizza, sport psychologist, 2002**

When, how, and to what end children play sports are issues that concern parents, community leaders, and child advocates in national and international organizations. When sociologists study youth sports, they focus on the experiences of children and how those experiences vary depending on the organization of programs and the social contexts in which the programs exist. Since the early 1970s, research done by sociologists, psychologists, and educators has influenced the ways that people think about and organize sport programs for children. Parents, coaches, and program administrators are increasingly aware of the issues they should consider when evaluating youth programs.

This chapter deals with five major topics:

1. The origin and development of organized youth sports
2. Major trends in youth sports
3. Differences between informal, player-controlled sports and formally organized, adult-controlled sports
4. Commonly asked sociological questions about youth sports, including
   - When are children ready to play organized competitive sports?
   - What are the dynamics of family relationships in connection with organized youth sports?
   - How do social factors influence youth sport experiences?
5. Recommendations for changing children's sports

An underlying question that guides our discussions of these topics is this: Are organized youth sports worth all the time, money, and effort put into them? I first asked this question when my son and daughter played sports during childhood, and I continue to ask it as I talk with parents and work with coaches and policymakers who have made extensive commitments to youth sports.

ORIGIN AND DEVELOPMENT OF ORGANIZED YOUTH SPORTS

During the latter half of the nineteenth century, people in Europe and North America began to realize that the social environment influenced child development. This led many people to organize the contexts in which children grew up. Their goal was to ensure that boys and girls would become productive adults in rapidly expanding capitalist economies.

It wasn't long before organized sports for young boys were organized and sponsored by schools, communities, and church groups. The organizers hoped that sports, especially team sports, would teach boys from working-class families to work together productively. They also hoped that sports would turn middle- and upper-class boys into tough, competitive men by providing them with learning experiences that would offset the "feminized" values learned from stay-at-home mothers. At the same time, girls were provided with activities that would teach them to be good wives, mothers and homemakers. The prevailing belief was that girls should learn domestic skills rather than sport skills, and this is what they were taught in schools and playground activities. There were exceptions to these patterns, but in most industrial nations after World War II, youth sport programs were organized in these ways.

The Postwar Baby Boom and the Growth of Youth Sports

The baby-boom generation was born between 1946 and 1964. Young married couples during these years were optimistic about the future and eager to become parents. As the first wave of baby boomers moved through childhood during the 1950s and 1960s, organized youth sports grew dramatically, especially in the United States. Public, private, and commercial sponsors funded programs. Parents also entered the scene, eager to have their sons' characters built through organized competitive sports. Fathers became coaches, managers, and league administrators. Mothers did laundry and became chauffeurs and short-order cooks so that their sons were always ready for practices and games.

Most programs were for boys eight to fourteen years old, and they were organized on the belief that playing sports would prepare boys to be occupationally successful in a competitive economy. Until the 1970s, girls' interests in sports were largely ignored in most countries. Girls were relegated to the bleachers during their brothers' games and, in the United States, given the hope of becoming high school cheerleaders. Then the women's movement, the fitness movement, and government legislation prohibiting sex discrimination all came together to stimulate the development of new sport programs for girls (see chapter 8). During the 1970s and early 1980s, these programs grew rapidly, to the point that girls had nearly as many opportunities as boys. However, their participation rates have remained lower than rates for boys—for reasons we will discuss in the section, "How Do Social Factors Influence Youth Sport Experiences?" (and in chapter 8).

Participation in organized youth sports is now a valued experience in the process of growing up in most wealthy nations. Parents and communities that have the resources to sponsor, organize, and administer programs have created a variety of youth sports for their children. Some parents question the benefits of programs in which winning seems to be more important than overall child development, whereas other parents seek out the win-oriented programs, hoping their children will become the winners.

Some parents also encourage their children to engage in noncompetitive physical activities outside of organized programs, and many children participate in these activities as alternatives to adult-supervised organized sports. Research shows that a variety of so-called alternative sports have become increasingly popular in the lives of children in many countries (Midol and Broyer, 1995; Rinehart, 2000; Rinehart and Grenfell, 2002; Rinehart and Syndor, 2003).

> More than 40 million children participate in organized sports in the United States, a cultural phenomenon known as much for its excesses as its successes.
> —Bill Pennington,
> *New York Times*, 2003

Social Changes Have Influenced the Growth of Organized Youth Sports

Since the 1950s, an increasing amount of children's free time and sport participation has occurred in organized programs supervised by adults. This growth is related in part to changes in the ways that people define family and childhood in societies where individualism and material success are highly valued. The following five changes are especially relevant.

First, the number of families with both parents working outside the home has increased dramatically, especially since the early 1970s. This has created a growing demand for organized and adult-supervised after-school and summertime programs. Organized sports have been especially popular because many parents believe they offer their children opportunities to simultaneously have fun, learn adult values, become physically fit, and acquire status among their peers.

Second, since the early 1980s, there have been significant changes in what it means to be a "good parent." Good parents, in the minds of many people today, are those who can account for the whereabouts and actions of their children twenty-four hours a day, every day. This expectation is a new component of parenting ideology, and in recent years it has led many parents to seek organized, adult-supervised programs for their children. Organized sports are favored because they involve adult leadership, and have predictable schedules, and provide parents with measurable indicators of their children's accomplishments. When their children succeed, parents can claim that they are meeting their responsibilities. In some cases, mothers and fathers feel that their moral worth as parents is associated with the visible achievements of their children in sports—a factor that further intensifies parental commitment to youth sports (Coakley, 2006; Dukes and Coakley, 2002).

Third, there has been a growing belief that informal, child-controlled activities are often occasions for children to cause trouble. In its extreme form, this belief leads adults to view children as threats to social order. This leads them to see organized sports as ideal activities because they keep children occupied, out of trouble, and under the control of adults.

Fourth, many parents now see the world outside the home as dangerous for their children. They regard organized sports as safe alternatives to informal activities that occur away from home. Even when sports have high injury rates and coaches use methods that border on abuse, parents still feel that organized programs are needed to protect their children (Gorman, 2005; Nack and Munson, 2000; Nack and Yaeger, 1999; Pennington, 2005).

Fifth, the visibility of high-performance and professional sports has increased people's awareness of organized competitive sports as a valued part of culture. As children watch sports on television, listen to parents and friends talk about sports, and hear about the wealth and fame of popular athletes, they often see organized youth sports, especially those modeled after professional sports, as attractive activities. And when children say they want to be gymnasts or basketball players, parents often look for the best-organized programs in those sports (see figure 5.1). Therefore, organized youth sports have become popular because children see them as enjoyable and culturally valued activities that will gain them acceptance from peers and parents alike.

Together, these five social changes have boosted the popularity of organized youth sports in recent decades. Knowing about these changes helps us understand why parents are willing to invest so many family resources into the organized sports participation of their children. The amount of money that parents spend on participation fees, equipment, travel, personal coaches, high-performance training sessions, and other things defined as necessary in many programs has skyrocketed in recent years (Ferguson, 1999; Giordana and Graham, 2004; King, 2002; Moore, 2002; Poppen, 2004; Sokolove, 2004a; Wolfe, 2003). For example, when my students and I recently interviewed the parents of elite youth hockey players who traveled to Colorado for a major tournament, we discovered that the families had spent $5000 to $20,000 per year to support their sons' hockey participation. As they added up their expenses, many of them shook their heads and said, "I can't believe we're spending this much, but we are." And then they quickly explained that it was worth it because their son would benefit from the experience.

One of the problematic issues raised by these changes is that mothers and fathers in working-class and lower-income households are increasingly defined as irresponsible or "bad" parents because they cannot pay the financial price to put their children in supervised after-school sport programs, as wealthier parents do. Furthermore, they are not as likely to have the time and other resources needed to serve as volunteers and coaches for youth sport programs. In this way, organized sports for children become linked to political issues and debates about family values and the moral worth of parents in lower-income households.

MAJOR TRENDS IN YOUTH SPORTS TODAY

In addition to their growing popularity, youth sports are changing in five socially significant ways. *First*, organized programs have become

FIGURE 5.1   When children have schedules that are full of organized youth sports, they have little time to be with their parents. The irony is that many parents spend more time making it possible for their children to play sports than they spend with their children.

increasingly privatized. This means that more youth sports today are sponsored by private and commercial organizations, and fewer are sponsored by public, tax-supported organizations.

Second, organized programs increasingly emphasize the "performance ethic." This means that participants in youth sports, even in recreational programs, are encouraged to evaluate experiences in terms of developing technical skills and progressing to higher personal levels of achievement.

Third, there has been an increase in the number of private, elite sport-training facilities, which are dedicated to producing highly skilled and specialized athletes who can move up to higher levels of competition.

Fourth, parents have become more involved in and concerned about the participation and success of their children in organized youth sports. This has made youth sports into serious activities for adults and children, and adults are more

likely to act in extreme ways as they advocate the interests of their children.

Fifth, participation in alternative, action sports has increased. This means that many young people prefer unstructured, participant-controlled sports such as skateboarding, in-line skating, snowboarding, BMX biking, Frisbee, jumping rope, and other physical activities that have local or regional relevance for children.

These five trends have an impact on who participates in organized youth sports and the experiences that children have when they play sports. This is discussed in the following sections and in the box "Organized Youth Sports and the Goals of Sponsors."

The Privatization of Organized Programs

Privatization is an interesting and sometimes alarming trend in youth sports today. Although

reflect on SPORTS

Organized Youth Sports and the Goals of Sponsors
How Do Politics Affect Sport Participation?

The purposes of organized youth sports often vary with the goals of sponsors. Forms of sponsorship differ from one program to another, but they generally fall into one of the following four categories:

1. *Public, tax-supported community recreation organizations.* This includes local parks and recreation departments and community centers, which traditionally have offered a range of free or low-cost organized sport programs for children. These programs are usually inclusive and emphasize overall participation and general physical skill development as it relates to health and enjoyment.

2. *Public, nonprofit community organizations.* These include the YMCA, the Boys and Girls Club, the Police Athletic League (PAL), and other community-based clubs, which traditionally have provided a limited range of free or low-fee organized sport programs for children. The goals of these programs are diverse, including everything from providing children from particular neighborhoods a "wholesome, Christian atmosphere" for playing sports to providing "at-risk children" with activities to keep them off the streets. A few professional sport franchises and wealthy pro athletes in a few U.S. cities are now funding these organizations out of their profits and salaries.

3. *Private, nonprofit sport organizations.* These include organizations such as the nationwide Little League, Inc., Rush Soccer (rushsoccer.com), and local organizations operating independently or through connections with larger sport organizations, such as national federations. These organizations usually offer more exclusive opportunities to selective groups of children, generally those with special skills from families who can afford relatively costly participation fees.

4. *Private commercial clubs.* These include gymnastics, tennis, skating, soccer, and many other sport clubs and training programs. Many of these organizations have costly membership and participation fees, and some emphasize intense training, progressive and specialized skill development, and elite competition. Because these sponsors exist for different purposes, the youth sports that they provide are likely to appeal to different people and offer different types of experiences. Therefore, their impact on children and families is also likely to vary (King, 2002). This makes it difficult to generalize about what happens in organized youth sports and how participation affects child development and family dynamics.

When there are cuts in government spending, one of the first things to be dropped or scaled back is public, tax-supported youth sport programs—the type in category 1. Wealthy people seldom object to this because they have the money to fund private programs and pay membership fees in commercial programs. However, cutting public programs has a range of effects. It limits opportunities available to children from low-income families and funnels those with strong interests and top skills into one or two sports for which public programs remain. Additionally, it creates a market for private, commercial programs that cater to those with the money to pay for their services.

This information shows that local and national politics have an impact on who participates in organized youth sports and the type of participation opportunities available. Many communities continue to face the question of whether organized youth sports ought to be funded through local taxes. *What do you think?*

organized sports have become more popular in recent years, there has been a decline in publicly funded programs with free and open participation policies. When local governments face budget

crises because of federal and state tax cuts, various social services, including youth sports, often are downsized or eliminated. Some publicly funded programs have tried to survive by imposing participation fees, but many have been forced to drop programs altogether. In connection with these changes, middle- and upper-middle-class parents have organized private sport clubs and leagues for their children. These organizations depend on fund-raising, membership dues, and corporate sponsorships. They offer sport opportunities for children in well-to-do families and neighborhoods, but they are too expensive and inconveniently located for children in low-income families and neighborhoods.

Private, for-profit sport programs also have become major providers of youth sports as public programs have declined in number. These commercial programs are usually selective and exclusive, and they provide few opportunities for children from low-income households. The technical instruction in these programs often is good, and they provide regulated skills training for children from wealthier families. Through commercial programs, some parents hire private coaches for their children at rates of $35–$150 per hour (Giordano and Graham, 2004; King, 2002; Poppen, 2004; Sokolove, 2004a; Wolff, 2003).

Two negative consequences are associated with this trend toward privatizing youth sports. *First*, privatized programs reproduce the economic and ethnic inequalities that exist in the larger society. Unlike public programs, they depend on the resources of participants rather than entire communities. Low-income and single-parent families often lack money to pay for dues, travel, equipment, and other fees. This in turn creates or accentuates ethnic segregation and social-class divisions in communities. *Second*, as public parks and recreation departments cease to offer programs, they often become brokers of public parks and rent them out to private sport programs. The private programs that use public parks often do not have commitments to gender equity or other policies of inclusion that are a key part of public programs. For example, if 83 percent of the participants in private programs are boys and 17 percent are girls, as was the case in Los Angeles in the late 1990s, taxpayers face a situation in which they directly subsidize the perpetuation of gender inequity.

When privatization occurs, market forces become primary factors shaping who plays youth sports under what conditions. Wealthy people do not see this as a problem because they can pay for their children to play under the conditions that they choose. But people with few economic resources find themselves in a double bind: They cannot pay to support their children's activities, and they are often defined as negligent parents because their children do not experience the same successes as their wealthier peers. There are obvious problems associated with privatization, and they disproportionately affect poor people with little political power; therefore, they receive little attention.

> They're talented, terrific players, but I don't see the joy. They look tired. They've played so much year-round, they are like little professionals.
>
> —Bruce Ward, Director, physical education/athletics, San Diego Public Schools, 2003

Emphasis on the Performance Ethic

The performance ethic has become increasingly important in youth sport programs. This means that performance becomes a measured outcome and an indicator of the quality of the sport experience. *Fun* in these programs comes to be defined in terms of becoming a better athlete, becoming more competitive, and being promoted into more highly skilled training categories. Often, the categories have names that identify skill levels, so there may be gold, silver, and bronze groups to indicate a child's status in programs. Many parents like this because it enables them to judge their child's progress and prove to themselves and others that they are "good parents." (Review the box "Organized Youth Sports and the Goals of Sponsors," p. 126.)

Private and commercial programs emphasize the performance ethic to a greater degree than do public programs, and many market themselves as "centers of athletic excellence." This approach attracts parents willing and able to pay high fees for membership, participation, and instruction. Another way to sell private programs to parents who can afford the cost is to highlight successful athletes and coaches who have trained or worked in the program.

Parents of physically skilled children are attracted to programs emphasizing the performance ethic. They sometimes define fees and equipment expenses, which can be shockingly high, as *investments* in their children's future. They are concerned with skill development, and as their children get older, they use performance-oriented programs as sources of information about college sports, scholarships, and networks for contacting coaches and sport organizations. They approach their children's sport participation rationally and see clear connections between participation and their children's future development, educational opportunities, and success in adult life.

Of course, the application of the performance ethic is not limited to organized sports; it influences a range of organized children's activities (Mannon, 1997). Childhood in some segments of wealthy societies has been changed from an age of exploration and freedom to an age of preparation and controlled learning. Children's sports reflect this larger trend (Sokolove, 2004a; Wolfe, 2003).

New, Elite, Specialized Sport-Training Programs

The emphasis on performance is also tied to a third trend in youth sports—the development of elite, specialized training programs (King, 2002; Sokolove, 2004a; Wolfe, 2003). Many private and commercial programs encourage exclusive attention to a single sport because it is necessary for program owners and staff to capture year-round fees for memberships. Commercial programs have year-round operating expenses in the form of staff salaries and the rent and utilities

paid for facilities, so they depend on membership fees through the year to meet expenses and show a profit for owners.

Therefore, they develop rationales to convince parents and athletes that they must make year-round commitments to participation. As more parents accept these rationales, "high-performance" training schools, clubs, and programs continue to grow (see imgacademies.com). Commercial programs in gymnastics, figure skating, ice hockey, soccer, tennis, volleyball, lacrosse, and other sports now boast an explicit emphasis on making children into headline-grabbing, revenue-producing sport machines. Children in these programs even become marketing tools for program managers and symbols of the moral worth of parents, who pay the bills and brag to friends about their children's accomplishments and how much they have done to make their children successful (Dukes and Coakley, 2002; Grenfell and Rinehart, 2003; Mahany, 1999; Rinehart and Grenfell, 1999).

Children in high-performance training programs work at their sports for long hours week after week and year after year (King, 2002; Wolff, 2003). They compete regularly and often generate revenues (directly and indirectly) for their coaches and families. They appear on commercial television, attract people to expensive spectator events to watch them perform, and are contracted to endorse products. In a sense, they become child laborers because the livelihoods of coaches and other adults often depend on their performances (Donnelly, 1997, 2000). All this occurs without government regulations, which might protect the child athletes' interests, bodies, health, and overall psychosocial development.

Existing child labor laws in many postindustrial societies prevent adults from using children as sources of financial gain in other occupations, but there are no enforceable standards regulating what child athletes do or what happens to them. Coaches need no credentials. They can use fear, intimidation, and coercion to turn a few children into medal-winning athletes and damage other, "less talented" children in the process. Parents can live off their children's earnings, and

As publicly funded youth sports are downsized or eliminated, private clubs provide participation opportunities. Unfortunately, membership fees in these club-based programs are too expensive for many families. Additionally, many children may not enjoy the emphasis on the performance ethic that is common in many club programs. (*Source:* Travis Spradling, *Colorado Springs Gazette*)

commercial events can be scheduled around their talents. The results of this situation are sometimes frightening (Coakley, 1994; Coakley and Donnelly, 2004; Ryan, 1995).

When Bela Karolyi was hired in late 1999 to coordinate the U.S. women's gymnastics team, one of his former student-performers, 1996 Olympic medal winner Kerri Strug said this about her former coach:

> He knows how to get the most out of each child. I think a lot of his motivation is fear. When I messed up, I was more worried about what he would think than about messing up. (in Raboin, 1999, p. 2A)

Strug fought through pain in her final vault to help the U.S. team win a gold medal in the 1996

Summer Olympics. In 1999 she had second thoughts about her life as a gymnast:

> Bela had complete control of everything in your life—your workouts, your eating, your sleeping. . . . I look back now and say, "That was crazy. That's not America." But it was Bela's way or no way. And he was a coach who got you where you wanted to go. (Strug, 1999, p. 73)

Karolyi explains this way of handling children in the following way:

> Sometimes the preparation is so hard, so intense . . . [t]he crying, the screaming. . . . We are not in the gym to be having fun. The fun comes at the end, with the winning and the medals. (in O'Brien, 1992, p. 52)

Dominique Moceanu, another member of the 1996 team, had a slightly different story to tell. In 1998 she disclosed that her father-coach had subjected her to mental and physical abuse as she trained. She said, "Most of the time . . . he'd hit me because I was gaining weight or wasn't doing well in the gym" (in Raboin, 1998, p. 2C). Moceanu's troubles were accentuated because her father had lost nearly all of the money that she had earned as a gymnast-laborer. Are there ethical issues that should be considered in connection with this approach to sport participation? Are children being used and abused? Are children being harmed physically, psychologically, and socially? Sociologists, some parents, and others now are asking serious questions about how this new emphasis on elite training affects the health and development of children (American Academy of Pediatrics, 2000; Gorman, 2005; Pennington, 2005; Sokolove, 2004a).

> **I can't believe how you're playing! You're giving these guys hope; your job is to destroy their hope!**
>
> —Football coach to eleven-year-old players, 2001

Increased Involvement and Concerns Among Parents

Youth sports have become serious business in many families. The notion that good parents today must control the actions of their children twenty-four hours a day and carefully promote and monitor their children's development has changed parents' lives over the past two generations. Many parents now feel compelled to find the best organized youth sport programs for their children and ensure that their children's interests are being met in those programs.

Even though many factors influence child development today, many people attribute the success or failure of children entirely to their parents. When children are successful in sports, their parents are seen to be doing the right thing as parents. When Tiger Woods began winning tournaments, everyone labeled Earl Woods, his father, as a good and wise parent. The same thing occurred with Richard Williams, the father of Venus and Serena Williams. When children succeed, parents are labeled "good parents" and even asked by other parents how they did it. When a child fails, people question the moral worth of the parents.

Under these conditions, a child's success in sports is especially important for many parents. Youth sports are highly visible activities and become sites where dads and moms can establish and prove their moral worth as parents. This increases the stakes associated with youth sports.

This link between parents' moral worth and their children's sports achievements leads many parents to take youth sports seriously.

The stakes associated with youth sports are increased even further among parents who hope that their children might earn college scholarships, professional contracts as athletes, or social acceptance and popularity in school and among peers. When parents think in these terms, the success of their children in youth sports is linked to anticipated social and financial payoffs.

As the moral, financial, and social stakes associated with youth sport participation have increased, youth sports have become sites for extreme actions among some adults (Engh, 1999; Nack and Munson, 2000). Parents may be assertive and disruptive as they advocate the interests of their child with coaches and youth sport program administrators. Some are obnoxious and offensive as they scream criticisms of coaches, referees, players, and their own children. A few have even attacked other people over sport-related disagreements.

In one of the most extreme cases, a father from Reading, Massachusetts, attacked and beat to death another father in connection with events that occurred during an open skating session at an ice rink. This case was defined as an example of "rink rage" and covered in terms of one hockey dad killing another hockey dad. Subsequent coverage of extreme, disruptive, or belligerent actions by parents has led many people to think that there is a general epidemic of out-of-control youth sport parents.

This case and others have led to calls for parent education combined with new rules and enforcement procedures to control adults associated with youth sports. These are appropriate strategies, but to be successful they must be administered with an understanding of the context in which parenting occurs today. As long as parents' moral worth is linked with the achievements of children in youth sports and as long as financial and social payoffs are associated with success in sports, parents will be deeply concerned about their children's youth sport participation. Furthermore, if people continue to believe that it takes only a family to raise a child, parents will not receive more support from community institutions. This leaves them in a position where they must advocate the interests of their children. If they don't, who will? Under this condition, many parents feel that it is their moral obligation to get in the face of anyone standing in the way of their child's happiness and success in sports.

Increased Interest in Alternative Sports

As organized programs have become increasingly exclusive, structured, and performance oriented, some young people have sought alternatives, which allow them to engage more freely in physical activities on their own terms. Because organized youth sports are the most visible settings for children's sport participation, these unstructured and participant-controlled activities are referred to as alternative sports—alternatives, that is, to organized sports. Alternative sports, or "action sports" as many now refer to them, encompass a wide array of physical activities done individually or in groups. Their popularity is based in part on children's reactions against the highly structured character of adult-controlled, organized sports. For example when legendary skateboarder Tony

Many children seek alternatives to adult-controlled youth sports. Some of these are related to the "extreme" sports seen in televised events and the videotapes that are made, duplicated, and circulated by the participants themselves. When you create your own sports, you have experiences very different from that of organized youth sports. (*Rocky Mountain News*)

Hawk was asked why he chose to skateboard rather than do other sports, he said, "I liked having my own pace and my own rules . . . and making up my own challenges" (in Finger, 2004, p. 84).

When I observe children in action sports, I am regularly amazed by the physical skills that they have developed without adult coaches and scheduled practices and contests. Although I am concerned about injury rates and the sexism that often is a part of these activities, I am impressed at the discipline and dedication of children who seek challenges apart from adult-controlled sport settings. The norms in these participant-controlled activities are complex, and they vary from one location to another (Rinehart and Grenfell, 2002).

Mark Shaw, winner of the first International Mountain Board Championships in 2000, explains a widely accepted norm that has made many of these activities attractive to children. He says that, when he goes to areas where there are other skateboarders and mountain boarders, he feels that it is important to be "a positive influence as a skater." He teaches tricks, gives helpful hints to less experienced board riders, and values the friendships and sense of community created around the sports. He explains, "I look forward to helping young skaters . . . at the park each weekend almost as much as I look forward to skating and my own progression on the board" (2002, p. 3). Many children find this orientation to be more engaging than what they perceive or experience in competitive youth sport programs.

Increased participation in alternative sports is so widespread that media companies and corporations wishing to turn children into consumers have invented competitive forms of these sports and now hype them as high-risk and "extreme" sports. These sponsored events, such as the X Games, Gravity Games, and the Dew Action Sports Tour provide exposure and material support for athletes willing to display their skills in a televised format that is or at least appears to be highly organized and competitive. Although participants in these events are teens and young adults, many spectators are children. Children use images from media events to inform what they do when they play action sports, but we need research on the ways that this occurs and its implications in the lives of young people. Adult intervention in these activities has been limited to the provision of facilities such as skateboard parks and occasional words of advice regarding safety (Merrill, 2002). But will the future bring adult skateboard coaches and organized programs? I'd bet on it, but I'd also bet that children will always seek opportunities to play sports on their own terms.

DIFFERENT EXPERIENCES: INFORMAL, PLAYER-CONTROLLED SPORTS VERSUS ORGANIZED, ADULT-CONTROLLED SPORTS

Since the late 1970s, my students and I have interviewed many children about their sport experiences and watched children play sports in different settings. We've learned that individual children define and interpret personal experiences in many ways. But we've also discovered that experiences among children differ, depending on whether sports are informally organized and controlled by the players themselves or are formally organized and controlled by adults.

Our findings indicate that informal, player-controlled sports are primarily action centered, whereas formal, adult-controlled sports are primarily rule centered. This means that, when children create their own activities and games, they emphasize movement and excitement. But when they play sports that are organized and controlled by adults, the adults emphasize learning and following rules. The following sections provide more complete descriptions of these two types of participation settings.

Informal, Player-Controlled Sports

We've observed informally organized, player-controlled sports in backyards, parks, vacant lots, and school playgrounds, and we've interviewed hundreds of children. We found that when children create games and play on their own, they are interested in four things:

1. Action, especially action leading to scoring
2. Personal involvement in the action
3. A challenging or exciting experience (for example, a close score in a competitive contest)
4. Opportunities to reaffirm friendships during games

Informal games usually had two to twelve players, all or mostly boys. The players often knew each other from games played previously. In most cases, they formed teams quickly, using skill differences and friendship patterns as criteria for choosing teams. Initiating and maintaining games usually involved complex dynamics; success depended on the players' abilities to manage interpersonal relationships and make decisions accepted as fair by their peers.

Games and game rules often resembled those used in organized programs, but they contained modifications to maximize action, scoring, and personal involvement, while keeping the scores close. Action-producing strategies involved eliminating free throws in basketball, keeping throw-ins to a minimum in soccer, dropping yardage penalties in football, and slowing the speed of pitches so that all batters would hit the ball in softball and baseball. Similar action-producing rules existed in other informal games, and they generally resulted in extremely high scores.

Personal involvement was maximized through rule qualifications and handicap systems. Restrictive handicaps were sometimes used to keep highly skilled players from dominating games, whereas other handicaps advantaged less skilled players. Less skilled players used "do-over" or "interference" calls to get second chances or compensate for the effects of their mistakes on the outcomes of games. This saved them personal embarrassment and preserved their integrity as contributing members of their teams. It also kept game scores close. The overuse of these special rules was usually discouraged through jests and teasing.

Personal involvement was also promoted by unique game rules. In baseball there was a rule against called strikes so that everyone had a chance to hit—which meant that fielders had chances to make catches and other action-packed plays. In football every team member was eligible to receive a pass on any play. When children were asked to name the biggest source of fun in their games, they almost always referred to hitting, catching, kicking, scoring, or another form of action in which they were personally involved.

Maintaining order in informal games depended on the extent to which players were committed to maintaining action. Usually, when children were personally involved in the game, they were more committed to maintaining action. Social control strategies were used most often to keep players from disrupting action in the games. Players joked around and even ignored rules, but

norm violations were allowed unless they interfered with the flow of action.

Our observations of these games uncovered many performance styles and "moves," and these were accepted as normal if they did not disrupt action in the games. The players with the greatest skill also had the most freedom to be creative because they usually could do so without upsetting game action or interfering with the personal involvement of other players.

Social status among players was important because it determined which individuals became involved in decision-making processes during the games. The older or more skilled players usually had the highest status. Disagreements were usually resolved in creative ways and seldom destroyed the games. When children played together often, they became more skilled at solving conflicts.

A word of caution: these summary descriptions of informal sports do not apply to all occasions when children create their own games. Problems in informal games do occur. Bigger and stronger children occasionally exploit smaller and weaker ones. Girls sometimes are patronized or dismissed when they try to play with groups of boys, and children excluded from games often feel rejected by their peers.

Additionally, the dynamics of games usually vary with the availability of play spaces and equipment. For example, when a large group uses the only basketball court in a neighborhood, the games exclude many children who want to play. The team that wins takes on challengers, rather than giving up the court to others, and those with less developed skills are not given concessions when it comes to participation. Taking turns is rare when there are more players than spaces to play. However, when there are many courts and only a few players, the goal is often to accommodate everyone's interests so that nobody leaves and forces the game to end. This is a major reason that the informal games of children in low-income areas with few facilities and resources are often different from the games played by children in higher-income areas where

Informal games usually emphasize action, personal involvement, close scores, and the reaffirmation of friendships. These boys and girls often play games with each other, and they have developed creative strategies for resolving conflicts. (*Source:* Jay Coakley)

facilities are more plentiful and there is little or no competition for space (Carlston, 1986).

Clearly, then, external conditions in the society as a whole have important effects on the way children play informal games. Most of the children who we observed and interviewed were from neighborhoods where competition for space was not a major issue.

Formal, Adult-Controlled Sports

Our observations and interviews done in connection with formally organized, adult-controlled sports focused on children between eight and twelve years old. The data indicated that, even though the children valued action and personal involvement, they were concerned about playing well and winning games. Most apparent in these games was that they were strictly regulated by formal rules. Adults, including coaches, managers, umpires, referees, scorekeepers, timekeepers, and other game officials enforced these rules.

Children in these sports often were concerned with the positions they played on their teams. They even referred to themselves as "defensive halfbacks" or "offensive ends," as "centers" or "left wingers," as "catchers" or "right fielders." The importance of positions was also emphasized by the coaches and spectators, who encouraged players to "stay in position" during games. This happened regularly in all sports in which the players were constantly on the move, such as soccer and basketball.

Adult-controlled schedules governed organized sports. Individual playing time varied by skill levels, and less skilled children played least often. Every player was in the game for at least a short time, but the children whose playing time was low often seemed uninterested in what occurred on the field or court. The highly skilled players showed strong interest in games and expressed disappointment when they were taken out of the lineup.

A consequence of adult control and organization was the visible absence of arguments and overt displays of hostility between players from opposing teams. There were occasional arguments between officials and coaches or spectators and between teammates. Arguments between teammates usually were caused by a player's inability to remember game rules, stay in position, or carry out the strategies developed by the adults.

Adult control and **formal structure** (that is, *established rules plus roles or positions*) kept children organized, but they also seemed to limit visible displays of affection and friendship during the games. This made it difficult to determine which children were friends. However, interpersonal relationships among the players had little to do with how the games were played because players made so few decisions.

The major purpose of game rules was to standardize the competition and control the players. Rules and rule enforcement regularly caused breaks in the action, but the players did not seem to resent this. The only signs of displeasure came when delays were caused by penalties called against a player's team. Rule enforcement (social control) in these games was based on players' self-control and obedience, but it ultimately rested in the hands of adults: coaches, referees, and game officials. Adults usually applied the rules universally and seldom made exceptions, even when there were differences in players'

abilities and characteristics. The coaches' strict application of rules restricted players' freedom, but players seldom violated rules.

When deviance occurred, it was more often caused by players forgetting or not knowing what to do than by blatantly ignoring the rules. On the playing field, rule infractions usually were accompanied by formal sanctions, even if they did not affect game action or outcomes. Off the field, rules varied from one team to another, and violations usually involved "joking around" or exhibiting a lack of interest in the game or the team. Responses to these actions also varied. Coaches and parents used verbal and nonverbal sanctions to control players, preserve the organization of the game, and maintain the authority of referees and coaches.

The children in organized sports were serious about their games, and they wanted to win although they were seldom obsessed with winning. Those most concerned with winning were the highly skilled players and members of the most successful teams. Although they had other goals, the principal goal of most players was to have fun. However, they usually knew their win–loss record and the place of their team in league standings. The players were disappointed when they did not log the playing time that they thought they deserved. Playing time was very important because it was related to the children's reputations among peers. Status on the teams, however, usually depended on relationships with coaches.

Finally, the games in organized sports were extremely stable. Games did not end until the rules said they were over, regardless of the quality of play or enjoyment among the players. Adults' whistles, along with verbal encouragement, commands, and advice, were ever present in these games.

Analysis of Differences

The personal experiences of children in these two sport forms are very different. Informal

In organized sport programs for children, it is the adults who determine and enforce the rules,

plan strategies and call plays,

solve problems,

and wait anxiously for results. (*Source:* Jay Coakley)

sports are action centered, whereas organized sports are rule centered. Which of these experiences is more valuable in the development of children? The answer to this question is important to children and the adults who invest so much time, money, and energy in organized programs.

Research on this issue indicates that each experience makes different positive contributions to the lives of children, and neither experience is without problems. However, people traditionally overrate the contributions of participation in organized sports and underrate the contributions of participation in informal sports (Schultz, 1999).

Playing informal sports clearly involves the use of interpersonal and decision-making skills. Children must be creative to organize games and keep them going. They encounter dozens of unanticipated challenges requiring on-the-spot decisions and interpersonal abilities. They learn how to organize games, form teams, cooperate with peers, develop rules, and take responsibility for following and enforcing rules. These are important lessons, many of which are not learned in adult-controlled organized sports.

Patricia and Peter Adler (1998) spent eight-years studying the everyday lives of children and adolescents in their community, and they concluded that informal sports provide experiences involving cooperation, planning, organizing, negotiating, problem solving, flexibility, and improvisation. Their examples of how children do these things are impressive. Although we do not know how or to what extent the learning that occurs in these informal sports carries over to other settings, we can assume that children are influenced by their experiences.

Playing organized sports, on the other hand, involves different experiences. Organized sports help children learn to manage relationships with adult authority figures. Children also learn the rules and strategies used in activities that are defined as important in the culture, and through their participation, they often gain status that carries over to other parts of their lives. When they play organized sports, they learn about formal structures, rule-governed teamwork, and adult models of work and achievement (Adler and Adler, 1998). A possible problem in organized sports is that children may learn to view the world in passive terms, as something that is given rather than created. If this occurs, children grow up thinking they are powerless to change the world in which they live.

It is important to recognize that some games fall between the two types described in this section. For example, there are informal games in which an adult provides subtle guidance to children, who control most of what occurs. There are also organized games in which adults let children handle many things on their own. These "hybrids" are valuable contexts for learning. The adults in such games often say that it takes tact and patience to put up with children's mistakes and oversights. They also say that it is a joy to see the creativity and compassion shown by many children, who respond to adult suggestions and subtle encouragement. International soccer star, Brandi Chastain observes that a problem today is that "children in sports are often overly organized." She says that informal games are unique because they give children "the opportunity to be independent, creative, and self-motivated" Furthermore, children are more likely to develop a love of physical activity and sports when they "dictate the place, the time, the rules, and the structure—or lack of it" in their play (2004, p. 125).

SOCIOLOGICAL QUESTIONS ABOUT YOUTH SPORTS

Dozens of questions could be raised in this section, and I've chosen three that people who work with children ought to be able to answer as they plan programs and make policies related to youth sports.

When Are Children Ready to Play Organized Competitive Sports?

Parents often ask readiness questions. They wonder: Should I sign my four-year-old up for T-ball, put my six-year-old on a competitive swim team, and let my ten-year-old participate in a state gymnastics tournament? Some parents want to give their children an early start on an imagined path to athletic glory; some don't want their children to fall behind peers in skills development; and some just want their children to have healthy fun and a positive body image. Scholars in motor learning, physical education, exercise physiology, psychology, and sociology provide answers to readiness questions. Sociological answers often reflect interactionist research done by researchers who study social development during childhood. This work indicates that children *begin* at about eight years old to develop the cognitive and social abilities that they must have to understand the complex relationships in competitive sports. Among most children, these abilities are not fully developed until about twelve years old.

Anyone who has watched two teams of seven-year-old soccer players knows about these developmental issues. Most children younger than twelve play "beehive soccer": After the opening kick, there are twenty bodies and forty legs surrounding the ball, and they follow the ball around the playing field like a swarm of bees following its queen. Everyone is out of position, and all players usually stay that way for the entire game. Meanwhile, the coaches and parents loudly plead with them to "Stay in position!" and "Get back where you belong!" However, determining where you belong in most sports is difficult. Positions change, depending on the placement of teammates and opponents relative to the location of the ball. Understanding the concept of position requires the ability to do three things simultaneously: (1) mentally visualize the ever-changing placements of teammates and opponents over the entire field, (2) assess their relationships to each other and to the ball, and (3) then decide where you belong. The ability to think through these three things and accurately determine where you should be on the field develops gradually in connection with social experience and cognitive maturation.

Parents and coaches become frustrated when children fail to understand positions and strategies. When adults don't take into account the cognitive and social development patterns during childhood, they mistakenly think that children are not concentrating or trying hard. This frustrates children who *are* doing the best they can at their level of psychosocial development.

"Beehive soccer" and its equivalents in other sports are avoided in two ways. *First*, the games children play can be altered to focus on skills and expression rather than competition and team strategies. In other words, games can be revised to fit children's needs and abilities (Morris and Stiehl, 1989; Torbert, 2004, 2005). This is a preferred strategy.

Second, children can be systematically conditioned to respond in certain ways to certain situations during competitive games and matches. This requires that coaches create game situations during practices so that each player can rehearse individual tactical responses to each situation, over and over, again and again. This makes practices boring, but it generally helps teams win games. However, in the long run, it is not a preferred strategy because it often destroys much of the action and personal involvement that children value in sports.

Just imagine how many ground balls a coach must hit to infielders on a children's baseball or softball team to teach them where to throw the ball with different numbers of outs and different numbers of opponents on base. I tell my students that I will buy dinner for any one of them and three of their friends if they can find me a ten-year-old who can determine without adult guidance what to do in the following situation: The child is playing left field. There is one out, with opposing runners at first and second base. The batter hits a long line drive, which falls beyond and between the right fielder and the center fielder. Everyone on the team now has a position to which he or she should move. Where should the left fielder go? If the left fielder had the ability to put him- or herself simultaneously in the positions of eight teammates and three base runners, he or she would run in toward third base to back up the third-base person. This would be done in case of an overthrow from the second-base person, who should have moved to the relay position in short right-center field. Ten-year-olds cannot figure this out by themselves. They must be conditioned to do it because they do not yet have the ability to fully understand complex sets of relationships among

> I play to win. I don't play to play. If I find out I have a team that's going to be 0–8, I'll go with a different team.
>
> —Nick, age ten, hockey player, Lake Forest, Illinois, 1999

three or more people. By the way, where should the pitcher go in this situation? How about the first-base person? It is very unlikely that a coach can teach all these things without making baseball boring for children.

Children are not born with the ability to compete or cooperate with others. Nor are they born with the ability to visualize complex sets of social relationships between teammates and opponents. They must learn these things, and the learning occurs in connection with a combination of social experiences and the development of abstract thinking abilities. This learning cannot be forced. It occurs only as children move from a stage in which they see the world from an egocentric viewpoint to a stage in which they can see the world through the eyes of many others at once. This ability gradually emerges between the ages of eight and twelve years old in most children. Therefore, organized sports for children younger than twelve should be controlled and modified to accommodate this gradually emerging ability. In the meantime, the main emphasis should be on developing physical skills and basic cooperation. All children must learn to cooperate before they can compete with each other in positive ways. If they don't know how to cooperate, competitions often degenerate into chaos.

Finally, those of us who ask the question "When should children play organized competitive sports?" generally live in cultures in which scientific approaches to childhood development are popular and people have the time and resources to organize children's activities. *Youth sports are a luxury.* They cost money and take time; therefore, many people cannot afford them. This is true even in wealthy countries among families with few resources. Many children around the world simply include movement and physical play in their lives as they grow up in their cultures. Deciding when to begin organized sports is not an issue for them or their parents because their lives are seriously constrained by a lack of resources. Therefore, it is important to be aware

of poverty and its impact on children's lives as we discuss questions related to youth sports.

What Are the Dynamics of Family Relationships in Connection with Organized Youth Sports?

Organized youth sports require time, money, and organizational skills, and these usually come from parents. Therefore, playing organized sports is often a family affair. However, few sociologists have done research on how youth sport participation affects family relationships.

Anecdotal information and a few studies indicate that youth sports can bring family members together in supportive ways or create problems in family relationships. Parents may become so emotionally involved with sports that they put pressure on their children or fail to see that their children perceive their encouragement as pressure to play well and stay involved in sports. When children feel such pressure, they face a triple dilemma: (1) If they quit sports, they fear that their parents may withdraw support and attention; (2) if they play sports but do not perform well, they fear their parents will criticize them; (3) if they perform well, they fear that their parents will treat them like "little pros" and never let them do other things.

When sociologist Mike Messner (1992) interviewed former elite male athletes, he heard about similar dilemmas. Many men in his study remembered that early sport experiences enabled them to connect with their fathers, who were otherwise away from home and emotionally distant from them. As young boys, they wanted to please and receive attention from their fathers. However, they often found that the father–child togetherness they had in sports did not involve real intimacy and it did not carry over into their lives away from sports. Despite this, many of the men remembered feeling that they had to stay in sports and become good athletes to maintain relationships with their fathers. This can occur with daughters as well.

There is a parental division of labor associated with youth sports. Mothers provide a wide range of off-the-field support, such as watching the "little kids," whereas fathers do the coaching and league administration, especially when players are ten-years old or older. (*Source:* Jay Coakley)

Organized youth sports have an impact on families and family relationships in other ways as well. Research shows that organized sport programs for children could not exist without the volunteer labor of parents, especially mothers (Chafetz and Kotarba, 1999; Thompson, 1999a,b). Mothers drive children to practices and games, fix meals at convenient times, launder dirty training clothes and uniforms, and make sure that equipment is ready. They raise funds for teams and leagues; purchase, prepare, and serve food during road trips and postgame get-togethers; form and serve on committees that supervise off-the-field social activities; and make phone calls about schedules and schedule changes. Mothers also manage the activities of brothers and sisters who are not playing games, and they provide emotional support for their child-athletes when they play poorly or when coaches or fathers criticize them. Fathers also provide labor, but it is devoted primarily to on-the-field and administrative

matters such as coaching, field maintenance, and league administration.

When parental labor occurs in this pattern, youth sports reproduce a gendered division of labor in families, communities, and the minds of children, especially the boys who are treated as "son-gods" as they play organized sports. More research is needed on this and other aspects of family dynamics that exist in connection with youth sports. For example, we know little about fatherhood and sports, a topic that is important to consider as expectations for parents become more demanding and wives demand more assistance from their husbands (Coakley, 2006).

How Do Social Factors Influence Youth Sport Experiences?

Children make choices about playing sports, but they have little control over the context in which they make their choices. Many factors, including parents, peers, and the general social and cultural contexts in which they live, influence the alternatives from which they choose and how they define and give meaning to their choices. For example, children from low-income, inner-city backgrounds generally have many fewer sport participation opportunities than other children. Children with able bodies have more opportunities and receive more encouragement to play sports than do children with disabilities. Choosing to play a contact sport, such as football, is seen by most people around the world to be more appropriate for boys than for girls. Boys who want to figure skate do not receive the same encouragement from peers as girls receive. Racial and ethnic stereotypes often influence the sport participation choices made by people who learn to associate certain sports and physical skills with various skin colors and cultural backgrounds (Coakley, 2002; Harrison and Lawrence, 2004; L. Harrison, 1995; Harrison et al., 1999; Harrison et al., 2004; Lewis, 2003).

None of these statements is earthshaking. People know these things. They know that, as children make sport choices and give meaning to their experiences, they and the people around them are influenced by prevailing cultural beliefs about age, gender, sexuality, race and ethnicity, ability and disability, and social class. This is how social forces influence youth sport experiences. This is highlighted in the "Breaking Barriers" box on pages 142–143.

When Patricia and Peter Adler (1998) did their eight-year study of white, upper-middle-class children and adolescents, they found that playing sports fit into the lives of boys and girls in different ways. For example, athletic ability, coolness, toughness, and being "smooth" in social relationships were key determinants of the popularity of the boys. Very high or very low academic performance often subverted popularity among the boys. Girls' popularity depended primarily on their families' social status, the freedoms granted to them by parents, their physical appearance and "beauty habits," their abilities to manage relationships with boys

and female peers, and their grades in school. The Adlers note that criteria for popularity sometimes shift slightly when young people enter junior high school (about age twelve in most U.S. school districts), but they do change dramatically.

These popularity criteria were linked with sport participation choices in interesting ways. Boys and the girls in the Adlers' study had many opportunities to play informal sports and organized sports at all levels of competition. However, girls were less likely than boys to play informal and alternative sports. This is because girls do not receive as much encouragement, approval, and social rewards for doing these activities as boys receive in preadolescent culture. Furthermore, boys often control the ways that informal games are organized and played, and boys seldom treat girls as equals in these settings. In the Adlers's study, the girls played organized sports almost at the same rate as the boys, but in junior high school, the girls dropped out of sports at a higher rate than the boys did. The girls who excelled at sports often stayed involved, but those with average or mediocre physical skills usually dropped out. Overall, girls felt that playing sports was not required for acceptance and status among peers.

Other research also shows that sport choices and experiences are influenced by dominant definitions of gender in society. These definitions influence early childhood experiences when it comes to physical activities (White et al., 1992). For example, in the United States, fathers play with their sons more often and in more physically active ways than they play with their daughters. Furthermore, the physical activity messages that most young boys receive differ from the messages many young girls receive, both inside and outside family settings (Beal, 1994; Hargreaves, 1994; Hasbrook, 1999). Because of these messages, most children have definite ideas about their physical skills and potential before they even think about playing sports. For example, boys are more likely than girls to *think* they are better than they actually are as athletes. This

breaking BARRIERS

Mainstreaming Barriers
Will They Let Me Play with My Brace?

Ally was born with a physical impairment—no fine motor movement in her left hand and a left leg that was stabilized by a brace as she learned to walk. Ally didn't see her impairments as problems because she never experienced life without them. In her eyes, her body was simply a fact of life. Like other children, she developed physical skills and learned about her limits. After playing soccer with her parents and sisters and watching her older sister play on a team, she said she wanted to be on a team, and asked, "Will they let me play with my brace?"

Ally's brace had never been an issue in her family. But Ally observed sports on television, went to high school and college volleyball and basketball games, and watched her parents and sister play in local leagues. Not seeing athletes with braces caused her to wonder if people would let her play with one. Growing up in a society where images of athletes reflect a "cultural fantasy" of bodies that conform to ideal standards of beauty and ability (Thomson, 2002), Ally wondered if there was space for a girl who deviated from those standards enough to need a brace.

The public, community-sponsored youth soccer program where Ally lived was covered by the Americans with Disability Act (ADA), signed into law in 1990 by President George H. W. Bush. When applied to youth sports, this law states that public programs and private programs open to the public cannot exclude children with disabilities unless there are direct threats to the health and safety of able-bodied participants. The threats must be real, based on objective information, and unavoidable even after reasonable efforts are made to eliminate them. In Ally's case, it was easy to follow the law: Pads were put on her brace, and the soccer league did not have to make accommodations that would cause "undue burden" or a "fundamental alteration of the program" (Block, 1995).

According to the ADA, if there were tryouts for a team, the coach could not cut Ally because she had a disability, but Ally *could* be cut for skills-related reasons. Her coaches could not say that all players must be able to run without a limp to play on the team, but they could say that any child who could not run the length of the field would be cut.

As youth sports programs increasingly stress a performance ethic, children with disabilities lack the requisite skills to play on mainstream organized teams.

affects their self-confidence and willingness to be physically active and express an interest in playing youth sports. Overall, girls learn to minimize the physical space that they occupy, sexualize their bodies through modifying appearance and movement, and accept the notion that boys are physically superior to them. And boys learn to present themselves as physically big and strong, act in ways that claim physical space around them, and assume power and control over girls in sports (Hasbrook, 1999; Hasbrook and Harris, 1999).

Gender-related expectations may be one of the reasons why boys' ball games often dominate the space on elementary school playgrounds and in other public places. This pattern extends through the life course. For instance, observe the playing fields and gyms on a college campus and measure the amount of time that young men or young women appropriate those spaces for themselves. It is often difficult to change these male-dominant patterns because they are deeply rooted in the culture as a whole. In the case of children, it is important to focus on variations in their experiences rather than simply looking for differences related to gender, ethnicity, ability, and social class. As we see how experiences vary, we learn how social forces interact with each

This is why few children with disabilities are mainstreamed in youth sports, even though they are routinely mainstreamed in classrooms.

Although most people define this approach as reasonable, it leaves children with disabilities two options if they wish to play sports: Find an adapted program, or play informal games in which peers are willing and able to develop adaptations. Unfortunately, many communities lack public programs adapted for children with disabilities, and local peer groups seldom have experiences that enable them to quickly or easily include a child with disabilities in their informal games.

Research indicates that in light of these two options most children with disabilities are relegated to the sidelines. Without someone to advocate their interests, they become observers rather than participants. This is noted by a ten-year-old boy with cerebral palsy who explains that his peers "like me but . . . if I'm trying to get in a game without a friend, it's kind of hard" (in Taub and Greer, 2000, p. 406). Without a friend who has enough power with peers and enough experience with disabilities to facilitate a process of adaptation and inclusion, this ten-year-old doesn't play sports. Other children describe their experiences in these terms: "[Kids] try and shove me off the court, tell me not to play," "they just don't want me on their team," and "there's a couple of people that won't let me play" (in Taub and Greer, 2000, p. 406). Such experiences deny children with disabilities access to contexts in which friendships are formed and nurtured and to activities that have "normalizing" effects for children growing up in a culture where sports are defined as socially and self-validating activities.

As we consider how to eliminate barriers that prevent mainstreaming in sports, think of these statements made by children with cerebral palsy:

> [Playing games] makes me feel good 'cause I get to be with everybody, . . . and talk about how our day was in school while we play.
>
> Playing basketball is something that I can do with my friends that I never thought I could do [with them], but I can, I can! (in Taub and Greer, 2000, pp. 406 and 408)

Eliminating barriers to mainstreaming is challenging. But we can if we use our abilities creatively and compassionately.

other and influence children's lives on and off the playing field.

RECOMMENDATIONS FOR IMPROVING YOUTH SPORTS

Improving Informal, Alternative, and Action Sports

Informal, alternative, and action sports are unique because they are not controlled directly by adults. Many children opt for these sports because they seek activities without organized structures and adult control. Further, there are ways that adults can foster safety and participation opportunities for children interested in action sports. For example, instead of passing laws to prohibit skateboarding or in-line skating, adults can work with young people to design and provide safe settings for them to create their own activities. If adults are not supportive of alternative sport forms, their children will use the extreme models of the X Games, Gravity Games, and other made-for-TV spectacles as sole sources of inspiration.

The challenge for adults is to be supportive and provide guidance without controlling alternative sports. Children need their own spaces in which they can be creative and expressive while they engage in physical activities. Adult guidance is crucial in making those spaces safe and open for as many children as possible—boys and girls as well as children with disabilities and from various ethnic and social class backgrounds.

Improving Organized Sports

When considering improvements for organized youth sports, most people agree that programs should meet the needs of the children who participate in them. This means that children are valuable sources of information about possible changes. If children seek fun emphasizing action, involvement, close scores, and friendships in their informal games, it makes sense that organized programs also should emphasize these things. The following recommendations are based on this assumption.

Increasing Action   Children emphasize *action* in their games. Much activity occurs around the scoring area, and scoring is usually so frequent that it is difficult to keep personal performance statistics. Organized sports, although they contain action, strongly emphasize rules, order, standardized conditions, and predictability. The strategy of many organized teams is to prevent action, rather than stimulate it. Parents and coaches often describe high-scoring games as undisciplined free-for-alls caused by poor defensive play. The desired strategy in the minds of many adults is to stop action: Strike out every batter (baseball and softball), stall the game when you are in the lead (soccer and basketball), and use a safe running play for a 3-yard gain (football). These tactics may win games, but they limit action and scoring—the things that children define as the most exciting aspects of playing sports.

It's easy to increase action and scoring in most sports, as long as adults do not view game models as sacred and unchangeable. Bigger goals, smaller playing areas, and fewer rules are the best means

to increase action. Why not double the width of goals in soccer and hockey, make all players eligible to receive passes and carry the ball in football, and use a 6-foot basket in a half-court basketball game?

Many adults resist changes that they think will alter game models—that is, the models used in elite, adult sports. They want children to play "the real thing" and they forget that children are more interested in having fun than mimicking adults following institutionalized rules.

Increasing Personal Involvement   Children do not sit on the bench in informal games. They use rule qualifications and handicap systems to maximize personal involvement and promote action. Less skilled players may not contribute to the action as much as their more skilled peers, but they play the whole game. If they are treated badly or excluded, they leave without being branded as quitters or given lectures on commitment by their parents.

In organized games, playing time is often limited for all but the most skilled players, and the substitution process creates problems for coaches and pressure on players. Specialization by position further restricts involvement by limiting the range of experiences for players. Improvements would involve rotating players to different positions and coordinating group substitutions with opposing teams. Team size could be reduced (as already done in many leagues for very young children) to create more opportunities for players to be involved in the action. Batting lineups for baseball and softball could include all team members, regardless of who plays positions in the field. In ice hockey, games could be played across the width of the rink, thereby allowing three times as many teams to compete at the same time. In basketball, first-string teams could play a half-court game at one basket, while second-string teams played at the other basket, and a combined score would determine the winner. These and many other revisions of games would increase personal involvement.

Many sport programs for younger children have decreased the size of playing fields and teams. This soccer program has three-on-three teams, there are no goalies, and no scores are recorded although some parents keep track of scores and team records. The four- and five-year-olds in the league are most interested in running around and kicking the ball somewhere, even if it's in the wrong direction. (*Source:* Jay Coakley)

Creating Close Scores   "Good games" are those for which the outcomes are in doubt until the last play; double-overtime games are the best. Lopsided scores destroy the excitement of competition. Children realize this, so they usually keep their informal games close. Because motivation depends on perceived chances for success, a close game usually keeps children motivated and satisfied. Just like adults who use handicaps to keep competition interesting in bowling, golf, and other sports, children adjust their games to keep them close.

In organized games, lopsided scores are common, and team records are often uneven. Keeping players motivated under these circumstances is difficult. Coaches are forced to appeal to pride and respect to motivate players in the face of lopsided scores and long, losing seasons. Ironically, when coaches urge players to develop a "killer instinct"

by taking big leads during games, it often undermines motivation among all players in the long run.

Many adults hesitate to make changes that affect the outcomes of games, but some possibilities are worth consideration. For example, they could encourage close scores by altering team rosters or by using handicap systems during games. The underdog could be given an advantage such as extra players or the right to use five downs, five outs, or a bigger goal. Many changes could keep games close; however, when game models are viewed as unchangeable, possibilities are not discussed, even though children make such changes when they play informal games.

Maintaining Friendships   When children play informal and alternative sports, the reaffirmation of friendships is important. Friendships influence processes of selecting teams and the dynamics of problem-solving processes during games and activities. Organized sports provide contexts for making friends, but players need more than adult-controlled practices and games to nurture relationships with teammates and peers on other teams.

To foster friendships, coaches could help groups of players plan game strategies or coach practices. They could enable players to talk and interact with opponents in supportive ways during games. Too often, relationships between opponents are impersonal or hostile, and players don't learn that games have a human component that is central to having fun in competitive relationships. Most important, players should be expected to enforce game rules so that they understand why rules are necessary and how collective action depends on cooperation related to following rules. Many people claim that self-enforcement would never work (although it does in tennis). However, if organized programs do not teach young people how to cooperate to the extent needed to play games on their own, then those programs are *not* worth our time and effort. If young people do not learn how to play games without coaches and referees, how can adults claim that sports teach young people leadership, discipline, decision-making skills, or character?

Improving High-Performance Sport Programs

Many of the worst problems in youth sports occur in high-performance programs. To deal with these problems, sociologist Peter Donnelly (1993) has called on the governing bodies of all sports to do two things:

1. Change their policies, procedures, and rules to account for the rights and interests of children.
2. Create less controlling sport environments designed to promote children's growth, development, and empowerment.

Because people in sport organizations often have vested interests in maintaining the status

quo, Donnelly advocates that some form of child labor laws be developed and enforced so that children might be protected from overzealous parents and coaches (see figure 5.2). Journalist Joan Ryan picked up on Donnelly's points when she studied girls in elite gymnastics and figure skating. She suggested the following:

> Since those charged with protecting young athletes so often fail their responsibility, it is time the government drops the fantasy that certain sports are merely games and takes a hard look at legislation aimed at protecting elite child athletes. (1995, p. 15)

This is a suggestion that deserves serious consideration as overuse and other injury rates increase among children in these programs. Past experience in the United States and many other nations indicates that, when the status and

"How many times have I told you to practice your basketball before you even think of homework?"

FIGURE 5.2   The fame and fortune of some professional athletes may encourage some parents to overemphasize youth sports in the lives of their children. Might this turn young athletes into "child workers"?

incomes of adults depend on the work or performance of children, children need formal protection from an agency that is concerned with their well-being more than the medals and championships they win.

PROSPECTS FOR IMPROVING YOUTH SPORTS

Many youth sport programs have made changes that reflect a concern for the needs and well-being of children. Research identifies excellent models for making creative and progressive changes in youth sports (Chalip and Green, 1998; Morris and Stiehl, 1989; Murphy, 1999; Torbert, 2004; 2005). However, the approach most often used to guide changes in youth sports is grounded in functionalist theory (see chapter 2) and focuses primarily on increasing the efficiency and organization of existing programs and maximizing the physical skills of athletes.

A functionalist orientation often leads to an emphasis on coaching education programs and tough rules regulating the actions of parents, spectators, players, and coaches. But at the same time, it also leads to increased emphasis on the performance ethic and more tournaments, playoffs, and championships that take children around the country for the sake of creating sport "résumés." Furthermore, as local programs align with national organizations, the people who run those organizations decide how to define "improvements" and what should be changed in youth sports. Most of these organizations run programs that are commercial and "excellence oriented," and they appeal to parents who mistakenly equate excellence in sports with overall child development. Even parents who don't make this mistake find themselves in a bind because the national organizations that now control many local programs also monitor the "feeder" process leading onto teams at higher competitive levels. And parents know that if their children drop out at eleven years old, they will fall behind and never get back into the feeder tracks through which players are chosen for high school teams, college scholarships, and even professional contracts.

Coaching education programs could be a tool for changing this trend in youth sports. Most coaching education emphasizes putting athletes' needs ahead of winning, but it never teaches coaches how to critically assess the sports programs or general organizational contexts in which they work with young people. It does not teach coaches how to make structural changes in programs or create alternatives to existing programs. Instead, coaching education generally assumes that existing youth sport programs are pretty good, but they could be better if coaches were more organized and used more applied sport science as they work with child athletes. The dependence

"I'll say this only once, Dad. You turn on the camera, I walk off the court."

FIGURE 5.3 Many children who play sports do not enjoy videotapes of their games, meets, and matches. They would rather remember their experiences in their own terms. Too often, the tapes are used to identify mistakes and make youth sports more important than children want them to be.

on win–loss records to measure coaching effectiveness intensifies this approach.

One thing to be avoided in coaching education is a "technoscience approach" emphasizing control and skill development rather than human development. If this happens, coaches become "sports efficiency experts" rather than teachers who help young people become responsible and informed decision makers about physical activity and sports in their lives. Unfortunately, I know of no organized youth sport program or coaching education program with a mission statement declaring that the goal is to help child athletes become decision makers who control their sport lives and the contexts in which they play sports. Such a mission statement would be based on critical rather than functionalist theory.

summary

ARE ORGANIZED YOUTH SPORT PROGRAMS WORTH THE EFFORT?

Although physical activities exist in all cultures, organized youth sports are a luxury. They require resources and discretionary time among children and adults. They exist only when children are not required to work and only when adults believe that experiences during childhood influence overall growth and development. Youth sports have a unique history in every society in which they exist. However, they characteristically emphasize experiences and values defined as important in the societies in which they exist.

The growth of organized sports in North America and much of Europe is associated with changes in the family that occurred during the latter half of the twentieth century. Many parents now see organized sports as vehicles to control children and ensure that boys and girls have access to important developmental experiences.

Major trends in youth sports today include the privatization of organized programs, an emphasis on the performance ethic, the development of high-performance training programs, and more involvement by and concern among parents. In response to these trends, some children have turned to informal, alternative, and action sports.

Children's sport experiences vary with levels of formal organization and the extent to which they are participant controlled or adult controlled. The dynamics of sport participation and the lessons learned during participation are different in informal games than in organized youth sports. Involvement across a range of participation settings is best for the overall development of children. Interactionist research in the sociology of sport helps us understand that, prior to eight years old, children do not have the developmental abilities to fully participate in organized competitive sports, especially team sports in which complex strategies are used. Such abilities are not fully developed until twelve years of age in most children. Research also describes and helps us understand some of the family dynamics associated with organized youth sports, especially in terms of how they affect family relationships, family schedules, and the lives of mothers and fathers. Studies guided by critical theories illustrate how social factors influence youth sport experiences, including the participation choices available to children and the meanings given to various sport experiences.

Recommendations for improving organized youth sports emphasize that there should be action, involvement among all participants, exciting competition, and opportunities for children to form and nurture friendships with peers—just as there are in many informal games. Adults inhibit the prospects for change because they often have vested interests in maintaining programs as they are currently organized. This is especially true in high-performance sport programs, even though these are the ones in which improvements are most needed. Coaching education programs could facilitate critical thinking among those who work most directly with children in these programs, but coaching education is based on functionalist rather than critical approaches to sports.

No sports program can guarantee that it will make children into models of virtue, but the adults who organize and control youth sports can make improvements to existing programs. This means that organized sports for children *are* worth the effort—when the adults put the children's interests ahead of the programs' organizational needs and their own needs to gain status through their association with successful and highly skilled child athletes.

 See the OLC, www.mhhe.com/coakley9e, for an annotated list of readings related to this chapter. The OLC also contains a key concept list, a review test, and other helpful features.

WEBSITE RESOURCES

Note: Websites often change. The following URLs were current when this book was printed. Please check our website (www.mhhe.com/coakley9e) for updates and additions.

www.mhhe.com/coakley9e   Click on chapter 5 to find information on studying gender in children's sports, observation guide for studying a youth sport event; in-depth discussion of when children are ready to play sports; materials on parent–child relationships and youth sports; discussion of social factors influencing youth sports.

http://ed-web3.educ.msu.edu/ysi   The site of the Institute for the Study of Youth Sports at Michigan State University; the institute sponsors research on the benefits and detriments of participation in youth sports, produces educational materials, and provides educational programs for coaches, officials, administrators, and parents; useful links to other sites.

www.nays.org   The site of the National Alliance for Youth Sports, a nonprofit organization with the goal of making sports safe and positive for America's youth; links to other youth sport sites.

www.righttoplay.com   Right To Play, headquartered in Toronto, Canada, is an international humanitarian organization that uses sport and play to encourage the overall health and development of children in high-poverty regions of the world; the focus is on community development in connection with sport programs, and it provides a practical evaluation system that youth sport administrators can use to assess programs and teams, identify and anticipate problems among spectators and with coaches and players, and provide corrective action when there are problems.

http://deepfun.com/junkyard-sports.html   This site, maintained by Bernie De Koven, contains practical descriptions of how play and games can be done in any environment by using creativity rather than special equipment.

www.sportsparenting.org/csp   The site of the Center for Sports Parenting, a web-based program that offers immediate and practical guidance to parents, coaches, educators, administrators, officials, and others involved in youth sports.

www.momsteam.com   Information at this parents' site is designed to create a safer, saner, less stressful, and more inclusive youth sports experience; it is directed at mothers of children in organized youth sport programs.

www.sportinsociety.org/uys.html   The site of the Urban Youth Sports Program of the Center for the Study of Sport in Society; focuses on issues in Boston, but it provides a useful conceptual model for what might be done in other cities to overcome barriers that limit youth sport participation and to increase opportunities for healthy development.

www.youth-sports.com   A general site for information, advice, and instructional products for parents, coaches, and children involved in youth sports.

www.aahperd.org/naspe/template.cfm?template= specialinterest-ysc.html   Site of the Youth Sport Coalition, a subgroup of the National association for Sport and Physical Education; it provides leadership to those who work with children and youth in sport; the site provides helpful links including one through which a new Youth Sport Report Card can be downloaded for use by parents and program administrators.

(Mark Reis, *Colorado Springs Gazette*)

DEVIANCE IN SPORTS

Is It Out of Control?

WHERE DO ACCEPTABLE practices end and cheating begin? Why is it okay for a cyclist to sleep in an oxygen tent but not okay to inject EPO?

—Paula Parrish, journalist, 2002

IF I HADN'T HAD the injections [of painkillers], I don't think I would have been able to skate.

—Johnny Weir, two-time U.S. figure skating champion, 2005

 Online Learning Center Resources

Visit *Sports in Society*'s Online Learning Center (OLC) at **www.mhhe.com/coakley9e** for additional information and study material for this chapter, including

- Self-grading quizzes
- Learning objectives
- Related websites
- Additional readings

_____

A complete outline is available online at www.mhhe.com/coakley9e.

IT'S NO SECRET what's going on in baseball. At least half the guys are using steroids. They talk about it. They joke about it. . . . At first I felt like a cheater. But I looked around, and everybody was doing it.

—**Ken Caminiti, Major League Baseball player, 2002**

BEING TOO MORALISTIC about our games is like going to the circus and being indignant about how the clowns act.

—**Dan Le Batard, ESPN journalist, 2005**

Deviance among athletes, coaches, agents, and others connected with sports have attracted widespread attention in recent years. Daily media reports of on-the-field rule violations and off-the-field criminal actions have led some people to conclude that deviance in sports is out of control. News about widespread drug and substance use among athletes has intensified this perception. Because many people believe that sports build character, every case of deviance in sports leads them to be disappointed and believe that the moral fabric of society itself is eroding. They often conclude that money and greed, combined with a lack of discipline and self-control, have destroyed the purity of sport and the existence of sportsmanship.

Because many people have come to this conclusion, the purpose of this chapter is to examine deviance in sports. We focus on four questions as we deal with this issue:

1. What problems do we face when we study deviance in sports?
2. What is the most useful way to define *deviance* when studying sports in society?
3. Are rates of deviant actions among athletes (on and off the field), coaches, and others connected with sports out of control?
4. Why do some athletes use performance-enhancing substances, and is there a way to control substance use in sports?

These questions direct our attention to important issues in the study of sports in society.

PROBLEMS FACED WHEN STUDYING DEVIANCE IN SPORTS

Studying deviance in sports presents problems for four reasons. First, *the types and causes of deviance in sports are so diverse that no single theory can explain all of them.* For example, think of the types of deviance that occur just among male college athletes: talking back to a coach at practice, running wind sprints to the point of vomiting, violating rules or committing fouls on the playing field during a match or game, taking megadoses of performance-enhancing substances in the locker room, hazing rookie team members by demeaning them and forcing them to do illegal things, binge drinking and fighting in bars, harassing women, engaging in group sex, sexual assault, turning in course-work prepared by others, betting on sports, playing with painful injuries and using painkillers to stay on the field, destroying hotel property during a road trip after an embarrassing loss or a difficult win, and going home over a holiday to meet agents who have given money to their parents and bought a luxury SUV for them to use when they return to campus. This diverse list includes only a sample of cases reported for one group of athletes at one level of competition over the past decade. The list would be more diverse if we included all athletes and if we were to list types of deviance among coaches, administrators, team owners, and spectators.

Second, *actions that are accepted in sports may be deviant in other spheres of society, and actions accepted in society may be deviant in sports.* Athletes are allowed and even encouraged to do things that are outlawed or defined as criminal in other settings. For example, some of the things that athletes do in contact sports would be classified as felony assault if they occurred on the streets; boxers would be criminals outside the ring. Ice hockey players would be arrested for actions they define as normal during their games. Racecar drivers would be ticketed for speeding and careless driving. Speed skiers and motocross racers would be defined as irresponsible if not deviant outside their sports. However, even when serious injuries or deaths occur in sports, criminal charges usually are not filed, and civil lawsuits asking for financial compensation are generally unsuccessful.

Coaches treat players in ways that most of us would define as deviant if teachers treated students or employers treated employees similarly. Team owners in North American professional

It is difficult to study deviance in sports because athletes often engage in actions that would not be accepted in other settings. For example, actions that are acceptable in boxing, hockey, football, and other sports would get you arrested or sued if you were to engage in them off the field. (*Source: Colorado Springs Gazette*)

sports clearly violate the antitrust laws that apply to other business owners. Fans act in ways that would quickly alienate friends and family members in other settings or lead people to define them as mentally deranged.

On the other hand, if athletes take the same drugs or nutritional supplements used by millions of nonathletes, they may be banned from their sports and defined as deviant, even by people using those drugs and supplements. Athletes who miss practices or games due to sickness or injury often are defined as deviant by coaches and teammates. Certain college athletes violate rules if they hold jobs during the school year, and coaches may punish players who fail to attend class. Youth league players may be benched for a game if they miss practice to attend a family picnic.

Norms in sports often are different from norms in other social worlds, and responses to deviance by athletes may be different from responses to others who engage in deviance. For example, athletes often are praised for their extreme actions that risk health and well-being and inflict pain and injury on others, whereas non-athletes would be defined as deviant for doing the same things. We tend to view the motives of people in sports, especially athletes, as positive because their actions are directed toward the achievement of success for their team, school, community, country, or corporate sponsor. Therefore, those actions, even when they clearly overstep generally accepted limits in society as a whole, may be tolerated or even praised rather than condemned. Athletes often are seen as different and deviant in ways that evoke fascination and awe rather than repulsion and condemnation. Most sociological theories about deviance do not adequately explain many actions that occur in sports and the meanings given to them.

Third, *deviance in sports often involves an unquestioned acceptance of norms, rather than a rejection of norms.* Much of the deviance in sports does not involve a rejection of commonly accepted norms and expectations for action. Sports involve exciting experiences and powerful social processes, which encourage extreme actions among athletes. These actions, even when they are tolerated or seen as entertaining, are also seen as falling outside the range of normal acceptance in society. However, they may not be punished because they exaggerate ideals such as commitment, sacrifice, dedication, and a desire to achieve goals. Ironically, this leads many people to see athletes as role models, even as they push or exceed normative limits.

Unlike deviance in other settings, deviance in sports often involves an unquestioned acceptance of and extreme conformity to norms and expectations. For example, most North Americans see playing football as a positive activity. Young men are encouraged to "be all they can be" as football players and to live by slogans such as "There is no *I* in t-e-a-m" and "No pain, no gain." They are encouraged to increase their weight and strength so that they can play more effectively and contribute to the success of their teams. When young men go too far in conforming to expectations and use banned substances to become bigger and stronger, they become deviant (Neyer, 2000).

This type of "overdoing-it deviance" is dangerous, but it is based on a desire to fit in and maintain an athlete identity through excessive dedication and commitment. This is sociologically different from *antisocial deviance* grounded primarily in alienation and a rejection of norms. Athletes accept without question the norms that define what it means to be an athlete, and their deviance often involves overconformity to those norms, not a rejection of them. Therefore, taking

a drug to meet expectations in sports is very different from taking a drug to escape reality and expectations. The athlete overconforms when taking drugs to improve performance and gain acceptance from teammates; the alienated youth underconforms when mainlining heroin. This difference is important when we study and try to explain the origins of deviance in sports.

Fourth, *training and performance in sports are now based on such new forms of science and technology that people have not yet developed norms to guide and evaluate the actions of athletes and others in sports.* Science and medicine once used only to treat people who were ill are now used regularly in sports. The everyday challenge of training and competition in sports often pushes bodies to such extremes that continued participation requires the use of new medical treatments and technologies just to stay on the field. For example, the use of nutritional supplements has become a standard practice in nearly all sports. As one high school athlete explains, supplements "are as much a fixture in sports participation as mouthguards and athletic tape" (in Mooney, 2003, p. 18). Ingesting substances thought to enhance performance is simply part of being an athlete today. This is why the athletic departments at the University of Texas and Texas A&M spent over $200,000 on supplements just for their football players in 2005. But even without support from athletic departments, athletes buy supplements online and at local stores, not because they want to take shortcuts, but because they want to be all they can be in sports.

Count the ads for performance-enhancing substances in any recent issue of the magazines *Muscle Media* and *Muscle and Fitness*. The motto for these ads seems to be "Strength and high performance are just a swallow away"! Of course, corporations encourage this approach when they use athletes' bodies to promote products and corporate images in terms of strength and machinelike efficiency (Hoberman, 1995). In the meantime, it has become much more difficult to determine just what actions are deviant and what actions are accepted parts of athletic training.

DEFINING AND STUDYING DEVIANCE IN SPORTS: THREE APPROACHES

Approaches to identifying, defining, and controlling deviance in sports vary depending on the theoretical framework used. We focus on approaches based on functionalist theory, conflict theory, and a combination of interactionist and critical theories.

Using Functionalist Theory: Deviance Disrupts Shared Values

According to functionalist theory, social order is based on shared values. Shared values give rise to shared cultural goals and shared ideas about how to achieve those goals. Deviance occurs when actions demonstrate a rejection of cultural goals and/or the accepted means of achieving them. In other words, deviance involves a departure from cultural ideals: the greater the departure, the more disruptive the action, the greater the deviance. Conversely, conformity to cultural ideals reaffirms the social order and is seen as the foundation of ethics and morality.

Most functionalists see deviance as a result of faulty socialization or inconsistencies in the organization of society. Deviance occurs because people have not learned and internalized cultural values and norms or because there are conflicts and strains built into the structure of society. Therefore, reforming socialization processes and eliminating structural conflicts, strains, and inconsistencies in social systems is the best control for deviance.

Deviance in sports, according to a functionalist approach, deviance occurs when an athlete rejects the goal of improving skills or the expectation that the means to achieve goals is to work harder than others. A problem with this approach is that it becomes difficult to identify deviance when there is a lack of agreement about the importance of various goals. For example, if I think that the goal in sports is to play fair but you think that it is to win, then I will see any violation of the rules as deviant, whereas you will see some violations as "good fouls" if they contribute to winning. If I regard sports as a form of play in which intrinsic satisfaction is the reason for participation but you regard sports as "war without weapons" fought for external rewards such as trophies and cash prizes, then I will see violent actions as deviant, whereas you will see them as signs of courage and commitment. Because we don't share beliefs about the ideals of sports, we don't define *deviance* in the same way.

Another problem with a functionalist approach is that it leads many people to think that controlling deviance always calls for policies and programs that increase conformity. This usually involves establishing more rules, making rules more strict and consistent, developing a more comprehensive system of detecting and punishing rule violators, and making everyone more aware of the rules and what happens to those who don't follow them (see figure 6.1). This approach often

"If they had more rules and better enforcement, all this deviance would stop."

FIGURE 6.1 Many people use a functionalist approach when they think about deviance in sports. They call for more rules and better enforcement. This approach has only limited usefulness in sports today.

AT YOUR *fingertips* For more information, on violent actions in sports, see Chapter 7.

subverts creativity and change, and it assumes that all conformity, especially extreme conformity, is a cultural ideal. This assumption is questionable because obsessive and excessive conformity can be dangerous, a possibility discussed in the section on interactionist and critical theories (p. 157).

Despite these problems, many people use a functionalist approach when they discuss deviance in sports. When actions don't match their ideals they define them and their perpetrators as deviant. The solution, they say, is to "get tough," make punishments more severe, and throw out the "bad apples." This solution is based on the idea that people violate rules because they lack moral character and that "normal" people in normal situations are not deviant. This approach may be useful when people are unaware of norms, but it ignores the influence of powerful social processes in sports and leads people to label athletes unjustly as moral failures when, in fact, most athletes are "hyperconformers" whose main fault is that they have not learned to critically assess norms or set limits on what they will do to conform to norms in sport. We will say more about this throughout the chapter.

Using Conflict Theory: Deviance Interferes with the Interests of Wealthy People

According to conflict theory, social order is based on economic interests and the use of economic power by those who own the means of production in society. Therefore, social norms reflect the interests of those people, and any actions, ideas, or people violating those norms are defined as deviant.

Those who use this approach assume that all people act in their own interests and that people in power use their position to turn their ideas of right and wrong into the official definitions of

conformity and deviance in a society. Those who lack economic power in society have nothing to say about the content or enforcement of rules and they are more likely to be identified as deviant than people with wealth and power. Furthermore, legal processes are organized so that people who lack power don't have the resources to resist being labeled as deviant when their actions do not conform to the standards of the rule makers.

Conflict theorists assume that rules in sports reflect the interests of owners and sponsors and ignore the interests of athletes and most fans. Therefore, they see deviance among athletes as a result of rules that discriminate against them and force them to follow the expectations of those in power, even though their health and well-being may be harmed in the process. Athletes are viewed as victims of a profit-driven system, in which progressive change requires rejecting and remaking the rules.

A problem with conflict theory is that deviance in sports is always assumed to be the result of biased norms and law enforcement processes controlled by wealthy owners and sponsors who convince everyone that their rules are the only rules. For instance, conflict theorists cannot explain why deviance exists in nonrevenue-producing sports in which the athletes themselves may be in positions of power and control. Furthermore, many athletes voluntarily use dangerous growth hormones and other substances because they seek acceptance from teammates, not sponsors and team owners. Therefore, it is unlikely that all deviance in sports would disappear if athletes were in charge. Athletes should have more control over their sport participation, but without the critical consciousness needed to eliminate the profit motive and transform sports, it is unlikely that shifting more power to athletes would eliminate deviance in sports. Explaining all forms of deviance in economic terms is difficult. Although the commercialization of sports and financial motives may account for certain forms of deviance, other factors and dynamics must be considered to understand why deviance occurs in sports that are neither commercialized nor driven by profit motives.

Using Interactionist and Critical Theories: Deviance as a Social Construction

Although functionalist and conflict theories call attention to socialization and economic factors, they overlook the possibility that much of the deviance in sports involves overconformity to the norms that athletes use to evaluate themselves and others.

Most people who violate rules in sports can't be classified as morally bankrupt, as functionalists often conclude, or as exploited victims, as conflict theorists often conclude. For example, it is not accurate to say that young people lack moral character when they accept without qualification the notion that athletes are dedicated to the game and willing to do what it takes to become and remain an accepted participant of a sport culture, even if it means going beyond normal limits as they train. Nor is it accurate to define all athletes who engage in deviance as passive victims of an exploitive, profit-driven sport system; after all, athletes participate in the creation and maintenance of the norms that guide their decisions and actions in sports. This means that we need an alternative explanation of deviance in sports, an explanation that takes into account the experiences of athletes within the actual contexts in which they play sports.

In searching for such an explanation, most sociologists now use a constructionist approach based on interactionist and critical theories. This approach focuses on two issues: (1) the meanings that people give to actions, traits, and ideas and (2) the ways that people use those meanings to "construct" their definitions of what and who is deviant. It acknowledges that norms change over time and from situation to situation so that it is possible for something or someone to be considered deviant at one time or place and not at other times and places. For example, Arnold Schwarzenegger took steroids to help him win seven Mr. Universe and seven Mr. Olympia titles

between the late 1960s and 1980 and then used his reputation and enhanced body to become an action hero in films, but he is not considered deviant by most people today because steroids were legal in bodybuilding in the 1960s and 1970s. However, most voters in California used a constructionist approach to deviance as they elected Schwarzenegger as their governor—they decided that it was not appropriate to use today's norms to judge actions in the past as unethical or criminal.

People who assume that social reality contains absolute truths about right and wrong and good and evil reject a constructionist approach to deviance. They believe that unchanging moral truths are the foundation for all norms. Therefore, every norm represents an ideal, and every action, trait, or idea that departs from that ideal is deviant, immoral, or evil. When this "absolutist" approach is used, deviance becomes increasingly serious as the departure from the ideal increases. For example, if using drugs violates an absolute principle of fairness in sports, any use of drugs at any time or place would be deviant, and if the drug use continued, use over time would be defined as immoral or evil. People using an absolutist approach do not accept that norms and deviance are social constructions. They cling to the notion of absolute moral truths and use it to divide the world into good and evil and to make decisions about deviance and social control in everyday life. For example, media commentators who discuss criminal cases or drug use in sports often use an absolutist approach when they say without qualification that athletes today lack moral character to the point that they cannot distinguish right from wrong.

A CONSTRUCTIONIST APPROACH TO DEVIANCE IN SPORTS

Deviance always involves violating a norm. But sociologists using a constructionist approach say that a definition of deviance must take into account the process of *identifying* and *responding to* actions, traits, and ideas. Therefore, they define

deviance as *an action, trait, or idea that falls outside a range of acceptance as determined by people with the power to enforce norms in a social world.* This definition emphasizes the following points about deviance:

1. Norms are socially constructed as people interact with each other and determine a range of accepted actions, traits, or ideas that are consistent with their values; norms *do not* represent absolute ideals against which all actions are evaluated. This point is illustrated in Figure 6.2 where line A shows that norms are constructed in ways that permit variations within accepted limits so that everyone is not required to act, look, and think exactly alike to conform to values and avoid being labeled as deviant. Line B, on the other hand, illustrates an absolutist approach in which every norm is based on an ideal that identifies a specific action, trait, or idea as right, good, and moral; and any departure from the ideal represents a degree of deviance, immorality, or perversity.

2. Deviance is socially constructed as people negotiate the limits of what they will accept and then identify the actions, traits, and

ideas that go beyond those limits. This is illustrated in line A by the two "limit lines" that separate socially accepted or "normal" actions, traits, and ideas from those that are unacceptable, or deviant.

3. Power relations influence the process of negotiating normative limits because limits are seldom meaningful unless they can be enforced. Therefore, people who possess the power to administer sanctions (that is, punishments or rewards) generally have the most influence in determining normative limits.

4. Most actions, traits, and ideas in a social world fall into a normally accepted range, and those that fall outside this range involve deviant underconformity *or* deviant overconformity as illustrated in Figure 6.3.

Figure 6.3 is useful when trying to understand deviance in sports, especially the use of performance-enhancing substances and other extreme actions that most people in society define as outside the normal range of acceptance because they jeopardize health and well-being. The figure depicts a normal bell-shaped curve. The horizontal line below the curve represents a continuum of actions, traits, and ideas that encompasses cases

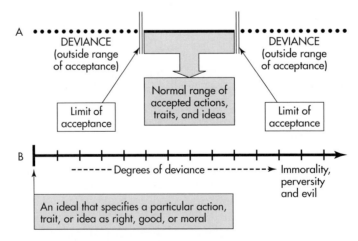

FIGURE 6.2 Norms set limits but permit a range of acceptable actions, traits, or ideas.

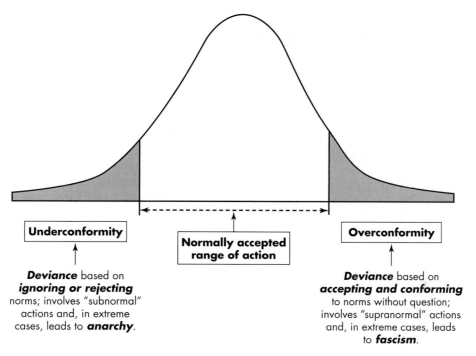

Underconformity

Normally accepted range of action

Overconformity

Deviance based on ***ignoring or rejecting*** norms; involves "subnormal" actions and, in extreme cases, leads to ***anarchy***.

Deviance based on ***accepting and conforming*** to norms without question; involves "supranormal" actions and, in extreme cases, leads to ***fascism***.

FIGURE 6.3   Two types of deviance in sports. Most actions in sports fall within a normally accepted range in society as a whole. Deviance occurs when actions, traits, or ideas go beyond normative limits on either side of this range. Deviance that involves underconformity is grounded in different social dynamics than deviance that involves overconformity. Most discussions of deviance in sports focus on athletes or others who engage in deviant underconformity by ignoring or rejecting norms. Generally overlooked or misinterpreted are cases of deviant overconformity that occur when the actions, traits, and ideas of athletes and coaches involve such extreme and unquestioned normative conformity that they endanger themselves and others.

of extreme underconformity on the left to cases of extreme overconformity on the right.

Actions, traits, and ideas that fall into a normally accepted range are located in the middle of the bell curve to show that they occur with the most frequency. The height of the curve represents the frequency of actions along the continuum. The shaded areas at each end of the continuum represent deviance—that is, actions that fall outside the limits of what is normally accepted in society. **Deviant underconformity** consists of *actions based on ignoring or rejecting norms,* whereas **deviant overconformity** consists of

actions based on uncritically accepting norms and being willing to follow them to extreme degrees. Both types of deviance can be dangerous.[1] For example,

---

[1]Some social scientists (Heckert and Heckert, 2002, 2004, 2006; Hughes and Coakley, 1991; Irwin, 2003; West, 2003) use the terms *negative deviance* and *positive deviance* to refer to deviant underconformity and deviant overconformity, respectively. The term *positive deviance* does *not* imply that such deviance is good or beneficial to self or others. In fact, positive deviance involves extreme actions, traits, and ideas that often are unhealthy and dangerous. Additionally, this discussion focuses on actions only; a more detailed discussion of deviance in sports would also focus on traits and ideas.

extreme, widespread underconformity leads to lawlessness or anarchy in a group or society, whereas extreme, widespread overconformity leads to blind obedience or fascism as people accept without question a rigid belief system or the commands a charismatic leader. Both anarchy and fascism are dangerous.

Deviant Overconformity in Sports

Research shows that deviant overconformity occurs often in sports. For example, when Keith Ewald and Robert Jiobu (1985) studied men seriously involved in bodybuilding or competitive distance running, they concluded that some of the men displayed classic characteristics of deviance in the form of unquestioned overconformity to norms related to training and competition. This occurred when the bodybuilders and distance runners followed these norms to such an extent that family relationships, work responsibilities, and/or physical health were affected negatively, yet they never questioned what they were doing or why they were doing it.

This study was done over twenty years ago, and it identified a form of deviance that is even more common today. Many elite athletes prepare so intensely for their sports that they ignore the needs of family members. As former NFL player Matt Millen says, "You have to be selfish, getting ready for a game that only a handful of people understand. It's tough on the people around you. . . . It's the most unspoken but powerful part of the game, that deep-seated desire to be better at all costs, even if it means alienating your family or friends." Millen also says that, whenever athletes enter high-level sports, they want to make the cut and stay involved, and "they will doing anything to accomplish that goal, even if it means sacrificing their own physical or mental well being" (in Freeman, 1998, p. 1). Bette McKenzie (1999), a daughter of an NHL player and a former wife of an NFL player, agrees. She notes that her ex-husband's deviant overconformity to the norms of professional

football interfered with family relationships so much that it was a key factor in their divorce.

Research has identified other forms of deviant overconformity, such as self-injurious overtraining, unhealthy eating behaviors and weight-control strategies among female athletes in intercollegiate and other elite amateur sports and among men in wrestling,[2] extreme dedication to training among ultramarathon bicyclists (Wasielewski, 1991) and triathletes (Hilliard and Hilliard, 1990), and uncritical commitments to playing sports with pain and injury.[3]

When we use a critical, constructionist approach to study deviance in sports, we see that it is important to distinguish between actions that show indifference toward norms or a rejection of norms, on the one hand, and actions that show an uncritical acceptance and overconformity to norms on the other hand. This approach forces us to examine sports cultures and the social dynamics that occur in them. For example, athletes in high-performance sports are often encouraged to overconform to a set of norms that they then use to evaluate themselves and others as they train and compete (Donnelly, 1996b; Howe, 2004; Ingham et al., 1999, 2002; Johns, 1997; Waldron and Krane, 2005). Because of this, much of the deviance among athletes (and coaches) involves *unquestioned acceptance of* and *overconformity to* norms embodied in the ethos of contemporary power and performance sports.

---

[2]See Beals, 2000; Davis, 1999; Donnelly, 1993; Franseen and McCann, 1996; Hawes, 2001; Johns, 1992, 1996, 1997, 2004; Johns and Johns, 2000; Sundgot-Borgen, 2001; Thompson and Sherman, 1999; also see Wilmore, 1996, for a review of thirty-five studies.

[3]See Curry, 1993; Cotton, 2005a; Curry and Strauss, 1994; Grant, 2002a, 2002b; Haney and Pearson, 1999; Howe, 2004; Ingham et al., 2002; Keown, 2004; P. King, 2004; Lyons, 2002; Nixon, 1993a, 1993b, 1994a, 1994b, 1996a, 1996b; Peretti-Watel et al., 2004a, 2004b; Pike and Maguire, 2003; Schefter, 2003; White and Young, 1997; Wood, 2004; Young and White, 1995; Young, 2004; Young et al., 1994.

<table>
<tr></tr>
</table>

reflect on SPORTS

Just (Over)do It
The Sport Ethic in Nike Ads

Nike and other corporations use advertising strategies in which they depict and glorify deviant overconformity to the norms of the sport ethic. They assume that this attracts attention and sells products.

In 1996 during coverage of the Olympic Games in Atlanta, a Nike ad in *Sports Illustrated* asked boldly, "Who the Hell Do You Think You Are? Are You an Athlete?" The text in the ad answered this question with words that echo the norms of the sport ethic:

> Because if you are [an athlete], then you know what it means to want to be better, to want to be the best. And if you are [an athlete], then you understand it's not enough to just want to be the best. You can't just sit around and BS about how much you want it. Show me how much you want it. . . . Dare to do what it takes to be the best. And then, whether you win, lose, or collapse on the finish line, at worst you'll know exactly who you are. If You Can't Stand the Heat, Get Out of Atlanta!

In 1999 Nike ran ads showing the disfigured bodies of athletes who had pushed limits in their sports (Bryant,

1999). The background tune, Joe Cocker's "You Are So Beautiful," was chosen to glorify these bodies, which were seriously injured and left permanently scarred or disfigured. Of course, the ad showed only the bodies of athletes who had recovered enough to play again. Erased from coverage were images of athletes whose injuries had ended their careers and left them with permanent, inglorious impairments for the rest of their lives.

More recent ads for everything from cars to soft drinks show young people, usually young men, in extreme sports engaging in actions that clearly fall outside the range of normal acceptance. The images and narratives in these ads show that people in corporate advertising understand the sport ethic and the tendency among athletes to overconform to its norms. These ads are problematic because they glorify and encourage dangerous forms of deviance.

What do you think?

....

The Sport Ethic and Deviance in Sports

When Bob Hughes and I studied athletes and coaches in the late 1980s, we found that there were four norms that were especially important in their lives. We referred to these as the **sport ethic**—that is, *a set of norms accepted as the dominant criteria for defining what is required to be defined and accepted as an athlete in power and performance sports.* The sport ethic constitutes the normative core of high-performance sport culture and consists of the following four norms:

1. *An athlete is dedicated to "the game" above all other things.* This norm stresses that athletes must love "the game" and prove it by giving it priority over all other interests. This is done by having the proper attitude, demonstrating unwavering commitment, meeting the expectations of fellow athletes,

making sacrifices to play the game, and facing the demands of competition without question. Coaches' pep talks and locker room slogans are full of references to this norm.

A college football player who had ten knee operations in six years and continued to play the game he loved between each operation explained this norm with these words: "I've told a hundred people that if I got a chance to play in the NFL, I'd play for free. It's never been about money. It's never been about anything but playing the game" (in Wieberg, 1994, p. 8C). When NBA player Alonzo Mourning faced a life-threatening kidney disease and played while waiting for a transplant, all-star player Jason Kidd said, "For him to come out and almost kill himself to just play the game that he loves, it just

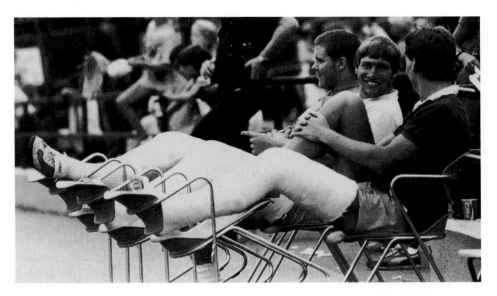

Athletes overconform to the norms of the sport ethic to demonstrate commitment and courage. This leads to high rates of injury in certain sports. These injured football players put their bodies on the line for their team. Coaches and teammates praise their unquestioned acceptance of the norms of the sport ethic. (*Source:* Bobette Brecker, University of Colorado Media Relations)

shows the kind of person 'Zo is" (in Canavan, 2003, p. D3). There are many similar examples of athletes who prove their dedication to and love of "the game" by paying a price to play. Retired athletes say that they want to give back to the game because they care so much about it, despite having disabilities caused by their careers.

2. *An athlete strives for distinction.* The Olympic motto *Citius, Altius, Fortius* (swifter, higher, stronger) captures the meaning of this norm. Being an athlete means relentlessly seeking to improve and achieve perfection. Winning symbolizes improvement and establishes distinction; losing is tolerated only because it increases the desire to win and magnifies winning as a sign of distinction in the culture of high-performance sports. Breaking records is the ultimate achievement because it shows that athletes are a special group

dedicated to climbing the pyramid, reaching for the top, pushing limits, excelling, exceeding others, and being the best they can be no matter what it takes. This norm is highlighted by a former U.S. gymnast who explained that "the harder you train, the more pounding the body takes. . . . We're clearly pushing the envelope. All it takes is one or two gutsy guys to exceed the difficulty level, then everyone tries it" (in Becker, 1999, p. 4E). Justin Wadsworth, the top U.S. Nordic skier in the 30-kilometer race, pushed his body so hard during the 2002 Olympics in Salt Lake City that he suffered internal bleeding due to his exertion. From his hospital bed he said, "It's pretty special to push yourself that hard," and his coaches and fellow athletes agreed with him (Berger, 2002).

3. *An athlete accepts risks and plays through pain.* According to this norm, an athlete does not

give in to pressure, pain, or fear. Willingly accepting risks is a sign of being a true athlete; and playing under pressure is expected. The norm is that athletes don't back down from challenges; they willingly accept the increasing risk of failure and injury as they ascend the pyramid of competitive sports.

The language used in sports is full of references to this norm. When asked about playing with serious injuries and pain, NFL running back Ricky Williams explained that "every Sunday, an NFL player plays through pain that would make the average human cry and stay home from work for a few days. . . . The measure of a football player isn't how well he performs on Sunday but how well he performs in pain" (in Williams, 1999, p. 80). Similarly, when NBA player Allen Iverson was asked about playing with excrutiating shoulder pain he said, "This is what I do. It kills me to sit and watch a game. It kills me. . . . My teammates need me . . . they just need me. . . . And I need to be with my teammates" (in *Denver Post*, 2 March 2000, p. 4D). Connecting dedication to playing with pain, NBA player John Amaechi says that "The only difference between the guy who has passion and the one who doesn't is that it's much easier to work and push through the pain if you have it and much harder if you don't" (in Le Batard, 2002, p. 85). Furthermore, coaches look for players willing to take risks and play through pain; they like injured players in the lineup because it shows teammates that overconformity to the norms of the sport ethic is valued on their teams.

4. *An athlete accepts no obstacles in the pursuit of possibilities.* This norm stresses "the dream" and the obligation to pursue it without question. An athlete doesn't accept obstacles without trying to overcome them and beat the odds; dreams are always seen as achievable *if* a person gives in to no obstacles while pursuing them. Overconformity to this norm was clearly illustrated by Buddy Lazier, who won the Indianapolis 500 while driving with a broken back. Despite his injury, he trained four hours a day, seven days a week. After the race, his father said, "He absolutely never said quit. He was not going to be robbed of this opportunity" (in Ballard, 1996, p. A1). Lazier accepted no limits in pursuing his dream; surgery on the crushed disks pressing on his nerves waited until after the race. Champion boxer Lucia Rijker (who starred in the film *Million Dollar Baby*) stated this norm succinctly as she trained for a $1 million championship match against Christy Martin: "I use obstacles as wood on a fire" (in Blades, 2005, p. 96).

To understand the connection between the sport ethic and deviance in sports, three points must be kept in mind. *First*, the norms of the sport ethic are widely accepted in cultures in which people believe that it is important to be dedicated to what you do, strive for improvement, make sacrifices to achieve goals, push yourself even when things are difficult or painful, and pursue dreams despite obstacles. For example, in the United States these norms are taught to children by parents, incorporated into academic curricula, emphasized in motivational speeches and self-help books, and portrayed on posters hung on office walls. *Second*, it is expected that those who wish to be accepted as athletes in sport cultures will conform to these norms. *Third*, people with power in sports take great care to control deviant underconformity, but they often ignore or encourage overconformity, even though it may lead to injuries and have long-term negative implications for the health and well-being of athletes. Therefore, in the culture of high-performance sports, these norms are accepted uncritically, without question or qualification, and often followed without recognizing limits or thinking about the boundaries that separate normal from deviant.

Alberto Salazar, a great marathoner, discussed the dangerous consequences of deviant overconformity when he coached middle-distance runner Mary Decker Slaney during the mid-1990s. Slaney had undergone nineteen sport-related surgeries and was living in constant pain at the time. Salazar explained that

> The greatest athletes want it so much, they run themselves to death. You've got to have an obsession, but if unchecked, it's destructive. That's what it is with [Slaney]. She'll kill herself unless you pull the reins back. (in Longman, 1996, p. B11)

Salazar's warning shows that dangerous forms of deviance occur when athletes do not critically assess the sport ethic and the context in which deviant overconformity becomes commonplace. This lack of critical assessment allows this type of deviance to exist even though it is one of the biggest problems in sports today.

Deviant underconformity is also a problem, but when athletes reject norms or refuse to take them seriously, they are immediately reprimanded or dropped from teams. Players who underconform to the norms of the sport ethic are not accepted as athletes by others associated with high-performance sports. But reactions to deviant overconformity are different. When players overconform to the norms of the sport ethic, they are praised and hailed as models, even if they risk their safety and well-being in the process. Media commentators glorify these athletes, praising those who play with broken bones and torn ligaments, endure surgery after surgery to play the game, and willingly submit to injections of painkilling drugs to stay in the game. Spectators often express awe when they hear these stories, even though they realize that athletes have surpassed normative boundaries as defined in the society as a whole. According to

Robert Huizinga, a former NFL team physician and past president of the NFL Physicians Society, many sport fans today "want people to play hurt, and when someone doesn't play hurt, he's no longer our hero" (in King, 1996, p. 27). Fans like to see deviance as long as it reaffirms an acceptance of values; they condemn deviance when it is based on a rejection of values. This was demonstrated when NFL player Ricky Williams quit in the "prime" of his career as a running back and fans condemned him for not staying in a game that had brutalized his body for over a decade. This led Williams to ask the following questions in an interview:

> When is it OK for me to stop playing football? . . . When my knees went out? When my shoulders went out? When I had too many concussions? . . . When is it OK? I'm just curious, because I don't understand. When is it OK to not play football anymore? (*60 Minutes*, CBS, 19 December 2004)

In light of the way that many people respond to the actions and traits of athletes, it is not surprising that many of them uncritically overconform to the norms of the sport ethic without question or qualification, even when it creates problems, causes pain, disrupts family life, jeopardizes health and safety, or shortens their life expectancy (Safai, 2003; Tracey and Elcombe, 2004). This type of deviance raises interesting and important sociological questions.

Why Do Athletes Engage in Deviant Overconformity?

Many athletes overconform to the norms of the sport ethic, but some do not. The main reasons for overconformity are these:

1. Playing sports is so exciting and exhilarating that athletes will do almost anything to stay involved.
2. Being selected to play high-performance sports often depends on a perceived

willingness to overconform to the norms of the sport ethic; coaches praise overconformers and use them as models on their teams.

3. Exceeding normative boundaries infuses drama and excitement into people's lives because it increases the stakes associated with participation and bonds athletes together in the form of a "bunker mentality" that encourages putting one's body on the line for teammates and expecting them to do the same.

For these reasons, athletes often use cases of deviant overconformity as standards to define and evaluate their sport experiences. Nike and Gatorade do this in TV commercials (see the box "Just (Over)do It") by highlighting athletes who throw up, shed blood, collapse from exhaustion, break bones, and morph into su-perbeings as part of regular train-ing and competition. "Just doing it" is fine, even commendable, but "just overdoing it" until you vomit, bleed, lose consciousness, need surgery, or die is generally defined as deviant. However, most athletes don't see overcon-formity to the sport ethic as deviance because it is required to reaffirm their identities as athletes and retain membership in a special group, sepa-rated from normal everyday people who live boring lives and never push the edge of the envelope. When Writer Tom Wolfe (1979) studied astronauts and fighter pilots, he found that pilots who overconformed to norms similar to those constituting the sport ethic, they were defined as having "the right stuff" to move up the pyramid and become one of a special few in the world. Dangerous overconformity, said Wolfe, was a small price to pay to live such an exciting life.

Of course, not all athletes are equally likely to overconform to the sport ethic. Bob Hughes

and I hypothesize that those most likely to do so include

1. Athletes who have low self-esteem or are so eager to be accepted as athletes that they will do whatever it takes to be acknowledged by their peers in sport.
2. Athletes who see achievement in sports as their only way to get ahead, gain respect, and become significant in the world.
3. Male athletes who link together their identities as athletes and as men so that being an athlete and being a man become one and the same in their minds.

Therefore, athletes whose identities or future chances for recognition and success depend exclusively on sport participation are most likely to engage in deviant overconformity. An athlete's vulnerability to group demands, combined with the desire to gain or reaffirm group membership, is a critical factor underlying deviant over-conformity. This is why some coaches create team environ-ments that keep athletes in a per-petual state of adolescence, a time in life characterized by identity insecurities and a strong depen-dence on acceptance by peers. This encourages a never-ending quest to confirm identity and elim-inate self-doubt by going overboard to follow team norms and be accepted by athlete-peers. This dependency-based commitment fuels over-conformity to the sport ethic, making it common for athletes to willingly sacrifice their bodies and play with reckless abandon. When coaches use this strategy they promote dangerous forms of deviance. If coaches were concerned with con-trolling all forms of deviance in sports, they would help athletes set limits for conformity to the norms of the sport ethic; they would also en-courage athletes to ask themselves why they do what they do and how their lives as athletes are connected with the rest of their lives. If athletes

> I feel like I've been coached that way my whole life—to play dirty and to play mean.
> —Jeremy Shockey, NFL player (in Lieber, 2003, p. 1C)

do not learn to set such normative limits, their participation in sports often subverts the process of building character.

Deviant Overconformity and Group Dynamics

Being an athlete is a social as well as a physical experience. At elite levels of competition, special bonds form between athletes as they conform to the norms of the sport ethic. When people join together and collectively dedicate themselves to a goal and willingly make sacrifices and endure pain in the face of significant challenges, they often create a social world in which overconformity to the sport ethic becomes "normalized," even as it remains deviant in society as a whole (Albert, 2004; Curry, 1993; Pike, 2004). As athletes in high-performance and high-risk sports collectively overconform to the norms of the sport ethic, the bonds between them become extraordinarily powerful. This is because their overconformity sets them apart and separates them from the rest of the community. It also leads many athletes to assume that people who are not high-performance athletes cannot understand them and their lives. Athletes may appreciate fan approval, but fans cannot reaffirm their identity as an athlete because fans don't really know what it takes to pay the price day after day, face risk and pain, subordinate one's body and total being to the needs of the team, and do anything required to be among a select few who can perform as no others in the world can perform. Only other athletes understand this, and this makes everyone else peripheral to an athlete's life in sports.

The separation between athletes and the rest of the community makes the group dynamics associated with participation in high-performance sports very powerful. However, they are not unique. Other selective and exclusive groups, usually groups of men, experience similar dynamics. Examples are found in the military, especially among Special Forces units. Former soldiers sometimes

talk about these dynamics and the powerful social bonds formed while they faced danger and death with their "teams." Tom Wolfe (1979) explains that trusting your life to fellow pilots when a small mistake or misjudgment means death creates special bonds, along with feelings that you and your peers are special. These bonds may exist in fraternities and sororities, where "pledges" voluntarily submit to systematic hazing processes designed to emphasize that membership in this special group must be earned by paying the price. In fact, hazing rituals have long been part of the initiation into groups that see themselves as special and separate from the rest of the community. Sport teams often have preseason hazing rituals, during which rookies must obey the commands of team veterans, no matter how demeaning, sickening, painful, or illegal the "mandated" actions are (Alfred University, 1999; Bryshun and Young, 1999; Hawes, 1999a; Wieberg, 2000a, 2000b). The bonds in these groups and the need for group acceptance and approval can be so strong that they prevent group members from reporting deviant and criminal forms of hazing to people outside the group.

As high-performance athletes endure the challenges of maintaining their membership in select groups and teams at the highest level of accomplishment in their sports, they develop not only extremely strong feelings of unity with other athletes but also the sense that they are unique and extraordinary people. After all, they are told this day after day by everyone from coaches to team boosters to autograph seekers. They read it in newspapers and magazines, and they see it on TV and the Internet.

When the sense of being unique and extraordinary becomes extreme, as it does among many high-profile athletes in certain settings, it may be expressed in terms of pride-driven arrogance, an inflated sense of righteousness and power, and a public persona that communicates superiority and even insolence. The Greeks used the word **hubris** to describe this *expression of self-importance and the accompanying sense of being separate from and above the rest of the community*. Hubris is so common in some sports that it has become a key dimension of the public personas of many athletes. A few athletes even market it and use it to attract attention and make people remember them, whereas others may be very selective in choosing when to express it.

The point in this section is that the social processes that exist in many sports, especially elite power and performance sports, do three things:

1. They bond athletes together in ways that encourage and normalize deviant overconformity.
2. They separate athletes from the rest of the community at the same time that they inspire awe and admiration from people in the community.
3. They lead athletes to develop hubris, which simultaneously bonds athletes together, separates them as a group from the rest of the community, and sometimes creates among them a sense of entitlement.

As we understand the impact of these social processes on athletes, we see that much of the deviance in sports is less motivated by winning or making money than by a desire to play the game, successfully claim an identity as an athlete, and maintain membership in an elite athletic in-group. This is not to say that winning and money are irrelevant, but they don't explain why deviant overconformity often is as high among athletes who know they will never win championships or sign big contracts as it is among athletes who can make big money and win championships (see figure 6.4). These athletes, just like their more talented and moneymaking peers, are motivated by the belief that being a "real athlete" means taking risks, making sacrifices, and paying the price to develop skills, stay in the game, and be accepted by other athletes, even if they are not champions.

This means that the roots of deviant overconformity in sports go deeper than individual desires to win or make money. In fact, they are grounded in the social organization of sports,

FIGURE 6.4 Winning is important to athletes. But winning and standing on the victory podium is usually secondary to the goal of being defined and accepted as true athletes by their peers in sports.

processes of identity development, and the failure of people in sports to effectively control deviant overconformity. Fines and jail sentences seldom control this form of deviance. Throwing out the so-called bad apples may help in the short run, but the social processes that operate in the social world of many sports guarantee that next season the crop in the apple orchard will look the same.

Deviant Overconformity and Deviant Underconformity: Is There a Connection?

After identifying deviant overconformity in sports, there are additional issues that require investigation. These include the following:

- If the social bonds created in sports are powerful enough to normalize deviant overconformity that jeopardizes health and well-being, are they powerful enough to foster other forms of deviance?
- If the actions of athletes separate them from the rest of the community, do athletes come

to disdain or disrespect nonathletes to the point that they might be likely to harass or assault them?

• If athletes develop hubris, might they feel entitled to the point of concluding that community standards and rules do not apply to them?

• If people in the community view athletes with awe and fascination because of their displays of deviant overconformity, are those people less likely to enforce laws and other community standards when athletes, especially high-profile athletes, violate them?

Research is needed on these questions. My sense is that long-term overconformity to the sport ethic creates social conditions and group dynamics in sports that encourage notable forms of deviant underconformity such as binge drinking, academic cheating, group theft and property destruction, drunken and careless driving, sexual harassment, physical assault, spousal abuse, and sexual assault. The possible connection between these two types of deviance is identified by an NFL football player who proudly said, "Hey, I have no problem sharing women with my teammates. These guys go to battle with me" (in Nelson, 1994, p. 144).

This player's comment may be shocking, but it is consistent with other cases. For example, it is common for male high school and college athletes to maintain group silence after witnessing teammates gang rape a woman (Curry, 1991, 1996, 1998; Lefkowitz, 1997). Groups of athletes have mercilessly taunted and harassed other students, whom they defined as "unworthy" of respect because of how they looked or dressed (ESPN, 1999). Hazing rituals have subjected prospective teammates to demeaning and even criminal treatment—coercing rookies to steal, drink to the point of passing out, harass others, urinate on each other, drink urine, hold each other's genitals, appear nude in public, and endure

various forms of sodomy, beatings, and brandings (Hawes, 1999b).

The awe and adulation accorded to athletes who entertain others as they push and exceed normative limits in sports on the field have, in some cases, interfered with the enforcement of laws and community standards off the field. Kathy Redmond, founder of the National Coalition Against Violent Athletes, has noted that people in society do not "want to admit that this athlete whom we live vicariously through . . . is capable of deviant behavior" (*USA Today*, 1998, p. C3). For example, boosters and fans who express "get-tough-on-crime" attitudes have threatened women who are alleged assault and rape victims of athletes (Benedict, 1997; Lipsyte, 1998). This occurred to the victim of an alleged sexual assault by NBA player Kobe Bryant; it occurred to a woman who was a placekicker on the University of Colorado football team when she alleged that a fellow player raped her; it occurred to a woman who said that she had been raped multiple times by University of Colorado players and recruits. Furthermore, these cases are difficult to prosecute when police officers ask athletes for autographs during the process of arresting them, and judges rule on cases involving athletes who play on teams representing their alma mater or teams for which the judges have season tickets.

Controlling Deviant Overconformity in Sports

Deviant overconformity presents special social control problems in sports. Coaches, managers, owners, and sponsors—people who exercise control of sports—often benefit when athletes accept without question and overconform to the norms of the sport ethic. These people often see athletes who willingly engage in deviant overconformity as a blessing, not a curse. Athletes see their overconformity to the sport ethic as proof of their dedication and commitment rather than a form of deviance, and people associated with sports often see it as a factor that contributes to wins and high TV ratings. This is why those who control sports are unwilling to discourage this type of deviance, even though they know that it is outside of normative boundaries.

The issue of social control is further complicated by the tendency to promote overconformers into positions of power and influence in sports. Because they have proved they will do anything it takes as players, these people are seen as ideal candidates for certain jobs in sports, especially coaching jobs. This creates a situation in which deviance and ethical problems among athletes are rooted in the organization of sports and in athletes' relationships with each other and with coaches and managers.

Controlling deviant overconformity is difficult. It requires that parents, coaches, and sport administrators teach athletes to set limits as they play sports. This of course conflicts with accepted practices in sports. Controlling deviant underconformity is less difficult because it is quickly identified by authority figures, and everyone understands that it will be punished. Deviant overconformity, however, is more subversive because it is widely ignored. For example, when a fourteen-year-old gymnast is late for practice, her coach immediately sanctions her for being deviant. However, when the same gymnast loses weight and becomes dangerously thin as she strives for distinction and pursues her dream, many coaches, parents, and judges don't see possible deviance as much as they see the mind-set of a champion and the culture of excellence in the gym—that is, until stress fractures or anorexia interfere with competition and put their athlete-daughter in the hospital.

The control of deviant overconformity requires that people associated with sports raise critical questions about the goals, purpose, and organization of sports, as well as the ways that coaches and others enforce the norms of the sport ethic. In the absence of these questions, dangerous

forms of deviance will persist, including the use of performance-enhancing substances. Unfortunately, many coaches encourage deviant overconformity as they tell athletes that the team is their family and that family members put their bodies on the line for each other when they go to battle. Similarly, fostering the belief on teams that "outsiders are out to get us" and that "we have to stick together because nobody understands us" clearly promotes hubris and further separates athletes from the surrounding community and its laws.

The most effective strategy for controlling deviant overconformity is to encourage athletes to set limits that respect their health and use sport participation as a means of connecting more meaningfully with the rest of the community. This also could be an important step in controlling deviant underconformity because it would make athletes feel less like outsiders and help them identify with the community so they would not see themselves as above the law. A major barrier to controlling deviant overconformity is that sport fans want athletes to exceed normative limits and put their bodies on the line. Fans see this as entertaining. But they can't have it both ways—if fans want deviant overconformity, it will sometimes come in forms that make them uncomfortable.

RESEARCH ON DEVIANCE AMONG ATHLETES

Headlines and media coverage of deviance among athletes are common, but systematic studies are rare. Lists of arrest records and criminal charges filed against athletes attract attention, but they don't tell us if deviance is out of control in sports, if there is more deviance today than in the past, if deviance involves overconformity or underconformity, or what causes deviance in sports. Most media reports blame deviance on the character weaknesses of athletes and the financial greed of people associated with sports. Generally ignored is the possibility that deviance could be related

There is no evidence that rates of deviance on the field are higher
today than in the past. What is different today is the media coverage
and video technology, which enable us to see rule violations in
slow motion, stop action, and replay after replay after replay.
Actually, many forms of deviance were more prevalent and blatant
eighty years ago when the technology of enforcement was limited.
(*Source:* Peter Cosgrove, AP/Wide World Photos)

to the culture and organization of sports or the
social dynamics that exist in social worlds created
around sports.

When we discuss deviance among athletes, it
is important to distinguish the actions that occur
on the field and in the immediate realm of sports
from the actions that occur off the field and away
from sports. They are related to different types
of norms and rules, and they have different
causes and consequences.

Deviance on the Field and in the Realm of Sports

This type of deviance includes cheating (such as using the spitball or corking a bat in baseball), gambling, shaving points, throwing games or matches, engaging in unfair conduct, fighting, taking illegal performance-enhancing drugs, and generally finding ways to avoid rules of the game. Some people claim that these types of deviance have become serious today because the personal and financial stakes have become so great in sports. But historical research indicates that cheating, dirty play, fighting, and the use of violence are less common today than in the days before television coverage and high-stakes commercialization (Dunning, 1999; Guttmann, 2004; Maguire, 1988; Scheinin, 1994). This research also shows that sports today are more rule governed than in the past and that on-the-field deviance today is more likely to be punished and publicly criticized. Therefore, it is a mistake to blame deviance in sports today on money and TV, as some people do.

Comparing rates of on-the-field deviance among athletes from one time period to another is difficult because rules and enforcement standards change over time. Research shows that athletes in most sports interpret rules very loosely during games and they create informal norms, which stretch or bend official rules (Shields and Bredemeier, 1995). But this is not new. Athletes have done this ever since umpires and referees have enforced rules. In fact, athletes in organized sports traditionally "play to the level" permitted by umpires and referees—that is, they adjust their actions according to the ways that referees enforce rules. However, this does not mean that players ignore rules or that deviance is out of hand. Nor does it mean that we ought to ignore deviance when it occurs.

The perception that deviance on the field and in the realm of sports is increasing also exists today because there are more rules now than ever before and sports are more rule governed now than in the past. Rulebooks in sport organizations show that there are thousands of rules today that did not exist a generation ago in sports. The National Collegiate Athletic Association (NCAA) and other sport-governing organizations have thousands of rules and regulations in official handbooks, and every year more rules are added. International sport organizations now provide catalogues of banned substances. Today, there are more ways to be deviant in sports than at any time in history! Furthermore, the forms of surveillance used today and the increased emphasis on rule enforcement means that more rule violators are caught today than ever before.

Finally, evidence shows that athletes in power and performance sports expect and engage in certain forms of on-the-field deviance such as, "good fouls" and "cheating when you can get away with it" (Anonymous, 1999; Pilz, 1996; Shields et al., 1995). This is most prevalent at higher levels of competition, it increases with the number of years that people play sports, and it is more common among men than women. These patterns are consistent with other research suggesting that participation in power and performance sports does not generally promote moral development or moral decision making (Stoll and Beller, 1998; 2000). However, no historical studies show that deviance on the field and in the realm of sports is more common than in the past, and deviance doesn't seem to be out of control today. However, deviance does exist in sports; *it is a problem*. It ought to be studied, and efforts should be made to control it without violating individual rights and principles of due process. The only form of sport-related deviance that is more prevalent today than in the past is the use of banned performance-enhancing substances. This is clearly a serious problem, and it will be discussed later in the section on "Performance-Enhancing Substances: Deviant Overconformity in Sports."

Deviance off the Field and Away from Sports

Off-the-field deviance among athletes receives widespread media attention. When athletes are arrested or linked to criminal activity, they make headlines and become lead stories on the evening news. Media reports of bar fights and assault charges appear regularly (Starr and Samuels, 2000).

Research doesn't tell us if rates of off-the-field deviance have gone up or down or if general crime rates are higher among athletes than among comparable people in the general population. However, there have been studies of (1) delinquency and sport participation among high school students, (2) academic cheating and excessive alcohol use among high school and college athletes, and (3) particular felony rates among athletes.

Delinquency Rates   Research on high school students shows that delinquency rates among athletes are usually lower than rates for other students from similar backgrounds. With a couple of exceptions, this general finding seems to hold for athletes in various sports, athletes in different societies, and both boys and girls from various racial and social-class backgrounds (see Miracle and Rees, 1994, for a summary of these studies; McHale et al., 2005; Miller et al., 2002).

The problem with most of these studies is that they don't take into account that students with histories of deviance may not try out for sport teams, that coaches may cut them when they do try out, or that athletes may receive preferential treatment enabling them to avoid being labeled a delinquent. It is also possible that forms of deviance among some athletes are obscured by a façade of conformity—conforming to norms in public and violating them in private where they are never publicly detected (Miracle and Rees, 1994).

Even when sport programs are designed as "interventions" for "at risk youth," success is difficult to achieve. In a review of this issue, Doug Hartmann (2003) notes that we lack a clear theory to explain how and why we might expect sport-based intervention programs to be effective in reducing delinquency or producing other positive effects. Most of these programs have little effect because they do nothing to change the unemployment, poverty, racism, poor schools, and other delinquency-related factors that exist in most neighborhoods where sports for at risk youth are offered (Coakley, 2002).

We know from chapter 4 (pp. 100–104) that we cannot make generalizations about athletes because sport experiences vary from program to program and sport participation constitutes only a part of a person's experiences. Therefore, when someone says that "playing sports kept me out of trouble," we need to investigate what that means and if there are ways to organize sports and sport experiences that provide young people with opportunities to identify positive alternatives for their lives. Until more of this research is done, we must say that sport participation creates neither "saints nor sinners," although both may play sports. This issue is discussed further in the box "Is Sport Participation a Cure for Deviant Behavior?"

Academic Cheating   Despite highly publicized cases of college athletes having their coursework completed by "academic tutors," the charge that college athletes generally engage in academic cheating more often than other students has never been studied systematically.

If we compared athletes with other students, we might find comparable rates but different methods of cheating. A varsity athlete may be more likely to hand in a paper written by an "academic tutor," whereas other students would obtain papers from files maintained at a fraternity house, from an online site, or from a professional writer hired by the student's father (Kristal, 2005). However, when a regular student is caught turning in a bogus paper, the case will not make national news, the student will not be rebuked publicly by people around the nation, the reputation of the university will not be questioned in the national media, and no faculty members will be fired for failing to police students effectively.

Might varsity athletes cheat more often because the stakes associated with making particular grades are so much higher for them than for other students? This is possible but we need studies comparing athletes with other students who would lose their scholarships or job opportunities if they did not maintain minimum grade point averages. Might some varsity athletes cheat less because they are watched more closely and have more to lose if they are caught? This, too, is possible.

Alcohol Use and Binge Drinking Underage and excessive alcohol consumption in high school and college is not limited to athletes. However, data collected through the 1990s indicated that male and female intercollegiate athletes engaged in more alcohol use, abuse, and binge drinking than other male and female students (Bacon and Russell, 2004; Eccles and Barber, 1999; Naughton, 1996a; Wechsler et al., 1997; Wechsler and Wuethrich, 2002). Recent data collected from junior and senior high school students in the United States suggest that rates of alcohol use may be lower among teens under eighteen years old who play on sport teams than among teens who do not play on teams (SAMHSA, 2002).

This may mean that norms related to alcohol use are different among junior and senior high school athletes than among college athletes or that young people under eighteen years old who play sports are monitored and controlled by their parents and other adults more closely than other young people or college athletes are controlled and monitored.

Research on this topic is important because alcohol use and abuse is related to other forms of deviance. Studies are needed to see if the group dynamics of alcohol use and binge drinking at the college level are related to the dynamics underlying overconformity to other group norms among athletes. Slamming drinks and getting drunk with fellow athletes may not be very different, sociologically speaking, from playing with pain to meet the expectations of teammates: "Have another shot of tequila—it's what we teammates who take risks together are doing tonight. Are

you a part of this special group or not?" Again, research is needed to see if, why, when, and how often this occurs.

Felony Rates Widely publicized cases of assault, hard-drug use, and driving under influence (DUI) in which male athletes are the offenders have created a growing sense of urgency about the need for systematic studies of these forms of deviance. At this point, research is scarce, and the studies that do exist report mixed findings (see Crosset, 1999, for a review and critique of research on sexual assault, in particular).

Another problem with studies of felony rates is that the data on arrest rates for athletes are seldom compared with arrest rates in the general population or in populations comparable to the athletes in age and race. For example, after a study by Jeff Benedict and Don Yaeger (1998) reported that 21.4 percent of a sample of NFL players had been arrested at least once for something more serious than minor crimes since the year they started college, most people were horrified. However, a follow-up study by crime statistics experts Alfred Blumstein and Jeff Benedict (1999) showed that 23 percent of the males living in cities of 250,000 or more people are arrested for a serious crime at some point in their lives, usually during young adulthood; the arrest rate for whites is 14 percent, and for blacks it is 51 percent. When they focused on the crimes of domestic violence and nondomestic assault and compared NFL players with young adult males from similar racial backgrounds, Blumstein and Benedict discovered that the annual arrest rate for NFL players was less than half the arrest rate for males in the general population. This pattern was nearly the same when the rate for white NFL players was compared with the rate for young, white men generally, and the rate for black NFL players was compared with the rate for young black men generally.

When Blumstein and Benedict compared arrest rates for property crimes, NFL players had distinctively lower rates than the rest of the population, a finding the researchers explained partly in terms of the salaries made by NFL players. However, their overall conclusion was that, when NFL players are compared with young men in the general population, their off-the-field deviance does not seem to be out of control. Of course, this does not mean that deviance among athletes is not a problem or that professional sport leagues and universities should not take actions to control it.

Benedict also collected data on NBA players during the 2001–2002 season and found that 40 percent of them had a police record involving a serious crime—a lower rate than young black men in the general population. After doing over four hundred interviews, reviewing police records, and searching court documents, Benedict focused on the issue of sexual assault and concluded that the social world of NBA basketball is organized so that it is "nearly impossible for a rape victim to file a criminal complaint against an NBA player without being labeled a groupie or a gold digger." He suggested that "it takes a victim nothing less than Snow White to obtain a conviction in a sexual assault case against a celebrity athlete and emerge with a reputation still intact" (Benedict, 2004, p. 29). The incidence of assault and sexual assault among male athletes is an especially important topic and it is discussed in chapter 7.

Off-the-Field Deviance: A Final Comment
The point of this section is that off-the-field deviance among athletes does not seem to be out of control. Although research is scarce, existing studies contradict the attention-grabbing headlines that we often see and hear in the news. Research suggests that delinquency and crime rates among athletes may not be higher than they are for comparable peers. At the same time, rates for alcohol abuse, binge drinking, and certain forms of assault may be higher among athletes. But until we have good theories to explain these data, we can only speculate on why these patterns exist.

Why Focus on Deviance Only Among Athletes?

This chapter focuses almost exclusively on deviance among athletes. This is an important issue. However, athletes are not the only people in sports who violate norms. The following list identifies other examples of sport-related deviance:

- Coaches who hit players, treat them inhumanely, use male players' insecurities about masculinity to motivate them, sexually

When a black NBA player loses his temper, throws a ball in anger, and appears ready to fight, many people "see" deviance and worry about it. When a white coach does similar things—throws towels, chairs, rolled-up programs, and appears ready to fight—many people "see" him (Bobby Knight, for example) as a legend, as an authority figure who controls subordinate players with tactics that might be defined as criminal if a teacher used them in the classroom. How do people define deviance in sports? Are race and roles (authority) related to these definitions? These questions must be answered for a full understanding of deviance in sports. (*Source:* Jake Schoellkopf; AP/Wide World Photos)

AT YOUR *fingertips* For more information, on violations and enforcement of Title IX law, see pages 238–242.

harass women in and out of sports, subvert efforts to follow Title IX law that mandates equal participation opportunities for girls and women in sports, and violate NCAA or other organizational rules

- High school and college program administrators who operate sport programs that do not provide athletes with proper health and accident insurance or ignore infractions of university or NCAA rules (Zimbalist, 1999)
- Sport team owners who violate antitrust laws, collude with each other to depress player salaries, and deliberately mislead city officials and voters to obtain public money to build stadiums and arenas
- Sport administrators (including those on the International Olympic Committee and related organizations) who take bribes and gifts in return for favors and who violate public trust and organizational principles by making decisions clearly based on their personal interests (see Jennings, 1996a, 1996b; Jennings and Sambrook, 2000).
- Judges and other officials in events such as figure skating, gymnastics, and boxing who take bribes or make agreements with others to alter the outcomes of events
- Media promoters and commentators who deliberately distort and misrepresent sport events so that they can generate high television ratings or newspaper/magazine sales
- Agents who mislead athletes, misrepresent themselves, or violate rules as they solicit

college student-athletes and represent professional athletes

- Parents/spectators who berate, taunt, and fight with each other, referees, and players as they watch their children in youth sports
- Spectators who attack or throw objects at athletes, fight with each other, destroy property as they mourn a loss or celebrate a win, place illegal bets on sports, and sell forged autographs of athletes

Some of these and other examples of deviance are discussed in chapters 5, 7, 8, and 11–14.

PERFORMANCE-ENHANCING SUBSTANCES: DEVIANT OVERCONFORMITY IN SPORTS

Stories about athletes using performance-enhancing substances are no longer shocking; they appear regularly in the media. However, many people do not know that drug and substance use in sports has a long history.[4] Athletes have taken a wide variety of everyday and exotic substances over the years, and substance use has never been limited to elite athletes. Data suggest that, if today's drugs had been available in past centuries, athletes back then would have used them as frequently as athletes use them today (Hoberman, 1992, 2004; Todd, 1987). This makes it difficult to blame all drug use on the profit motive, commercial interests, television, and the erosion of traditional values.

Research also suggests that drug and substance use by athletes generally is not the result of defective socialization or lack of moral character because many users and abusers are the most

> How different is steroid use from cosmetic surgery for the male TV newsies reporting these stories, from Botox for actresses, beta blockers for public speakers[?]
> —Robert Lipsyte, journalist, 2005

[4]See the Sports in Society website (www.mhhe.com/coakley9e) for a summary of this history.

reflect on SPORTS   Is Sport Participation a Cure for Deviant Behavior?

We often hear that sports keep kids off the streets and out of trouble and build character in the process, and then we hear about athletes who get into trouble and prove that years of playing sports have not turned them into models of character. How do we make sense out of this conflicting information? Fortunately, research can help.

A study by sociologist Michael Trulson (1986) suggests that *only certain types of sports and sport participation* can lower delinquency rates among young people. Trulson worked with thirty-four young men, ages thirteen to seventeen, who had been classified as delinquents. He tested them for aggression and personality adjustment and divided them into three

groups matched on important background characteristics. For six months, each group met three times a week for training sessions with the same instructor. Group 1 received traditional tae kwon do training, taught with a philosophy emphasizing respect for self and others, the importance of physical fitness, self-control, patience, perseverance, responsibility, and honor. Group 2 received "modern" martial arts training, emphasizing free-sparring and self-defense techniques; and the coach provided no philosophy in connection with the physical training. Group 3 received no martial arts training but jogged and played basketball and football under the instructor's coaching and supervision.

Off-the-field deviance among athletes may decrease if athletes are taught a philosophy of nonviolence, respect for self and opponents, self-control, confidence in their abilities, and responsibility. This can happen in a variety of sports, even those involving heavy physical contact. (*Source:* McGraw-Hill)

Trulson's findings indicated clear changes in group 1. After six months, the young men in this group had fewer delinquent tendencies, less anxiety and aggression, improved self-esteem and social skills, and more awareness of commonly held values. Those in group 2 had increased delinquent tendencies and were more aggressive and less adjusted than when the study began. Those in group 3 showed no change in delinquent tendencies or on most personality measures, but their scores on self-esteem and social skills improved over the six months.

THE MORAL OF THE STORY

Sport participation might keep kids out of trouble when it emphasizes (1) a philosophy of nonviolence, (2) respect for self and others, (3) the importance of fitness and control over self, (4) confidence in physical skills, and (5) a sense of responsibility. When these five things are absent, sport participation will seldom keep young people out of trouble. Simply taking kids off the streets is just the beginning. If they play sports that emphasize confrontation, dominating others, using their bodies as weapons, and defining masculinity or success in terms of conquest, we *cannot* expect rates of deviance to decrease.

Changing behavior is a complex process, and to do it in connection with sport participation requires a clear program of intervention in the lives of young people. This doesn't mean that all sports must be turned into treatment programs, but it does mean that playing sports can't be expected to keep kids out of trouble unless participation connects them with people who can support them and advocate their interests and provides them with opportunities to make choices that do not involve deviance.

A WORD OF CAUTION

A study by sociologist Eldon Snyder (1994) suggests that, when athletes form special bonds with each other, become arrogant about their unity and uniqueness, and become subjectively separated from the rest of the community, sport participation may be associated with deviance. Snyder did a qualitative analysis of a case in which nine varsity athletes at a large university were arrested after committing dozens of burglaries over two years. Seven of the athletes were on the men's swim team, one was on the track team, and one was a former member of the women's swim team (and dating one of the men); they all came from middle-class families.

Snyder examined records, testimony, and court documents in the case, including statements by athletes, parents, lawyers, and others. He did *not* conclude that sport participation had *caused* these young people to be deviant. Instead, he concluded that playing sports had created the bonds and dynamics out of which the deviance of this group of college athletes emerged. Snyder had no final explanation for why these young people did what they did, but he noted that sport participation certainly did not deter deviance in their case. This conclusion is consistent with Peter Donnelly's (1993) research showing that certain forms of binge deviance sometimes occur among elite athletes, especially after major competitions, at the end of their seasons, and following retirement.

A FINAL NOTE

These studies show that neither virtue nor deviance is *caused* by sports and sport participation. Sports are sites where young people often have powerful and exciting physical and social experiences. When experiences are organized so that young people receive thoughtful guidance from adults who can help them develop self-respect and become connected to the rest of the community, good outcomes are likely. However, when playing sports separates athletes from the rest of the community and fosters overconformity to the norms of the sport ethic, good outcomes are unlikely. Bonds formed among athletes can take them in many directions, including deviant ones. Sport programs are effective only when they enable people to live satisfying lives in the world beyond sports; simply taking people off the streets for a few hours a week so that they can bounce basketballs does little more than provide temporary shelter. *What do you think?*

dedicated, committed, and hard-working athletes in sports. Nor are all substance users helpless victims of exploitive coaches and trainers, although coaches and trainers who push the sport ethic without question may indirectly encourage the use of performance-enhancing substances. Instead, most substance use and abuse seems to be an expression of uncritical acceptance of the norms of the sport ethic. Therefore, it is grounded in overconformity—the same type of overconformity that occurs when injured distance runners continue training, even when training may cause serious injuries; when young female gymnasts control weight by cutting their food intake to dangerous levels; and when NFL players use painkilling drugs and risk their already injured and surgically repaired bodies week after painful week (Freeman, 2002).

Apparently, many athletes enjoy playing their sports so much that they will do whatever it takes to stay involved and meet the expectations of their fellow athletes. Of course, they seek on-the-field success, enabling them to avoid being cut or eliminated, but the desire to win is usually secondary to the desire to play and be accepted as an athlete. This means that most athletes will do whatever it takes to pursue their dreams. As long as some athletes are willing to take performance-enhancing substances to gain the edge that they need, others will use similar substances to stay competitive, even if it's against their better judgment.

These dynamics, all connected with overconformity to the sport ethic, operate at various levels of sports—from local gyms, where high school athletes work out, to the locker rooms of professional sport teams—and among women and men across a wide variety of sport events, from the 100-meter sprint to the marathon and from tennis to football.

Defining and Banning
Performance-Enhancing Substances

Defining *performance-enhancing substances* is difficult. They can include anything from aspirin to heroin; they may be legal or illegal, harmless or dangerous, natural or synthetic, socially acceptable or unacceptable, commonly used or exotic. Furthermore, they may produce real physical changes, psychological changes, or both (see figure 6.5).

Problems with definitions are faced whenever a sport organization develops an antidrug or no-doping program. For example, until 1999, the International Olympic Committee (IOC) defined doping in this way:

> [Doping is] the administration of or use by a competing athlete of any substance *foreign* to the body or any *physiological substance* taken in *abnormal quantity* or taken by an *abnormal route of entry* into the body with the *sole intention* of increasing in an *artificial* and *unfair* manner his/her performance in competition. When necessity demands *medical treatment* with any substance that, because of its nature, dosage, or application, is able to boost the athlete's performance in competition in an artificial and unfair manner, this too is regarded by the IOC as doping. (USOC, 1992, p. 1, italics added)

"Is this what those hormones are supposed to do, Carl?"
....

FIGURE 6.5   The negative side effects of various combinations of substances are difficult to identify. Controlled studies of banned substances are difficult to do because it may not be ethical to experiment with the same dosages that athletes use. This means that the side effects of many substances are unknown.

This definition may sound good, but the IOC had difficulty defining all the terms in italics. For example, what is a substance "foreign" to the body, and why are the "foreign" substances of aspirin and ibuprofen not banned, whereas the "natural" hormone testosterone and naturally grown marijuana are banned? What is an "abnormal" quantity or an "abnormal" route of entry? Why are megadoses of vitamins not banned, whereas small amounts of decongestants are banned? Why can athletes be stripped of medals when they swallow medications without intending to enhance performance, whereas other athletes keep their medals after having intravenous needles inserted into their veins to be rehydrated during competitions?

With scientific discoveries being made every day and applied to sports, what is artificial and what is unfair? Why are needles permitted to drain fluid from the knees of NFL players and inject their bodies with painkillers, whereas the same needles are considered dangerous and artificial when used to inject a cyclist's or distance runner's own "natural" red blood cells into a vein (blood boosting)? Why isn't the electronic stimulation of muscles banned? Isn't it artificial? Is it fair to compete with knees strengthened with surgically inserted synthetic ligaments after natural ligaments were torn beyond repair? Why are biofeedback and other psychological technologies defined as "natural" and "fair," whereas certain naturally grown herbal teas are defined as "unnatural" and "unfair"? Are vitamins natural? Amino acids? Caffeine? Human-growth hormone? Gatorade? Protein drinks? Creatine? Eyeglasses? What if an athlete could wear contacts that would boost vision acuity from 20-20 to 20-5?

How about so-called natural herbs, chemicals, and compounds now stacked floor to ceiling in stores that sell nutritional supplements with the promise of performance enhancement? Is it natural to deprive yourself of food to make weight or meet the demands of a coach who measures body fat every week and punishes athletes who eat "normal" diets? Should athletes who binge and purge, become anorexic, or exercise in saunas

wearing rubber suits to lose weight be considered normal? In fact, what is normal about any of the social, psychological, biomechanical, environmental, and technological methods of manipulating and changing athletes' bodies and minds in today's high-performance sports? Are big-time college football players deviant when saline solutions are dripped into their veins through intravenous needles in a pregame locker room to minimize the threat of dehydration on a hot playing field? Isn't this performance-enhancing? Is it normal, safe? How about twelve-year-old gymnasts and sixteen-year old football players who pop a dozen anti-inflammatory pills every day so that they can train through pain? Are they deviant? Are they different from hockey players who pop a dozen Sudafed pills (containing pseudoephedrine) to get "up" for the game or baseball players who use the antifatigue drug modafinil?

How about NFL players who became addicted to painkillers after being regularly injected by team physicians? Why do we call athletes heroes when they use an intravenous procedure to play in ungodly heat or take large injections of painkilling drugs to keep them training and playing and then condemn the same athletes when they take drugs to help them build muscles damaged by overtraining or take other drugs to help them relax and recover after their bodies and minds have been pushed beyond limits in the pursuit of dreams?

Why do many athletes see the use of drugs as a noble act of commitment and dedication, whereas many spectators see it as a reprehensible act of deviance yet pay big money to watch athletes do superhuman things requiring extreme training regimes and strategies made possible only by drugs or random genetic mutations? These and hundreds of other questions about what is artificial, natural, foreign, fair, and abnormal show that any definition of *doping* will lead to endless debates about the technical and legal meaning of terms (Shapin, 2005). For this reason, the IOC changed its definition of doping in 1999.

Now the Olympic Movement Anti-Doping Code defines doping as

> (1) the use of an expedient (substance or method) which is potentially harmful to athletes' health and/or capable of enhancing their performance, or (2) the presence in the athlete's body of a Prohibited Substance or evidence of the use thereof or evidence of the use of a Prohibited Method. (USADA, 2001, p. 4)

However, even this simplified definition, along with the thirty pages in which prohibited substances and prohibited methods are described, raises many questions.

Meanwhile, physicians, pharmacists, chemists, inventors, and athletes continue to develop new and different aids to performance—chemical, "natural," and otherwise. For example, Anthony Almada and former partner Bill Phillips, founders of EAS (Experimental and Applied Sciences), a major supplement producer and distributor, made many millions of dollars by knowing all the loopholes in every sport's drug policy and creating substances that fit through the holes. Now we have a seemingly endless game of scientific hide and seek, which persists despite new definitions and drug policies. This game will become even more heated and controversial as scientists manipulate the brain and nervous system and use genetic manipulation and engineering to improve athletic performance. With new performance-enhancing technologies, we are approaching a time when defining, identifying, and dealing with doping and drugs will be only one of many strategies for manipulating athletes' bodies and improving performance (Bjerklie and Park, 2004).

Further complicating decisions about which substances to ban is confusion about their effects on athletic performance. Ethical and legal considerations have constrained researchers who study the impact of megadoses and multiple combinations of substances that are "stacked and cycled" by athletes. Athletes learn things in

> **We've taught illegal tactics to survive.**
> —Billy Tubbs, basketball coach, Texas Christian University (in Wolff, 2000, p. 47)

locker rooms faster than scientists learn them in the lab, although the validity of locker room knowledge is questionable at best. Furthermore, by the time researchers have valid information about a substance, athletes have moved on to others, which are unknown to researchers. This is why most athletes ignore "official statements" about the consequences and dangers of doping—the statements are about two to five years behind the "inventors" who supply new substances.

As the market for substances and the wealth of athletes have grown, so have the labs that are dedicated to "beating the system" with "designer drugs," undetectable substances, and masking agents that hide certain molecules in the testing process. For example, IGF-1 (Insulin-like growth factor-1) is a muscle builder that can be injected directly into the bloodstream. It improves strength development and it is undetectable with current tests. The same is true for dozens of other "designer substances" rumored to be available for the right price (Assael, 2003, 2005; Sokolove, 2004b).

The Internet has made information about and access to substances immediately available to athletes around the world (www.t-nation.com, www.musclemedia.com/, www.getbig.com, www.elitefitness.com, and www.muscleandfitness.com/). Magazines, such as *Muscle Media* (published by Bill Phillips, a founder of EAS), provide dozens of references to these sites. Most athletes know that even though sport organizations have drug policies, the people who control those organizations are not eager to find drug users because too many positive tests would jeopardize the billions of dollars that corporate sponsors and TV networks pay for events that are promoted as "clean and wholesome" (*ESPN The Magazine*, 2005; Jennings and Sambrook, 2000). This lack of enforcement led the U.S. Congress to become involved in 2004 when it was discovered that many baseball players used anabolic steroids and a wide array of amphetamines. Defining steroid use in professional sports as a national public-health crisis, Congress passed the *Anabolic Steroid Control Act of 2004*. As a result, both anabolic steroids and prohormones were added to the list of controlled substances so that possession, as of January 20, 2005, became a federal crime.

This law and the threat of additional legislation led Major League Baseball to initiate a drug testing program with relatively strong penalties. However, testing remains a challenge in most sport organizations (Keating, 2005). In fact, if there were a law that mandated random testing of all professional athletes across all major sports by an independent enforcement agency, it would cost over $10 million per year to enforce in the NFL alone. It would cost billions of dollars to test all international, Olympic-level, intercollegiate, and high school athletes over the next decade.

Finally, some people ask why drugs should be banned in sports when they are widely accepted in society and used to improve performance or treat conditions that interfere with performance at home, work, or play. The majority of adults in most wealthy, high-tech societies use tranquilizers, pain controllers, mood controllers, antidepressants, decongestants, diet pills, birth control pills, insulin, caffeine, nicotine, sleep aids, and alcohol. Doctors readily prescribe prohormone and hormone therapies to improve strength and counteract the negative effects of aging; these include thyroid hormone, testosterone (patches, gels, injections, and pills now taken by over 2 million men in the United States alone; Noonan, 2003), anabolic steroids, human growth hormone (HGH), HGH stimulants, androstenedione, DHEA, and creatine.[5] Every six months, the list

changes and grows longer as new discoveries are made and new supplements are manufactured. In fact, if people really did say no to drugs, life in most Western societies would change dramatically. When a fifty-five-year-old man takes HGH to maintain strength so that he can outperform others in his highly paid job, why shouldn't his twenty-five-year-old son take HGH to perform in the NFL (Weise, 2003)?

These issues lead to an important question: Why control athletes in ways that other people are not controlled? After all, do colleges have rules banning caffeine and other drugs that students use so that they can study all night and be mentally primed to take a biology test? Do teachers make students sign an oath to avoid drugs that might enable them to perform better in a course? Do employers tell executives not to use hormone therapies that will keep them fit for work? Do wives tell their husbands not to take Viagra, Cialis, Levitra, or other substances that elevate sexual performances? Why should athletes be tested and denied access to substances, when others competing or working for valued rewards are often encouraged to take similar substances? As these questions are asked, it remains difficult to define drugs, doping, and substance abuse in sports.

Why Is the Challenge of Substance Control So Great in Sports Today?

Many factors contribute to the tendency among today's athletes to seek substances for the edge that they need to pursue their dreams and stay involved in the sports they love and the jobs for which they are paid. These factors include the following:

1. *The visibility and resources associated with sports today have fueled massive research and development efforts devoted to performance-enhancing substances.* Entrepreneurs and corporations have tied the development of performance-enhancing substances to the general realm of "alternative medicine" and now use it to make quick and substantial

---

[5]Dehydroepiandrosterone (DHEA) is a hormone widely available over the counter in most countries. It is a product of the adrenal glands, and it stimulates the production of testosterone. Some athletes and people over age forty take it to maintain lean body mass. At this time, it is not a widely banned substance for athletes. Creatine is a compound produced by the liver, kidneys, and pancreas. It facilitates the renewal of anaerobic energy reserves, delays the onset of fatigue during intense exercise, and cuts recovery time between workouts (Kearney, 1999).

profits. These substances are especially profitable because aging baby boomers (the massive population cohorts born between 1946 and 1964) see these substances as health aids. This creates a market consisting of 70 million Americans that pushes the supplement industry to make available an ever-expanding array of substances.

2. *People in postindustrial societies are deeply fascinated with technology and how they can use it to push or extend human limits.* Advertising that promotes hyperconsumption as a lifestyle in society encourages this fascination. Athletes, because they live in social worlds characterized by a "culture of excellence," hear those messages loud and clear. Like many of us, they see consumption as the way to pursue their dreams, and because they are willing to overconform with the norms of the sport ethic, they become hyperconsumers of whatever it takes to stay on the field.

3. *The rationalization of the body has influenced how people conceptualize the relationship between the body and mind.* People in postindustrial societies see the body as a malleable tool serving the interests of the mind. Separating the body from the mind is common in cultures with Judeo-Christian religious beliefs, and it leads people to objectify their own bodies, view them as machines, and use them as tools for doing what the mind has determined. Using substances to improve the performance of the body fits with this orientation. This orientation also leads athletes to use their minds to ignore physical pain and injury (Grant, 2002a, 2002b).

4. *There is a growing emphasis on self-medication.* People in wealthy postindustrial societies increasingly seek alternatives to mainstream medicine. They use friends, ads, and the Internet for medical information, and they are open to experimenting with substances that can be purchased online and over the counter without licensed medical advice or approval. In the United States, the Dietary Supplement Health and Education Act of 1994 deregulated "nutritional" and performance-enhancing substances and allowed them to be produced, distributed, and consumed without testing and approval by the U.S. Food and Drug Administration (FDA). This was great for business, but it flooded the market with untested products and boosted self-funded, self-medication—which also increased profits for health insurance companies that do not pay for untested therapies.

5. *Gender relations are changing in contemporary society.* As traditional ideas about masculinity and femininity have been challenged, the threat of change has fueled a desire among some men to do whatever it takes to develop a physique that reaffirms an ideology of male strength and power. At the same time, the promise of change has fueled a desire among many women to revise their notions of femininity and do whatever it takes to achieve strength, power, and physical ability and to lose weight at the same time. Therefore, men and women define performance-enhancing substances as valuable in their quests to preserve or challenge prevailing gender ideology.

6. *The organization of power and performance sports encourages overconformity to the norms of the sport ethic.* Many sports are organized so that continued participation at the level needed to sustain an "athlete identity" requires competitive success—*making the cut*, so to speak. The desire to maintain participation makes winning personally important to athletes and fuels their search for performance-enhancing substances.

7. *Coaches, sponsors, administrators, and fans clearly encourage deviant overconformity.* Athletes who make sacrifices and put their bodies on the line for the sake of the team, the school, the community, or the nation are defined as heroes. Athletes realize this and many willingly take substances as they "do

their duty." For example, a former NFL player who had twenty-nine surgeries during his career, including twenty on his knees, used these words to explain how he remained in the game that he loved and trained every day to play: "You name it, I've taken it—in excess. Too much at times. But that's the way you get through" (in Schefter, 2003, 6J).

8. *The performance of athletes is closely monitored within the social structure of elite sports.* Elite sports today emphasize control, especially control over the body; conformity, especially to the demands of a coach; and guilt, especially when one does not meet the expectations of fellow athletes and sponsors, parents, schools, communities, clubs, and corporations. The desire to control one's body plus the need to meet performance expectations is a powerful incentive to do whatever it takes to remain an elite athlete.

When these eight factors are combined, access to substances and the willingness to use them are high. Such conditions exist today, and this makes it more difficult than ever to control substance use.

Drug Testing as a Deterrent

Drug testing is controversial. There are powerful arguments for and against it. The arguments in favor of testing are these:

1. Drug testing is needed to protect athletes' health and reduce the pressures that they feel to take substances to keep up with competitors. In elite cycling, the blood-boosting drug EPO has been implicated in the deaths of about twenty riders from Europe since 1988 (Zorpette, 2000). EPO causes a person's blood to thicken and clot, and it can be fatal when taken in high doses. In professional wrestling steroids are suspected in forty deaths among wrestler-performers under the age of forty between 1997 and mid-2002; ten of those deaths occurred in

the first six months of 2002 (Marvez, 2002). Furthermore, the use of steroids and other substances may partially account for the rising injury toll in certain sports in which severe muscle and tendon tears and bone fractures are common (Keating, 2004b; Verducci, 2002). Other serious health risks are associated with various substances, including ephedrine; steroid precursors, such as androstenedione; diuretics; epogen; and beta-blockers (Meyer, 2002a).

2. Drug testing is needed to achieve a level playing field where competitive outcomes reflect skills and training rather than access to substances. Many athletes and spectators believe that some of the most visible and talented athletes today owe part of their success to drugs. This damages the integrity of sports and jeopardizes sponsorships, television rights fees, and the willingness of spectators to buy tickets and pay cable fees so that they can see games.

3. Requiring people to submit to drug tests is legally justified because the actions of those who take substances affect the lives of other people. Furthermore, the U.S. Supreme Court ruled in 2002 that schools could conduct drug tests on all students involved in sports and other extracurricular activities because drug use by schoolchildren is a serious national problem and because schools have "custodial responsibilities" for their students (Lewin, 2002). When the U.S. Congress discussed the Professional Sports Responsibility Act of 2005, its goals was to mandate uniform testing and sanctions partly because it would protect children who use athletes as role models.

4. Drug testing is part of normal law enforcement because drug use is illegal and must be controlled, as other criminal acts are controlled. This means that punishments must be clearly explained, fairly administered, and severe enough to deter future substance use.

5. Drug tests must be expanded to anticipate genetic engineering because genetically altered athletes will change the meaning of sports and athletic achievements. According to one member of the World Anti-Doping Agency's (WADA) special committee on "gene doping," genetic manipulation will lead to "the end of sport as we know it. Sport will be a circus of unbelievable performances" (in Swift and Yaeger, 2001, p. 91). Unless testing is used to discourage genetic manipulation, sports will be replaced by spectacle, and athletes will become pawns in video game-like contests controlled by genetic engineers competing against each other to produce the best-performing bodies.

The arguments against testing are equally powerful. They emphasize the following points:

1. Testing is ineffective because athletes are one step ahead of rule makers and testers (see figure 6.6). By the time certain substances are banned and tests are developed to detect them, athletes are taking new substances that tests cannot detect or are not calibrated to detect (Assael, 2005; Zorpette, 2000; Sokolove, 2004b). Don Catlin, head of the UCLA lab that does all the tests for WADA says, "You may think testing is wonderful and great, but . . . [athletes] have little trouble beating the test and there are many doctors telling them how to do it" (in Patrick, 2005). The NFL policy, reputedly the toughest in pro sports, was described by the founder of a supplement company as having "numerous loopholes." He noted that "athletes are out there looking for anything to give them an edge. And there are always people out there to fill that need" (in Saunders, 2005).

2. Requiring people to submit to drug tests without cause violates rights to privacy and sets precedents for invasive testing programs that produce medical and biological information that could be used against a person's interest apart from sports (Malloy and Zakus, 2002). If protocols for future tests require blood samples, muscle biopsies, genetic testing, and DNA analysis, test results could lead some people to be stigmatized as "impure," "contaminated," or abnormal for medical or biological reasons.

3. Drug tests are expensive and drain resources that could be used to fund health education programs for athletes. The test administered to athletes in Olympic sports by the recently formed United States Anti-Doping Agency (USADA) and the WADA costs well over $300 per athlete every time it is administered. Testing 100,000 potential Olympic athletes around the world once a year would cost about $30 million. Furthermore, athletes taking substances are unlikely to be deterred by a test administered only once a year, especially if it is set up to detect only a limited number of substances. High schools face similar cost issues. In a school district with 10,000 high school students, in which 4000 students play sports, a basic test for illegal street drugs costs $15 to $20 per student, or $60,000 for the district. A test for a limited range of performance-enhancing substances given once per year would cost the district at least $250,000. Furthermore, athletes could still take the substances during the off-season while they train and then stop prior to the season when they would be tested. This would teach athletes nothing about health and how to set health priorities in sports.

4. Drug tests often cannot detect substances that are designed to match substances naturally produced by the body. EPO (erythropoietin), HGH (human growth hormone), IGF-1 (insulin-like growth factor-1), and testosterone are powerful performance enhancers produced by the body, and normal levels of these substances

"Don't worry, honey. Most of these are legal, some can't be tested for, others mask the ones they can test for, and some are too new for the tests!"

FIGURE 6.6   Some athletes take vast amounts of various substances in many combinations. The industries that produce performance-enhancing substances have stayed ahead of the testers in sports, and they will probably continue to stay ahead.

vary from person to person.[6] This makes it difficult to determine an amount of each substance that would be considered illegal

---

[6]EPO (erythropoietin) is a protein hormone that is produced by cells in the kidneys. It promotes the production of red blood cells, the cells that carry oxygen. Therefore, it can be useful to endurance athletes looking to increase the oxygen-carrying capacity of their blood. HGH (human growth hormone) is a hormone produced naturally by the pituitary gland, and it stimulates physical growth in children. However, it can be used to increase muscle mass and overall strength in adults, and some adults take it in the belief that it slows the aging process. IGF-1 (insulin-like growth factor-1) is a protein that helps muscles grow and repair themselves when they are damaged. It can be used to reduce muscle-recovery time after strenuous workouts.

for all bodies. And, once legal levels are determined, athletes who test positive frequently use lawsuits to challenge the limits in individual cases (Zorpette, 2000).

5. Drug tests provide an incentive for developing forms of genetic engineering that alters physical characteristics related to performance (Assael, 2005; Longman, 2001; Parrish, 2002; Sokolove, 2004b; Sweeney, 2004; Swift and Yaeger, 2001; Zorpette, 2000). When genetic engineering occurs, it will make steroids and other drugs obsolete. Gene therapies are seen as crucial treatments to deal with the negative effects of aging and to cure or reduce the symptoms of certain diseases. These therapies will make "gene

This "Athlete Anti-Doping Passport" is used by the United States Anti-Doping Agency and the World Anti-Doping Agency— independent testing organizations contracted to conduct tests for all Olympic sports. The passport must be carried by Olympic athletes and presented to the doping-control officer who conducts tests. All test results are recorded in this document, which contains the athlete's photo and a signed pledge not to violate the ideals of the Olympic movement. (*Source:* Jay Coakley)

doping" possible for athletes—therapies to enhance muscle size, strength, and resiliency. Gene doping and other forms of genetic manipulation will be difficult if not impossible to detect, and tests will cost at least $1000 per athlete (Sweeney, 2004). Chuck Yesalis, a professor at Penn State who has studied drugs in sports for many years, argues that drug testing will be made irrelevant by "genetic engineering" (in Patrick, 2002, p. 6C).

In the face of arguments for and against drug testing, many athletes have mixed feelings about testing policies and programs. They realize that political and economic interests can cloud the validity and reliability of testing programs. They also know that drug testing is an enormously complicated bureaucratic process and that mistakes can occur at many points. This has already provoked legal challenges to test results. These challenges are complicated because they often cross national borders where judicial processes and definitions of individual rights and due process are inconsistent. In the meantime, athletes know that fellow athletes continue to overconform to the sport ethic and seek creative ways to push their bodies to new limits in the pursuit of dreams.

When drug testing is done by the same organizations that promote and profit from sports, athletes have good reason to have mixed feelings. Promoting, profiting, and policing just don't go together. To avoid conflicts of interest, international athletes in Olympic sports are tested by "independent" agencies formed in 1999. WADA conducts random, unannounced tests around the world. The USADA conducts similar tests on U.S. athletes wherever they are training around the world. These two agencies work together. However, part of the funding for the USADA comes from the U.S. Olympic Committee. This causes some people to wonder about how independent the agency is, despite clear statements about agency integrity made by the spokespeople for the USADA and WADA. Both agencies have an educational emphasis, which may be more important than the tests they conduct, if educational programs are expanded to emphasize the control of all forms of deviant overconformity in elite sports. But this is unlikely.

Controlling Substance Use in Sports: Where to Start

Today's athletes, like their counterparts in the past, seek continued participation and excellence in sports. When they overconform to norms promoting sacrifice and risk in the pursuit of distinction and dreams, they are not likely to define the use of performance-enhancing substances as deviant. Even Ben Johnson, the Canadian sprinter who lost his gold medal for the 100-meter sprint in the 1988 Seoul Olympics, said this in 1993: "You can never clean it up. People are always gonna be doing something. They feel good about themselves, and they feel it's right to do it" (in Fish, 1993, p. A12). A physician who works with athletes makes Johnson's point in another way; he observes that "athletes don't use drugs to escape reality—they use them to enforce the reality that surrounds them" (DiPasquale, 1992, p. 2).

A central point in this chapter is that athletes use performance-enhancing substances not because they lack character, as might be concluded when using functionalist theory or an absolutist approach to deviance; nor do they use them because they are victims of biased and coercive rules, as might be concluded when using conflict theory. The solutions based in these approaches are unsatisfactory. Tougher rules and increased testing have not been effective, and changing the organization of sports so that athletes made and enforced rules would not necessarily lead to the elimination of dangerous substances.

As long as athletes accept without question or qualification the norms of the sport ethic, they will voluntarily try or take anything to remain in sports. Moral panics over drug use and oversimplified solutions will not stop athletes from using substances they see as essential in maintaining their identities and their exciting experiences as athletes.

Drug use and future forms of genetic manipulation can be controlled only when the people associated with sports critically assess the norms of the sport ethic in ways that lead them to set limits on conformity to those norms (Shogan and Ford, 2000). In light of this approach, recommendations for controlling substance use in sports should begin with the following changes:

- *Critically examine the deep hypocrisy involved in elite power and performance sports.* How is it possible to encourage athletes to stop using performance-enhancing substances when federations and teams approve the use of legal performance-enhancing drugs and procedures? Using creatine, painkillers, massive injections of vitamin B-12, hydration therapies, and pure oxygen is condoned if not encouraged by coaches and teams. This is also the case for playing with pins in broken bones, with high-tech "casts" to hold broken bones in place during competition, and using special harnesses to restrict the movement of injured joints. These practices are common, and they foster a sport culture in which the use of performance-enhancing substances is defined as logical and courageous.
- *Establish rules indicating clearly that certain risks to health are undesirable and unnecessary in sports.* When fourteen-year-old girls who

Technology Barriers
That's an Act, Not Sports

Marlon Shirley runs faster and jumps further than any person has ever run or jumped with a below-the-knee amputation. In 2003 after winning a gold medal in the 100-meter dash at the 2000 Paralympics in Sydney and setting a world record in the long jump in 2002, he became the first person in the T44 category (below-the-knee amputee) to break eleven seconds in the 100-meter dash.

When Oscar Pistorius edged out Marlon Shirley while setting a world record in the 200 meters, both runners were sponsored by Team OSSUR, the company that makes their carbon-fiber Flex-Foot® Cheetah prosthesis. The Flex-Foot replicates the hind leg of the cheetah whose small profile foot extends and reaches out to paw at the ground while the large thigh muscles pull the body forward. These prosthetic legs will return about 95 percent of the energy put into them by the runners' upper legs; a human lower leg can return about 200 percent of the energy put into them. OSSUR researchers want to duplicate the running power of a human leg. (*Source:* David Biene; Photo courtesy of Ossur, www.ossur.com)

compete with training-induced stress fractures in elite gymnastics are turned into national heroes and poster children for corporate sponsors, we promote deviant overconformity in sports. This sets up athletes for permanent injuries and disabilities. This is clearly unnecessary, and sport organizations should not allow it to occur.

When he was six years old, Shirley lost his left foot and ankle in a lawnmower accident at the children's home where he lived. During high school, he had a second amputation on the same leg after fracturing a bone in his stump as he tried to dunk a basketball (Price, 2005). Not long after that, as he set a record in the high jump at an open track meet in Idaho, he was spotted by a coach who had worked with Paralympians. Shirley then began training and running as a pro. His success brought him prize money and an offer to become a spokesperson for Ossur, a company in Iceland that makes racing prostheses (see photos on pp. 17 and 188).

With a carbon-fiber prosthesis designed to match the movements of a human foot, Shirley continued to win medals and set records. In Athens his goal was to win five gold medals—in the long jump, the 100- and 200-meter dashes, and the 4-by-100 and 4-by-400 relays. However, seventeen-year-old Oscar Pistorius from South Africa outran him in the 200-meter dash. Pistorius was born without a fibula in both legs, and during infancy had his legs amputated just below his knees. Shirley beat Pistorius in the 100-meter dash, but he tore his right hamstring at the finish line and could not compete in the other three events.

As Shirley trains for the 2008 Paralympic Games in Beijing, he regularly hears about Pistorius, now known as "the fastest person on no legs." In 2004 Pistorius ran the sixth fastest 400 meters ever by a South African, able-bodied or (dis)abled. In 2005 he competed against able-bodied runners in a Grand Prix event sponsored by the International Association of Athletics Federations (IAAF), the world governing body for track and field.

When Marlon Shirley runs, his prosthetic leg is designed to match the length of his other leg. But when Oscar Pistorius runs, how long should his legs

be? Shirley and others, including a former Paralympian and current prosthetist who fit Pistorius for his dual carbon-fiber legs before the 2004 Games in Athens, think that the legs he raced on during the Paralympics were longer than the legs he had earlier in the summer. The prosthetist claims that the original legs made Pistorius 6 feet, 1 inch tall, but his height in Athens was at least 6 feet, 3 inches. Pistorius and his current prosthetist disagree, saying he was actually shorter than he should have been.

This issue raises the question of what counts as deviance when technology improves faster than governing bodies can make rules? With lightweight carbon fiber and rapid changes in prosthetic foot design, we may soon see a race in which a person with prosthetic legs has an advantage over runners with flesh and blood legs. Marlon Shirley wants to see how tall Oscar Pistorius will be in Beijing. But he is not the only one concerned. Neither the International Olympic Committee (IOC) nor the IAAF prohibits (dis)abled runners from competing in the Olympics or IAAF World Championships. And there are no rules about the length of prosthetic legs for someone with no legs.

Some say that if Pistorius comes to Beijing at 6 feet, 6 inches tall, he will find himself in court rather than on the track. But others would want him to run in the hope that he could come close to breaking Michael Johnson's stunning world record 200-meter time of 19.32 seconds set at the 1996 Olympics in Atlanta. Shirley says that if a 6 foot, 6 inch tall Pistorius runs the 200-meters in 20 seconds or less, it would be cool, although he quickly adds, "But that's an act, not sports" (in Price, 2005, p. 58). Then again, as sports and technology merge, what will count as sports and how will they be distinguished from "acts"? Will rules create technology barriers for athletes with disabilities in the future? Should they?

- *Establish rules stating that injured athletes are not allowed to play until certified as "well" (not simply "able to compete") by two independent physicians apart from doctors hired by teams and sport* *organizations.* Too many team physicians and trainers have divided loyalties because they are paid by teams or by medical organizations that have contracted with teams or leagues (*ESPN*

The Magazine, 2005; Pipe, 1998; Polsky, 1998; Safai, 2003)). Trainers and physicians also must be able to identify the ways that athletes hide injuries and be prepared to negotiate strategies for healthy recoveries.

• *Establish educational programs for young athletes.* Young people should be taught to define *courage* in terms of recognizing limits and accepting the discipline necessary to accurately and responsibly acknowledge the consequences of deviant overconformity and sports injuries. Learning to be in tune with one's body rather than to deny pain and injury is important in controlling the use of potentially dangerous performance-enhancing substances.

• *Establish codes of ethics for sport scientists.* Too many sport scientists assist athletes as they overconform to the norms of the sport ethic, rather than helping them raise critical questions about how deviant overconformity is dangerous to their health and development. When they do this, the scientists become part of the problem rather than the solution. For example, sport psychology should be used to help athletes understand the consequences of their choices to play sports and reduce the extent to which guilt, shame, and pathology influence participation and training decisions. This is the alternative to the technique of "psycho-doping," which encourages deviant overconformity by making athletes more likely to give body and soul to their sports without carefully answering critical questions about *why* they are doing what they are doing and *what* it means in their lives.

• *Make drug education part of larger deviance and health education programs.* Parents, coaches, league administrators, managers, trainers, and athletes should participate in formal educational programs in which they consider and discuss the norms of the sport ethic and how to prevent deviant overconformity. Unless these people understand their roles in reproducing a culture supportive of substance use and abuse, the problems will continue. Such a program would involve training to do the following:

• Create norms regulating the use of new and powerful technology and medical knowledge that go beyond the use of drugs.

• Question and critically examine values and norms in sports, as well as set limits on conformity to those values and norms.

• Teach athletes to think critically about sports so that they understand that they can make choices and changes in sports.

• Provide parents, coaches, and athletes with the best and most recent information available on performance-enhancing technologies so that they can make informed decisions about if and how they will be used.

We now face a future without clearly defined ideas about the meaning of achievement in sports in light of (1) new financial incentives to set records and win events, (2) the new importance of sport participation in the lives and identities of many young athletes, (3) the new technologies, which clearly enhance performance, and (4) the new forms of corporate sponsorship, which make image as important as ability.

Therefore, we need *new* approaches and guidelines. Old approaches and guidelines combined with coercive methods of control will not work. Trying to make sports into what we believe they were in the past is futile. We cannot go back to an imagined past. We face new issues and challenges, and it will take new approaches to deal with them effectively (Smith, 2005). As described in Breaking Barriers, pages 188–189, this is evident in the Paralympics where new technologies have created a number of challenges related to fairness.

Widespread participation is needed in this process of dealing with new issues and challenges, or powerful entities, such as transnational corporations, will appropriate sport culture and the bodies of athletes as sites for delivering their messages about success, performance, efficiency, winning, and enduring pain for the sake of achieving goals. We are already headed in that direction, and we are traveling at a pace that makes it difficult to put on the breaks or change directions. But change remains possible if we work to create it.

summary

IS DEVIANCE IN SPORTS OUT OF CONTROL?

The study of deviance in sports presents challenges due to four factors: (1) The forms and causes of deviance in sports are so diverse that no single theory can explain all of them; (2) actions, traits, and ideas accepted in sports may be defined as deviant in the rest of society, and what is permitted in society may be defined as deviant in sports; (3) deviance in sports often involves uncritically accepting norms rather than rejecting them; (4) training in sports has incorporated such new forms of science and technology that people have not had the opportunity to develop norms to guide and evaluate the actions of athletes and others in sports.

Widely used conceptual frameworks in sociology don't offer useful explanations of the full range of deviance in sports, nor do they offer much help in devising ways to control it. Problems are encountered when functionalist theory is used. Functionalists define deviance as the failure to conform to ideals, and deviants are seen as lacking moral character. But ideals are difficult to identify, and athletes often violate norms as they go overboard in their acceptance of them, not because they lack character.

Similarly, problems occur when conflict theory is used. Conflict theorists define deviance as actions violating the interests of people with money and power, and deviants are seen as exploited victims of the quest for profits. But people with power and money don't control all sports, and it is not accurate to define all athletes as victims.

A constructionist approach using interactionist and critical theories seems to be most useful when explaining much of the deviance in sports today. Such an approach emphasizes that the dynamics of sport participation are grounded in the social worlds created around sports and that people in sports make choices and can act as agents of change in sports and the culture as a whole. The use of a constructionist approach in this chapter highlights the distinction between cases of deviant underconformity and overconformity. Such a distinction is important because the most serious forms of deviance in sports occur when athletes, coaches, and others overconform to the norms of the sport ethic—a cluster of norms that emphasizes dedication to the game, making sacrifices, striving for distinction, taking risks, playing with pain and injury, and pursuing dreams. When little concern is given to setting limits in the process of conforming to these norms, deviant overconformity becomes a problem.

Research supports this explanation. Most on-the-field and sport-related actions fall within an accepted range; when they fall outside this range, they often involve overconformity to the norms of the sport ethic. Rates of off-the-field deviance among athletes are generally comparable with rates among peers in the general population; when rates are high, as they are with binge drinking and sexual assault, they often are connected with the dynamics and consequences of overconformity to the sport ethic.

The use of performance-enhancing substances is a form of deviance that is reportedly widespread among athletes, despite new rules, testing programs, educational programs, and strong punishments for violators. Historical evidence suggests that recent increases in rates of use are due primarily to increases in the supply and range of available substances rather than changes in the values and moral characters of athletes or increased exploitation of athletes. Most athletes through history have sought ways to improve their skills, maintain their athlete identity, and continue playing their sports, but today their search is more likely to involve the use of widely available performance-enhancing substances.

Despite new enforcement efforts by sport organizations, athletes using performance-enhancing substances have generally stayed one jump ahead of the rule makers and testers. When one drug is banned, athletes use another, even if it is more dangerous. If a new test is developed, athletes switch to an undetectable drug or use masking drugs to confuse testers. The use of HGH, blood doping, testosterone, and many new substances still escape detection, and testing programs are often problematic because they are expensive and often violate privacy rights or cultural norms in many societies. However, many people are strongly committed to testing, and new testing procedures have been developed. The prospect of "gene-doping," or performance-enhancing genetic manipulation, will present significant challenges for testing in the future. In the meantime, testers are struggling to stay ahead of athletes who continue to overconform to the norms of the sport ethic.

Controlling deviant overconformity requires a critical assessment of the norms and social organization of sports. A balance must be struck between accepting and questioning norms and rules; people in sports must critically qualify norms and rules and set limits on conformity so that athletes who engage in risky and self-destructive actions are not defined and presented as heroes. Everyone in sports should question existing norms and create new norms related to the use of medical science and technology.

An effective transformation of sports also requires that all participants be involved in a continual process of critical reflection about the goals, purpose, and organization of sports. Controlling deviance requires an assessment of the values and norms in sports, as well as restructuring the organizations that control and sponsor sports. Critical assessment should involve everyone, from athletes to fans. It is idealistic but it is worth trying.

> **OLC** See the OLC, www.mhhe.com/coakley9e, for an annotated list of readings related to this chapter. The OLC also contains a key concept list, a review test, and other helpful features.

WEBSITE RESOURCES

Note: Websites often change. The following URLs were current when this book was printed. Please check our website (www.mhhe.com/coakley9e) for updates and additions.

www.mhhe.com/coakley9e   Click on chapter 6 for information on the history of performance-enhancing drug use and drug testing in high-performance sports and for information on recent cases of athletes testing positive for certain drugs.

www.sportslaw.org   The Sports Lawyers Association often refers to deviance in sports in terms of the legal issues raised; this site lists articles and recent cases.

www.alfred.edu/news/html/hazing_study.html   A report of the National Survey of Initiation Rites and Athletics for NCAA Sports; excellent source of hazing data from U.S. colleges, universities, and high schools.

www.physsportsmed.com/issues/1998/0jun/pipe.htm   An article calling for physicians to act assertively to control deviance in sports by reviving ethics in sports and encouraging athletes to minimize risk-taking behaviors on the field.

www.ncava.org   National Coalition Against Violent Athletes; provides news, statistics, updates, and information about prevention programs.

www.sports.findlaw.com   This site contains a list of the "Tarnished 20" rankings, which identify universities where people associated with sport programs have violated rules; has a Student-Athlete Center where NCAA rules are simplified.

www.usantidoping.org   The site of the official substance-testing agency in the United States; online materials illustrate how the agency is presenting regulatory and educational materials to athletes and others.

www.wada-ama.org   The site of the official worldwide drug- and substance-testing agency; online materials illustrate how the agency is presenting regulatory and educational materials.

www.wada-ama.org/web/standards_harmonization/code/list_standard_2004.pdf   The World Anti-Doping Code: the 2004 Prohibited List, International Standard, updated 17 March 2004, 10 pages.

www.cces.ca/pdfs/CCES-ADV-2004WADAProhibitedList-E.pdf   The site of the Canadian Centre for Ethics in Sport, the 2004 WADA Prohibited List: Summary of Revisions.

http://bodybuilding.com/store/hardcore.htm   The site lists more than 200 producers of "nutritional supplements," chemical compounds, and what many consider to be performance-enhancing drugs; this is where bodybuilders and athletes who cannot afford designer drugs choose among over 200 different substances to aid their training and stay ahead of drug testers.

http://bodybuilding.com/store/hgh.html   The site provides information on HGH and other substances for which there are no tests being used in most sports.

www.t-nation.com/   The site of Testosterone Nation; widely used by people who take bodybuilding compounds and drugs, seek information on what drugs to use, how to obtain them, and what others say about them.

http://multimedia.olympic.org/pdf/en_report_817.pdf   The IOC Anti-Doping Rules Applicable to the 2004 Athens Olympic Games, 4 June 2004, 25 pages.

http://www.champion-nutrition.com/champion/   Click on "products" to see a few of the hundreds of substances available for people wanting to build strength and mass, boost endurance, and recover more rapidly from hard workouts.

www.ahcpr.gov/clinic/evrptfiles.htm#ephedra   Ephedra and ephedrine for weight loss and athletic performance enhancement: clinical efficacy and side effects, by Paul G. Shekelle Rockville, MD: U.S. Dept. of Health and Human Services. Agency for Healthcare Research and Quality, 2003. 2v. ISBN 1587631350 (v1, Evidence report and evidence tables; v2, Appendices) (Evidence report/technology assessment no. 76).

www.SportsEthicsInstitute.org   A nonprofit corporation that fosters critical information and discussions about ethical issues in sports; site provides news, information, and links to online resources.

www.espn.go.com/special/s/drugsandsports   This site provides basic information on a variety of drugs used by athletes; ESPN regularly includes on its site information about deviance in sports as it hits the news.

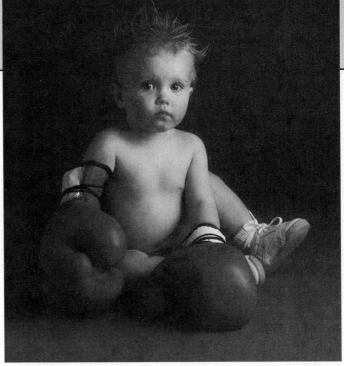

(McGraw-Hill)

chapter
7

VIOLENCE IN SPORTS

How Does It Affect Our Lives?

WITH THE SMART COACH, fighting is a tool. . . .
Fighting can be used to inspire your team, send
a message, change momentum.

> —Barry Melrose, ESPN hockey announcer,
> 2002

THE FIRST THING on our mind is to be violent . . .
and rip someone's head off.

> —Marcus Stroud, NFL player, 2005

 Online Learning Center Resources

Visit *Sports in Society*'s Online Learning Center
(OLC) at **www.mhhe.com/coakley9e** for additional information and study material for this
chapter, including

- Self-grading quizzes
- Learning objectives
- Related websites
- Additional readings

A complete outline is available online
atwww.mhhe.com/coakley9e.

THERE'S A TIME to fight and a time not to. . . .
You've got to be smart about it.

Kris Mallette, professional hockey player, 2004

I DON'T WANT TO SOUND LIKE I'm bragging,
because I'm not, but back [in the 1960s, when I
played basketball] the violence was much more
intense.

—Satch Sanders, former NBA player, 1999

AT YOUR *fingertips* For more information on deviance in sports, see Chapter 6.

Discussions of violence in sports, like discussions of deviance, are often connected with people's ideas about the moral condition of society as a whole. When violence occurs in sports, many people are quick to use it as an indicator that the moral foundation of society is eroding and that people, especially children, are learning a warped sense of morality as they watch athletes and use them as models for their own actions.

Statements about violence in sports are often confusing. Some people say that violence is an inherent part of many games, whereas others say that it destroys the dynamics of games. Some people say that violence in sports reflects natural tendencies among males in society, whereas others say that men use violence in sports to promote the idea that physical size and strength is a legitimate basis for maintaining power over others. Some say that violence in sports is worse today than ever before, whereas others say it is less common and less brutal than in the past.

Contradictory statements and conclusions about violence in sports occur for four reasons. *First*, many people fail to define important terms in their discussions. They use words such as *physical, assertive, tough, rough, competitive, intense, intimidating, risky, aggressive, destructive*, and *violent* interchangeably. *Second*, they may not distinguish players from spectators, even though the dynamics of violence differ in these two groups. *Third*, they categorize all sports together, despite differences in meaning, purpose, organization, and amount of physical contact involved. *Fourth*, they may not distinguish the immediate, short-term effects of experiencing or watching violence in sports from more permanent, long-term effects.

The goal of this chapter is to enable you to include information based on research and theories in your discussions of violence in sports. Chapter content focuses on five topics:

1. A practical definition of *violence* and related terms
2. A brief historical overview of violence in sports
3. On-the-field violence among players in various sports
4. Off-the-field violence among players and the impact of sports violence on their lives apart from sports
5. Violence among spectators who watch media coverage of sports, attend events in person, and play sport video games

In connection with the last three topics, I will make suggestions about how to control violence and limit its consequences on and off the field.

WHAT IS VIOLENCE?

Violence *is the use of excessive physical force, which causes or has the potential to cause harm or destruction.* We often think of violence as actions that are illegal or unsanctioned, but there are situations in which the use of violence is encouraged or approved in most groups or societies. For instance, when violence involves deviant underconformity based on a rejection of norms in society, it is often classified as illegal and sanctioned severely. However, when violence occurs in connection with enforcing norms, protecting people and property, or overconforming to widely accepted norms, it may be approved and even lauded as necessary to preserve order, reaffirm important social values, or entertain spectators. Therefore, violence is often, but not always, accepted and defined as legitimate when soldiers, police, and athletes are perceived to be protecting people, reproducing accepted ideologies, or pursuing victories in the name of others.

When violence occurs in connection with the widespread rejection of norms, it is often described as anarchy. When it occurs in connection with extreme methods of social control or extreme overconformity to norms, it often is associated with a sense of moral righteousness even when it produces harmful or destructive consequences. Under certain political conditions, this latter expression of violence is tied to fascism and fascist leaders.

In the case of sports, pushing a referee who penalizes you or a coach who reprimands you is violence based on a rejection of norms. These actions are defined as illegal and punished severely by teams and sport organizations, even if the referee or coach was not seriously injured. However, it is different when a football player delivers a punishing tackle, breaking the ribs or blowing out the knee of an opposing running back after his coach told him to be aggressive and put his body on the line for the team. Such violence involves conformity to norms and is often defined as appropriate, accepted by fans, highlighted on video replays, and approved by teammates and many other football players. The player might feel righteous in being violent, despite the harmful consequences, and would not hesitate to be violent again. His violence would not be punished because it conforms to norms endorsed in the social world of football. Furthermore, his ability to do violence and to endure it when perpetrated by others would be used to affirm his identity as an athlete and a football player.

The term **aggression** is used in this chapter to refer to *verbal or physical actions grounded in an intent to dominate, control, or do harm to another person.* Aggression is often involved in violence, but some violence occurs without aggressive intent. This definition allows us to distinguish aggressive actions from other actions that we might describe as assertive, competitive, or achievement oriented. For example, a very competitive person may use violence during a game without the intent to dominate, control, or harm others. However, there is often a difference between being aggressive and simply being assertive or trying hard to win or achieve other goals. The term **intimidation** is used to refer to *words,*

gestures, and actions that threaten violence or aggression. Like aggression, intimidation is used to dominate or control another person. These definitions will help focus our discussion, but they will not eliminate all conceptual problems.

VIOLENCE IN SPORTS THROUGH HISTORY

Violence is not new to physical activities and sports (Dunning, 1999; Guttmann, 1998; 2004). As noted in chapter 3, so-called blood sports were popular among the ancient Greeks and throughout the Roman Empire. Deaths occurred regularly in connection with ritual games among the Mayas and Aztecs. Tournaments during medieval and early modern Europe were designed as training for war and often had warlike consequences. Folk games were only loosely governed by rules, and they produced injuries and deaths at rates that would shock and disgust people today. Bearbaiting, cockfighting, dog fighting, and other "sporting" activities during those periods involved the treatment of animals that most people today would define as brutal and violent.

Research indicates that, as part of an overall civilizing process in Europe and North America, modern sports were developed as more rule-governed activities than the physical games in previous eras (see figure 7.1). As sports became formally organized, official rules prohibited certain forms of violence that had been common in many folk games. Bloodshed decreased, and there was a greater emphasis on self-control to restrict physical contact and the expression of aggressive impulses often created in the emotional heat of competition (Dunning, 1999).

Social historians, who study these changes, also explain that rates of sports violence do not automatically decrease over time. In fact, as actions and emotional expression have become more regulated and controlled in modern societies, players and spectators view the "controlled" violence in sports as exciting. Furthermore, the processes of

"Now that we've invented violence, we need a sport to use it in."

FIGURE 7.1   Violence in sports is not new. However, this does not mean that it is a natural or inevitable part of sports.

commercialization, professionalization, and globalization have given rise to new forms of instrumental and "dramatic" violence in many sports. This means that goal-oriented and entertainment-oriented violence has increased, at least temporarily, in many Western societies. Sociologist Eric Dunning (1999) notes that violence remains a crucial social issue in modern sports because their goal is to create tension rather than relieve or discharge it. Additionally, violent and aggressive sports serve, in patriarchal societies, to reproduce an ideology that naturalizes the power of men over women. Overall, historical research shows that sports are given different meanings by time and place and that we can understand violence in sports only when we analyze it in relation to the historical, social, and cultural context in which it occurs.

VIOLENCE ON THE FIELD

Violence in sports comes in many forms, and it is grounded in social and cultural factors related to the sport ethic, commercialization, gender ideology and ideas about masculinity, the dynamics of social class and race, and the strategies used in sports. Violence also has significant consequences for athletes and presents challenges to those who feel that it should be controlled. Each of these topics is addressed in this section.

Types of Violence

The most frequently used typology of on-the-field violence among players was developed by the late Mike Smith, a respected Canadian sociologist (1983; see Young, 2000, 2002a). Smith identified four categories of violence associated with playing sports:

1. *Brutal body contact.* This includes physical practices common in certain sports and accepted by athletes as part of the action and risk in their sport participation. Examples are collisions, hits, tackles, blocks, body checks, and other forms of forceful physical contact that can produce injuries. Most people in society define this forceful physical contact as extreme, although they don't classify it as illegal or criminal, nor do they see a need to punish it. Coaches often encourage this form of violence. As one coach said after a big playoff victory in high school football, "We preached to the kids all week that we had to get back to what we do best—playing smash-mouth football" (in Trivett, 1999, p. 30C).

2. *Borderline violence.* This includes practices that violate the rules of the game but are accepted by most players and coaches as conforming to the norms of the sport ethic and representing commonly used competitive strategies. Examples are the "brush back" pitch in baseball, the forcefully placed elbow or knee in soccer and basketball, the strategic bump used by distance runners to put another runner off stride, the fistfight in ice hockey, and the forearm to the ribs of a quarterback in football. Although these actions are

expected, they may provoke retaliation by other players. Official sanctions and fines are not usually severe for borderline violence. However, public pressure to increase the severity of sanctions has grown in recent years, and the severity of punishments has increased in some sports.

3. *Quasi-criminal violence.* This includes practices that violate the formal rules of the game, public laws, and even the informal norms used by players. Examples are cheap shots, late hits, sucker punches, and flagrant fouls that endanger players' bodies and reject the norm of respecting the game. Fines and suspensions are usually imposed on players who engage in such violence. Most athletes condemn this form of violence and see it as a rejection of the informal norms of the game and what it means to be an athlete.

4. *Criminal violence.* This includes practices that are clearly outside the law to the point that athletes condemn them without question and law enforcement officials may prosecute them as crimes. Examples are assaults that occur after a game and assaults during a game that appear to be premeditated and severe enough to kill or seriously maim a player. Such violence is relatively rare although there is growing support that criminal charges ought to be filed when it does occur. This support grew recently after a hockey player intentionally smashed an opponent's head with his stick. The act was such a blatant and dangerous assault that a fellow player known for his on-ice violence said, "He's lost the respect of every player in the league."

Sociologist Kevin Young (2002a, 2004b) has noted that this is a useful general typology but that the lines separating the four types of violence shift over time as norms change in sports and societies. Furthermore, the typology fails to address the origins of violence and how violent acts are related to the sport ethic, gender ideology, and the commercialization of sports. Despite these weaknesses, this typology enables us to make distinctions between various types of violence discussed in this chapter.

Violence as Deviant Overconformity to the Norms of the Sport Ethic

In Pat Conroy's novel *The Prince of Tides* (1986), there is a classic scene in which the coach addresses his team and describes the ideal football player. He uses words that many athletes in heavy-contact sports have heard during their careers:

> Now a real hitter is a headhunter who puts his head in the chest of his opponents and ain't happy if his opponent is still breathing after the play. A real hitter doesn't know what fear is except when he sees it in the eyes of a ball carrier he's about to split in half. A real hitter loves pain, loves the screaming and the sweating and the brawling and the hatred of life down in the trenches. He likes to be at the spot where the blood flows and the teeth get kicked out. That's what this sport's about, men. It's war, pure and simple. (p. 384)

Not all coaches use such vivid vocabulary because they know it can inspire dangerous forms of violence. However, there are coaches and team administrators who seek athletes who think this way. For example, during a recent NFL draft, a reporter observed that the coach of the team in his city was seeking "cold-blooded defenders who smile when quarterbacks bleed" (Kiszla, 2001, p. 3D).

When athletes think this way, violence occurs regularly enough to attract attention. Journalists describe it, sociologists and psychologists try to explain it, and athletes brag or complain about it. When an athlete dies or is paralyzed by on-the-field violence, the media present stories stating that violence is rampant in sports and in society, and then they run multiple replays or photos of violent acts knowing that this will increase their ratings or sales.

Although players may be concerned about brutal body contact and borderline violence in

Violence is often connected with overconformity to the norms of the sport ethic. This high school rugby jacket presents violence as part of team culture. By associating violence with excellence, players learn what is expected on the field, even if they do not feel comfortable with brutal body contact and borderline violence. (*Source:* Jay Coakley)

their sports, they generally accept them. Even players who don't like them may use them to enhance their status on teams and popularity among spectators. Athletes whose violence involves overconformity to the sport ethic become legends on and off the field. Athletes who engage in quasi- and criminal violence often are marginalized in sports, and they may face criminal charges, although prosecuting such charges has been difficult and convictions are rare (Young, 2000, 2002a, 2004b, 2007a).

Violence as deviant overconformity is also related to insecurities among athletes in high-performance sports. Athletes learn that "you're only as good as your last game," and they know that their identities as athletes and status as team members are constantly tested. Therefore, they often take extreme measures to prove themselves, even if it involves violence. Violence becomes a marker of self-worth and leads other athletes to reaffirm your identity. This is why athletes who don't play in pain are defined as failures, whereas those who do are defined as courageous. Playing in pain and with injuries honors the importance of the game and it expresses dedication to teammates and the values in high-performance sport culture.

It is important to understand that violent expressions of overconformity to the sport ethic are not limited to men although it is more common among male athletes than female athletes. Women also overconform to the norms of the sport ethic, and, when they play contact sports, they face the challenge of drawing the line between physicality and violence. For example, when sociologist Nancy Theberge (1999) spent a full season studying the sport experiences of women on an elite ice hockey team in Canada, she discovered that the women loved the physicality of hockey, even though body checking was not allowed. As one woman said,

> I like a physical game. You get more fired up. I think when you get hit . . . like when you're fighting for a puck in the corner, when you're both fighting so you're both working hard and maybe the elbows are flying, that just makes you put more effort into it. (in Theberge, 1999, p. 147)

The experience of dealing with the physicality of contact sports and facing its consequences creates drama, excitement, strong emotions, and special interpersonal bonds among female athletes as it does among men. Despite the risk and reality of pain and injuries, many women in contact sports feel that the physical intensity and body contact in their sports make them feel alive and aware. Although many women are committed to controlling brutal body contact and more severe forms of violence, the love of their sport and the excitement of physicality can lead to violence grounded in overconformity to the norms of the sport ethic.

Commercialization and Violence in Sports

Some athletes in power and performance sports are paid well because of their ability to do violence on the field. However, it is difficult to argue that commercialization and money in sports cause athletes to be violent. Violent athletes in the past were paid very little, and athletes in high schools, colleges, and sport clubs today are paid nothing, yet many of them do violence, despite the pain and injuries associated with it.

Commercialization and money have expanded opportunities to play certain contact sports in some societies, and media coverage makes these sports and the violence they contain more visible than ever before. Children watch this coverage and may imitate violent athletes when they play informal games and organized youth sports, but this does not justify the conclusion that commercialization is the cause of violence in sports.

Football players and athletes in other heavy-contact sports engaged in violence on the field long before television coverage and the promise of big salaries. Players at all levels of organized football killed and maimed each other at *rates* that were far higher than the death and injury rates in football today. There are more injuries in football today because there are more people playing football. This is a serious problem that must be addressed, but to think that it is caused mainly by commercialization and money is a mistake.

This is an important point because many people who criticize sports today blame violence and other problems in sports on money and greed. They claim that, if athletes were true amateurs and played for love of the game instead of money, there would be less violence. However, this conclusion contradicts research findings, and it distracts attention from the deep cultural and ideological roots of violence in particular sports and societies. This means that we could take

AT YOUR *fingertips* For more information on commercialization, see pages 373–381.

money away from athletes tomorrow, but violence would be reduced only if there were changes in the culture in which athletes, especially male athletes, learn to value and use violence in sports.

Many people resist the notion that cultural changes are needed to control violence because it places the responsibility for change on all of us. It is easy to say that wealthy and greedy team owners, athletes without moral character, and TV executives seeking high viewer ratings are to blame for violence in sports. But it is more difficult to critically examine our culture and the normative and social organization of the sports that many people watch and enjoy. Similarly, it is difficult for people to critically examine the definitions of *masculinity* and the structure of gender relations that they have long accepted as part of the "natural" order of things. But these critiques are needed if we wish to understand and control violence in sports.

The point in this section is that commercialization is not the *primary* cause of violence in sports. But money is not irrelevant. Consider the following statements made by a boxer and two football players:

> I'm challenging Laila Ali. . . . Kicking [her] butt will be a walk in the park. . . . And if she wants a rematch, I'll dust her off again. (Jacqui Frazier-Lyde in Farhood, 2000, online)

> I want to hurt him. . . . I love to see people bleed. I do my talking [in the NFL] by hitting my man, throwing him on the ground, jumping on him. (Orlando Brown in Montville, 1999, p. 100)

> The first thing on our mind is to be violent and disruptive and rip someone's head off. (Marcus Stroud in Fleming, 2005, p. 66)

These are three among dozens of similar statements from popular sports publications. They express the language and rhetoric that has come to be used in certain commercial sports. The most extreme examples of this rhetoric are in professional wrestling. Therefore, when images of intimidation are used by Jacqui Frazier-Lyde (daughter of former heavyweight boxing champion Joe Frazier) as she challenges Laila Ali (daughter of Muhammad Ali) to a prize fight with a big payoff and when NFL players tell reporters that they want to hurt one another and rip someone's head off, their violent rhetoric tells us less about the way they *play sports* than it does about how they want us to *think* they play sports.

Professional athletes are entertainers, and they now use a promotional and heroic rhetoric that presents images of revenge, retaliation, hate, hostility, intimidation, aggression, violence, domination, and destruction. These images attract attention and serve commercial purposes. The NFL, the NHL, and even the NBA use these images to hype their games. They sell videos that present image after image of glorified violence in slow-motion close-ups accompanied by the actual sounds of bodies colliding, bones and tendons snapping on impact, and players gasping in agony and pain. In true promotional fashion, the same media companies that sell or promote these videos also publish articles that condemn violence and violent players. Their marketing people know that violence *and* moral outrage about violence attracts audiences and generates profits.

Does this commercially inspired rhetoric represent the real on-the-field orientations of

Both men and women are capable of violence on and off the playing field. However, women may not connect violent actions to their identities in the same way that some men do. Prevailing definitions of *masculinity* lead many people to feel that violence is more "natural" for men than for women, and it may lead men to feel comfortable with violence in their sports. (*Source:* Beth A. Keiser, AP/World Wide Photos)

athletes, or is it part of a strategy to create personas and attract attention, which have commercial value? Research is needed on this, but my sense is that most athletes don't relish hurting opponents and seeing them bleed. At the same time, some athletes have become experts at using violent rhetoric to enhance the entertainment value of what they do and the events in which they participate. It is part of the spectacle dimension of sports, similar to dramatic storylines delivered by paid announcers, sexy cheerleaders and halftime dancers, and toy tomahawks for the symbolic "chopping" of opponents.

However, it raises this question: How far can the spectacle be emphasized before people conclude that a particular sport has lost its authenticity as a game and has become a planned confrontation devoid of play? Professional wrestling (WWE) has crossed this line, and so did the XFL, the short-lived extreme football league sponsored by the same people who own the WWE. People may be willing to watch violence in the context of an authentic game, but they may not pay to watch violence week after week apart from the goal-oriented game that legitimizes it.

Violence and Masculinity

Violence in sports is not limited to men. However, research based on critical feminist theory indicates that, *if we want to understand violence in sports, we must understand gender ideology and issues of masculinity in culture.* Sociologist Mike Messner explains:

> Young males come to sport with identities that lead them to define their athletic experience differently than females do. Despite the fact that few males truly enjoy hitting and being hit, and that one has to be socialized into participating in much of the violence commonplace in sport, males often view aggression, within the rule-bound structure of sport, as legitimate and "natural." (1992, p. 67)

Messner notes that many male athletes learn to define injurious acts as a necessary part of the

game, rather than as violence, as long as they are within the rules of the game and within the informal norms the players use to judge and evaluate each other.

In many societies today, participation in power and performance sports has become an important way to prove masculinity. Boys discover that, if they play these sports and are seen as being able to do violence, they can avoid social labels such as *pussy, lady, fag, wimp,* and *sissy* (Ingham and Dewar, 1999). In a review of the research on this issue, Phil White and Kevin Young (1997) note that, if a boy or young man avoids these sports, he risks estrangement from his male peers.

Boys and men who play power and performance sports learn quickly that they are evaluated in terms of their ability to do violence in combination with physical skills (Lance, 2005). This learning begins in youth sports, and by the time young men have become immersed in the social world of most power and performance sports, they accept brutal body contact and borderline violence as part the game as it is played by "real" men. For example, when Ozzie Guillen, manager of the Chicago White Sox, was asked to comment about some of his players who complained about a vicious collision between a teammate and the catcher on the opposing team, he said, "If we don't like it, [we should] go and play softball or go play tennis. I don't want them to be a bunch of ladies playing this game" (*Denver Post*, 2004). When gender is viewed in these terms, the ability to do violence becomes "one of the cornerstones of masculinity" (White and Young, 1997, p. 9).

A tragic example of the connection between masculinity and violence in sports occurred at a Massachusetts hockey rink a few years ago. As a few boys practiced hockey skills during an informal skating session, a father watching the skaters became angry because his son failed to stick up for himself when other boys pushed him around. The father entered the rink and told his son that he had to "be a man" on the ice. The boy turned away and walked to the locker room as his father continued to harass him. Another father passed

breaking BARRIERS | Ideological Barriers
The Hit Isn't Real Unless It Bends Steel

Murderball is unique. It is four-on-four competition with players in wheelchairs customized to function like minichariots: angled wheels, bucket seats, safety harnesses, and protective metal bars that shield legs and feet during crashes. Using a volleyball and a basketball court, the teams engage one another in a contest that resembles a mix of rugby, team handball, and football organized by an X Games promoter.

In the Paralympics, murderball is officially called wheelchair rugby. Many people call it quad rugby because participants have quadriplegia or limited use of three or four limbs. Each of the twelve members of a team is rated in terms of upper-body muscle function, from 0.5 to 3.5 (least impaired). During games the four players on the court from each team may not exceed a cumulative rating of 8.0 points. Participation is open to men and women, but men only comprise most teams. During the four eight-minute quarters, points are scored when a player possessing the ball crosses the opponents' end line.

Wheelchair rugby was invented in Canada (1981) and first played in the Paralympics in 1996. It

Wheelchair rugby, aka quad rugby and murderball, is played in the Paralympics. These are the Portland Pounders, one of the many teams in North America. Some participants use a highly masculinized vocabulary to describe the intimidation and violence that occur in games. Wheelchair rugby challenges stereotypes about people with a disability, but it also reaffirms a gender ideology in which manhood is defined in terms of the ability to do violence. When sports embody contradictory ideological themes making clear sense of them is difficult. (*Source:* Jason E. Kaplan Photography, Portland, Oregon)

by and told his fellow dad to ease up because it was a minor incident. This further irritated the angry father, and he punched the man who gave him the unwanted advice. He exited the rink, but he came back, found the man whom he had punched, and beat him to death in the lobby of the rink, in front of a few children, mothers, and a rink employee.

This case was covered in the media as an extreme example of parental "rink rage," but it was never discussed as an issue related to particular ideas about masculinity in American society. The father, who was later convicted of voluntary manslaughter, first became enraged when his son failed to meet his definition of what a man should be on the ice, and then he killed another man immediately became popular among people with quadriplegia, especially those who favored power and performance sports involving heavy contact. Paul Davies, a former player and now manager of the British national team, describes wheelchair rugby as "a real in your face sport [resembling] chess with violence" (BBC Sport Academy, 2005).

Many wheelchair rugby players have impairments caused by accidents in risky activities, including high-risk sports. They like wheelchair rugby because it differs from other sports in the Paralympics. When players and other insiders refer to the sport as murderball, it implies a closer connection to able-bodied heavy-contact sports than there is for other Paralympic sports.

Some athletes say that murderball allows them to express their aggression and therefore gain a sense of control over their bodies. But as one member of the U.S. team said, "Of course, you're gonna have healthy aggression and unhealthy aggression." And then one of his teammates added, "But when you can use your body and your chair just to go knock the shit out of somebody, it helps" (in Anderson, 2005; from the documentary film, *Murderball*).

Although other Paralympic sports are organized so that violence is inconsistent with the strategy and rhythm of participation, some athletes with disabilities want to play a sport involving violence and use their ability to do violence to reaffirm their identities as athletes and men. For example, when the U.S. team faced Canada in the gold medal game of the 2002 Wheelchair Rugby World Championships, the coach

reminded the players that, "It's not buddy-buddy time anymore, guys." And when a member of the U.S. team was asked about their goal for the 2004 Paralympics in Athens, he quickly replied, "We're not going for a hug, we're going for a f___ing Gold Medal" (in *Murderball*, 2004). "Hugs" are associated with the Special Olympics, which are organized to emphasize play and personal accomplishment among athletes with intellectual disabilities. There is little emphasis on competitive success and none on dominating opponents in the Special Olympics. Volunteer coaches, in fact, are known for giving athletes hugs when they complete an event, regardless of the outcome.

Many Paralympians, using the ideology of ableism, want to distance themselves from the Special Olympics because it doesn't match dominant sport forms in society and it perpetuates the idea that people with disabilities cannot play "real" sports—that is, the sports played by able-bodied athletes. **Ableism** is a *web of ideas and beliefs that people use to classify bodies perceived as unimpaired as normal and superior and bodies perceived as (dis)abled as subnormal and inferior*. This ideology is widespread in society and many people, including some with disabilities, use it to evaluate themselves and others. Similarly, some murderball athletes use traditional gender ideology to connect power, status, and male identity with the ability to do violence. As expressed through words on a player's tee-shirt: "The hit isn't real unless it bends steel" (Grossfeld, 2005). This is not surprising because none of us lives outside the influence of ideology.

who had said that the issue was minor. This case highlights the problems associated with a gender ideology that leads people to think that masculinity is proved by doing violence in sports.

When women do violence in sports, it may be seen as a sign of commitment or skill, but it is not seen as proof of femininity. Dominant gender ideology in many cultures links manhood with

the ability to do violence, but there is no similar link between womanhood and violence. Therefore, female athletes who engage in violence do not receive the same support and rewards that men receive—unless they wrestle in the WWE or skate on a roller derby team where the sport personas of female athletes are constructed to shock or titillate spectators (Berra, 2005; Blumenthal,

2004). The emergence of women's boxing provides a context in which female athletes are rewarded for doing violence, but most female boxers do not feel that doing violence in the ring makes them more of a woman than the boxers they defeat. Overall, none of us lives outside the influence of ideology. This point is highlighted in connection with a rapidly growing sport that participants call murderball. Officially known as wheelchair rugby, murderball is the focus of Breaking Barriers on pages 204–205.

The Institutionalization of Violence in Sports

Certain forms of violence are built into the culture and structure of particular sports (Guilbert, 2004). Athletes in these sports learn to use violence as a strategy, even though it may cause them pain and injury. Controlling institutionalized violence is difficult because it requires changes in the culture and structure of particular sports—something that most people in governing bodies are hesitant to do. These are the topics discussed in the following sections.

Learning to Use Violence as a Strategy: Non-contact Sports   In some noncontact sports, participants may try to intimidate opponents, but violence is rare. For example, tennis players have been fined for slamming a ball to the ground in protest or talking to an official or opponent in a menacing manner. Players in noncontact sports are seldom, if ever, rewarded for violent actions. Therefore, it is doubtful that playing or watching these sports teaches people to use violence as a strategy on the field.

Some athletes may use violent images as they describe competition, but they don't have actual opportunities to convert their words into deeds. For example, a sprint cyclist on the U.S. cycling team used violent images as he described his approach to competition on the track:

> I am really aggressive out there. I pretty much hate the guy I'm racing. It wouldn't matter if it were my brother. . . . I want to destroy the guy.

> End it quick. Boom. One knockout punch. (in Becker, 1996, p. 4E)

Of course, cycling does not allow him to physically destroy or punch a competitor, but the language he used had violence built into it.

Men who play noncontact sports use violent images in their descriptions of competition much more often than women use them. The use of a "language of violence" is clearly linked to masculinity in most cultures. Women may use it on occasion, but men use it more frequently. It may be that many women realize that a language of violence reaffirms a version of gender ideology that privileges men, works against their interests, and subverts the health and well-being of everyone in society.

Learning to Use Violence as a Strategy: Men's Contact Sports   Athletes in power and performance sports that involve heavy physical contact learn to use intimidation, aggression, and violence as strategies to achieve competitive success on-the-field. Success in these sports depends on the use of brutal body contact and borderline violence. Research shows that male athletes in contact sports readily accept certain forms of violence, even when they involve rule-violating behaviors, and that, as the amount of physical contact increases in a sport, so does this acceptance (Pilz, 1996; Shields and Bredemeier, 1995; Weinstein et al., 1995; White and Young, 1997). These athletes routinely disapprove of quasi-criminal and criminal violence, but they accept brutal body contact and borderline violence as long as it occurs within the rules of the game. They may not intend to hurt, but this does not prevent them from doing things that put their bodies and the bodies of opponents in jeopardy.

In boxing, football, ice hockey, rugby, and other heavy-contact sports, athletes also use intimidation and violence to promote their careers, increase drama for spectators, and enhance the publicity given to their sports and sponsors (see figure 7.2). These athletes realize that doing violence is expected, even if it causes harm to themselves

SIDELINES

"When are you gonna learn when it's necessary to use unnecessary roughness?"

FIGURE 7.2 In men's contact sports, players sometimes learn physical intimidation and violent behaviors as strategies. Both have been used to win games and build reputations.

and others. This was illustrated in 2004 when Brad May, the general manager of the NHL Vancouver Canucks, promised that his team would go after an opposing player who had injured one of their players in a previous game. May stated, "There's definitely a bounty on his head . . . It's going to be fun when we get him" (in Sadowski, 2005, p. 7C). In the game that followed May's comment, a Canucks player wrapped his left arm around the target player's neck, punched his head repeatedly, and slammed him to the ice. This "fun" resulted in a broken neck, a closed head injury, and deep cuts on the face of the victim. The Canucks were fined $250,000, and the attacking player was suspended, causing him to lose $502,000 of his $6.8 million salary. The victim sustained serious physical and neurological damage and has not played hockey since being attacked. The attacker was charged with criminal assault and, after pleading guilty, was sentenced to twelve months of probation and eighty hours of community service; additionally, he was prohibited from ever playing against the person he attacked, but he currently plays in the National Hockey League (NHL) and earns a multimillion-dollar salary.

Violence is also incorporated into game strategies when coaches use players as designated agents of intimidation and violence for their teams. These players are called "enforcers," "goons," and "hit men," and they are expected to protect teammates and strategically assist their teams by intimidating, provoking, fighting with, or injuring opponents.

The violence of these enforcers and goons is an accepted part of certain sports, including hockey and basketball. For example, former Los Angeles Laker player Rick Fox regularly played the role of enforcer on the basketball court. To do it right, he says, "You have to look within and find the evil that's inside of you. It's not the kind of talk you want your kids to hear, but we're grown men" (in AP, 2000).

Some players continue to act as enforcers, and they are still paid for doing violence. However, every time they maim or come close to killing someone on the ice, court, or playing field, people raise questions about this form of institutionalized violence in sports. Football, basketball, and baseball have taken actions to control certain forms of institutionalized violence, but hockey has been slow to do so. Once violence is built into the culture, structures, and strategies of a sport, controlling or eliminating it is difficult.

Learning to Use Violence as a Strategy: Women's Contact Sports   Information on violence among girls and women in contact sports remains scarce even though more women are participating in them (Lawler, 2002). This creates the possibility for cases of violence among female athletes, but there are few studies that tell us if and why this is true.

Women's programs have undergone many changes over the past thirty years. They have become more competitive with a greater emphasis on power and performance and higher stakes associated with success. Today, as women become increasingly immersed in the social world of elite power and performance sports, they become more tolerant of rule violations and aggressive actions on the playing field, but this pattern is less clear among women than men (Nixon, 1996a, 1996b; Shields and Bredemeier, 1995; Shields et al., 1995).

"We know of no biological reasons that would prevent women from using intimidation and violence or being as physically aggressive as men" (Dunn, 1994). However, most girls and women become involved in and learn to play sports in ways that differ from the experiences of most boys and men. As women compete at higher levels, they often become similar to men in the way they embrace the sport ethic and use it to frame their identities as athletes. Like men, they are willing to dedicate themselves to the game, take risks, make sacrifices, pay the price, play with pain and injury, and overcome barriers. However, it is rare for them to link toughness, physicality, and aggression to their gender identities. In other words, women do not tie their ability to do violence to their definitions of what it means to be a woman in society. Similarly coaches don't try to motivate female athletes by urging them to "go out and prove who the better woman is" on the field. Therefore, at this time, women's contact sports are less violent than men's contact sports.

With this said, there are many research questions that have not been answered: Do elite female athletes develop the same form of hubris (pride-based arrogance) that many elite male athletes develop? If so, how is it linked to their identities, and how do they express it in sports? Do female athletes use a rhetoric of violence when they talk about sports? Some studies suggest that they don't (Nelson, 1994, 1998; Theberge, 1999; Young and White, 1995), but more information is needed. A good place to start might be with the women now playing heavy-contact sports

> **Becky Zerlentes took a shot to the head above her left eye, then staggered forward and fell to the canvas. . . . [She] never regained consciousness and died, becoming the first female boxer to die in a sanctioned event.**
>
> —*CBS News,* 5 April 2005

such as football, ice hockey, rugby, and boxing or participating in dramatic spectacles such as professional wrestling.

Pain and Injury as the Price of Violence

Many people think about sports in a paradoxical way: They accept violence in sports, but the injuries caused by that violence make them uneasy. They seem to want violence without consequences—like the fictionalized violence they see in the media and video games in which characters are involved in brutal actions but not really injured. However, sports violence is real, and it causes real pain, injury, disability, and even death (Dater, 2005; Farber, 2004; Rice, 2005; Smith, 2005b; Young, 2004).

Ron Rice, an NFL player whose career ended when he tackled an opponent, discusses the real consequences of violence. The brutal body contact of the tackle left him temporarily paralyzed and permanently disabled. He remembers that "before I hit the ground, I knew my career was over. . . . My body froze. I was like a tree that had been cut down, teetering, then crashing, unable to break my fall." Reminiscing about his life as a football player, Rice says that he was "programmed from a very young age to live and think a certain way," to be a warrior who keeps going no matter what (Rice, 2005). He did just that, and today he lives with chronic pain in his neck, wrists, hands, ankles, knees, and back, the toll of doing violence to others and enduring it in return. Rice says, "I'm 32 now, . . . These injuries are a part of my life. And I got off easy compared to a lot of these guys" (Rice 2005, p. 83).

Research on pain and injury among athletes helps us understand that violence in sports has real consequences. As noted in chapter 6, studies indicate that professional sports involving brutal body contact and borderline violence are among the most dangerous workplaces in the occupational world (Nixon, 2000; Waddington, 2000a, 2000b; White, 2004; White and Young, 1997; Young, 1993, 2000, 2004a). The same could be said about high-profile power and performance intercollegiate sports in which 80 percent of male and female athletes sustain at least one serious injury while playing their sports and nearly 70 percent are disabled for two or more weeks (Nixon, 2000). Rates of disabling injuries vary by sport, but they are high enough in many sports to constitute a serious health issue. The "normal" brutal body contact and borderline violence in contact sports regularly cause arthritis, concussions, bone fractures, torn ligaments, and other injuries. In other words, the violence inherent in power and performance sports takes a definite toll on the health of athletes (Young, 2004a).

Research shows a close connection between dominant ideas about masculinity and the high rate of injuries in many sports. Ironically, some power and performance sports are organized so that players feel that their manhood is up for grabs. Men who define *masculinity* in terms of physically dominating others often use violence in sports as an expression of this code of manhood. As long as athletes do not critically examine issues related to gender and the organization of their sports, they will mistakenly define *violence* as action that adds "value" to their lives rather than restricting, limiting, and sometimes threatening their lives.

Controlling On-the-Field Violence

The roots of violence on the playing field are deep. They are grounded in overconformity to the sport ethic, processes of commercialization, and definitions of *masculinity*. Therefore, many of the men who control and play power and performance sports resist efforts to control violence. They have come to think that their identities depend on approving of and doing violence and that competitive success in sports depends on the use of strategic violence.

Brutal body contact is the most difficult type of violence to control. It is grounded in the culture of power and performance sports and dominant gender ideology. Unfortunately, about 90 percent of the serious injuries in power and performance sports occur *within the rules* of those sports. This means that many men pay the price for their destructive definitions of *sports* and *masculinity*.

Efforts to control brutal body contact require changes in certain sports cultures and gender ideology. This requires relentless strategies that call attention to the dangers and absurdity of the actions and the language that men and women use to reproduce violent sport cultures and the gender ideology that supports them. People should demand and keep accurate records and publish information on injuries on a team-by-team, league-by-league, and sport-by-sport basis. Parents should be informed of these rates before they enlist their children in the service of reproducing patriarchy and a gender ideology that jeopardizes health and development. People should also calculate the cost of injuries due to brutal body contact and other types of violence in terms of medical expenses, lost work time and wages, days missed in college classes, disability payments, family problems, and even loss in life expectancy. This will help us understand better the connections between sport participation and health.

It is less difficult to control borderline, quasi-criminal, and criminal violence in sports, although many people continue to resist taking necessary actions. Enforcers (players hired explicitly for their ability to do violence on the field) should be eliminated by suspending them without pay, prohibiting teams from replacing suspended players, and fining coaches and team owners for the violence of their players. Unless these or similar actions are taken, owners will simply replace one headhunting enforcer with another. When team owners and league officials think that violence boosts their profits, they have little incentive to control it unless they lose money when their

Controlling brutal body contact and certain forms of borderline violence is difficult. In basketball, for example, there is a fine line between a "hard foul," as encouraged by many coaches, and a flagrant or intentional foul, as defined by league rules. However, when enforced consistently, rules can limit some forms of violence. (*Source:* Chuck Burton, AP/Wide World Photos)

players cross the line. Suspensions prevent players from doing what they love to do, and if they cannot be replaced on rosters, the suspensions also hurt coaches and team owners, who have some of the power needed to discourage violence on the field.

VIOLENCE OFF THE FIELD

When athletes in contact sports are arrested for violent crimes, many people assume that their violence off the field is related to the violent strategies they have learned to use on the field.

For example, *New York Times* columnist Robert Lipsyte says,

> Felony arrests among pro and college [male] athletes may or may not be rising, but better reporting makes it clear that many of them cannot turn off their aggressive behavior at the buzzer. (1999, p. 11)

Jessie Armstead, a linebacker in the NFL, says making the transition from a violent playing field to life off the field is not easy for many players:

> When you think about it, it is a strange thing that we do. During a game we want to kill each other. Then we're told to shake hands and drive home safely. Then a week later we try to kill each other again. (in Freeman, 1998, p. 1)

John Niland, a former NFL player, supports this:

> Any athlete who thinks he can be as violent as you can be playing football, and leave it all on the field, is kidding himself. (Falk, 1995, p. 12)

These quotes suggest that the violence used strategically on the field carries over into athletes' lives off the field. However, research on the carry-over issue is difficult to do, and good studies are rare. When people refer to statistical correlations that show a relationship between playing certain sports and high rates of off-the-field violence, it does not prove that playing violent sports causes people to be violent outside of sports. There are other issues that must be considered before we can talk about causality.

First, the people who choose to play sports that involve violent actions may already be inclined to use violence in their lives, either to establish status or cope with problems. Playing violent sports doesn't make them violent as much as it attracts them because they already feel comfortable about doing violence. *Second*, off-the-field violence among athletes may be due to unique situational factors encountered by some athletes. For example, athletes with reputations as tough players may be encouraged by others to be tough on the streets. Others may even challenge them to fight

because of their reputations in sports. This sometimes occurs when athletes who grew up in neighborhoods with high crime rates return home and find that they have been identified as "marks" by locals who push drugs or run scams to make money. If athletes hang out in those neighborhoods, they may also attract locals who define them as "sellouts" to big money and corporate sponsors. Some of these locals would like nothing better than to take the athletes down a notch or two. If trouble occurs and an athlete is arrested for fighting in these circumstances, it is not accurate to say that their actions were caused by what they learned in sports.

Some evidence suggests that male athletes with many years of experience in power and performance sports are more likely than recreational athletes or people who don't play sports to approve of off-the-field violence and to use violence when they play other sports (Bloom and Smith, 1996). Such evidence is useful, but it does not indicate if violence in a certain sport is the cause or the effect of violence that occurs in other spheres of the players' lives.

Assaults and Sexual Assaults by Athletes

Highly publicized cases of assault, sexual assault, rape, gang rape, and even murder that involve athletes who play power and performance sports have led many people to think that the violence in those sports carries over to personal relationships off the field, especially relationships with women. Athletes are public figures and celebrities, so when they are accused, charged, arrested, or tried, people hear and read about it time and time again—as was the case with sexual assault charges filed against NBA player Kobe Bryant. Although people have studied arrest rates and other aspects of particular reported incidents, there is little information on what athletes do compared to similar groups of young men or women who are not high-profile athletes (Benedict, 1997, 1998, 2004; Lefkowitz, 1997; Robinson, 1998). Research on the conversations and biographies of athletes

Do athletes perpetrate sexual assaults at a higher rate than other men? It's difficult to answer this question because victims may not report assaults, prosecutors may not file charges, "settlements" may be reached before criminal prosecution, and verdicts may be debated after trials have been held. Asking this question, as in the case of sexual assault charged filed against Kobe Bryant, often distracts attention from the fact that violence against women is a serious social and cultural problem in the United States, not simply a sport problem. (*Source:* Andy Cross, AP/Wide World Photos)

has presented important information suggesting that the social worlds created around men's power and performance sports subvert respect for women and promote the image of women as "game" to be pursued and conquered (Curry, 1991, 1996, 1998; Lefkowitz, 1997; Messner and Stevens, 2002; Nack and Munson, 1995; Reid, 1997). However, as noted in chapter 6, data on the arrest records of NFL players do not support the carryover hypothesis (Blumstein and Benedict, 1999).

How do we make sense of these seemingly contradictory pieces of information? In a critical

assessment of the debate about male athletes' violence against women, sport sociologist Todd Crosset (1999) reviewed all the published research on the issue. His review indicated that male intercollegiate athletes, in particular, seem to be involved in more sexual assaults than other male students, but the differences are not statistically significant in any study and differences often are related to other factors, which makes the data difficult to interpret. Crosset explains that when people conclude that the hypermasculine world of men's power and performance sports causes male athletes to engage in violence against women, they overlook important cultural and ideological issues related to sexual assault and distract attention away from the following important points:

- Violence against women occurs regularly and is a serious problem.
- Some male athletes have perpetrated sexual assault and rape, but nearly all violence directed against women is perpetrated by heterosexual men who are not currently playing competitive sports.
- We must understand the problem of violence against women within the context of U.S. culture and the forms of gender relations that exist in sports and other spheres of society if we wish to significantly cut the rates of sexual assault and rape.

Building on the framework developed by Crosset and combining it with other research on patterns of violence in all-male groups, I hypothesize that a combination of the following factors accounts for male athletes' violence against women:

1. Support from teammates and fellow athletes for the use of violence as a strategy for being a "man" and controlling women in their lives
2. Perceived cultural support for using physical domination to establish an identity as a man and an athlete and enhance one's status among certain male peers
3. Social bonds created among athletes who engage in deviant overconformity to the norms of the sport ethic, strong feelings that people outside sports cannot understand athletes or their experiences in sports, and a strong sense of hubris (pride-driven arrogance) among some elite athletes
4. Collective hubris among team members who believe that people outside the fraternity of elite athletes do not deserve respect, that outsiders should defer to the wishes of elite athletes, and that elite athletes live outside the norms of the general community

5. The taken-for-granted belief among athletes that women, apart from their own mothers and sisters, are celebrity-obsessed "groupies" who can be exploited for sexual pleasure without consequences
6. Institutional (team, athletic department, university, community) support for elite athletes, regardless of their actions
7. Institutional failure to hold elite athletes accountable when they violate community norms and rules

Research is needed on the relevance of these factors in an overall theory of assault and sexual assault perpetrated by male athletes. It appears that assaults perpetrated by athletes are most commonly directed toward women, gay men, and "cocky straight" men in the community who publicly challenge an athlete's assumed status and privilege. These are people who have characteristics directly opposed to the athletes' definitions of their own worth as athletes and as men. It may be true that rates of certain forms of violence are higher among athletes than others, but we need research to help us understand violence *in the full social and cultural contexts in which it occurs*.

As noted in chapter 6, the norms and group dynamics in certain all-male sport groups encourage athletes to demean and humiliate those who don't come close to matching what they see as their own unique, elite status. In other words, off-the-field violence is not simply on-the-field violence that carries over to the rest of life. Instead, it is action grounded in complex social processes related to the social worlds in which athletes live, define their identities, and deal with their social relationships. As athletes are increasingly being separated from the rest of the community, these processes become more important, if we wish to explain assault rates among athletes. The fact that elite athletes today are more separate from the rest of the community (on campus and in town) than ever before is an important issue. Until this separation is institutionally bridged or eliminated, assaults will continue to be a problem.

When discussing this issue, it is important to remember that even if studies indicated that male athletes had higher sexual assault rates than other categories of people, this would not change the fact that "nonathletes" perpetrate nearly all violence, including violence against women. Jackson Katz, a violence prevention expert, explains that it would be useful to explain why some male athletes assault women, but this is only part of what we need to know when trying to answer the main question of why "stockbrokers, teachers, priests, auto mechanics, and Ivy League students also commit rape" (Katz, 2003). People from all racial and ethnic groups, social classes, and occupational groups perpetrate violence. But one thing is apparent: Men commit nearly all rapes.

Finally, the focus on athletes should not distract attention away from other sport-related assault issues. For example, sexual assaults, including statutory rape, by coaches have a greater impact in sports and on people's lives than sexual assaults by athletes (Brackenridge, 2001; Brackenridge and Fasting, 2003; Fasting et al., 2004). In a series of articles, the *Seattle Times* (2003) reported that 159 coaches in the state of Washington (where only 2 percent of the U.S. population lives) were fired or reprimanded for sexual offenses between 1993 and 2003. These ranged from harassment to rape, nearly all involved heterosexual male coaches victimizing girls, and nearly 60 percent of these coaches continued to coach or teach after the misconduct was known. Research by journalists showed that even though official sanctions were given in 159 cases, most reports of misconduct were neither investigated by school authorities nor reported to the police. Even when coaches admitted misconduct, the incidents were kept secret if they agreed to leave their jobs. Cases in private sport clubs are especially problematic because clubs have no regulation or oversight, and most parents trust coaches even when they are suspicious of misconduct (Willmsen and O'Hagan, 2003). Overall, the issues of assault and sexual assault go far beyond the realm of sport. They are part of a larger issue in many societies, especially in the United States where rates of violence in general and rape in particular are high compared to similar nations.

Control Versus Carryover

Is it possible that athletes learn things in sports that help them control violent actions off the field? Does sport participation teach people to control violent responses in the face of adversity, stress, defeat, hardship, and pain?

This possibility was explored in research that found a decrease in aggressive tendencies among male juvenile delinquents who received training in the philosophy and techniques of tae kwon do (Trulson, 1986; summarized in chapter 6). The philosophy emphasized respect for self and others, confidence, physical fitness, self-control, honor, patience, and responsibility. Similar young men who received martial arts training *without* the philosophy actually measured higher on aggressive tendencies after a training period, and young men who participated in running, basketball, and football with standard adult supervision didn't change at all in terms of their aggressive tendencies.

French sociologist Loïc Wacquant studied these issues for three years as he trained and "hung out" at a traditional, highly structured, and reputable boxing gym in a Chicago neighborhood. During that time, he observed, interviewed, and documented the experiences and lives of more than fifty men who trained as professional boxers at the gym. He not only learned the craft of boxing but also became immersed in the social world in which the boxers trained. He found that the social world formed around this gym was one in which the boxers learned to value their craft and to become dedicated to the idea of being a professional boxer; they also learned to respect their fellow boxers and to accept the rules of sportsmanship that governed boxing as a profession. In a low-income neighborhood where poverty and hopelessness promoted intimidation and violence all around them, these boxers accepted taboos against fighting outside the ring, they avoided street fights, and they internalized the controls necessary to follow a highly disciplined daily training schedule.

When Wacquant (1995a) asked the boxers about the connection between boxing and violence, the responses he heard challenged popular beliefs. Two of those responses are as follows:

> Boxin' doesn't jus' teach you violence. I think, boxin' teaches you discipline an' self-respect an' it's also teachin' you how to defen' yourself. . . . Anybody who feels that it teaches you violence is a person tha's really a, a *real incompetent mind* I think. (Twenty-four-year-old night security guard who trained at the gym for eight years, pp. 494–95)

> Man, the sports commentators an' the writers and stuff, they don't know nuthin' abou' the boxin' game. *They ignorant.* I be embarrassed to let somebody hear me say [chuckles in disbelief], "Boxing teach you violence." . . . Tha's showin' *their* ignorance. For one thin', they lookin' at it from a spectator point of view . . . on the *outsi' lookin' in,* but [the boxer's] *insi' lookin out.* (Twenty-eight year-old part-time janitor, seven years in the ring, p. 489)

These statements are not meant to support professional boxing. However, the boxers' statements, along with other findings in the studies by Trulson and Wacquant, suggest that participation in sports, even martial arts and boxing, can teach people to control violence. Of course, this depends greatly on the conditions under which sport participation occurs. *If* the social world formed around a sport promotes a mind-set and norms emphasizing nonviolence, self-control, respect for self and others, physical fitness, patience, responsibility, and humility (the opposite of hubris), then athletes *may* learn to control violent behavior off the field. Those most likely to benefit seem to be young men who lack structured challenges and firm guidance as they navigate their way through lives where there are many incentives to engage in violence.

Unfortunately, many sports are not organized around these norms. Instead, most sport cultures emphasize hostility, physical domination, and a

Some sports, even at the youth level, use symbols and language that encourage orientations supportive of violence. Coaches award skull-and-crossbones decals, as shown on this player's helmet, to players who make "big hits" and intimidate the opposition. (*Source:* Jay Coakley)

willingness to use one's body as a weapon. They are also organized to produce hubris, separate athletes from the community, and encourage athletes to think that others do not deserve their respect.

More studies are needed to understand the social worlds of athletes in particular sports; the meanings that athletes attach to their actions; and the place of violence in sport cultures. Similarly, we need to know more about issues of identity, group dynamics among athletes, ideological issues, and social factors associated with the incidence of violence. The aggression and violence learned in certain sports do not inevitably carry over to

reflect on
SPORTS

Violence on the Field
Does It Distort Our Ideas About Gender?

"Men are naturally superior to women": This is a contentious statement today. However, many people still believe it, mostly because the hierarchical structure of gender relations depends on the extent to which people in a society accept it as true.

The ideology of male superiority represented by boxers, football players, and other men in heavy-contact sports links them and their sports to millions of other men around the world (Burstyn, 1999). Violence in sports reaffirms beliefs that there should be hierarchical distinctions between men and women and people of different social classes.

Power and performance sports emphasize *difference* in terms of physical strength, they emphasize *control* through the domination of others, and they emphasize *status* as dependent on victories over others. This serves to "naturalize" hierarchical differences and reaffirm the belief that power differences are inevitable and that success depends on one's rank compared to others. These beliefs are perpetuated through the stories that people tell about power and performance sports and the way that victories and championships have been won by using strength and strategy to overcome or dominate others, often using violence in the process (Burstyn, 1999).

The ideology formed around these beliefs is so important in U.S. culture that male boxers are paid up to $50 million dollars for three to thirty-six minutes of brutalizing one another. Heavyweight boxers are paid more than any other athletes in the world because they promote the idea that one-on-one violent confrontations are "nature in action" and that only the strongest and most violent survive (although they often lose millions of brain cells in the process).

Boxing and other power and performance sports celebrate, among other things, the use of strength and violence in a quest for victory over others. At the same time, they reproduce an ideology of masculinity stressing the same factors.

The irony in this approach is that, if gender were really based exclusively in biology and nature, there would be no need for sports to reaffirm the importance of gender in people's lives. Gender would be something that "just comes naturally," even without painting our children's bedrooms different colors and spending so much time and effort making sure that they are taught about gender differences. If differences are natural, why is there a need to reinforce them through socialization and laws? The answer is that the actions and orientations of males and females don't

other relationships and settings, nor does sport participation automatically teach people to control violence. Instead of looking for examples of carryover or control, perhaps we should look for cultural connections between sports and ideologies associated with high rates of violence. This is discussed in the box "Violence on the Field."

VIOLENCE AMONG SPECTATORS

Do sports incite violence among spectators? This is an important question because sports capture widespread public attention around the

world and spectators number in the billions. To answer this question, it is necessary to distinguish between watching sports on television and attending events in person, to understand the emotional dynamics of identifying with teams and athletes, and to know how spectators use sports to give meaning to people and places.

Violence Among Television Viewers

Most sport watching occurs in front of the television. Television viewers may be emotionally expressive during games and matches. They may even get angry, but we know little about whether come naturally. This is why power and performance sports are favored by people whose privilege depends on maintaining a gender ideology that emphasizes sex differences.

Sociologist Michael Messner discovered this when he asked a thirty-two-year-old man in a professional job what he thought about the recent promotion of a woman to a high position in his organization. The man replied with these words:

> A woman can do the same job I do—maybe even be my boss. But I'll be *damned* if she can go out on the [football] field and take a hit from Ronnie Lott. (1992, p. 168; Lott was a football player with a reputation for hitting others very hard)

Messner noted that, even though this man could not "take a hit" from Lott either, he identified with Lott as a man and used that identification to claim that men are superior to women because they have "superior" ability to do violence.

Some men celebrate sports in which violence and aggression are common because these sports reaffirm a gender order in which men are privileged over women. These often are the same people who reject rules against fighting. For example, when rules were passed to partially limit fighting in hockey, Tie Domi,

a player with a reputation for being violent, complained: "If you take out fighting, what comes next? Do we eliminate checking? Pretty soon, we will all be out there in dresses and skirts" (Domi, 1992, p. C3). Domi's point was that, unless men can do violence in hockey, there will be nothing that makes them different from women, and the perception is that nothing is worse for a man than being like women—except, perhaps, being gay.

What happens to gender ideology when women play power and performance sports and use violence on the field? On the one hand, this contradicts the ideological notion that women are frail and vulnerable. On the other hand, it reaffirms values and experiences that have worked to the disadvantage of many women. This is why many women feel that it is wise for them to avoid the emphasis on physical domination so characteristic in men's sports. Many women have learned that there are ways to be strong and assertive without being aggressive and violent.

The social impact of the ideology reproduced by sports goes far beyond the actions of athletes. It affects the cultural context in which we all live—sometimes in questionable ways. *What do you think?*

their anger is expressed through violence directed at friends and family members at home.

We also do not know much about violence among those who watch televised sports in more public settings such as bars and pubs. Most viewers are supportive of each other and restrict their emotional expressions to verbal comments. When they do express anger, they nearly always direct it at the players, coaches, referees, or commentators for the televised event rather than fellow viewers. Even when fellow viewers define outbursts of emotions as too loud or inappropriate, their efforts to settle a fan down are supportive rather than aggressive. When fans from opposing teams are in the same bar, there are usually other sources of mutual identification, which keep them from identifying each other as targets of aggression, and they tend to confine expressions of their differences to verbal comments.

Since the mid-1990s, there has been an increase in cases when people, usually men who have been watching sports in a bar or other public place, gather in crowds after the favored team wins a big game or championship. Predicting if and when celebratory violence will occur is difficult, but a combination of heavy alcohol consumption and the presence of television cameras are apparent factors that increase its likelihood.

This woman attends all the games of the New England Patriots. She displays a mask that infers violence, but what does it really mean? Does she condone violence on the field, violence as a basis for defining masculinity, the use of violence generally, or is she simply fitting in with a crowd that often cheers when brutal body contact and borderline violence occurs in NFL games? Determining the connection between sports and violence in society as a whole is difficult. (*Source:* Robert E. Klein, AP/Wide World Photos)

The belief that watching sports is associated with violence has led some people to wonder if watching sports—the Super Bowl, for example—leads to domestic violence in a community or the nation as a whole. During the 1990s, a journalist misleadingly reported that women's shelters filled on Super Bowl Sunday because of increased domestic violence on that day. Subsequent statements and research proved this wrong (Cohen 1994; Sachs and Chu, 2000), but the belief con-

tinues to persist. The anger caused by something in a televised sport event *could* be a factor in particular cases of domestic violence. However, violence in the home is a complex phenomenon, and to blame it on watching sports overlooks more important factors. Furthermore, we don't know enough about the ways that spectators integrate televised sport content into their lives to say that watching sports does anything in particular (Coakley, 1988–89; Crawford, 2004).

Violence at Sport Events

Spectators attending noncontact sport events seldom engage in violence. They may be emotionally expressive, but violence directed at fellow fans, players, coaches, referees, ushers, or police is rare. The attack and wounding of Monica Seles in 1993 stands out as one of the only violent incidents at a noncontact sport event, and that had more to do with celebrity stalking than with sports. Of course, there are occasions when fans use hostile words or engage in minor skirmishes when someone unintentionally drops a drink onto another person's head, but such cases of violence are usually controlled effectively by the fans themselves.

Spectators attending contact sports tend to be vocal and emotional, but most of them have not been involved in violent actions (see figure 7.3). However, crowd violence occurs with enough regularity and seriousness in certain sports to be defined as a problem for law enforcement and a social issue for which it would be helpful to have an explanation (Briggs, 2004; Upton, 2005; Young, 2002b; 2007b).

Historical Background   Media reports of violent actions at sport events around the world, especially at soccer matches in Europe and college football games in the United States, have increased our awareness of crowd violence. However, crowd violence is not new. Data documenting the actions of sport spectators through the ages are scarce, but research suggests that

FIGURE 7.3   We need research on so-called celebratory riots. Research on other forms of collective action suggests that celebratory riots may not be as spontaneous and unplanned as many people think.

spectator violence did occur in the past and much of it would make crowd violence today seem rare and tame by comparison (Dunning, 1999; Guttmann, 1986, 1998; Scheinin, 1994; Young, 2000).

Roman events during the first five centuries of the first Christian millennium contained especially brutal examples of crowd violence (Guttmann, 1986, 1998; 2004). Spectators during the medieval period were not much better, although levels of violence decreased in the late medieval period. With the emergence of modern sports, violence among sport spectators decreased further, but it remained common by today's standards. For example, a baseball game in 1900 was described by a journalist in this way:

> Thousands of gunslinging Chicago Cubs fans turned a Fourth of July doubleheader into a shoot-out at the OK Corral, endangering the lives of players and fellow spectators. Bullets sang, darted, and whizzed over players' heads as the rambunctious fans fired round after round whenever the Cubs scored against the gun-shy Philadelphia Phillies. The visiting team was so intimidated it lost both games . . . at Chicago's West Side Grounds. (Nash and Zullo, 1989, p. 133)

This newspaper account goes on to report that, when the Cubs scored six runs in the sixth inning of the first game, guns were fired around the stadium to the point that gun smoke made it difficult to see the field. When the Cubs tied the score in the ninth inning, fans again fired guns, and hundreds of them shot holes in the roof of the grandstand, causing splinters to fly onto their heads. As the game remained tied during three extra innings, fans pounded the seats with the butts of their guns and fired in unison every time the Phillies' pitcher began his windup to throw a pitch. It rattled him so much that the Cubs scored on a wild pitch. After the score, a vocal and heavily armed Cubs fan stood up and shouted, "Load! Load at will! Fire!" Fans around the stadium emptied the rest of their ammunition in a final explosive volley.

Between 1900 and the early 1940s, crowd violence was common: Bottles and other objects were thrown at players and umpires, and World Series games were disrupted by fans angered by umpires' calls or the actions of opposing players (Scheinin, 1994). Players feared being injured by spectators as much as they feared the "bean balls" thrown regularly at their heads by opposing pitchers. During the 1950s and 1960s, high school basketball and football games in some U.S. cities were sites for local youth gang wars. Gang members and a few students used chains, switchblade knives, brass knuckles, and tire irons to attack each other. During the late 1960s and early 1970s, some high school games in Chicago were closed to the public and played early on Saturday mornings because the regularly scheduled games had become occasions for crowd violence, much of it related to racial and ethnic tensions in the city.

These examples are not meant to minimize the existence or seriousness of crowd violence today. They are mentioned here to counter the argument that violence is a bigger problem today than in the past, that coercive tactics should be used to control unruly fans, and that there is a general decline of civility among fans and in society as a whole (Jayson, 2004; Saporito, 2004; Wolfe, 2005). Some spectators do act in obnoxious and violent ways today. They present law enforcement challenges and interfere with the enjoyment of other fans, but there is no systematic evidence that they are unprecedented threats to the social order or signs of the decline of civilization as we know it.

Celebratory Violence   Oddly enough, some of the most serious and destructive crowd violence occurs during the celebrations that follow victories in important games. Until recently, when middle-class, white college students tore down expensive goalposts after football victories or ransacked seats and threw seat pads and other objects on the field, it was treated as displays of youthful exuberance and loyalty to the university or community. However, in the wake of injuries and mounting property damage associated with these displays, local and university authorities have banned or limited alcohol sales in stadiums and arenas, and they now use police and security officials to prevent fans from rushing onto the playing field when games end. Cases of celebratory violence still occur, but new social control

methods have been reasonably successful in stopping them from happening *inside* the stadium.

Controlling celebratory violence is especially difficult when crowds gather in multiple locations throughout a city. Local police are usually prepared to anticipate celebratory crowds around the stadium, but effective control depends on specialized training, advance planning, and officers who can intervene without creating backlash in the crowd. Breakdowns are relatively common in the face of massive crowds and uncertainty about what might happen. For instance, when thousands of Boston Red Sox fans gathered to celebrate winning the World Series in October 2004, a Boston police officer carelessly shot a projectile filled with pepper spray at a crowd and hit a young woman in the eye. She died of head injuries caused by the impact. In most cases, however, deaths occur when crowds move suddenly and trample people or when people are pushed in the way of vehicles with drivers trying to escape the situation.

Sociologists have studied crowds and crowd dynamics, but scholars in the sociology of sport usually don't have the resources to study sport-related celebratory violence (see figure 7.4).

"Hey, watch it, pal! You stepped on my foot."

FIGURE 7.4   The language used by some spectators often refers to violence, but it is not known if such language actually incites violent actions.

However, if celebratory violence continues to occur at the current rate, there will be resources for law enforcement research. Furthermore, professional sport teams will develop strategies to defuse violence through announcements by highly visible players and respected coaches, bar owners will be asked to control drinking and contain the movement of their customers, and universities will attempt to control the binge drinking that accompanies most celebratory violence. The goal will be to facilitate the formation of norms that discourage violence in connection with celebrations.

Research and Theories About Crowd Violence

Researchers in the United States have done many studies of violence, but they have generally ignored violence at sport events. Apparently, this form of violence has not been seen as significant enough to attract research attention. The research that does exist has focused primarily on issues of race relations, and little attention has been given to other issues.

European scholars, especially those from Great Britain, have done most of the research on crowd violence, and their studies have focused almost exclusively on soccer and "soccer hooliganism." Studies grounded in social psychological theories have emphasized that displays of intimidation and aggression at soccer matches have involved ritual violence, consisting of fantasy-driven status posturing by young males who want to be defined as tough and manly (Marsh, 1982; Marsh and Campbell, 1982). These studies are interesting, and they describe classic examples of ritualistic aggression, but they have understated the serious and occasionally deadly violence perpetrated by soccer fans, especially during pre- and postgame activities.

Research inspired by various forms of conflict theory has emphasized that violence at soccer matches is an expression of the alienation of disenfranchised working-class men (Taylor, 1982a, 1982b, 1987). In addition to losing control over the conditions of their work lives, these men also feel that they have lost control of the recently commercialized clubs that sponsor elite soccer in England. This research helps us understand that certain forms of violence may be associated with class conflict in society, but it does not explain why violence at soccer matches has not increased proportionately in connection with the declining power of the working class in England.

Research inspired by interactionist and critical theories has emphasized a variety of factors, including the importance of understanding the history and dynamics of the working-class and youth subcultures in British society and how those subcultures have been influenced by the professionalization and commercialization of society as a whole and soccer in particular (Clarke, 1978; Critcher, 1979). However, the data presented in this research are not very strong, and more work is needed to develop critical analyses of crowd violence across various situations.

Much of the recent research on soccer violence has been based on figurational theory an explanatory framework that is grounded in a synthesis of approaches based on biology, psychology, sociology, and history. Much of this work, summarized by Dunning (1999), Dunning et al. (1988, 2002), and Young (2000), emphasizes that soccer hooliganism is grounded in long-term historical changes, which have affected working-class men, their relationships with each other and their families, and their definitions of community, violence, and masculinity. Taken together, these changes have created a context, or social figuration, in which soccer represents the collective turf and identity of people in local communities and the identity of the British people as a whole. Soccer then becomes a site for defending and/or asserting community and identity through violence. This research has provided valuable historical data and thoughtful analyses of the complex social processes of which soccer hooliganism is a part. It has also been used as a guide by those who have formulated recent policies of social control related to soccer crowds in England and around Europe.[1]

As the police have become more sophisticated in anticipating violence associated with soccer crowds, young men, some of whom may not be avid soccer fans, take it as a challenge to outsmart the police and create discord and violent confrontations with rival groups. Research indicates that current forms of hooliganism involve semiorganized confrontations that are strategically staged to avoid arrest. At the same time, the police play the role of umpire between groups and attempt to confine confrontations to spaces where they are prepared to deal with them and make arrests before serious injuries and property damage occur (Armstrong, 2006; Brown, 1998; Dunning et al., 2002; Giulianotti and Armstrong, 2002). Cell phones, handheld GPS devices, and other forms of communications technology used to formulate on-the-spot strategies and escape detection and arrest fuel this cat-and-mouse scenario. The police use similar technologies combined with surveillance cameras to contain violence. The dynamics associated with this form of violence are not related to sports to the same degree that so-called hooliganism was in the past. Today, soccer matches and tournaments are not the focus of those involved in the violence; instead, men simply use soccer matches as occasions for seeking excitement through violence.

General Factors Related to Violence at Sport Events

Crowd violence at sport events is a complex social phenomenon related to three factors:

1. The action in the sport event itself
2. The crowd dynamics and the situation in which the spectators watch the event
3. The historical, social, economic, and political contexts in which the event is planned and played

VIOLENCE AND ACTION IN THE EVENT   If spectators perceive players' actions on the field as violent, they are more likely to engage in violent acts during and after games (Smith, 1983). This point is important because spectators' perceptions often are influenced by the way in which events are promoted. If an event is hyped in terms of violent images, spectators are more likely to perceive violence during the event itself, and then they are more likely to be violent themselves. This leads some people to argue that promoters and the media have a responsibility to advertise events in terms of the action and drama expected, not the blood and violence.

Research by Daniel Wann and his colleagues (1999; 2001a, b; 2002; 2003; 2004) has shown that the perceptions and actions of spectators heavily depend on the extent to which they identify with teams and athletes. Highly identified fans are more likely than others to link their team's performance to their own emotions and identities. Although, by itself, this does not cause violence, it predisposes fans to take action if and when they have opportunities to do something that they think might help their team. This is important because teams and venues encourage fans to believe that they can motivate home team players and distract visiting team players. Although most fans restrict their "participation" to cheering, stomping, and waving objects, some fans and groups of fans systematically harass and taunt opposing players.

Taunts from fans are not new, but they have become increasingly obscene and personal in recent years. Players are expected to ignore taunts, but there are occasions when they have gone into the stands to attack an obnoxious fan. This has occurred more often in Latin America and Europe than in North America, but it appears to be increasing in the United States and Canada. In 2005 there was a highly publicized case when

---

[1]Theories of violence at soccer games in Europe are too complex to explain in this chapter. Those interested in this topic should consult the following: Armstrong, 1998, 2006; Brown, 1998; Dunning, 1999; Dunning et al., 1988, 2002; Giulianotti and Armstrong, 2002; Pilz, 1996; Weed, 2001.

When fans perceive violence on the field, they are more likely to be violent during and after games. Therefore, one of the most effective ways to control fan violence is to control the violence that occurs on the field of play. However, the belief that violence and the possibility of violence attract fans provides a commercial incentive to allow certain forms of violence to occur in professional sports. (*Source:* Tony Gutierrez, AP/Wide World Photos)

three NBA players on the Indiana Pacers fought with fans during a game with the Detroit Pistons after a fan hit a player with a cup of liquid and ice thrown from the stands. The cup was thrown following an incident of brutal body contact on the court. For a few moments, many people feared a major riot, but players, coaches, security officers, and fans intervened to prevent an escalation of violence. As a result, the three visiting players involved in the fight were suspended for a total of 128 games and forfeited about $11 million dollars of salary between them. Two of these players were charged with assault and battery, two players from the Pistons also were suspended for

multiple games, the Indiana Pacers paid to the NBA a fine of nearly $3 million, and two fans were charged with minor crimes and one had his season tickets revoked.

This incident created discussions nationwide in the United States. In sociological terms, it highlighted the need to manage player–fan relationships more carefully. This is a challenge under current circumstances. Fans pay high prices for tickets, they are encouraged to be emotionally involved in the action, they expect players to give them their money's worth, and they often detest what they perceive as arrogance displayed by highly paid players. To complicate matters, over

90 percent of fans are white, and over 75 percent of the players are black (in the NBA); this frames the expectations and perceptions of fans and the attitudes of players in potentially volatile racial terms. From the players' perspective, there is a strong sense of vulnerability when standing amidst 20,000 fans who could kill or main them in minutes if a mass brawl occurred. For example, a Pacers' player who was suspended for thirty games and lost $1.7 million in salary for coming to the aid of his teammate said this:

> I regret the incident . . . But I never regret helping my teammate. We shine together; we go down together. If my teammate feels threatened, I'm going to be there for him. . . . I protect my brother, my family. . . . Players understand [what I mean]. If you were a player, you would too. (in Le Batard, 2005d, p. 14)

This quote emphasizes the strong bonds between athletes who overconform to the norms of the sport ethic and these bonds lead athletes to protect each other if there are confrontations with fans.

Also important in the sport event are the calls made by the officials. Data suggest that when fans believe that a crucial goal or a victory has been "stolen" by an unfair or clearly incompetent decision made by a referee or an umpire, the likelihood of violence during and following the event increases (Murphy et al., 1990). This is why it is important to have competent officials at crucial games and matches and why it is important for them to control game events so that actions perceived as violent are held to a minimum.

The knowledge that fan aggression may be precipitated by a crucial call late in a close, important contest puts heavy responsibility on the officials' shoulders. For example, the brawl at the Detroit–Indiana NBA game occurred after a flagrant foul by a Detroit player. The officials had allowed players to continue the rough play that had characterized the game, even though there was less than a minute to play and the Pacers were winning by 15 points. Would the brawl have occurred if the officials had controlled the game differently in the final quarter? We don't know, but the question emphasizes that officials are important when it comes to controlling violence.

VIOLENCE, CROWD DYNAMICS, AND SITUATIONAL FACTORS   The characteristics of a crowd and the immediate situation associated with a sport event also influence patterns of action among spectators. Spectator violence is likely to vary with one or more of the following factors:

- Crowd size and the standing or seating patterns among spectators
- Composition of the crowd in terms of age, sex, social class, and racial/ethnic mix
- Importance and meaning of the event for spectators
- History of the relationship between the teams and among spectators
- Crowd-control strategies used at the event (police, attack dogs, surveillance cameras, or other security measures)
- Alcohol consumption by the spectators
- Location of the event (neutral site or home site of one of the opponents)
- Spectators' reasons for attending the event and what they want to happen at the event
- Importance of the team as a source of identity for spectators (class identity, ethnic or national identity, regional or local identity, club or gang identity)

We do not discuss each factor in detail, but the following comparison of two game situations illustrates how many of them might be related to spectator violence.

The *location of an event* is important because it influences who attends and how they travel. If the stadium is generally accessed by car, if spectators for the visiting team are limited due to travel distance and expense, and if tickets are costly, it is likely that people attending the game have a vested interest in maintaining order and avoiding violence. On the other hand, if large groups of people travel to the game in buses or trains and if tickets are relatively cheap and many of the spectators are young people more interested in creating a memorable experience than simply seeing a game, confrontations between people looking for exciting action increase, as does the possibility of violence. If groups of fans looking for excitement have consumed large amounts of alcohol, the possibility of violence increases greatly.

If spectators are respected and treated as paying guests rather than bodies to be controlled and if stadium norms emphasize service as opposed to social control, people are less likely to engage in defensive and confrontational actions, which could lead to violence. If the stadium or arena is crowded and if the crowd itself is composed mostly of young men rather than couples and families, there is a greater chance for confrontations and violence, especially if the event is seen as a special rivalry whose outcome has status implications for the schools, communities, or nations represented by the teams.

Spectator violence, when it does occur, takes many forms. There have been celebratory riots among the fans of the winning team, fights between fans of opposing teams, random property destruction carried out by fans of the losing team as they leave town, panics incited by a perceived threat unrelated to the contest itself, and planned confrontations between groups using the event as a convenient place to face off with each other as they seek to enhance their status and reputation or reaffirm their ethnic, political, class, national, local, or gang identities.

Whenever thousands of people gather together for an occasion intended to generate collective emotions and excitement, it is not surprising that crowd dynamics and circumstances influence the actions of individuals and groups. This is especially true at sport events where collective action is easily fueled by what social psychologists call *emotional contagion*. Under conditions of emotional contagion, norms are formed rapidly and may be followed in a nearly spontaneous manner by large numbers of people. Although this does not always lead to violence, it increases the possibility of potentially violent confrontations between groups of fans and between fans and agents of social control, such as the police.

VIOLENCE AND THE OVERALL CONTEXT IN WHICH EVENTS OCCUR   Sport events do not occur in social vacuums. When spectators attend events, they take with them the histories, issues, controversies, and ideologies of the communities and cultures in which they live. They may be racists who want to harass those they identify as targets for discrimination. They may come from ethnic neighborhoods and want to express and reaffirm their ethnicity or from particular nations and want to express their national identity. They may resent negative circumstances in their lives and want to express their bitterness. They may be members of groups or gangs in which status is gained partly through fighting. They may be powerless and alienated and looking for ways to be noticed and defined as socially important. They may be young men who believe that manhood is achieved through violence and domination over others. Or they may be living lives so devoid of significance and excitement that they want to create a memorable occasion they can discuss boastfully with friends for years to come. In other words, when thousands of spectators attend a sport event, their actions are grounded in factors far beyond the event and the stadium.

When tension and conflict are intense and widespread in a community or society, sport events may become sites for confrontations. For example, some of the worst spectator violence in the United States has been grounded in racial tensions aggravated by highly publicized rivalries between high schools whose students come from different racial or ethnic backgrounds (Guttmann, 1986). Where housing segregation has led to heavily segregated schools, the racial and ethnic conflicts within communities have contributed to confrontations before, during, and after games. Gangs, some of whose members have weapons, may stake out territories around a sport stadium so that sport events become scenes for displays of gang power. Similarly, when the "ultras," organized groups of fans prevalent in Italy during the 1990s, attended soccer games, they often used violence to express their loyalty to peers and the teams they followed (Roversi, 1994).

Finally, it must be noted that nearly all crowd violence involves men. This suggests that future research on this topic must consider the role of masculinity in crowd dynamics and the actions of particular segments of crowds (Hughson, 2000). Female fans generally do not tip over cars and set them on fire or throw chairs through windows during so-called celebratory riots. They may become involved in fights, but this is relatively rare. Crowd violence may be as much a gender issue as it is a racial or social class issue, and controlling it may involve changing notions of masculinity as much as hiring additional police to patrol the sidelines at the next game.

Controlling Crowd Violence Effective efforts to control spectator violence are based on an awareness of each of the three factors previously discussed. *First,* the fact that perceived violence on the field positively influences crowd violence indicates a need to control violence among players during events. If fans do not define the actions of players as violent, the likelihood of crowd violence decreases. Furthermore, fans' perceptions of violence are likely to decrease if events are not hyped as violent confrontations between hostile opponents.

Players and coaches could make public announcements that might defuse hostility and emphasize the skills of the athletes involved in the event. High-profile fans for each team could make similar announcements. The use of competent and professionally trained officials is also important. When officials maintain control of a game and make calls the spectators define as fair, they decrease the likelihood of spectator violence grounded in anger and perceived injustice. Referees also could meet with both teams before the event and explain the need to leave hostilities in the locker rooms. Team officials could organize pregame unity rituals involving an exchange of team symbols and displays of respect between opponents. These rituals could be given media coverage so that fans could see that athletes do not view opponents with hostility. These strategies conflict with media interests in hyping games as wars, so we are faced with a choice: the safety of fans and players versus media profits and gate receipts for team owners. Until now, media profits and gate receipts have been given priority.

Second, an awareness of crowd dynamics and the conditions that precipitate violence is critical. Preventive measures are important. The needs and rights of spectators must be known and respected. Crowd-control officials must be well trained so that they know how to intervene in potentially disruptive situations without creating defensive reactions and increasing the chances of violence. Alcohol consumption should be regulated realistically, as has been done in many facilities around the world. Facilities should be safe and organized, to enable spectators to move around while limiting contact between hostile fans of opposing teams. Exits should be accessible and clearly marked, and spectators should not be herded like animals before or after games. Encouraging attendance by families is important in lowering the incidence of violence.

Third, an awareness of the historical, social, economic, and political issues that often underlie crowd violence is also important. Restrictive

Fearing mass violence, this officer aims pepper spray at the fans, mostly males, who occupied the field after a major college football game. When fans are emotional and sometimes inebriated, the best strategy is to contain them and then disperse them in small groups in different directions. Using pepper spray may incite as many people as it subdues. (*Source:* Mark Hall, AP/Wide World Photos)

law-and-order responses to crowd violence may be temporarily effective, but they will not eliminate the underlying tensions and conflicts that often fuel violence. Policies dealing with oppressive forms of inequality, economic problems, unemployment, a lack of political representation, racism, and distorted definitions of *masculinity* in the community and in society as a whole are needed. These are the factors often at the root of tensions, conflicts, and violence. As noted in the box "Terrorism," dealing with the threat of political terrorism at sports events also requires an awareness of these factors on a global level. It may be that war is another factor that creates the tensions that precipitate sport-related violence.

Also needed are efforts to establish connections between teams and the communities in which they are located. These connections can defuse potentially dangerous feelings among groups of spectators or community residents. This does not mean that teams merely need better public relations. There must be *actual* connections between the teams (players) and the communities in which they exist. Effective forms of community service are helpful, and team owners must be visible

reflect on SPORTS

Terrorism
Planned Political Violence at Sport Events

The visibility of sport events and the concentration of many people in one place make sport venues a possible target of terrorist attacks. After the murderous attacks on the World Trade Center and the Pentagon on 9/11/01 and events that have followed, people in the United States have a heightened awareness of terrorism and its possible impact on their lives.

Since 9/11, those in charge of sport events have initiated security measures at arenas and stadiums. Spectators often are searched as they enter venues, and rules regulate what they may bring into events. However, most security changes take place behind the scenes in the form of bomb searches, electronic surveillance, and undercover tactics.

As sport teams and venues deal with security issues, their costs have increased between a few thousand dollars at smaller venues to well over $50,000 per event at larger venues. Furthermore, professional teams and some college teams face significant increases in the premiums that they pay for liability insurance. For example, an NFL stadium that was insured by a $250,000 annual premium prior to 9/11 now requires over $1 million in premiums for the same coverage (Hiestand, 2002). During the 2004 Summer Olympic Games in Athens, nearly $1.5 billion was spent on security.

Although the threat of political terrorism may be new in the minds of people in the United States, others around the world have lived for many years with the threat and reality of terrorism. Furthermore, terrorism has occurred in connection with sports in the past. For instance, during the early morning hours of September 5, 1972, members of a Palestinian terrorist group called Black September entered the Olympic Village in Munich, Germany. Dressed in athletic warm-up suits and carrying sport bags containing grenades and automatic weapons, they entered a bedroom that housed Israeli athletes participating in the Summer Olympic Games. They shot and killed a wrestling coach and a weightlifter and captured nine other Israeli athletes, one of whom was from the United States.

After a twenty-one-hour standoff and a poorly planned rescue attempt, seventeen people were dead—ten Israeli athletes and one coach, one West German police officer, and five terrorists. The remaining terrorists were sought out and killed by Israeli commandos. The Olympics were suspended for a day, but events resumed and the closing ceremonies occurred as planned. About $2 million had been spent on security during the Olympics in Munich; thirty-two years later Athens spent 750 times that amount.

Although the terrorism in Munich has been remembered by those responsible for planning subsequent Olympic Games, it has seldom been mentioned in the media coverage of subsequent Olympics. The reasons for overlooking this event are complex, but it is clear that many people do not want their favorite sport events disrupted or defined in connection with the nasty realities of everyday life, even though sports cannot be separated from the world in which they exist.

Because terrorism occurs regularly, it is useful to remember that sports cannot be separated from the policies, events, and material conditions of life that create deeply felt resentment and hatred around the world. This means it is in everyone's interest to learn more about the world and how peace might be achieved. This takes time and commitment on our part, and it won't be easy to change the conditions that precipitate terrorism. In the meantime, none of us can escape the threat of terrorism, not even at the sport events that we attend. *What do you think?*

supporters of community events and programs. Teams must develop programs to assist in the development of local neighborhoods, especially those around their home stadium or arena.

The goal of these guidelines is to create anti-violence norms among spectators and community residents. This is difficult but more effective than using metal detectors, moving games to remote locations, hiring hundreds of security personnel, patrolling the stands, using surveillance cameras, and scheduling games at times when crowds will be sparse. Of course, some of these tactics can be effective, but they destroy part of the enjoyment of spectator sports. Therefore, they are last resorts or temporary measures taken only to provide time to develop new spectator norms.

summary

DOES VIOLENCE IN SPORTS AFFECT OUR LIVES?

Violence is certainly not new to sports. Athletes through history have engaged in actions and used strategies that cause or have the potential to cause injuries to themselves and others. Furthermore, spectators through history have regularly engaged in violent actions before, during, and after sport events. However, as people see violence in sports as something that can be controlled, they deal with it as a problem in need of a solution.

Violence in sports ranges from brutal body contact and borderline violence to quasi-criminal and criminal acts. It is linked with deviant overconformity to the sport ethic, commercialization, and cultural definitions of *masculinity*. It has become institutionalized in most contact sports as a strategy for competitive success, even though it causes injuries and permanent physical impairments among athletes. The use of

enforcers is an example of institutionalized violence in sports.

Controlling on-the-field violence is difficult, especially in men's contact sports, because it is often tied to players' identities as athletes and as men. Male athletes in contact sports learn to use violence and intimidation as strategic tools, but it is not known if the strategies learned in sports are carried over to off-the-field relationships and situations. Among males, learning to use violence as a tool within a sport is frequently tied to the reaffirmation of a form of masculinity that emphasizes a willingness to risk personal safety and a desire to intimidate others. If the boys and men who participate in certain sports learn to perceive this orientation as natural or appropriate, then their participation in sports may contribute to off-the-field violence, including assault and sexual assault. However, such learning is not automatic, and men may, under certain circumstances, even learn to control anger and their expressions of violence as they play sports.

The most important impact of violence in sports may be its reaffirmation of a gender ideology that assumes the "natural superiority of men." This ideology is based on the belief that an ability to engage in violence is part of the essence and reality of being a man.

Female athletes in contact sports also engage in aggressive acts, but little is known about how those acts and the willingness to engage in them are linked to the gender identities of girls and women at different levels of competition. Many women seem to prefer an emphasis on supportive connections between teammates and opponents and regulation of the power and performance aspects of sports. Therefore, aggression and violence do not occur in women's sports as often or in connection with the same dynamics as they occur in men's sports.

Violence among spectators is influenced by violence on the field of play, crowd dynamics, the situation at the event itself, and the overall historical and cultural contexts in which spectators give meaning to their lives and the world around them. Isolated cases of violence are best controlled by improved crowd management, but chronic violence among spectators usually signals that something needs to be changed in the culture and organization of sports and/or the social, economic, and political structures of a community or society.

Terrorism in the form of planned, politically motivated violence at sport events is rare, but the threat of terrorism alters security policies and procedures at sport venues. The terrorist attack at the 1972 Olympic Games reminds us that global issues influence our lives, even when we attend our favorite sport events. Just as violence in sports affects our lives, the social conditions in the rest of our lives affect violence in sports.

See the OLC, www.mhhe.com/coakley9e, for an annotated list of readings related to this chapter. The OLC also contains a key concept list, a review test, and other helpful features.

WEBSITE RESOURCES

Note: Websites often change. The following URLs were current when this book was printed. Please check our website (www.mhhe.com/coakley9e) for updates and additions.

www.mhhe.com/coakley9e   Click on chapter 7 for information and critique of instinct theory and frustration-aggression theory as applied to violence in sports; discussion of cultural patterning theory and violence associated with sports.

http://www.un.org/sport2005/   The site for the U.N. International Year for Sport and Physical Education 2005; also a link to the Sport for Development and Peace report entitled, "Sport as a Tool for Development and Peace: Towards Achieving the United Nations Millennium Development Goals" (33 pages).

http://www.un.org/Depts/dhl/resguide/r58.htm Links to two U.N. resolutions: "Building a Peaceful and Better World Through Sport and the Olympic Ideal" (A/RES/58/6) and "Sport as a Means to Promote Education, Health, Development and Peace" (A/RES/58/5).

www.findarticles.com/p/search?tb=art&qt= Violence+in+sports+%2F+Analysis   Find Articles is a good site on many topics; this site lists dozens of articles from popular and academic sources, but it is up to the user to decide which ones are worthwhile because many are just polemical condemnations of violence, not analysis of why it happens and what might to done to control it.

www.answers.com/topic/violence-in-sports Encyclopedia-like information about violence in sports; good links to sites on specific topics.

http://encyclopedia.lockergnome.com/s/b/ Violence_in_sports   Similar to the preceding site.

www.sportinsociety.org/mvp.html   Mentors in Violence Prevention (MVP) is a gender violence prevention and education program based at Northeastern University's Center for the Study of Sport in Society; it enlists high school, collegiate, and professional athletes in the effort to prevent all forms of men's violence against women.

www.ed.gov/databases/ERIC_Digests/ed316547.html Summary of basic information about violence in sports; created by ERIC, the Educational Resources Information Center.

www.ncava.org   National Coalition Against Violent Athletes; news, statistics, updates, and information about prevention programs.

www.harassmentinsport.com   Sport Canada sponsors this site, which provides information and links to sites on sexual harassment in sports.

http://conventions.coe.int/Treaty/EN/ cadreprincipal.htm   The site for the Council of Europe; Document 120 contains the council's official position on "spectator violence and misbehavior at sports events and in particular at football matches."

www.noviolence.com   This site presents a campaign to curb fan violence in soccer stadiums; links to other useful sites, as well as information about the campaign.

www.footballhooligans.org.uk   Links and commentary discussing the myths and the reality of disruptive and violent actions in connection with soccer around the world, especially in Europe.

(Marc Piscotty, *Rocky Mountain News*)

GENDER AND SPORTS

Does Equity Require Ideological Changes?

EVERY GIRL SHOULD BE given the opportunity to participate in a sport she loves. The experience will teach her valuable lessons . . . and will give her confidence to strive for success in sport and life.

> —Julie Foudy, former captain of the U.S.
> National Soccer Team and president of the
> Women's Sports Foundation, 2002

I DON'T WANT to be seen as a woman golfer breaking barriers. I just want to do something different. I want to make people think.

> —Michelle Wie, professional golfer, 2005

 Online Learning Center Resources

Visit *Sports in Society*'s Online Learning Center (OLC) at **www.mhhe.com/coakley9e** for additional information and study material for this chapter, including

- Self-grading quizzes
- Learning objectives
- Related websites
- Additional readings

A complete outline is available online at
www.mhhe.com/coakley9e.

ALL MY LIFE, I believed that I couldn't show
weakness. I couldn't pull myself out if I was
hurt, I couldn't let people say, "She's just a
girl." . . . I had to be tougher [than men],
because only then did you get respect.

—**Lauren Arase, goalie for NCAA
soccer champions**

FEMALE GENETIC lottery winners become
supermodels. Male genetic lottery winners play
professional basketball.

—**Peter De Jonge, author of sports
books, 2003**

Gender and gender relations are central topics in the sociology of sport. It is important to explain why most sports around the world have been defined as men's activities, why half the world's population generally was excluded or discouraged from participating in many sports through history, and why there have been dramatic increases in women's participation since the mid-1970s. To explain these things we must understand the relationship between sports and widespread beliefs about masculinity, femininity, homosexuality, and heterosexuality.

Discussions and research on gender relations and sports usually focus on two interrelated issues. One is fairness and equity, and the other is ideology and power. *Fairness and equity issues* revolve around topics such as

- Sport participation patterns among girls and women.
- Gender inequities in participation opportunities, support for athletes, and jobs in coaching and administration.
- Strategies for achieving equal opportunities for girls and women.

Ideology and power issues revolve around topics such as

- The production and reproduction of gender ideology in connection with sports.
- The ways in which prevailing gender ideology constrains people's lives and subverts the achievement of gender equity.
- The cultural and structural changes required to achieve gender equity and democratic access to participation in sports.

The goal of this chapter is to discuss these two sets of issues and show that, even though many people deal with them separately, they go hand in hand in our lives. We cannot ignore either one if we define sports as important in the lives of human beings.

PARTICIPATION AND EQUITY ISSUES

The single most dramatic change in sports over the past two generations is the increase in participation among girls and women. This has occurred mostly in wealthy postindustrial nations, but there have been increases in some developing nations as well. Despite resistance against change, more girls and women now participate in sports than ever before.

Reasons for Increased Participation

Since the mid-1960s, five interrelated factors account for the dramatic increases in sport participation among girls and women:

1. New opportunities
2. Government legislation mandating equal rights
3. The global women's rights movement
4. The health and fitness movement
5. Increased media coverage of women in sports

New Opportunities   New participation opportunities account for most of the increased sports participation among girls and women over the past three decades. Prior to the mid-1970s, many girls and women did not play sports for one simple reason: Teams and programs did not exist. Young women today may not realize it, but the opportunities they enjoy in their schools and communities were not available to many of their mothers or any of their grandmothers. Teams and programs developed since the late 1970s have inspired and supported interests ignored in the past. Girls and women still do not receive an equal share of sport resources in most organizations and communities, but their increased participation clearly has been fueled by the development of new opportunities. Many of these opportunities owe their existence to some form of political pressure or government legislation.

Government Legislation Mandating Equal Rights   Although many people complain about government regulations, literally millions of girls and women would not be playing sports today if it were not for local and national legislation mandating equal rights. Policies and rules calling for gender equity exist today mostly because of persistent political action focused on raising legal issues and pressuring political representatives. Activist individuals and groups often have been feminists committed to achieving fairness in society. For example, the U.S. Congress passed Title IX of the Educational Amendments in 1972 only after years of lobbying by concerned citizens. Title IX declared that *no person in the United States shall, on the basis of sex, be excluded from participation in, be denied the benefits of, or be subjected to discrimination under any educational program or activity receiving federal financial assistance.* This law made sense to most people when it was applied to classes and courses, but when it was applied to sports it faced strong resistance.

The men who controlled athletic programs in high schools and colleges thought that sharing half of all sport resources with women was an outrageous and subversive idea, and they delayed the enforcement of Title IX for nearly seven years after it became law. Many men and some women claimed that equity was unfair because men would have to share the privilege and resources that they assumed belonged to them. This is discussed in the box "Title IX."

Governments in many nations now have laws and policies that support equal rights for girls and women in sports. Women around the world have formed the International Working Group on Women and Sport (the IWG; see www.iwg-gti.org) to promote the enforcement of these laws and policies and pressure resistant governments and international groups to pass equal rights legislation of their own. Political power in these nations and organizations rests in the hands of men, and they often think that if girls and women played sports it would disrupt their ways of life and violate important moral principles grounded in nature and/or their religious beliefs.

The women and men working to produce changes in these settings have had to be persistent and politically creative to achieve even minor improvements. Progress has been made in some nations, but at least half the women in the world today lack regular access to sport participation opportunities.

The Global Women's Rights Movement   The global women's movement over the past forty years has emphasized that females are enhanced as human beings when they develop their intellectual *and* physical abilities. This idea has encouraged women of all ages to pursue their interests in sports, and it has inspired new interests among those who, in the past, never would have thought of playing sports (Fasting, 1996).

The women's movement also has initiated and supported changes in the occupational and family roles of women. These changes have in turn provided more women the time and resources they need to play sports. As the goals of the women's movement have become more widely accepted and as male control over the lives and bodies of women has weakened, more women choose to play sports. More changes are needed, however, especially in poor nations and among low-income women in wealthy nations, but the choices now available to women are less restricted than they were a generation ago.

The global women's movement has fueled both national and international political action. Many politically influential women's sport organizations have emerged in connection with the women's movement. For example, the Women's Sport Foundation in the United States and similar organizations in other nations have become important lobbyists for change. The IWG emerged from a 1994 conference, which brought women delegates from eighty countries to Brighton, England, to discuss "women, sport, and the challenge of

The global women's rights movement has enabled some women to become world-class athletes. The skills of top female athletes are demonstrated clearly in major international events such as soccer's World Cup and the Olympic Games. (*Source:* Michael Caulfield, AP/Wide World Photos)

change." After three days of discussion and debate, the delegates unanimously passed a set of global gender equity principles now known as the "Brighton Declaration." This document, updated and reaffirmed at world conferences on women in sport in Windhoek, Namibia (1998), Montreal, Canada, (2002), and Kumamoto, Japan (2006), continues to be used by people as they pressure governments and sport organizations to create new opportunities for girls and women in sports.

Lobbying efforts by representatives from these and other organizations led to the inclusion of statements related to sports and physical education in the official Platform for Action of the United Nation's Fourth World Conference on Women, held in Beijing, China, in 1996. These statements called for new efforts to provide sport

AT YOUR *fingertips* For more information on the media coverage of women in sports, see pages 428–433.

and physical education opportunities to promote the education, health, and human rights of girls and women in countries around the world. What began as inspiration based in the women's movement has become a widely accepted global effort to promote and guarantee sport participation opportunities for girls and women. However, a Fifth World Conference on Women has not been scheduled yet because the goals of the 1996 conference are far from being achieved in 2006.

The Health and Fitness Movement Since the mid-1970s, research has made people more aware of the health benefits of physical activities (Sabo et al., 2004). This awareness has encouraged women to seek opportunities to exercise and play sports. Although much of the publicity associated with this movement has been influenced by traditional ideas about femininity and tied to the prevailing feminine ideal of being thin and sexually attractive to men, there also has been an emphasis on the *development of physical strength and competence.* Muscles have become increasingly accepted as desirable attributes for women of all ages. Traditional standards for body image remain, as illustrated by clothing fashions and marketing strategies associated with women's fitness, but many women have moved beyond those standards and focused on physical competence and the good feelings that go with it rather than trying to look like anorexic models in fashion magazines.

Many companies that produce sporting goods and apparel also have recognized that women can be serious athletes. They continue to sell apparel and equipment, but they now focus on function in their designs and marketing approaches. For example, they have produced ads that appeal to women who see sport participation and achievements as

symbols of independence and power. In the process, they have encouraged and supported sport participation among girls and women at the same time that they do the opposite in other ads (Wearden and Creedon, 2002).

Increased Media Coverage of Women in Sports
Even though women's sports are not covered as often or in the same detail as men's sports, girls and women now can see and read about the achievements of female athletes in a wider range of sports than ever before. This encourages girls and women by publicly legitimizing their participation (Heywood and Dworkin, 2003). This was evident in the United States after its national soccer team won the World Cup in 1999. The media images in the coverage of that event were very powerful and inspirational to girls and women. It was also evident when women in boxing and other contact sports saw the film *Million Dollar Baby* and felt encouraged by watching a woman boxer being taken seriously as an athlete and a human being (Blades, 2005; Cohen, 2005).

As girls grow up, media images help them envision possibilities for developing athletic skills. This is important because the media present so many other images and messages that emphasize versions of femininity that are inconsistent with playing sports and being identified as a serious athlete. For example, visions of being an athlete can be clouded by the *Sports Illustrated* swimsuit edition that evokes rave reviews from men when images of women connect thinness, vulnerability, and nonathletic bodies with sex appeal and heterosexual femininity. But despite mixed messages, media coverage of everything from professional women's basketball to synchronized swimming helps girls and young women conclude that sports are human activities, not male only activities.

Media companies, like their corporate counterparts that sell sporting goods, now realize that women make up half the world's population and therefore half the world's consumers. NBC, the company that televised the 1996 Olympic Games in Atlanta, experienced high ratings when it

Title IX
Can a Law Create Gender Equity?

Title IX is a U.S. law prohibiting gender discrimination in schools that receive federal funds through grants, scholarships, or other support for students. Passed in 1972, the law states that federal funds can be withdrawn from a school engaging in intentional gender discrimination in the provision of curriculum, counseling, academic support, or general educational opportunities; this includes interscholastic or varsity sports.

Title IX has benefited many girls and women, but it remains a controversial law among those who think that men should not give up previously unquestioned preferences that advantaged them and excluded women from sports for nearly a century. (*Source: Rudolpho Gonzalez, Rocky Mountain News*)

On the thirtieth anniversary of this law, a reporter asked tennis star Jennifer Caprioti what she thought of Title IX. Caprioti looked puzzled and said that she had never heard of it. This surprised many people because the law is responsible for the dramatic growth of sport participation opportunities for girls and women in the United States. But Caprioti, twenty-six years old in 2002, was born four years after Title IX passed. She grew up benefiting from the law without knowing that she owed much of her career to it.

BEFORE TITLE IX: PLAY DAYS AND CHEERLEADERS

Prior to 1972, sports were almost exclusively a "guy thing" in American schools. In 1971 there were 3.7 million boys and 295,000 girls playing varsity high school sports. For every 12.5 boys on teams, there was 1 girl on a team. Similarly, out of every dollar spent on high school teams, girls received 1 cent, and boys received 99 cents.

In colleges, 180,000 men and 32,000 women played on intercollegiate teams in 1971; 1 of every 10 male college students and 1 of every 100 female students played intercollegiate sports. Women's programs received only 1 percent of the athletic budget, even though the student fees of female students and the tax money of female workers were used to fund a sizable proportion of the intercollegiate athletic programs.

In the pre–Title IX era, most girls and women played sports only on annual "play days" when track and field events were scheduled for them. Of course, girls did have opportunities to be cheerleaders for the boys' and men's teams, and they could be in pep clubs and attend games as spectators. But very few had chances to play on teams like the ones provided for boys and men. If you know women older than fifty (in 2007), ask them to tell you about those days.

TITLE IX: A HISTORY OF RESISTANCE AND PROGRESS

In 1972 Congress decided to update the 1964 Civil Rights Act, which prohibited discrimination based on "race, color, religion, or national origin" in public education, public facilities, publicly funded programs, and private companies engaged in interstate commerce. Congress wanted to extend the law to prohibit gender discrimination in public education, so they passed the Education Amendments to the Civil Rights Act, and President Nixon signed it.

Title IX was a section of the Amendments that applied to educational opportunities in schools. Its purpose was to eliminate gender-based barriers to all programs defined as "educational." When Title IX was passed, it wasn't controversial. The women's movement and the civil rights movement were in full swing, and most people wanted their daughters to have the same educational opportunities as their sons. But, when people realized that Title IX could be applied to sport programs, sparks began to fly.

Gender equity sounded good in theory, but when the men who controlled and played interscholastic and intercollegiate sports realized that they would have to share their educational experiences with girls and women, many of them objected and claimed that Title IX was unfair to them. What was *equity*, the men wanted to know. Did the law mean that boys and men had to share the 99 percent of the athletic budget that they used for their programs? How much of the 99 percent would they have to share? Equity did not mean a 50-50 split, did it? Was it fair to make boys and men share if it meant giving up opportunities they had come to expect and define as "rightfully" and "naturally" theirs? Did it mean that girls and women should have the same number of sport teams that boys and men had? Should just as many girls and women be playing on varsity teams as boys and men? Such were the questions used to delay progress toward equity.

The men who controlled sports and organized them around their values and experiences saw equity as radical, subversive, disruptive, and potentially destructive. They said that they didn't know the legal meaning of *equity*, so the U.S. Department of Education's Office of Civil Rights (OCR) developed a clarification of Title IX. In the meantime, the NCAA tried to subvert the law because its executives knew that if they had to treat women as equals their control of all

sport resources would be jeopardized. Dividing budgets, teams, and scholarships by two was a mathematical challenge that they resisted.

After receiving nearly 10,000 comments, questions, and complaints about Title IX, the OCR published legal clarifications in 1975. Officials told high schools that they had one year to comply with the regulations, and universities were given three years to comply. But resistance to the law continued to grow as male athletes, coaches, and athletic directors complained that they did not know how the OCR would decide if equity existed in their programs. In response, the OCR in 1979 established three legal tests to assess compliance with Title IX. According to OCR enforcement guidelines, a school is in compliance with Title IX if it meets *any one* of the following three tests:

1. *Proportionality test.* Equity exists when a school has the same proportion of women playing sports as there are women enrolled as full time (undergraduate) students. Therefore, if women are 51 percent of students in the school, women should make up between 46 percent and 56 percent of varsity athletes.
2. *History of progress test.* Equity exists when a school has a history and continuing practice of expanding its sport programs for female athletes.
3. *Accommodation of interest test.* Equity exists when a school demonstrates that its sports program fully accommodates the interests female students and potential students (that is, younger students in the region).

This three-part test did not eliminate resistance to Title IX, but it gave women a legal basis for filing lawsuits against schools that did not provide equitable opportunities to play sports. This in turn led Title IX opponents to contact President Ronald Reagan, lobby Congress, and file suits to overturn the law. In 1984 one of those suits reached the U.S. Supreme Court. In a split decision, the justices ruled that Title IX applied *only* to programs that *directly* received money from the federal government and, because varsity sports did not directly receive federal funds, the law *did not* apply to

reflect on SPORTS

Title IX (*Continued*)
Can a Law Create Gender Equity?

them. Immediately, the OCR dropped its investigations of nearly 800 complaints against schools charged with violating Title IX.

Title IX was not enforced between 1984 and 1987. Then the U.S. Congress passed the Civil Rights Restoration Act in 1987. Among other things, this act declared that Congress intended Title IX to apply to sport programs because they were part of the overall educational programs at schools. President Reagan promptly vetoed the law, but Congress overrode Reagan's veto in 1988. In 1990 the OCR provided a more detailed guide that explained what *equity* meant in all aspects of athletic programs, such as scholarships, facilities, scheduling, coaching, and other forms of support for athletes, teams, and athletic programs.

In 1992 the Supreme Court ruled that a person could be awarded monetary damages if she (or he) proved that a school intentionally violated Title IX. This marked a major turning point because it meant that schools could be forced to pay damages if they lost a Title IX case. Prior to 1992, a school that violated Title IX could only be required to eliminate gender inequities in the future, without being financially liable for past discrimination. This limited the effectiveness of Title IX because no school had ever lost federal funds for violating the law; the OCR had always been more interested in fixing inequities than punishing schools. As of 2006, this record has not changed: *No school has ever lost a penny of federal money, even though the majority of them have been in violation of the law for more than thirty years!*

After 1992 Title IX was easier to enforce, and the law gained credibility among many Americans in 1994 when Congress passed the Equity in Athletics Disclosure Act. This act required any university with students receiving financial aid from the federal government to provide an annual report containing data on athletic participation, staffing, and budgets for all men's and women's sports. The purpose of this report was to enable prospective students to see the actual numbers related to equity in schools that they might choose to attend. These data, available online at http://ope.ed.gov/athletics/index.asp, have shined a bright light on universities and made their equity/inequity records public.

Since 1994 there has been slow progress toward gender equity in high schools and universities. Resistance to Title IX remains strong among people with vested interests in certain men's sports. For example, Brown University objected on legal grounds to the three-part test, but the legality of the test was upheld in a 1996 court decision. After the Brown case, the OCR clarified for the third time the meaning of the three-part test. In 1997 it clarified the ways that sexual harassment violated Title IX, and in 1998 it clarified the meaning of equity related to athletic scholarships. Resistance to Title IX hit another peak in 2001 after the election of George W. Bush. Some Bush supporters thought he would support a critical review of Title IX. They joined with others, including representatives of men's teams that had been cut from intercollegiate sport programs since 1981. They argued that Title IX created a system of "preferences" for girls and women and unfairly hurt men's sports in the process. Men had been hurt, they argued, because athletic departments cut men's teams to meet the proportionality test of Title IX. They said that men should not be forced to give up resources or opportunities to achieve gender equity.

In response to this argument, President Bush appointed his Secretary of Education to chair a fifteen-member Commission on Athletic Opportunity (CAO). The CAO was charged with determining if Title IX should be modified so that men would not be adversely affected by efforts to achieve equity. Members had heated discussions during their meetings, and the CAO report was controversial when it was released in 2003.

Advocates of girls' and women's sports criticized the report because the commission's recommendations

> **Parity in funding must be more than a goal. It must be a reality. That means more money for operating women's sports programs. . . . Justice often comes with a price tag.**
>
> —Donna Shalala, former U.S. Secretary of Health and Human Services, 2002

were confusing and contradictory. Opponents of Title IX were hopeful that the recommendations would protect all men's teams. As people debated the recommendations, Ted Leland, the athletic director at Stanford University and cochair of the commission said, "Let us remember, the commission is not the last word on Title IX. Rather, [it] is the first step in what will be a long process." What Leland forgot to say was that the process of achieving gender equity was already thirty years old in 2003, and that hundreds of steps had already been taken.

After the report was released, a U.S. district court judge ruled against the National Wrestling Coaches Association and their claim that Title IX created a gender-based quota system that forced schools to cut men's teams. The judge ruled that Title IX provided flexible guidelines for achieving equity, and it could not be blamed when men's teams were cut. Schools, he explained, cut teams for many reasons, such as budget constraints, liability costs, lack of specialized training spaces, and other factors unrelated to gender equity. In the wake of this decision and in the face of an upcoming presidential election in which parents of daughters who played sports would be voting, the Bush administration decided not to announce any changes in Title IX. However, people continued to debate the law.

In 2005 the Supreme Court heard a crucial Title IX case and ruled in a 5–4 split decision that a coach who was fired after reporting Title IX violations at his school has the right to sue the school and try to prove that he was fired for complaining of sex discrimination (www.pbs.org/newshour/bb/law/jan-june05/scotus_3-29.html). This decision was important because it protected "whistle-blowers" who identify inequities. However, a week before this decision, the U.S. Department of Education released a letter stating that with approval from the Bush administration it was changing its interpretation of Equity Test 3—the "accommodation of interest test." The new interpretation indicated that all schools are presumed to comply with this test if they conduct a web-based survey of students and do not find a pattern of unmet interests among female students or if a sport in which women express interest is not played by other schools in the area.

This move by the Bush administration angered Title IX advocates because it ignored the CAO report and required women to prove the existence of unmet interest to achieve equity. This, they argued, was a flawed methodology for many reasons: (1) Students don't take online surveys seriously, (2) women often don't express interests in sports in the same ways that men express their interests, (3) women interested in a sport would not enroll in a school that did not have the sport, (4) college teams recruit athletes for specific sports rather than waiting for them to show up and prove their interest, (5) men's teams have never depended on the results of "interest surveys," and (6) higher education is supposed to provide contexts in which students develop new interests and skills in addition to extending existing interests and skills. As I write this, it is difficult to know how this change in Title IX enforcement will affect progress toward gender equity. But it is likely that some schools will use it as a loophole to avoid dealing with inequities in affirmative ways, and a few others will use it to fully explore and nurture the sport participation interests of women.

THE SOCIOLOGY OF TITLE IX

As you read this, the story of Title IX continues. It tells us that the law can be a powerful tool for making changes in society. Between 1971 and 2004, for example, the number of girls playing varsity high school sports increased from 295,000 to about 2.95 million—a 1000 percent increase! Instead of 1 of every 27 high school girls playing on teams, now 1 in 3 play. The number of women playing on all intercollegiate teams (in four-year schools) has increased from 32,000 to about 160,000—more than a 500 percent increase! Today, over 5 percent of all women in college play intercollegiate sports. At the same time, there are over 4 million boys playing high school sports and 240,000 men playing in college (see chapter 14 for data on participation over time). Also important is that many of these boys and men have learned to see and respect women

Title IX (*Continued*)
Can a Law Create Gender Equity?

Although sexualized images of cheerleaders are presented in men's professional sports, many young women at the high school level view cheerleading as a sport in its own right. If cheerleaders were considered athletes, many schools would achieve gender equity. However, in some schools, such a change might reaffirm the very definitions of *femininity* that perpetuate inequities. (*Sources:* Mary Bowden [left]; Dennis Coakley [right])

targeted women during its 175 hours of coverage. Many men complained about this, but Olympic coverage since 1996 has continued this approach of covering female athletes and acknowledging female viewers.

Women's sports will continue to be covered in the media, and this will influence the images that all of us associate with women's sports and the achievements of female athletes. The most influential coverage occurs when female athletes demonstrate physical skills and present body images and forms of self presentation that push

traditional ideas and beliefs about the characteristics and potential of women on and off the field (Lafferty and McKay, 2004; Thomsen et al., 2004).

Reasons to Be Cautious When Predicting Future Participation Increases

Increases in the sport participation rates of girls and women have not come easily, and they will not be given up without a fight. They are the result of dedicated efforts by many individuals and groups. Progress has been remarkable, but gender as athletes—something that boys and men in 1971 seldom had a chance to learn.

The story of Title IX also demonstrates that laws do not exist in a social and cultural vacuum. All laws depend on popular support and a commitment to enforce them. When laws threaten vested interests, ideology, or deeply held principles, people will resist them, especially if they have the power to do so. This means that the histories of certain laws involve extended struggles over what people think is important and how they want to organize their lives. Developing consensus about these things is seldom easy.

The fact that laws, like sports, are social constructions means that they can be changed. When Title IX was passed in 1972, the time was right to make the case for gender equity in education. Many people were ready and eager to embrace it. But enforcement was bound to evoke resistance among those whose privilege was threatened. Sport programs have generally reaffirmed and reproduced male privilege, so it is not surprising that many men have strongly resisted gender equity in sports. Nor is it surprising that people continue to question Title IX.

Some people argue that inequities today exist only because girls and women are not as interested in sports as boys and men are. Others argue that more changes are needed and that differences in interest result from other inequities related to socialization, encouragement, and a general cultural devaluation of women's sports relative to men's sports. Young women, they say, are discouraged when they are told that they play like men if they excel in sports or if their programs are second class. Some people question the use of the proportionality test in universities because the ratio of female to male students has gone from 40:60 to nearly 60:40 over the last forty years, and this means that women should receive more than half of all resources and opportunities in sports. Some people say that if high school cheerleading were considered a sport, most schools could achieve equity. Others argue that cheerleading reaffirms traditional definitions of femininity and discourages the very cultural changes needed to build increased interest in sports among girls and women.

These and other issues are discussed throughout this book. However, sports continue to be "social places" organized in ways that privilege boys and men over girls and women. Therefore, struggles over Title IX will last long into the future. *What do you think?*

Note: Materials in this section are based on many sources; most of these are summarized in Suggs (2005) and Carpenter and Acosta (2005).

....

equity does not exist yet in many sport programs in most parts of the world. Furthermore, there are seven reasons to be cautious about the pace and extent of future sport participation increases:

1. Budget cuts and the privatization of sport programs
2. Resistance to government regulations
3. Backlash among people who resent changes that threaten dominant gender ideology
4. Underrepresentation of women in decision-making positions in sports
5. Continued emphasis on "cosmetic fitness"
6. Trivialization of women's sports
7. Homophobia and the threat of being labeled "lesbian"

Budget Cuts and the Privatization of Sport Programs Gender equity is often subverted by budget cuts. Compared with programs for boys and men, programs for girls and women often are vulnerable to cuts because they are less well established, they have less administrative and community support, and they have less revenue-generating potential. Overall, they often are seen as less important by many sponsoring organizations. As one woman observed, "It seems like the only time women's programs are treated equally is when cuts must be made."

Because sport programs for girls and women often are relatively new, they have start-up costs that long-standing and well-established programs for boys and men do not have. Therefore, "equal" budget cuts cause women's programs to fail at a faster pace than men's programs because they haven't developed institutional support or market presence. Many programs for boys and men are less vulnerable because they have had more than one hundred years to develop legitimacy, value, support, and an audience. Today, many of them can raise funds to sustain themselves, whereas many girls' and women's programs cannot.

As public tax-supported programs are cut, sport programs often become privatized. This has a negative impact on sport participation opportunities for girls and women, especially those in low-income households. Public programs are accountable to voters, and they are regulated by government rules related to equal rights and opportunities. Private programs are accountable to the needs of their dues-paying members, and this means that they are influenced by market forces more than commitments to equal rights and opportunities.

When free and affordable public programs are cut, people must buy sport participation from private providers. This is easy for females from well-to-do backgrounds: They just buy what they want and private providers seek their business. "Free-enterprise sports" are great for people with money. But they are not "free" for people on tight budgets nor are they "enterprising" in providing opportunities for women with low salaries and little discretionary money. Private programs serve only people who can buy what they sell. When money talks, poor people are seldom heard, and poor girls and women are silent. Therefore, future participation increases may be unevenly distributed among girls and

women, and those who lack resources may suffer participation setbacks in the future (Braddock et al., 2005; Sabo et al. 2004). Research also shows that when the quality of sport programs is poor, as often occurs when there is a lack of public funding, girls lose interest and don't take sport participation seriously (Cooky, 2004).

Setbacks have already occurred in some U.S. public schools as they cut sports, especially in low-income areas. In some schools where cuts have occurred, booster organizations provide funds and facilities for boys' sports, such as football, but they often ignore girls' sports (Wieberg, 2004a). They don't follow Title IX law because they are private organizations and receive no support from the federal government. Similarly, when the city of Los Angeles cut some of its public sport programs and let private organizations run sport programs in public parks, the new programs served four times as many boys as girls. The organizations claimed that boys wanted to play sports but girls did not, and state, county, and city programs are not covered by Title IX because they are not defined as "educational." Los Angeles struggled for over five years to deal fairly with this (in)equity dilemma, and in 2005 the California State Legislature passed a law requiring that all city and county sport programs be gender balanced. But California is the only state with such a law.

Resistance to Government Legislation   Those who benefit from the status quo often resist government legislation that mandates changes. This is certainly true in the case of Title IX as some people claim that it represents government interference in everyday life. They also say that if girls and women were really interested in sports, there would be opportunities for them and that laws interfere with a more basic and natural order related to gender and sports (Gavora, 2002; Knudson, 2005).

These people would like to turn back the clock, and they have influenced some political discussions about Title IX and the decisions about Title IX enforcement made in 2005 by the Bush administration. This resistance to government legislation has a long history in the United States, and it is not likely to go away.

Backlash Among People Who Resent Changes That Threaten Dominant Gender Ideology

When women play certain sports, they become strong. Strong women challenge the prevailing gender ideology that underlies the norms, legal definitions, and opportunity structures that frame the conditions under which men and women form identities, live their lives, and relate to each other. Those who are privileged by the prevailing gender ideology in society see strong women as a threat. They seek to discredit most women's sports and strong female athletes, and they call for a return to the "good ol' days," when men played sports and women watched and cheered.

A variation of backlash occurred in 2002 after Martha Burk, head of the National Council of Women's Organizations, which represents 6 million members and 160 organizations, wrote to Hootie Johnson, chairman of the Augusta National Golf Club. Burk asked Johnson to open the Augusta Club to women members. The all-male club is very prestigious. It hosts the annual Masters Golf Tournament, and its members receive public attention and have their status boosted by worldwide media coverage of the Masters event. Johnson used the following words to describe how he felt about Burk's request:

> We will not be bullied, threatened or intimidated. We do not intend to become a trophy in their display case. . . . There may well come a day when women will be invited to join our membership, but that timetable will be ours, and not at the point of a bayonet. (in Brennan, 2002 p. 3C)

Johnson strongly objected to any changes threatening a dominant gender ideology that supported the power and privilege of men. Therefore, he would not make concessions to a woman's organization by asking his club to abandon its male-only membership policy. Giving in to a request by women was ideologically intolerable for him,

and he and his peers succeeded in demonizing Burke by calling her a "radical feminist." The club continues its policy of gender exclusion, and the media have dropped the story.

Private clubs have the right to maintain policies of gender (or racial) exclusion, but Johnson's response was indicative of backlash by a powerful man against equity claims that challenged the male-dominated status quo (Nylund, 2003; S. Roberts, 2004). To the extent that other men in positions of power in sport organizations think this way, progress toward gender equity will be slowed.

Underrepresentation of Women in Decision-Making Positions in Sports

Despite increased sport participation among girls and women, women have suffered setbacks in the ranks of coaching and sport administration in women's programs. For example, in the years immediately following the passage of Title IX in the United States, there was a decline in the number and proportion of women head coaches and administrators (Acosta and Carpenter, 2004; Carpenter and Acosta, 2005; Parkhouse and Williams, 1986). As women's sports changed and became more important in high schools and colleges, men replaced female coaches and administrators.

Many men do a good job of coaching and administering women's sports, but unless girls and young women see women in decision-making positions in their programs, they will be reluctant to define sports and sport participation as important in their futures. If women are not visible leaders in sport programs, some people conclude that women's abilities and contributions in sports are less valued than men's. This conclusion certainly limits progress toward gender equity (Ligutom-Kimura, 1995).

Continued Emphasis on "Cosmetic Fitness"

There are competing images of female bodies in many cultures today. Girls and women receive confusing cultural messages that they should be "firm but shapely, fit but sexy, strong but thin"

(Markula, 1995). Although they see images of powerful female athletes, they cannot escape the images of fashion models whose bodies are shaped by food deprivation and multiple cosmetic surgeries. Girls and women also hear that physical power and competence are important, but they see disproportionate rewards going to women who look young, vulnerable, and nonathletic. They are advised to "get strong but lose weight." They learn that muscles are good but too many muscles are unfeminine. They are told that athletic women are attractive, but they see men attracted to professional cheerleaders and celebrity models with breast implants and airbrushed publicity photos. They also see attractive athletes, such as Russian tennis player Maria Sharapova "packaged and sold as the . . . giggly gal who just wants to have fun: Hillary Duff with a forehand" (Glock, 2005). Therefore, they may conclude that even if you're a good athlete, it is hot looks that bring fame. And they know that Anna Kornikova turned her looks, not her success in tennis, into fame, and they see that her fame has lasted far longer than her tennis skills would have lasted.

Despite cultural messages that promote athletic performance, they are outnumbered and outhyped by cultural messages promoting appearance and beauty (Hargreaves, 1994; Heywood and Dworkin, 2003). Effective commercial messages for everything from makeup to clothing are based on the well-established marketing assumption that insecurities about appearance promote consumption, whereas positive body image does not. Therefore, even many ads that show women doing sports are carefully staged to make women feel insecure rather than confident about their bodies.

A related cultural message is that being buff is in but only when it attracts men. For example, when the U.S. Women's Soccer team was described as "Babe City" by a popular U.S. TV talk-show host, it was clear that, underlying all the adulation of strong, physically competent women, there was the inference that men still

These Barbie dolls are a classic example of sport images mixed with the notion of cosmetic fitness. The beauty myth remains strong in popular ideas about femininity. Does Barbie reproduce those myths? (*Source:* Jay Coakley)

retain the prerogative to judge women by their appearance and assess women's bodies as objects of men's pleasure (A. Solomon, 2000). Even when Brandi Chastain pulled off her soccer shirt in spontaneous jubilation after scoring a shootout goal to win the 1999 World Cup and revealed a sport bra, people sexualized Chastain and her action—even though women have worn such bras for years as they've worked out, and male soccer players for decades have pulled off their shirts when celebrating goals. It was as if many people in 1999 did not have a frame of reference to see Chastain's gesture as a joyous celebration of achievement rather than a titillating striptease to please or shock everyone

(Caudwell, 2003; Chastain, 2004; Schultz, 2004; A. Solomon, 2000).

Messages about feminine and sexy bodies are so powerful that some women avoid sports until they are thin enough to look "right" and wear the "right" clothes; other girls and women combine participation with pathogenic weight-control strategies to become dangerously thin. Research shows that some female athletes use laxatives, diet pills, diuretics, self-induced vomiting, binges, and starvation diets in conjunction with their training (Beals, 2000; Hawes, 2001; Johns, 1997; Madison and Ruma, 2003; Wilmore, 1996). This increases the probability of injuries, jeopardizes health, and keeps alive the idea that women must conform to media-based beauty standards or be rejected by men and women who use those standards to evaluate females of all ages.

Although most female athletes do not develop eating disorders, they may choose sports and/or monitor their appearance and actions in light of the standards of cosmetic fitness. Overall, the tensions between cosmetic fitness and being strong and physically skilled create for many girls and women the challenge of negotiating the meanings they and others give to their bodies (Dworkin, 2001; Garrett, 2004; Heywood and Dworkin, 2003; Shakib, 2003; Wedgewood, 2004; Young, 1998). This challenge is especially daunting for female athletes with disabilities, as explained in "Breaking Barriers," page 248.

When the goal of playing sports is cosmetic fitness, women may define their participation as a means of achieving an unrealistic body image, burning calories so that they can eat without guilt, or punishing themselves when they've eaten too much (Krane et al., 2001). Additionally, young women seeking cosmetic fitness sometimes drop out of sports if they gain weight while they train, and others drop out after they achieve weight-loss goals. Overall, it appears that cultural messages

> **If I wanted to wear a bikini I would have chosen to play beach volleyball.**
> —Solveig Gulbrandsen, professional soccer player, Norway (in Christenson and Kelso, 2004)

about cosmetic fitness will interfere with future increases in sport participation.

Trivialization of Women's Sports "Okay. Women play sports, but they are not as good as men and people want to see the best." Statements like this assume that "real" sports involve "manly" things, such as intimidation, violence, and physical domination over others, and that women's sports are second rate. This orientation is widespread enough that it interferes with achieving gender equity in sports (Laurendeau, 2004; Vincent, 2004).

Power and performance sports are historically grounded in the values and experiences of men, and they use evaluative standards that disadvantage women. Women play football, but they don't hit as hard as men do. They play basketball, but they don't dunk. They play hockey, but they don't check or fight. They do sports, but they don't do them as men do them. Therefore, they don't do them well enough to receive equal support. A high school senior who played on his schools' basketball team expressed the foundation for this "gender logic": "Watching the girls' basketball team is like watching elementary-school kids trying to play. It's not exciting. I mean you watch them because it's your kids out there playing. But it's not exciting" (Shakib and Dunbar, 2002, p. 363).

An extension of this "logic" was used in 2004 by the president of FIFA, the world-governing body for soccer, when he told international women players that more spectators would watch them if they would wear tighter shorts (Christenson and Kelso, 2004). He assumed that the women's game was trivial, compared with the men's game, and using sex appeal would make it more fan friendly.

When enough people trivialize women's sports by dismissing competent female athletes or defining them primarily as sex objects, it is

Narrative Barriers
I Was Too Ashamed of My Body

Anna was born with underdeveloped arms and feet. Despite encouragement and support from a close friend, she resisted going to the gym and becoming involved in sports. She explained her resistance in the following way:

> I really wanted to go—inside, I was dying to be physical, to have a go at "pumping iron." . . . But at the time I just couldn't say yes. . . . I was too ashamed of my body. . . . It was the same thing with swimming. I just couldn't bear the thought of people looking at me. I felt *really* vulnerable. (in Hargreaves, 2000, p. 187)

Anna's fear of her body being seen and judged is not unique. Negotiating the meanings that we and others give to our bodies is a complex and challenging process. But in contemporary cultures it is more challenging for women than men and for people with disabilities than their able-bodied peers.

In cultures where femininity is tied to physical attractiveness and sexual desirability, the women who accept dominant gender ideology often make choices that interfere with sport participation. For example, a young woman with an amputated leg may choose a prosthesis that is more natural looking, rather than one that is more functional and better suited to sport participation. As one woman explained, "It's one thing to see a man with a Terminator leg. . . . It may inspire people to say, 'Cool.' But body image for women in this country is model thin and long sexy legs" (in Marriott, 2005). In agreement, Nick, a twenty-year-old college student who lost his legs after contracting a rare bacterial disease at summer camp when he was fourteen, says, "I love my Terminator legs," and he doesn't think twice about plugging them into the nearest electrical outlet when they run short on their charge.

Although Nick loves his "Terminator legs," negotiating the meaning given to one's body is more challenging for men with disabilities than for most able-bodied men. This is especially true when they accept a gender ideology that ties masculinity to power and the ability

to outperform or dominate others. For example, after filling his car with gas and putting his wheelchair in the back, Mark had trouble starting his car. A man who had just driven up behind him laid on his horn and shouted obscenities. Mark said that before the accident that paralyzed his legs "I would have got out of the car and . . . laid him out, but now I'm useless . . . This is why I say my manhood has been shattered" (in Sparkes and Smith, 2002, p. 269).

Although Mark did not use the same words that Anna used, he also felt vulnerable. When men with disabilities feel vulnerable, some may do what Anna did and avoid sport participation, whereas others may view sport as a site for asserting or reaffirming masculinity.

Sociologists Brett Smith and Andrew Sparkes (2002) point out that people create identities, including feminine and masculine identities, through narratives—that is, the stories that they show and tell others about themselves. Their research indicates that playing power and performance sports is a masculinizing narrative—a story in which manhood is constructed through physical accomplishments and dominance over other men. Such narratives are the foundation of dominant gender ideology.

When alternative or oppositional narratives are not available to women with disabilities, they often avoid sports because sports don't contain femininity narratives. Similarly, some men like Mark may avoid sports for fear that they will not be able to overpower other men. Therefore, males and females with disabilities would benefit if they had access to new, counternarratives that construct gender in less constraining terms (Thomas, 1999). When there are multiple ways to be a woman or a man, people with visible disabilities have more options for negotiating the meanings that they and others give to their bodies. Maybe this would enable Anna to become more physical and have a go at pumping iron. And maybe it would enable Mark to accept help and still feel like a man.

difficult to generate gate receipts and commercial sponsorships to sustain elite and professional programs. This is why the Women's United Soccer Association (WUSA) and other professional women's sports have not been successful. Even though most people know they should not say that a person "throws like a girl" when he or she doesn't throw well, many people continue to think that playing like women is by definition second rate. This form of trivializing women's sports and female athletes continues to interfere with achieving gender equity at all levels of sport.

Homophobia and the Threat of Being Labeled "Lesbian" **Homophobia** is *a generalized fear or intolerance of lesbians, gay men, and bisexual people* (Griffin, 1998). It is based on the notion that homosexuality is deviant or immoral, and it supports prejudice, discrimination, harassment, and violence directed toward those identified or believed to be homosexual or bisexual. Homophobia is a powerful cultural factor that has discouraged many girls and women from playing certain sports or making sports an important part of their lives.

Homophobia causes some parents to steer their daughters away from sports that they believe attract lesbians and away from teams or programs in which lesbians are believed to play or coach. Homophobia and public expressions of homophobic discourse influence and often limit the sport participation choices available to women (Dworkin, 2003; Howe, 2003; Veri, 1999). When women fear the label of *lesbian* or fear being associated with lesbians, they sometimes avoid certain sports, limit their commitment to sports, de-emphasize their athletic identities, or emphasize their heterosexuality. Closeted lesbians may fear the loss of secrecy so much that they limit their relationships with others and become lonely and isolated in the process (Bredemeier et al., 1999; Griffin, 1998; Lenskyj, 2003; Swoopes, 2005).

Heterosexual men may use homophobic discourse to tease female athletes and control all women who are intimidated by it. This occurs in some high schools and colleges, and it can cause women to become defensive and give sport participation a lower profile in their lives. Effectively challenging homophobic discourse and forcing others to confront their homophobia is a daunting task. Some people, gay and straight, are good at this, but most people lack the experience to do it effectively.

In the meantime, many female athletes go out of their way to emphasize traditional feminine attributes and even say in interviews that being an athlete is not nearly as important as eventually getting married, settling down, having children, and becoming a nurturing homemaker. Like athletes, people who market women's sports often avoid acknowledging lesbians for fear that it will decrease attendance among potential spectators who are homophobic. Players know this and often say that if a woman wants to make a team, she better grow her hair long and talk about wanting to be married and have children. As one international player said, it is well known that team officials "don't want a bunch of dykes representing our country" (Hall, 2002, p. 200).

Homophobia affects all women, lesbian and straight alike; it creates fears, it pressures women to conform to traditional gender roles, and it silences and makes invisible the lesbians who manage, coach, and play sports (Griffin, 1998; Hall, 2002; Lenskyj, 1999; Nelson, 1998).

Gender and Fairness Issues in Sports

Sport participation among girls and women will not continue to increase automatically. Without continued efforts to achieve gender equity, there is a tendency in most cultures to give priority to men's sports and male athletes. This is because sport worlds are usually organized to be the following:

1. *Male dominated* so that the characteristics of men are used as standards for judging qualifications

2. *Male identified* so that the orientations and actions of men are used as standards for defining what is right and normal

3. *Male centered* so that men and men's lives are the expected focus of attention in sport programs, stories, legends, and media coverage

Therefore, female athletes, coaches, officials, and administrators are considered qualified if they play or do their jobs "like a man." If a woman in sports does not think and act like a man, she is not likely to be defined as right or normal. And when people talk about athletes and sports in such a social world, it is assumed that they are talking about men and men's sports unless they specify otherwise—such as saying that they are talking about women's teams, women's records, the best female athletes, the Women's Final Four, the Women's World Cup, and so on.

The impact of social organization that is male dominated, male identified, and male centered is illustrated through a review of information on sport participation, support for athletes, and jobs for women in sports.

> It's unfortunate that [some golf clubs have policies that exclude women and minorities], but it's just the way it is.
> —Tiger Woods, professional golfer (in Dodd, 2002, p. 1C)

Participation Opportunities: Organized and Mainstream Sports Prior to the early 1970s, most people did not question the male-dominated/identified/centered organization of sports. They believed that females were naturally frail and unsuited for most sport participation. When girls and women were encouraged to be physically active, they were steered into figure skating, ice dancing, gymnastics, swimming, tennis, golf, and other sports that were assumed to not require strength, power, and speed—the traits associated with masculinity. Some girls and women ignored these assumptions and played sports involving strength, power, and speed—and they lived with the consequences, which often involved some form of social rejection. But overall, there were limited opportunities for girls and women to play sports.

Over the past fifty years, female athletes demonstrated clearly that notions of female frailty were grounded in ideology rather than nature. They expanded ideas about what girls and women could and should be encouraged to do in sports. Today, most people in the United States and many nations agree that women should have opportunities to play sports. But there continue to be disagreements about girls and women playing certain contact sports, playing certain sports with men, and having access to the same resources that men have.

These disagreements have perpetuated inequities in participation opportunities in many international sports. For example, there are still fewer sports for women than for men in the Olympics and other international events. Although important changes have occurred since the early 1980s, female athletes remain underrepresented in international competitions. The data in figure 8.1 and table 8.1 illustrate that women in the modern Summer Olympic Games have always had fewer events than men have had, and there have always been fewer women participants than men. The International Olympic Committee (IOC), which from 1894 to 1981 had no women members, did not approve a women's 1500-meter run until the 1972 Games in Munich. It was not until the 1984 Games in Los Angeles that women were allowed to run the marathon. Women waited until 1988 to run the Olympic 10,000-meter race and 1996 to run the 5000-meter race. But despite these changes, the French Minister of Sports observed at the start of this century that "women's involvement in sports [around the world] is characterized by deep inequalities."

Equity sometimes is difficult to achieve because of fundamentalist religious beliefs in certain cultures. For example, strict Islamic beliefs in certain nations forbid women from publicly exposing any surface of their bodies to the sight of men. Women in traditionally Catholic nations have not faced moral restrictions, but they've often lacked the power and resources to play sports traditionally played by men only. Women in traditional and poor societies often face barriers that preclude or discourage sport participation as well as limit the extent to which any woman could take sports seriously enough to train at an elite level. These barriers are both ideological and structural. In other words, they are related to (1) *webs of ideas and beliefs* about what is and isn't appropriate for girls and women to do (*gender ideology*) and (2) the organization of *opportunities* and the distribution of *resources* to take advantage of opportunities (*social structure*).

Opportunities to play professional sports always have been scarce for women. Until recently, many people did not believe that spectators would pay to watch women play anything but "ladylike" sports in which they competed alone (figure skating, golf) or with nets separating the opponents and preventing physical contact (tennis, volleyball). Norms in some countries began to change in the 1980s, but many people still doubted that spectators would pay to watch women play sports that went beyond the limits

AT YOUR *fingertips* For more information about gender equity related to participation, see pages 58–85 and 512, 515, and 518–521.

of dominant definitions of *femininity*. Although these limits have been pushed and broken, there remains "cultural encouragement" to highlight traditional notions of femininity. Therefore, many female athletes are still referred to as "ladies," and any recognition of the participation of lesbians is carefully erased in the media profiles of teams and leagues. The media emphasis is on heterosexual habits, lifestyles, and "looks"; children and husbands are made visible and discussed often. Homophobia continues to shape the public image of women's sports, and lesbians have been made invisible despite their strong presence in many sports. Opportunities for women at the professional level will continue to be limited until ideas and beliefs about femininity expand to embrace multiple notions of womanhood.

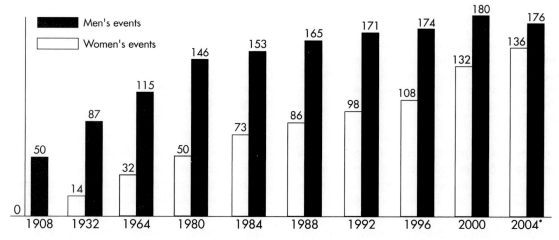

*Twelve events in 2004 were mixed, or open to both men and women. These twelve have been added to both totals for men and women. This procedure of adding mixed events to the total events for women and men was also used for each of the other Olympics in this graph.

FIGURE 8.1 Number of Summer Olympic events open to women and to men, 1908–2004

Table 8.1   Male and female athletes in the modern Summer Olympic Games, 1896–2000

Year	Place	Countries Represented	Male Athletes	Female Athletes	Percent Female
1896	Athens	14	241	0	0.0
1900	Paris	24	975	22	2.2
1904	St. Louis	12	645	6	0.9
1908	London	22	1971	7	1.8
1912	Stockholm	28	2359	48	2.0
1916	Olympics scheduled for Berlin canceled (World War I)				
1920	Antwerp	29	2561	65	2.5
1924	Paris	44	2954	135	4.4
1928	Amsterdam	46	2606	277	9.6
1932	Los Angeles	37	1206	126	9.5
1936	Berlin	49	3632	331	8.4
1940	Olympics scheduled for Tokyo canceled (World War II)				
1944	Olympics canceled (World War II)				
1948	London	59	3714	90	9.5
1952	Helsinki	69	4436	519	10.5
1956	Melbourne	72	2938	376	11.3
1960	Rome	83	4727	611	11.4
1964	Tokyo	93	4473	678	13.2
1968	Mexico City	112	4735	781	14.2
1972	Munich	122	6075	1059	14.8
1976	Montreal	92	4824	1260	20.7
1980	Moscow	81	4064	1115	21.5
1984	Los Angeles	140	5263	1566	22.9
1988	Seoul	159	6197	2194	26.1
1992	Barcelona	169	6652	2704	28.9
1996	Atlanta	197	6806	6806	34.0*
2000	Sydney	199	6582	4069	38.2
2004	Athens	201	6452	4412	40.6

Source: www.olympic.org/uk/games/index_uk.asp.

*Twenty-six countries sent only male athletes to the 1996 Summer Games.

Note: These data show 108 years of gradual progress toward gender equity. At this rate, the 2016 or 2020 Summer Games may have equal numbers of men and women. The number of athletes participating in 1976, 1980, and 1984 was lower than expected, due to boycotts.

Participation Opportunities: Informal and Alternative Sports   Gender and fairness issues are not limited to formally organized, mainstream sports. Informal games often have gender dynamics that present girls and women with special challenges for gaining access to participation and claiming identities as athletes. Similar challenges exist in alternative sports, both informal and formal. This is because boys and men generally control who plays and who is defined as a "fellow" athlete.

Regardless of where informal sport participation occurs—backyards, driveways, local parks, school playgrounds, gyms and playing fields at high schools and universities, or on the streets—the contexts are male dominated/identified/centered. This often discourages the participation of girls and women, and it creates a situation in

Girls and women are eager participants in alternative sports such as climbing. However, in many "action sports," boys and men control who plays and who is defined as an athlete, and girls and women are seldom treated seriously in those sports unless they do things like the boys and men do them. (*Source:* Jay Coakley)

which they must be exceptionally good athletes and have clever inclusion strategies to be given the chance to play and be accepted as an athlete by male peers. In many cases, the best inclusion strategy is to be "sponsored" by an influential boy or man who vouches for a girl's or a woman's "right" to demonstrate what she can do as an athlete. Laws such as Title IX do not apply to these settings. Therefore, changes come more slowly than they do in formal sport settings such as school-sponsored varsity sports.

Forms of excluding or restricting the participation of girls and women in informal sports have received little attention in the sociology of sport. However, we do know that girls and women face unique participation and identity challenges in both informal and alternative

sports and that there are equity and fairness issues related to who plays under what conditions (Wheaton and Beal, 2003). The most important consequence of these issues is that many girls and women feel that they are not welcome to develop and display their skills. This leads many boys and men to say that they should receive priority when using sports facilities or resources because girls and women are not interested in sports. It's a "Catch-22" situation for girls and women: They have fewer opportunities than men to develop interests and skills, and then they are denied opportunities to play because they have fewer interests and skills!

Research on alternative sports shows that they are clearly organized around the values and experiences of boys and young men (Anderson,

1999; Honea, 2007; Rinehart and Syndor, 2003). Observations at nearly any open, noncommercial skateboard park will reaffirm this point. Girls and young women are usually spectators, "skate Bettys" (perceived as "groupies" with boards), or they are cautious participants earning the right to be taken seriously (Beal and Weidman, 2003)— and a disproportionate number of girls are in-line skaters, which puts them lower in the skateboard park status hierarchy. The few girls who do claim space for themselves in bowls or ramp areas have earned the "right" to participate, but they have done so on terms set by the boys. As one hard-core mountain biker noted as he described expert women riders: "Testosterone is contagious" (in Bridges, 2003, p. 181). In sociological terms, this means that to be accepted as an authentic athlete in alternative sports, a female must perform "like a guy."

Alternative sports have emerged in connection with the lifestyles of boys and young men who value, among other things, facing one's fears, taking risks, and pushing normative limits. The boys and young men in these sports say that inclusion is based on skill, guts, and aggressiveness, not gender. But when pressed on this point, one skater said with a swagger, "It takes too much coordination for a girl, and it's too aggressive" (in Beal and Weidman, 2003, p. 345). Therefore, the girls who are identified as athletes in the "extreme" versions of alternative sports are those who demonstrate "Kodak Courage"—that is, enough skill and guts to attempt and occasionally accomplish creative and dangerous unique tricks that others want to see in person or on film (Kay and Laberge, 2003).

The consequences of the male-dominated/identified/centered culture and organization of alternative sports are seen in media-created, corporate-sponsored versions such as the X Games, Gravity Games, and Dew Action Sport Tour (Kilvert, 2002). For example, there were fifty-six female athletes in the 1995 X Games but only twenty-six in 2003; in 2005 only four of the fifty-four *invited* participants were females. The August 2005 Dew Action Sport Tour had no females on the invited list of participants. Patterns vary from one alternative sport to another, but gender inclusion is relatively rare in the case of participation opportunities.

Support for Athletes   Female athletes in most North American high schools and colleges seldom receive the same support enjoyed by the boys and men. This is also the case in sport-sponsoring organizations around the world. Historically, serious inequities have been in the following areas:

- Access to facilities
- Quality of facilities (playing surfaces, locker rooms, showers, and so on)
- Availability of scholarships*
- Program operating expenses
- Provision and maintenance of equipment and supplies
- Recruiting budgets*
- Scheduling of games and practice times
- Travel and per diem expenses
- Opportunity to receive academic tutoring*
- Numbers of coaches assigned to teams
- Salaries for administrators, coaches, trainers, and other staff
- Provision of medical and training services and facilities
- Publicity for individuals, teams, and events

Inequities in some of these areas remain a problem in schools at all levels of education, but they also are a problem in many community programs.

When they exist in community programs, they often go undetected unless someone digs through data from public, nonprofit, and private programs. Access to facilities, the number of programs available, and the staff assigned to programs are the most likely areas of inequity in community-based sports in North America and around the world.

---

*These apply primarily to U.S. colleges and universities.

Most people today realize that a lack of support for female athletes subverts sport participation among girls and women. For well over a century, men built their programs, shaped them to fit their interests and values, generated interest in participation, sold them to sponsors, and marketed them to potential spectators. During this time, public funds and facilities, student fees, and private sponsorships were used to start and maintain programs for boys and men. Girls and women want only the same treatment. Mary Jo Kane, director of the University of Minnesota's Tucker Center for Research on Girls and Women, says, "Women are not asking for a handout, we're just asking for an investment. Just put the same investment in us that you put into men. Then we'll see what happens" (in Lamb, 2000, p. 57). For those who believe in fairness, it is difficult to argue with this point.

Jobs for Women in Coaching and Administration Most sport programs are controlled by men. Although women's programs have increased in number and importance around the globe, women often have lost power over them. Data at all levels of competition show that women do not have equal opportunities when it comes to jobs in coaching and administration. Women are especially underrepresented at the highest levels of power in sports. A twenty-seven-year study by Vivian Acosta and Linda Carpenter (2004; Carpenter and Acosta, 2005) documents gender trends for U.S. college coaching and administration:

- When Title IX became law in 1972, women coached 90 percent of women's teams; by 1978, the proportion dropped to 58 percent; by 2004, it dropped further to 44 percent.
- Between 2000 and 2004, there were 624 new jobs for head coaches of women's teams; men received 463 (74 percent) of these jobs, whereas women received 161 (26 percent).

- Women administered 90 percent of women's athletic programs in 1972 and 19 percent in 2004; 18 percent of all women's programs in 2004 had *no* women administrators.
- In 2004 there were 3356 administrative jobs in NCAA *women's athletic programs*. Men held (65 percent) of those jobs, whereas women held 35 percent.
- The women's programs that had female athletic directors in 2004 also had a higher proportion of women coaches.
- The decline in the proportion of female coaches and administrators generally has been most dramatic at the highest levels of competition and in the highest-paying jobs.
- Women held only 12 percent of the full-time sports information director positions in universities in 2004 and 30 percent of athletic trainer positions.
- Women accounted for less than 2 percent of men's team coaches, and most of those worked with gender-combined teams in swimming, cross-country, and tennis.

Table 8.2 presents longitudinal data on the proportion of women coaches for the ten most popular women's intercollegiate sports in 2004. Only soccer had a higher proportion of women coaches in 2004 than it had in 1977, and the gain was less than 1 percentage point. Six of the other nine sports showed at least a 15 percentage–point decline in the proportion of women coaches between 1977 and 2004. What would men say if 80 percent of the administrators and two-thirds of the coaches *in men's programs* were women and only 2 percent of the coaches in women's programs were men? They would be outraged! They would file lawsuits and demand affirmative action programs to achieve fairness—and they would be justified in doing so.

The coaching and administration situation is much the same in other nations and on a global level. Systematic data on coaches are not easy to collect from nation to nation, but over 80 percent of all national team coaches are men. The IOC,

Table 8.2   Percentage of women coaches for the ten most popular women's intercollegiate sports in all NCAA divisions, 1977–2004

Sport	1977	1987	1997	2002	2004	Percentage Point Change, 1977–2002
Basketball	79.4	59.9	65.2	62.8	60.7	−15.7
Volleyball	86.6	70.2	67.8	57.3	59.5	−27.1
Cross-country	35.2	18.7	20.7	21.3	22.0	−13.2
Soccer	29.4	24.1	33.1	30.7	30.1	+0.7
Softball	83.5	67.5	65.2	65.1	64.8	−18.7
Tennis	72.9	54.9	40.9	34.5	34.6	−38.3
Track	52.3	20.8	16.4	19.0	19.7	−32.6
Golf	54.6	37.5	45.2	39.2	41.7	−12.9
Swimming/diving	53.6	31.2	33.7	23.0	25.6	−28.0
Lacrosse	90.7	95.1	85.2	85.9	86.2	−4.4

Modified from Acosta and Carpenter (2005). In 2004, 44 percent of the coaches of women's teams were women. This is the lowest representation of women as coaches of women's teams in the history of college sports. In 1972, women coached 90 percent of all women's teams, but there were far fewer teams.

the most powerful administrative body in global sports, had had *no* women members from 1896 until 1981. In response to widespread charges of sexism, the IOC in 1997 announced that its goal was to have 10 percent of all decision-making positions in the IOC, all National Olympic Committees (NOCs), and all International Governing Bodies (NGBs) of sports held by women by the end of 2000; by 2005 women would hold 20 percent of those positions. However, in 2005 the IOC membership was composed of 106 men and 10 women, and its executive committee had 13 men and 1 woman. Therefore, as of 2005 they had not reached their goal for 2000. The NOCs and NGBs have worse records than the IOC, especially in their most powerful positions (White and Henry, 2004). The goal of having women in 20 percent of the decision-making positions in sport organizations around the world by 2005 was not reached, and at the current rate of change, it will not be reached for many years in many nations and many sports.

The reasons for the underrepresentation of women in coaching and administrative positions in women's sports have been widely debated and studied (McKay, 1997, 1999; Pastore et al., 1996;

Wilkerson, 1996). The major reasons appear to include the following:

- Men use well-established connections with other men in sport organizations to help them during the job search and hiring process.
- Compared with men, most female applicants for coaching and administrative jobs do not have the strategic professional connections and networks to compete with male candidates.
- Job search committees often use ideologically-based evaluative criteria, making it likely that female applicants for coaching and administrative jobs will be seen as less qualified than men.
- Support systems and professional development opportunities are scarce for women who want to be coaches or administrators and for women already in coaching and administrative jobs.
- Many women know that it is difficult to work in athletic departments and sport organizations that have corporate cultures organized around the values and experiences of men (see Figure 8.2).

SIDELINES

©1982 M.T.F.-T.W.S.-Lakewood. CO

FIGURE 8.2 Women traditionally have been expected to play support roles for men in sports as well as in society at large. This is changing but these roles are still present in the gendered social structures of many societies.

- Sport organizations are seldom organized in family-friendly ways.
- Sexual harassment is more often experienced by women than by men, and female coaches and administrators often feel that they are judged by more demanding standards than men are.

These factors affect aspirations and opportunities. They influence who applies for jobs, how applicants fare during the hiring process, how coaches and administrators are evaluated, who enjoys their job, and who is promoted into higher-paying jobs with more responsibility and power.

People on job search committees seek, interview, evaluate, and hire candidates who they think will be successful in sport programs that are male dominated/identified/centered. After looking at objective qualifications, such as years of experience and win–loss records, search committee members subjectively assess such things as a candidate's abilities to recruit and motivate players, raise money, command respect in the community (among boosters, fans, sport reporters), build toughness and character among players, maintain team discipline, and "fit" in the athletic department or sport organization.

None of these assessments occurs in a vacuum, and some are influenced by gender ideology in addition to the facts. Although people on search committees do not agree on all things, many think in terms that favor men over women (Hovden, 2000). This is because coaching and other forms of leadership in sports often are seen to be consistent with traditional ideas about masculinity: If you "coach like a girl," you are doing it wrong; if you "coach like a man," you are doing it right. In a male-dominated and identified organizational culture, this is taken for granted.

Under these conditions, women are hired only when they present compelling evidence that they can do things as men have done them in the past. In sport programs and athletic departments where men have routinely been hired and women have been ignored, there may be pressure to recruit and hire women so that charges of discrimination can be deflected. When a woman is hired in such circumstances, it is often said that, *"We had to hire a woman."* But the more accurate statement is this: *"We've favored men for so long that people were going to rightfully accuse us of gender discrimination if we didn't hire a woman or two."*

When women are hired, they are less likely than men to feel welcome and fully included in sport organizations. Therefore, they often have lower levels of job satisfaction and higher rates of job turnover (Pastore et al., 1996). When turnover occurs, some people accuse women of being secretive and defensive and not having what it takes to survive in the "real" world of sports. But this ignores that expectations for coaches and administrators have been developed over the years by men who often had wives who raised their children, provided them and their teams with emotional support, hosted social events for teams and boosters, coordinated their social schedules, handled household finances and maintenance, made sure they were not distracted by family and household issues, and faithfully attended games season after season. If female coaches and administrators had the opportunity to build programs and coach teams under similar circumstances, job satisfaction would be high

AT YOUR *fingertips*   For more information on jobs and mobility in sports, see pages 343–355.

and turnover would be low, and there would certainly be child care provided for the children of coaches and administrators (McKay, 1999).

Finally, some sport organizations have records of being negligent in controlling sexual harassment and responding to complaints from women who wish to be taken seriously in the structure and culture of sport organizations and programs. This means that people in the programs must critically assess the impact of male-dominated/centered/identified forms of social organization on both males and females. Unless this is done and changes are made, gender equity will never exist in the ranks of coaching and administration.

Strategies to Achieve Equity

Most men support the idea of gender equity, but few of them are willing to give up anything to achieve it. This resistance has forced proponents of gender equity to ask governments for assistance or to file lawsuits. Governments have been helpful, but they often are slow to respond. Legal actions have been effective, but lawsuits involve costs and long-term commitments. Therefore, Donna Lopiano, former executive director of the Women's Sport Foundation (WSF), has identified strategic political organization and pressure as the key for achieving gender equity. This involves the development of grassroots organizations to systematically support and publicize sport programs for girls and women. As these organizations publicly recognize the achievements of female athletes and their sponsors, more people will see the value of women's sports and join their efforts to achieve equity. The WSF and other organizations have facilitated this process with their resources, and they have been effective in fostering progressive changes.

Lopiano (1991) also has urged people in sport organizations to use the following strategies to promote gender equity:

- Confront discriminatory practices in your organization and become an advocate for female athletes, coaches, and administrators.
- Insist on fair and open employment practices in your organization.
- Keep track of equity data and have an independent group issue a public "gender equity report card" every three to four years for your organization or program.
- Learn and educate others about the history of discrimination in sports and how to recognize the subtle forms of discrimination that operate in sport worlds that are male dominated, male identified, and male centered.
- Object to practices and policies that decrease opportunities for women in sports and inform the media of them.
- When possible, package and promote women's sports as revenue producers, so there will be financial incentives to increase participation opportunities for women.
- Recruit female athletes into coaching by establishing internships and training programs.
- Use women's hiring networks when seeking coaches and administrators in sport programs.
- Create a supportive work climate for women in your organization and establish policies to eliminate sexual harassment.

These are useful suggestions. They emphasize a combination of public relations, political lobbying, pressure, education, and advocacy. They are based on the assumption that increased participation and opportunities for women will not come without struggle and that favorable outcomes depend on organization and persistence. More important, they have already produced varying degrees of change in many organizations.

Those who use critical and critical feminist theories to study sports in society have argued that gender equity cannot be achieved in contexts that are organized by men who are unwilling to critically assess dominant gender ideology. Therefore, real equity requires cultural and structural changes in existing sports and sport programs combined with the development of new models of sport participation and sport organizations that acknowledge the values and experiences of women (Birrell, 2000; Nelson, 1998; Theberge, 2000a). This is discussed below in the section "Ideology and Power Issues."

Girls and Women as Agents of Change   Some people assume that women are empowered when they play sports and that empowered women become effective agents of gender equity in sports and in society as a whole. Research supports this claim but only to a point (Eitle and Eitle, 2002; Stoelting, 2004).

Sport participation provides girls and women with opportunities to connect with the power of their bodies. This is important because social life sometimes is organized to encourage girls and women to see themselves as weak, dependent, and powerless. Additionally, many images of women in society present the female body as an object to be viewed, evaluated, and consumed, and girls and women learn to objectify their bodies as they view and assess themselves through the eyes of others (Fredrickson and Harrison, 2005; Young, 1990). Because identity and a personal sense of power are partly grounded in one's body and body image, sport participation can help women overcome the feeling that their bodies are objects. Furthermore, the physical skills and strength often gained through sport participation go beyond simply helping a woman feel fit. They also can make her feel less vulnerable, more competent and independent, and more in control of her physical safety and psychological well-being (see Blinde et al., 1994; Chastain, 2004; Ference and Muth, 2004; Frederickson and Harrison, 2005; Pelak, 2002, 2005b; Roth and Basow, 2004; Theberge, 2000a; Wedgewood, 2004).

Empowerment does not occur automatically when a girl or woman plays sports, nor is a sense of empowerment always associated with a desire or an ability to actively promote fairness and equity issues in sports or other spheres of life. Feeling competence as an athlete does not guarantee that women will critically assess gender ideology and gender relations or work for fairness and equity in sports or society at large. For example, some female athletes express negative attitudes toward feminism and distance themselves from social activism related to women's issues. In other words, those who play elite-level sports are not likely to be "boat rockers" critical of the gender order (McClung and Blinde, 1998; Young and White, 1995). There are four possible reasons for this:

1. Female athletes may feel that they have much to lose if they are associated with civil and human rights issues for women because others might identify them as ungrateful or marginalize them by tagging them with labels such as *radical*, *feminist*, or *lesbian*.
2. The corporation-driven "celebrity feminism" promoted through media sports today focuses on individualism and consumption rather than everyday struggles faced by ordinary girls and women who want to play sports but also are concerned with obtaining child care, health care, and a decent job (Cole, 2000b).
3. The "empowerment discourses" associated with fitness and sports often emphasize individual self-empowerment through physical changes that enhance feminine beauty (Eskes et al., 1998; MacNeill, 1999); they do not emphasize social or cultural changes.
4. Female athletes, even those with high media profiles and powerful bodies, have little control over their own sport participation and little political voice in sports or society as a whole (Lowe, 1998).

Similarly, women hired and promoted into leadership positions in major sport organizations are expected to promote power and performance sports in society. The men who control many sport organizations are not usually eager to hire women

Developing physical skills often improves health and provides girls and women with a sense of empowerment. This is true for Reshma, a seven-year-old in Dhaka, Bangladesh. But if the culture and social structure in Bangladesh do not provide Reshma with opportunities to express her sense of empowerment as a woman, beating all the boys in this race will not enable her to participate in society as they will when they become adults. (*Source:* Photo courtesy of The Hunger Project; www.thp.org/)

who put *women's issues* on the same level as *sport issues*. Of course, not all female leaders become uncritical cheerleaders for power and performance orientations in sports and society. However, it takes effort and courage to critically analyze sports and use one's power to change the culture and structure of sports. But without this effort and courage, gender inequities tend to persist.

Boys and Men as Agents of Change   Gender equity is not just a woman's issue. Equity also involves creating options for boys and men to play sports that are not based exclusively on a power

and performance model. Sports that emphasize aggression and domination often encourage orientations and actions that lead to chronic injuries, an inability to relate to women, fears of intimacy with other men, homophobia, and a compulsive concern with comparing oneself with other men in terms of what might be called "life success scores" (Burstyn, 1999; White and Young, 1997).

Sports privilege men over women, but they also privilege some men over others. When men realize that some sports constitute cultural contexts that constrain and distort their relationships with one another and with women, they are more inclined to view sports critically. Bruce Kidd, a former Olympic runner and now a physical educator and social scientist, used his experiences to suggest the following:

> Through sports, men learn to cooperate with, care for, and love other men, in [many] ways, but they rarely learn to be intimate with each other or emotionally honest. On the contrary, the only way many of us express fondness for other men is by teasing or mock fighting. (1987, p. 259)

Men who want to move beyond an expression of fondness based on teasing and mock fighting have good reason to join with those women concerned with critically assessing dominant sport forms in their society (Anderson, 2005; Pronger, 1999).

Facing Football: A Challenge for Equity Strategies In the box "Title IX" on pages 238–243, I did not mention that one of the primary obstacles to achieving gender equity in high school and college sport programs is the place of high-profile football teams in the culture and structure of high school and university athletic programs. Strategies for achieving equity and fairness often come up short in the face of football.

High schools and colleges with large football programs often fail to meet equity goals because of the size and cost of football teams. When teams have 80 to 120 team members, award eighty-five scholarships, employ multiple coaches, and have high operational costs, there is little chance for a women's sport program to match the men's program in terms of budget and number of athletes. For example, the vast majority of Division 1 universities spend more on football than they spend for all women's sport teams (Keating, 2002a). This is why very few universities meet the Title IX proportionality test.

The reason I need sports in my life is that it's the only aspect of my existence that I understand completely. . . . And this is true for a lot of men. . . . It is the only subject that allows us to see—or at least feel—the truth

—Chuck Klosterman, journalist, 2003.

Despite this, university officials resist cutting the size and budgets of football teams—even though all but about seventy big-time football programs lose money every year. This management decision puts many athletic directors in a position where they must cut expenses by cutting nonrevenue-producing men's teams such as wrestling, gymnastics, and diving.

The men on these teams feel that they are victims of Title IX. But more accurately, they are victims of a noncreative management strategy that gives unquestioned priority to football. Blaming Title IX is easier than challenging football because the culture and structure of the entire athletic department often revolves around football; women's sports and other men's sports are powerless in comparison. But defining the loss of men's teams as a men-versus-women conflict makes more sense to many men than challenging the sport (football) that reproduces the gender ideology that many of them have used to define their identities and status since they were boys.

When football is the "cultural and structural centerpiece" in schools and surrounding communities, gender equity is chronically out of reach. The irony of this is that some of the best-funded intercollegiate women's sport programs exist in the sixty to seventy universities where big-time Division 1 football generates so much money that the athletic department is resource rich. However, unless the university is in one of the six conferences that automatically participates in the Bowl Championship Series (BCS), the football team usually loses money and depends on support from boosters whose identities are deeply grounded in football and the ideologies it reproduces. These ideologies do not support strategies to achieve gender equity. For example, when a booster of a Georgia high school football team was asked about participation opportunities for girls in the high school, he had this to say:

> We got girls in the band. The cheerleaders are girls. Half the people in the stands are girls. We hold graduation in the stadium, and half the graduates are girls. Our managers are girls; our statisticians are girls. (in Fish and Milliron, 1999)

According to his gender ideology, football puts everyone in his or her proper place in the school: boys on the field, physically battling opponents for competitive success, with girls on the sidelines, cheering them on and maintaining an attractive appearance. Many people don't agree with this booster, but those who do agree with him often control resources for sports. This means that strategies for achieving equity must focus on ideology issues and the distribution of power in sports.

IDEOLOGY AND POWER ISSUES

Ideology often is so deeply rooted in our social worlds that we seldom think about it and almost never raise questions about it. We take it for granted and use it as a form of "cultural logic" to make sense of the world. This is especially the case with gender ideology.

Gender is a central organizing principle of social life, and gender ideology influences how we think of ourselves and others, how we relate to others, and how social life is organized at all levels, from families to societies. It influences what we wear, how we walk, how we present ourselves to others, and how we think about and plan for our future. Most people take gender ideology as a "given" in their lives; they do not question it because it is so deeply rooted in their psyches and the way they live their lives.

The tendency to ignore ideology is a serious problem when we deal with gender equity in sports. The achievement of equity requires changes in the gender ideology that has been used to organize, play, and make sense of sports.

The following sections critically examine the prevailing gender ideology in society, its effects on our lives, its connection with sports, and some strategies for changing it as well as how power is distributed in sports.

Gender Ideology in Society

Gender ideology varies from culture to culture. In most societies in which men have been privileged in terms of legal status, formal authority, political and economic power, and access to resources, gender ideology is based on a *simple binary classification model*. According to this model, all people are classified into one of two **sex categories:** *male or female* (see figure 8.3). These categories are defined in biological terms, and they are conceptualized to highlight difference and opposition; they are commonly identified as "opposite sexes." All people in the male category are believed to be naturally different from all people in the female category, and they are held to different normative expectations when it comes to feelings, thoughts, and actions. These expectations outline the basis for the ways that people define and identify **gender**—that is, *what is considered masculine and what is considered feminine in a group or society*. This classification and interpretation model is so central to the way that many people see the world that they resist thinking about gender in new ways and they often feel uncomfortable when people do not fit neatly into one sex category or the other.

It takes dedication and hard work to maintain a simple binary classification model because it is inconsistent with biological evidence showing that anatomy, hormones, chromosomes, and secondary sex characteristics vary in complex ways and cannot be divided neatly into two sex categories, one male and one female. As biologist Anne Fausto-Sterling explains, "A body's sex is simply too complex. There is no either/or. Rather, there are shades of difference" (2000, p. 3). Real bodies have physiological and biological traits,

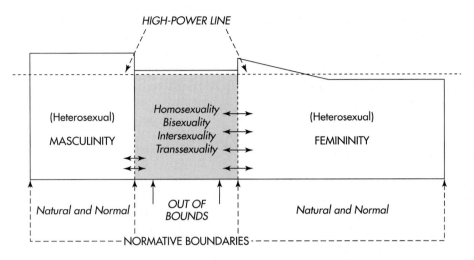

HIGH-POWER LINE

(Heterosexual)
MASCULINITY

Homosexuality
Bisexuality
Intersexuality
Transsexuality

(Heterosexual)
FEMININITY

Natural and Normal

OUT OF
BOUNDS

Natural and Normal

NORMATIVE BOUNDARIES

Note: Heterosexual masculinity and heterosexual femininity are depicted as separate, nonoverlapping categories. Each has clearly marked normative boundaries that limit what is defined as normal. The "FEMININITY" category is wider than the "MASCULINITY" category because girls and women have more latitude in what they can do without being out of bounds. Other forms of sexuality are in a gray area that many people define as being outside the normative boundaries of the two gender categories widely perceived as "natural." People in this gray area include lesbians, gay men, bisexuals, the intersexed, and transsexuals.

The short double arrows (↔) indicate two processes: (1) movement into and out of the categories of heterosexual male and female and (2) efforts to push normative boundaries to make space for different expressions of masculinity and femininity, create new sexual categories, or to transcend sexual categories by making them socially irrelevant.

The "high-power line" indicates that heterosexual men are more likely to occupy high-power and influential positions, such as heads of state, members of the Senate and Congress, CEOs, and top-level leaders and decision makers in religious organizations, education, media, and sports. The high-power line can also be viewed as a representation of the "glass ceiling" for women, although a few women have cracked through it in certain spheres of social life.

FIGURE 8.3 The two-category gender classification model: a representation of gender construction in U.S. culture.

which are distributed along continua related to these dimensions of biochemistry and appearance.

This natural sexual variation does not fit with a binary classification model. Therefore, when people are born with physical traits that don't fit ideology-based definitions of *male* and *female*, genitals and reproductive organs usually are surgically "fixed" to make them fit (Fausto-Sterling, 2000).

Hormones vary from one person to the next, and both men and women have testosterone and estrogen in their bodies. However, testosterone is identified as a "male hormone" and estrogen as a "female hormone." This way of thinking about and referring to hormones is misleading, but it enables people to maintain their two-category gender classification model without asking critical questions about it.

Even chromosomal patterns do not always fit neatly into two distinct categories. Nor do secondary sex characteristics, which vary greatly. But we do our best to cover variations with sex-appropriate clothes and forms of body management that highlight characteristics that identify us as male or female. Most people spend considerable time, energy, and money to ensure that their physical characteristics and appearance fit general expectations based on the two-category gender classification model. Those who ignore these expectations risk being marginalized or treated as if they are "out of gender bounds" (Fenstermaker and West, 2002). A woman who does not remove natural hair growth above her upper lip or on other parts of her body risks being ridiculed, and a slender man with "fine" features who does not avoid wearing clothes defined as effeminate risks serious ridicule in many situations.

Physical variation is real, and to say that all variation can be reduced to two separate and "opposite" categories forces biology to fit socially constructed definitions of what males and females are "supposed to be" in physical terms (Butler, 2004).

Being "Out of Bounds": A Problem for Gays and Lesbians

Another problem created by a binary classification model is that the model comes with relatively fixed ideas and expectations about how men and women are supposed to think, feel, and act. These ideas and expectations emphasize *difference*, and they are the foundation for gender. A binary gender classification model is based on the assumption that heterosexuality is natural and normal and that those who express feelings, thoughts, and actions that do not fit neatly into the two socially constructed categories of masculine and feminine are "out of bounds" when it comes to gender (review figure 8.3).

When gender ideology is based on this classification model, many people, including gay men, lesbians, bisexuals, and transsexuals don't fit into either of the two categories, so they usually are defined as deviant. A two-category model provides no legitimate social space or recognition for those who are neither heterosexual males nor heterosexual females. This, in turn, serves as a foundation for **homophobia,** *a general fear and/or intolerance felt for those who are "out of bounds" in the classification model.*

Power in Society: Gender Ideology in Action

Another important aspect of a binary classification model is that the two categories are seldom equal. As represented in figure 8.3, males have access to higher levels of privilege, power, and influence than females have, and men occupy the highest levels of power and influence in greater numbers than women do. However, there is a social and personal cost that comes with access to and possession of power.

When a two-category gender classification model exists in cultures that emphasize equal rights and freedom of expression, the accepted range of feelings, thoughts, and actions for men often is more restricted than it is for women. This means that the normative boundaries associated with masculinity are more restrictive and more closely regulated than the normative boundaries associated with femininity. Masculine characteristics are believed to be consistent with positions of power and influence; therefore, men have more to lose collectively if they do not conform to gender expectations. This is why men strictly police their gender boundaries and sanction those who push or move outside them. Women, on the other hand, have less to lose and more to gain if they push boundaries, although they must do so carefully.

What this means in everyday life is that men have less social permission to express the feelings, thoughts, and actions associated with femininity than woman have to express the feelings, thoughts, and actions associated with masculinity. This is why boys are teased for being "sissies," whereas girls are praised for being "tomboys"; it's also why male ballet dancers and interior designers are less likely to be socially accepted in society than are female rugby players and women in Congress (Laberge and Albert, 1999).

To demonstrate this point, ask the women in a gender-mixed group how many of them have bought clothing for themselves in a men's store or the men's section of a department store; most will say they have done so. Then ask the men how many of them have bought clothing for themselves in a women's store or a women's section of a department store and listen to the laughter caused by the tension of thinking about the question. The responses illustrate that men face more restrictive normative boundaries related to gender than women face. However, the payoff for men is that they have more access to power, although some men have more access than others.

Challenging Gender Ideology: Blurring the Old Boundaries   A binary classification model has socially constructed normative boundaries. However, not everyone accepts or conforms to them. The double arrows in figure 8.3 represent efforts by men and women to push, erase, pass through, and revise normative boundaries. Of course, women do more pushing and passing through than men, although there are potential costs associated with challenging gender boundaries (that is, "gender bending"). However, as boundary pushers and crossers raise issues that promote revised definitions of *masculinity* and *femininity*, the normative boundaries for women and men change. Change comes slowly though because most people have vested interests in the two-category gender classification model. After all, they have learned to use the model as a guide for perceiving and making sense of themselves, their relationships, and the world around them.

For example, when Annika Sorenstam became the first woman to compete on the traditionally male only PGA Tour, a PGA golfer was threatened and declared, "I'll do what men do, and she should do what women do" (*Newsweek*, 2004, p. 122). After Sorenstam beat him by three strokes, his assumptions about sex differences and male superiority were shown to be wrong but he could use football to maintain his ideas about gender and male superiority (Caudwell, 2003; Messner, 1992). Similarly, when golfer Michelle Wie played in her first men's tournament in 2005, an analyst for the Golf Channel wondered if her presence would turn the PGA into "a freak show" (Kensler, 2005).

Gender Ideology in Sports

Ideas and beliefs about gender are a crucial part of the foundation on which sports are organized, promoted, and played. Sports are sites for reaffirming beliefs about male–female *difference* and valorizing masculine characteristics. At the same time, women's sports often are marginalized because they are not seen as "real" or as good as men's sports, and female athletes sometimes are marginalized or seen as deviant because they violate femininity norms. Sports also are sites for challenging and revising gender ideology, a fact that makes gender interesting to study when trying to understand sports in society.

Celebrating Masculinity   Gender is not fixed in nature. Therefore, gender ideology grounded in a binary classification model can be preserved only if people work hard to police gender boundaries and maintain them through myths, rituals, and everyday cultural practices. People must "do" gender to keep the model viable, and the model is most effectively maintained when gender categories become embodied dimensions of people's lives—that is, when they are built into the way people move and experience the world with and through their bodies (Fenstermaker and West, 2002). This is how and why sports become important in connection with gender (Messner, 2002).

Sports have been important sites and activities for preserving gender ideology in most cultures. The meaning of gender and its application in people's lives have been symbolized and powerfully presented in the bodily performances that occur in sports. Men's achievements in power and performance sports have been used as evidence of men's aggressive nature, their superiority over women, and their rights to claim social and physical space as their own. Sociologist Doug Hartmann explains this issue in this way:

> [Sport] makes male advantages and masculine values appear so normal and "natural" that they can hardly be questioned. Therein may lie the key to the puzzle connecting men and the

Traditional gender ideology is reproduced in many men's sports. Some of those sports inspire fantasies and symbols of a heroic manhood in which playing the role of warrior is the substance of being a man. Do these fantasies and symbols influence how these boys define *masculinity*? (*Source:* Jay Coakley)

seemingly innocent world of sports: they fit together to tightly, so seamlessly that they achieve their effects—learning to be a man, male bonding, male authority, and the like— without seeming to be doing anything more than tossing a ball or watching a Sunday afternoon game. (2003b, p. 20)

Hartmann's words help us understand why Bruce Kidd (1987) describes sports stadiums and domed arenas as "men's cultural centers." These facilities, often built with public funds, host events that present a manhood based on aggression, physical power, and the ability to intimidate and dominate others. A Major League Baseball coach emphasized this when he was asked about the orientations of male professional athletes. He stated that "the bottom line is . . . you're dealing with the male ego. It's not just about winning. . . . It's about dominating" (in Armstrong, 2000, p. 3D). In this way, sports reproduce a gender ideology that privileges the

interests of men and favors a particular form of manhood.

Political scientist Varda Burstyn (1999) explains that the major men's sports in most societies provide people with a vocabulary and a set of stories that erase diverse and contradictory masculinities and present a homogenized manhood in which the heroic warrior is the model of a real man. For example, when television sports announcers give special recognition to a male athlete, they often refer to him as "a warrior."

Girls and Women as Invaders   When girls and women play certain sports, they are seen to be invaders of male turf. This is why they've been excluded from some sports at the same time they've been encouraged to play sports that emphasize grace, beauty, and coordination. Through most of the twentieth century, this exclusion was rationalized by experts and educators, who told women that if they played strenuous sports, they

AT YOUR *fingertips* Go to the OLC for a discussion of these myths.

would damage their uteruses and breasts and experience problems endangering their abilities to give birth and nurture their children (Coakley, 1990). Today's college students laugh at these myths from the past because they have information that refutes them. However, it has taken many years to refute the myths and challenge traditional gender ideology. Unfortunately, myths continue to be widely believed in cultures where literacy rates are low and men control the production and distribution of knowledge.

The legacy of traditional gender ideology has not disappeared, even in postindustrial societies (McGarry, 2005). Journalist Joan Ryan writes about this in the following description of women's gymnastics and figure skating:

> Talent counts, but so do beauty, class, weight, clothes and politics. The anachronistic lack of ambivalence about femininity in both sports is part of their attraction, harkening back to a simpler time when girls were girls, when women were girls for that matter: coquettish, malleable, eager to please. In figure skating especially, we want our athletes thin, graceful, deferential and cover-girl pretty. We want eyeliner, lipstick and hair ribbons."
> (1995, p. 5)

Figure skating and gymnastics are the highest spectator-rated women's sports because they present athletes in ways that do not force viewers to deal with the ideologically threatening issues of sexuality, power, and gender relations. As sports columnist Mark Kiszla thought about these issues in 2005, ten years after Ryan's analysis, he made the following observation:

> America forces women to play sports by a different set of rules. Points are awarded for beauty. The trophy does not really shine unless she looks sexy

holding it. Acting like a lady is more important than winning. Isn't it about time we declare our independence from the dumbing-down of female sports? (2005, p. 1B)

One result of this dumbing-down approach was highlighted by fifteen-year-old Tara Lipinski as she trained for what was to be her gold medal figure skating performance in the 1998 Winter Olympics in Nagano, Japan. In response to a journalist's question, she said that her most difficult challenge was maintaining the strength and power needed to do seven triple jumps in a routine while still looking cute, soft, and feminine. Trying to meet that challenge has forced many female athletes to play by rules that lead to serious injuries. Lipinski, for example, suffered a serious hip injury that forced her to retire before she was twenty years old—but she looked cute when she went down with the injury.

When female athletes challenge traditional gender ideology, they have pushed gender boundaries to make more cultural space for girls and women in sports. Julie Foudy, cocaptain of the 1999 Women's World Cup U.S. soccer team, pushed boundaries when she was told she looked like a tomboy. She said, "All right call me a tomboy. Tomboys get medals. Tomboys win championships. Tomboys can fly. Oh, and tomboys aren't boys" (*WOSPORT Weekly*, 1999). Foudy's statement expanded notions of femininity in society. However, some young women still hear messages indicating that being a tomboy violates expectations for heterosexual attractiveness, lifestyles, and self-presentation. Playing most sports is widely accepted today, but the cuteness of being a tomboy still begins to fade during adolescence. If young female athletes do not conform to dominant definitions of *femininity*, they may experience certain forms of social rejection or less credit than they deserve.

FOREVER "LADIES"?   Female athletes deal with the consequences of traditional gender ideology in various ways (Cox and Thompson, 2000; Harris, 2005; Krane et al., 2004). For example,

reflect on **SPORTS**   ## Female Bodybuilders
Expanding Definitions of Femininity?

Female bodybuilders have been described as powerful women, unfeminine freaks, the ultimate hard bodies, new women, gender benders, entertainers, and side-shows for real sports. Descriptions have varied over time and from one group to another as gender ideology has changed.

Until the late 1970s, there was no such thing as competitive women's bodybuilding. It didn't exist because it so totally contradicted dominant definitions of femininity and what people saw as "natural" muscular development for women. The first bodybuilders challenged those definitions of femininity, pushed boundaries of social acceptance, and raised questions about what is natural and normal when it comes to the bodies of women (Lowe, 1998).

Many people continue to see female bodybuilders as rebels, deviants, and freaks of nature. According to the gender ideology used by most people, females are the "weaker sex" when it comes to muscles and strength. Leslie Heywood, a lifelong athlete and currently a professor of English and a bodybuilder, explains that female bodybuilders challenge this ideology and threaten dominant ideas about gender and nature. She describes women's bodybuilding as

> an in-your-face confrontation with traditional roles, an unavoidable assertion of . . . unequivocal self-expression, an indication of women's right to be, for themselves . . . not for anyone else. In a culture that still mostly defines women's purpose as service for others, no wonder female bodybuilding is so controversial. (1998, p. 171)

Therefore, bodybuilders have been accused of being unfeminine because they are "too muscular," too like men. Of course, not everyone accepts this gender ideology, and for those seeking new or expanded definitions of femininity, women's bodybuilding provides exciting and provocative new images. These images challenge notions of "female frailty" and raise questions about the biology of gender difference.

Like others who challenge hegemonic ideologies, female bodybuilders have discovered that careful strategies are required to change widely accepted ideas. The first female bodybuilders were careful to be "feminine" and not "too muscular." They emphasized a toned, symmetrical body displayed through carefully choreographed graceful moves. Their goal was to stay within the boundaries of femininity as determined by contest judges. However, even this approach presented problems because definitions of femininity have never been set permanently. Definitions changed and judges could not provide unchanging guidelines for what type of body symmetry was needed to look "feminine" and what exactly was "too muscular."

Many female bodybuilders have been frustrated as they try to anticipate changing guidelines (Lowe, 1998). For example, one bodybuilder observed that

> When you compete, your muscularity is all, but the judges insist on [us] looking womanly. They try to fudge the issue with garbage about symmetry, proportion and definition. What they really want is tits and ass. (in Bolin, 2003, p. 115)

Some bodybuilders try to live with the confusion caused by dominant ideas about gender by making clear distinctions between how they present themselves during competitive posing and what they do in their workouts (Bolin, 1998, 2003). In the gym, they focus on bodywork and muscle building. As Heywood notes, "The gym remains a place where the female body, unlike other places, can, by getting strong, earn a little respect" (1998, p. 187). Serious training overrides concerns about how gender is defined outside the gym. Workouts are not "gendered," and bodybuilders, both women and men, train in similar ways.

The public arena of competitive posing is different, and the women try to neutralize the socially imposed stigma of having too many muscles. They

In women's bodybuilding, there is clear tension between muscularity and femininity. It is created when a woman's muscles places her outside normative boundaries. This tension did not exist for Arnold Schwarzenegger when he was judged the most muscled man in the world. Muscles and masculinity go together in ideological terms, but women with muscles cause ideological confusion, even when they wear long hair and ponytails, polish their nails, and accessorize with "feminine" jewelry. Would you vote for this woman as your state governor in 2016? (*Source:* Steve Wennerstrom, *Women's Physique World Magazine*)

use "femininity insignias" to carefully construct a presentation of self that highlights the "look" of dominant femininity as it is defined today. They may dye their hair blonde, wear it in a long, fluffy style, and adorn it with a ribbon. They manicure fingernails and toenails and polish them or glue on false fingernails. They employ makeup artists, carefully choose posing bikinis for color and material, wear earring studs and an engagement or wedding ring, shave all body hair, and perhaps use plastic surgery to soften the contours of their faces. When they pose, they may walk on their toes, use graceful dance moves, and smile incessantly. They try to be seen with husbands or male friends, and they cautiously flirt with male judges. They do all this to appear "natural" according to dominant definitions of femininity (Bolin, 2003).

Of course, none of this is natural in biological terms. When female bodybuilders walk on stage, the femininity insignias they inscribe on their bodies contrast with their muscularity to such an extent that it is difficult for anyone who sees them not to realize that femininity is a social construction rather than a biological fact. The contestants in women's events today are clearly more muscled than 99 percent of the men in the world, and they challenge the notions that women are the "weaker sex" and that femininity implies frailty and vulnerability.

Female bodybuilders provide living examples that nature is more variable than prevailing gender ideology would indicate. In the process, they make it possible for women to view muscles and strength as a source of personal empowerment. This empowerment focuses on personal change rather than the development of progressive and collective politics among women, but those personal changes serve to challenge dominant definitions of femininity. At the same time, women who are "too muscular" repulse many people. *What do you think?*

young women who play contact and power sports sometimes discover that, unless they are seen as "ladylike," the *tomboy* label may change to *lesbian*. Therefore, they sometimes try to be more feminine by wearing hair ribbons, ponytails, makeup, dresses, hose, heels, or engagement or wedding rings; by saying how they like to party with heterosexuals in heterosexual clubs; and by making statements about boyfriends or husbands and their desire to eventually settle down and have children. In the absence of these heterosexualized "femininity insignias," some people define women in contact and power sports as threats to their ideas about "nature" and morality. This illustrates how the two-category gender classification model fuels homophobia in sports and the lives of female athletes (Griffin, 1998; Krane, 1996). The dynamics of this process are discussed in the box "Female bodybuilders."

The pressure to be "forever ladies" was intensified in the mid-1960s through the late 1990s when many international sport events, including the Olympics, demanded that female competitors take "gender tests" to prove that they were women (see www.pponline.co.uk/encyc/0082.htm). The assumption was that, if they were really good in sports, they might not be real women! At first, the female athletes were required to present themselves, naked, to a panel of doctors. But the all-male IOC decided that for the 1968 Olympics in Mexico City they would use a Barr body test to establish the gender of female athletes. Each competitor had cells scraped from inside her cheek so that a testing lab could determine if she had a female, or XX, chromosome profile. But chromosome profiles don't always match the socially constructed two-gender classification model used by IOC officials. For example, some people with only one X chromosome grow up as females, others have two X

> **Gender is much more than a biochemical construct. It's bizarre to think you can determine whether someone is male or female based on [lab] tests.**
>
> —Andrew Pipe, former president of the Canadian Academy of Sports Medicine and chair of the Canadian Center for Ethics in Sport (in Lehrman, 1997).

chromosomes and one Y and grow up as men, and there are "XX males and XY females whose sex doesn't match their chromosomes" (Lehrman, 1997). This meant that some athletes who had lived their lives as women failed the Barr body test and were disqualified from the Olympics. This surprised the parents and friends of the athletes who knew that they were women.

Most female athletes continued to object to gender testing, and the tests were eliminated by most international sport organizations in the 1990s. However, all 3500 female athletes at the Olympic Games in Atlanta were required to take the Barr body test or show their "fem card" from a previous test certifying that they were "real" women. The IOC continued testing through 1999 but dropped it before the 2000 Sydney Games in response to protests and research that challenged the test's validity.

SPORTS AS SITES FOR CHANGE Although female athletes still live with the consequences of traditional gender ideology and homophobia, their achievements have challenged certain ideas and beliefs and encouraged many people to think in new ways about masculinity, femininity, and gender relations (Theberge, 2000a). When this occurs, women's sports are important sites for pushing the normative boundaries of *femininity*. For example, author Leah Cohen points out that "any girl who boxes challenges, unwittingly or not, the idea of what it means to be a girl in our culture" (2005, p. xiii). In some cases, female athletes even encourage people to question the validity of the two-category gender classification model and rethink the meaning of gender in society. For example, in 2004 IOC executive board members revised their thinking about gender when they approved a proposal to allow athletes who have undergone sex change operations to participate in the Olympics (Hui, 2004). The athletes must have had their new gender legally recognized and had postoperative hormone therapy for at least two years. Although this decision assumes a two-gender classification model, it recognizes that gender is changeable. This is a significant change that now applies worldwide in international sports.

Gender Ideology: The Challenge of Being Gay or Lesbian in Sports

When a two-category classification model is used to define *gender*, the identities and actions of gay men, lesbians, bisexuals, and transsexuals (GLBTs) are outside normative boundaries (refer to Figure 8.3, p. 263). Therefore, GLBTs are sometimes feared, marginalized, or seen as oddities or sinners. They may be harassed and, in extreme cases, physically attacked (Smith, 2005b; Wertheim, 2005).

Discussions about the identities and lives of those who live outside normative boundaries established in connection with a two-gender classification model sometimes evoke strong emotions, defensive reactions, and moral judgments. Exceptions to this exist when people don't accept such a model or define *gender* in normative terms that reflect the reality of people's lives (see figure 8.4).

The same is true in sports. GLBTs play sports but they are seldom recognized. When discussions do occur, many people express ambivalence, mixed feelings, and inconsistencies. For example, a 2005 survey in the United States indicated that 78 percent of the respondents in a nationally representative sample agreed that, "It is OK for gay athletes to participate in sports, even if they are open about their sexuality" (NBC/USA Network, 2005). But about one in four said that openly gay athletes would hurt their teams and sport and would cause them as fans to enjoy the sport less and care less about the athletes. Forty-four percent agreed that homosexual behavior was a sin, half said that media coverage of gay athletes would cause negative reactions, over 60 percent agreed that "America is not ready to accept gay athletes," and nearly 70 percent said that being openly gay would hurt an athlete's career. Additionally, about 40 percent of youth sport coaches

FIGURE 8.4 Gender ideology is changing. However, when men or women become seriously involved in sports that challenge the two-category gender classification model, some people may tease or discourage them.

and 20 percent of college and professional coaches thought it is inappropriate for homosexuals to work in sports.

Acceptance of GLBTs has increased in society as a whole *and* in sports (Anderson, 2000, 2002, 2005). Today, there are teams and sport programs in which GLBTs are accepted and supported by heterosexual athletes and coaches, and there are more teams and programs exclusively for those with sexualities that are not heterosexuals (Elling et al., 2003). But significant challenges remain for both lesbian and gay athletes, and even when acceptance occurs, it is defined on terms set by heterosexual athletes, not terms preferred by gay and lesbian athletes (Anderson, 2002). Therefore, many GLBT athletes remain closeted, pass as heterosexual, cover their identity, or selectively reveal identity to trusted others and in situations where their sexuality is accepted (Griffin, 1998). Because of different levels of acceptance, identity management strategies often differ between athletes in women's and men's sports.

> Being a gay icon is a great honor for me. I'm quite sure of my feminine side.
>
> —David Beckham (in Wahl, 2003)

Lesbians in Sports   Acceptance of homosexual, bisexual, and transsexual athletes is greater in women's than men's sports. When the first high-profile female athletes came out as lesbians in the 1980s, they were the focus of praise, hostility, and endless media discussions and debates. When tennis star Martina Navratilova came out, it is estimated that she lost over $10 million in endorsement contracts—a major price to pay back in the 1980s. Today, she receives endorsement offers *because* of her sexuality. As other top-level female athletes come out today, they face short-term media attention, some negative reactions from fans and other athletes, and the personal challenges that most women face when they come out with friends and family (Griffin, 1998). But they are also likely to find people who will support them, even if most corporations are hesitant to sign them to endorsements (Swoopes, 2005).

Pat Griffin's groundbreaking book *Strong Women, Deep Closets: Lesbians and Homophobia in Sports* (1998) provides clear evidence that "sports and lesbians have always gone together" (p. ix). She notes that this evidence has been ignored in the popular consciousness, largely because of cultural myths about lesbians. Although most myths have been challenged and discredited, some remain. For example, some people think that lesbians are predatory and want to "convert" others to their "way of life," which is imagined to be strange, immoral, or downright evil. To the extent that lesbian athletes fear such people, they may turn inward and experience isolation and loneliness. When heterosexual athletes believe these myths or even wonder about their veracity, they avoid lesbian athletes and coaches; when coaches and administrators believe them, they are less likely to hire and promote lesbians in coaching and sport management.

Some women's sports and teams are characterized by a "don't ask, don't tell" atmosphere in which lesbians work to hide their identity so that they may play the sports they love without being marginalized or harassed. However, such a strategy has costs, and it does not encourage changes that might defuse and even eliminate homophobia in women's sports. Ethics educator Pat Griffin (1998) makes a good case for being open and truthful about sexual identity, but she also notes that open lesbians must be prepared to handle everything from hostility to cautious acceptance when they come out. She notes that handling challenges is easier when friends, teammates, and coaches provide support; when there are local organizations that challenge homophobia and advocate tolerance; and when there is institutionalized legal protection for gays and lesbians in organizations, communities, and society.

Gay Men in Sports   In men's sports, changes are not as visible as in women's sports. The culture of many men's sports continues to support a vocabulary of exclusion, marginalization, and homophobia, but this vocabulary does not always predict the responses of heterosexual athletes when a teammate comes out (Anderson, 2005; Bull, 2004). Men's sports have always been key sites for celebrating and reproducing dominant ideas about masculinity. Playing sports has been a rite of passage for boys to become men, and many people define male athletes in contact and power sports as the epitome of what it means to be a heterosexual man in society. Therefore, there is much at stake in maintaining the silence about gay men in sports and in discouraging gay male athletes from revealing their identities. This is necessary to maintain the integrity of existing normative gender boundaries and the privilege that is available to some men as long as the two-gender classification model is widely accepted (Pronger, 1999, 2002). Therefore, men in locker rooms use a vocabulary that reaffirms the norms of heterosexual masculinity. Policing gender boundaries preserves the glorified status of male athletes and men's access to power and influence in society as a whole.

It is due to these issues that the message to boys and men in sports is loud and clear: "Don't be a fag," and "don't play like a girl." The message to gay males of all ages is also clear: "Don't challenge the two-category gender classification model because it works for us men and has given some of us privilege and power in sports and in society." These messages create a combination of commitment to the cult of masculinity and deep fears of homosexuality in men's sports (Anderson, 2005; Tuaolo, 2002).

These messages also create a context in which boys and men feel ashamed about feelings of affection toward other men and feel compelled to mimic violent caricatures of masculinity to avoid being labeled "fags" (Messner, 1996). This maintains the norm that "real" men play with pain and injuries, never admit that they are afraid, and never, never confide affectionately in other men,

even—or especially—when they care deeply for another man. Instead, connections between male athletes are expressed through bell-ringing head-butts, belly bashers, arm punches, forearm crosses, fist touching, and other ritualistic actions that disguise and belie intimacy.

The power of gender ideology among male athletes is illustrated with a simple example: The first man to come out as gay in a major men's team sport will be guaranteed a spot in sport history. He will be seen as a hero by closeted and openly gay men of all ages. He will be on every talk show on television and radio. His website will receive millions of hits. Corporations that market to the gay demographic will knock his door down with endorsement deals. He will be an overnight celebrity and eventually defined as a hero in the company of Jackie Robinson, Mohammed Ali, and others who stood up for a principle that would later be taken for granted in the culture as a whole.

So why are dozens, even hundreds, of high-profile athletes taking a pass on this status and fame? Research by sociologist Eric Anderson (2005), who in 1993 was the first openly gay male high school coach in the United States, indicates that all male athletes, including gays, have learned to see themselves in strict ideological terms and they conform to the norms of hegemonic masculinity in cultlike ways, even when they would benefit by leaving the cult. This explanation makes sense, and it highlights the point that problems for gay athletes are ultimately grounded in a sport culture organized around a two-category gender classification model. Therefore, solutions rest in finding strategies to change gender ideology and the ways we do sports.

Strategies for Changing Ideology and Culture

Gender equity in sports ultimately depends on transforming gender ideology, including ideas and beliefs about *masculinity* and *femininity*, and changing the ways we do sports in society. These are complex and challenging tasks.

***Alternative Definitions of* Masculinity**   Dominant gender ideology today normalizes and naturalizes the idea that masculinity involves aggressiveness and a desire to physically dominate others. Men with the power and willingness to do whatever it takes to dominate others are lionized and defined as heroes in sports, business, and politics. Men seen as nurturing and supportive of others are defined as weak and emasculated.

As boys and men apply this ideology to their lives, they learn to view manhood in terms of things that jeopardize the safety and well-being of themselves and others. They may ride the tops of elevators, drive cars at breakneck speeds, play various forms of "chicken," drink each other under the table, get into fights, use violence in sports as indicators of manhood, use dangerous substances to build muscles, avoid interacting with women as equals, keep sexual scores in heterosexual relationships, and physically control girlfriends and wives. Some men learn that size and toughness allow them to violate norms and control others through fear and physical coercion.

Despite the dangers and socio-emotional isolation caused by this ideology, male athletes are seldom criticized for using it to guide their words and actions in sports. Coaches do not make athletes run laps for hitting someone too hard or showing no feeling when they have blown out someone's knee, knocked someone unconscious, or paralyzed—even killed—an opponent (as in boxing). Instead, coaches want athletes who can hurt others without hesitation or remorse and simply see it "as part of the game." But in the larger social and cultural context, does this ideology destroy men's ability to empathize with others and feel their pain, even the pain of opponents? Does it discourage the development of intimate and supportive relationships with other men or with women? Does it lead to high assault and sexual assault rates in society?

The frightening record of men's violence suggests that it would be useful to answer these questions and create new cultural space for alternative definitions of *masculinity*. The dual notion that hormones irrationally drive boys and that "boys will be boys" continues to be closely associated with seriously dangerous actions in many societies around the world. If dominant forms of sport in today's society prevent people from questioning and transforming this gender ideology, it is important to critically examine sports in society. When Joe Ehrmann, a former NFL player and currently a successful high school coach, did this, he decided that "masculinity ought to be defined in terms of relationships and taught in terms of the capacity to love and be loved" (in Marx, 2004, p. 4). Ehrmann's goal is to tear down traditional masculinity and establish in his players a commitment to empathy, inclusion, and integrity so that they can change their communities for the better. This is an example of an alternative definition of *masculinity* on a football team.

***Alternative Definitions of* Femininity**   The experiences of many female athletes also suggest a need to develop additional definitions of *femininity*. This process has already begun but requires commitment to maintain. For example, how are girls socialized to avoid objectifying their bodies to the point that they refrain from becoming physically skilled in a wide range of sports? We know that parents and others monitor the bodies and actions of girls more closely than they do for boys, even during infancy. Does this pattern of protectiveness continue through the entire life course and, in the process, limit physical skill development and participation in sports? Research suggests that it does (Frederickson and Harrison, 2005; Young, 1990). Therefore, alternative definitions of *femininity* are needed. This does not mean that girls and women should become like men as much as they should explore and connect with the power of their

As new ideas about femininity have been accepted, girls and women have become involved in sport settings where they were previously excluded. Only a small number of parents and coaches in this youth football league had problems when this girl excelled as a defensive end on one of the teams. (*Source:* Jay Coakley)

bodies across many activities, including competitive sports. In the past, large and/or strong girls and women without traditionally feminine characteristics and mannerisms have challenged the two-gender classification model, and sport seems to be a context for extending this challenge to the point of transforming gender ideology. If this occurs, there will be new femininities that recognize and support more women than are now supported by traditional notions of femininity.

Changing The Way We Do Sports Gender equity involves more than socially constructing new ways to define and perform masculinity and femininity. It also depends on changes in how

sports are defined, organized, and played. New and creative sport programs, new vocabularies to describe those programs, new images that people can associate with sports, and new ways to evaluate success and enjoyment in sports are the foundation of such changes (Burstyn, 1999; Hargreaves, 2000). When women and men who participate in sports as athletes, coaches, and administrators can critically assess sports and sport organizations from the inside, changes are more likely to occur (see chapter 16).

One strategy for achieving gender equity is to develop new programs that change how we do sports. Possibilities include the following:

1. Programs that promote lifetime sport participation and emphasize combinations of

competition and partnership, individual expression and teamwork, and health and skill development

2. Programs that embody an ethic of care and connection between teammates and opponents (Duquin, 2000)
3. Programs that provide coaching and administrative opportunities for lesbians, heterosexual women, and gay men, thereby adding new voices in decision-making processes, expanding ideas about the organization and purpose of sports, and opening sports to a wider range of participants
4. Programs bringing boys and girls, men and women, and heterosexuals and GLBTs together in shared sport experiences that promote new ideas about gender and sports in society

New programs are useful, but strategies to effect change requires that people realize that there may be political challenges associated with them. These include the following:

1. When women's sport programs are structured differently than men's programs, it is difficult to determine if there are equal opportunities for girls and women.
2. New sport programs for girls and women run the risk of being perceived as "second class," thereby perpetuating notions of female inferiority.
3. New sport programs are difficult to promote, and it is easier to apply pressure for equal resources in schools and other organizations when asking for comparable programs rather than new ones.
4. Sports that do not reproduce dominant gender ideology often are devalued and defined as "not real" and are (under)funded accordingly.

In the long run, gender equity depends on maintaining both approaches simultaneously.

This means that changes will occur if those who participate in existing sports can envision and work toward creating alternatives for the future. Likewise, those who envision and favor new sport forms will contribute to changes if they establish credibility and gain access to the power and resources needed to develop new programs.

All of us participate in ideological and cultural change when we critically assess how we talk about and do sports. This occurs when we do the following:

- Eliminate the language of difference and domination associated with sports and sport participation.
- Refrain from using labels such as *sissy*, *tomboy*, *fag*, and *wimp* in conversations and relationships.
- Object to coaches who motivate young men by telling them to go out and prove their masculinity on the playing field.
- Speak out against language that bashes gays and demeans women.
- Discourage the use of military metaphors that masculinize descriptions of sports (for example, "throwing long bombs," "he/she is a warrior," "putting in the big guns," and "punishing opponents").

Rule changes in sports are also useful strategies to achieve gender equity. For example, rules to restrict violence in hockey, football, rugby, and soccer create contexts where female athletes are more likely to be taken seriously. Men will object to this by saying such rules make sports into "girls' games," but such comments only reaffirm that the rules are necessary. Similarly, rules that support rituals that bring opponents together in ways that emphasize partnership rather than hostility and rivalry can provide images that change ideas about the goals and purposes of sports.

Gender equity depends on seeing and doing sports that reflect the values and experiences of everyone, including women and the men who don't identify themselves in terms of the dominant definition of *masculinity*. Therefore, gender equity does not automatically mean that the goal is to have girls and women play sports just as men have played them. Full equity means that people have a wide range of choices when it comes to organizing, playing, and giving meaning to sports.

summary

DOES EQUITY REQUIRE IDEOLOGICAL CHANGES?

Sport participation among females has increased dramatically since the late 1970s. This is the result of new opportunities, equal rights legislation, the women's movement, the health and fitness movement, and increased publicity given to female athletes.

Despite this recent trend of increased participation, gender equity is far from being achieved, and future increases in sport participation among girls and women will not be automatic. In fact, there are reasons to be cautious when anticipating more changes in the future. These reasons include budget cuts and privatization of sports, resistance to government policies and legislation, backlash in response to changes favoring strong women, a relative lack of female coaches and administrators, a cultural emphasis on cosmetic fitness among women, the trivialization of women's sports, and the existence of homophobia.

More women than ever are playing sports and working in sport organizations, but gender inequities continue to exist in participation opportunities, support for athletes, jobs for women in coaching and administration, and informal and alternative sports. This is because sports have traditionally been organized to be male dominated, male centered, and male identified.

Even when sport participation creates feelings of personal empowerment among women, the achievement of full gender equity is impossible without a critical analysis of the gender ideology used in sports and society as a whole. Critical analysis is important because it gives direction to efforts to achieve equity and it shows that there are reasons for men to join women in trying to achieve equity.

The major point of this chapter is that gender equity in sports is integrally tied to ideology and power issues. Gender equity will never be complete or permanent without changes in how people think about masculinity and femininity and in how sports are organized and played.

Dominant sport forms in society are currently based on a two-category gender classification model, which leads to the conclusion that girls and women are by definition inferior to boys and men. The gender ideology based on this classification model includes beliefs about male–female differences that "naturalize" the superiority of men over women and erase the existence of gay men, lesbians, bisexuals, and transsexuals from cultural images about sports and athletes. Therefore, sports celebrate a form of masculinity that marginalizes women and many men. As this form of masculinity is celebrated through sports, sexism and homophobia are built right into the structure of sports and sport organizations.

When gender ideology and sports are organized around the values and experiences of heterosexual men, real and lasting gender equity depends on changing dominant definitions of masculinity and femininity and the way we do sports. Useful strategies include developing new sports and sport organizations and changing existing sports from the inside and through outside actions and pressure.

Changes also depend on strategies such as these: using new ways to talk about sports, developing new rules to control violence and injuries and foster safety for all players, and creating new rituals and orientations based on the pleasure and participation approach to sports rather than the power and performance approach. Unless gender ideology and sports change, gender equity will never be completely and permanently achieved. This is why those interested in gender equity in sports should be interested also in gender and gender-relation issues outside of sports.

 See the OLC, www.mhhe.com/coakley9e, for an annotated list of readings related to this chapter. The OLC also contains a key concept list, a review test, and other helpful features.

WEBSITE RESOURCES

Note: Websites often change. The following URLs were current when this book was printed. Please check our website (www.mhhe.com/coakley9e) for updates and additions.

www.mhhe.com/coakley9e   Click on chapter 8 for a discussion of cheerleaders, myths about the impact of strenuous exercise on women, and other gender issues.

http://raw.rutgers.edu/womenandsports/Websites/index.htm   A valuable gateway site for women in sports links.

http://webpages.charter.net/womeninsport/   This site contains R. Vivian Acosta and Linda Jean Carpenter's latest report on gender equity in U.S. universities; summary data are presented on pages 255–256.

www.womenssportsfoundation.org/   The site of the most recognized sport organization for women in the United States; contains excellent links to many sites.

http://education.umn.edu/tuckercenter/resources/bibliographies/homophobia.htm   The Tucker Center for Research on Girls and Women in Sport lists references to research on gender and

sports, including studies that focus specifically on homophobia and sport.

www.gssf.co.nr/   The site of the Gender Sport and Society Forum, a site maintained by Emma Rich, at Loughborough University in England; contains an excellent bibliography of recent published books and articles on gender and sports, among other helpful resources.

www.statusofwomen.ca.gov/doc.asp?id=640   Title IX athletics compliance at California's public high schools, community colleges, and universities, by Margaret Beam, Bonnie Faddis, and Patricia Ruzicka. Portland, RMC Corporation for the California Postsecondary Education Commission, March 22, 2004, 55 pages.

www.titleix.info/index.jsp   The site of I Exercise My Rights, a public service, informational campaign that helps people understand the spirit and the legal letter of Title IX; it has links to descriptions of legal cases and other resources related to girls and women in sports.

http://www.savetitleix.com/   This site dedicated to providing information about challenges to Title IX and what is being done to resist them.

www.feminist.org/sports/   Numerous links to sites dealing with girls and women in sports; links include many sites related to gender equity.

www.iwg-gti.org   The site of the International Working Group on Women and Sport; contains information on programs, policy issues, and problems faced by girls and women in more than one hundred nations.

www.aahperd.org/nagws/   The National Association for Girls and Women in Sport is an active organization advancing gender equity in U.S. schools; has information on Title IX.

http://outsports.com/   Outsports.com is based in Los Angeles, and its goal is to provide a full range of information for the gay sports community; links to current news and other stories about gays and lesbians in sports. If a professional athlete in one of the major men's team sports ever came out, it would be covered on this site.

www.HomophobiaInSports.com   The Project to Eliminate Homophobia in Sport is a collaborative effort involving seven leading national organizations; its mission is to create an educated public that respects all athletes and sports-affiliated personnel regardless of sexual orientation and gender identity/ expressions.

http://www.xtremecentral.com/WASN/ WASNintro.htm   The site of the Women's Aggressive Skating Network, but it may change to the Women's Alternative Sports Network; designed to showcase "Outrageous Women Doing Incredible Things."

(Jay Coakley)

RACE AND ETHNICITY

Are They Important in Sports?

SPORTS CAN BRING KIDS together. It can also
pull them apart by feeding the misconception
that race predetermines what athletes can or
cannot do.

—Michael Dobie, journalist (2000, p. 335)

 Online Learning Center Resources

Visit *Sports in Society*'s Online Learning Center
(OLC) at **www.mhhe.com/coakley9e** for additional information and study material for this
chapter, including

- Self-grading quizzes
- Learning objectives
- Related websites
- Additional readings

A complete outline is available at www.mhhe.com/coakley9e.

THE SPORTS INDUSTRY is a white and male-dominated institution. Historically, black women have [not been] a real threat to the system, because we are women, and women do not have real power.

—**Colette D. Winlock, former U.S. track star (2000)**

ATHLETES ARE LIMITING themselves by what they see in the mirror. We become slaves to our stereotypes. Athletes of all races commit the same error.

—**Mark Kiszla, sports columnist, *Denver Post*, 2005**

Sports involve complex issues related to race and ethnicity. These issues are increasingly relevant as global migration and political changes bring together people from different racial and ethnic backgrounds and create new challenges for living, working, and playing together. The challenges created by racial and ethnic diversity are among the most important ones that we face in the twenty-first century (Edwards, 2000).

Ideas and beliefs about race and ethnicity influence self-perceptions, social relationships, and the organization of social life. Sports reflect this influence and are sites where people challenge or reproduce racial ideologies and existing patterns of racial and ethnic relations in society. As people make sense of sports and give meaning to their experiences as athletes and spectators and the experiences of others, they often take into account skin color and ethnicity. The once-popular statement, "White men can't jump," is an example of this.

Not surprisingly, the social meanings and the experiences associated with skin color and ethnic background influence access to sport participation, decisions about playing sports, and the ways that people integrate sports into their lives. People in some racial and ethnic groups use sport participation to express their cultural identity and evaluate their potential as athletes. In some cases, people are identified and evaluated as athletes because of the meanings given to their skin color or ethnic background.

Sports also are cultural sites where people formulate or change ideas and beliefs about skin color and ethnic heritage and then use them as they think about and live other parts of their lives. This means that sports are more than mere reflections of racial and ethnic relations in society; they're also sites where racial and ethnic relations happen and change. Therefore, it is important to study sports if we want to understand the dynamics of racial and ethnic relations.

This chapter will focus on the following topics:

1. Definitions of *race* and *ethnicity*, as well as the origins of ideas about race in contemporary cultures

2. Racial classification systems and the influence of racial ideology in sports
3. Sport participation patterns among racial and ethnic minorities in the United States
4. The dynamics of racial and ethnic relations in sports

DEFINING *RACE* AND *ETHNICITY*

Discussions about race and ethnicity are confusing when people don't define their terms. In this chapter, **race** refers to *a population of people who are believed to be naturally or biologically distinct from other populations.* When people identify a racial population, they use or infer a classification system that divides all human beings into distinct categories, which are believed to share genetically based physical traits passed from one generation to the next. Therefore, race involves a reference to physical traits, but it is ultimately based on a classification system that people develop around the meanings that they give to particular traits (see the section "The Origins of Race and Racial Ideologies" for further explanation).

Ethnicity is different from race because it refers to *a particular cultural heritage that is used to identify a category of people.* Ethnicity is *not* based on biology or genetically determined traits; instead, it is based on cultural traditions and history. This means that an **ethnic population** is *a category of people regarded as socially distinct because they share a way of life, a collective history, and a sense of themselves as a people.*

Confusion sometimes occurs when people use the term *minority* as they talk about racial and ethnic populations. In sociological terms, a **minority** is *a socially identified population that suffers disadvantages due to systematic discrimination and has a strong sense of social togetherness based on shared experiences of past and current discrimination.* Therefore, all minorities are *not* racial or ethnic populations, and all racial and ethnic populations are *not* minorities. For example, whites in the United States often are identified as a race, but they would not be a minority unless another racial or ethnic population had the power to subject them to systematic discrimination, which would put the population as a whole at a collective disadvantage in American society. Similarly, Polish people in Chicago are considered an ethnic population, but they are not a minority. Mexican Americans, on the other hand, are an ethnic population that also is a minority due to historical and current discrimination experienced by Mexicans and Mexican Americans.

African Americans often are referred to as a race because of the special meanings people have given to skin color in the United States; additionally, they are referred to as an ethnic group because of their shared cultural heritage. This has led many people to use *race* and *ethnicity* interchangeably without acknowledging that one is based on a classification of physical traits and the other on the existence of a shared culture. Many sociologists avoid this confusion because they realize that "race" has always been based on the social meanings that people have given to physical traits. These meanings, they say, have been so influential in society that shared ways of life have developed around them. Therefore, the focus in sociology today is on ethnicity rather than race, except when sociologists study the social consequences of the ideologies that have been organized around the idea of race.

This information about race is confusing to most people in the United States because they have been socialized to take for granted that race is a biological reality. To be told that race is based on social meanings rather than biological facts is difficult to understand. This issue is clarified in the next section.

THE ORIGINS OF RACE AND RACIAL IDEOLOGIES

Human diversity is a fact of life, and people throughout history have always categorized one another, often using physical appearance and cultural characteristics to do so. However, the idea that there are distinct, identifiable races is a recent invention. Europeans developed it during the seventeenth century as they explored the world and encountered people who looked and lived unlike anything they'd ever known. As they colonized regions on nearly every continent, Europeans developed classification systems to distinguish the populations that they encountered. They used the term *race* very loosely to refer to people with particular religious beliefs (Hindus), language or ethnic traditions (the Basque people in Spain), histories (indigenous peoples such as New World "Indians" and "Aborigines"), national origins (Chinese), and social status (chronically poor people, such as Gypsies in Europe or the Untouchables in India).

Ideas about race emerged in connection with religious beliefs, scientific theories, and a combination of political and economic goals (Omi and Winant, 1994). However, people have gradually come to use the term *race* to identify populations that they believe are naturally or biologically distinct from other populations. This shift to a biology-based notion of race occurred as light-skinned people from northern Europe sought justification for colonizing and exercising power over people of color around the world. Intellectuals and early scientists facilitated this shift by developing "objective" racial classification frameworks that enabled them to "discover" dozens of races, subraces, collateral races, and collateral subraces—terms they used as they analyzed the physical variations of people in colonized territories and other regions of the world.

"Scientific" analyses combined with the observations and anecdotal stories told by explorers led to the development of racial ideologies. As noted in Chapter 1, **racial ideology** consists of *a web of ideas and beliefs that people use to give meaning to specific physical traits such as skin color and to evaluate people in terms of how they are classified by race.* The racial classification models developed in Europe were based on the assumption that the appearance and actions of white Europeans were normal and that deviations from normal were strange, primitive, or immoral. In this way, "whiteness" became the standard against which the appearance and actions of *others* ("those people") were measured and evaluated.

Between the seventeenth and early twentieth centuries, whites used this racial ideology to conclude that people of color around the world were primitive beings driven by brawn rather than brains, instincts rather than moral codes, and impulse rather than rationality. This in turn enabled whites to colonize and subsequently exploit, subjugate, enslave, and even murder dark-skinned peoples without guilt or the sense that they had sinned (Hoberman, 1992; Smedley, 1997, 1999; Winant, 2001). Racial ideology also led some whites to view people of color as pagans in need of spiritual salvation. They worked to "civilize" and save souls, and in the process, dark-skinned people came to be known as the "white man's burden." Over time, these racial ideologies were widely accepted, and whites used them to connect skin color with other traits including intelligence, character, and physical characteristics and skills.

> Science has a long and disreputable history of making false extrapolations from inconclusive hard data—extrapolations that merely parrot the prejudices of the age.
>
> —Gary Kamiya, executive editor, *Solon* (2000, online)

Racial Ideology in the United States

Racial ideology in the United States is unique. It emerged during the seventeenth and eighteenth centuries as proslavery colonists developed justifications for enslaving Africans. By the early nineteenth century, many whites believed that race was a mark of a person's humanity and moral worth. Africans and Indians, they concluded, were subhuman and incapable of being civilized. By nature, these "colored peoples" were socially, intellectually, and morally inferior to light-skinned Europeans—a fact that was unchangeable (Smedley, 1997). This ideology became popular for three reasons. *First*, as the need for political expansion became important to the newly formed United States, the (white) citizens and government officials who promoted westward territorial expansion used racial ideology to justify killing, capturing, and confining "Indians" to reservations. *Second*, after the abolition of slavery, white Southerners used the "accepted fact" of black inferiority to justify hundreds of new laws that restricted the lives of blacks and enforced racial segregation in all public settings; these were called Jim Crow laws (DuBois, 1935). *Third*, scientists at prestigious universities, including Harvard, did research on race and published influential books and articles that claimed to "prove" the existence of race, the "natural superiority" of whites, and the "natural inferiority" of blacks.

The acceptance of this ideology was so pervasive that the U.S. government established policies to remove Native Americans from valued lands, and in 1896 the U.S. Supreme Court ruled to legalize the segregation of people defined as "Negroes." The opinion of the court was that "if one race be inferior to the other socially, the Constitution of the United States cannot put them on the same plane" (U.S. Supreme Court, *Plessy* v. *Ferguson*, 1896). This ruling has influenced race relations from 1896 until today much more than slavery has because it led to hundreds of laws, political policies, and patterns of racial segregation that connected whiteness with privilege, full citizenship and voting rights, and a combination of social, intellectual, and moral superiority over people of color.

As patterns of immigration changed between 1880 and 1920, people came to the United States from Ireland, southern Europe (Italy, Greece, Sicily), China, Japan, and Israel. At the same time, dominant racial ideology was used to link whiteness with American identity. Therefore, the question of who counted as white was often hotly debated as immigrant populations tried to claim American identities. For example, Irish, Jewish, Italian, Japanese, Chinese, and western

Asian populations were considered through the late 1800s and early 1900s to be nonwhite and therefore unqualified for U.S. citizenship. Some people objected to being classified as "colored" and took cases all the way to the Supreme Court to prove that they had ancestral links to "real" white people. But it took some of these populations many years to establish or prove their whiteness because whites carefully policed racial boundaries to maintain their privilege in U.S. culture and society. The traditional belief that whiteness is a pure and innately special racial category has, through the twentieth century, created a deep cultural acceptance of racial segregation and inequality and strong political resistance to policies that are designed to deal with the existence and legacy of these facts of American life.

The Trouble with Race and Racial Ideology

Research since the 1950s has produced increasing evidence that the concept of race is not biologically valid (Omi and Winant, 1994). This point has received powerful support from the Human Genome Project, which demonstrates that external traits such as skin color, hair texture, and eye shape are not genetically linked with patterns of internal differences among human beings. We now know that there is more biological diversity within any one human population than there is between any two populations, no matter how different they seem on the surface (AAA, 1998; Williams, 2005). Noted anthropologist Audrey Smedley (2003) explains that the idea of race has had a powerful impact on history and society, but it has little to do with real biological diversity among human beings. This is because it is based on categories and classifications that people have developed for social and political reasons. Therefore, race is a myth based on socially created ideas about variations in human potential and abilities that are assumed to be biological.

This conclusion is surprising to most people in the United States because they have learned to "see" race as a fact of life and use it to sort people into what they believe to be biology-based racial categories. They have also used ideas and beliefs about race to make sense of the world and their experiences. This is because racial ideology is so deeply rooted in U.S. culture that many people see race as an unchangeable fact of nature that cannot be ignored when it comes to understanding human beings, forming social relationships, and organizing social worlds.

When racial ideology is put aside, we see that definitions of race and approaches to racial classification vary widely across cultures and over time. Thus, a person classified as black in the United States, would not be considered to be "black" in Brazil, Haiti, Egypt, or South Africa where approaches to racial classification are different than they are in the United States. For example, Yannick Noah, a pop singer and former professional tennis player, is classified as white in Cameroon because his mother is a light-skinned woman from France, but he is classified as black in his native France because his father is a dark-skinned man from Cameroon in Central West Africa. Brazilians use over one hundred different terms when asked to identify their race. Less than 5 percent of Brazilians classify themselves as black, even though people in the United States would say that half of all Brazilians are black according the way they define race. Additionally, definitions of race have varied from one U.S. state to another so that through much of the twentieth century some people would be legally classified as black in one state but as white if they moved to another state; and definitions within states have changed over time as social norms have changed (Davis, 2001). These cultural and historical variations indicate that race is a social construction instead of an objective, unchanging biological fact.

Another trouble with race is that racial classification models involve making racial distinctions related to *continuous traits* such as skin color and other physical traits that exist in all people. Height is a good example of a continuous physical trait: Everyone has some height, and height varies along a continuum from the shortest person in the world to the tallest. But if we wanted to classify all human beings into particular height categories, we would have to decide where and how many lines we should draw along the height continuum. To do this, we would have to form social agreements about the meanings we wanted to give to various heights. Therefore, in some societies a 5 foot, 10 inch tall man would be classified as tall, whereas "tall" in other societies might mean 6 feet, 5 inches or more. To make classification matters more complicated, people in particular societies sometimes change over time their ideas about what they consider to be short or tall, as Americans have done through the twentieth century. Additionally, evidence clearly shows that the average height of people in different societies changes over time as diets, lifestyles, and height preferences change, even though height is a physical, genetically based trait for individuals (Bilger, 2004). This is why the Japanese now have an average height nearly the same as Americans, and northern Europeans have surpassed Americans in average height.

Skin color also is a continuous physical trait. It varies from *snow white* at one end of the skin color continuum to *midnight black* on the other, with an infinite array of color shades in between. When skin color is used to identify racial categories, the lines drawn between races are based on the meanings that are given to skin color by the people who are doing the classifying. Therefore, the identification of races is based on social agreements about where and how many racial dividing lines to draw; it is not based on objective biological division points. For example, racial classification in the United States was traditionally based on the "one-drop rule." This meant that a person with any black ancestor was classified as "Negro" (black) and could not be considered white in legal terms even if he or she appeared to be white. This approach to racial classification was based on decisions that served to perpetuate slavery, maintain the "purity" of the white race, discourage white women from forming sexual relationships and having children with black men, deny interracial children legal access to the property of their white parent, and guarantee that white men would retain power and privilege in society (Davis, 2001). The one-drop rule was based on a social agreement among white men, not on some deep biological significance of "black blood."

The trouble with using the one-drop rule to define race is that "mixed-race" people are erased in U.S. history and in sports. Additionally, it has created confusing social and identity issues. For example, when golfer Tiger Woods was identified as "black," he said he was "Cablinasian"—a term he invented to explain that he is one-fourth Thai, one-fourth Chinese, one-fourth African American, one-eighth Native American, and one-eighth white European (Ca-bl-in-asian = *Ca*ucasian + *Bl*ack + *In*dian + *Asian*). However, when people use the one-drop rule, they ignore diverse ancestry and identify people as black if they are not "pure" white, with qualifications in the case of those who also have Asian or Latino ancestry. This is why mixed-race persons in sports are constantly described as black, even though a parent or multiple grandparents are white.

To say that race is a social construction does not deny the existence of physical variations between human populations. This is obvious to all of us. However, when scientists have identified biologically meaningful variations, such as those related to disease or responses to drugs, they do not fit into the skin color–based racial classification models used in the U.S. and some other cultures. Additionally, scientists now realize that physiological traits, including genetic patterns, are also related to the experiences of particular individuals as well as the long-term experiences of particular populations.

Even though race is not a valid biological concept, its social significance has profoundly influenced the lives of millions of people for three centuries. This has occurred as people have developed webs of ideas and beliefs around race.

Tiger Woods is only one-fourth African American, yet he is often identified as black because of the way race has been defined by most people in the United States. Annika Sorenstam, a highly talented Swedish golfer, is defined as white, even though her physical characteristics are quite different from those of Italians, Greeks, and others commonly described as whites according to the racial classification system used by many people in the United States. (*Source:* Mark J. Terrill, AP/Wide World Photos)

In the process, racial ideologies have become deeply embedded in many cultures. These ideologies change over time, but at any point in time they influence people's lives.

The primary trouble with racial ideologies is that their primary purpose over the last three centuries has been to justify the oppression and exploitation of one population by another (Smedley, 1997, 1999). Therefore, they have led to and supported **racism,** or *attitudes, actions, and policies based on the belief that people in one racial category are inherently superior to people in one or more other categories.* In extreme cases, racial ideology has been used to support racist beliefs that people in certain populations are (1) childlike beings in need of external control, (2) subhuman beings

that can be exploited without guilt, (3) forms of property that can be bought and sold, or (4) evil beings that should be exterminated through **genocide,** or *the systematic destruction of an identifiable population.*

Another trouble with racial ideologies is that they foster the use of **racial stereotypes,** or *generalizations used to define and judge all individuals in a particular racial category.* Because stereotypes provide ready-made evaluative frameworks for making quick judgments and conclusions about others, they are widely used. They are used most often by people who do not have the opportunity or aren't willing to learn about and interact with those who have different race-related experiences. Knowledge undermines racial stereotypes and gradually subverts the ideologies that support them and the racism that accompanies them.

Race, Racial Ideology, and Sports

None of us is born with racial ideology. We acquire it over time as we interact with others and learn to give meanings to physical character-istics such as skin color, eye shape, the color and texture of hair, or even specific bodily movements. These meanings become the basis for classifying people into racial categories and associating cat-egories with particular psychological and emo-tional characteristics, intellectual and physical abilities, and even patterns of action and lifestyles. This process of making race and racial meanings is built into the cultural fabric of many societies, including the United States. It occurs as we in-teract with family members, friends, neighbors, peers, teachers, and people we meet in our every-day lives. General cultural perspectives as well as images and stories in children's books, textbooks, popular films, television programs, video games, song lyrics, and other media content influence it. We incorporate these perspec-tives, images, and stories into our lives to the extent that they fit with our experiences.

The influence of race and racial ideologies in sports has been and continues to be significant in the United States (Brown et al., 2005; Buffington, 2005; Woodward, 2004). For example, through the nineteenth and much of the twentieth century when African Ameri-cans engaged in clearly courageous acts, many whites used racial ideology to conclude that such acts among blacks were based on ignorance and desperation rather than *real* character. Some white people went so far as to say that blacks did not feel pain in the same way whites did and that this permitted them to engage in superhuman physical feats and endure physical blows as in the case of boxers (Mead, 1985). Many whites con-cluded that the success of blacks in sports was

> The challenge in sports in the 21st Century is going to be diversity.
> —Harry Edwards,
> sociologist/activist (2000)

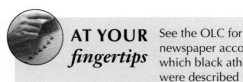

AT YOUR *fingertips*   See the OLC for newspaper accounts in which black athletes were described in blatantly racist terms.

meaningless because black athletes were driven by animal instincts instead of heroic and moral character. For example, when legendary boxer Joe Louis defeated a "white" Italian for the heavyweight championship of the world in 1935, the wire service story that went around the world began with these words:

> Something sly and sinister and perhaps not quite human came out of the African jungle last night to strike down [its opponent]. . . (cited in Mead, 1985, p. 91)

Few people today use such blatantly racist lan-guage, but traditional ideas about race continue to exist. Therefore, when eight blacks line up in the Olympic finals of the 100-meter dash or play in an NBA All-Star game, many people talk about "natural speed and jumping abili-ties," and some scientists want to study bodies wrapped with dark skin to discover what underlying physical traits allow them to per-form well—that is, *better than whites*.

On the other hand, when white athletes do extraordinary physical things, dominant racial ideology leads people to conclude that it is either expected or a result of fortitude, intelligence, moral character, strategic preparation, coachability, and good organization. Therefore, few people want to study bodies wrapped in white skin when all the finalists in multiple Olympic Nordic (cross-country skiing) events are "white." When white skiers from Austria and Switzerland—countries half the size of Colorado, with one-twentieth the population the United States—win nearly all World Cup championships year after year, peo-ple don't say that the genetic traits of the white population explain their success. Everyone already knows why the Austrians and Swiss are such good skiers: They live in the Alps, they learn to ski before they go to preschool, they grow up in a culture in which skiing is highly valued, they have many opportunities to ski, all their friends ski and talk about skiing, they see fellow Austrian and Swiss skiers winning races and making money in highly publicized (in Europe) World Cup competitions, and their cultural heroes are skiers.

Racial ideology focuses attention on *social* and *cultural* factors when the athletes are white. This is why people don't do studies to find genes that give Canadian hockey players strong ankles, instinctive eye-hand-foot coordination, and the ability to endure cold climates. Racial ideology prevents people from seeing whiteness as an issue in these cases because in a white-dominated culture whiteness is the taken-for-granted standard against which everything else is viewed.

When dominant racial ideology serves as the cultural foundation of a white-dominated, white-identified, and white-centered society, the success of white athletes is seen as "normal." At the same time, the success of black athletes is a "problem" in need of an explanation focused on dark-skinned bodies. This was the approach taken in 1997 when the white editors of *Sports Illustrated* titled a feature-length cover story, "What Happened to the White Athlete?" (Price, 1997). The story was based on their sense that blacks had taken over sports and white athletes were fast disappearing. However, data ignored by the story indicted that black athletes played only a limited number of the most visible and best revenue-producing sports (for white owners and media companies), whereas white athletes made up all or nearly all participants in dozens of other sports from the youth to professional levels. This illustrates that when racial ideology influences how topics are chosen and stories are told in the media, race-related ideas and beliefs become self-perpetuating, even when they portray reality in distorted and inaccurate terms.

Like the rest of us, scientists don't live or do their research outside the influence of ideology. For example, when people study human performance, it is important for them to understand how racial ideology influences the research questions that they ask, the people who they study, the data that they collect, and the analysis and interpretation of the data. This is because scientific "truth" depends on the facts that we choose to examine, the way that we classify those facts, and the theories that we use to analyze and interpret facts. Therefore, racial ideology can exert significant influence on knowledge about racial difference as well as the processes through which people give meanings to physical traits and use those meanings to organize their lives. This issue is discussed further in the box "'Jumping Genes' in Black Bodies."

Racial Ideology and a Sense of Athletic Destiny Among African American Men Does racial ideology influence how African Americans interpret their own physical abilities and potential as athletes? This is a controversial question. Statements by athletes and coaches combined with research suggests that many young blacks, especially men, grow up believing that the black body is special and superior when it comes to physical abilities in certain sports (Harrison and Lawrence, 2004; Harrison et al., 2004; Lawrence, 2005; Liddle, 2003; Stone et al., 1997, 1999). This belief might inspire some young people to think that playing certain sports and playing them better than anyone else in the world is part of their biological and cultural destiny. This inspiration is intensified when young blacks feel that their occupational future might involve low-wage, dead-end jobs on the one hand or riches and respect gained from slam dunks, end-zone catches, or Olympic sprint victories on the other hand. Even boxing might look better than a demeaning, minimum-wage job!

Figure 9.1 outlines a hypothesized sociological explanation of the athletic achievements of African American male athletes. The top section

In U.S. culture, may African American men grow up taking sports, especially basketball and football, very seriously. This youth player learned by age eleven not to smile when presenting himself as an athlete. His father told him to look serious and tough in the photo. (*Source:* Jay Coakley)

of figure 9.1 shows that racial stereotypes about innate physical abilities among blacks have been a part of U.S. history. When this fact is combined with limited opportunities in mainstream occupations and access to opportunities to develop skills in certain sports, many young blacks are motivated to play those sports; indeed, over time, they come to believe that it is their destiny to play them better than anyone else, especially whites (see the middle section of figure 9.1). If this sense of destiny is strong and pervasive enough, it could push blacks to accomplish great things and set records in certain sports (see the last section of figure 9.1).

This sense of personal and cultural destiny could be a powerful force driving millions of African Americans to dedicate the very fabric of their being to achieving greatness in certain sports. Is this what has led to the notable achievements of African American men in basketball, football, track, and boxing? Is this the reason why they have won medals in certain Olympic events for many years? Is this why African American women are following in their brothers' footsteps in certain sports? Former NBA player Charles Barkley, an outspoken observer of sports in U.S. culture, claims that the answer to these questions is yes. He says that we "have a society now where every black kid in the country thinks the only way he can be successful is through athletics. People look at athletes and entertainers as the sum total of black America" (in McCallum, 2002, p. 34).

In addition to Barkley's anecdotal analysis, historical evidence supports the power of a perceived sense of biological cultural destiny on an entire population. Three centuries ago, when whites from the small nation of England felt that it was their biological and cultural destiny to colonize and rule other parts of the world, they were driven to such a degree that they conquered over one-half of the globe as they formed the British Empire! This frightening and notable achievement dwarfs the achievements of blacks in certain sports. Furthermore, it is clear that this achievement was due to a combination of historical, cultural, and social factors rather than the genetic ancestry of white British people, although some whites in Europe and North America still believe that their genes account for the power and privilege they have achieved in global affairs. When social worlds are organized to foster a sense of destiny among particular people, *it shouldn't be surprising when they achieve notable things in the pursuit of their perceived destiny.*

The Challenge of Escaping Racial Ideology in Sports   The most effective way to defuse racial ideology is to bring people from different ethnic backgrounds together under conditions that

When these three social and cultural conditions are added together:

A long history of racial ideology that has emphasized
"black male physicality" and innate, race-based physical abilities among blacks
+
A long history of racial segregation and discrimination, which has limited
the opportunities for black men to achieve success and respect in society
+
The existence of widespread opportunities and encouragement
to develop physical skills and excel in a few sports

There are two intermediate consequences:

Many blacks, especially young men, come to believe
that it is their biological and cultural destiny to become great athletes.
+
Young black men are motivated to use every opportunity
to develop the skills they need to fulfill their destiny as athletes.

The resulting hypothesis is this:

This sense of biological and cultural destiny, combined with
motivation and opportunities to develop certain sport skills,
leads some black males, especially those with certain physical
characteristics, to be outstanding athletes in a few sports.

Note: This hypothesis has not been tested systematically, and it is not meant to ignore physical traits. Furthermore, it does not assume that black men and/or black women exclusively possess the particular traits required for success in certain sports.

FIGURE 9.1   A sociological hypothesis for explaining the achievement of black male athletes.

enable them to deal with one another as individuals and discover that ideologies obscure important aspects of people and the realities of their lives. However, when ethnic segregation exists, as it does in U.S. schools, for example, there is a tendency for black males to be "tagged" in a way that subverts their success in claiming identities that don't fit expectations based on racial ideology. For example, educator Amanda Godley (1999a) studied student interactions in a California high school and discovered that, when black male student-athletes excelled in academic work and were placed in honors classes, other students and teachers identified them as *athletes* rather than *honors students*. At the same time, Asian and white athletes in these classes were clearly identified as honor students rather than as athletes. Data on black female honors students who played on school sport teams were inconclusive, but those who did not play sports were identified by others and by themselves as honors students, rather than in race-related terms. In other words, racial ideology has a uniquely powerful impact on identity dynamics for black males in American culture.

Educator C. Keith Harrison has found similar identity dynamics on major university campuses. As two black male college athletes in one of his studies noted, "Everyone around perceives us being there only for our physical talents," and "Everything is white [on campus], only sports [are] for blacks" (1998, p. 72). This is not a new phenomenon (Adler and Adler, 1991), but its consequences are still frustrating for black men who want to expand their social identities beyond sports, or who don't even play sports.

More research is needed on this issue, but it seems that, when being a black male is combined with playing sports, it is difficult for some men to escape the subtle racial ideology that encourages people to tie race and sports together in the identity politics that exist in certain settings (T. Brown et al., 2003). This suggests that racial ideology enforces a student-versus-athlete dichotomy for black males and some black females who excel at sports. If this occurs, the connections between these individuals and other students, teachers, and the institution of the school will be constrained in ways that lead them to be academically marginalized. We need to know more about the conditions under which this occurs and how it affects everyone involved.

Many visible African Americans have pointed out the urgency of the need to know these things. Former NBA player Charles Barkley has noted that "sports are a detriment to blacks" because too many blacks channel their energies into sports

at the expense of developing other important skills. This, he says, "is a terrible, terrible thing, because that ain't even one-tenth of what we are" as a people (in McCallum, 2002, p. 34). This point is made in more specific sociological terms by prize-winning author John Edgar Wideman—the father of Jamila Wideman, who played basketball at Stanford and in the WNBA. He says,

> Basketball also functions to embody racist fantasies, to prove and perpetuate "essential" differences between blacks and whites, to justify the idea of white supremacy and rationalize an unfair balance of power . . . between blacks and whites. (in Lipsyte, 2001a, p. S13)

Wideman's point is not that blacks should avoid playing basketball or any other sport. He only wants to emphasize that when current racial ideology is accepted uncritically it distorts perceptions among blacks and whites in ways that perpetuate the racial status quo and undermine the possibility of creating a fair and just society. Wideman's point also emphasizes that racial ideology supports stereotypes about the abilities of blacks and whites that have become so widely accepted that people use them to assess the potential and abilities of themselves as well as others, and this is especially the case when it comes to sports (see also Stone et al., 1997, 1999 for empirical verification of this point).

Racial Ideology and Sport Choices Among Whites
A few years ago, I invited five children to be on a youth sports panel in my sports in society course; all were white ten- to twelve-year-olds who were heavily involved in sports. During the discussion, a sixth-grade boy known in his nearly all-white elementary school for his sprinting and basketball skills was asked if he would play those sports in junior high school. Surprisingly, he said no. When asked to explain, he said, "I won't have a chance because the black kids will beat me out." He said this did not upset him because he would play soccer and run the mile in track. He also said that he'd never played sports with black peers in elementary school, but he had watched TV and

seen blacks play basketball and win Olympic sprint medals.

About the same time that this sixth-grader was using racial ideology to make sport participation decisions, a white male voted the best football and basketball player in the entire state was asked by a local sportswriter what sport he would play in college, given that he was recruited in both sports by many top universities. The young man said, "I guess, right now, I'd take football because it's more unique to be a 6-6 quarterback . . . than a 6-6 *white* forward." His decision about sports and college selection clearly took into account his whiteness and racial ideology as it applies to sports.

Both of these young people, one twelve and the other eighteen years old, watched sports on television and listened to people discuss the abilities of athletes. In the process, they developed ideas about race, physical abilities, and their chances for success in various sports. Their whiteness, a taken-for-granted characteristic in

Racial ideology operates in complex and diverse ways. In some cases, it influences whites to avoid the sports in which blacks have a record of excellence. This way of thinking did not influence the white teenager on this team, nor does it influence whites in Europe where racial ideology does not discourage them from playing basketball. (*Source:* Courtesy of Preston Miller)

"Jumping Genes" in Black Bodies
Why Do People Look for Them, and What Will It Mean if They Find Them?

When people seek genetic explanations of achievements by black athletes, many of us who study sports in society question why their search begins and where it will take us. The search for "jumping genes" is a good example. Our questions about research on this issue are based on two factors: (1) many current ideas about the operation and effects of genes are oversimplified and misleading, and (2) jumping is much more than a simple physical activity.

OVERSIMPLIFIED AND MISLEADING IDEAS ABOUT GENES

Most people have great hopes for genetic research. They see genes as the building blocks of life that will enable us to explain and control everything from food supplies to human feelings, thoughts, and actions. These hopes have led to research seeking "violence genes" in people who are violent, "intelligence genes" in people who are smart, "power and endurance genes" in people who run fast and far, and "jumping genes" in people who play basketball. Many people assume that, if we find the key gene, we can explain and control the thoughts and actions that it "causes."

According to Robert Sapolsky (2000), a professor of biology and neurology at Stanford University, this notion of the "primacy of the gene" leads to deterministic and reductionist views of human action and social problems. The actions of human beings, he explains, cannot be reduced to particular genetic factors. Even though genes are important, they do not work independently of the environment. Research shows that genes are activated and suppressed by many environmental factors; furthermore the *effects* of genes in our bodies are mediated by environmental factors as well.

Genes are neither autonomous nor the sole causes of important, real-life outcomes associated with our bodies and what we do with them. Some chemicals that exist in cells and other chemicals (such as hormones), which come from other parts of the body, regulate genes. Furthermore, many external environmental factors influence regulatory processes. For example, when a mother rat licks and grooms her infant, these actions are environmental stimuli that initiate biochemical events, which turn on genes related to the physical growth of the infant rat. Therefore, say geneticists, the operation and effects of genes cannot be separated from the environment that turns them on and off and influences the expression of genetic effects. Sapolsky is hopeful about genetic research, but he explains that, as we learn more about genes, we also learn more about the environment and the connections between the two.

Genes do not exist and operate in environmental vacuums. This is true for genes related to diseases and genes related to jumping. Furthermore, we know that physical actions such as jumping, running, and shooting a basketball all involve one or more clusters of multiple genes. Explaining athletic performance would require studying "at least 124 genes and thousands, perhaps millions, of combinations of those genes," and this would provide only part of an explanation (Farrey, 2005). The rest would involve research on why people choose to do certain sports, why they practice, why they are motivated to practice and excel, how they are recognized and identified by coaches and sponsors, and how they are able to perform under particular conditions.

This means that discovering jumping genes would be exciting, but it would *not* explain why one person jumps higher than another, *nor* would it explain why people from one population jump, on average, higher than people from other populations. Furthermore, no evidence shows that particular genes related to jumping or other complex sport performances vary systematically with skin color or any socially constructed ideas about race and racial classifications.

JUMPING IS MORE THAN A PHYSICAL ACTIVITY

Jumping is not simply a mechanical, springlike action initiated by a few leg muscles exploding with power. Instead, it is a total body movement involving the neck, shoulders, arms, wrists, hands, torso, waist, hips, thighs, knees, calves, ankles, feet, and toes. Jumping also involves a timed coordination of the upper and lower body, a particular type of flexibility, a "kinesthetic feel," and a total body rhythm. It is an act of grace as much as power, a rhythmic act as much as a sudden muscular burst, an individual expression as much as an exertion, and it is tied to the notion of the body in harmony with space as much as simply the overcoming of resistance with the application of physical force.

Athletes in different sports jump in different ways. Gymnasts, volleyball players, figure skaters, skateboarders, mogul skiers, BMX bikers, wakeboarders, basketball players, ski jumpers, high jumpers, long jumpers, triple-jumpers, and pole vaulters all jump, but techniques and styles vary greatly from sport to sport and person to person in each sport. The act of jumping in societies where skin color and ethnic heritage have important social meanings is especially complex because race and ethnicity are types of performances in their own ways. These performances involve physical expressions and body movements that are integrally related to the cultural–kinesthetic histories of particular groups. Gerald Early (1998) notes in his article, "Performance and Reality: Race, Sports, and the Modern World," that playing sports is an *ethnic performance* because the relevance and meaning of jumping vary from one cultural context to another. For example, jumping is irrelevant to the performances of world leaders, CEOs of major corporations, sport team owners, coaches, doctors, and college professors. The power and influence possessed by these people and the rewards they receive do not depend on their jumping abilities. This is why the statement that "white men can't jump" is irrelevant to most whites, including every U.S. president and vice president in American history, nearly all senators, CEOs, and geneticists (Myers, 2000). Outside of a few sports, jumping ability has nothing to do with success in everyday life or achieving positions of power and influence. White CEOs making tens of millions of dollars a year don't care that someone says they can't jump. As Public Enemy rapped in the 1998 movie *He Got Game*, "White men in suits don't *have* to jump."

To study the physical side of jumping, sprinting, and distance running is important if it helps us understand human biology more fully. But this research will not provide all the answers to who jumps well in sports. Such answers also depend on our understanding of the historical, cultural, and social circumstances that make jumping and running important in some people's lives and why some people work so hard to develop their jumping and running abilities. It is not wrong to hypothesize that there may be genes related to jumping, but it is naïve to assume that they operate independent of environmental factors or that they are connected with skin color or socially constructed approaches to racial classification. Knowledge about genes is important, but it probably will never tell us much about the complex physical and cultural performance of slam dunks orchestrated by NBA players Amare Stoudemire (United States), Yao Ming (China), Dirk Nowitzki (Germany), and Manu Ginobili (Argentina). Nor will it tell us much about the vertical leaps and amazing hang time of the white European or the Chinese and Japanese volleyball players who have won so many international events. Nor will it tell us why whites have always won America's Cup yacht races (see figure 9.2) *What do you think?*

"*Of course, white folks are good at this. After 500 years of colonizing the world by sea, they've been bred to have exceptional sailing genes!*"
....

FIGURE 9.2 This statement is laughable when made about whites. However, some whites have made similar statements about blacks, and racial ideology has encouraged some scientists to use these statements as a basis for developing research hypotheses. This is one way that culturally based ideas about race influence research questions and distort interpretations of data.

the rest of their lives, strongly influenced decisions about their athletic futures. Ironically, they voluntarily limited their options because of their skin color—although they had so many options that this did not bother them.

This may be why the official times of white runners in certain sprints and long-distance road races have actually become slower since the 1950s and 1960s. Whites' genes have not changed, but their perceived choices and motivation have changed as African Americans and Africans have become successful participants in these events (Bloom, 1998; George, 1994; Merron, 1999; Weir, 2000). For example, when Tim Layden, a *Sports Illustrated* journalist, returned to the high school that inspired the 2000 film *Remember the Titans*, he noted that the football team at the school was no longer racially integrated as it was in 1971, the year depicted in the film. One of the players on the 2002 team told Layden that "most white kids around here wouldn't even think of coming out for football. They think it's a black sport" (Layden, 2002, p. 79).

Research suggests that racial ideology and the stereotypes that they spawn influence sports participation choices and how people perform in sports (Harrison and Lawrence, 2004; Harrison et al., 1999; Stone et al., 1997, 1999), but this is a tricky issue to study. Racial ideology exerts subtle and indirect influence that often is difficult to detect. Therefore, researchers must use creative methods to examine how it affects people's lives and the organization of the social worlds in which people make choices.

Racial Ideology, Gender, and Social Class

There are complex interconnections between racial and gender ideologies in the social world of sports. For example, research suggests that the implications of racial ideology are different for black men than for black women (Bruening, 2005; Bruening et al., 2005; Corbett and Johnson, 2000; Daniels, 2000; Majors, 1998; Smith, 2000; A. Solomon, 2000; Winlock, 2000). This is true

partly because the bodies of black men have historically been viewed and socially constructed differently than the bodies of black women.

Many whites in the United States have grown up fearing the power of black male bodies, being anxious about their sexual capacities, and being fascinated by their movements. Ironically, this aspect of racial ideology has created circumstances in which black male bodies have come to be valuable entertainment commodities, first on stage in music and vaudeville theater and later on athletic fields. Black female bodies, on the other hand, have been socially constructed in sexualized terms that have not made them valuable entertainment commodities in sports (Corbett and Johnson, 2000; Winlock, 2000).

Race and gender have influenced the lives of African American men in another way. Because they have systematically been denied opportunities enabling them to be successful breadwinners and providers for wives and families, some African American men have developed a presentation of self that is described as "cool pose." This presentation of self is organized around "unique, expressive, and conspicuous styles of demeanor, speech, gesture, clothing, hairstyle, walk, stance, and handshake" (Majors, 1998, p. 17). It emerges out of the frustration, self-doubt, anger, and marginalization in schools and the mainstream economy that has emasculated many African American men.

Cool pose is all about achieving a sense of significance and respect through *interpersonal* strategies when one is denied significance and success in jobs, politics, and education. Cool pose is also about being tough, detached, and in control. Cool pose says different things to different people. To the white man, it says, "Although you may have tried to hurt me time and time again, I can take it (and if I am hurting or weak, I'll never let you know)." It also says, "See me, touch me, hear me, but, white man, you can't copy me" (Majors, 1986, pp. 184–85). Cool pose also is an interpersonal strategy through which masculinity is portrayed by black boys and men who face status threats in everyday life. It is even used in this way by first- and second-graders in inner-city U.S. schools (Hasbrook, 1999; Hasbrook and Harris, 1999).

Educator Richard Majors, cofounder of the National Council of African American Men, suggests that cool pose has become part of the public personas of many black males in the United States and an integral part of the sports in which many athletes are black men. Is this how personal style has become such a big part of basketball? Is this why some black athletes are known for their "talk" as well as physical skills? Do black men use cool pose to intimidate white opponents? Does cool pose sell tickets and create spectator interest in college basketball, the NBA, and football? Do people go to see dunks and other moves inscribed with the personas of the black men who perform them? Is cool pose the result of what happens when black men face oppressive racial and gender ideologies and the realities of class relations in the American economy? We don't know, but it is worth seeking answers these questions (see Wilson, 1999).

Black female athletes face some of the same challenges faced by black men. However, Donna Daniels, an African American studies scholar from Duke University, suggests that physical appearance norms for females in predominantly white cultures have been racialized so that black female athletes exist outside the norm. Therefore, they must carefully "monitor and strategize about how they are seen and understood by a public not used to their physical presence or intellect, whether on the court, field, or peddling a product" (2000, p. 26). If they are not careful, there is a danger that people will interpret their confidence and intelligence as arrogance and cockiness or as an indication that they are "too black." This means that they must tone down their toughness and appear amicable and nonthreatening—much like Oprah Winfrey—lest they be defined as outsiders.

The marketing people at the WNBA were so sensitive to this issue that, when they first promoted the league, they presented ad after ad highlighting black players who had modeling contracts or newborn babies (Banet-Weiser, 1999; A. Solomon, 2000). When lip gloss and babies were not used, the ads depicted nicely groomed black female players in nurturing and supportive roles, especially with children.

At the same time, the NBA is using the sounds and images of urban hip-hop to recruit young males as fans. They know that about 70 percent of the young people who consume elements of hip-hop culture are whites and that they can use it to market the NBA across ethnic groups. As they do this, they also are careful not to alienate existing season-ticket holders, most of whom are relatively wealthy white men who may see hip-hop as too urban, too street, too tattooed, too cornrowed—"too black" for them (Hughes, 2004; Long and McNamee, 2004; Platt, 2002; Simons, 2003; Zirin, 2004). This is the major reason for the NBA "dress code" established in 2005 by Commissioner David Stern. But things may change over time in the NBA as changes occur in the cultural definitions of gender and race. Such is the case in all sports.

As social conditions change, so do ideas and beliefs about race and the bodies of athletes. Boxers today are more apt to be Latino than black. Large numbers of upper-middle-class whites now play the Native American game of lacrosse, and Africans are widely recruited by previously all-white men's soccer clubs in Europe. At the same time, white Americans have been replaced by young women from Russia at the top levels of professional tennis, NBA recruiters have established training programs in China, and Major League Baseball (MLB) is now full of stars from the Dominican Republic, Japan, and Korea. The USA Men's Basketball team struggled against Latin American and European teams to win only a bronze medal in the 2004 Olympics, and over 25 percent of the NBA All-Stars in 2005 were born outside the United States. To explain these things, we must understand social and cultural changes along with shifts in racial, ethnic, gender, and political ideologies. Information on genes may not help much, if at all, when developing our theories.

SPORT PARTICIPATION AMONG ETHNIC MINORITIES IN THE UNITED STATES

Sports in the United States have long histories of racial and ethnic exclusion (Bretón, 2000; Brooks and Althouse, 2000; Corbett and Johnson, 2000; Harrison, 1998; Hartmann, 2004; 2003; C. R. King, 2004a; Miller and Wiggins, 2003; Niiya, 2000; Wiggins, 2003). Men and women in all ethnic minorities traditionally have been underrepresented at all levels of competition and management in most competitive sports, even in high schools and community programs. Prior to the 1950s, the organizations that sponsored sport teams and events seldom opened their doors fully to African Americans, Latinos, Native Americans, and Asian Americans. When members of minority groups played sports, they usually played among themselves in games and events segregated by choice or by necessity (Giles, 2004; Miller and Wiggins, 2003; Niiya, 2000; Powers-Beck, 2004; Ruck, 1987).

Sport Participation Among African Americans

Prior to the 1950s, most whites in the United States consistently avoided playing with and against blacks. Blacks were systematically excluded from participation in white-controlled sport programs and organizations because whites believed that blacks didn't have the character or fortitude to compete with them. Since the 1950s, the sport participation of blacks has been concentrated in a limited range of sports. Even today, 40 million black Americans are underrepresented in or absent from most sports at most levels of competition. This is often overlooked because people watch college and professional football and basketball, Major League Baseball, Olympic track and field, and boxing and see

black athletes. However, these sports make up only four of the forty-four men's and women's sports played in college, four of the dozens of sports played at the international amateur level, and five of the dozens of professional sports in the United States. There is a similar pattern in Canada and in European countries with strong sporting traditions.

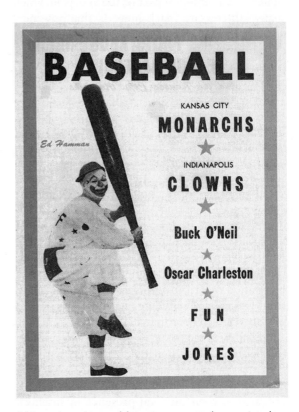

African American athletes were not taken seriously by most white people through much of the twentieth century. To make money playing sports, they often had to present themselves to fit the racial stereotypes held by whites. The Indianapolis Clowns baseball team and the Harlem Globetrotters basketball team joked around and acted in childlike ways so that whites would pay to watch them. Racism seemed to allow cultural space for blacks to be entertainers for the enjoyment of whites, but blacks faced exclusion in other spheres of social life, including sports. (*Source:* American Memory Collection)

Many people forget that there is a virtual absence of black athletes—male or female— in archery, auto racing (NASCAR, Formula-1, and Indy car), badminton, bowling, canoeing/ kayaking, cycling, diving, equestrian events, field hockey, figure skating, golf, gymnastics, hockey, motocross, rodeo, rowing, sailing, shooting, alpine and Nordic skiing, soccer, softball, swimming, table tennis, team handball, tennis, volleyball, water polo, yachting, most field events in track and field, and all of the action sports that are covered in the X Games and similar alternative sport events. How many black medal winners have there been in the Winter Olympics? When have black athletes been profiled in the X Games and NASCAR auto racing, two of the most rapidly growing media sports today? Someone who knows about race and sports might write an article in *Sports Illustrated* asking, "Why are there no black athletes?"

The exceptions to this pattern of exclusion stand out because they *are* exceptions. The underrepresentation of blacks in this long list of sports is much greater than the underrepresentation of whites in sports such as basketball and football. Additionally, there are proportionately many more whites who play basketball and football in high school and college than there are blacks who play tennis or golf at those levels. Finding black drivers at an Indy-car or NASCAR race is impossible, and even though all the drivers, support personnel, and nearly 100 percent of the spectators are white, nobody refers to these sports as white events. In a *white-centered* cultural setting where the lives of whites are the expected focus of attention, it is not even noticed that these sports are exclusively white. And in a *white-dominated* and *white-identified* setting where the characteristics of whites are used as the standards for judging qualifications, black athletes must play, drive, think, and act like whites to be accepted as participants who are doing it the right way. But this is often the case for anyone breaking a long-standing barrier related to race, ethnicity, or gender.

Through U.S. sports history, the participation of black females has been severely limited and has received little attention, apart from that given to occasional Olympic medal winners in track events. Black women suffer the consequences of gender and racial ideologies. Apart from a handful of studies, little is known about the unique experiences of African American female athletes, even those participating today (Bruening, 2005, ; Bruening et al., 2005; Corbett and Johnson, 2000; Green, 2000; Smith, 2000).

Overall, sport participation rates in middle- and upper-middle-income white communities in the United States are much higher than those in most predominantly black communities, especially those where resources are scarce. Racial ideology causes many people to overlook this fact. Many people see only the black male athletes who make high salaries in high-profile sports and then assume that they have "taken over" sports and that discrimination is gone. This exemplifies how dominant racial ideology influences what people see in their social worlds and what they define as problems.

Sport Participation Among Native Americans

There are 4.5 million Native Americans and Alaskans in the United States (including those who identify as Native American plus one other "race"). Although the U.S. census counts Native Americans as a single population, they comprise dozens of diverse cultural groups. The differences between many of these cultural groups are socially significant. However, most non-Native Americans tend to erase these differences by referring generally to "Indians" and envisioning stereotypical habits and dress—long hair, feathers, buckskin, moccasins, bows and arrows, riding horses, and being half naked, even in cold climates.

Native American sport participation patterns are diverse. They vary with cultural traditions, socioeconomic status, and whether they live on or off reservations. For example, participation patterns are heavily affected by a poverty rate of

26 percent (and up to 50 percent on some reservations)—at least twice the poverty rate in the United States as a whole. Many sports in traditional Native American cultures combine physical activities with ritual and ceremony (Keith, 1999; King, 2004a; Nabokov, 1981; Oxendine, 1988; Powers-Beck, 2004). For example, Native Americans from several western states commemorated the nearly 200 Cheyenne and Arapaho people killed by regional government troops in 1864 by organizing a 187-mile run from Sand Creek, the site of the massacre, to Denver. Forty Northern Arapaho people participated in the run, which was held in connection with a prayer vigil for the men, women, and children who were killed in the surprise attack at dawn (Frazier, 1999).

Although Native Americans have made significant achievements in certain sports over the past century, public recognition has often been limited to those few who have been standout athletes on the football and baseball teams of government-sponsored reservation schools and training schools. For example, when Jim Thorpe and his teammates at the Carlisle School, a segregated government training school, defeated outstanding mainstream college teams in 1911 and 1912, they attracted considerable attention (Bloom, 2000; Oxendine, 1988). Apart from a few successful teams and individual athletes in segregated government schools, Native American participation in most sports has been limited (Draper, 2005). It is subverted by poverty, poor health, lack of equipment and facilities, and a lack of understanding by those who control sports.

Native Americans who could play intercollegiate sports often fear being cut off from their cultural roots and identities. For example, Billy Mills, gold medalist in the 10,000-meter race at the 1964 Olympics, explains that becoming immersed in sport programs that provides no acknowledgment of or support for your culture is "like walking death." He speaks for many traditional Native Americans when he says that "if you go too far into [white] society, there's a

fear of losing your Indianness. There's a spiritual factor that comes into play. To become part of white society you give up half your soul" (in Simpson, 1996, p. 294). Native Americans who learn the culture of their people often feel an uncomfortable tension between the dominant American culture and their way of life. They say that when you leave your customs, religious ceremonies, families, and community behind, you must be prepared to live without those things that have made you who you are (Bloom, 2000; Clancy, 1999; Draper, 2005). This is a challenge that most people in any culture would not accept.

Cultural tensions are intensified for Native Americans attending schools or watching games between teams with names such as Indians, Redskins, Redmen, and Savages and with mascots that run around and mimic stereotypes of "Indians." Playing sports under such conditions involves giving up much more than half one's soul (see the box "Identity Theft?"). To see a distorted or historically inappropriate caricature of a Native American on the gym wall of a school where students have no knowledge of local or regional native cultures means swallowing cultural pride; repressing anger against insensitive, historically ignorant non-Native Americans; and giving up hope of being understood in terms of personal feelings and cultural heritage.

Native American athletes also face challenges when their cultural orientations do not match orientations in the power and performance sports of many high schools. Through the years, some white coaches who have worked with Native American students on certain reservations have used strategies to systematically strip them of traditional cultural ideology emphasizing cooperation and replace it with a Euro-American ideology emphasizing competition.

Some coaches frustrated by the nonaggressive orientations of certain populations of Native Americans have tried to instill a "killer instinct" in their football, basketball, and track athletes. For example, a high school football coach in Arizona complained that students at Hopi High

School "aren't used to our win-at-all-costs, beat-the-other-man mentality. Their understanding of what it means to be a good Hopi goes against what it takes to be a good football player." When the coach was asked how he handled the situation, he said, "[I did] exactly what the missionaries tried to do—de-Indianize the Indians" (in Garrity, 1989, p. 12).

When Native Americans don't give up their cultural souls voluntarily, some white coaches ask for them in the name of winning and cultural assimilation. Other coaches simply avoid recruiting Native American athletes because they don't want to risk bringing a student who will not fit in with teammates and campus culture. This is a problem that affects many Native American high school basketball players, a sport that is very popular among young Native Americans and one in which many excel (Draper, 2005).

Fortunately, Native American sport experiences do not always involve dramatic cultural compromises. Some Native Americans play sports in contexts in which their identities are respected and supported by others (Bloom, 2000; Clancy, 1999; King, 2003; King and Springwood, 2001a, 2001b; Paraschak, 1995, 1999; Schroeder, 1995). In these cases, sports provide opportunities for students to learn about the cultural backgrounds of others. In other cases, Native Americans adopt Euro-American ways and play sports without expressing any evidence of their cultural heritage; they accommodate the dominant culture and use it to guide their participation, even if they don't agree with or accept all of it. In some cases, they redefine participation to fit their cultural beliefs. This is a strategy that has been used by many ethnic minorities who participate in the sports developed by and for people in the dominant culture.

Sport Participation Among Latinos and Latinas

Latinos include people from diverse cultures. They may share language, colonial history, or Catholicism, but their cultures and group histories vary greatly. Mexican Americans constitute the largest Latino group in the United States, followed by Puerto Ricans, Cubans, other Central and South Americans, and people from Spain. Overall, Latinos constitute the largest ethnic minority population in the United States—about 44 million people in 2006.

Most scholars and journalists in the past have ignored the experiences of Latino athletes. Stereotypes about Latinos vary from one region of the United States to another, but all of them are misleading generalizations. For example, one MLB scout explained that most Mexicans and Mexican Americans in Major League Baseball were pitchers because

> Mexicans have bad foot speed. It's a genetic type thing. They have a different body type. Most have good hands and good rhythm. That's why they dance so well. Rhythm is important in baseball, it means agility. (in Beaton, 1993, p. 11)

At the same time, millions of soccer fans know that foot speed is not lacking among Mexicans. Another baseball scout used a slightly different stereotype about Mexicans when he stated, "Mexicans, because of their Indian blood, can run to New York and not stop. Just not fast" (in Beaton, 1993, p. 11).

Stereotypes about the genetic makeup of Mexicans are not applied to Cubans, Venezuelans, or Dominicans, whose success in baseball is legendary. Additionally, stereotypes often change when Latinos are classified as black. This shows that the black-or-white approach to racial classification traditionally used in the United States is both inaccurate and misleading. Furthermore, stereotypes about Mexican Americans ignore that Mexico itself is a multiethnic society, with nearly 110 million people who have a combination of Spanish, Indian, English, German, French, and various Central American ancestries. To use them to explain the success or failure of Latino athletes creates confusion and perpetuates misinformation. Studying these stereotypes is important,

reflect on SPORTS

Identity Theft?
Using Native American Names and Images in Sports

Using stereotypes to characterize Native Americans is so common that most people don't realize they do it. When people take Native American images and names, claim ownership of them, and then use them for team names, mascots, and logos, sports perpetuate an ideology that trivializes and distorts the diverse histories and traditions of native cultures. No other ethnic population is subject to this form of cultural identity theft. As sportswriter Jon Saraceno, exclaims, "Can you imagine the reaction if any school dressed a mascot in an Afro wig and a dashiki? Or encouraged fans to show up in blackface?" (2005, p. 10C).

To understand this issue, consider this story told by the group, Concerned American Indian Parents:

> An American Indian student attended his school's pep rally in preparation for a football game against a rival school. The rival school's mascot was an American Indian. The pep rally included the burning of an Indian in effigy along with posters and banners labeled "Scalp the Indians," "Kill the Indians," and "Let's burn the Indians at the stake." The student, hurt and embarrassed, tore the banners down. His fellow students couldn't understand his hurt and pain.

This incident occurred in a public school in 1988, twenty years after the National Congress of American Indians initiated a campaign to eliminate stereotypes of "Indians" in U.S. culture. In 1970 there were about 3000 schools using Native American images, names, logos, and mascots for their sport teams. However, as Native Americans have struggled for over three decades to reclaim their identities and gain control over how they are represented by others, over 2000 schools changed their names and mascots. They realized that it was not right to assume ownership of the names and identities of other human beings and use them to promote themselves. However, hundreds of schools and a few professional teams still do this (King, 2004b; King and Springwood, 2001a, 2001b). Therefore, twenty years after this incident, there are teams still named "Indians," "Savages," "Warriors," "Chiefs," "Braves," "Redskins," "Red Raiders," and "Redmen" (not women!). And many have mascots who pretend to be Indians by dressing in war bonnets

Chief Illiniwek, the mascot of the University of Illinois, has provoked debates for nearly two decades. The president and Board of Trustees say they honor "Indians" when a white student cross-dresses as an "Indian" and does choreographed "native" dance routines. The NCAA says that ethnic cross-dressing and the historically inaccurate Indian head logo are "hostile and abusive." But there are state legislators and university trustees who insist that they will continue fighting to use "their" chief. (*Source:* Ted S. Warren, AP/Wide World Photos)

and war paint, brandishing spears and tomahawks, pounding tom-toms, intoning rhythmic chants, and mimicking religious and cultural dances. Schools still put "their" Indians on gym walls and floors, scoreboards, and the dozens of products that they sell. This is done, they say, as a "harmless" tradition that "honors" the "Indians" from whom they have taken images and identities. Is it possible to honor someone you don't know and won't listen to?

What if the San Diego Padres' mascot were a fearsome black-robed missionary who walked the sidelines swinging an 8-foot long rosary and carrying a 9-foot long faux-crucifix? And what if he led fans in a pumped up rendition of Gregorian chant as spectators held up plastic crucifixes covered with the team logo and chanted with him? People would be outraged because they know the history and meaning of Christian beliefs, objects, and rituals. Therefore, if more Americans knew the histories, cultural traditions, and religions of the 500 Native American tribes and nations in the United States today, they wouldn't think of using Native American names and allowing naïve students to dress in costumes containing feathers and other items defined as sacred in the animistic religious traditions of many Native Americans. Nor would they allow fans to mimic sacred chants or engage in war-whooping, tomahawk-chopping cheers based on fuzzy memories of "cowboy and Indian" movies in which the Indians always lost their land, lives, and dignity.

Many public school officials and state legislators realize that using public money to fund schools that misrepresent an ethnic minority whose ancestors were massacred, ordered off their lands at gunpoint, and confined to reservations by government representatives is adding insensitivity to cruelty and a long history of broken promises (treaties) made to Native Americans. They also realize that romanticizing a distorted version of the past by taking the names and images of people who currently experience discrimination, poverty, and the negative effects of stereotypes is the height of white privilege and hypocrisy. Therefore, some states and school districts now have policies banning such practices.

In 2003 the National Collegiate Athletic Association (NCAA) recommended that all universities using American Indian names, mascots, or logos review their practices and assess if they were inconsistent with the NCAA's stated commitment to cultural diversity. The NCAA realized that allowing students to dress up as Indians and mimic Native American dances and chants at games was hypocritical. In 2005 the NCAA took things a step further and banned the display of Native American names, logos, and mascots at all NCAA playoff games and championships and gave member institutions a timeline for changing how they represented their teams. But then NCAA officials made an exception for Florida State University (FSU) when it claimed they had "permission" to use the Seminole name and logo image in an honorable way. FSU honors the Seminoles by having a white European American student paint his face, put on a headband and a colorful shirt, carry a feather-covered spear, and ride into the football stadium on a horse named Seminole. And at www.nolesstore.com, FSU fans can honor *their* "'nole," as they call "their Indian," by buying products with the painted and feathered "Seminole face" on them. These products include floor mats, welcome mats, stadium seats, napkins, paper plates, and other things that allow fans and their friends to wipe their feet on the image that they "honor" and put it on the floors of their car. Then they can sit on the Seminole face as they watch a game and wipe their mouths and eat off it as they tailgate. Sales profits go to the university, not the Seminole people. But the NCAA allows this in the name of honoring "Indians" in a manner consistent with their commitment to diversity!

This is not surprising in light of other cases. For example, in 2005 the California State Legislature passed a bill banning the use of "Redskins" as a public school nickname because many Native Americans consider it the equivalent of *nigger, spic, kike, chink, slope,* and *camel jockey;* Governor Schwarzenegger vetoed the bill, however, saying it was a trivial issue. In 1999 a panel in the U.S. Patent and Trademark Office ruled that "Redskins," "Redskinettes," and the logo of a feathered "Redskin" man as used by the NFL team in Washington, D.C. "disparaged" Native Americans. The panel canceled six exclusive trademarks, which meant that the NFL no longer owned exclusive rights to the "Redskins" name and logo. But in 2003 a federal district court judge overturned the panel's ruling.

Continued

Identity Theft? (*Continued*)

Although this decision is under appeal (in early 2006), the NFL team in the capital city of the government that has broken all but one of over 400 treaties with Native Americans still controls its "Redskins." For many Native Americans, this is a slap in the face and symbolizes the history of oppression that they've experienced in the United States.

Some people have argued that "petty insults" such as this are "functional" because they "actually promote cultural survival by bringing Indians together in solidarity against the dominant culture" (Brown, 2003). However, if some school named their team the "Fighting Coakleys" and used a silly caricature of my deceased son as their mascot and logo, I would be enraged, even if it brought my family together to fight a common foe. I have not trademarked our family name nor images of my son, but does that mean others are free to use them exclusively for their purposes and say that they are honoring us in the process? All identity theft is wrong. *What do you think?*

but there is a need for research on the cultural, political, economic, and social factors affecting the sport experiences of Latinos. In other words, theories are most helpful when they focus on ethnic relations issues and avoid assumptions based on genetic predispositions and abilities.

Latinos in North American Baseball   Research by anthropologist Alan Klein (1991) indicates that young Latinos who want to play professional baseball in the United States are generally recruited and trained in the baseball academies that major league teams maintain in Latin American countries. The destinies of these players are controlled by scouts and coaches associated with these academies. Once players sign contracts to play in North America, they face significant cultural adjustments and language problems; they also face the strain of living in a society where few people understand their cultural backgrounds (Bretón and Villegas, 1999; Klein, 1991). This is partly why 90 to 95 percent of all Latino players who sign contracts never make it to the major leagues. Even those lucky enough to make minor league teams often are cut after a year or two. Rather than return home to face the embarrassment of failure, they stay in the United States as undocumented workers, doing low-wage

work. Writer Marcos Bretón notes that "these castoffs represent the . . . rule rather than the exception in the high-stakes recruitment of ball players from Latin America and the Caribbean" (2000, p. 15), but their stories remain untold on ESPN and the sports pages of newspapers.

Despite the difficulties faced by most Latino players, baseball remains popular in Latin America, and major league teams maintain academies because Latin America provides a pool of cheap baseball labor. Established Latino stars are well paid, but young players are signed for a fraction the money paid to new players born and trained in the United States. As a vice president of one major league team noted, it costs less to sign five Latin American players than one player from the United States. This "boatload mentality" partly explains why over one of every four players on major league teams are Latinos and nearly 40 percent of all minor league baseball players were Latin Americans in 2006.

This "boatload mentality" also creates other problems for Latino players. For example, when Major League Baseball instituted new drug-testing policies in 2005, twenty-four of the forty-seven players who tested positive were Latinos, most of whom spoke little English, did not know all the substances on the list, and came from

Lisa Fernandez, probably the best player in softball history, led the U.S. team to three gold medals (Atlanta, Sydney, and Athens). Her father was born in Cuba and played baseball there; her mother was born in Puerto Rico and played stickball after moving to New York. Fernandez continues to be an inspiration for many Latinas who play sports.
(*Source:* Elaine Thompson, AP/Wide World Photos)

countries where taking vitamins, supplements, and over-the-counter drugs is common in the absence of accessible medical care (Jenkins, 2005; LeBatard, 2005c). Furthermore, drugs are less regulated in Latin America compared to the United States. Many substances, including anabolic steroids, are available over the counter, and the cheapest steroids are those used by ranchers and farmers to increase the growth of their animals. Therefore, when young baseball players want to gain strength and speed as they pursue their dreams and hope to support their families and as they listen to advice offered by unethical scouts, they may take these drugs, even when the bottles are labeled, "for veterinary use only." When tested in the United States, some of these players are defined as drug users and punished, often as examples that baseball is tough on drugs. This of course destroys the dreams that Latino players have worked for many years to achieve.

"Mexicanos" in Texas High School Football
Anthropologist Doug Foley studied Mexican-Anglo relations associated with high school football in a small Texas town. He explained that working-class Mexicano males (*vatos*) rejected sport participation but used Friday night football games as occasions for publicly displaying their "style" (cool pose?) and establishing social reputations in the community. Foley (1990a, 1990b, 1999a) described how the Mexicanos protested a homecoming ceremony that gave center stage to Anglos and marginalized Mexicanos, how the Mexicano players defied the coaches when the Anglo players were given high-status positions on the team, and how the Mexicano coach resigned in frustration when faced with the bigotry and contradictory expectations of powerful Anglo boosters and school board members.

Foley concluded that despite being a site for resistance against prevailing Anglo ways of doing things in the town, high school football ultimately perpetuated the power and privilege of the local Anglos. As long as Mexicanos saw and did things the Anglo way, they were accepted; raising issues did nothing to make Anglos accommodate Mexicanos' values and experiences.

Latinas in U.S. Sports   Research on Latinas in the United States shows the diversity of the traditions and norms that revolve around gender and sport participation for girls and women from various Latin cultures (Acosta, 1999; Jamieson,

1998, 2005; Sylwester, 2005a, 2005b, 2005c). First-generation Latinas in the United States often do not receive parental support to play sports. Parents may feel that playing sports is contrary to their cultural traditions and prevents their daughters from doing household tasks such as caring for siblings, assisting with meal preparation, and cleaning house—none of which their brothers are expected to do. Furthermore, playing sports is a luxury in households where meeting expenses is a struggle and transportation to practices and games is unavailable or costly.

Second- and third-generation Latinas face fewer constraints in their families. Their parents often see sports as developmentally important and are willing to use family resources to fund their daughters' sport participation. However, talented high school players often remain hesitant to play intercollegiate sports if it means going to a college far from home where there is little support for their Latina identities and traditions. Kathleen Jamieson's (1998, 2005) research describes some of the unique identity-management experiences of Latina intercollegiate athletes who must bridge a cultural divide as they live, study, and play with others who know little about merging cultural identities and managing relationships in two cultural spheres.

Young Latinas are more likely than their peers in past generations to see good athletes who look like them. Sometimes, there is media coverage of Latinas in golf, softball, soccer, and other sports. But most of their inspiration comes from older sisters and neighbor girls who play sports. Research on the experiences of Latinas is important because it helps us understand more fully the dynamics faced by young women caught up in the experience of immigration and making their way in a new society and culture. At this point, we know that first-generation Latinas face more constraints than Latinas in second- and third-generation families. However, we know little about the experiences of these young women as they combine family life with school, sports, and jobs. And we know almost nothing about adult Latinas who play sports in local leagues. These women often use their participation to maintain regular contact with relatives and friends in the United States and Mexico. This makes sports such as soccer and softball important in their lives and in their overall ability to adjust to life in the United States.

Research on the sport experiences of Latinos and Latinas is important because they constitute the fastest growing ethnic population in the United States. Physical educators and coaches in schools benefit from this research as do people in commercial sports where there is an emphasis on attracting Latino fans. For example, the economic success of professional soccer in much of the United States depends on being sensitive to the interests and orientations of Latino athletes and spectators. Latinos are eager to have their cultural heritage recognized and incorporated into sports and sport experiences in the United States and into the awareness of their fellow citizens (Otto, 2003).

Sport Participation Among Asian Americans

There were nearly 16 million people with Asian and Pacific Island backgrounds in the United States as of mid-2006. The global migration of labor has brought people from many Asian cultures to the United States and other nations around the world. In the United States, most Asian Americans live on the West Coast and in cities where they have been attracted by job opportunities. However, the cultural heritage and the individual histories of Asian Americans are very diverse. This diversity is often ignored in media coverage and sometimes ignored in research.

Although Chinese and Japanese people in the United States have long played sports in their own communities (Niiya, 2000), the recent success and popularity of a few Asian and Asian American athletes has raised important issues about ethnic dynamics in sports. For example, the popularity of Yao Ming of the Houston Rockets in the NBA and several Japanese and

The popularity of Apolo Ohno has been linked to his exciting athletic skills, his "action sport" persona, and his mixed ethnic heritage. He was raised by his Japanese father and is clearly aware of his combined Japanese and Euro-American background. As more people forge their own hybrid ethnic identities, public figures like Ohno will be viewed in positive ways. (*Source:* Amy Sancetta, AP/Wide World Photos)

Korean baseball players highlights the extent to which many Asians and Asian Americans have embraced sports associated U.S. culture. Safeco Field, home of the Seattle Mariners and star player Ichiro Suzuki, now has so many Japanese spectators at baseball games that signs in the stadium are posted in both Japanese and English. Research is now needed to examine the impact of these players on ethnic relations in the stadiums and communities where they live and play.

The success of speed skater Apolo Anton Ohno, figure skaters Kristi Yamaguchi and Michelle Kwan, NBA player Yao Ming, and MLB player

Ichiro Suzuki suggests that it is possible for athletes from a range of Asian backgrounds to develop a strong fan base in the United States. Although some transnational corporations have been hesitant to offer endorsement contracts to these athletes, a growing number of companies now see some of these athletes as having global commercial appeal and value. For example, Apolo Ohno's mixed ethnic heritage (half Japanese and half Euro-American), combined with his "soul patch" chin whiskers and his unassuming but confident "action sport" persona, caught the attention of teen fans and the media during the 2002 and

2006 Winter Olympics. His popularity, anchored in his exciting athletic performances, may also be tied to how he has seemingly forged a hybrid ethnic identity with which he is comfortable. This is attractive to many people who have done the same or face the challenge of doing so in the United States where living with a mixed ethnic heritage is an increasingly common experience.

The participation of Asian-born athletes in elite sports has elicited prejudiced statements from some athletes. When Shaquille O'Neil was playing for the Los Angeles Lakers in 2003, he responded to a journalist's question about playing against Yao Ming by saying, "Tell Yao Ming, 'ching-chong-yang-wah-ah-so.'" Pro golfer Jan Stevenson, a native of Australia and current resident in Florida, said in 2003 that Asian women golfers "are killing our tour." She explained that the Asian pros didn't promote women's golf because they lacked emotional expressiveness, refused to speak English, even when they could do so, and rarely spoke to fans and reporters (Adelson, 2003; Blauvelt, 2003). Public comments such as these are rare, but they point to the challenges faced when people from different cultural and ethnic backgrounds participate in sports that are organized around the cultural orientations and traditions of Europeans and North Americans. (See discussions of globalization in chapter 13, pp. 456–468.)

At this point, research is needed on how images of Asian and Asian American athletes are taken up and represented in the U.S. media and in the minds of people around the country. Research is also needed on the dramatic rise in popularity of various martial arts in the United States. Karate, judo, tae kwon do, and other sports with Asian origins have become especially popular among children. Has participation in these martial

arts had an impact on children's knowledge and awareness of Asian cultures, on ethnic relations in elementary schools, and on the stereotypes used or challenged among children and others who participate in these sports? Or have these sport forms become so Americanized that their Asian roots are lost or ignored by participants?

The experiences and sport participation patterns of Asian Americans differ, depending on their immigration histories. Chinese Americans and Japanese Americans whose families have lived in the United States for four or more generations have experiences that are clearly different from those of recent Vietnamese, Thai, Cambodian, Indian, and western Asian immigrants and their children. Research must be sensitive to these differences and the ways that they influence sport participation patterns and experiences. Gender issues also are important to study across a range of sports (Wong, 1999). Applied research is needed to assist coaches in high schools with Asian American students.

Anthropologist Mark Grey (1999) dealt with some of these issues in his study of high school sports and relations between immigrants from Southeast Asia and the established residents of Garden City, Kansas. Grey reports that the immigrant students often had a difficult time fitting into sports organized around the values and experiences of European Americans. When these newcomers did not try out for football, basketball, baseball, and softball, they were seen by many local residents as unwilling to become "true Americans." This created tensions that contributed to the social marginalization of Asian students and families. It is possible that this pattern also exists in other communities although not enough is known about it or other patterns.

> We're in the 21st century in a global society. We have to be sensitive to images, thoughts, behaviors that affect other cultures—cultures that we now know we were misinformed about.
> —Dr. Frances Carroll, University of Illinois, Board of Trustees (in Wise, 2003)

In contrast to Grey's research, third- and fourth-generation Asian American families often are integrated into community life in the United States and play the same sports that other members of the community play. In fact, some Asian American young people have used sports to express their assimilation into U.S. culture and reaffirm social relationships with peers. Again, research is needed on how and when this occurs in multiethnic neighborhoods and schools and in areas where there are few Asian and Asian American students.

THE DYNAMICS OF RACIAL AND ETHNIC RELATIONS IN SPORTS

Racial and ethnic relations in most sport settings are better today than in the past, but many changes are needed before sports are a model of intergroup fairness. The challenges faced today are different from the ones faced twenty years ago, and experience shows that they will always be a part of social life. When one set of challenges are met, a new social situation is created, and it presents its own challenges. For example, once racial and ethnic segregation is eliminated and people come together, there is the challenge of living, working, and playing with people who have diverse experiences and cultures. Meeting this challenge requires a commitment to equal treatment, *plus* learning about the perspectives of others, understanding how they define and give meaning to the world around them, and then determining how to form and maintain relationships while respecting differences, making compromises, and supporting one another in the pursuit of goals that may not always be shared. None of this is easy, and challenges are never met once and for all time.

Many people think in fairy-tale terms when it comes to racial and ethnic relations: They believe that opening a door so that others may enter a social world is all that's needed to achieve racial and ethnic harmony. However, coming together is just the first step in a never-ending process of nurturing relationships, producing a representative culture, and sharing power with others. Racial and ethnic diversity brings potential vitality and creativity to a team, organization, or society, but this potential does not automatically become reality. It requires constant awareness, commitment, and work to achieve and maintain it.

The following sections deal with three major challenges related to racial and ethnic relations in sports today: (1) eliminating racial and ethnic exclusion in sport participation, (2) dealing with and managing racial and ethnic diversity by creating an inclusive culture on sport teams and in sport organizations, and (3) integrating positions of power in sport organizations.

Eliminating Racial and Ethnic Exclusion in Sports

Why are some sports characterized by disproportionately high rates of participation by racial and ethnic minorities, whereas others have little or no racial or ethnic diversity? When sociologist Harry Edwards (1973) answered this question in the early-1970s, he said that certain sports had built-in incentives for eliminating racial segregation. These incentives included the following:

1. The people who control teams that make money when they win games benefit financially when they do not exclude players who can help them win games.
2. The individual performances of athletes can be measured in concrete, objective terms that are less likely to be influenced by racial ideology than is the case in other occupations.
3. Sport teams are organized so that all players benefit when a teammate performs well, regardless of the teammate's skin color or ethnicity.

4. When athletes play well on a sport team there is no expectation that they will be promoted into leadership positions where they have control over other players.

5. The success of most sport teams does not depend on friendships and off-the-field social relationships between teammates, so players are not expected to befriend teammates from racial or ethnic backgrounds different from their own.

6. When ethnic minority athletes are signed to a contract, they remain under the control of (white) coaches, managers, administrators, and owners in the organizational structure of a sport or sport team.

These six incentives offset the threats that whites often perceive when they consider racial and ethnic desegregation in non-sport situations and organizations. When the people who controlled professional and major revenue-producing intercollegiate teams realized that they could benefit financially from recruiting ethnic minority players without giving up power and control or upsetting the existing structure and relationships in their sports, they began to do so.

Desegregation has come more slowly in sports lacking these incentives. This is why golf, tennis, swimming, and other sports played in private clubs where social interaction is personal and often involves relationships between males and females have been slow to welcome racial and ethnic diversity. As the degree of social closeness increases in any setting, including sports, people are more likely to enforce various forms of exclusion. When others define exclusion as unfair and challenge it, racial and ethnic conflict often occurs. The history of this conflict in the

> **Diversity does not breed interaction.**
> —Tim Layden, journalist, *Sports Illustrated* (2001)

United States is well documented, and it shows that policies of racial and ethnic exclusion in many sports are changed only when government legislation makes them illegal or when civil rights lawsuits threaten the financial assets of people and organizations that have proven histories of discrimination.

Informal practices of racial and ethnic exclusion still remain in some private sports clubs. This is why in 2006 it was difficult to name more than a few African American women and men playing in the major professional golf and tennis tours. This is also part of the reason why Tiger Woods (only one-fourth African American) along with Venus and Serena Williams have received so much publicity during their careers. Golf and tennis in the United States are composed almost exclusively of whites, and many of them want to show that the blatantly racist and exclusionary policies of the past no longer exist today. However, even in 2006, nearly sixty years after Jackie Robinson broke the color line in Major League Baseball, college and professional golf and tennis have few African American players. Progress over the past twenty-five years has been negligible. Private golf and tennis clubs in the United States have many more black, Latino, and Asian people working in low-wage service jobs than playing on courses and courts and watching their children take lessons. However, the most significant forms of racial and ethnic exclusion today occur at the community level where they are hidden behind policies that tie sport participation to fees and access to personal transportation. Some communities claim to have open sport programs when in reality there are few facilities where racial and ethnic minorities live, when fees preclude participation, and when there is no convenient access to the transportation required for participation. This is one of the points made in Breaking Barriers on page 311.

Point-of-Entry Barriers
We Are Out There

Toni Davis was training for the 2004 Paralympics in Athens. As a swimmer, she'd heard about Martiza Correia, a new member of the Athens-bound U.S. Olympic team. Correia had broken U.S. swimming records held by the highly touted Amy Van Dyken and Jenny Thompson in the 50- and 100-meter freestyle. When Davis looked online for information about the new record-setting swimmer, she discovered that Correia was also an African American. Davis was heartened and said to herself, *"We are out there."*

When Davis referred to "we," she meant *black swimmers*. As a former intercollegiate athlete, she knew that a black person on a swim team caused many people to do a double take. She also knew that when people saw her—a black swimmer with only one arm—they often did a triple take.

Davis says that she gets more looks for having one arm than for being black, but she knows that race influences choices and opportunities in sports. "I'm not afraid to speak out and get black swimmers more attention, more participation," she says, but "I also want to get more notice for the Paralympics" because many people don't know it exists. "What we need to do for minority kids," Davis explains, is to have a program that is "low-cost but gets them into the water, [and] gets them the instruction they need . . . to find out if they have the ability" (quotes in Schaller, 2005).

Davis knows that sport participation always has a point of entry—a point at which a person is hooked up with an opportunity. In the case of people with a disability, the point of entry is often connected with rehabilitation or occupational therapy programs, medical care and treatment, or a local network of friends and family.

Taking advantage of an entry opportunity is most likely when people from ethnic minority backgrounds see others in a program who will understand them and with whom they can identify. If everyone in a program, including administrators and coaches, is white, most ethnic minority people, especially those with a disability, will think twice before taking the first step toward participation. "Fitting in" is always an issue when it comes to joining up and trying out.

This means that point-of-entry issues have complex dynamics related to race, ethnicity, health care, medical insurance, trusting medical providers, transportation, and the "look and feel" of disability sport programs. If ethnic diversity and a sense of inclusiveness are not apparent, people of color may conclude that they will be seen as "different." Playing sports is fun, but it becomes tedious when forced to deal with people doing triple takes when they see you.

Eliminating point-of-entry barriers related to race and ethnicity is a major challenge in sports for people with disabilities. As in most sport organizations, there is a need to open coaching and administrative positions to men and women from traditionally underrepresented ethnic minorities. Inclusiveness must be apparent so that prospective participants can see people who look like them. Additionally, there is a need to create new entry points that are part of the structure of everyday life in neighborhoods and communities where ethnic minorities live and work. Churches, schools, hospitals, medical clinics, and veteran organizations are sites at which institutionalized entry points can be created. Once they exist, more people from ethnic minority backgrounds will know that "we are out there."

As public programs are dropped and more sports become organized by nonprofit and commercial organizations, there is a tendency for class-based patterns of exclusion to seriously restrict participation by people in some racial and ethnic groups. Even though this form of exclusion is different from exclusion based solely on race and ethnicity, its effects are much the same, and they are more difficult to attack on the grounds that they violate civil rights. Eliminating forms of exclusion related to socioeconomic status that overlap with race and ethnicity will be one of the most difficult challenges of this century.

Dealing With and Managing Racial and Ethnic Diversity in Sports

As sports become more global, as teams recruit players from around the world, and as global migration creates pressures to develop racially and ethnically sensitive policies related to all aspects of sports, there will be many new racial and ethnic challenges faced by players, coaches, team administrators, and even spectators. It is naïve to think that the racial and ethnic issues that exist around the world today have no impact on sports or that sports can effectively eliminate these issues once and for all time. A brief look at sports and racial issues in U.S. Major League Baseball illustrates this point.

History shows that, after Branch Rickey signed Jackie Robinson to a contract with the Brooklyn Dodgers in 1946, there were many new challenges faced by Rickey, Robinson, the Dodger organization, players throughout the league, other baseball teams in the National League, and spectators attending baseball games. Rickey had to justify his decision to sign a black player to many people, including his partners in the Dodger organization and other baseball team owners. Robinson had to endure unspeakable racism by opponents, spectators, and racists in the general population. To control his anger and depression, he needed support from Rickey, his coach, and his teammates.

As thousands of African American fans wanted to see Robinson, the Dodgers and other teams had to change their policies of racial exclusion and segregation in their stadiums. Teammates were forced to decide if and how they would support

Eliminating racial exclusion is important as when Jackie Robinson joined the Brooklyn Dodgers in 1947. However, this does not end the challenges associated with racial and ethnic relations. After desegregation, there are new challenges associated with managing intergroup relations on teams and integrating positions of power in sport organizations. (*Source:* American Memory Collection)

Robinson on and off the field. The team's coach had to manage interracial dynamics that he had never faced before. Who would be Robinson's roommate on road trips? Where would the team stay and eat in cities where hotels and restaurants excluded blacks? What would he say to players who made racist comments that could destroy team morale? None of these questions required answers in the past because Major League Baseball had been all white.

Baseball fans who had never socialized across racial lines were forced to come to terms with sitting next to someone from a different race. Stadium managers had to deal with the challenge of serving food to people with different tastes and traditions; white, working-class service workers had to come to terms with serving black customers—something that most of them had never done before. Journalists and radio announcers had to decide how they would represent Robinson's experiences in their coverage—if they would talk about the racism of other players, or if they would pretend that race was not an issue, even though it was crucial in much of what they saw.

Of course, these are only a few of the new challenges faced *after* the desegregation of Major League Baseball. As these challenges were met, new and different challenges emerged. As other black players entered Major League Baseball, teammates began to racially segregate themselves in the locker room and their social lives. Successful black players could not buy homes in segregated white areas of the cities where they played. When black players challenged records set by whites, they received death threats, and stadium security became an issue. Some teams became racially divided. Black players felt disadvantaged in team politics because all the coaches, managers, trainers, and owners were white. Even the positions that blacks and whites played fit patterns tied to racial ideologies: Blacks played outfield positions, requiring speed and quick reactions, whereas whites played the positions believed to require intelligence and decision-making skills.

"I love it when they line dance after they score a touchdown!"

FIGURE 9.3 Experiences and traditions vary from one racial or ethnic group to another. What happens when people from various groups bring their experiences and traditions to sports and use them to guide how they play or how they celebrate on-the-field success? If white players from the University of Texas did a line dance after scoring a touchdown, would the NCAA make a rule prohibiting it?

These position placements, or "stacking" patterns, prevented most blacks from playing the positions that led players to be identified as good candidates for coaching jobs after they retired.[1] The lack of black general managers and coaches remains an issue in baseball today.

This example of one professional sport illustrates that racial and ethnic issues are never settled permanently. Challenges met today create new challenges tomorrow. For example, NHL hockey coaches often have players from five or more national and cultural backgrounds. These players sometimes hold negative racial and ethnic stereotypes at the same time that they have customs that other players and staff may define as strange (see figure 9.3).

---

[1]"Stacking" is discussed in detail and illustrated with diagrams at the *Sports in Society* website, www.mhhe.com/coakley9e.

Translators are used on hockey and baseball teams, cultural diversity training is needed, coaches must learn new ways to communicate effectively, and the marketing departments for teams must learn how to promote an ethnically diverse team to predominantly white, European American fans. Ethnic and cultural issues enter into sponsorship considerations and the products sold at games. Cultural and ethnic awareness is now an important qualification for employees who handle team advertising and sponsorship deals.

These and related issues are central to the success of teams in Major League Soccer in the United States because some have a strong base of Latino spectators—well over 25 percent of all fans for teams in California, Colorado, Florida, Texas, and New York City. The commercial success of soccer in the United States depends partly on attracting ethnic spectators to games and television broadcasts. Spanish-speaking announcers are crucial, and deals must be made with radio and television stations that broadcast in Spanish. This challenge will also face women's professional soccer if it is revived in the United States.

Teams in the NFL and NBA now face situations in which 70 to 85 percent of their players are black, whereas 90 to 95 percent of their season-ticket holders are white. Many people are aware of this issue although there have been few public discussions about it. Race is not something that people in the United States feel comfortable talking about in public settings, even though they do talk about it in private, often among friends from the same racial or ethnic background. Research shows that avoiding discussions of race and ethnicity is not due to personal prejudices or underlying racism as much as it is due to a civic etiquette that discourages public discussions of these issues (Eliasoph, 1999). This etiquette keeps racial and ethnic issues "off the table" and prevents people from discussing them thoughtfully and publicly—even in many college classrooms.

Sport teams in Western Europe increasingly face the challenge of coping with new racial and ethnic tensions created by high rates of migration from Africa and Eastern Europe. These challenges are related to matters of national identity, labor migration, and citizenship status. Populist leaders in some nations don't want their national teams to include players whose ancestors may have come from another country, and some fans use players with African or South Asian backgrounds as scapegoats for social and economic problems in their lives. These issues will not go away anytime soon in Europe, North America, or other parts of the world. Challenges related to managing racial and ethnic relations are here to stay although they will change over time.

Integrating Positions of Power in Sport Organizations

Despite progressive changes in many sports, positions of power and control are held primarily by white, non-Latino men. There are exceptions to this, but they do not eliminate pervasive and persistent racial and ethnic inequalities related to power and control in sports. Data on who holds positions of power change every year, and it is difficult to obtain consistent information from sport teams and organizations.

Fortunately, Richard Lapchick (2005c) at the Institute for Diversity and Ethics in Sport at the DeVos Sport Business Management Program at the University of Central Florida publishes regularly a *Racial and Gender Report Card* for sport organizations. It contains data on the racial and ethnic composition of players in major professional team sports and an analysis of the number and types of jobs held by women and people of color in major professional and major university sports organizations. The report covers everyone from owners and athletic directors to office staff and athletic trainers.

The data in table 9.1 were drawn from seven of the many tables in the 2004 *Report Card*. The table focuses on men's professional sports because

Table 9.1   Who plays, who coaches, and who has the power: Race and ethnicity in major men's team sports in North America, 2003–2004.

League		Players (%)	Assistant Coaches (%)	Head Coaches (%)	VPs (%)	General Manager* (%)	CEO/ President (%)	Major Owners (%)
NBA:	Whites	22	71	63	88	83	90	96
	Blacks	76	29	37	8	17	10	4
	Latinos	1	0	0	3	0	0	0
	Asians	<1	0	0	0	0	0	0
	Others[†]	0	0	0	0	0	0	0
NFL:	Whites	29	67	91	89	94	100	100
	Blacks	68	30	9	10	6	0	0
	Latinos	<1	2	0	1	0	0	0
	Asians	1	0	0	0	0	0	0
	Others	<1	1	0	0	0	0	0
MLB:	Whites	63	73	77	89	94	100	97
	Blacks	9	12	10	4	3	0	0
	Latinos	26	13	13	4	3	0	3
	Asians	2	1	0	3	0	0	0
	Others	0	0	0	0	0	0	0
NHL:[‡]	Whites	98	100	100	96	100	100	94
	Blacks	<1	0	0	3	0	0	0
	Latinos	<1	0	0	0	0	0	0
	Asians	<1	0	0	1	0	0	6
	Others	<1	0	0	0	0	0	0
MLS:	Whites	64	64	100	100	100	100	NA[§]
	Blacks	17	11	0	0	0	0	NA
	Latinos	14	5	0	0	0	0	NA
	Asians	1	0	0	0	0	0	NA
	Others	4	4	0	0	0	0	NA

Source: Lapchick (2005c).

*These men are responsible for the day-to-day operation of teams (no women were in this position).

[†]"Others" consist of Native Americans and people who are unidentifiable by race or ethnicity.

[‡]Data are for 2002–2003 because the 2004–2005 season was canceled.

[§]NA means "Not Applicable" because the MLS is a monopoly with investor/franchise holders rather than owners.

patterns in those sports are representative of patterns in other sports organizations. The percentages in the table describe the racial and ethnic composition of players, assistant coaches, head coaches, vice presidents, chief operating officers and general managers, team chairmen and presidents, and team owners. The data show that the percentages of black assistant and head coaches and chief operating officers in the NBA surpass the percentage of blacks in the general population (13 percent in 2003). This is also true for the assistant coaches in the NFL and Major League Baseball. Only in the position of head coach in Major League Soccer do Latinos match or surpass their percentage in the general population (13 percent in 2003). Therefore, apart from these positions, whites are overrepresented in every power position in the major men's professional sports in the United States. Blacks are overrepresented among players in a few sports, but they generally play under the control and management of whites (Hughes, 2004).

Patterns are similar in most other sport organizations at nearly all levels of competition. For example, during the 2003 WNBA season, 61 percent of the players were black and 3 percent were Latina, but 72 percent of all assistant and head coaches were white. Eighty percent of the top administrators were white, 15 percent were black, and 5 percent were Latina. At the same time, about 95 percent of all athletic directors in NCAA colleges and universities were white. At the main NCAA offices, about 80 percent of all administrative personnel are white, and 20 percent are black. In college sports, Division I basketball is the only sport in which black men are well represented in coaching. The latest information for 117 Division I football teams indicates that there were only five black head coaches at the start of the 2005–2006 season—a situation previously described by Tyrone Willingham, an African American and the former the head coach at the University of Notre Dame, as "criminally wrong, to be honest about it" (in Price, 2002b, p. 40). When he made this statement, Willingham realized that blacks held less than 4 percent of all head coaching jobs at NCAA schools—1058 out of a total of 22,895 jobs. He and others said that the employment record of universities is embarrassing and in need of immediate attention (this is discussed further in chapters 10 and 14). Notre Dame fired Willingham in 2004, even though his athletes had a nearly perfect graduation and conduct record under his leadership and even though his teams won 60 percent of their games while playing one of the most difficult schedules in college football.

Black, Latino, and Asian players at all levels of sports are aware that whites have a disproportionate share of power and control in sports. When they see good minority candidates passed over as white candidates are selected for important jobs in sport organizations, they question the attitudes and orientations of owners and other decision makers in sports. They know that there is a difference between desegregating sports to make more money and being inclusive to the point of sharing power in sport organizations. The data suggest that full inclusion in the form of sharing power has not yet occurred.

Apart from general racial issues in sports, the underrepresentation of blacks and other minorities in coaching and administration jobs has been widely publicized since the mid-1980s. Although this issue will be discussed further in chapter 10, it is important to note that blacks and Latinos hired as coaches have generally had longer and more productive playing careers than the whites who are hired as coaches (Rimer, 1996). Many white coaches had mediocre or unimpressive playing careers, and some have unimpressive past coaching records as well. Meanwhile, minority candidates with similar or better playing careers are routinely passed over as coaching candidates in a range of sports. It seems that, because coaching and administrative abilities cannot be measured as objectively as playing abilities, the subjective feelings of those doing the hiring come into play when coaching and top management candidates are assessed (Lavoie and Leonard, 1994).

Prospects for Change

People do not give up racial and ethnic beliefs easily, especially when they come in the form of well-established ideologies rooted deeply in their cultures. Those who have benefited from dominant racial ideology often resist changes in the relationships and social structures that reproduce it. This is why certain expressions of racism have remained a part of sports.

Sports may bring people together, but they do not automatically lead them to adopt tolerant attitudes or change long-standing policies of exclusion. White team owners, general managers, and athletic directors in the United States worked with black athletes for many years before they ever hired black coaches. It often requires social and legal pressures to force people in power positions to act more affirmatively in their hiring practices. In the meantime, blacks and other ethnic minorities remain underrepresented in coaching and administration.

Although there is resistance to certain types of changes in sports, many sport organizations are more progressive than other organizations when it comes to many aspects of racial and ethnic relations. However, good things do not happen automatically or as often as many think; nor do changes in people's attitudes automatically translate into changes in the overall organization of sports. Challenging the negative beliefs and attitudes of individuals is one thing; changing the relationships and social structures that have been built on those beliefs and attitudes is another thing. Both changes are needed, but neither occurs automatically just because sports bring people together in the same locker rooms and stadiums.

Racial and ethnic relations will improve in sports only when those who have power work to bring people together in ways that confront and challenge racial and ethnic issues. This means that changes must be initiated and supported by whites as well as members of ethnic minorities, or else they will fail (Oglesby and Schrader, 2000). It has never been easy for people to deal with racial and ethnic issues, but if it can be done in sports, it would attract public attention and possibly inspire changes in other spheres of life.

Change also requires a new vocabulary to deal with racial and ethnic diversity in social life and promote inclusive practices and policies. A vocabulary organized around the belief that skin color or ethnicity signifies a unique biological essence only perpetuates racial and ethnic discrimination. In connection with sports, there is a need for research to go beyond documenting racial and ethnic performance differences and explain how social and cultural factors, including racial ideologies, create and perpetuate differences. Simply documenting differences without explaining them

The Irish Football Association began in 2000 to use soccer as a site for eradicating the Protestant-versus-Catholic sectarianism that has led to decades of violence and terrorism in Northern Ireland. Aaron Hughes, captain of Northern Ireland's National Soccer Team, and his teammates work with young people to promote equality and diversity. The team motto is "Sectarianism and racism in Northern Ireland Football is not welcome and will not be tolerated." (*Source:* Mike Collins, Irish Football Association, Northern Ireland)

too often reproduces the very racial ideologies that have caused hatred, turmoil, and confusion in much of the world for nearly 300 years. This is why many scholars in the sociology of sport now ask research questions about the meanings that people give to physical and cultural characteristics and how those meanings influence actions, relationships, and social organization.

The racial and ethnic diversity training sessions used over the past two decades have produced some changes, but promoting positive changes in intergroup relations today requires training leaders to create more inclusive cultures and power structures in sport organizations. This means that training sessions should go beyond athletes and include everyone from team owners and athletic directors to the people in middle management, coaching, marketing, and public information. One of the problems with diversity-training sessions in the past is that they were directed at low-level employees who often did not take them seriously because they did not see their superiors taking them seriously.

Even people who are sensitive to diversity issues require opportunities to learn new things about the perspectives of those whose experiences and cultures are different from our own. This means that effective training sessions are organized, in part, around the perspectives of racial and ethnic minorities. This is an essential strategy if positive changes are to occur. When making things better means doing them to fit the interests of those currently in power, real change is unlikely.

summary

ARE RACE AND ETHNICITY IMPORTANT IN SPORTS?

Racial and ethnic issues exist in sports, just as they exist in most other spheres of social life. As people watch, play, and talk about sports, they often take into account ideas about skin color and ethnicity. The meanings given to skin color and ethnic background influence access to sport participation and the decisions that people make about sports in their lives. *Race* refers to a category of people identified through a classification system based on meanings given to physical traits among humans; *ethnicity* refers to collections of people identified in terms of their shared cultural heritage. Racial and ethnic *minorities* are populations that have endured systematic forms of discrimination in a society.

The idea of race has a complex history, but it has served as the foundation for racial ideology, which people use to identify and make sense of racial differences. Racial ideology, like other social constructions, changes over time as ideas and relationships change. However, over the past century in the United States, dominant racial ideology has led many people to assume that there are important biological and cognitive differences between blacks and whites and that these differences explain the success of blacks in certain sports and sport positions.

Racial ideology has influenced the ways that many people connect skin color with athletic performance. At the same time, it has influenced the ways that some whites make sport participation decisions and the ways that many people explain the performance of black males who excel in sports. Race, gender, and class relations in American society have combined to create a context in which black males emphasize a personal presentation of self that has been described as "cool pose," a stylized persona that has added to the commodity value of the black male body in sports and enabled some black athletes to use widely accepted ideas about race to intimidate opponents, especially white opponents, in sports.

Sport participation patterns among African American, Native American, Latino, and Asian American populations each have unique histories. Combinations of historical, cultural, and social factors have influenced those histories. However, sport participation in ethnic minority populations usually occurs under terms set by the dominant ethnic population in a community or society. Minority populations are seldom able to use sports to challenge the power and privilege of the dominant group, even though particular individuals may experience great personal success in sports.

The fact that some sports have histories of racially and ethnically mixed participation does not mean that problems have been eliminated. Harmonious racial and ethnic relations never occur automatically, and ethnic harmony is never established once and for all time. As current problems are solved, new relationships and new challenges are created. This means that racial and ethnic issues require regular attention if challenges are to be successfully anticipated and met. Success also depends on whether members of the dominant ethnic population see value in racial and ethnic diversity and commit themselves to dealing with diversity issues alongside those who have different ethnic backgrounds.

Sports continue to be sites for racial and ethnic problems. However, it is important to acknowledge that, despite problems, sports can also be sites for challenging racial ideology and transforming ethnic relations. This happens only when people in sports plan strategies to encourage critical awareness of ethnic prejudices, racist ideas, and forms of discrimination built into the cultures and structures of sport organizations. This awareness is required to eliminate ethnic exclusion in sports, deal with and manage ethnic diversity, and integrate ethnic minorities into the power structures of sport organizations. Without this awareness, ethnic relations often become volatile and lead to overt forms of hostility.

See the OLC, www.mhhe.com/coakley9e, for an annotated list of readings related to this chapter. The OLC also contains a key concept list, a review test, and other helpful features.

WEBSITE RESOURCES

Note: Websites often change. The following URLs were current when this book was printed. Please check our website (www.mhhe.com/coakley9e) for updates and additions.

www.mhhe.com/coakley9e   Click on chapter 9 for discussion guides for *Hoop Dreams* and *In Whose Honor;* brief readings on the history of racial desegregation in U.S. sports, and stacking in the NFL and Major League Baseball.

http://www.pbs.org/race/000_General/ 000_00-Home.htm   The site for the three-part series, *Race—The Power of An Illusion*, first shown in 2004; the site contains information for students and instructors; each part of the series is summarized in links provided through this site. Also there are many resources links for those wishing to explore the topic of race in more detail.

http://home.earthlink.net/~prometheus_6/ RaceReadings.htm   This site contains a series of short essays dealing with race; the essays are authored by people from many academic disciplines. They are very helpful for anyone wishing to understand race as a concept and as a lived experience.

www.sportinsociety.org/rgrc.html   See the *Racial and Gender Report Card*—a research document that analyzes hiring practices in major sports organizations in the United States.

www.sportinsociety.org/ptw.html   Project TEAMWORK is a diversity awareness and conflict-resolution program that teaches high school students to combat discrimination.

http://racerelations.about.com/cs/raceandsports   A general site with links to articles on diversity and other sources that cover race and ethnicity-related issues in sports.

www.shipbrook.com/jeff/ChiefWahoo/   A humorous and serious look at the mascot/logo of the MLB team in Cleveland. The video at this site highlights points made in this chapter.

www.nativeculturelinks.com/mascots.html   This site contains links to websites and articles related to the issue of Indian mascots used by sports teams.

www.fightingwhites.org/   Official site of the Fighting Whites basketball team that was organized in 2002 by a group of Native American and non-Native American students at the University of Northern Colorado; the team played intramural basketball and chose this name to highlight the issue of stereotyping American Indians in sports symbolism.

www.bus.ucf.edu/sport/cgi-bin/site/sitew.cgi?page=/ ides/media.htx   The site containing news releases from the Institute for Diversity and Ethics in Sport; data on graduation rates for university teams in postseason tournament and bowl games, and on other diversity patterns in intercollegiate sports.

10

(John Sutherland)

SOCIAL CLASS

Do Money and Power Matter in Sports?

PUBLIC SCHOOLS in the wealthiest neighborhoods win state team championships at more than twice the rate of schools in the least wealthy neighborhoods . . . Private schools . . . won almost as many championships as the most wealthy public schools.

—*USA Today* survey (Brady and Sylwester, 2004a, 2004b, 2004c)

 Online Learning Center Resources

Visit *Sports in Society*'s Online Learning Center (OLC) at **www.mhhe.com/coakley9e** for additional information and study material for this chapter, including

- Self-grading quizzes
- Learning objectives
- Related websites
- Additional readings

A complete outline is available at
www.mhhe.com/coakley9e.

LUXURY BOXES AND CLUB seat sections are the
gated communities of sport stadiums.

> —**Spectator assessing Invesco Field, new
> stadium of the NFL's Denver Broncos, 2002**

GROWING UP IN the Robert Taylor Homes [in
Chicago], you have three choices. You can be
a gangbanger, a rapper or a basketball player.

> —**Jay Straight, college student and basketball
> player (in Berger, 2004)**

People like to think that sports transcend issues of money, power, and economic inequalities. They see sports as open to everyone, watch them on "free" television, and define success on the playing field in terms of ability and hard work. However, all organized sports depend on material resources, and those resources must come from somewhere. Therefore, playing, watching, and excelling in sports depend on resources supplied by individuals, families, governments, or corporations.

More than ever before, it takes money to play sports and receive the training needed to develop sport skills. Tickets are expensive and spectators often are segregated by social class in the stadium: The wealthy and well connected sit in club seats and luxury suites, whereas fans who are less well off sit in other sections, depending on their ability to pay for premium tickets or buy season tickets. It even takes money to watch sports on television when events air on cable channels that often have hefty monthly subscriber fees or pay-per-view charges. This means that sports and sport participation are closely connected with the distribution of economic, political, and social resources in society. Money and power do matter in sports.

Many people also believe that sports are avenues for economic success among people from all social classes. Rags-to-riches stories are common when people talk about athletes. However, these beliefs and stories distract attention from how sports often reflect and perpetuate existing economic inequalities in society.

This chapter deals with matters of money and wealth, as well as larger sociological issues related to social class and socioeconomic mobility. Our discussion will focus on the following questions:

1. What is meant by *social class* and *class relations*?
2. How do social class and class relations influence sports and sport participation?
3. Are sports open and democratic in the provision of economic and career opportunities?
4. Does playing sports contribute to occupational success and social mobility among former athletes?

SOCIAL CLASS AND CLASS RELATIONS

Social class and the related concepts of social stratification, socioeconomic status, and life chances are important when studying social worlds. This is because economic resources are related to power in society, and economic inequalities influence nearly all aspects of people's lives.

Social class refers to *categories of people who share an economic position in society based on a combination of their income (earnings), wealth (possessions), education, occupation, and social connections.* People in a particular social class also share similar **life chances**—that is, they share *similar odds for achieving economic success and gaining economic power in society.* Social classes exist in all industrial societies because life chances are not equally distributed across all populations.

Social stratification is the concept that sociologists use when referring to *structured forms of economic inequalities that are part of the organization of everyday social life.* In other words, when compared with people from upper social classes, people from lower–class backgrounds have fewer opportunities to achieve economic success and gain economic power. Children born into wealthy, powerful, and well-connected families are in better positions to become wealthy, powerful, and well-connected adults than are children born into poor families that lack influence and social networks connecting them with educational and career opportunities.

Most of us are aware of economic inequalities in society. We see them all around us and on television in programs like MTV's *Cribs* (the contemporary young people's version of a previous program, *Lifestyles of the Rich and Famous*). We know they exist and influence people's lives, but there are few public discussions about the ways that social class influences our views of ourselves and others, our social relationships, and our everyday lives (Perrucci and Wysong, 2003). In other words, we do not discuss **class relations**—that is, the many *ways that social class is incorporated into everyday life in society.* In schools and the media, we hear about the importance of equal opportunities, but we learn little about the ways that people in upper socioeconomic classes use their income, wealth, and power to maintain their privileged positions in society and pass that privilege from one generation to the next. Instead, we hear about those who have moved up and out of lower socioeconomic classes through hard work and strong character and about "millionaires next door" and "regular guys" who are CEOs making tens of millions of dollars a year. But we learn little about the oppressive effects of poverty and the limited opportunities available to those who lack economic resources, access to good education, and well-placed social connections. Those stories, say the executives that produce the news on commercial television and in other commercial media, are too depressing to tell, and people don't like to hear them. However, social-class differences are real, they have real consequences for life chances, they affect nearly every facet of people's lives, and all of this is clearly documented by valid and reliable data (Domhoff, 2002; Kozol, 1991; Perrucci and Wysong, 2003; Sernau, 2005).

> We are already in a situation where we are expecting children to play games they cannot afford to watch.
> —Harry Edwards, sociologist/social activist (2000)

People in many postindustrial societies, especially the United States, are uncomfortable with critical discussions of social class and class relations (hooks, 2000; Sage, 1998). The myth of equality in many democratic societies discourages such discussions, even though we are aware of class and class relations in our lives. This is especially true when it comes to sports and sport participation in which we like to think that money and class-based privilege does not matter.

The discussion of social class and class relations in this chapter is grounded in critical theories.

The focus is on economic inequality, the processes through which it is reproduced, the ways that it serves the interests of those with wealth and economic power, and how it affects what happens in sports and the lives of people associated with sports.

SPORTS AND ECONOMIC INEQUALITY

Money and economic power exert significant influence on the goals, purpose, and organization of sports in society (Gruneau, 1999; Sugden and Tomlinson, 2000; Tomlinson, 2007). Many people believe that sports and sport participation are open to all people and that inequalities related to money, position, and influence don't spill over into the organized games we play and watch. However, formally organized sports could not be developed, scheduled, or maintained without economic resources. Those who control money and economic power use them to organize and sponsor sports. As they do so, they give preference to sport forms that reflect and maintain their values and interests.

The wealthy aristocrats who organized the Olympic Movement and sponsored the modern Olympic Games even used their power to establish a definition of *amateur* that privileged athletes from wealthy backgrounds around the world. This definition excluded athletes from working-class backgrounds, who could afford to train only if they used their sport skills to help them earn a living. The definition of *amateur* has been revised over the years so that more people can participate in sports. However, money and economic power now operate in different ways as training opportunities for developing high-level skills has become increasingly privatized in many countries. Additionally, powerful corporations use the Olympics to expand profits by linking their logos and products to particular athletes and global sport images that serve their interests.

Elite and powerful groups in society always have had considerable influence over what "counts as sport" and how sports will be organized and played. Even when grassroots games and physical activities become formally organized as sports, they are not widely sponsored or promoted unless they can be used to promote the interests and ideologies of those with money and economic power in society. For example, ESPN organized and televised the X Games to fit their corporate interests and orientations rather than those of the athletes, although the athletes have struggled to have their concerns taken into account. Similarly, the informal games played by people of all ages often depend on the availability of facilities, equipment, and safe play spaces. These are more plentiful in the everyday lives of people from upper- and upper-middle-income families and neighborhoods. Low-income families and neighborhoods often lack the resources and well-maintained public spaces needed to initiate and sustain informal activities; they do not have large lawns at their homes, cul-de-sacs without traffic, or well-maintained parks where they can play. This is why it is important that we understand the dynamics of class relations when we study sports and patterns of sport participation.

The Dynamics of Class Relations

One way to understand the dynamics of class relations is to think about how age relations operate in sports. Consider this: Even though children are capable of creating their own games, adults intervene and develop youth sport programs. These programs are organized around the ideas and orientations that adults think are best for their children. As noted in chapter 5, adults possess the *resources* to develop, schedule, and maintain organized youth programs that reflect their ideas of what children should be doing

and learning as they play. Children often enjoy adult-controlled, organized sports, but their enjoyment occurs in a framework that is determined by adults and serves to legitimize and reproduce the power that adults have over the lives of children.

An example of age relations occurs when the actions of children in organized sports deviate from adult expectations. The adults use their power to define deviance, identify when it occurs, force children to comply with rules, and convince children that it is in their best interest to play sports "the right way," which, of course, is the adults' way. When children comply and meet adult expectations, they are told that they have "character," and they receive rewards. This is why many adults like coaches who are autocratic and controlling. Such coaches reaffirm the cultural belief that the world is a better place when adults have full and strict control over young people and when young people consent to that control. In this way, sports reproduce a hierarchical form of age relations, in which adult power and privilege are defined as natural, normal, and necessary aspects of social life.

Class relations work in similar ways. People in the upper social classes have the resources to organize and promote the sports and sport forms that support their ideas about "good character" and the way that social life ought to be organized. One of the first things that people do when they obtain power in a social world is to make sure that "character" is defined in terms that fit their interests and match the characteristics that they possess. For example, if wealthy and powerful people play sports in exclusive clubs, it is important that everyone believe that this is the way that society and sports should be organized and that wealthy and powerful people deserve their privilege to play sports as they do. In addition to playing on their terms, people with resources also can create and sponsor forms of organized sports that reinforce ideologies that support and legitimize existing economic relationships and the class structure of society. This is partly why popular spectator sports around the world are presented in ways that emphasize competition, individualism, highly specialized skills, the use of technology, and dominance over opponents. The people who benefit from an emphasis on these values and cultural practices have usually been successful in convincing most people in society to believe that this is how sports should be organized and presented. Visions of sports that emphasize partnership, sharing, open participation, nurturance, and mutual support are outside of popular consciousness because most people have accepted that sports are sports only when they stress individual achievement through competition and the consumption of technology and equipment that can be used to outscore and dominate others.

Class Ideology in the United States

Sociologists define **class ideology** as a *web of ideas and beliefs that people use to understand economic inequalities, identify themselves in terms of their class position, and evaluate the manner in which economic inequalities are and should be integrated into the organization of social worlds*. The dominant class ideology in the United States has long been organized around a belief in the American Dream and the idea that the United States is a meritocracy.

The American Dream is *a hopeful vision of boundless economic opportunities to succeed and consume in ways that lead to individual fulfillment and happiness*. A belief in this dream focuses attention on individual aspirations and consumption and often blurs class distinctions and the hard economic realities faced by many people. The uniquely American belief that "you can be anything you want to be, regardless of your current class position," leads most people to dream about the future instead of critically examining the social and economic forces that influence their current economic circumstances. It also discredits

those who are poor because poverty is defined as a sign of individual failure, laziness, and general character defects.

Belief in the American Dream is complemented by the idea that the United States is a meritocracy. A **meritocracy** *is a form of social organization in which rewards and positions of leadership and power are earned when people prove that their characteristics and abilities are superior to those of others*. The idea that the United States is a meritocracy legitimizes the economic inequalities that are inevitably created in a capitalist economy. In a meritocracy, it is assumed that power and success are associated with strong character and smart choices, whereas failure is associated with weak character and poor choices. Class ideology in the United States emphasizes that economic success (winning) is proof of individual ability, worth, and character. People who uncritically accept this ideology and use it to give meaning to their lives often engage in an endless quest for victories and status. They measure success in terms of how many "things" they can acquire and how they rank relative to their peers when it comes to "life scores." A locker-room slogan born of this class ideology is, "When you're satisfied with your performance, you're finished." This and similar ideas drive market economies and enable people with wealth and power to preserve and extend their resources.

When people in a society adopt an ideology that links competitive success with moral worth, they assume that "you get what you deserve, and you deserve what you get." This advantages those who have more wealth and economic power than others, and it promotes the idea that economic inequality in society is necessary if society is to operate efficiently. This ideology is usually reproduced through the sports sponsored by corporations that are financially profitable. These corporations favor sports that promote competition as a "natural" way to allocate rewards and define winners as those who deserve valued rewards. This, of course, is how

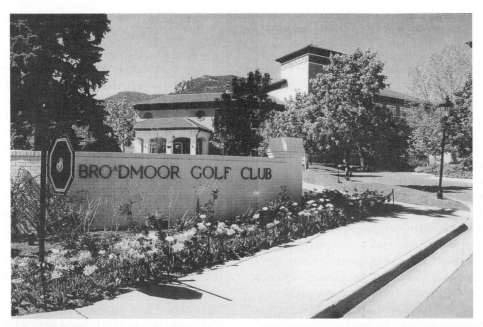

An ideology of achievement through competitive success infers that being wealthy and powerful (winning) is proof of individual abilities, moral worth, and character. Exclusive sports clubs such as this one highlight this ideology. Therefore, they promote the interests of powerful and wealthy people and, at the same time, provide them with luxurious places to play sports. (*Source:* Jay Coakley)

sports come to be connected with class relations in society.

Class Relations and Who Has Power in Sports

Sport decisions are made at many levels, from neighborhood youth sport programs to the International Olympic Committee. Although scholars who study sports in society identify those who exercise power in various settings, they usually do not develop lists that rank powerful people in sports. But such lists do exist. For example, *The Sporting News,* a national weekly newspaper in the United States, publishes an annual list of "the most powerful people in sports." The list ranks those who have had the greatest influence on elite-level sports in the United States during the previous year. Although people outside the United States may be included, their rank reflects their influence on sports from a U.S. perspective.

Table 10.1 identifies the *Sporting News* "Top 25" people from the list for 2004 and indicates their ranks in 1990,1996, and 2000. The "Top 25" includes twenty-six people (two men were ranked number 7), plus four white men identified as "emperors" because they have vast power over sports around the world. Of these thirty people, all are men; twenty-seven are white, two are black, and one is Chinese. There are ten executives from media organizations, nine from professional sport organizations, four from sponsoring corporations; two from sport management companies, one agent, and three athletes. The nine men (eight white and one black) who control professional sport organizations have power partly because they deal with the ten white men who control media organizations that broadcast games and pay them fees for the rights to broadcast their games. It is clear that in addition to structural factors, such as access to wealth and control of major corporations, gender and racial ideology also influence who has power in sports. When it comes to power in sports, it's a white man's world.

It is interesting that there are no coaches on the list and only three athletes. Few athletes, even when they are highly paid, have influence that matches the influence of people who control sport organizations or multibillion-dollar corporations, especially media corporations. We can understand more about the dynamics of power in sports by taking a closer look at three of the four white men identified as "Emperors" by *The Sporting News:* Brian Roberts, Rupert Murdoch, and Chuck Dolan.

Brian Roberts is president and CEO (chief executive officer) of Comcast Corporation. If you watch televised sports in Chicago, Philadelphia, Baltimore/Washington DC, Dallas, Detroit, or northern California, you watch Comcast's *SportsNet.* Comcast also owns the Golf Channel and Outdoor Life Network, which televises the Gravity Games and the Tour de France. It has a national television show, *Out of Bounds,* and plans to take market share away from ESPN's *SportsCenter.* It owns the Philadelphia 76ers (NBA) and Philadelphia Flyers (NHL) and their arenas, along with minor league teams and smaller sport facilities. Comcast is the largest distributor of the NFL Network, linked to 50 million homes, and its *SportsNet* channels broadcast local games in regions around the nation. Combined with its broadband cable subscribers, it is one of the three most powerful media corporations in the United States and among the most powerful in the world. Over 70 million people think about Comcast every month when they pay their cable bills. Roberts's power will increase when sport programming comes through the Internet. But it will decrease if people can convince legislators that their communities should have wireless access to the Internet as a low-cost public service, despite the interests of cable and DSL corporations.

Rupert Murdoch is chairman of DirecTV and chairman and CEO of News Corporation. As a major owner of these companies, he is the most powerful media person in the world. His ownership includes Fox Network, DirecTV (the

Table 10.1 The Top 25 in *The Sporting News'* "Power 100," 2004*

Rank	Name	Position	Organization	1990 Rank	1997 Rank	2000 Rank
	Brian Roberts[†]	Chairman/CEO	Comcast Corporation	NR[‡]	NR	NR
	Rupert Murdoch[†]	Chairman/CEO Chairman	News Corporation DirecTV	NR	6	3
	Chuck Dolan[†]	Chairman	Cablevision	34	NR	11
	Jim Dolan[†]	President/CEO	Cablevision	NR	40	11
1	Paul Tagliabue	Commissioner	NFL	3	16	2
2	Brian France	Chairman/CEO	NASCAR	NR	NR	65
3	Bud Selig	Commissioner	Major League Baseball	11	22	3
4	David Stern (2003: 6)	Commissioner	NBA	5	8	8
5	George Bodenheimer (2003: 1)	President Co-chair	ESPN & ABC Sports Disney Media Networks	NR	NR	12
6	Ted Forstmann	Chairman	IMG	NR	NR	NR
7	August Busch IV	President	Anheuser-Busch, Inc.	NR	NR	9
	Tony Ponturo	VP, Global Media and Marketing	Anheuser-Busch, Inc.	NR	26	9
8	David Hill	Chairman/CEO	FOX Sports Television Group	NR	30	31
9	Dick Ebersol	Chairman	NBC Sports	2	1	10
10	Phil Knight	Chairman	Nike	46	2	5
11	Kobe Bryant	Guard	Los Angeles Lakers	NR	NR	NR
12	Roger Goodell	Exec. VP/COO	NFL	NR	NR	38
13	Paul Fireman	Chairman/CEO	Reebok	NR	NR	NR
14	Curt Schilling	Pitcher	Boston Red Sox	NR	NR	NR
15	George Steinbrenner	Owner	New York Yankees	NR	NR	6
16	Scott Boras	Agent	Self-employed	NR	NR	36
17	Gene Upshaw	Exec. director	NFLPA	NR	NR	NR
18	Mark Shapiro	Exec. VP of Programming and Production	ESPN	NR	NR	14
19	Jacques Rogge	President	International Olympic Committee	NR	NR	51
20	Bob Kain	Co-CEO	IMG	NR	NR	22
21	Bruce McMillan	Exec. VP of Worldwide Studios	Electronic Arts	NR	NR	NR
22	Ed Goren	President/exec. producer	FOX Sports	NR	NR	18
23	Bill France, Jr.	Vice chairman Chairman	NASCAR International Speedway Corp.	40	NR	20
24	Yao Ming (2003: 25)	Center	Houston Rockets	NR	NR	NR
25	Steve Bornstein	President/CEO	NFL Network	NR	NR	NR

*At the close of every year, the editors of *The Sporting News* rank the one hundred most powerful people in U.S. sports during the year.
[†]These four white men are not ranked because they were described as "Emperors" who controlled broadcast and cable television empires and sport teams. Their power transcends the everyday decisions in sports, so they were simply put at the top of the list far above everyone else.
[‡]NR means "Not Ranked."

largest U.S. satellite TV provider), Fox News Channel, Fox Sports Net, Fox Soccer Channel, Fox Sports en Español, Fox Sports en Latinoamérica, SkySports (United Kingdom), and cable, broadcast, Internet, and satellite systems and channels (such as the National Geographic Channel) across Asia, Europe, Latin America, and Australia. Murdoch's companies decide what soccer games will be seen by billions of people in more than 160 nations. News Corp also owns hundreds of major newspapers and major and minor sport teams around the world. It has television contracts with all the major professional men's sports in the United States. It is largely responsible for the national popularity of NASCAR, and it has had close working relationships with Disney and other major media companies that fear being conquered by Murdoch's empire. Murdoch's decisions influence the sports that become popular and the sports that don't receive media coverage and come to be defined as "second class." His companies make things happen and prevent things from happening in sports. On any given day, Murdoch can deliver a message or programming to over 70 percent of the world's population. No other person on earth can make such a claim.

Charles Dolan is the founder and chairman of Cablevision, and his son, James, is CEO. Cablevision's regional sports channels televise many sports to millions of subscribers in the United States. In 2004 his company controlled much of the sports landscape in New York, owning the New York Knicks (NBA), Madison Square Garden, and the New York Rangers (NHL). Cablevision televises the games played by major New York area teams, including the Knicks, Nets, Mets, Yankees, and Rangers. Dolan and his company used their power to prevent the building of a new stadium in Manhattan; he didn't want it to compete with his Madison Square Garden. His ads and his influence contributed to the failed bid by New York City to host the 2012 Olympic Games. So he had power in 2004 and was hated in July 2005! But because he collects more money from

cable subscribers than any other cable operator, he has stayed rich and powerful through it all, and his company is still 100 percent family owned, a fact that increases his power considerably— unless New York and other eastern seaboard cities would develop low-cost wireless Internet systems for their citizens.

Descriptions of others on the list clearly indicate that economic wealth and power do matter in sports. Those who control economic resources around the world make decisions that influence the visibility of sports, the ways in which they are organized, and the images and meanings associated with them. Although these decisions do not ignore the interests of common folk around the world, their main purpose is to establish and expand the power and profitability of the organizations represented by the decision makers. Therefore, sports tend to revolve around the meanings and orientations valued by those with economic resources and power while providing enjoyable and entertaining experiences to people like you and me.

This is why some critical theorists have described sports as cultural vehicles for developing "ideological outposts" in the minds of people around the world: When transnational corporations become the primary providers of popular pleasure and entertainment, they can use the very things that give people joy and excitement to deliver messages about what should be important in people's lives. This is a clear manifestation of class relations and the process of hegemony at work.

SOCIAL CLASS AND SPORT PARTICIPATION PATTERNS

In all societies, social class and class relations influence who plays, who watches, who consumes information about sports, and what information is available in the mainstream media. Involvement with sports goes hand in hand with money, power, and privilege. Organized sports are a luxury item in the economies of many nations, and

The sports played by young people from low-income households often occur in public places such as this public school playground. Young people from upper-income backgrounds usually have the resources to purchase access to privately owned sport facilities and spaces. This results in different sport experiences and different sport participation patterns from one social class to another in society. (*Source:* Tini Campbell)

they are most prevalent in wealthy nations where people have discretionary money and time (see chapter 11).

In all societies, it is people in high-income, high-education, and high-status occupational groups that have the highest rates of active sport participation, attendance at sport events, and even watching of sports on television (Booth and Loy, 1999; Donnelly and Harvey, 1999; Scheerder et al., 2002; T. Wilson, 2002). For example,

Olympic athletes and officials always have come from more privileged groups in society (Collins and Buller, 2003; Kidd, 1995). This was noted in a 1996 analysis of U.S. Olympic teams across all sports:

A sport by sport breakdown of recent U.S. Olympic teams shows a movement split by both class and race. Although in theory anyone can earn a spot in the Olympics, the reality of the process is far different. Lack of funding and access at the developmental level creates a team and a system tilted toward segregation. (*Atlanta Journal/Constitution*, 1996, p. H7)

This pattern is even more prevalent today than it was in 1996, and it also exists in many professional sports in the United States and other countries.

Even the health and fitness movement, which often has been described as a grassroots phenomenon in the United States and Canada, is confined primarily to people who have higher-than-average incomes and educations and work in professional or managerial occupations. People in lower-income categories may do physical labor, but they don't run, bicycle, or swim as often as their high-income counterparts. Nor do they play as many organized sports on their lunch hour, after work, on weekends, or during vacations. This pattern holds true throughout the life course, for younger and older people, men and women, racial and ethnic groups, and for people with disabilities: Social class is related strongly to participation, regardless of the category of people in question.

Other aspects of sports participation patterns can also be explained in terms of class relations. The long-term impact of economic inequality on people's lives has led to connections between certain sports and the lifestyles of people with differing amounts of wealth and power (Bourdieu, 1986; Dukes and Coakley, 2002; Laberge and Sankoff, 1988). For the most part, these connections reflect patterns of sponsorship and access to participation opportunities. For example, wealthy people have lifestyles that routinely include golf, tennis, skiing, swimming, sailing, and other sports that are self-funded and played at exclusive clubs and resorts. These sports often involve the use of expensive facilities, equipment, and/or clothing, and they have come to be associated with "class" as people with money and power define it. The people who engage in these sports usually have control over their work routines, so they often have the freedom to take the time needed to participate, or they can combine participation with their work, such as going to the club, gym, game (luxury box), and tournament with business associates. They even use the company credit card to pay for these things, and the company then deducts a portion of the expenses so it pays less income tax thereby decreasing federal and state tax receipts that could be used to fund sport programs for people who don't own golf club memberships.

The lifestyles of middle-income and working-class people, on the other hand, tend to include sports that by tradition are free and open to the public, sponsored by public funds, or available through public schools. When these sports involve the use of expensive equipment or clothing, participation occurs in connection with some form of financial sacrifice. For instance, buying a motocross bike means working overtime for six months and not taking a vacation this year.

The lifestyles of low-income people and those living in poverty seldom involve regular forms of sport participation, unless a shoe company sees them outplaying all the other twelve-year-olds on a local playground. Life chances clearly vary by social class, and when people spend much of their time and energy coping with the challenges of everyday life, they have few resources left to develop lifestyles that revolve around sport participation. Spending money to play or watch sports is a luxury that many people cannot afford. At the same time, those who are successful in the economy like sports because they reaffirm a class ideology that works to their advantage. This is partly why they are willing to spend thousands of dollars each year to buy club memberships, season tickets, and luxury suites or have their companies buy them.

Homemaking, Child Rearing, and Earning a Living: Class and Gender Relations in Women's Lives

The impact of social class on everyday lives often varies by age, gender, race and ethnicity, and

Public Money and Private Profits
When Do Sports Perpetuate Social Inequality?

The dynamics of class relations sometimes have ironic twists. This is certainly true in connection with the ways in which sports have been used as vehicles for transferring public monies collected through taxes into the hands of wealthy individuals and corporations in the private sector. For example, during the 1990s, over $15 billion of public money in the United States was used to build sport stadiums and arenas, which now generate revenues for wealthy individuals and powerful corporations that own professional sport team franchises and develop real estate around those facilities (Brown et al., 2004; Cagan and deMause, 1998; Curry et al., 2004; Eitzen, 2003; Friedman et al., 2004).

Furthermore, wealthy investors often purchase the tax-free municipal bonds that cities sell to obtain the cash to build these facilities. This means that while city and/or state taxes are collected from the general population to pay off the bonds, wealthy investors receive tax-free returns, and team owners use the facilities built by taxpayers to make large amounts of money. When sales taxes are used to pay off bonds, people in low- and middle-income brackets pay a higher percentage of their annual incomes to build the stadiums than people in higher-income brackets.

According to a U.S. senator who reviewed a study done by the nonpartisan Congressional Research Service, this method of financing stadiums through tax-exempt bonds "amounts to little more than a public housing program for millionaire team owners and their millionaire employees [athletes]" (Welch, 1996, p. A1). He also asked, "Do [Americans] have enough money to finance stadiums for [wealthy team] owners . . . at the same time we are cutting Head Start Programs [for low-income children]?" (in Brady and Howlett, 1996, p. 13C). Nearly ten years later, Republican Senator John McCain stated that, "owners have too much political power in major cities. I mean, how else could they get the people to build stadiums for 'em" (in Keating, 2004)

To make matters worse, the average residents whose taxes build the stadiums and arenas usually cannot afford to buy tickets. Corporate accounts are used to buy so many tickets to professional games that teams raise prices to match the demand. Corporations don't mind paying higher prices because they claim a portion of the cost as a business deduction on their taxes. Ironically, this means that tax revenues decline and the government has less money to support programs that might benefit average taxpayers. At the same time, average residents are priced out of the ticket market. If they do manage to save enough money to buy tickets, they find that the luxury suites have pushed the average seats so far away from the action that they have a hard time seeing what's going on (see figure 10.1). Meanwhile, team owners misleadingly blame price increases on players' salaries.

The dynamics of class relations do not stop here. After contributing public money to build nice new stadiums and arenas, local and state governments often give discounted property tax rates to team owners and their real estate partners who develop areas around the new stadium or arena. Property taxes are the main source of revenues for public schools, so urban public schools often have to do with less because the teams are making more. Meanwhile, the teams set up a few charity programs for "inner-city kids" and occasionally send players to speak at urban schools. Then the local sports media describe team owners and millionaire athletes as great public servants! When teachers complain about this scam, local editorials and letters to the editor accuse the schools of wasting public money, even though the schools are falling apart.

This method of transferring public money into the hands of wealthy individuals has occurred during a time when social services for the unemployed and working poor are being cut. When Carl Pohlad, the owner of the Minnesota Twins baseball team, was asked about this, he said, "Sports is a way of life, like

"I thought they said 'Sport brings everyone together' when they used our tax money to build this place!"
....

FIGURE 10.1   As they sit in the distant bleachers and spot wealthy people in luxury boxes and club seats, these fans discover that the dynamics of social class operate in ways that privilege some people more than others. To say that "sports unite the social classes" is to ignore the dynamics that often separate people from different social-class backgrounds.

eating. People say, 'You should pay to feed the homeless.' But the world doesn't work that way" (Cagan and deMause, 1998: 162).

WHAT ABOUT JOBS CREATED BY SPORTS?

Jobs are always created when $300–$800 million is spent in a city. But those jobs also would be created if the arenas and stadiums were privately financed. Furthermore, when cities spend public money to build stadiums for professional teams, they create far fewer jobs than they would create through other forms of economic development. The congressional study cited previously found that *each new job* created in connection with the state-financed $222 million football stadium that opened in Baltimore in 1998 cost about $127,000. Meanwhile, the cost of creating one job through the Maryland economic development fund was about $6250. Thus, for every 100 jobs created by the new stadium, about 2,100 jobs could have been created if public money had been invested in other development projects. This is because sport facilities do not employ many people. Stadiums and arenas sit empty most of the time, and most of the jobs they generate are low paying and seasonal. If they were good investments, team owners would build stadiums and arenas with their own money!

WHO ELSE BENEFITS?

Sport team owners are not the only wealthy and powerful people who benefit when tax money is used to construct stadiums and arenas. New publicly financed sport facilities increase property values in urban areas in which major investors and developers can initiate profitable projects. Others also may benefit as money trickles down to the rest of the community, but the average taxpayers who fund the facilities will never see the benefits enjoyed by the few. When new stadiums and arenas are vehicles for transferring public money to powerful individuals and private corporations, it is an example of class relations operating in sports. *What do you think?**

---

*The pros and cons of using public money to build stadiums and arenas are discussed further in chapter 11, pages 384–388.

geographic location. For example, women in family situations are less likely than their male counterparts to be in positions enabling them to negotiate the time and resources needed to play sports (Thompson, 1999a, 1999b). For example, when a married woman with children joins a soccer team that schedules practices late in the afternoon, she may wonder if its okay with her family because she is the family chef, chauffeur, and tutor. "Time off for good behavior" is not a principle that applies to married women with children.

On the other hand, married men with children usually have more freedom to make such decisions. When they play softball or soccer after work, their wives may delay family dinners, keep dinners warm until they arrive home, or even go to the games and watch them play. Women in middle- and lower-income families most often feel the constraints of homemaking and child rearing. Without money to pay for child care, domestic help, and participation fees, these women have few opportunities to play sports. They also lack time, a car to take them to where sports are played, access to gyms and playing fields in their neighborhoods, and the sense of physical safety that they need to leave home and travel to where they can play sports. Because many sports require multiple participants, the lack of resources among some women affects others. This is also true for men, but women from middle- and lower-income families are more likely than their male counterparts to lack the network of relationships out of which sport interests and participation emerge and come to be supported.

Women from upper-income families often face a different situation. They have resources to pay for child care, domestic help, carryout dinners, and sport fees. They participate in sports by themselves and with friends and family members. Their social networks include other women

> My only brother was not required to help out around the house, but was encouraged to go out and play football with his friends.
>
> —Dr. Beatriz Vélez (2003)

who also have resources to play sports. Women who grow up in these families play sports during their childhoods and attend schools with good sport programs. They seldom experience the same constraints as their lower-income counterparts, even though their opportunities may not equal those of upper-income men.

The sport participation of girls and young women also may be limited when they are asked to shoulder responsibilities at home. For example, in low-income families, especially single-parent and immigrant families, teenage daughters often are expected to care for younger siblings after school until after dinner when their mothers get home from work. According to one girls' team coach in a New York City high school, "It's not at all unusual that on a given day there may be two or three girls who aren't [at practice] because of responsibilities at home" (Dobie, 1987). The coach also explained that child-care duties keep many girls from going out for teams. His solution was to coordinate a cooperative child-care program at practices and games, so that girls from low-income families could meet family expectations *and* play sports. However, when coaches are not so creative and accommodating, some girls drop out to meet responsibilities at home (Sylwester, 2005a).

Boys and girls from higher-income families seldom have household responsibilities that force them to drop out of sports. Instead, their parents drive them to practices, lessons, and games; make sure they have all the equipment they need to play well; and then give them cars so that they can drive themselves to practices and games.

The implications of class dynamics become very serious when health and obesity issues are considered. Limited opportunities to exercise safely and play sports are part of a series of factors contributing to a rapid rise in obesity, diabetes, and heart disease, especially among girls and women from low-income households (NHANES, 2002).

The availability of facilities, safe spaces, transportation, and sports programs all vary by social class, and the girls and women in low-income households experience the effects of social class in different and more profound ways when it comes to involvement in physical activities and sports.

Being Respected and Becoming a Man: Class and Gender Relations in Men's Lives

Boys and young men learn to use sports to establish a masculine identity, but the dynamics of this process vary by social class. For example, in a qualitative analysis of essays written about sports by fifteen- to sixteen-year-old French Canadian boys in the Montreal area, Suzanne Laberge and Mathieu Albert (1999) discovered that ideas about sports and masculinity varied among the upper-class, middle-class, and working-class boys. The upper-class boys connected sports participation with masculinity because they saw sports as an arena in which they could learn to be leaders, and leadership was important in their definition of masculinity. The middle-class boys connected sports participation with masculinity because they saw sports as an arena for sociability and opportunities to gain acceptance in male groups, thereby confirming their manhood. The working-class boys connected sports participation with masculinity because they saw sports as an arena for displaying tough, hypermasculine actions and personas, which represented their conception of manhood.

Sociologist Mike Messner has noted that, in U.S. culture, "the more limited a boy's options appear to be, and the more insecure his family situation, the more likely he is to make an early commitment to an athletic career" (1992, p. 40). In other words, the personal stakes associated with playing sports are different and greater for boys from low-income backgrounds than they are for boys from high-income backgrounds. Messner found that former elite male athletes from low-income backgrounds often saw sport participation as a way to obtain "respect." However, this

was not as important among males from middle-class backgrounds. One former athlete who later became a junior high school coach explained this difference in the following way:

> For . . . the poorer kids, [sports are] their major measuring stick. . . . They constantly remind each other what they can't do in the sports arena. It's definitely peer-acceptable if they are good at sports—although they maybe can't read, you know—if they are good at sports, they're one of the boys. Now I know the middle- and upper-class boys, they do sports and they do their books. . . . But as a whole, [they put] less effort into [sports]. (in Messner, 1992, pp. 57–58)

This coach suggested that social class factors create social conditions under which young men from lower-income backgrounds often have more at stake when it comes to playing sports. What he didn't mention is that the development of sport skills often requires material resources that do not exist in low-income families. Therefore, unless equipment and training are provided in public school athletic programs, young men from low-income groups stand little chance of competing against upper-income peers, who can buy equipment and training if they want to develop skills—except in two or three sports (football, basketball, and track) that are still provided in many public schools in lower-income areas.

In fact, young people from upper-income backgrounds often have so many opportunities to do different things that they may not focus on sport to the exclusion of other activities. For someone who has a car, nice clothes, money for college tuition, and good career contacts for the future, playing sports may be good for enhancing popularity, but it is not perceived as a necessary foundation for economic survival (Messner, 1992). Therefore, young men from middle- and upper-income backgrounds often choose to disengage gradually from exclusive commitments to becoming professional athletes. When these young men move through adolescence and into adulthood, opportunities often take them in a variety of directions. Playing sports may be important to them, but not like it is for young men from working-class and low-income families. This is clearly illustrated in the next section.

Fighting to Survive: Class, Gender, and Ethnic Relations Among Boxers

Chris Dundee, a famous boxing promoter, once said, "Any man with a good trade isn't about to get himself knocked on his butt to make a dollar" (in Messner, 1992, p. 82). What he meant was that middle- and upper-class males see no reason to have their brain cells destroyed in a quest to get ahead through a sport such as boxing. Of course, this is why nearly all boxers always come from the lowest and most economically desperate income groups in society and why boxing gyms are located in low-income neighborhoods, especially low-income minority neighborhoods, where desperation is often most intense and life piercing (Wacquant, 2004).

The dynamics of becoming and staying involved in boxing have been studied and described by French sociologist Loïc Wacquant (1992, 1995a, 1995b, 2004). As noted in chapter 7, Wacquant spent over three years training and hanging out at a boxing gym in a black ghetto area in Chicago. During that time, he documented the life experiences of fifty professional boxers, most of whom were African Americans. His analysis shows that the motivation to dedicate oneself to boxing can be explained only in terms of a combination of class, race, and gender relations. Statements by the boxers themselves illustrate the influence of this combination:

> Right [in the area where I lived] it was definitely rough, it was dog-eat-dog. I had to be a mean dog . . . young guys wan'ed to take yer money and beat ya up an' you jus' had to fight or move out the neighbo'hood. I couldn't move, so I had to start fightin'. (in Wacquant, 1992, p. 229)

> I used to fight a lot when I was younger *anyway so*, my father figure like, you know, [said] "If you gonna fight, well why don't you take it to a gym where you gonna learn, you know, a little more

> basics to it, maybe make some money, go further and do somethin' . . . insteada jus' bein' on the streets you know, and fightin' for nothing." (in Wacquant, 1992, p. 229)

The alternative to boxing for young men in this area was often the violence of the streets. When Wacquant asked one boxer where he'd be today if he hadn't started boxing, he answered with these words:

> If it wasn't for boxin,' I don't know where I'd be . . . Prob'ly in prison or dead somewhere, you never know. I grew up in a tough neighbo'hood, so it's good for me, at least, to think 'bout what I do before I do it. To keep me outa the street, you know. The gym is a good place for me to be every day. Because when you're in d'gym, you know where you are, you don' have to worry about getting' into trouble or getting shot at. (in Wacquant, 2004, p. 239)

Wacquant explains that most boxers know they would not be boxing if they had *not* been born as poor minority persons or if they had excelled in school. A trainer-coach at the gym explained the connection between social class and boxing when he said, "Don't nobody be out there fightin' with an MBA" (in Wacquant, 1995a, p. 521). Wacquant sees the men he studied as being tied to boxing in the form of a "coerced affection, a captive love, one ultimately born of racial and class necessity" (1995a, p. 521). Many of the boxers realized that, despite their personal commitment to boxing, their sport involved exploitation. As one boxer noted, "Fighters is whores and promoters is pimps, the way I sees it" (in Wacquant, 1995a, p. 520).

When Wacquant asked one boxer what he would change in his life, the boxer's answer represented the feelings of many of his peers at the gym:

> I wish I was born taller, I wish I was born in a rich family, I . . . wish I was smart, an' I had the brains to go to school an' really become somebody real important. For me I mean I can't stand the sport, I hate the sport, [but] it's carved inside of me so I can't let it go. (in Wacquant, 1995a, p. 521)

Boxing has long been a sport for men from low-income groups. As a long-time boxing coach says, "If you want to know who's at d'bottom of society, all you gotta to do is look at who's boxin'" (in Wacquant, 2004, p. 42). (*Source:* McGraw-Hill)

Even though the boxers were attached to their craft, over 80 percent didn't want their children to become boxers. For example, one said,

> No, no fighter wants their son [to box], I mean . . . *that's the reason why you fight, so he won't be able to fight.* . . . It's too hard, jus' too damn hard. . . . If he could *hit the books* an' study an' you know, with me havin' a little background in school an' stuff, I could help him. My parents, I never had nobody helpin' me. (in Wacquant, 1995a, p. 523)

These mixed feelings about boxing were pervasive; the men were simultaneously committed to and repulsed by their trade.

We can understand the sport participation of these men only in terms of the social-class contexts in which they lived their lives and how those contexts influenced their identities as black men. For them, boxing and the gym where they practice their craft provide a refuge from the violence, hopelessness, and indignity of the racism and poverty that framed their lives since birth. As a French sociologist looking at the United States, Wacquant concludes that being a young, poor, black man "in America is no bed of roses" (2004, p. 238). This, he says, is the major reason that they excel in the few sports in which they've had opportunities to play.

Class Relations in Action: Changing Patterns in Sports Participation Opportunities

In chapter 5, we noted that publicly funded youth sport programs are being cut in U.S. communities facing government budget crises. The same thing is occurring with high school sports in school districts with high proportions of low-income families (see chapter 14). Varsity sport programs are being cut back or eliminated in many poor school districts. When this occurs, fewer young people from low-income backgrounds have opportunities to participate in sports such as baseball and football, each of which requires playing fields that are relatively large and expensive to maintain. Meanwhile, basketball grows in popularity among low-income boys and girls because a school can offer basketball as long as it can maintain a usable gym. However, maintaining a usable gym is a serious problem in some inner-city schools where overcrowding has caused gyms to be turned into classroom space.

School sport programs in middle- and upper-income areas also may be threatened by financial problems. But, when this occurs, "participation fees" paid by athletes and their families are used to maintain them. These fees, sometimes as high as $250 per sport, guarantee that opportunities to participate in varsity programs will continue

for those young people lucky enough to be born into families living in relatively wealthy areas. Furthermore, when school sport programs do not measure up to the expectations of those with economic resources, as is currently the case with soccer, volleyball, lacrosse, and ice hockey, they either vote to use public funds or simply use private funds to build new fields and facilities, hire coaches, and run high-profile tournaments at which college coaches look for athletes they might recruit with scholarships. When tax revolts led by upper-middle-income people cause public programs to disappear, people with money simply buy a wide range of privatized sports participation opportunities for their children. This nationwide trend highlights the importance of social class. When it comes to sport participation, the socioeconomic status of the family you are born into has never been more important—participation is a family affair and is driven by family resources. This often is the case for people with disabilities, as explained in "Breaking Barriers," page 340.

When we compare the availability and quality of school and club sport programs by social class, we see as *savage inequalities* according to long-time educator Jonathan Kozol (1991, 2002). These inequalities decrease the life chances of young people living with the legacy of poverty and racism. The dynamics of this process were portrayed in the award-winning documentary film, *Hoop Dreams* (1994). The film shows the differences between high school sport programs in poor urban areas and wealthy suburban areas. Basketball teams in the urban schools didn't play at night or on weekends, as the suburban schools did; the public urban schools couldn't afford the overtime janitorial costs, so their games were played on weekday afternoons after school (Joravsky, 1995). Other differences were related to the quality of equipment and practice facilities, the availability of uniforms, the existence of junior varsity teams, the size of the gym and its seating capacity, the quality of locker-room facilities, heating and air conditioning in the gym, transportation to away games, the number

Children in middle-class suburban areas often have safe streets on which they can play. The boys in this cul-de-sac have access to many portable basketball goals, and they often recruit friends to play full-court games in the street. Of course, they also play roller hockey, soccer, baseball, and football, and they water-ski behind boats owned by families in the neighborhood. Sports may be important in their lives, but they are not seen as a means of economic survival. (*Source:* Jay Coakley)

of coaches, the number and quality of referees, access to training-room support, and game attendance.

With funds being cut and coaches laid off, people in poor neighborhoods cannot maintain sport programs, so they look to outside funding sources such as corporations. But corporations tend to sponsor only those sports that promote their images. A shoe company may support basketball rather than other sports because basketball's popularity makes it effective in the company's marketing and advertising programs. Corporate funding usually emphasizes certain sports to generate product visibility through media coverage and high-profile state and national tournaments. NFL and NBA funding, for

Resource Barriers
I'm Trying to Make Do

Stories about space-age materials like Kevlar and carbon fiber are heartening. These and other high-tech materials are used to make light, fast racing chairs, running prostheses shaped like a cheetah's leg, and racing mono-skis that can be maneuvered down steep slopes.

This technology is seductive for those who see it for the first time. So seductive, that they often overlook the person and focus on the device (Belson, 2002). However, as most athletes know, technologies are only as good as the people who use them. And as many people with disabilities know, adaptive technologies for sports often are prohibitively expensive.

Diane Cabrera discovered the cost of adaptive technology when she lost her leg to cancer in 2001. The bill for her prosthesis was $11,000, and her HMO covered only $4000 per year. She spread payments over two years and struggled to find $2200 for co-pays related to diagnostics, fitting, tuning, and maintenance. When she needed a new leg socket a few years later, she put it off because her original prosthesis no longer fit correctly and she couldn't afford a new one. When asked about her situation, Diane said with resignation, "I'm trying to make do right now."

"Making do right now"—that's a common strategy for many people who need prostheses. Unless you are wealthy or have insurance that covers more than $1500 a year for prosthetic limbs, you quickly learn to "make do." This is because most below-the-knee prosthetics cost $6000 to $8000. An arm or an above-the-knee prosthetic leg costs $10,000 to $15,000 (Sweeney, 2005). Prosthetic limbs and adaptive devices for sports involve additional costs. Sport prosthetics require replacement every year or two, and other prosthetic limbs should be replaced every four to six years. Racing wheelchairs cost about $4000, and Kevlar wheels push the cost up to $6000.

The cost of equipment is a real barrier to sport participation among many people with disabilities. Accentuating resource barriers in the United States are the following facts (McKay, 2005; U.S. Department of Labor, 2005):

- The unemployment rate among nearly 50 million people with disabilities is three times higher than the rate among people without disabilities; the rate among 33 million people with "serious or significant" disabilities is the highest of any category of Americans—about 70 percent of working-age people.
- Thirty-five percent of people with disabilities report they are working full or part time compared to 78 percent of people without disabilities.
- People with disabilities are three times more likely than people without disabilities to live in households making less than $15,000 per year.
- People with disabilities are less likely to have regular access to transportation and more likely to go without needed medical care than people without disabilities.

These are the realities of social class and disability in the United States. Federal government assistance for people with disabilities has been cut in recent years, states have not been able to pick up the slack, charity is spotty and uneven, and community programs are scarce, even if people have transportation to play sports regularly.

For young elite athletes, there are a few sponsorships available from companies that develop and manufacture prostheses and other adaptive technologies. This is one way for a select few to bypass resource barriers. But for others who don't have wealthy and connected advocates the barriers are formidable. Their goal is simply "to make do right now."

• •

example, emphasizes tackle football for boys and basketball. League executives may be concerned about poor children in inner cities, but they also realize that, if the schools are not training the

next generation of football and basketball players, they must do so with their programs. Sports continue to exist, but they exist on terms that meet corporate interests. When this happens, the link between sports and class relations becomes especially apparent.

Class Relations in Action: The Cost of Attending Sport Events

It is still possible to attend some sports events for free. High school and many college events in the United States remain affordable for many people, and in some communities the tickets for minor league sports are reasonably priced. But tickets to most major intercollegiate and professional events are beyond the means of many people, even those whose taxes are being used to pay for the facilities in which the events are played. The cost of attending these events has increased far beyond the rate of inflation over the past fifteen years.

Table 10.2 shows that, between 1991 and 2004, the average ticket prices for Major League Baseball, the NFL, the NBA, and the NHL increased 129 percent, 117 percent, 142 percent,

and 99 percent, respectively. During the same time period, inflation was 41 percent. Ticket prices increase as new stadiums and arenas are built to attract wealthier spectators. Team owners want to "capture" the people who have money to spend. Therefore, these new facilities are shopping malls built around a playing surface. They house expensive luxury suites and sections of club seating, where upper-income spectators have special services available to them: wait staff, special food menus, private restrooms, televisions, telephones, refrigerators, lounge chairs, temperature controls, private entrances with no waiting lines or turnstiles, special parking areas, and other things that make going to a game no different than going to a private club.

As ticket prices increase and as spectators are increasingly segregated by their ability to pay, social class and class relations become more evident in the stands. Spectators may cheer at the same times and experience similar emotions,

Table 10.2   Escalating ticket prices versus inflation in the United States, 1991–2004

	AVERAGE TICKET PRICE				Thirteen-Year Increase (%)
	1991 ($)	1996 ($)	2001 ($)	2004 ($)	
Major League Baseball	8.64	11.20	19.00	19.82	129
National Football League	25.21	35.74	50.02	54.75	117
National Basketball Association	23.24	31.80	51.34	56.13*	142
National Hockey League	24.00†	34.75	47.70	47.85*	99†
Minor League Baseball	NA	NA	NA	6.01‡	NA
				Inflation rate, 1991–2004 = 41.4%§	

Source: Adapted from data in Team Marketing Report www.teammarketing.com.

*The Team Marketing Report did not include for 2004 the average premium ticket price for NBA and NHL games in its basic average ticket price. Therefore, I assumed that 10 percent of NBA and NHL tickets cost the premium price and recomputed the average, assuming a 17,000-seat facility. The premium ticket prices for NBA games was $153.80 and for NHL games was $86.35. Also, the NBA averages do not take into account the special luxury club seating sections located under certain stadiums where celebrities and the superwealthy watch the game on large high-definition screens while they "wine and dine" and do other things in private at an extremely high cost.

†These are estimates because no NHL data were available prior to 1994.

‡This is a new figure added to the Team Marketing Report; it does not include children's ticket prices, which average about 30 cents less than adult ticket prices.

§Ticket prices increased at more than three times the official rate of inflation as measured by the U.S. government officials at w1.jsc.nasa.gov/bu2/inflation/nasa/inflateNASA.html.

but social-class differences in society are seldom transcended at the events, and if they are, they become reality as soon as people leave the stadium.

For middle- and working-class fans wanting to resist rising prices, class relations often subvert their efforts. This is because people in luxury boxes, club seats, and other exclusive seats are not eager to be identified with fans who cannot afford high-priced tickets and concessions. Wealthy spectators use expensive tickets as status symbols with their friends and business associates. They *want* class distinctions to be preserved in connection with attending games, and they are willing to pay, for example, over $1500 per ticket for NBA courtside seats in New York and Los Angeles to conspicuously display their status and experience the game without mixing with average fans. Attendance and seating at many events, from the opening ceremonies at the Olympics to the NFL Super Bowl, also are tied to conspicuous displays of wealth, status, and influence. As long as this is the case, efforts to make games affordable to the people whose taxes build the facilities will fail.

GLOBAL INEQUALITIES AND SPORTS

When we discuss social class and sports, it is essential to think beyond our own society. Inequalities exist at all level of social organization—in families, groups, organizations, communities, societies, and the world. Global inequalities related to per capita income, living standards, and access to developmental resources are the source of the most serious problems that we face today. Research clearly shows that the gap between the richest and poorest nations is growing wider. For example, people in the United States, *on average*, spend about $60 per day to live as they do—and this includes everyone, even newborns. In the thirty-nine nations classified as "less developed countries" (LDCs), people spend about 58 cents a day to live as they do. In terms of consumption, an average person in the United States spends

about 100 times more than nearly half the individuals in the world spend per day. But this understates standard-of-living differences between Americans and people in LDCs because the U.S. gross domestic product (GDP = money generated by the economy) is over 125 times higher than the GDPs in an average LDC.

Another way to look at social class in global terms is to determine how many of the 6.6 billion people (as of mid-2006) live on less than $1 or $2 a day, an amount that international organizations agree is clearly below basic subsistence levels in any country, regardless of cost of living. As of 2004, about 1.2 billion lived on less than $1 per day, and an additional 2 billion people lived on less than $2 per day. In total, nearly half the world's population lived in poverty—that is, on less than $2 per day (Gore, 2002, 2004; www.globalisationguide.org/03.html). As a point of comparison, the *median* income in U.S. households containing four people was about $64,000 in 2003 (Cleveland, 2005).

The meanings given to this global gap between the wealthy and poor differ depending on the ideologies that people use to guide their understanding of world affairs. But apart from ideological interpretations, it is clear that half the people in the world have few resources to use on anything but basic survival. Those who are not sick or disabled may engage in physical play or games, but they don't have resources for organizing and playing sports as we know them. Therefore, half the people in the world see the sports played in the United States and other postindustrial nations as "dreamlands." They cannot understand why Tiger Woods can make $86,370,407 in 2004, an amount that is spent over an entire year by nearly 200,000 poor people in their country (Freedman, 2005). Neither would it be understood by people in other countries who make less than $1 an hour producing the balls, shoes, and other equipment and clothing used by most Americans who play sports, including professional athletes (Weiner, 2004).

When there is a dirt soccer pitch or basketball surface in a community in one of these countries,

After hearing about the millions of dollars that Lance Armstrong's cycling team spent on technology to prepare for the 2005 Tour de France, people in wealthy societies generally forget that sports are a luxury item. At least half the people in the world do not have regular access to the time, resources, equipment, or spaces enabling them to play sports. This little boy lives in Nairobi, Kenya, and this is his sport. (*Source:* Karel Prinsloo, AP/Wide World Photos)

it often attracts young people who may have seen a televised soccer or basketball game. This has not escaped the people who scout for new talent for U.S. colleges or professional soccer and basketball teams in wealthy nations. According to a *Sports Illustrated* article (Wahl, 2004), those scouts are "on safari for 7-footers." When they find a prospect, they know that he will not have an agent and will sign a contract for little money in "Western" terms,and also will appreciate a chance to experience "dreamland." Only a few of

these prospects have made it to the NBA or other top professional leagues. And the irony is that some of them have found themselves nearly penniless after using most of their incomes to keep the people in their home village from starving. But the owners of the teams they played for usually made money from their labor as players. This is one of the ways that class relations operate on a global scale.

ECONOMIC AND CAREER OPPORTUNITIES IN SPORTS

Do sports and sport organizations provide opportunities for upward social-class mobility in society? **Social mobility** is a term used by sociologists to refer to *changes in wealth, education, and occupation over a person's lifetime or from one generation to the next in families*. Social mobility can occur in downward or upward directions. On a general level, career and mobility opportunities exist in sports and sport organizations. However, as we consider the impact of sports on mobility in the United States, it is useful to know the following things about sport-related opportunities:

1. The number of career opportunities in sports is limited, and the playing careers of athletes are short term.
2. Opportunities for women are growing but remain limited on and off the field.
3. Opportunities for blacks and other ethnic minorities are growing but remain limited on and off the field.

These points are discussed in the following sections.

Career Opportunities Are Limited

Young athletes often have visions of becoming professional athletes, and their parents may have similar visions. But the chances of turning these visions into reality are quite low. The actual odds for a person to become a college or professional athlete vary greatly because people use so many different methods to calculate them. For example, the odds of becoming a professional athlete may be calculated for high school or college athletes in a particular sport, for high school or college athletes from particular racial or ethnic groups, or for any male or female in a particular age group of the total population in a society. The calculations may be based on the number of players in the top league in a sport, such as the NHL in hockey, or they may take into account that professional hockey leagues are in Europe and minor league professional teams are in North America. The calculations may or may not take into account the number of NHL players that come from different countries. This is important because few NHL players have ever played on a U.S. high school varsity team, and about 75 percent of current NHL players grew up outside the United States, most in Canada.

The point here is that all estimates of the odds of making it in the pros must be qualified, and many estimates reported in the media are inaccurate. The data in table 10.3 represent computations made by the NCAA in 2004. As you view the data in the table, read the footnotes to understand the limitations of these calculations. The data indicate that playing at the professional level is a long shot. In fact, if you saw similar odds for a horse at a racetrack, you would never bet on it unless you had money to burn—and, if you placed a bet with such bad odds, people would look at you as if you were crazy.

In addition to poor odds, professional sport opportunities are short term, averaging three to seven years in team sports and three to twelve years in individual sports. This means that, after playing careers end, there are about *forty additional years* in a person's work life. Unfortunately, many people, including athletes, coaches, and parents, ignore this part of reality.

The media focus on the best athletes in the most popular sports, and they have longer playing

Table 10.3 Estimated probability of competing in athletics beyond the high school interscholastic level*

Student-Athletes	Men's Basketball	Women's Basketball	Football	Baseball	Men's Ice Hockey	Men's Soccer
High school student-athlete	549,500	456,900	983,600	455,300	29,900	321,400
High school senior student-athlete	157,000	130,500	281,000	130,100	8,500	91,800
NCAA student-athlete	15,700	14,400	56,500	25,700	3,700	18,200
NCAA freshman roster positions	4,500	4,100	16,200	7,300	1,100	5,200
NCAA senior student-athlete	3,500	3,200	12,600	5,700	800	4,100
NCAA student-athlete drafted	44	32	250	600	33	76
Percent high school to NCAA	2.9%	3.1	5.8	5.6	12.9	5.7
Percent NCAA to professional	1.3	1.0	2.0	10.5	4.1	1.9
Percent high school to professional	0.03[†]	0.02	0.09	0.5	0.4	0.08

Source: NCAA, 2004, online at www.ncaa.org/research/prob_of_competing/probability_of_competing2.html#m_ice_hockey.

*These numbers, based on estimated data, are very rough approximations of reality. For example, the numbers for NCAA players do not take into account players at non-NCAA schools, players from other countries who are recruited by NCAA schools, players in North American professional leagues who have not attended high school or college in the United States, or U.S. high school and college players that play professional sports in other countries. Therefore, the odds of a U.S. high school or college athlete making it to the next levels of competition in these sports are worse than these numbers suggest. To see how these numbers were calculated, go to www.ncaa.org/research/prob_of_competing/probability_of_competing2.html#methodology.

[†]How to read the last line: For men's basketball, 3 of every 10,000 high school players will be drafted by the NBA, or 1 of every 3333 (but this does not mean they will sign pro contracts); for women's basketball, it is 2 in 10,000 high school players, or 1 of every 5000; and for men's football it is 9 of every 10,000 high school football players, or 1 of every 1100.

careers than others in their sports. Little coverage is given to those who play for one or two seasons before being cut or forced to quit for other reasons, especially injuries. We hear about the long football careers of popular quarterbacks, but little about the numerous players whose one-year contracts are not renewed after their first season. The average age of players on the *oldest* NFL team in 2004 was less than twenty-eight years old. This means that few players older than thirty are still in the league. Much more typical than thirty-year-olds contemplating another season are twenty-three-year-olds trying to deal with the end of their professional playing careers.

Finally, many professional athletes make less than their peers in nonsport occupations. For example, 86 of the 331 players in Major League Soccer in 2005 made less than $20,000 per year (Bell, 2005). Another 57 players made less than $30,000, and many others had salaries less than $50,000. Elementary school teachers who have trained in their occupations for as many years as these soccer players make more money, have more security and stability, and usually have a pension plan. But the teachers have less fame.

Opportunities for Women Are Growing but Remain Limited

Career opportunities for female athletes are limited relative to opportunities for men. Tennis and golf provide opportunities for women; however, the professional tours for these sports draw athletes from around the world. For women in the United States, this means that the competition to make a living in these sports is great. There were more than 1000 players who competed in Women's Tennis Association (WTA) tournaments in 2005, but relatively few of them were American. For example, only 13 of the 100 top-ranked players in July 2005 were American, and those ranked beyond the top 100 made less than $100,000 of prize money during the year and most did not cover their expenses for the year (www.wtatour.com/thewtatour/). In the Ladies

Professional Golf Association (LPGA), about one-third of the players and 40 percent of the top money winners are from nations other than the United States (www.lpga.com/default_rr.aspx). Fewer than 70 women from the United States make enough prize money to cover their expenses as professional golfers.

There are expanding opportunities in professional basketball, soccer, volleyball, figure skating, bowling, skiing, bicycling, track and field, and rodeo, but the number of professional female athletes remains very low, and only a few women make large amounts of money. For example, it took nineteen years for Aleta Still, the top money winner in the history of bowling, to make $1 million in total earnings for her career, whereas NFL quarterback Peyton Manning made twice that amount in each game he played during the 2004 season—a comparison that says much about opportunities, gender, and cultural values.

Professional leagues for women now exist in basketball, soccer, and beach volleyball, but they provide career opportunities for fewer than 400 athletes at any given point in recent years. The Women's United Soccer Association (WUSA), employed about 170 players for the two years it operated, and about 40 of those players were from outside the United States (Wieberg, 2005b). The combined salaries for *all* WUSA players during the 2002 season was $6.76 million, which was less than the annual salary of most individual star players on European men's teams.

In the WNBA, the pay is a fraction of what men in the NBA make. The minimum salary for players with one to three years experience is $30,600; for players with four or more years of experience, it is $43,700. No WNBA player has a salary more than $89,000, the amount that Shaquille O'Neill makes in about thirteen minutes of one game. In fact, the total payroll for all WNBA players in 2004 was about $8.8 million, the amount that O'Neill makes in the first twenty-six games of the 2005 season. For every dollar that an NBA player makes, a player in the WNBA makes about 1 cent (see figure 10.2).

"Ah, the glamorous life of a spoiled, overpaid professional athlete!"

....

FIGURE 10.2   Only a few professional athletes achieve fame and fortune. Thousands of them play in minor and semipro leagues in which salaries are low and working conditions poor.

There are about ninety players in the six-team National Women's Basketball League, and they generally make less than $10,000 for a twenty-four-game season. Additionally, the future of the WNBA and NWBL are tenuous. There are opportunities in European basketball and soccer, but they are limited and salaries are unimpressive. Actually, most high school teachers make as much as many pro women basketball players. Overall, the advice for women who aspire to make a living as professional athletes is have a backup plan and be ready to use it.

What about other careers in sports? There are jobs for women in coaching, training, officiating, sports medicine, sports information, public relations, marketing, and administration. As noted in chapter 8, most of the jobs in women's sports continue to be held by men, and women seldom are hired for jobs in men's programs, except in support positions. In the United States, when men's and women's high school or college athletic programs are combined, men become the athletic directors in nearly all cases. Women in most postindustrial nations have challenged the legacy of traditional gender ideology, and some progress has been made in various administrative

positions in some sports organizations (Lapchick, 2005c). However, a heavily gendered division of labor continues to exist in nearly all organizations (McKay, 1997, 1999). In traditional and developing nations, the record of progress is negligible, and very few women hold positions of power in any sports organizations (Rintala and Bischoff, 1997; White and Henry, 2004).

Job opportunities for women have not increased as rapidly as women's programs have grown. This is partly due to the persistence of traditional ideas about gender and the fact that Title IX does not have precise enforcement procedures when it comes to equity in coaching and administration. Title IX enforcement focuses almost exclusively on athletes, and it has not had as much impact on equity in other aspects of sport organizations (Matson, 2004). Therefore, a pattern of gender underrepresentation exists in nearly all job categories and nearly all sport organizations. For example, in U.S. colleges and universities, the men and women who coach women's teams make less money than the men who coach men's teams. This is true in nearly all sports, even those that do not generate revenues. According to the most recent NCAA data (see NCAA, 2004), the 25,300 full- and part-time head coaches and assistants of women's teams in 1033 colleges and universities received combined salaries that were an estimated $245.3 million less than the combined salaries of the 30,279 coaches of men's teams.[1] This difference does *not* include incentives and other perks received mostly by male coaches of high-profile football and basketball teams.

When the salaries of NCAA coaches are compared in each Division, the coaches of men's teams in Division I have average salaries that are 55 percent greater than coaches of women's Division I teams. In Division II, the coaches of men's teams make an average of 30-percent

---

[1]I used NCAA data and extrapolated them to all 327 Division I, 282 Division II, and 424 Division III schools, even though all schools did not respond to the NCAA gender equity survey.

more than coaches of women's teams. And in Division III, the coaches of women's teams make an average of 2 percent more than coaches of men's teams, but the salaries for all coaches in Division III are so low that this difference amounts to less than $100 per year. Only 44 percent of all coaches of women's teams are women, so the men coaching women's teams also experience the effects of these salary differences.

Opportunities for women in sports will continue to shift toward equity, but people continue to resist the ideological changes that would open the door to full equity. In the meantime, there will be gradual increases in the number of women coaches, sports broadcasters, athletic trainers, administrators, and referees. Changes will occur more rapidly in community-based recreation and fitness programs and in high school and college programs where salaries are low and in certain sport industries that target women as consumers and need women employees to increase their sales and profits. But the gender ideology used

Of the fifty highest paid (including endorsements) athletes in the world in 2004, Serena Williams was the only woman on the list, and she made less than one-fourth of what Tiger Woods made and less than one-half of what Andre Agassi made. In 2005 Maria Sharapova—an attractive white, blond Russian who won Wimbledon in 2004 and received $20 million in endorsements for 2005—overtook Serena Williams. Only thirteen of the top one hundred money winners on the WTA Tour in 2005 were from the United States. (*Source:* Amy Sancetta, AP/Wide World Photos)

by influential decision makers *inside* many sports organizations will continue to privilege those perceived as tough, strong, competitive, and aggressive—and men are more likely to be perceived in such terms.

Many women who work in sport organizations continue to face the burden of dealing with organizational cultures that are primarily based on the values and experiences of men. This contributes to low job satisfaction and high job turnover among women. Professional development programs, workshops, and coaching clinics have been developed since the late 1990s to assist women as they live in and try to change these cultures in ways that will make them more inclusive. However, equity requires that many men in sports and sport organizations change their ideas about gender and its connection with sports and leadership. (McKay, 1997).

Opportunities for African Americans and Other Ethnic Minorities Are Growing but Remain Limited

The visibility of black athletes in certain spectator sports often has led to the conclusion that career opportunities for African Americans are abundant in U.S. sports. Such beliefs have been supported by testimonials from successful black athletes who attribute their wealth and fame to sports. However, the extent to which job opportunities for blacks exist in sports has been greatly overstated. Very little publicity is given to the actual number and proportion of blacks who play sports for a living or make a living working in sport organizations. Also ignored is the fact that sports provide very few career opportunities for black women.

A review of professional spectator sports shows few blacks in any pro sports apart from boxing, basketball, football, baseball, and track. Some of the most lucrative sports for athletes remain almost exclusively white. Tennis, golf, hockey, and auto racing are examples. My best guess is that fewer than 6000 African Americans, or about

1 in 6660, are making a very good living as professional athletes. Data from the U.S. Department of Labor indicates that, in 2004, 18,640 African American men and women were classified as "athletes, coaches, umpires, and related workers." In the same year, 50,630 African Americans were physicians and surgeons, 44,840 were lawyers, and 69,388 were college and university teachers. Therefore, there were thirty-six times more African Americans working in these three prestigious professions than African American athletes in top-level professional sports; and nine times more African American doctors, lawyers, and college teachers than African Americans working in all of sports. Furthermore, physicians, lawyers, and college teachers have greater *lifetime* earnings than most athletes whose playing careers, on average, last less than five years and whose salaries outside top pro leagues rarely exceed $50,000 per year. Department of Labor statistics for 2004 indicate that the median (that is, half make more and half make less) incomes of male doctors and surgeons, lawyers, and college teachers were $97,500, $88,900, and $60,400, respectively; but for athletes, coaches, umpires, and related workers, it was only $41,184. Therefore, an African American male college student today has a ten times better chance of becoming a doctor, lawyer, or college teacher than being employed in sports and will make 50 to 100 percent more in those nonsport professions.

Despite the dismal odds of becoming a professional athlete, young blacks often aspire to reach that goal. Of course, this does not mean that they ignore other goals as they pursue their sport dreams, but it does suggest a need to emphasize that educational goals and career opportunities outside of sports should not be ignored (Collins, 2004; Early, 1991; Edwards, 1993; Hoberman, 1997; McCallum, 2002; Platt, 2002; Sailes, 1998). With the sport images that come into the lives of young people every day, sport dreams can be very seductive, especially when other dreams are absent. Unfortunately, some young African Americans see so little hope and justice in the world around them that they focus on televised images of successful black athletes in the NFL and NBA. Those images are powerful because they are among the only positive images of black men that they see regularly in the media.

Employment Barriers for Black Athletes   When sports were first desegregated in the United States, blacks faced **entry barriers:** They had to be outstanding athletes with exemplary personal characteristics before they were given professional contracts (see Kooistra et al., 1993). Prejudices were strong and team owners assumed that players, coaches, and spectators would not accept blacks unless they made immediate, significant contributions to a team. Black athletes with average skills were passed by. The result was that black athletes had performance statistics surpassing those of whites, a fact that often reproduced white stereotypes about black physicality.

As entry barriers declined between 1960 and the late 1970s, new barriers related to retention took their place. **Retention barriers** existed when experienced black players did not have contracts renewed unless they had significantly better performance records than white players at the same career stage (Lapchick, 1984). This pattern existed through the early 1990s (Kooistra et al., 1993). But since that time, it appears that such retention barriers no longer exist (Leonard, 1995). Race-based salary discrimination existed in most sports immediately following the time when they were desegregated, but there is no evidence that it exists today in any of the major team sports (Singh et al., 2003). This is because performance can be measured, tracked, and compared to the performances of other players. Objective statistics are now kept on nearly every conceivable dimension of an athlete's skill. Agents use these statistics when they represent players in salary negotiations. Agents receive a percentage of players' salaries, so they have a built-in incentive to make sure that racial discrimination does not affect contracts for any of their players. Furthermore, an awareness of past racial discrimination in sports generally makes most people sensitive to issues of fairness related to salaries.

Employment Barriers in Coaching and Off-the-Field Jobs   In 1987 the long-time director of player personnel for the Los Angeles Dodgers said that blacks are excluded from coaching and administrative jobs in baseball because they "lack the necessities" to handle such jobs. This attitude explained why, during the thirty years he shaped the coaching and management staff on the Dodgers, the team never had a black person in the positions of general manager, field manager, pitching coach, or third-base coach (the most influential coach on a baseball team).

The Los Angeles Dodgers were one of many teams with such a record in the 1980s and 1990s. For example, when the Dallas Cowboys won the Super Bowl in 1994, a press release issued by a national black organization (the NAACP) accused the team of having plantation-like hiring practices. Seventy-five percent of the players on the team were African American, whereas all eleven of the top administrators were white men (Shropshire, 1996). This led Jesse Jackson to form the Rainbow Coalition for Fairness in Athletics, which began to work with the Center for the Study of Sport in Society (CSSS) to put pressure on professional and college sport teams to increase the representation of ethnic minorities and women in administrative and staff positions.

Since 1994, the pace at which blacks have been included in positions of power and responsibility has varied from one sport to another. There has been slow progress in most sport organizations, especially those associated with college and professional football. Even in 2002, when nearly 70 percent of the players on NFL rosters were black, only 6 percent of the head coaches were black—two out of thirty-two. This led lawyers Johnnie Cochran, Jr., and Cyrus Mehri (2002) to file a report in which they demanded that the NFL make systematic changes in the recruitment and hiring process so that qualified black candidates for head coach positions would be treated fairly.

Black men and women are seriously underrepresented in coaching at the college and professional levels in U.S. sports. Mike Davis, head basketball coach at Indiana University, is one of a growing number of black male coaches in college basketball and football. Opportunities for black women coaches, however, remain scarce. (*Source:* NCAA Photos)

The data presented by Cochran and Mehri showed that, between 1986 and 2001, black head coaches outperformed their white counterparts, yet they were hired less often and fired more quickly. An expert panel assembled by ESPN used these data to conclude that the lack of minority head coaches was the most serious problem facing the NFL in 2002 (Cochran and Mehri, 2002).

The general patterns in the NFL also exist in big-time college football. This caused Floyd Keith, the executive director of the Black Coaches Association, to issue a report to the NCAA and to begin forming alliances with other civil rights organizations. This report, and the one by Cochran and Mehri, caused many people to speculate about the reasons for the persistent underrepresentation of blacks in head coaching jobs in football. The following is an explanation given by *Sports Illustrated* writer Frank Deford:

> Football coaches are executives. . . . [T]he people who hire football coaches probably fail at getting to know young black coaching candidates, there is almost surely some kind of submerged racism, which presumes that, sure, a black man can handle a little basketball club, but a heavy-duty football operation is really too complicated to trust to a minority. (2002, p. 2A)

Clarence Underwood, a former athletic director at Michigan State University, explained that "the old boy network" accounted for the persistence of what he described as "an insidious pattern of racial discrimination." He also noted that the powerful white boosters in college football "want to see someone who looks like them, someone they can rub elbows with at the country club" (in Moran, 2002a, p. 2A). Others agreed by pointing out that a college football coach must be able to mingle with and be readily accepted by powerful white alumni and wealthy team supporters. The coach must raise funds from corporations and wealthy donors, nurture their continued support, play golf with them, and fit into their social settings. Therefore, even when a black coach is the best person for the job on the field, he may not be seen as the best candidate for the job as a whole (Moran, 2002a, 2002b).

Research in sociology has shown that, when CEOs (chief executive officers) and COOs (chief operating officers) recruit candidates for top-management positions, they often look for people who think as they do so that they can work closely and supportively (Cunningham and Sagas, 2005). This is why they often hire fraternity brothers, fellow alumni from college, or people they have known for many years. Such people are "known quantities" because they have familiar and shared backgrounds and are perceived as predictable and trustworthy. Therefore, if the CEO is a white male, he may question the job qualifications of candidates from racial or ethnic backgrounds different from his—backgrounds he may know little about. He may wonder if he could trust them to be supportive and fit in with others. If he has *any* doubts, conscious or unconscious, he will choose the candidate most like himself. These dynamics exist in sports and other organizations, and if they continue, minority men and all women will remain underrepresented in power positions in sports. For example, in 2004 the percentage of African American coaches in NCAA Divisions II and II was about the same as the percentage of *women coaching men's teams* in those two divisions (just under 4 percent) (Lapchick, 2005c).

Opportunities for Ethnic Minorities The dynamics of ethnic relations in every culture are unique (see chapter 9). Making generalizations about ethnic relations and opportunities in sports is difficult. However, dominant sport forms in any culture tend to reproduce dominant cultural values and the social structures supported by those values. This means three things: (1) Members of the dominant social class in a society may exclude or define as unqualified those who have characteristics and cultural backgrounds different from their own, (2) ethnic minorities often must adopt the values and orientations of people in the dominant social class if they want to be hired and promoted in sport organizations, and (3) the voices of ethnic minorities are seldom represented in the stories that people tell one another about themselves. In any case, blacks are likely to perceive that they have fewer career opportunities than their white counterparts, and they may have higher levels of job dissatisfaction (Cunningham and Sagas, 2005).

People in the United States with Latino, Asian, or Native American backgrounds also are underrepresented in many sports and sport organizations (Lapchick, 2004, 2005c). One reason for this is that many people still feel uncomfortable with ethnic diversity in situations in which they must trust coworkers. This is due to a lack of knowledge about people from various ethnic backgrounds and

about the ways that ethnic diversity can make positive contributions to the operation and overall culture of an organization. Exceptions to this are found in Major League Baseball and Major League Soccer teams that have many Latino players and a fair representation of Latinos in management. However, neither Asians nor Native Americans fare very well in any U.S. sport organizations, except in a few lower-level staff positions, partly because they are perceived as having little sports knowledge and experience, regardless of the reality of their lives (Lapchick, 2004, 2005c).

SPORT PARTICIPATION AND OCCUPATIONAL CAREERS AMONG FORMER ATHLETES

What happens in the occupational careers of former athletes? Do they have career patterns that are different from the patterns of those who have never played competitive sports? Is sport participation a stepping-stone to future occupational success and upward social mobility? Does playing sports have economic payoffs after active participation is over?

These are difficult questions to answer, and only a few studies have compared former athletes with others on issues related to social class and social mobility. Those studies suggest that, as a group, the young people who had played sports on high school and college teams experienced no more or less occupational success than others from comparable backgrounds. This does not mean that playing sports has never helped anyone in special ways; it means only that there have been no consistent research findings indicating that former athletes have a systematic advantage over comparable peers when it comes to future occupational careers and social-class position.

Research done a decade ago may not tell us what is happening today because the meaning and cultural significance of sport participation changes over time, and those changes may be related to career processes in some way. However, past research suggests that, *if* playing sports is connected to career success, it may operate in one or more of the following ways (see Coakley, 1983 and 1998, p. 317, for references to thirty of these studies):

- Playing sports under certain circumstances (see the following numbered list) may teach young people *interpersonal skills*, which carry over into various jobs and enable them to be successful in jobs that require those skills.
- Some people with power and influence may define former athletes as good job prospects and give them opportunities to develop and demonstrate work-related abilities, which serve as the basis for career success.
- Individuals who were very high-profile athletes may be able to use their reputations to obtain certain jobs and be successful in them.
- Playing sports under certain circumstances (see the following numbered list) may connect athletes with others who can help them get good jobs after they retire from sports.

After reviewing all the research on this topic, my sense is that playing sports is positively related to occupational success and upward mobility when it does the following things:

1. Increases opportunities to complete academic degrees, develop job-related skills, and/or extend knowledge about the organization and operation of the world outside of sports.
2. Increases support from significant others for *overall* growth and development, not just sport development.
3. Provides opportunities to make friends and develop social contacts with people outside of sports and sport organizations.
4. Provides material resources and the guidance needed to use those resources to create or nurture career opportunities.
5. Expands experiences in ways that foster the development of identities and abilities unrelated to sports.
6. Minimizes risks of serious injuries that restrict physical movement or require extensive and expensive medical treatment.

These is not a surprising list of conditions. It emphasizes that playing sports can either constrict or expand a person's overall development (see chapter 4). When expansion occurs, athletes often develop work-related abilities and connections that lead to career opportunities and success. When constriction occurs, the development of work-related abilities and career opportunities are likely to be limited.

Highly Paid Athletes and Career Success After Playing Sports

Conclusions about sport participation, career success, and social mobility must be qualified in light of the dramatic increases in the salaries of *some* professional athletes over the past twenty to thirty years (see chapter 11). Before the late 1970s, few athletes made enough money in sports to pave their way into other careers after they retired. However, a few athletes today make enough money in a few years to finance any one of a range of career alternatives after they retire from sports—if they do not throw their money away or hire irresponsible agents to manage it.

Of course, many professional athletes have short careers or play at levels at which they do not make much money (see figure 10.3). When they retire, they must deal with the challenge of entering another career and making a living. Many experience patterns of success and failure similar to the patterns experienced by comparable others who did not play sports. Their post-sport careers may not enable them to drive new cars, travel to exciting places, or read their names in newspapers every week, but this does not mean they are failures or victims of sports.

As noted in chapter 4, retirement from sports is best described as a process rather than a single event, and most athletes don't retire from sports on a moment's notice—they gradually disengage and shift their priorities over time. Although many athletes disengage smoothly from sports, develop other interests, and move into relatively satisfying occupational careers, some do encounter adjustment problems that interfere

FIGURE 10.3 Only a few former athletes can cash in on their athletic reputations. The rest must seek opportunities and work just like the rest of us. Those opportunities vary, depending on qualifications, experience, contacts and connections, and a bit of luck.

with occupational success and overall life satisfaction.

When sociologist Mike Messner interviewed former elite athletes, he found that those who had been heavily involved in sports since childhood encountered serious adjustment problems as they tried to make the transition out of sports. A former NFL player highlighted these problems with the following explanation:

> [When you retire] you find yourself scrambled. You don't know which way to go. Your light . . . has been turned out. . . . Of course you miss the financial deal, but you miss the camaraderie of the other ballplayers. You miss that—to be an elite, to be one of a kind. . . . The game itself . . . the beating and all that . . . you don't really miss. You miss the camaraderie of the fellas. There's an empty feeling. . . . The one thing that has been the major part of your life is gone. . . . You don't know how people are going to react to you. . . . You wonder and question. (in Messner, 1992, pp. 120–21)

The two challenges that face many retiring athletes are (1) reconstructing identities in terms of activities, abilities, and relationships that are not directly related to sport participation and (2) renegotiating relationships with family

and friends so that new identities can be established and reaffirmed. Messner's study also indicated that young men from low-income families were more likely to have problems when retiring from sports because they had fewer material resources to use in the transition process and they were more likely to have identities deeply rooted in sports. The men from middle-class backgrounds, on the other hand, had greater material resources and support that enabled them to take advantage of opportunities and social connections; and they were less likely to have identities exclusively rooted in sports.

Studies also have shown that adjustment problems are more likely when an injury forces retirement from sports (Coakley, 1983b; Swain, 1999; Weisman, 2004). Injuries complicate retirement and tie it to larger issues of health and self-esteem. Injuries also disrupt life plans by throwing off the timing of retirement and forcing a person into life-changing transitions before they are expected. This is not surprising, and athletes often need career-related assistance when this occurs.

When athletes have problems making a transition out of sports into careers and other activities, it would be helpful if they received support from the sport organizations that benefited from their labor, especially when the athletes never made enough money to make the transition less problematic (Dacyshyn, 1999). Some sport organizations, including universities and national governing bodies, are beginning to do this through career transition programs that involve workshops focusing on career self-assessments, life skills training, career planning, résumé writing, job search strategies, interviewing skills, career placement contacts, and psychological counseling. In many cases, it is helpful just to have guidance in identifying the skills learned in sports and the ways that they are transferable to other settings or jobs.

Athletic Grants and Occupational Success

Discussions about sport participation and social mobility in the United States often include references to athletic scholarships. Most people believe that these grants-in-aid are valuable mobility vehicles for many young people. This belief raises many questions: How many students receive athletic scholarships, as opposed to other forms of financial assistance? How much are athletic scholarships worth to those who receive them? Who receives them and how many recipients would not attend college without them?

Answering these questions has become possible since 1994 when Congress passed the Equity in Athletics Disclosure Act. This forced most colleges and universities to inform people about what was going on in their athletic departments. The data that are reported annually indicate that the actual number of *full* athletic scholarships is often exaggerated. This occurs for the following reasons:

1. High school students who receive standard recruiting letters from university coaches often tell people they are anticipating *full* scholarships when in fact they may receive only partial aid or no aid at all.
2. College students receiving tuition waivers or other forms of partial athletic aid sometimes lead people to believe that they have full scholarships.
3. Athletic scholarships are awarded one year at a time and may not be renewed for certain athletes, who may continue their education while people believe they have scholarships.
4. Many people simply assume that college athletes, especially at big universities, all have scholarships when this is not true.

These factors cause people to think that sport participation has more relevance for upward mobility than it actually does.

According to NCAA data, there were 5.75 million undergraduate students in NCAA institutions in 2003. Table 10.4 shows that 377,651 (6.6 percent) of these students were on intercollegiate teams. Division I and II schools had 70,244 scholarships to award; they could award full scholarships or partial athletic aid with these resources. Of 232,473 Division I and II athletes,

132,758 athletes, or about 58 percent of them, received some amount of athletic aid, but most received only partial scholarships. According to NCAA sources, an estimated 17,561 athletes—4.7 percent of all NCAA athletes—received full scholarships (tuition, room, and food). The remaining 52,683 scholarships were split in various ways between 115,197 athletes—30.5 percent of all intercollegiate team members. The fact that surprises most people is that about 65 percent of all intercollegiate athletes receive no athletic aid.

Another way of making sense of the data in table 10.4 is to say that among all undergraduate students in NCAA schools, only .3 percent of them have full athletic scholarships, and only 2.3 percent of all undergraduates receive some form of athletic aid. Clearly, far fewer students receive full athletic scholarships than is commonly believed. In fact, academic scholarships amount to many millions of dollars more than the total amount of athletic scholarships, even though many high school students and their parents think otherwise.

Class and racial relations are heavily connected with athletic scholarships. In many universities, black men from middle- and lower-income families play on teams that generate the revenues that are used to pay for the athletic scholarships given to athletes in nonrevenue sports. At the same time, these men may feel socially isolated on campus and in the local community. If this feeling of isolation subverts the opportunities that expand experiences and social networks, then playing sports is not likely to contribute to career success. The few football and basketball players who sign big contracts distract attention away from this more important aspect of class and racial relations.

When athletic aid goes to financially needy young people who focus on learning and earning their degrees, sport participation increases their chances for career success. But how many of the students who receive athletic scholarships, full or partial, would not be able to attend college without them? A portion of scholarship recipients certainly would attend college without them. This

Table 10.4 Athletes, students receiving athletic aid, and number of full scholarships available to schools in NCAA Divisions I, II, and III, by gender (2003)*

	MEN			WOMEN		
Division	**All Athletes**	**No. of Full Scholarships**	**Athletes with Athletic Aid**	**All Athletes**	**No. of Full Scholarships**	**Athletes with Athletic Aid**
Division I (N = 327)	87,015	29,888	47,579	68,670	23,577	38,160
Division II (N = 282)	46,078	9,729	27,495	30,710	7,050	19,524
Division III (N = 424)	83,910	0	0	61,268	0	0
Total	217,003	39,617	75,074	160,648	30,627	57,684

Summary:

- All NCAA athletes: 377,651
- Number of full scholarships: 70,244 (Over 50,000 of these are split between two or more athletes.)
- Athletes with athletic aid: 132,758
- Percentage of all athletes with aid: 35%
  - Division I men: 55%
  - Division I women: 56%
  - Division II men: 60%
  - Division II women: 64%
  - Division III men: 0%
  - Division III women: 0%
  - All men: 35%
  - All women: 36%
- Percentage of all athletes with full scholarships: 4.7% (17,561)
- Athletes with no athletic aid: 244,893 (65%)

Source: Adapted from NCAA data (NCAA, 2004).

does not mean that athletic aid is unjustified, but it does mean that athletic scholarships contribute to little upward social mobility in society.

summary

DO MONEY AND POWER MATTER IN SPORTS?

Social class and class relations are integrally involved in sports. Organized sports depend on resources. Those who provide those resources do so in ways that fit their interests and foster ideas supportive of economic arrangements that work to their advantage. This is why the dominant sport forms in the United States and other nations with market economies promote an ideology that is based on the idea that "you always get what you deserve, and you always deserve what you get (meritocracy)."

This ideology drives a combination of individual achievement and consumption, along with corporate expansion, in society. Using it leads to favorable conclusions about the character and qualifications of those who are wealthy and powerful, but it disadvantages the poor and powerless. Furthermore, using it leads to the conclusion that economic inequality in society is natural and beneficial.

Class relations also are connected with the ways that wealthy and powerful people around the world have become involved in sport team ownership, event sponsorship, and the media coverage of sports. Sport events are one of the vehicles these people can use to transfer public money into their own hands. As public funds build stadiums and arenas, people with wealth and power receive subsidies and income, which they use to maintain their privilege. At the same time, class relations have ideological implications in the sense that large segments of the population continue to see sports as enjoyable forms of entertainment brought to them by corporate sponsors. Although fans do not automatically see sports in the way that sponsors would like them to, most fans raise no critical questions about the ideology of success emphasized in media coverage of sports.

Sport participation patterns in society and around the world reflect the impact of material resources and social class on the ways in which people live their lives. Organized sports are a luxury that many people around the world cannot afford. Even in wealthy societies, sport participation is most common among those in the middle and upper classes. Patterns of sport participation throughout a society reflect class-based lifestyles, which emerge as people make decisions about how they will use the resources they do have.

Sport participation patterns also reflect the combination of class and gender relations, as in the case of lower-income girls and women who have low participation rates and lower-income men who see sports as a means of obtaining respect. Boxing provides an example in which class, gender, and racial relations come together in a powerful combination. The boxing gym provides a safe space, which takes minority men in poor neighborhoods away from the poverty, racism, and despair that spawn violence and desperate actions among their peers. The same social forces that lead minority men to choose boxing also give rise to variations of *hoop dreams* that captivate the attention of young ethnic minorities, especially black males. But even these dreams are now being

subverted as public schools in low-income areas are forced to drop some varsity sport programs for financial reasons.

Patterns of watching sports also are connected with social class and class relations. This is demonstrated by the increased segregation of fans in stadiums and arenas. Luxury suites, club seating, and patterns of season-ticket allocations separate people by a combination of wealth and power so that social class often is reaffirmed when people attend sport events.

Opportunities for careers that hold the hope of upward social mobility exist for some people in sports. For athletes, these opportunities often are scarce and short lived, and they reflect patterns of gender and ethnic relations in society. These patterns take various forms in the case of careers in sport organizations. Although opportunities in these jobs have become increasingly open over the past decade, white men still hold most of the top positions in sport organizations. This will change only when the organizational cultures of sport teams and athletic departments become more inclusive and provide new ways for women and ethnic minorities to participate fully in shaping the policies and norms used to determine qualifications in sports and to organize social relations at the workplace.

Research generally indicates that people who use sport participation to expand their social worlds and personal experiences often have an advantage when seeking occupational careers apart from sports. However, when sport participation constricts social worlds and personal experiences, it is likely to have a negative effect on later career success. The existence of these patterns varies by sport and by the resources that athletes can accumulate during their playing careers.

Retirement from athletic careers often creates stress and personal challenges, but most athletes move through the retirement process without experiencing *excessive* trauma or difficulty. Those who do experience difficulties are usually those whose identities and relationships have been built exclusively on and around sports. These people may need outside assistance as they make the transition into the rest of their lives and face the challenge of seeking jobs, maintaining satisfying occupational careers, and nurturing mutually supportive and intimate social relationships.

Athletic scholarships help some young people further their educations and possibly achieve career success, but athletic aid is relatively scarce compared with other scholarships and forms of financial aid. Furthermore, athletic scholarships do not always change the future career patterns of young people because many recipients would attend college without sport-related financial assistance.

In conclusion, sports are clearly tied to patterns of class, class relations, and social inequality in society. Money and economic power do matter, and they matter in ways that often reproduce existing patterns of social class and life chances.

OLC See the OLC, www.mhhe.com/coakley9e, for an annotated list of readings related to this chapter. The OLC also contains a key concept list, a review test, and other helpful features.

WEBSITE RESOURCES

Note: Websites often change. The following URLs were current when this book was printed. Please check our website (www.mhhe.com/coakley9e) for updates and additions.

www.mhhe.com/coakley9e   Click on chapter 10 for information on the "Top 25" from the 1996 and 2000 rankings made by *The Sporting News*, extended discussion of the odds of playing professional sports for people in various racial and ethnic groups, and references to films and to how *Hoop Dreams* is related to social class and class relations.

www.sportingnews.com/features/powerful   *The Sporting News*, a U.S. weekly, presents annual lists of the 100 most powerful people in sports; the lists are intended to be international, but they focus primarily on power in sports from a U.S. perspective, and they are only one picture of power in the world of sports.

www.ncaa.org/research/prob_of_competing/ probability_of_competing2.html#m_basketball   An NCAA page that contains computations of the estimated probability of competing in athletics beyond interscholastic sports; good information on the odds of playing in college and the pros.

www.finelinefeatures.com/hoop   The site for *Hoop Dreams*, a classic documentary film that provides a personalized look at social class and class relations issues in the lives of two young men living in a Chicago neighborhood.

http://www.teammarketing.com/   The Fan Cost Index provides information on ticket prices for all teams in MLB, NBA, NFL, NHL, and Minor League Baseball and computes an average for each league; also lists data for concession prices and how much it costs to take a family of four to a game and how much ticket prices and other costs have increased since the previous season.

www.teammarketing.com/links.cfm   This is a useful site because it has links to all major and minor league sport teams in the United States and Canada and lists tennis tournament information for the year.

www.bus.ucf.edu/sport/public/downloads/media/ides/ release_report.pdf   2004 Racial and Gender Report Card, compiled by Richard Lapchick, the Institute for Diversity and Ethics in Sports, 2005 (University of Central Florida, DeVos School of Business).

www.sportinsociety.org   The Center for the Study of Sport in Society posts Lapchick's most recent *Race and Gender Report Card*; this provides valuable information about patterns of fairness and discrimination in major sport organizations in the United States.

www.sportinsociety.org/sportscap.html   This site is designed to provide women, people of color, and people with disabilities with improved access to the sporting industry ranging from internships to high-level management, legal, and medical positions.

www.sportengland.org/resources/pdfs/ publicat%5FEng%5FJune03.pdf   Economists provide a report entitled "The Value of the Sports Economy in England: A Study on Behalf of Sport England"; it provides an example of how researchers study the economic impact of sport in an entire nation.

(*Source:* McGraw-Hill)

SPORTS AND THE ECONOMY

What Are the Characteristics of Commercial Sports?

IF ANOTHER PRO does a trick and you wanna keep your job, you better do it. . . . Everything [in skateboarding] is getting bigger, more dangerous.

—**Colin McKay, pro skateboarder**
(in Thompson, 2004)

 Online Learning Center Resources

Visit *Sports in Society*'s Online Learning Center (OLC) at **www.mhhe.com/coakley9e** for additional information and study material for this chapter, including

• Self-grading quizzes
• Learning objectives
• Related websites
• Additional readings

chapter outline

A complete outline is available online at
www.mhhe.com/coakley9e.

YOU'VE GOT TO GET these kids [who excel on
the court] in your product. You've got to get
these kids walking around being a Reebok
kid. . . . They will be your messengers.

—Sonny Vaccaro, Reebok representative
(in Alesia, 2004)

"THE N.B.A. BECAME the culture for young
people in Japan. These kids don't know so much
about the N.B.A., but they think the N.B.A. is a
cool brand.

—Hideki Hayashi, managing director,
NBA Japan, Inc. (in Belson, 2003)

Sports have been used as public entertainment through history. However, sports have never been so thoroughly commercialized as they are today. Never before have economic factors so totally dominated decisions about sports, and never before have economic organizations and corporate interests had so much power and control over the meaning, purpose, and organization of sports.

The economic stakes for athletes and sponsors have never been higher than they are today. The bottom line has replaced the goal line. As an editor at *Financial World* magazine notes, "Sports is not simply another big business. It is one of the fastest-growing industries in the U.S., and it is intertwined with virtually every aspect of the economy. . . . [Sports are] everywhere, accompanied by the sound of a cash register ringing incessantly" (Ozanian, 1995, p. 30).

Sports today are evaluated in terms of gate receipts, concessions and merchandise sales, licensing fees, media rights contracts, and website hits. Games and events are evaluated in terms of media criteria such as market share, ratings points, and the cost of commercial time. Athletes are evaluated in terms of their entertainment value as well as their physical skills. Stadiums, teams, and events are named after corporations and are associated with corporate logos instead of people and places that have local meaning.

Corporate interests influence team colors, uniform designs, event schedules, media coverage, and the comments of announcers during games and matches. Media companies sponsor and plan events, and they own a growing number of sport teams. Many sports are corporate enterprises, tied to marketing concerns and processes of global capitalist expansion. The mergers of major corporate conglomerates that began in the 1990s and now continue into the twenty-first century have connected sport teams and events with media and entertainment companies. The names of transnational corporations are now synonymous with the athletes, events, and sports that provide pleasure in the lives of millions of people.

Because economic factors are so important in sports, this chapter focuses on these questions:

1. Under what conditions do commercial sports emerge and prosper in a society?
2. What changes occur in the meaning, purpose, and organization of sports when they become commercial activities?
3. Who owns, sponsors, and promotes sports, and what are their interests?
4. What is the legal and financial status of athletes in commercial sports?

EMERGENCE AND GROWTH OF COMMERCIAL SPORTS

Commercial sports are organized and played to make money as entertainment events. They depend on a combination of gate receipts, concessions, sponsorships, the sale of media broadcasting rights, and other revenue streams associated with sport images and personalities. Therefore, commercial sports grow and prosper best under five social and economic conditions.

First, they are most prevalent in market economies where material rewards are highly valued by athletes, team owners, event sponsors, and spectators.

Second, commercial sports usually exist in societies with large, densely populated cities because they require high concentrations of potential spectators. Although some forms of commercial sports can be maintained in rural, agricultural societies, their revenues would not support full-time professional athletes or sport promoters.

Third, commercial sports are a luxury, and they prosper only when the standard of living is high enough that people have time and resources they can use to play and watch events that have no tangible products required for survival. Transportation and communications technologies must exist for sponsors to make money. Therefore, commercial sports are common in wealthy, urban, and industrial or postindustrial societies; they

Sports are played in all cultures, but professional sports seldom exist in labor-intensive, poor nations around the world. The Afghan horsemen here are playing buzkashi, a popular sport in their country, but Afghanistan lacks the general conditions needed to sustain buzkashi as a professional sport with paid athletes and paying fans. (*Source:* Efren Lukatsky, AP/Wide World Photos)

seldom exist in labor-intensive, poor societies where people must use all their resources to survive.

Fourth, commercial sports require *large amounts of capital* (money or collateral) to build and maintain stadiums and arenas in which events can be played and watched. Capital can be accumulated in the public or private sector, but in either case, the willingness to invest in sports depends on anticipated payoffs in the form of publicity, profits, or power. *Private* investment in sports occurs when investors expect financial profits; *public* investment occurs when political leaders believe that commercial sports serve their interests, the interests of "the public," or a combination of both (see chapter 13).

Fifth, commercial sports are most likely to flourish in cultures where lifestyles involve high rates of consumption and emphasize material status symbols. This enables everything associated with sports to be marketed and sold: athletes (including their names, autographs, and images), merchandise, team names and logos. When people express their identities through clothing, other possessions, and their associations with status symbols and celebrities, they will spend money on sports that are popular in their sphere of social life. Commercial sports depend on selling symbols and emotional experiences to audiences, and then selling audiences to sponsors and the media (Burstyn, 1999).

Class Relations and Commercial Sports

Which sports become commercialized in a society? As noted in chapter 10, priority is usually given to the sports that are watched or played by people who control economic resources in society. For example, golf is a major commercial sport in the United States, even though it does not lend itself to commercial presentation. It is inconvenient to stage a golf event for a live audience or to televise it. Camera placement and media commentary are difficult to arrange, and live spectators see only a small portion of the action. Golf does not involve vigorous action or head-to-head competition, except in rare cases of match play. Usually, if you don't play golf, you have little or no reason to watch it.

But a high proportion of those who *do* play golf are relatively wealthy and powerful people. They are important to sponsors and advertisers because they make consumption decisions for themselves, their families, their businesses, and thousands of employees who work under their supervision. They buy luxury cars and other high-end products for themselves; more important to advertisers, however, is that they buy thousands of company cars and computers for employees and make investment decisions related to pensions and company capital.

Golfers as a group have economic clout that goes far beyond their personal and family lives. This makes golf an attractive sport for corporations that have images and products that appeal to consumers with money and influence. This is why auto companies with high-priced cars sponsor and advertise on the PGA, LPGA, and Senior PGA tours. This also is why major television networks cover golf tournaments: They can sell commercial time at a high rate per minute because those watching golf have money to spend—their money *and* the money of the companies, large and small, that they control. The converse of this is also true: Sports attracting low- and middle-income audiences often are ignored by television or covered only under special circumstances. If wealthy executives bowled, we would see more bowling on television and more bowling facilities on prime real estate in cities.

Market economies always privilege the interests of those who have the power and resources to influence which sports will be selected for promotion and coverage. Unless people with power and resources want to play, sponsor, or watch a sport, it won't be commercialized on a large scale, nor will it be given cultural significance in society. A sport will not come to be known as a "national pastime" or become associated with ideal personal character, community spirit, civic unity, and political loyalty unless it favored by people with resources. This is why many people now describe football as "America's game" (Mihoces, 2002). It celebrates and privileges the values and experiences of the men who control and benefit from corporate wealth and power in North America. This explains why men pay thousands of dollars to buy expensive season tickets to college and professional football games, why male executives use corporate credit cards to buy expensive blocks of "company tickets" to football games, and why corporation presidents write hundred-thousand-dollar checks to pay for luxury boxes and club seats for themselves, friends, and clients. Football is entertaining for them, but more important, it reproduces an ideology that fosters their interests.

Women who want to be a part of the power structure often find that they must learn to talk football. Therefore, in the United States, seminars on sports are offered to women so that they can learn the language of football and other sports and use it to communicate with the men

> **I like being called a "Reebok kid" . . . It's cool with me.**
>
> —Star high school basketball player (in Alesia, 2004)

who have created organizational cultures and control their careers. If female executives don't go to the next big football game and take clients with them, they risk being excluded from the "masculinity loop" that constitutes the core of corporate culture and communication. When they go to work every Monday during the fall, they know that being able to "talk football" keeps them in touch with many of the men around them.

The Creation of Spectator Interest in Sports

What leads people to become sport spectators? Why do they look to sports for entertainment? These questions have multiple answers. However, spectator interest is related to four factors in modern and postindustrial societies: a general quest for excitement, a cultural emphasis on material success, early life experiences in sports, and easy access to sports through the media.

The Quest for Excitement   When social life becomes highly controlled and organized, people may become stuck in everyday routines to the point that they feel emotionally constrained. This leads to a search for activities that offer tension-excitement and emotional arousal. According to sociologists Eric Dunning and Norbert Elias, historical evidence suggests that this occurs in modern societies. Sports, they contend, provide activities in which rules and norms can be shaped to foster emotional arousal and exciting actions, thereby eliminating boredom without disrupting social order in society as a whole (Dunning, 1999; Elias and Dunning, 1986).

Sports generally are characterized by a tension between order and disruption. Managing this tension involves a challenge: Norms and rules in sports must be loose enough to break boredom, but not so loose that they permit violence or other forms of destructive deviance. When norms and rules are too controlling, sports are boring and people lose interest; when they are too loose, sports become sites for reckless and dangerous

behaviors, which can jeopardize health and social order. The challenge is to find and maintain a balance. This explanation of spectator interest raises the question, Why do so many people give priority to sports over other activities in their quest for excitement? Critical theorists suggest that answers can be found by looking at the connection between ideology and cultural practices. This leads us to consider other factors.

Success Ideology and Spectator Interest   Many people watch games or follow them in the media, but spectator involvement is highest among those who are committed to the ideas that success is always based on hard work and hard work always leads to success. Such ideas are part of class ideology in societies with capitalist economies (see chapter 10). These people who hold this ideology often use sports as a model for how the social world *should* operate. When sports promote the idea that success is achieved only through hard work and dedication to efficiency, these people have their beliefs and expectations reaffirmed, and they are willing to pay for that reaffirmation. This is why sport media commentators emphasize that athletes and teams make their own breaks and that luck comes to those who work hard. This also is why corporations use the bodies of elite athletes to represent their public relations and marketing images; the finely tuned bodies of athletes are concrete examples of efficiency, power, the use of technology, and the achievement of success (Hoberman, 1994). Under such ideological conditions, some high-profile, celebrity athletes make large amounts of money. Their very existence reaffirms a class ideology that reproduces privilege among powerful people around the world.

Youth Sport Programs and Spectator Interest   Spectator interest often is created and nurtured during childhood sport participation. When organized youth sport programs are publicized and made available to many young people in a society, commercial sports have a good chance to

Football is the most widely watched sport in the United States. It offers excitement in the form of rule-governed violence; it reaffirms the notion that success is achieved through competition and dominating opponents. Youth football teams are very popular, and more young men play high school football than any other sport. Football lends itself to media coverage during which replays, slow motion, and expert commentary are used to dissect plays and game plans. (*Source:* McGraw-Hill)

grow and prosper. With some exceptions, sport participation during childhood leads to spectator interests during adulthood. Children who learn to value sport skills, competition, and competitive success generally grow up wanting to watch "experts" compete with one another. For those who continue to participate actively in sports, watching the experts provides models for playing and improving skills. For those who no longer play sports, watching the experts maintains connections with the images and experiences of success that they've learned back when they played youth and interscholastic sports.

Media Coverage and Spectator Interest   The media promote the commercialization of sports (see chapter 12). They provide publicity and sustain spectator interest among many people. In the past, newspapers and radio did this, but television today has the greatest effect on spectator involvement. Tomorrow it is likely to be the Internet.

Television increases spectator access to events and athletes worldwide, and it provides a unique "re-presentation" of sports. It lets viewers see close-up camera shots of the action on the field and the athletes and coaches on the sidelines.

It replays selected action and shows it in slow motion, helping viewers become further immersed in the action.

On-air commentators serve as fellow spectators for the media audience, including those "interactive" spectators watching television while they are online with sports websites. Commentators dramatize and embellish the action and heighten identification with athletes. They provide inside stories, analyze strategies, describe athletes as personalities, and present the event in ways that magnify its importance.

Television recruits new spectators by providing a means of learning the rules and strategies of a sport without purchasing tickets. Furthermore, newcomers to a sport can do their learning at home with family and friends. Overall, television provides a painless way to become a spectator, and it increases the number of people who will buy tickets, regularly watch televised games, pay for cable and satellite sports programming, and even become pay-per-view customers in the future.

Economic Factors and the Globalization of Commercial Sports

Commercial sports have become global in scope for two reasons. *First*, those who control, sponsor, and promote them seek new ways to expand markets and maximize profits. *Second*, transnational corporations with production and distribution operations in multiple countries can use sports as vehicles for introducing their products and services around the world.

Sport Organizations Look for Global Markets

Sport organizations, like other businesses, wish to expand their operations into as many markets as possible. For example, profits for the NFL, NBA, NHL, and Major League Baseball (MLB) could expand significantly if the leagues were able to sell broadcasting rights to television companies worldwide and licensed merchandise (hats, shirts, jackets, and the like) to people in countries outside North America. This already occurs to some extent, but the continued commercial success of major sport organizations requires that they create spectators worldwide. Success also depends on using the media to export a combination of game knowledge and athlete identification. In this way, sport organizations become exporters of culture as well as products to be consumed. The complex export–import processes that occur in connection with sports are now topics studied by scholars in the sociology of sport (see chapter 13).

The desire for global expansion was the main reason why the NBA allowed its players to comprise the so-called Dream Team that played in the 1992 Olympics. The global media attention received by Michael Jordan, Magic Johnson, and other players provided the NBA with publicity worth many millions of dollars. This helped market NBA broadcasting rights and official NBA products worldwide. Today, the NBA finals and the NBA All-Star games are televised in nearly 200 countries every year, about one in four players in the league were born outside the United States, and there are NBA fans in over forty nations.

The spirit of global expansion has led NFL, NBA, NHL, and MLB teams to play games in Mexico, Japan, England, France, Germany, and Australia and to subsidize leagues and outreach programs for marketing purposes. This spirit is not new, nor is it limited to North American sport organizations. The International Olympic Committee (IOC) gradually has incorporated national Olympic committees from more than 200 nations and has turned the Olympic Games into the most successful and financially lucrative media sport events in history. Furthermore, the IOC, like some other powerful sport organizations, has turned itself and the Olympics into a global brand. This has had serious implications for the Paralympic Games, as explained in Breaking Barriers on page 366.

Soccer's FIFA (Fédération Internationale de Football Association) has a long history of global

Brand Barriers
There Was Nothing We Could Do

When is a flag not a flag? Dr. Jens Bromann discovered in 1983 that this is not a trick question. As a representative of athletes with a disability, he sat in a meeting called by Juan Antonio Samaranch, the newly elected president of the International Olympic Committee (IOC). Samaranch told Bromann and others from disability sport organizations that they could no longer use "Olympics" in any way and that the IOC would never include events for athletes with a disability in the Olympic Games.

Samaranch also declared that the Paralympics could no longer use Olympic symbols because the IOC was establishing the Olympics as a brand with commercial interests and goals. Then came the answer to the question: A flag is not a flag when it is a licensed logo to be used *only* by those who pay for the right to do so. As Bromann left the meeting, he told reporters that the Olympics had been branded and "there was nothing we could do" (Jennings, 1996).

Upset, but not wanting to cut ties with the IOC, Bromann and his peers turned their attention to the Games that they planned to have in Los Angeles, after the 1984 Olympic Games. But neither the Los Angeles Olympic Organizing Committee nor the United States Olympic Committee (USOC) would support them. So they held competitions in two locations: New York and Stoke Mandeville, England. They also formed the International Coordinating Committee of World Organizations for the Disabled (ICC) and made it the governing body for the Paralympic Games.

As ICC president, Bromann focused on organizing the 1988 Paralympic Games in Seoul, Korea. With support from Korean Olympic officials, the games were a huge success, bringing together over 3000 athletes from sixty-one nations. At the opening ceremonies, Bromann, who had once competed in sports for blind athletes, was presented with a flag that the Korean organizers designed for the Games. It was white and had five *tae-geuks*, or traditional Korean line symbols,

that resembled teardrops in the same positions and colors as the five interlocking rings on the Olympic flag. This was meant to show that the Paralympics were related to the Olympic movement and that Paralympians endured hardships to train and compete (Sheil, 2000).

The ICC reorganized in 1989 and would become the International Paralympic Committee (IPC) after the 1992 Paralympic Games in Barcelona, Spain. In the meantime, it used the five *tae-geuks* as its symbol, but this infuriated the IOC. The symbol, they declared, was too similar to their brand logo. In 1991 the IOC told the ICC to change the flag or face sanctions. This prompted noted author and journalist Andrew Jennings to ask sarcastically, "Sanctions against the disabled? What would they do? Shoot some guide dogs? Smash up a few wheelchairs?" (1996, p. 228). But the ICC knew exactly what sanctions meant: *No more funding from the IOC*.

To appease the IOC, a new symbol with 3 *tae geuks* was officially launched at the 1994 World Championships in IPC sports. The *tae-geuks* again appeared as three teardrops representing the Paralympic motto: "Mind, Body, and Spirit." It was used by the IPC through the 2004 Games in Athens. But in 2003, after years of failed attempts to gain full IOC recognition and support, the IPC decided to set itself apart from the IOC. It adopted a new symbol and flag to represent the unique purpose and identity of the Paralympic Games. It consisted of three elements in red, blue, and green—the colors most often used in national flags. The elements are known as *Agitos* (a Latin word meaning "I move"), and they appear to be in motion around a central point, representing a dynamic, global "Spirit in Motion," the new motto of the Paralympics. It emphasizes that the goal of the IPC is to bring athletes from all regions of the globe to compete. The Spirit in Motion flag will fly at the 2008 Paralympics in Beijing.

These are the flags that have been used by the Paralympics. Because of brand confusion that might discourage sponsors, the IOC demanded that the five-teardrop flag (A) be changed. The three-teardrop flag (B) was used between 1994 and 2004, and the new Spirit in Motion flag (C) will fly at the Beijing Paralympic Games in 2008 (*Source:* Flag images courtesy of the International Paralympic Committee).

With these changes, the IPC embraced a commercial model of sport as a survival strategy. Today, its flag is a licensed logo, like the five rings logo that is licensed by the IOC. This raises the question, Who will benefit from and who will be hurt by commercialization? Athletes who can attract an audience will certainly benefit, but will this inspire sport participation among those who cannot attract an audience or will it relegate them to the sidelines? Will there be resources for people who are not elite athletes. or will they see most resources going to top Paralympic athletes and say, "There's nothing we can do"? Hopefully not.

expansion, which predates the global expansion of any North American sports (Sugden and Tomlinson, 1998, 1999). Soccer/football teams such as Manchester United in England and Real Madrid in Spain have clearly used strategies to expand their global-marketing reach. They've been so successful that they are valued at a half billion dollars more than any North American sport team franchise (as of 2005). When Malcolm Glazer, a U.S. billionaire paid $1.47 billion to purchase 75 percent of Manchester United in 2005, he anticipated additional global expansion of the "Man U" brand. He had bought the Tampa Bay Buccaneers for $192 million in 1995 and saw the team value skyrocket to $779 million in 2004, so he knew that capitalist expansion could pay returns.

Corporations Use Sports as Vehicles for Global Expansion   Because certain sports capture the attention and emotions of so many people worldwide, corporations have been eager to sponsor them. Corporations need symbols of success, excellence, and productivity that they can use to create "marketing hooks" for their products and services and public goodwill for their policies and practices. For example, people around the world still associate Michael Jordan with the "Air Jordan" trademark copyrighted by Nike; and many people associate the Olympics with Coca-Cola. In the United States, the crowning Olympic achievement is to have your image associated with a product or brand. Status among many children depends on wearing expensive shoes and clothing with official logos and other sport images on them.

Companies whose profits depend on the sales of alcohol, tobacco, fast food, soft drinks, and candy are especially eager to have their products associated with the healthy image of athletes and sports (Dewhirst and Sparks, 2003). This enables them to counter negative publicity related to the nutritional value of their products. They want people to think that "if beer, cigarettes, sugar-based soft drinks, beef burgers, deep-fried foods,

Corporate branding is pervasive in sports today. Corporations that sell alcohol, tobacco, fast food, and candy are especially eager to sponsor sports because they want their products associated with activities defined as healthy and wholesome. (*Source: Colorado Springs Gazette*)

and candy bars bring us the sports we love, they can't be that bad for our health."

Scholars and sportswriters have identified Michael Jordan as a key figure in the process of corporations' using sports to boost bottom lines (Andrews, 2001; Andrews and Jackson, 2001). Jordan

> commercialized his sport and himself, turning both into brands for an emerging legion of sports marketers. . . . In his own way, Jordan . . . spread an ideology. It was that sports are not just games but tools for advertisers. It was that basketball isn't a playground thing, but a corporate thing. (in Weiner, 1999, p. 77)

We now live in an era of the transnational corporation. About half of the world's 100 largest economies (in terms of annual revenues) are corporations; the other half are nation-states (Anderson and Cavanagh, 2000). General Motors, Chevron-Texaco, Wal-Mart, Daimler-Chrysler, Exxon Mobile, Mitsubishi, Mitsui, and Ford Motor Company each has more economic resources and power than over 60 percent of all nations. The 200 largest corporations in the world control over one-third of the economic activity around the globe. The executives in these corporations make decisions that influence the economies of entire nations and even regions of the world. They affect who has jobs, the kinds of work people do, their salaries, working conditions, the products that they can buy, where they can buy them, and what they cost.

When these corporations enter the world of sports, they negotiate deals that promote their interests and increase their power. Their power over the last few decades has grown largely unchecked. Free-trade agreements now enable many companies to move capital at will and operate largely outside the laws of any single nation. As corporations and the multibillionaires who own or control them do business around the world, they need to create global images of themselves as both citizens and leaders. Sport serves as a site through which they can do this.

This is partly why corporations pay billions of dollars every year to sponsor sports and why they spend three times as much sponsoring sports as they do sponsoring the arts, festivals and fairs, and attractions in the United States. For example, General Motors and Coca-Cola together will spend over $2 billion to sponsor Olympic sports between 1998 and 2008. Like other transnational corporations, they want to promote the belief that enjoyment and pleasure in people's everyday lives depend on corporations and their products. Their goal is to use this belief as the foundation for *ideological outposts* in the minds of people around the world (see chapter 4). Corporate executives realize that they can use such outposts to defuse opposition to corporate policies and deliver ideological messages about what is and should be happening in the world. This is a useful strategy for global corporations that want to defuse resistance to products that may not be compatible with local attitudes and cultural practices. For example, when Coca-Cola and Kentucky Fried Chicken face anti-American attitudes in Islamic Pakistan, they can associate their products with international sports rather than U.S. culture and foreign policy.

When a Coca-Cola executive gave a presentation to IOC officials before the 1996 Olympic Games in Atlanta, he assumed that, after nearly eighty years of sponsoring the Olympics, the officials owed loyalty to Coke. So he told the officials the following:

> Just as sponsors have the responsibility to preserve the integrity of the sport, enhance its image, help grow its prestige and its attendance, so too, do you [in sports] have responsibility and accountability to the sponsor. (in Reid, 1996, p. 4BB)

The IOC officials knew that drinking cola was not consistent with the nutritional needs of elite athletes or the health goals of the Olympic movement. But after taking millions of sponsorship dollars from Coca-Cola, they did not resist the soft-drink executive's message. Coca-Cola had colonized their minds—the outposts were firmly established in most of their heads.

Outposts in Action: Branding Sports What do ranchers do when they want to prove that they own cattle? They brand them by burning logos into their hides. The brand is a mark of ownership and control. Corporations have done the same things with sports.

There are at least 175 major stadiums and arenas in North America that have sold naming rights to airlines, banks, brewers, and a bevy of companies selling cars, oil, auto parts, energy, soft drinks, and communications services and products. My favorites as of mid-2005 are Dunkin' Donuts Arena (Providence, Rhode Island), Dr. Pepper/Seven Up Ballpark (Frisco, Texas), ipayOne Center (San Diego, California), Papa John's Cardinal Stadium (Louisville, Kentucky), Monster Park (San Francisco, California), Pricecutter Park (Ozark, Missouri), and Whataburger Field (Corpus Christi, Texas). These rights are sold for a high of $195 million over thirty years (American Airlines Center, Dallas, Texas) to a low of $35,000 over ten years (Hawkinson Ford Field, Crestwood, Illinois). Most NFL, NBA and MLB stadiums sell naming rights for $3 million to $10 million per year. Deals usually are for ten to twenty years and often include signage in and around the venue, the use of luxury boxes and club seats, promotional rights for events, and exclusive concession rights (for example, the four Pepsi Centers in the United States sell only Pepsi products to fans). This benefits corporations, especially in major cities where a large billboard can cost up to $75,000 a month ($900,000 per year). Having a twenty-year "billboard" with "sport perks" for wealthy customers and friends is defined as a good investment by corporate executives.

The branding of sports also exists inside stadiums where nearly every available surface is sold to corporate sponsors. Surfaces without corporate messages are now defined as wasted space, even in publicly owned facilities. David Carter from the Sports Marketing Company in California says that corporations "desperately want to get into high schools, because they are getting a captive audience . . . that is about to make decisions of lifelong preference, like Coke versus Pepsi." Carter knows that schools need revenues, so he predicts that "commercialism is coming to a school near you: the high school cheerleaders will be brought to you by Gatorade, and the football team will be presented by Outback [Steakhouse]" (in Pennington, 2004, p.1).

As corporations brand public spaces, community identities are transformed into brand identities, and the physical embodiments of local traditions and histories are transformed into corporate ads that promote consumption and identify corporations as the source of pleasure and excitement in our lives. The public good is replaced by the corporate good, even in spaces owned by citizen-taxpayers, as illustrated in figure 11.1.

Sport events also are branded. College football fans in the United States watch the Tostitos Fiesta Bowl, FedEx Orange Bowl, Nokia Sugar Bowl, MPC Computers Bowl, GMAC Bowl,

"This is Pepsi McDonald at Spielberg Jurassic Park where the Microsoft Raiders will battle the Wal-Mart Titans. Team captains, Nike Jones and Budweiser Williams, prepare for the Franklin Mint Coin Toss, right after this message from our sponsor, GMC trucks—giving you power on demand!"

FIGURE 11.1 Televised versions of commercial sports have become inseparable from the logos and products of corporate sponsors. It is not too far fetched to imagine this scene in the near future.

Sheraton Hawaii Bowl, Insight Bowl, MasterCard Alamo Bowl, Chick-fil-A Peach Bowl, Vitalis Sun Bowl, AutoZone Liberty Bowl, Meineke Car Care Bowl, Capital One Bowl, Outback Bowl, Toyota Gator Bowl, and Pacific Life Holiday Bowl, among others. College football is thoroughly branded, as are the athletes who wear corporate logos on their shirts, shoes, helmets, and warm-up clothing.

In the United States, NASCAR auto racing has always been heavily branded. People watch Nextel Cup races named the Budweiser Shootout, Gatorade 125, Food City 500, Coca-Cola 600, Pepsi 400, Tropicana 400, EA Sports 500, Mountain Dew Southern 500, Sharpie 500, Subway 500, and UAW-GM Quality 500 (the only major race or sport event sponsored by a workers' organization instead of a corporation). Additionally, racecars are billboards with surface spaces purchased by companies selling products that often cannot be advertised on television, such as hard liquor and tobacco. This is why it was so important for NASCAR to be nationally televised—the liquor and tobacco companies wanted their brand names in front of a national audience from 125 to 600 times during a weekend race.

PGA golfers in 2005 competed in the Mercedes Championships, Merrill Lynch Skins Game, Shell Houston Open, Cialis Western Open, The Honda Classic, Chrysler Classic, Nissan Open, AT&T Pebble Beach National Pro-Am, Buick Invitational, and Sony Open, among many others. Men's pro tennis competed in the Mercedes Cup, the RCA Championships, and the Priority Telecom Open, among others. Professional women's tennis is called the Sony Ericsson WTA Tour, and players competed in the Porsche Tennis Grand Prix, Pilot Pen Tennis, Bausch & Lomb Championships, Family Circle Cup, NASDAQ-100 Open, and Volvo Women's Open.

Corporations brand teams worldwide in cycling, soccer, rugby, and many other sports. Seventime Tour de France winner Lance Armstrong and his cycling teammates ride for The Discovery Channel. Professional baseball teams in Japan are named after corporations, not cities. Players and even referees in most sports wear the corporate logos of sponsors on their uniforms. Because European soccer was televised for many years by public TV stations that had no commercials, corporations put their logos on the players themselves and all around the pitches (playing fields) so that spectators would see them constantly. This tradition continues. For example, in 2000, Vodaphone, the world's largest telecommunications company, paid $48 million to have their names on the uniforms of Manchester United, the most recognized and followed sport team in the world; in 2003 they paid $58 million to extend the deal another four years. Manchester United, with over 50 million fans worldwide, also has sponsorship deals with Nike ($450 million for thirteen years, 2002–2015), Fuji (photo/film), Lycos, Anheuser Busch, and Pepsi.

Corporate branders now give priority to sports that appeal to younger demographics. So there is the ESPN X Games, Dew Action Sport Tour, Van's Triple Crown (surfing, skateboarding, snowboarding), McDonald's All-American High School Basketball Game, the Sprite Rising Stars Slam Dunk Contest, and the Nike Hoop Summit.

Agents today tell celebrity athletes that they are brands in themselves and their goal is to merge with other commercial entities rather than simply endorse another company's products. Michael Jordan was the first to do this. He initially endorsed Nike products, gradually became a brand in his own right, and now has his own line of products in addition to "Air Jordan." Tony Hawk has done this with his own line of skateboards and other products. However, this strategy is possible only for those athletes whose celebrity is so great that it can be converted into a brand name.

In all other cases, it is corporations who choose who and what they wish to brand. For example, some athletes, as young as twelve years old, may be known as Nike, Adidas, or Reebok athletes. Corporate executives know that it is best to brand athletes as early as possible so that they can influence their lives and careers to promote corporate interests. This is why Nike signed Freddy Adu, currently a professional soccer player, to a $1 million endorsement contract when he was thirteen years old and gave seventeen-year-old high school senior LeBron James a $90 million contract before he was drafted by an NBA team.

The Super Bowl, too expensive for even a large corporation to brand on its own, is known as much for its ads as for the game itself. Corporate sponsors of the 2005 Super Bowl paid $2.4 million for thirty-second commercial spots during the telecast of the game. This generated over $140 million in revenues for Rupert Murdoch's Fox Network, which owned the 2005 television rights. Corporations paid this amount because they knew their ads would receive exposure beyond the commercial time during the game. Ads also would be previewed, summarized, highlighted, evaluated, and ranked in other media coverage, and they would be available for years on the Internet where people can see every ad starting with the 1969 Super Bowl. Anheuser-Busch (Budweiser) spent nearly $22 million for its commercial time during the 2005 game, not including the money spent to produce the commercials. Corporations have branded the Super Bowl to such an extent that it has been described as a program where the commercials are the entertainment, and the entertainment is the commercials.

Future forms of corporate branding are difficult to predict because it is hard to say where

people will draw the line and stop corporations from colonizing their lives. Ads during television coverage are now inserted digitally on the field, court, and other surfaces of arenas and stadiums so that viewers cannot escape them even when they record events and delete commercials. Corporations spend more of their advertising money today to purchase brand-placement rights, so their names, logos, and products appear directly in the content of sports. This means that we will see more branding of playing fields/spaces, uniforms, and athletes' bodies. For example, boxers

The goal of branding is to establish outposts in people's heads by connecting pleasure and excitement with corporations and their products. Corporations sponsor sports because many people are emotionally tied to athletes and teams. This man's emotional connections with the soccer club Manchester United is inscribed permanently on his body. Vodafone, the club's primary corporate sponsor, uses such connections to their advantage. (*Source:* Luca Bruno, AP/Wide World Photos)

have gone into the ring with henna tattoos of corporations on their backs. English soccer player Robbie Savage has an Armani logo tattooed on his arm. Action sport legend Shaun Palmer, arguably the best athlete in the world, has Cadillac tattoos because he likes old Cadillacs. However, what would happen if Cadillac used a photo of his body in one of their ads? Who owns Shaun Palmer's body and the images on its surface? Does he, the artist who created the tattoos, or Cadillac who owns copyrights on Cadillac images? There have already been lawsuits filed in cases like this, and we will see more in the future.

The Limits of Corporate Branding   Can corporations go too far in their branding of sports? People in New Jersey didn't resist when a local elementary school sold naming rights for its gym to ShopRite, a supermarket chain. Most high school and college sport programs have not resisted. Football fans didn't object when McDonald's was the Official Fast-Food Sponsor of the NFL from 1998 to 2005 or when the league dumped McDonald's to sign a new contract with Burger King. Olympic officials, dedicated to health and fitness, didn't turn down $65 million from McDonald's in a deal naming it the Official Restaurant of the 2004 and 2006 Olympics in Athens, Greece, and Torino (Turin), Italy. However, people did object when the CBS journalists wore Nike logos on their jackets as they covered the 1998 Winter Olympics in Nagano, Japan. Similarly, baseball fans were so upset in 2004 that Major League Baseball canceled a $3 million deal with Columbia Pictures that called for decorating bases, pitching mounds, and on-deck circles with spider-web patterns at fifteen home fields of teams playing games on the weekend before the release of *Spider Man 2*. But despite a few cases of resistance, sports generally are for sale, and corporations are willing buyers when deals boost their power and profits and promote consumption as a lifestyle.

Corporate executives realize that sports produce enjoyable and emotional identifications

AT YOUR *fingertips* See chapter 4, pages 112–113 for discussion of hegemony.

with athletes, teams, events, and places. Therefore, they think it makes economic sense to brand sports so that people will recognize corporate names and products and associate them with the things that provide excitement and pleasure in their lives (Pennington, 2004). In less than a generation, sports have been so thoroughly branded that many people, especially those under thirty years old, see it as "normal"—as the way it is and should be. Does this mean that corporations have established ideological outposts in people's heads to the point that they accept corporate power as inevitable and even desirable? If so, corporate hegemony is being maintained successfully, even if a few people say it is unwise to turn sports over to entities accountable only to market forces.

COMMERCIALIZATION AND CHANGES IN SPORTS

What happens to sports when they shift from being activities organized for players to being activities organized for paying spectators and sponsors? Do they change, and, if so, in what ways?

When a sport is converted into commercial entertainment, its success depends on spectator appeal. Although spectators have many reasons for watching sports, their interest usually is tied to a combination of four factors:

- Attachment to those involved ("Do I know or like players and/or teams?")
- The uncertainty of an event's outcome ("Will it be a close contest?")
- The risk or financial rewards associated with participating in an event ("How much money, ego, or personal safety and well-being is at stake in the contest?")

- The anticipated display of excellence, heroics, or dramatic expression by the athletes ("How entertaining are the players and/or teams?)

When spectators say they saw "a good game," they usually are talking about one in which (1) they were attached personally or emotionally to people involved, (2) the outcome was in doubt until the last minutes or seconds, (3) the stakes were so high that players were totally committed to and engrossed in the action, or (4) there were skilled, heroic, or dramatic performances. Events containing all four of these factors are remembered and discussed for many years.

Because attachment, uncertainty, high stakes, and performance attract spectators, successful commercial sports are organized to maximize the probability of all four factors. To understand how this affects sports, it is necessary to consider the impact of commercialization on the following:

1. The internal structure and goals of sports
2. The orientations of athletes, coaches, and sponsors
3. The people and organizations that control sports

Internal Structure and Goals of Sports

Commercialization influences the internal structure and goals of newly developed sports, but it has less influence on long-established sports. Among new sports developed explicitly for commercial purposes, it is clear that rules are designed to promote on-the-field action that will be defined as entertaining by a targeted audience.

Entertainment is not the only issue that influences the internal structure and goals of new sports, but it is the *primary* issue. This is apparent in the case of indoor soccer, arena football, beach volleyball, roller hockey, and commercial action sports. For example, rules in the X Games are designed to maximize "big air," dangerous and spectacular moves, and the technical aspects of equipment, often manufactured by event sponsors.

The rules in established sports also undergo changes to make the action more exciting and understandable for spectators, but the changes seldom alter the basic internal organization and goals of the sports. For example, rules in the NFL have been changed to protect quarterbacks, increase passing as an offensive strategy, discourage field goals, protect players from career-ending injuries, create automatic time-outs at the two-minute mark at the end of each half in the game, and establish game schedules that fit media needs and maximize exposure for teams and players.

Changes in all commercialized spectator sports usually do one or more of six things: (1) Speed up the action, (2) increase scoring, (3) balance competition, (4) maximize drama, (5) heighten attachment to players and teams, and (6) provide strategic breaks in the form of "commercial time-outs." A review of rule changes in many sports shows the importance of these factors. For example, the designated hitter position in baseball's American League was added to increase scoring opportunities and heighten the dramatic action. Soccer rules were changed to prevent matches from ending in ties. Tennis scoring was changed to meet the time requirements of television schedules. Golf tournaments now involve total stroke counts, rather than match play, so that big-name players will not be eliminated in the early rounds of televised events. Free throws were minimized in basketball to speed up action. Sudden-death overtime periods and shootouts were added to National Hockey League games so that outcomes would be clearly understood by spectators who define the meaning of an event exclusively in terms of who wins.

Although these changes are grounded in commercialization, they have not altered the internal structure and goals of long-established sports: Teams are still the same size with similar positions, and teams win when they score more runs, goals, or points than their opponents. Furthermore, some of these changes also reflect the concerns of athletes, who have more fun when there is more action, more scoring, and a closer contest. Players may object to TV time-outs, but they and their coaches anticipate them and now use them in game strategies. This is new, but the structures of their games have not changed.

Because sports are social constructions, they change in connection with shifts in social conditions and power relations in the society as a whole. This means that *people* have and always will establish rules for sports. And those people are always influenced by social and cultural conditions at the time that they make or revise rules. However, commercial issues are carefully considered today when changes are suggested, discussed, and made.

Another change that has come with commercialization is that many events today are organized intentionally as *total entertainment experiences.* There is loud music, attractive and rapidly changing video displays, cheerleaders and mascots that plan entertaining performances, light displays, and announcers who heighten drama with excited verbal descriptions of the action. As dedicated, long-time sports fans view these things, they may complain that the game has changed when it is actually the context surrounding the game that has changed.

Orientations of Athletes, Coaches, and Sponsors

Commercialized sports are characterized by a "promotional culture" (Gruneau and Whitson, 1993). Like other entertainment industries, they are geared to selling public performances to audiences and selling audiences to sponsors. Commercial sports are promoted through marketing hype based on stories, myths, and images created around players and teams. Athletes become entertainers and the orientations of nearly everyone in sports shift toward an emphasis on heroic actions and away from aesthetic actions.

The shift toward heroic orientations is necessary to attract a mass audience to buy tickets or watch televised events. Entertaining a *mass* audience is difficult because it contains many people who lack technical knowledge about the complex physical skills and strategies involved in a sport. Without technical knowledge, hype and drama become primary sources of entertainment for the audience. Hype and drama are easily understood, and spectators are entertained when athletes take risks and face clear physical danger. Spectators also are impressed by the dramatic expressions of athletes, and they are awed by athletes dedicated to the game and to victory, regardless of personal cost.

When spectators lack technical knowledge about football, for example, they are entertained more by a running back's end-zone dance after a touchdown than by the lineman's block that enabled the running back to score the touchdown. Those who know little about the technical aspects of ice skating are entertained more by triple and quadruple jumps than routines carefully choreographed and practiced until they are smooth and flawless. Without dangerous jumps, naïve spectators become bored because they are not aware of subtle differences in the skills of skaters. Those who lack technical knowledge about basketball are more likely to talk about a single slam dunk than the well-coordinated defense that enabled the team to win a game. Players know this and realize that their dunks will be shown on news replays, regardless of who plays a technically good game. Thus, dunkmania rules and fans are disappointed when they don't see "big jams" during games; they want to see the heroic more than the aesthetic aspects of sports (see figure 11.2).

Spectators without technical knowledge about a sport enjoy watching athletes project exciting or controversial personas, and they often rate performances in terms of a player's style as much as his or her technical proficiency. They are thrilled by long touchdown passes, not nine-minute touchdown drives made up of 3- to 4-yard runs. They want to see home runs, not sacrifice fly balls. They are more impressed by athletes who collapse as they surpass physical limits than by athletes who know their limits so well that

"If I create a football league like professional wrestling, it's bound to be popular."
....

FIGURE 11.2   When WWE owner Vince McMahon developed the XFL, he obtained a TV contract, but the league failed in its first season. Does this mean there are limits on the entertainment value of heroic orientations and actions?

they can play for years without going beyond them.

After observing many athletes in all the major sports in the United States, commentator Bob Costas has noted the following:

> The players have caught on to what the cameras want. They know what postures and noises will get them on air. [NBA players] know that cameras are under the basket. So a guy dunks the ball, looks right at the camera and screams (in Pluto, 1995, p. 275).

Costas understands that orientations change when players become entertainers. Players today even look at the replay screens and become spectators watching themselves.

Figure 11.3 illustrates that when a sport depends on entertaining mass audiences, the athletes, coaches, and team administrators often

revise their ideas about what is important in athletic performances. The danger of movement becomes important *in addition to* the beauty of movement; style and dramatic expression become important *in addition to* fundamental skills; pushing beyond personal limits becomes important *in addition to* exploring limits; and commitment to victory for the team and sponsor becomes important *in addition to* commitment to participation. When sports become commercialized, most people associated with them develop *heroic orientations* in addition to *aesthetic orientations;* they even describe games and matches as "showtime." This does *not* mean that aesthetic orientations cease to be important or that people are no longer impressed by beauty and skills in sports, but it does mean that heroic orientations enter the mix of what constitutes a good sport performance. Heroic actions are what attract a mass audience.

Many athletes realize the dangers associated with heroic orientations, and some even try to limit the emphasis on heroic actions in their sports. For example, some figure skaters want restrictions on the number of triple jumps required in skating programs. They worry that the quest for commercial success is putting their bodies on the line. Other skaters, however, adopt heroic orientations to please audiences and conform to shifts in the orientations of judges, coaches, and other skaters (Mihoces, 2005). Thus, it is not surprising that figure skaters train to hit a long succession of triple jumps and hope to perform occasional quad jumps without breaking bones or destroying the continuity of their skating programs. Aesthetic orientations still exist, but heroic orientations are becoming more central in defining the "quality" of figure skaters.

As the emphasis on heroic orientations becomes more central in a sport, so do concerns about representing sponsors. This has occurred in NASCAR racing since 2001 when NASCAR signed a $3.2 billion, eight-year television deal with four major television companies. Veteran driver Kyle Petty says that being a good racecar driver and being a good product representative

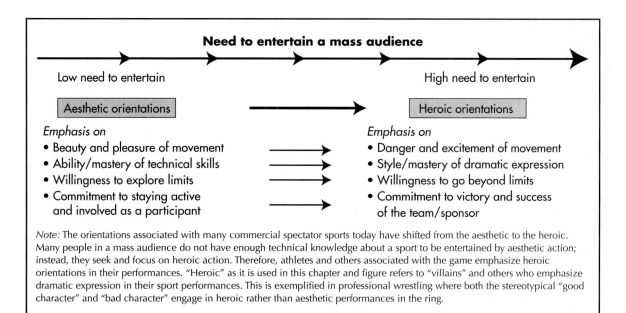

FIGURE 11.3 Shifting orientations: what happens when there is a need to entertain a mass audience.

are two different things and that most racing teams today walk a fine line "between performance and promotion." Petty knows that the mastery of technical racing skills is different from the mastery of dramatic expression. He observes that, on NASCAR racetracks today, "There's a lot of good looking guys out there who can walk and talk and chew gum and really sell products but they can't drive a race car" (in Jenkins, 2002, p. 2A).

Petty's critique does not mean that performance is no longer important. But it does mean that the "ability" of drivers is increasingly judged in terms of sponsors' interests. If a driver does not win races but boosts a sponsor's sales, the driver's team and car will stay on the track. If a driver consistently finishes well in races but does not boost the sponsor's bottom line, the driver may not be on the track in the future. According to one observer, this means that there are racers today "who can't drive a nail" but they continue to race "because they're good spokespeople for corporations" (Zengerle, 2002).

Sponsor sales, corporate stock values, and winning usually go hand-in-hand. Logo recognition increases as race-leading cars receive extensive camera coverage during races. Winning drivers show off their logo-laden racing suits as they pop corks on champagne bottles and receive kisses from attractive models in the winner's circle after the race. Winning drivers are interviewed and given opportunities to plug their sponsors as millions of people listen to what they say. However, if a sponsor sells Excedrin, it may not be as important for a driver to win as to tell fans how much he or she needs Excedrin for the headaches caused by losses. This is an extreme example, but the point is that driving fast and winning races is not the only way to promote a sponsor's bottom line. There are many ways to be a "steward of the brand."

NASCAR fans have observed that in the television coverage of races, announcers more heavily promote younger drivers. Darrell Waltrip, a former driver and now a television race analyst, says that car owners today "just need somebody to get

Raw Entertainment
Commercialization and Heroic Action

Professional wrestling is commercialization pushed to an extreme. It isolates elements of commercial sports and dramatizes them through parody and caricature (Atkinson, 2002; B. Maguire, 2005; Rinehart, 1998; Sammond, 2005). In the process, it abandons aesthetic orientations and highlights the heroic.

From the late 1990s through 2001, professional wrestling captured widespread spectator interest and was a smashing commercial success. It turnbuckled, leg locked, and jackhammered its way into popular culture around the globe (Leland, 2000; McShane, 1999). Professional wrestling events sold out stadiums nearly every night in North American cities. *Raw Is War* and *Smackdown!* were consistently the top-ranked programs on ad-supported cable television. Pay-per-view events regularly subscribed over half a million viewers at $30 per month and up to $50 for special events. Matches were televised in nine languages in 120 countries, wrestling videos were the number 1—selling "sports videos" in the world, and wrestling action figures outsold all other characters in popular culture. Boys finally had dolls they could play with!

Through 2001, pro wrestling was a mainstay on TBS, TNT, and USA Network with events televised four nights a week. Programs like *Monday Night Nitro* cut into the audience for both *Monday Night Football* and the *Finals of the NCAA Men's Basketball Tournament*. Most wrestling programs had viewer ratings consistently higher than NBA games and always higher than NHL games.

The popularity of professional wrestling was grounded in the *heroic orientations* of performers combined with storylines and wrestler personas that revolved around dramatic social issues such as the dynamics of social class, gender, ethnicity, and national identities in everyday life. In most cases, storylines and personas were performed by hypermasculine, heterosexual, and homophobic strong men who were arbitrarily victimized or privileged by greedy, underhanded corporate bosses or random, unpredictable events. The men were either supported or undermined by a conniving woman, represented as an alluring and vulnerable sex object or an exotic and heavily muscled dominatrix. Overall, events were staged to represent male fantasies and fears about sex and power and deep concerns about work in a world where men felt they were losing control (B. Maguire, 2005).

After late-2001, pro wrestling lost some of its popularity, but Linda and Vince McMahon, the daughter–father executive team that runs World Wrestling Entertainment (WWE), staged a comeback in 2004 and 2005. *Raw* (aka *Raw Is War*) and *Smack-Down!* boosted their ratings and remained popular with males between twelve and twenty-eight years old, a demographic segment that makes up two-thirds of the pro wrestling audience. *Raw* remains one of the most watched shows on cable television, and in 2005 the USA Network signed a deal to televise it for three years. In the meantime, pro wrestling has become popular worldwide. For example, The Wrestling Channel, a satellite channel available across Europe has seventeen hours of wrestling programs every day. The WWE and local wrestling programs are popular in Mexico and the rest of Central America where there is great interest in the Latinos that are regular performers in WWE matches.

Sociologist Brendan Maguire uses a functionalist approach to hypothesize that pro wrestling is popular because it "addresses the anxiety and angst associated with community breakdown, social disenchantment, and political correctness" (2005, p. 174). Therefore, if community ties are strong, social satisfaction is high, and social control is not overly constraining, people would not be so anxious that they would be entertained by dramatic parodies of heroic action. People who favor conflict theory would hypothesize that all commercial sports are spectacles that contain the seeds of their own destruction because they eventually become parodies of themselves. In the process, they

Professional wrestling emphasizes extreme heroic orientations with storylines that highlight hypermasculine, heterosexual, and homophobic strong men with personas that are staged in dramatic fashion. These action figures of WWE (formerly WWF) president Vince McMahon and wrestlers Ken Shamrock and the Undertaker were popular toys/dolls for young boys who were wrestling fans in 1999. In 2008 those boys will be fifteen to twenty-one years old. How did they play with their dolls in 1999? (Ask your male friends). (*Source:* Jay Coakley)

become so predictable that they are boring and so exploitive that they lose positive meaning.

The hypothesis most consistent with the approach used in this book is based on a combination of critical and interactionist theories. It suggests that the popularity of any cultural practice, including professional wrestling, depends on whether it reproduces dominant ideologies, especially those related to issues and attributes that people define as socially significant in their lives. In line with this hypothesis, the goal of those who produce commercial forms of entertainment is to provide people with pleasure and excitement without fostering opposition to the forms of social organization in which commercial entertainment thrives. In other words, commercial sports reproduce the status quo; they are likely to be supported by those who benefit from the status quo, and they are often opposed by those who question it. *What do you think?*

in the car that's charismatic, exciting and will drive the wheels off of it" (in Jenkins, 2002, p. 2A). Older drivers, he says, may be better and faster on the track, but they want more money to race, and they don't receive attention from the younger male demographic segment of the audience that the sponsors hope to attract. Furthermore, many sponsors feel that a new face, unconnected with other products in the past, is the best face to represent their products, so they support younger drivers with exciting personas and train them to represent their products without sounding like walking paid commercials, even though that is what they are.

What happens to a sport when heroic orientations are pushed to extremes? Are spectators willing to have aesthetic orientations abandoned in favor of the heroic? What would events be like if this happened? One way to answer this question is to study professional wrestling—a sport turned into spectacle in a quest to be entertaining. This is discussed in the box "Raw Entertainment."

The People and Organizations That Control Sports

Commercialization changes the ways that sports are controlled. When sports depend on the revenues they generate, the control center in sport organizations shifts away from the athletes and toward those who have the resources to produce and promote sports. Athletes in heavily commercialized sports generally lose effective control over the conditions of their own sport participation. These conditions are controlled by a combination of general managers, team owners, corporate sponsors, advertisers, media personnel, marketing and publicity staff, professional management staff, accountants, and agents.

The organizations that control commercial sports are designed to coordinate these people so that profits are maximized. This means that decision making in commercial sports reflect economic interests and have only incidental connections with the athletes involved. The power

to affect these decisions is grounded in resources that may not even be connected with sports. Therefore, athletes in many commercial sports find themselves cut out of decision-making processes, even when the decisions affect their health and the rewards they receive for playing.

As decision making in sport organizations moves further away from athletes, there is a need for athletes to develop strategies to represent their interests, financial and otherwise. As corporate interests come to dominate sports, athletes often discover that they must defer to the decisions of team owners, agents, advertising executives, media people, and corporate sponsors.

This has occurred repeatedly in ESPN's X Games as athletes have discovered that it is nearly impossible to maintain the spirit and norms of the sport culture that they have created when they participate under conditions controlled by a media company and corporate sponsors. A thirty-three-year-old former pro skateboarder identified this issue as he described what one of his friends did after he won an event in the X Games:

> He had this shirt on, this handmade shirt, that said ESPN down the side. For the "E" it said "Extreme," for the "P" it said "Profits"—the "S" was a dollar sign—and for the "N" it said "Network": Extreme Profit$ Network. And he wore that [to the awards ceremony] . . . got his little trophy, flipped the cameras off, threw [the trophy] into the audience, walked away and said, "I'll never ride in the X Games again." So, you've got certain guys that will really stay true to the roots of skateboarding . . . and then you've got others . . . that are pros competing [because] they've got kids and a family, so they've kind of gotta do that. It's a necessity to make a living. (in Honea, 2005, p. 162)

Like many athletes before them, the athletes in action sports are becoming resigned to the power of the media and corporate sponsors in their lives. They learn that to play commercialized sports, you must answer to the sponsors first.

This is not new. Commercialization has always brought with it a structure in which sponsors define the conditions of sport participation (Rinehart and Grenfell, 2002). Most Americans do not define this as an issue today because they accept the corporate branding of sports. But some people view commercialization in more critical terms, assessing more carefully the pros and cons of a commercial model in which corporations set the terms and conditions of playing sports at the highest levels of competition. Commercialization may not change the structure and goals inside their activities and games, but it dramatically changes the cultural and organizational contexts in which they are played.

OWNERS, SPONSORS, AND PROMOTERS IN COMMERCIAL SPORTS

Commercial sports are organized in different ways from one society to the next, but in all cases, owners, sponsors, and promoters control the conditions under which professional athletes perform. In this section, we focus on the overall control structure that exists in most visible professional sports in North America.

Professional Sports in North America

Professional sports are privately owned. The owners of many teams and franchises, from the smallest minor league teams to the top franchises in the NFL, NBA, NHL, and MLB, are individuals or partnerships. Large corporations, especially entertainment and real estate companies, own a growing proportion of the top teams and franchises (Harvey et al., 2001). Similarly, sponsors and event promoters range from individuals to large transnational corporations, depending on the size of the events.

Most people who own the hundreds of minor league teams in North America do not make much money. In fact, most are happy to break even and avoid the losses that are commonplace at this level of sports ownership. Also, many teams, leagues, and events have been financial

disasters over the past forty years. Four football leagues, a hockey league, a few soccer leagues, a volleyball league, four men's and five women's basketball leagues, a team tennis league, and a number of basketball and soccer teams have gone out of business, leaving many owners, sponsors, and promoters in debt. This list covers only the United States and doesn't include all those who have lost money on tournaments and special events.

Ownership of major professional sport franchises in North America is very different from ownership at other levels of pro sports. Franchise values at the end of 2004 ranged from about $108 million (Mighty Ducks of Anaheim in the NHL) to over $1.1 billion (Washington Redskins [sic] in the NFL). Owners are large corporations, partnerships, and very wealthy individuals whose assets range from hundreds of millions to many billions of dollars. Leagues are organized as monopolies, teams often play in publicly subsidized facilities, owners make good to excellent returns on their investments, and support from media companies and corporate sponsors almost guarantees continued financial success at this level of ownership.

Similarly, the large corporations that sponsor particular events, from major golf and tennis tournaments to NASCAR and Grand Prix races, know the costs and benefits that are involved. Their association with top events not only provides them advertising platforms but also connects them with clearly identified categories of consumers (see figure 11.4). Television companies also will sponsor events so that they can control their own programming, as in the case of ESPN's X Games.

Entertainment companies own teams and sponsor events so that they can control multiple aspects of the entertainment marketplace and link them together in mutually supportive ways—from Disneyland to ABC television to ESPN to the Anaheim Angels and Mighty Ducks to nationwide promotions at fast-food restaurants where action figures of sport celebrities are sold

"Winning at sports is easy when you own them and can prevent others from playing."

FIGURE 11.4 The growth and profitability of commercial sports around the world have little to do with athletes. Owners, sponsors, and media executives control sports today, and they make money when governments allow them to operate as cartels and keep competitors out of the game.

with meals for children. When the Disney-owned Anaheim Angels won the 2002 World Series, the victory parade was held in Disneyland, and Mickey Mouse was constantly standing by the coach and the most valuable player. This parade has become a tradition for the winning World Series teams, and Disneyland would like to maintain it as a publicity strategy.

Sport sponsorships enable companies that sell tobacco, alcohol, and foods with questionable nutritional value to link their products and logos to popular activities. Because people associate sports with healthy and strong bodies instead of cancer, heart disease, diabetes, obesity, tooth decay, and other forms of poor health related to their products, these companies are eager to be sponsors. It increases their legitimacy in society and defuses resistance to corporate policies, practices, and products.

Investments in sports and sport events are motivated by many factors. In some cases, investors are sports fans with money looking to

satisfy lifelong fantasies, build their egos, or socialize with celebrity athletes. Owning or sponsoring sports gain them more enjoyment and prestige than other business ventures, often making them instant celebrities in their cities. For example, a multimillionaire who owned part of the NFL's Atlanta Falcons between 1994 and 2004 described his experience by saying that "In 10 years, I had made five times my money and had a heck of a good time." Another wealthy man explained that he enjoys it because "owning a sports team is a label that differentiates one millionaire from another" (quotes in Heath, 2003, p. A1). Those who invest in sports seldom are so carried away with fun and fantasy that they forget business or capitalist expansion. They don't enjoy losing money or sharing power. They may look at their athletes as heroes, but they want to control them and maximize investment returns. They may be civic boosters and supporters of public projects, but they define the "public good" in terms that emphasize capitalist expansion and their business interests (Ingham and McDonald, 2003; Schimmel et al., 1993). They may not agree with fellow owners and sponsors on all issues, but they do agree on the need to protect their investments and maximize profits.

Team Owners and Sport Leagues as Cartels   The tendency to think alike has been especially strong among the team owners in the major North American sport leagues. Unity among these owners has led to the formation of some of the most effective cartels in North America. A **cartel** *is a centralized organizing group that coordinates the actions of a collection of people or businesses.* Therefore, even though each sport franchise in each league is usually a separate business, the team owners in each sport come together to form a cartel representing their collective interests (Downward and Dawson, 2000). The cartel is used to limit the extent to which teams compete against one another for players, fans, media revenues, and sales of licensed merchandise. It also is used to eliminate competition from other people who might form additional teams and leagues in their sports. When they succeed, as they usually have, the cartel becomes a **monopoly,** or *the one and only provider of a particular product or service.*

Each league (the NBA, the NFL, the NHL, and MLB) is also a **monopsony** because they have organized themselves to be *the single buyer of athletic labor in a particular sport.* This means that if a college football player wants to play professional football in the United States, he has one choice: the NFL. And the NFL, like the other leagues, has developed a system to force new players to negotiate contracts only with the team that drafts them. This enables owners to sign new players to contracts without bidding against other teams, which might be willing to pay particular players more money.

As a cartel, the owners prevent new leagues from being established and competing with them for players, and they also prevent new teams from entering their league without their permission. When permission is given, it involves conditions set by the cartel. For example, the new team owner is charged an entry fee to become a part of the league and must give back to the cartel some of the team's profits for a certain number of years. Since the 1960s when these fees were first assessed, they have escalated dramatically. For example, the Dallas Cowboys paid $600,000 to join the NFL in 1960, and the Houston Texans paid $700 million in 2002. These are just *entry fees,* divided among the existing owners. They do not include other start-up expenses, player salaries, and operating costs, nor do they include "infringement payments" made to existing teams in the same TV markets or the forfeiture of TV revenues during the first year(s) of operation (causing a $5 to $20 million annual loss, depending on the sport). Furthermore, a new owner can locate only in a

> **Being able to share the [team] ownership experience with clients is . . . a huge competitive advantage in business.**
> —Raul Fernandez, 10 percent owner, Washington Capitals (in Heath , 2004)

city approved by the cartel, and no current owner can move a team to another city without cartel approval.

Acting as a cartel, the owners in each sport league also collectively sell national broadcasting rights to their games and then share the revenues from national media contracts. This maintains the cartel's control over the condition under which fans can see televised games. This is why games are not televised in the home team's region when games are not sold out, and why cable and satellite fees are so high when fans wish to purchase access to more than the primary games telecast by media companies. Such a strategy enables team owners to make huge sums of money in their media contracts while forcing people to buy tickets to games. The U.S. Congress has approved this monopolistic method of doing business. From the owners' perspective, this guarantees relatively predictable revenues and gives them the power to influence television companies and the commentators working for those companies. This is why announcers sound like cheerleaders for the sports that their networks or cable channels pay to broadcast. Furthermore, team owners have also negotiated exclusive-use clauses in their contracts with the stadiums or arenas that they use, a strategy that effectively prevents new leagues and teams from using the stadiums or arenas that they need to make a profit. Potential competing leagues in each sport have been driven out of business because existing leagues are allowed to operate as cartels.

Being part of a legal cartel enables most team owners to make impressive sums of money over the past four decades. For example, in the mid-1960s, NFL teams were bought and sold for about $10 million; in 2004 the average franchise value was $732.6 million. That's an average per team capital gain of $722 million. That amounts to an average *annual* return of $24.4 million on an

AT YOUR *fingertips*   See chapter 12, page 414, for data on media rights fees.

original investment of $10 million. This is what a cartel does: It limits the supply of teams and drives up the value of existing teams. Of course, team owners do not count capital gains when they claim to be losing money and ask to raise ticket prices or force a city to build a new stadium so that they can be "competitive." When you are part of a cartel, you can get away with this.

Even though the NBA, the NFL, the NHL, and MLB are grouped together in this section, these leagues differ in many ways. These differences are complicated, and they change year to year as each league encounters new economic challenges and opportunities. For example, contracts with networks and major cable television companies vary by league. The NHL is the least successful in negotiating contracts, whereas the NFL and NBA (and NASCAR) have been the most successful in recent years.

Each league also has unique internal agreements regulating how teams can negotiate the sale of *local* broadcasting rights to their games. The NFL does not allow teams to sign independent television contracts for local broadcasts of their games, but MLB does. This creates significant disparities in the incomes of baseball teams. For example, in 2002 the New York Yankees sold their local rights for about $60 million, whereas the now defunct Montreal Expos sold theirs for about $500,000—120 times less than the Yankees made (Kaplan, 2002). Today, the media landscape is changing as leagues negotiate deals with satellite radio and begin online streaming of audio and video for games. This is why cable and satellite companies that own and broadcast sports are buying Internet companies with high-hit websites (Siklos, 2005); they want to guarantee that they will always have a piece of the sport media action.

The biggest differences between the major men's sport leagues are related to their contractual

agreements with the players' association in each league. Although each league gives players as few rights and as little money as possible, athletes have fought for over forty years to gain control over their careers and increase their salaries. This is discussed later in the section, "Legal Status and Incomes of Athletes in Commercial Sports."

Team Owners and Forms of Public Assistance

The belief that cities must have professional sports teams and big sports events to be "world class" has led to public support for sports owners and sports organizations (Silk, 2004). Most common is the use of public funds to build arenas and stadiums. As noted in chapter 10, "stadium socialism" enables wealthy and powerful capitalists to use public money for personal gain, but they call this "economic development," not "welfare."

Owners justify stadium subsidies and other public support for professional sport teams with five arguments (Lavoie, 2000):

1. A stadium and pro team creates jobs; those who hold the jobs spend money and pay taxes in the city.
2. Stadium construction infuses money into the local economy; this money is spent over and over as it circulates, generating tax revenues in the process.
3. The team attracts businesses to the city and brings in visitors who spend money.
4. The team attracts regional and national media attention, which boosts tourism and contributes to economic development.
5. The team creates positive psychic and social benefits, boosting social unity and feelings of pride and well-being in the local population.

These arguments often are supported by studies that are commissioned by team owners and promoters. However, *independent* studies, by liberal and conservative researchers, do *not* support

New Soldier Field, home of the Chicago Bears, was remodeled in 2001–2002 with private funds and $432 million of public money—a large government subsidy for a private, family-owned business. Promoted as a tourist destination, it has lost more money for taxpayers because the city maintains and manages it year-round—apparently, people don't like paying to tour an empty stadium. But the McCaskey family (and a few fellow owners) is very happy because the franchise value of the Chicago Bears increased from $362 million prior to the new facility to $785 million. (*Source:* Mike Smith of Aerial Views Publishing, October 5, 2003)

them.[1] Independent studies generally conclude the following:

1. Teams and stadiums create jobs, but apart from highly paid athletes and team executives, these jobs are low paying and seasonal. Football stadiums, for example, are used less than three weeks per year, and the ushers, parking lot attendants, ticket agents, and concessions workers don't make full-time living wages. Additionally, many athletes do not live in the city or spend their money there.

2. The companies that design and build stadiums are seldom local, and construction materials and workers on major projects often come from outside the region; they spend most of what they earn in other places.

[1]Studies of this issue are numerous; see Bandow, 2003; Bast, 1998; Brown et al., 2004; Cagan and deMause, 1998; Chapin, 2002; Curry and Schwirian, 2004; Delaney and Eckstein, 2003 Eckstein and Delaney, 2002; Friedman et al., 2004; Hudson, 2001; Noll and Zimbalist, 1997; Rosentraub, 1997; Silk, 2004; Smith and Ingham, 2003; Spirou and Bennett, 2003; Troutman, 2004; Weiner, 2000.

3. Stadiums attract other businesses, but most are restaurant and entertainment franchises headquartered in other cities. These franchised businesses often drive out locally owned businesses. Spectators come from out of town, but most live close enough to make day trips to games, so they don't spend much money outside the stadium and the immediate area.

4. Stadiums and teams generate public relations for the city, but this has mixed results for tourism because some people stay away from cities on game days. Most important, *regional* economic development often is limited by a new facility because fans who spend money at and around the stadium have fewer dollars to spend in their neighborhoods. A stadium helps nearby businesses, but it often hurts outlying businesses (Hudson, 2001). Spending $9000 on four NBA season tickets each year means that a family will spend less money on dinners and entertainment close to home.

5. A pro sport team makes some people feel better and may enhance general perceptions of a city, but this is difficult to measure. Additionally, feelings often vary with the success of teams, and some people are unimpressed by the male-oriented, heroic orientations that are glorified in some men's sports.

Independent researchers also note that positive things occur *whenever* a city spends $300 million to $800 million of public money on a project. However, they suggest that the public good might be better served if public money were spent on other things. For example, during the 1990s, the city of Cleveland spent nearly $1 billion of public money to build three sport facilities and related infrastructure. Inner-city residents during the same years pleaded with the city to install a drinking fountain in a park in a working-class neighborhood, and teachers held classes in renovated shower rooms in local public schools because there was no money to fund new educational facilities for inner-city students. The owners of the sport teams, however, received a fifty-year exemption on taxes related to their teams and facilities, as well as the equivalent of $120 million in tax abatements on other real estate development in the area around the stadiums (Bartimole, 1999). This meant that the city forfeits about $50 million in city and county tax revenues each year for the sake of professional sports. This is why new sport facilities don't cut poverty rates, improve schools, or increase the availability of safe, low-cost housing. Often, they simply force poor people to move to another area of town while developers build on condemned properties that they buy for little money.

Many people in Maryland realized the contradictions created when the state provided NFL owner Art Modell a new, rent-free stadium for the Baltimore Ravens while schools in Baltimore were rationing toilet paper and chalk, and students wore coats to class because schools could not pay heating bills. The Ravens owner responded with this statement:

> I feel for the schools. I feel for welfare. But look at the positive effects of pro football on a community, the emotional investment of people at large. You can't equate that with fixing up the schools. (in Brady, 1996, p. 19C)

The people who object to stadium subsidies seldom have the resources to oppose the well-financed, professionally packaged proposals developed by experienced political advisors hired by team owners. The social activists who might lead the opposition already deal full time with problems related to unemployment, underfunded schools, homelessness, poor health, drug use, and the lack of needed social services in cities. They cannot take leave from these tasks to lobby against using public money to benefit billionaire team owners and millionaire celebrity athletes. At the same time, local people are persuaded to think that team owners will abandon their city if they don't pony up public money to build a new facility with the requisite number of luxury suites and club seats. At the same time, sportswriters publish stories about the great public service of athletes who visit classes in dilapidated schools in the city.

When a new stadium or arena is built, the local team franchise value increases, and team owners are in a powerful negotiating position to get what they want when it comes to using the stadium for their own benefit. Their success has been so complete that *Financial World* magazine noted that "virtually every stadium is a money pit for taxpayers by any normal measure of return on investment" (Osterland, 1995, p. 107). From the local taxpayers' perspective, the result is that most families cannot afford to buy tickets to attend games in the stadiums built with their taxes.

When thinking about public subsidies to sport teams, it is useful to consider alternative uses of public funds. For example, my hometown of Colorado Springs used $6 million of public money in 2000 to construct a youth sport complex consisting of 12 baseball, softball, and T-ball fields of various sizes with bleacher seating; 10 soccer/football fields; 6 volleyball courts; an in-line skating rink; a batting cage (for baseball hitting practice); and multiple basketball courts. Meanwhile, nearly $300 million of tax money from six Denver metro counties was used to build the Denver Broncos owner Pat Bowlen a new stadium. Instead of doing this, the $300 million of public money could have built 600 baseball, softball, and T-ball fields; 500 soccer/football fields; 300 volleyball courts; 50 in-line skating rinks; 50 batting cages; and 250 basketball courts around the metro area.

Which of these two alternatives would best improve the overall quality of life in the metro area? The local facilities would be open seven days a week to everyone in the community for free or for nominal fees; the new stadium will host 72,000 people nine times a year at a cost of $70 a seat, and many local people will watch the games on TV. Some people prefer the former alternative, some the latter. But some of those

AT YOUR fingertips See the OLC—Additional Readings for chapter 11—for information on additional public benefits for team owners.

who prefer the latter have the resources to usually convince voters to build stadiums they will never visit rather than recreational facilities they could use year-round. This is hegemony in action.

Sources of Income for Team Owners   The owners of top pro teams in the major men's sports make money from (1) gate receipts, (2) media revenues, (3) stadium revenue, (4) licensing fees, and (5) merchandise sales. The amounts and proportions of each of these revenue sources vary from league to league.

The recent wave of new stadiums is the result of owners who demand venues that can generate new revenue streams. This is why new stadiums resemble a shopping mall built around a playing field. Sociologist George Ritzer (2005) describes them as "cathedrals of consumption" designed so that consumption is seamlessly included in spectator experiences (see figure 11.5). Owners see this as important because it enables them to capture a greater share of the entertainment dollar in a highly competitive urban market. For example, when Invesco Field at Mile High opened in Denver in 2001, it had the same number of seats as the old Mile High Stadium, but the new luxury suites, club seats, and nearly 400 concession outlets generated an additional $40 million per year for the Broncos owner, Pat Bowlen. No additional revenue went to the taxpayers who paid for nearly three-fourths of the stadium.

Stadiums are considered to have so much revenue-generating potential that the value of a franchise with a new stadium increases about 25 percent. This means that, if a city builds a

FIGURE 11.5 Recently built stadiums resemble shopping malls, and some fans see attendance as a shopping opportunity. They are a captive audience, and team owners want to capture as many of their entertainment dollars as possible. This fan has fallen for the lure of consumption to the point that he is less interested in the game than in buying products to prove he was there.

$400 million stadium for an NFL team that is valued at $500 million, the franchise value will increase about $125 million to $650 million. This increase goes directly to the owner when he or she sells the franchise. Owners realize that many people are not comfortable with this, so they make sure that announcers describe *their* team as *"your"* Denver Broncos, Cleveland Cavaliers, Detroit Red Wings, or Seattle Mariners (Sage, 1996). The owners are happy to support the illusion that the teams belong to the local community, as long as they collect all the revenues and walk away with all the capital gains when they sell teams.

Amateur Sports in North America

Amateur sports don't have owners, but they do have commercial sponsors and governing bodies that control events and athletes. Generally, the sponsors are corporations interested in using amateur sports for publicity and advertising purposes. The governing bodies of amateur sports operate on a nonprofit basis although they use revenues from events to maintain their organizations and power over amateur sports.

Centralized sport authorities administer amateur sports in most countries. They work with the national governing bodies (NGBs) of individual sports, and together they control events, athletes, and revenues. Sport Canada and the Canadian Olympic Association are examples of such centralized authorities; they develop the policies that govern the various national sport organizations in Canada.

In the United States, the organization and control of amateur sports are much less centralized. Policies, rules, fund-raising strategies, and methods of operating all vary from one organization to the next. For example, the major governing body in intercollegiate sports is the National Collegiate Athletic Association (NCAA). For amateur sports not connected with universities, the major controlling organization is the United States Olympic Committee (USOC). However, within the USOC, each of more than fifty separate NGBs regulates and controls a particular amateur sport. NGBs raise most of their own funds through corporate and individual sponsors, and each one sets its own policies to supplement the rules and policies of the USOC and IOC. The USOC has long tried to develop continuity in American amateur sports, but the NGBs and other organizations are very protective of their own turf, and they seldom give up power to regulate their sports; instead, they fight to maintain control over rules, revenues, and athletes. This has caused many political battles in and among organizations.

All amateur sport organizations share an interest in controlling two things: (1) *the athletes* in their sports and (2) *the money* generated from sponsorships and competitive events. Sponsorship patterns in amateur sports take many forms. Universities, for example, "sell" their athletic departments, consisting of all athletic teams and the bodies of athletes, to corporate sponsors in exchange for money, scholarships, equipment, and apparel. Corporations and universities usually enter these agreements outside of any democratic processes involving votes by students, athletes, or the taxpayers whose money funds the universities.

The NGBs of amateur sports long have depended on corporate sponsorship money to pay for athlete training, operating expenses, and competitive events. Corporate logos appear on the clothing and equipment of amateur athletes. In some cases, athletes sign deals as individuals, but they cannot do so when the deals might conflict with the interests of NGB sponsors. As this model of corporate sponsorship is increasingly used, the economics of sports becomes tied closely to the fortunes and fluctuations of market economies and large corporations. Corporations sponsor only sports that foster their interests, and economic conditions influence their ability and willingness to maintain sponsorships. For example, when the Women's United Soccer Association (WUSA) and its 180 professional athletes needed $20 million in 2003 to survive another year, Nike signed a $90 million endorsement deal with seventeen-year-old LeBron James and a $21 million deal with nineteen-year-old Carmelo Anthony, both basketball players who had not yet played in an NBA game. They decided that this was better for business than providing $20 million to WUSA and paying James and Anthony $91 million instead of $111 million. Or Nike could have reduced the $450 million deal they made with Manchester United, a men's soccer team in England, so as to support an entire women's soccer league. But corporations are about profits, not about (women's) soccer.

Corporate sponsorships also vary with changing economic conditions. For example, as rap artists become more popular than athletes with young consumers, shoe companies will reduce or cut sponsorships of high school teams, summer leagues and camps, athletic events, and individual athletes in favor of sponsoring rap concerts

and contests, rap groups in schools, and high-profile rap artists (McCarthy, 2005). Therefore, instead of signing a female athlete in 2005, Adidas signed rapper Missy Elliott to endorse "Respect Me" sneakers, bags, and jackets. And Reebok paid 50 Cent to endorse his GXT II cross-training shoe instead of looking for an athlete to endorse the shoe. NASCAR would face possible collapse if U.S. automakers decided that supplying hundreds of expensive, gas-guzzling cars to race teams would not create the marketing buzz they want (Jenkins, 2005). Such are the risks of depending on corporations.

LEGAL STATUS AND INCOMES OF ATHLETES IN COMMERCIAL SPORTS

When sports are commercialized, athletes are entertainers. This is obvious at the professional level, but it's true in other commercial sports such as big-time college football and basketball. Professional athletes are paid for their efforts, whereas amateur athletes receive rewards within limits set by the organizations that govern their lives. This raises two questions: (1) What is the legal status of the athlete-entertainers who work in "amateur" sports? (2) How are athlete-entertainers rewarded for their work? Many people don't think of athletes as workers, and they overlook owner–player relations in professional sports as a form of labor relations. This is because people associate sports with play in their lives, and they see sports as fun rather than work. However, when sports are organized to make money, players are workers, even though they may have fun on the job (Zimmer and Zimmer, 2001). This is not unique; many workers enjoy their jobs. But regardless of enjoyment, issues of legal status and fair rewards for work are important.

This section focuses on the United States and does not consider sports that collect gate receipts but never make enough money to pay for anything but basic expenses, if that. Therefore, we don't discuss high school sports, nonrevenue-producing college sports, or other nonprofit local sports in which teams sell tickets to events.

Professional Athletes

Legal Status: Team Sports   The legal status of athletes always has been the most controversial issue in professional team sports in the United States. Until the mid-1970s, professional athletes in the major sport leagues had little or no legal power to control their careers. They could play only for the team that drafted and owned them. They could not control when and to whom they might be traded during their careers, even when their contracts expired. Furthermore, they were obliged to sign standard contracts saying that they agreed to forfeit to their owners all rights over their careers. Basically, they were bought and sold like property and seldom consulted about their wishes. They were at the mercy of team owners, managers, and coaches. In all sports, this form of employee restriction was called the **reserve system** because it was *a set of practices that enabled team owners to reserve the labor of athletes for themselves and control the movement of athletes from team to team.*

As long as the reserve system was legal, owners could maintain low salaries and near total control over the conditions under which athletes played their sports. Parts of the reserve system continue to exist in professional sports, but players' associations in each of the major professional leagues for men have challenged the system in court and forced significant changes that increased their rights as workers. In any other business, a reserve system of this sort would violate antitrust laws. Companies cannot control employee movement from firm to firm, and they certainly cannot draft employees so that no other company can hire them, nor can they trade them to another company at will. But this type of reserve system is defined as legal in sports, and owners have used it for many years with minimal interference from any government agency. Team owners justify the

reserve system by saying that it's needed to maintain competitive balance between teams in their leagues. They argue that, if athletes could play with any team, the wealthiest owners in the biggest cities and TV markets would buy all the good athletes and prevent teams in smaller cities and TV markets from being winners. The irony of this argument is that team owners are capitalists who praise the free market but say it would destroy the business of sports! They embrace regulation and "sport socialism" to protect their power and wealth, and they form cartels to restrict athletes' rights and salaries, but they praise deregulation and capitalism whenever they have a chance.

Professional athletes always have objected to the reserve system, but it wasn't until 1976 that the courts ruled that professional athletes had the right to become *free agents* under certain conditions. This right allowed some players whose contracts had expired to seek contracts with other teams that could bid for their services. This change had a dramatic effect on the salaries of NBA and MLB players beginning in the late 1970s through today (see table 11.1).

Between 1976 and about 1991, team owners in the NFL and the NHL avoided much of the effect of this legal change by negotiating restrictions on free agency with players' associations. But players' unions have consistently mounted challenges to lift restrictions; therefore, owner–athlete relations change every time a new case is resolved or a new collective bargaining agreement (CBA) is negotiated and signed. Although team owners, league officials, and some fans dislike the players' unions/associations, they have enabled players to gain more control over their salaries and working conditions. Labor negotiations and players' strikes in professional team sports have focused primarily on issues of freedom and control over careers (although the media often focus on money as the only issue). As a result, free agency now exists for all players after they've been under contract for a certain number of years. Definitions of who qualifies as free agent and what that means differ slightly from league to league, but owners no longer have absolute control over players' careers.

Although it has been a struggle for professional team athletes to maintain their unions, they realize that there are crucial labor issues that must be negotiated every time they renew their CBA with the league (that is, team owners). At this time, the main issues negotiated in CBAs include the following:

1. The percentage of league revenues that are dedicated to "player costs" (salaries and benefits), and what counts as "league revenues"

2. The extent to which teams will share revenues with one another
3. Salary limits for rookies signing their first pro contract, salary restrictions for veteran players, and minimum salary levels for all players
4. The conditions under which players become free agents and the rights of athletes who are free agents
5. A salary cap that sets the maximum player payroll for teams and a formula determining the fines that an owner must pay if the payroll exceeds the cap

Table 11.1 Average salaries in major U.S. professional leagues, compared with median family income, 1950–2005*

| Year | SPORT LEAGUE | | | | | | Median U.S. Family Income[†] |
	NFL	NBA	WNBA	NHL	MLB	MLS	
1950	15,000	5,100		5,000	13,300	NA	4,000
1960	17,100	13,000		14,100	19,000	NA	5,620
1970	23,000	40,000		25,000	29,300	NA	9,867
1980	79,000	190,000		110,000	143,000	NA	21,023
1990	395,400	824,000		247,000	598,000	NA	35,353
2000	1,116,100	3,600,000	60,000	1,050,000	1,988,034	100,000	50,732
2004/05	1,330,000	4,500,000	51,770[‡]	1,434,783[§]	2,632,655	64,934	53,500

*Data on players' salaries come from many sources. Average salaries before 1971 are estimates because players' associations did not exist and teams were notorious for inconsistent payroll data and practices. Average salaries often differ from one source to another because some are based on rosters at the beginning of the season, whereas others are based on rosters at the end of the season. Differences also depend on how signing bonuses, prorated portions of those bonuses, and salary deferrals are included in salary computations.

[†]This represents total family income—parents and children in the same household. Half the families fall above the median, and half fall below. Data are from the U.S. Census; figures for 1950 and 2004 are estimates based on trends (http://www.census.gov/hhes/www/income/histinc/f07ar.html).

[‡]If every team paid up to the salary cap of $673,000, this would be the average salary. Some teams do not pay up to the cap, and some players make bonuses, so this figure is an estimate. The eighty players in the other professional women's basketball league (WNBL) have average salaries of about $4615 for a twenty-four-regular game season.

[§]There was no season in 2004–2005. This salary estimate for the 2005–2006 season assumes that average team payrolls are $33 million, an amount between the $39 million maximum and the $21.5 million minimum set by the new collective bargaining agreement.

Note: Players' salaries increased slowly from after World War II through the mid-1970s. During those years, pro athletes made from two to four times the median family income in the United States. After free agency was put in place in the 1970s, salaries began to skyrocket. As teams made more revenues from gate receipts and television rights, they were forced to compete for players and negotiate contracts with players' unions. Salaries increased dramatically as a result. In 2004 the ratios between salaries in the major men's professional sports and the median family income were 84:1 for the NBA; 49:1 for MLB; 32:1 for the NHL; 25:1 for the NFL; 1.2:1 for the MLS, and 1:1 for the WNBA.

6. A salary floor that sets the minimum payroll that a team owner must pay players
7. The conditions under which an individual player or team can request an outside arbitrator to determine the fairness of an existing or proposed contract
8. Changes in the rules of the game

To illustrate the importance of these eight factors, let's consider the contract signed in 2005 between the National Hockey League and the NHL Players Association after a 301-day lockout that canceled the entire 2004–2005 season. The contract was nearly 600 pages long, but these eight issues were central negotiating points, and they were resolved in the following way:

1. Player costs cannot exceed 54 percent of hockey-related revenue collected by all the teams, and if contracted salaries are greater than 54 percent, salaries are cut proportionately to meet the limit.
2. The ten teams that earn the most money must share some of their income with the ten teams that earn the least money (this is important to players because when teams share revenues, they have less incentive to pay salaries high enough to build winning teams).
3. Rookie players cannot be paid more than $850,000; a veteran player may not make over 20 percent of his team's payroll ($7.8 million in 2005–2006); and the minimum salary is $450,000, an important issue because 15 to 25 percent of all players in all pro leagues receive the minimum salary during any given year.
4. A player must be thirty-one years old to become an unrestricted free agent in 2005–2006. This age decreases by one year each season until the 2008–2009 season when a player must be twenty-seven years old or have a minimum of seven years experience in the league to become a free agent.
5. The maximum payroll for teams during the 2005–2006 season was $39 million (this is a

"hard cap," which means there are *no* exceptions for any team; a "soft cap" means that teams may exceed the maximum under certain conditions and subject to certain fines that are shared by "poorer" teams).
6. The minimum payroll for teams during the 2005–2006 season was $21.5 million.
7. Players and teams may request salary or contract arbitration (in other leagues, only players can request arbitration).
8. Hockey rules were changed to increase scoring and decrease the number of games ending in a tie score.

The hockey players were at a serious disadvantage when negotiating this contract because many NHL teams were losing money before they locked out the players when no CBA was reached in 2004. The players knew changes were needed, especially to salvage small-market teams in Nashville, Columbus, Raleigh, and San Jose and the six teams in Canada that had to pay player salaries in U.S. dollars even though most of their revenue was in Canadian dollars, which had been valued at 65 cents (U.S.) in early 2003 and 82 cents in mid-2005. Furthermore, ESPN had dropped the NHL media contract. These issues led the players to agree that all salaries be cut by 24 percent in addition to the other points they negotiated.

Players in the other top men's leagues generally negotiate their contracts under more favorable conditions. Therefore, they face less restrictive salary limits and can negotiate better terms on other issues. Owners and player are more agreeable when money is plentiful, but there always is a question about fairness when it comes to labor: What proportion of revenues should go to workers versus management/owners?

Athletes in most minor leagues and lower-revenue sports have few rights and little control over their careers. For players at this level, who far outnumber players in the top levels of professional sports, the pay is low, careers are uncertain, rights are few, and owners have the last word, although owners don't make large amounts of money.

Legal Status: Individual Sports   The legal status of professional athletes in individual sports varies greatly from sport to sport and even from one athlete to another. Although there are important differences among boxing, bowling, golf, tennis, auto racing, rodeo, horse racing, track and field, skiing, biking, and a number of recently professionalized alternative and action sports, a few generalizations are possible.

The legal status of athletes in individual sports largely depends on what athletes must do to train and qualify for competition in their sports. For example, few athletes can afford to pay for all the training needed to develop professional-level skills in a sport. Furthermore, they don't have the knowledge or connections to meet the formal requirements to become an official competitor in their sport, which may include having a recognized agent or manager (as in boxing), being formally accepted by other participants (as in most auto racing), obtaining membership in a professional organization (as in most bowling, golf, and tennis tournaments), or gaining a special invitation through an official selection group (as in pro track and field meets).

Whenever athletes need sponsors to pay for their training or have others help them meet participation requirements, their legal status is shaped by the contracts they sign with sponsors, agents, and the groups that regulate participation. This is why the legal status of athletes in individual sports varies so much.

Let's use boxing as an example. Because many boxers come from low-income backgrounds, they don't have the resources to develop high-level boxing skills or arrange official bouts with other boxers. Therefore, they need trainers, managers, and sponsors. The support of these people always comes with conditions that are written in formal contracts or based on informal agreements. In either case, they require the boxers to forfeit control over much of their lives and a portion of the rewards they may earn in future bouts. This means that few boxers, even those who win large amounts of money, have much control over their careers. They are forced to trade control over their bodies and careers for the opportunity to continue boxing. This is an example of how class relations operate in sports: when people lack resources, they cannot negotiate the conditions under which their sport careers occur.

The legal status of athletes in individual sports usually is defined in the bylaws of professional organizations such as the Professional Golf Association (PGA), the Ladies' Professional Golf Association (LPGA), the Association of Tennis Professionals (ATP), and the Professional Rodeo Cowboys Association (PRCA). Because athletes control many of these organizations, their policies support athletes' rights and enable them to control some of the conditions under which they compete. Without these organizations, athletes in these sports would have few rights as workers.

Income: Team Sports   Despite the publicity given to the supercontracts of some athletes in the NBA, the NFL, the NHL, MLB, and premier soccer leagues in Europe, salaries vary widely across the levels and divisions in professional team sports. For example, there are about 3500 Minor League Baseball players on 176 teams in North America, and they make from $150 a game at the lowest levels to a high of about $70,000 per year at the top minor league level. The same is true in minor league hockey where there are at least 2000 players. The average salary for a rookie running back in the nine-team Canadian Football League is about $23,000 for an eighteen-game season. The *median* salary of a player in Major League Soccer in the United States is $38,000; the *average* is about $65,000 because one player is paid $900,000, and a few others make about $500,000. WNBA players average about $52,000 per season, and those in the Women's National Basketball League average less than $5000 for a twenty-four-regular game season. Additionally, these are seasonal jobs with few benefits. Clearly commercialization is not as good for most athletes as it is for the special few (see figure 11.6).

SIDELINES

©1982 M.T.F.-T.W.S.-Lakewood, CO

"I make $20 million a year, and I don't feel guilty!"
....

FIGURE 11.6   Most athletes generate revenues that match their salaries or prize money. Like other entertainers, a few of them have benefited from national and international media exposure. Sport events are now marketed in connection with the celebrity status and lifestyles of high-profile athlete-entertainers.

To understand the range of income in pro sports, consider that during the 2005 baseball season the total salaries of 15 percent of MLB players were about the same as the total salaries of the other 85 percent. This is why the average (that is, *mean*) salary in Major League Baseball is about $2.63 million per year, whereas the *median* salary is less than one-third that amount at $850,000 per year. The big salaries for a few players drive up the average for the entire league. For example, when Peyton Manning, quarterback for the Indianapolis Colts, made $35,037,700 (including his signing bonus) in 2004, his salary was about the same as the combined salaries of sixty-one of his sixty-five teammates; the team's *average* salary was $1,397,109, but the *median* salary was only $384,400, meaning that thirty-three of the sixty-six players on the team had salaries less than $384,400 and that seventeen players made less than $300,000, as is the case with nearly 25 percent of all NFL players. In

team terms, there also are disparities. For example, the New York Yankees' payroll in 2005 was $12 million higher than the combined payrolls of five teams: Tampa Bay, Kansas City, Pittsburgh, Milwaukee, and Cleveland; and the salary of Yankees' Alex Rodriguez was only $4.2 million less than the entire Tampa Bay Marlins team. This is true in all the major men's professional leagues: About 15 percent of the players make enormous amounts of money, and nearly 30 percent make close to the minimum salary in their respective leagues.

The megasalaries in men's professional team sports did not exist before 1980. For example, when I graduated from college in 1966 with a degree in sociology, I had a job offer from a public agency, which would have paid me about 60 percent of the average salary of NBA players that year. Today, a new graduate with a bachelor's degree would be happy to find a job paying more than 1 percent of the average NBA salary.

The data in table 11.1 shows that players' average salaries have grown far beyond median family income in the United States. For example, players in 1950 made average salaries that were not much different from median family income at that time. In 2004–2005, the average NBA salary was eighty-four times greater than the median family income!

This disparity between players' salaries and general family income is why many fans no longer see the players as "workers" and why they do not side with them during strikes and lockouts. But siding with owners is also difficult because most of them make more than even the highest-paid players when you add their salaries and capital gains on franchise values. As of 2005, the percentage of league revenues that went to players was 57 percent in the NBA and MLB, 53 percent in the NHL, and 66 percent in the NFL. The owners used the rest of the annual revenue to cover other expenses and pay themselves. Each league has a team salary cap, and owners pay athletes only what they must to sign them to contracts. Contract amounts are shaped by the economics of the league and the CBAs that players' associations have with leagues.

The dramatic increase in salary at the top level of pro sports since 1980 is due to two factors: (1) changes in the legal status and rights of players, which have led to free agency and the use of a salary arbitration process, and (2) increased revenues flowing to leagues and owners. Salaries in each major men's team sport since 1970 show that increases in salary levels correspond closely with court decisions and labor agreements that changed the legal status of athletes and gave them bargaining power in contract negotiations with team owners. Unions and lawsuits have worked for some athletes, as they have for many workers in other industries.

Income: Individual Sports As with team sports, publicity is given to the highest-paid athletes in individual sports. However, not all players in these sports make enough money from tournament winnings to support themselves comfortably. Many golfers, tennis players, bowlers, track and field athletes, auto and motorcycle racers, rodeo riders, figure skaters, and others must carefully manage their money so that they do not spend more than they win as they travel from event to event. When tournament winnings are listed in the newspaper, nothing is said about the expenses for airfares, hotels, food, and transportation or about other expenses for coaches, agents, managers, and various support people. The top-money winners don't worry about these expenses, but most athletes in individual sports are not big money winners.

The disparity between the top-money winners and others has increased considerably on the men's and women's golf and tennis tours. In 2004 Tiger Woods made $6.4 million in prize money and $80 million in endorsements. Golfer Annika Sorenstam, who had a better golf year than Woods in 2004 made a total of $7.7 million in prize money and endorsements, less than 10 percent of Woods' annual earnings. Serena Williams, the only woman among the top fifty highest-paid athletes

in 2004, made $2.25 million in prize money and $20 million in endorsements (Freedman, 2005). But these are unique cases. Many people are surprised to learn that the top 15 to 20 players on the Women's Tennis Association (WTA) Tour make as much prize money as the other 1800 registered WTA players during the tour year.

The vast majority of men and women playing professional tennis, golf, and other individual sports do not make enough money to pay their competition expenses each year, although some have sponsors who pay for training and travel expenses. Some athletes with sponsors may be under contract to share their winnings with them. The sponsors/investors cover expenses during the lean years but then take a percentage of prize money when the athletes win matches or tournaments. This often occurs with boxers, most of whom never make enough money to live comfortably. Additionally, boxers have no unions, pensions, or health insurance. Journalist Jack Newfield notes that for every big-name boxer who becomes rich "there are 1000 you never hear of who end up with slurred speech, failing memory and an empty bank account" (2001, p. 14). In the United States, about ten boxers per year over the last half century have died due to boxing-related injuries, and few boxers have passed money to their heirs (Svinth, 2004).

Sponsorship agreements cause problems for professional athletes in many individual sports. Being contractually tied, for example, to an equipment manufacturer or another sponsor often puts athletes in a state of dependency. They may not have the freedom to choose when or how often they will compete, and sponsors may require them to attend social functions, at which they talk with fan-consumers, sign autographs, and promote products. For example, when Kim Clijsters (Belgium), the world's number 2–ranked tennis player, discovered that she would not be allowed to wear her sponsor's logo'd clothing during the 2004 Olympics, she withdrew from the games.

Overall, a few athletes in individual sports make good money, whereas most others struggle to cover expenses. Only when sport events are broadcast on television can athletes expect to compete for major prize money and earn large incomes, unless they are amateurs.

Amateur Athletes in Commercial Sports

The status of amateur athletes in commercial sports often is confusing and contradictory. Understanding their situation requires knowledge of their legal status and the restrictions they face when it comes to income related to their sports.

Legal Status of Amateur Athletes   The primary goal of amateur athletes is simple: to train and compete. However, achieving this goal has not always been easy because amateur athletes have little control over the conditions of their sport participation. Instead, control rests in the hands of amateur sport organizations, each setting rules that specify the conditions under which training and competition may occur. Although many rules ensure fairness in competition, others simply protect the power and interests of governing organizations and their leaders.

The powerlessness of amateur athletes in the United States led to the formation of the U.S. President's Commission on Olympic Sports in 1975. The commission's report was instrumental in the passage of the Amateur Sports Act of 1978. The Amateur Sports Act did not guarantee amateur athletes any rights, but it did create the USOC and clarified relationships among various sports organizations so that officials would be less likely to interfere with participation opportunities for athletes. Interference continues today, but it is less disruptive of training and competition than in the past.

The continued lack of power among amateur athletes is especially evident in U.S. intercollegiate sports. Even in revenue-producing college sports, athletes have few rights and no formal means of filing complaints when they've been treated unfairly or denied the right to play their

sports. The athletes are not allowed to share the revenues that they generate and have no control over how their skills, names, and images can be used by the university or the NCAA. For example, when college athletes become local or national celebrities, they have no way to benefit from the status that they've earned. They cannot endorse products or be paid when universities use their identities and images to promote events and sell merchandise.

Many amateur athletes recognize that they lack rights, but it has been difficult for them to lobby for changes. Challenging universities or the NCAA in court is expensive and would take years of a young person's life. Forming an athletes' organization would make it possible to bargain for rights, but bringing together athletes from many campuses would require resources. Additionally, some athletes have adjusted to their dependency and powerlessness and would be difficult to recruit into such an organization. The prospect of college athletes' engaging in collective bargaining to gain rights and benefits would be a serious threat to the structure of big-time college sports. Athletes often are treated like employees by coaches and athletic departments, but if they were legally defined as employees, they would be eligible for the same considerations granted to other workers in the United States. To suggest this makes coaches, athletic directors, and university presidents very nervous.

Although recent changes have called for the appointment of varsity athletes to certain NCAA committees, the likelihood of significantly increasing athletes' rights is not great. Athlete advisory committees now exist at the NCAA, conference, and campus levels, but there are no formal structures for effectively gaining more control over the conditions of training and competition. Coaches even call their athletes "kids," a word that puts them in a dependent status and keeps them there. The only way these "kids" will gain at least some control over their sport lives is for an outside group to develop a recognized athlete advocacy

The NCAA strictly limits the sport-related incomes of college athletes, even though the athletes may generate millions of dollars of income for their universities and the NCAA. Tickets to this Notre Dame football game cost the same as tickets to an NFL game, and television rights fees paid to Notre Dame are exceptionally high. However, the college athletes receive rewards that are a small fraction of the salaries received by NFL players. Universities make money on big-time football and men's basketball *only* because they have access to cheap athletic labor. (*Source:* Jay Coakley)

organization that represents athletes in their relationships with universities and the NCAA.

Amateur athletes in Olympic sports have made some strides to gain control over their training and competition, but as sports become more commercialized, the centers of power move further and further away from athletes. Athletes are now included on advisory boards for NGBs, but NGBs take a back seat to sponsors and media in the case of commercial events. The paradox for athletes is that, as they gain more resources to train and compete, the control of their training and competition moves further away from them. The exceptions are those athletes with national visibility and the individual power to negotiate support that meets their interests.

Income of Amateur Athletes   Amateur athletes in commercial sports face another paradox: They generate money through their performances, but they cannot directly benefit financially from participating in sports. Although American college athletes may receive limited athletic aid while they are students in good academic standing and elite international athletes may receive stipends for living expenses while they train, many amateur athletes receive no compensation, even when they create revenues. This is now new, but there are times now when amateurs compete in multimillion-dollar events such as the Olympics and big-time intercollegiate football and basketball. Even when it is clear that individual athletes generate $2 to $3 million for their universities, NCAA rules prohibit them from receiving more than one-year, renewable scholarships (Wieberg, 2004). Therefore, a football or basketball player from a low-income family can bring fame and fortune to a university for one to four years and never legally receive a penny beyond basic expenses for tuition, room, meals, and books, except in rare circumstances.

The unfairness of this situation for certain athletes promotes under-the-table forms of compensation. This has become so commonplace that some people in college sports say that the NCAA should revise its policies on compensation for athletes. However, developing a fair method of compensation is a challenge that has been beyond NCAA's capabilities so far. Therefore, some college athletes desiring fair compensation for their abilities and work leave college before graduation in the hope of playing professional sports.

International rules now permit athletes to be paid living expenses. However, they cannot make money *beyond* approved cost-of-living stipends and travel expenses related to training and competition. Therefore, if a sixteen-year-old gymnast on the U.S. national team takes money to be in an exhibition tour after the Olympics, she is not eligible to participate in NCAA college gymnastics. This also means she cannot receive athletic aid to attend college. Furthermore, if an Olympic figure skater participates in a professional skating competition, her amateur status may be revoked, even if she accepted no money. This would make

her ineligible for future Olympic competitions. This makes it difficult for many athletes from lower-income backgrounds to maintain amateur status and continue doing the sports they love (Sokolove, 2004c).

Questions about the fairness of this situation have been raised by an increasing number of athletes. University of Ottawa economist Mark Lavoie (2000) has noted that there may be a time "when the so-called amateur athletes will threaten to go on strike in order to get their share of the huge revenues generated by worldwide mega-events such as the Olympic Games" (p. 167).

summary

WHAT ARE THE CHARACTERISTICS OF COMMERCIAL SPORTS?

Commercial sports are visible parts of many contemporary societies. They grow and prosper best in urban, industrial societies with relatively efficient transportation and communications systems, a standard of living that allows people the time and money to play and watch sports, and a culture that emphasizes consumption and material status symbols. Spectator interest in commercial sports is based on a combination of a quest for excitement, ideologies emphasizing success, the existence of youth sport programs, and media coverage that introduces people to the rules of sports and the athletes who play them.

The recent worldwide growth of commercial sports has been fueled by sport organizations seeking global markets and corporations using sports as vehicles for global capitalist expansion. This growth will continue as long as it serves the interests of transnational corporations. As it does, sports, sport facilities, sport events, and athletes are branded with corporate logos and ideological messages promoting consumption and dependence on corporations for excitement and pleasure.

Commercialization leads to changes in the internal structure and goals of certain sports, the orientations of people involved in sports, and the people and organizations that control sports. Rules are changed to make events more fan-friendly. People in sports, especially athletes, emphasize heroic orientations over aesthetic orientations and use style and dramatic expression to impress mass audiences. Overall, commercial sports are packaged as total entertainment experiences for spectators, mostly for the benefit of spectators who know little about the games or events they are watching.

Commercial sports are unique businesses. At the minor league level, most of them do not generate substantial revenues for owners and sponsors. However, team owners at the top levels of professional sports have formed cartels to make their leagues into consistently effective sources of income.

Along with event sponsors and promoters, team owners are involved with commercial sports to make money while having fun and establishing good public images for themselves or their corporations and corporate products, policies, and practices. Their cartels enable them to control costs, stifle competition, and increase revenues, especially those coming from the sale of broadcasting rights to media companies. Profits also are enhanced by public support and subsidies, often associated with the construction and operation of stadiums and arenas.

It is ironic that North American professional sports often are used as models of democracy and free enterprise when, in fact, they have been built through carefully planned autocratic control and monopolistic business practices. As one NFL team owner said about himself and other owners, "We're twenty-eight Republicans who vote socialist." What he meant was that NFL owners are conservative individuals and corporations that have eliminated free-market competition in their

sport businesses and used public money and facilities to increase their wealth and power.

The administration and control of amateur commercial sports rest in the hands of numerous sport organizations. Although these organizations exist to support the training and competition of amateur athletes, their primary goal is to maintain power over athletes and control over revenue. Those with the most money and influence usually win the power struggles in amateur sports, and athletes seldom have the resources to promote their own interests in these struggles. Corporate sponsors are now a major force in amateur sports, and their interests strongly influence what happens in these sports.

Commercialization makes athletes entertainers. Because athletes generate revenues through their performances, issues related to players' rights and receiving revenues generated by their performances have become very important. As rights and revenues have increased, so have players' incomes. Media coverage has been key in this process.

Most athletes in professional sports do not make vast sums of money. Players outside the top men's sports and golf and tennis for women have incomes that are surprisingly low. Income among amateur athletes is limited by the rules of governing bodies in particular sports. Intercollegiate athletes in the United States have what amounts to a maximum wage in the form of athletic scholarships, which many people see as unfair when some athletes generate millions of dollars of revenue for their universities. In other amateur sports, athletes may receive direct cash payments for performances and endorsements, and some receive support from the organizations to which they belong, but relatively few make large amounts of money.

The structure and dynamics of commercial sports vary from nation to nation. Commercial sports in most of the world have not generated the massive revenues associated with a few high-profile, heavily televised sports in North America, Australia, Western Europe, and parts of Latin

America and eastern Asia. Profits for owners and promoters around the world depend on supportive relationships with the media, large corporations, and governments. These relationships have shaped the character of all commercial sports, professional and amateur.

The commercial model of sports is not the only one that might provide athletes and spectators with enjoyable and satisfying experiences. However, because most people are unaware of alternative models, they continue to express a desire for what they get, even though people with commercial and corporate interests largely determine it (Sewart, 1987). Therefore, changes will occur only when spectators and people in sports develop visions for what sports could and should look like if they were not shaped by economic factors.

> **OLC** See the OLC, www.mhhe.com/coakley9e, for an annotated list of readings related to this chapter. The OLC also contains a key concept list, a review test, and other helpful features.

WEBSITE RESOURCES

Note: Websites often change. The following URLs were current when this book was printed. Please check our website (www.mhhe.com/coakley9e) for updates and additions.

www.mhhe.com/coakley9e Click on chapter 11 for information on "outposts in action" and financial data on escalating franchise fees and franchise values, discussions of top athletes' salaries and endorsements, and why ticket prices to top events are increasing so rapidly.

www.fieldofschemes.com Representing the book of the same name by Joanna Cagan and Neil deMause; this site presents information from the book, monthly updates on stadium issues between 1998 and the present, and links to recent articles and related sites.

www.stadiumbattles.com/index.html The site related to *Public Dollars, Private Stadiums: The Battle over Building Sports Stadiums*, the book authored by Kevin J. Delaney and Rick Eckstein (2003); it provides links to sites dealing with current stadium issues.

http://sportsvenues.com/info.htm A business-oriented site that has lists of over 400 stadiums and arenas (excluding all universities) that are the homes of major and minor league teams in North America; provides data on luxury suites, club seats, and lists naming rights fees for 174 venues; additional information is for subscribers only.

www.sportengland.org/resources/pdfs/publicat%5FEng%5FJune03.pdf Economists provide a report entitled, "Value of the Sports Economy in England: a Study on Behalf of Sport England"; it provides an example of how researchers study the economic impact of sport in an entire nation.

www.bus.ucf.edu/sport/public/downloads/media/ides/release_report.pdf The site for *Racial and Gender Report Card, 2004*, compiled by Richard Lapchick (2005c).

www.teammarketing.com/fci.cfm?page=fci_mlb2004.cfm This site provides information on ticket prices for all teams in MLB, NBA, NFL, NHL, and Minor League Baseball, and computes an average for each league; also lists data for concession prices and how much it costs to take a family of four to a game, and how much ticket prices and other costs have increased since the previous season.

www.teammarketing.com/links.cfm A useful site because it has links to all major and minor league sport teams in the United States and Canada and lists tennis tournament information for the year.

http://www.forbes.com/lists/ Go to link for sport lists to see franchise values for all teams in MLB, NFL, NBA, NHL, and global soccer; each list of franchise values for leagues can be sorted by rank, team, current value, revenue, and operating income.

www.sportslaw.org/ The Sports Lawyers Association publishes the *Sports Lawyers Journal*; this site lists articles, many of which are devoted to the legal issues associated with the special legal context in which professional sport teams operate.

www.hockeyzoneplus.com/salair_e.htm This site has data on the business and economics of hockey in Canada and around the world; salary information for teams, NHL players, and players in nine leagues around the world, including the professional hockey league in Russia; information on the values of franchises, team ownership, attendance, and coaches' salaries, and other financial information; has not been updated to provide recent information.

www.nfl.com Any of the sites for professional sport leagues provide a picture of how they present themselves for commercial purposes; don't expect to find any critical information at these sites.

www.wwe.com This site illustrates an extreme example of "entertainment sport."

(Jay Coakley)

SPORTS AND THE MEDIA

Could They Survive Without Each Other?

ESPN HAS MADE a nation of highlight watchers out of us.

—**Barry Frank, vice president, IMG (global sport management), 2004**

ESPN HAS HAD a lot to do with the growth of mid-major and small [college] conferences, especially with exposure in football and basketball.

—**John Swofford, commissioner, Atlantic Coast Conference, 2004**

 Online Learning Center Resources

Visit *Sports in Society*'s Online Learning Center (OLC) at **www.mhhe.com/coakley9e** for additional information and study material for this chapter, including

- Self-grading quizzes
- Learning objectives
- Related websites
- Additional readings

A complete outline is available online at
www.mhhe.com/coakley9e.

OF THE MILLIONS [of dollars] that circulate in the media sport industry, only a small proportion is ever used to nurture grassroots sport. . . . [Elite] sport is now, more than ever, the playground of corporate capitalism.

—Gary Whannel, media scholar (2002)

IF [TEAMS AND TICKET PRICES] are chasing people out of the arena and onto their couches, it doesn't matter as long as those people are watching sports on television. Television is where corporate America makes its money.

—David Carter, sports marketing
consultant (2002)

The media, including newspapers, magazines, books, films, radio, television, video games, and the Internet, pervade culture. Although each of us incorporates media into our lives in different ways, the things we read, hear, and see in the media are important parts of our experience. They frame and influence many of our thoughts and conversations.

We use media images and narratives as we evaluate ourselves, give meaning to other people and events, form ideas, and envision the future. This does *not* mean that we are slaves to the media or passive dupes of those who control media content and the ways it is re-presented to us. The media don't tell us what to think, but they greatly influence *what we think about* and, therefore what we talk about in our relationships. Our experiences and our social worlds are clearly informed by media content, and if the media didn't exist, our lives would be different.

Sports and the media are interconnected parts of our lives. Sports programming is an important segment of media content, and many sports depend on the media for publicity and revenues. In light of these interconnections, five questions are considered in this chapter:

1. What are the characteristics of the media?
2. How are sports and the media interconnected?
3. What images and messages are emphasized in the media coverage of sports in the United States?
4. Do the media influence sport-related choices and actions?
5. What are the characteristics of sports journalism?

CHARACTERISTICS OF THE MEDIA

Revolutionary changes are occurring in the media. The personal computer and the emergence of the Internet have propelled us into a transition from an era of sponsored and programmed media for mass consumption into an era of multifaceted media content and experiences. The pace and

implications of this transition are significant, and college students are among those whose experiences are on the cutting edge of this media revolution. Although it is important to discuss new trends and explain what may occur in the future, our discussions should be based on a general understanding of the traditional media and their connections with sports.

In this chapter, we distinguish between print media and electronic media. **Print media** include *newspapers, magazines, fanzines, books, catalogues, event programs,* and even *trading cards:* words and images printed on paper. **Electronic media** include *radio, television, film, video games, the Internet,* and *online publications and representations*. Communications technology has given rise to multimedia publications that blur lines separating print media from electronic media, but it is still useful to make this distinction.

Taken together, the media provide *information, interpretation,* and *entertainment*. Sometimes they provide two or all three of these things simultaneously. However, entertainment goals are given higher priority than information and interpretation in commercial media as opposed to "public" media that does not depend on advertisers.

The media connect us with parts of the world and enable us to construct a version of that world. They bring us information, experiences, people, images, and ideas that would not otherwise be part of our everyday lives. However, media content is edited and "re-presented" by others: the producers, editors, program directors, technicians, programmers, camerapersons, writers, commentators, sponsors, and Internet site providers. These people provide information, interpretation, and entertainment based on their interest in one or more of five goals: (1) making profits, (2) shaping values, (3) providing a public service, (4) building their own reputations, and (5) expressing themselves in technical, artistic, or personal ways.

In nations where most of the media are privately owned and operated, the dominant interest is making profits. This is not the only interest, but often it is the most influential. For example, media expert Michael Real explains that there has been no greater force in the construction of media sport reality than "commercial television and its institutionalized value system [emphasizing] profit making, sponsorship, expanded markets, commodification, and competition" (1998, p. 17). Because the Internet will be a major force influencing media reality in the future, people with commercial interests are currently using their resources to control online access and content.

In nations where the popular media are controlled and operated by the state, the dominant interests are shaping values and providing a public service. However, state control of the media has steadily declined as television companies and newspapers have become privatized and as more people seek online access to information, interpretation, and entertainment.

Power relations in society also influence the priority given to the five goals that drive media content. Those who make decisions about content act as filters as they select and create the images and messages that they re-present in the media. In the filtering and representation process, these people usually emphasize images and narratives consistent with dominant ideologies in society as a whole. Thus, the media often serve the interests of those who have power and wealth in society. As corporate control of the media has increased and the media have become hypercommercialized, media content emphasizes consumerism, individualism, competition, and class inequality as natural and necessary in society. Seldom included in the content of commercial media is an emphasis on civic values, anticommercial activities, and political action (McChesney, 1999; Walker, 2005).

There are exceptions to this pattern, but when people use the media to challenge dominant ideologies, they can expect some form of backlash. This discourages counterhegemonic programming and leads people to censor media content in ways that defer to the interests of those with power. Even when there is legal protection for freedom of speech, as in the United States, those who work in the media often think carefully before representing images and messages that challenge the interests of those who have power and influence in society, especially when those people own the media or sponsor programs for commercial purposes.

This does not mean that those who control the media ignore what we consumers think or that media audiences are forced to read, hear, and see things unrelated to their interests. But it does mean that, apart from e-mail and the websites we create, we seldom have direct control over the content of what we read, listen to, and see in the media. The media re-present to us edited versions of information, interpretation, and entertainment. These versions are constructed primarily to boost media profits and maintain a culture and society in which commercial media can thrive. In the process, people who control the media are concerned with what attracts readers, listeners, and viewers within the legal limits set by government agencies and the preference parameters of individuals and corporations that buy advertising time. As they make programming decisions, they see audiences as collections of consumers that they sell to advertisers (see figure 12.1).

In the case of sports, those who control the media not only select which sports and events are covered but also decide what kinds of images and commentary are emphasized in the coverage (Andrews and Jackson, 2001; Bernstein and Blain, 2003; Brookes, 2002; Martzke and Cherner, 2004; Rowe, 2004a, 2004b; Whannel, 2002). When they do this, they play an important role in constructing the overall frameworks that we in media audiences use to define and incorporate sports in our lives.

Most people don't think critically about media content. For example, when we watch sports on

> Sport and the media must surely be the most potent combination of forces amongst the key factors in the globalization game. They have a unique synergy.
> —Robert Davies, chief executive, International Business Leaders Forum (2002b)

"Quick! Bring the camera—this crash will boost our ratings!

FIGURE 12.1   Media representations of sports are carefully selected and edited. Commentary and images highlight dramatic action, even when it is a minor part of an event. Some media people are quite effective in seeking out pain and tragedy because it attracts viewers.

television, we don't often notice that the images and messages we see and hear have been carefully designed to heighten the dramatic content of the event and emphasize dominant ideologies in American society. The pregame analysis, the camera coverage, the camera angles, the close-ups, the slow-motion shots, the attention given to particular athletes, the announcers' play-by-play descriptions, the color commentary, the quotes from athletes, and the postgame summary and analysis are all presented to entertain media audiences and keep sponsors happy.

Television commentaries (narratives) and images in the United States, for example, highlight action, competition, aggression, hard work, individual heroism and achievement, playing with pain, teamwork, and competitive outcomes. Television coverage has become so seamless in

its representations of sports that we often define televised games as "real" games, more real even than the games seen in person at the stadium. Magazine editor Kerry Temple explains:

> It's not just games you're watching. It's soap operas, complete with story lines and plots and plot twists. And good guys and villains, heroes and underdogs. And all this gets scripted into cliffhanger morality plays. . . . And you get all caught up in this until you begin to believe it really matters. (1992, p. 29)

Temple's point is more relevant today than in 1992. The focus on profits has accentuated an emphasis on soap opera storytelling as a means of developing and maintaining audience interest in both print and electronic media sports coverage. Media expert James Wittebols explains that sports programming has become "a never ending series of episodes—the results of one game create implications for the next one (or next week's) to be broadcast" (2004, p. 4). Sports rivalries are hyped and used as a basis for serializing stories through and even across seasons; conflict and chaos are highlighted in connection with an ever-changing cast of "good guys," "bad guys," and "redemption" or "comeback" stories; and the story lines are designed to reproduce ideologies favored by upper-middle-class media consumers—the ones that corporate sponsors want to reach.

Even though the media coverage of sports is carefully edited and re-presented in total entertainment packages, most of us believe that, when we see a sport event on television, we are seeing it "the way it is." We don't usually think that what we are seeing, hearing, and reading is a series of narratives and images selected for particular reasons and grounded in the social worlds and interests of those producing the event, controlling the images, and delivering the commentary (Crawford, 2004; McCullagh, 2002). Television coverage provides only *one* of *many* possible sets of images and narratives related to a sport event, and there are many images and messages that audiences do *not* receive (Knoppers and Elling,

2004). For example, if we went to an event in person, we would see something quite different from the images that are selected and re-presented on television, and we would develop our own descriptions and interpretations, which would be very different from those carefully presented by media commentators.

This point was clearly illustrated in the NBC coverage of the 1996 Olympics in Atlanta. NBC strategically created entertaining drama by representing what media analysts have described as "plausible reality" in their broadcasts. To do this, they deliberately withheld information so that they could frame events in their terms, even though they knew those terms were contrary to what was real for the athletes and others involved. They gave priority to entertainment over news and factual information. Former Olympic swimmer Diana Nyad, who was in Atlanta for the event, observed, "Compared to the TV audience, the people in Atlanta have seen a completely different Olympics" (National Public Radio, 1996). She also noted that television and other media coverage revolves around a focus on gold medals, which distorts the actual experiences and priorities of most of the athletes and spectators.

New York Times writer Robert Lipsyte (1996) describes televised sports as "sportainment," which is the equivalent of a TV movie that purports to be based on a true story but actually provides fictionalized history. In other words, television constructs sports and viewer experiences in important ways. And it happens so smoothly that most people believe that watching a game on television allows them to experience sports in a "natural" form. This is the goal of the directors, editors, and on-camera announcers who select images and narratives, frame them according to the stories they wish to tell, and make sure they do not offend sponsors in the process.

To illustrate this point, think about this question: What if all prime-time television programs were sponsored by environmental organizations, women's organizations, or labor organizations? Would program content be different than it is now?

Would the political biases built into the images and commentary be the same as they are now? It is unlikely that they would be the same, and we would be quick to identify all the ways that the interests and political agendas of the environmentalists, feminists, or labor organizers influenced images, narratives, and overall program content.

Now think about this: Capitalist corporations sponsor nearly 100 percent of all sports programming in the media, and their goals are to create consumers loyal to capitalism and generate profits for corporations and their shareholders.

The X Games were created by ESPN. ESPN is owned by ABC. ABC is owned by the Walt Disney Company. The power behind the X Games makes it difficult for the athletes to maintain the culture of their sports on their terms. (*Source:* Becky Beal)

However, we seldom question how this influences *what* we see in sports coverage, *what* we hear in commentaries, and *what* we do *not* read, see, and hear as we consume media sports.

Whether we know it or not, our experiences as spectators are heavily influenced—that is, "mediated"— by the decisions of those who control the media. Those decisions are influenced by social, political, and economic factors—including dominant ideologies related to gender, race, and class (see chapters 8 through 10). We explore this issue in the section "What Ideological Themes Underlie Media Images and Narratives?"

Characteristics of the Internet

The Internet extends and radically changes our media connections with the rest of the world because it gives us virtual access to potentially unlimited and individually created and chosen information, interpretation, and entertainment. Being online is partly like having open voice, video, and text connections with everyone in the world also online. Some of these connections allow real-time interaction, and others provide posted text and images, which we can access on our own terms and in our own time frame.

In the case of sports, the Internet extends our access to sport content. We can interact with fellow fans in chat rooms, ask questions of players and coaches, identify scores and statistics, and we can play online games that either simulate sports or are associated with real-time sport events around the world. We can even *create* media content to match our interests and the interests of others worldwide. This gives us a form of control that radically alters media experiences and mediated realities (Crawford, 2004).

Most people interested in sports use the Internet as an extension of the existing media. They visit team sites, listen to live-game audio, and most recently, pay for game video streaming from television feeds. Although subscriber fees are charged for video coverage, the Internet may soon provide access to all televised games in the world. This concerns the five media companies

that control most media content worldwide; they want to control access to this content and be able to sell Internet audiences to other corporations who wish to advertise products and services. At the same time, sport leagues such as the NFL contemplate streaming games on their own sites, bypassing media companies and collecting subscription fees without a "middleman."

The major sociological question related to the Internet is this: Will it democratize social life by enabling people to freely share information and ideas, or will it become a tool for corporations to expand capital, increase consumption, reproduce ideologies that drive market economies, and maintain the belief that they are the major source of pleasure and excitement in our lives? The answer to this question will emerge as we struggle over issues of Internet access and how Internet use will be funded and incorporated into our lives. For example, giant cable and satellite companies have already convinced state legislatures to pass laws making it illegal for communities in some states to establish wireless connectivity as a public service for all citizens. These companies want the Internet to be forever a toll road on which they charge and collect the tolls rather than a publicly maintained information highway attached to a local street system.

Other sociological questions deal with the dramatic growth in Internet-based "Fantasy Leagues" and sport gambling. The first fantasy sport league was invented in 1979 by a baseball fan. It didn't require the Internet, but most fantasy sport participants today use Internet sites to play. If we use the NFL as an example, playing fantasy football makes every participant an owner who constructs his or her own pro football team by taking turns with other owners and choosing real NFL players for the positions on their fantasy team. The weekly performance statistics of the players on an owner's team roster are converted into points so that each owner can compete against one or more owners of other teams. Websites are designed to accumulate relevant statistics for all NFL players each week and compute scores for owners' teams in particular leagues. This is how it works for about 12 million "owners" who played fantasy football in 2005 and about 4 million who play fantasy baseball, hockey, and basketball season after season.

The average fantasy team owner is a white male (93 percent) about forty years old with a college degree, and an annual household income of about $80,000. Collectively, owners spend over $2 billion annually to obtain data about players and compete in online leagues. Individually, each owner devotes about three hours per week to managing his or her team, and a portion of this occurs during work hours (Ballard, 2004; Petrecca, 2005; Wendel, 2004).

Fantasy football, baseball, NASCAR, basketball, hockey, and other sports completely change the way these men and a few women consume sports (Levy, 2005; Wendel, 2004). They care little about teams or team records because they focus on the performances of their players who are on many different teams in a sport. Therefore, many "owners" also subscribe to expensive cable and satellite television "sport packages" that give them access to broadcasts of every game played in the league in which they own fantasy teams. They watch their players, add up their points, scout other players, compare statistics, consider trades with other owners, and decide who they should put in their starting lineups. Fantasy sports combine the Internet and other media and turn many sport fans into avid media sport consumers. Being a fantasy owner provides the white men who constitute over 90 percent of all participants with a sense of power and control, and it connects them with others who share their interests and backgrounds (Levy, 2005).

The Internet also is connected with gambling on sports. Most bets related to sports are made informally with family members, friends, and coworkers. Formal gambling on sports goes back centuries (Cashmore, 2007) and continues today at horse and dog tracks and in Las Vegas–based "sport books" in which people can place legal bets on nearly every possible outcome in sport events—number of points, who scores first, points in first half or second half, who beats the point

spread, and so on. The Internet has increased access to both legal and illegal sport gambling opportunities. It doesn't cause people to gamble, but it makes it very easy to do so twenty-four hours a day, seven days a week. This is partly because there are many offshore websites that now take bets from people in the United States, even though what they are doing would be illegal if it occurred within U.S. borders. A credit card is all that is needed to bet online.

Online sport gambling is especially popular among male college students who have access to the Internet and feel that they know more about sports than other people (Brown, 2000; Crist, 1998; Jenkins, 2000; Layden, 1995a, 1995b, 1995c). Gambling changes the way people consume media sports because their bets often involve point spreads. Point spreads are determined by bookies, who want to make sure that they don't take too many bets on a particular outcome in a sport event and find themselves unable to cover the money that must be paid to winners. This means that when a person bets on Miami University who is favored by 21 points in a football game with Iowa State, Miami must win by more than 21 points for the person to win the bet. This makes the game exciting even if it's one sided because all the betters are concerned with the final score rather than who wins or loses.

Despite gambling debts that have destructive consequences for a growing number of people, betting on sports is not generally seen as an important moral or legal issue. Many people are accustomed to buying lottery tickets and participating in state-sponsored gambling activities, so they don't take seriously restrictions that limit or ban betting on sports.

Overall, issues related to access will cause the Internet to be contested terrain well into the future as people struggle over the rights of users to share information and ideas. Sports leagues and teams will use the Internet more widely in the future, but they will charge fees for access to events for which they have also sold media rights to television and radio. Furthermore, sponsors of the TV and radio broadcasts will oppose Internet

reflect on SPORTS

"Win at Any Cost"*
Video Games as Simulated Sports

Video games that simulate sports have become so realistic that some athletes even use them to train. The games offer high-definition graphics, intense interactivity, control of the action, and opportunities to create, train, and be your own player competing with and against "real" players.

Organized video game sports tournaments attract thousands of players worldwide, many of whom identify themselves as cyberathletes and participate in the Cyberathlete Professional League (CPL). They train regularly, have fans and agents, and if they are high-profile players, endorse products related to the games. Since 1997 the CPL has sponsored about fifty major international tournaments and awarded over $3 million in prizes to competitors.

John Madden, known to football fans over the age of forty as a former NFL coach and longtime NFL commentator (recently on *Monday Night Football*), is known to the under-forty-year-old game player as a video game brand. Madden NFL games are among the most popular video products on the market. When Madden was asked to comment on the video game craze, he said that designers have made video games that look so much like the games on television that television producers are now using special lenses and filters on cameras at NFL games to make television images look like video game images.

When developers create games, they consult top athletes so that game situations and players' movements are lifelike simulations. Most top players cooperate with game developers because they want their moves and actions accurately portrayed in the video game. Even unique mannerisms related to their dramatic on-field personas are filmed so that they can be included in the action just as they are in "real" commercialized sports.

The graphics in EA Sports™ Madden NFL have become increasingly realistic, and television producers now use camera filters to make real-time games appear more like video As this occurs, simulations begin to merge with representations of sports. (© 2005 Electronic Arts, Inc.; © 2005 NFL Players; reproduced with permission)

Professional team coaches now worry that video games are so popular among their players that they are distractions from real games. According to an ESPN report, some NFL and NBA players would rather play video game sports than watch televised real-time games. On the other hand, NASCAR, Formula One, and Indy Car video games are so realistic that some racecar drivers use the games to prepare for the split-second responses required during actual races. Game designers want to create for players the audio, visual, and emotional experiences matching those of the athletes.

The financial stakes associated with creating realistic and entertaining games are significant. This constantly pushes designers to refine graphics, action, and game possibilities. It also leads them to talk with potential sponsors about product placements and advertisements built into the story lines and actions in the games. As more young people play these games

_____

*Online promotion for Blitz: The League
(www.midway.com/rxpage/Game_Blitz:TheLeague.html).

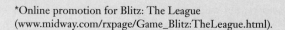

and watch fewer television broadcasts, corporations see video games as tools for developing outposts in the heads of game players and fostering their commitment to a lifestyle based on consumption (Richtel, 2005). Product placement in games is now a major advertising venue and a valuable source of revenue for game designers.

A major issue for game developers is obtaining the rights to use the names and images of athletes and sport leagues in their games. Madden NFL 06, for example, was produced by EA Sports with permission from the NFL and the NFL Players Association, which receive rights fees from the sales of the games. But this also means that NFL officials had to approve everything in the game. Midway Games, on the other hand, developed Blitz: The League, a video game modeled after pro football without buying rights from the NFL. Therefore, they cannot use NFL players' names or images or any reference to the NFL. But they also have the freedom to design the game without NFL approval. This allows them, for example, to include images of blood and gory injuries, near-naked cheerleaders, dirty hits, in-your-face celebrations after big plays, drug use (for energy and strength), and off-field controversies (Ives, 2004) that might titillate game players.

Meanwhile, a small but growing number of children are being introduced to sports through video games. They learn rules and game strategies as they play. They see the moves involved in a sport as they manipulate images in the games, and their initial emotional experiences in certain sports are felt in front of computer monitors or televisions rather than on playing fields. For those of us in the sociology of sport, this raises important research questions: After playing video sports for two years, will six-year-olds be willing to listen to whistle-blowing coaches when they are accustomed to being in complete control of players, game strategies, and game conditions? Will children bring new forms of game knowledge to the situations in which they play informal and formally organized games? How will that knowledge influence the games they play? Will some children simply stay home in front of their monitors and televisions as they control their own games without having to accommodate the wishes of teammates or obey the commands of coaches? Will they know that, when they do this, they are taking for granted the ideologies of the people who developed the games they play? To whom are game developers accountable other than market forces?

Adult game players outnumber children who play, and the majority of players are males between the ages of 12 and 30. Many male college students are regular game players to the point that status in certain dorms reflects prowess in video game sports. Playing these games also provides regular social occasions similar to those provided by "real" sport events.

As high-speed Internet connections become more widespread, cybersports will become more popular. Technology now enables players to compete with opponents around the world and even form teams with rosters of players who have never met one another in person. Spectators can watch games online and even listen to the voices of the players as they compete. If bookies developed betting odds and took bets on video sport game outcomes, it would not be surprising.

At this point, studies of simulated sports and video games are rare. We know little about the experiences of players, the social settings created around the games, and what players learn about themselves and others during their experiences. Future research is likely to be inspired by many questions such as the following: Will playing video games influence how people play real-time sports? Will the norms in real-time sports be influenced by players' experiences in simulated sports? Will children be introduced to sports through video games rather than informal games? If so, will video game experiences influence what they will expect in real-time games? Will game designers and manufacturers eventually have more power than the big media companies today? *What do you think?*

coverage that interferes with selling products and services to sport audiences.

As technology improves over the next decade, it may be possible for a grandparent to see a grandchild playing in a high school basketball game simply by paying a fee to the high school website. High school students could film the game, do the commentary, and produce their own coverage for small audiences of distant friends and relatives. Such a possibility could lead to many creative forms of sport media coverage and income for high schools and their instructional technology curriculum. Furthermore, being a spectator could become a more active and creative experience for online fans who may have opportunities to participate directly in the construction of media reality. How this will change the reality of mediated sports and our experience of them remains to be seen.

The future is difficult to predict. Will people choose 500-channel, high-definition digital television over the medium of the Internet? Will InternetTV become widespread so that people can have both? Will the economics of technology and the "digital divide" between technology haves and have-nots segregate spectators even further by social class? Will the culture of the Internet favor some people over others, or will it enable all spectators to create realities that fit their interests and preferences?

Answers to these questions depend on the social, political, and economic forces shaping the future of the Internet. Economic forces guarantee that the first people to enjoy new spectator experiences and realities will be those who can buy the hardware, software, and bandwidth to move around the Internet at will. Social class will influence Internet access to spectator experiences because broadband providers overlook lower-income neighborhoods because they say it doesn't pay to invest there. But progressive public policies and programs could mandate the provision of access in these neighborhoods or provide them with wireless access as a pubic service, thereby blurring class differences in future access

to the Internet. This, however, depends on the public good being given priority over the corporate good when it comes to online access.

Characteristics of Video Games and Virtual Sports

Sports also come into our lives through video games and virtual experiences. Sport video games are popular in wealthy nations, and some people have even participated in virtual sports of various types although most virtual sports are experimental and not available for general participation.

The images in digital games have become increasingly lifelike, and those who play them have uniquely active spectator experiences, even when they occur in solitude. Social science research has focused mostly on violence and gender issues, and there is little information about the actual experiences of people who play video games modeled after "real" sports.

It is clear that people who play sport video games have different experiences than those who watch televised sport events. For example, golf fans can match their video golf skills with the physical skills of pro golfers by going online and golfing on the same course as Tiger Woods or other high-profile players whose shots have been represented and archived through digitized images. This is a new media experience, and research has not been done to show how people integrate such experiences into their lives.

Those who play video sports games are usually regular consumers of standard sport media events. Their interest in and enjoyment of the video games are tied to their knowledge about a sport, sport teams, and athletes. However, the experience of digital gaming will change as more people play one another on the Internet in organized tournaments while others watch.

Sport teams and individual athletes will sell interactive video games to fans who want to pretend that they are managing the New England Patriots in simulated NFL games, controlling David Beckham's body as he plays on a soccer team in the United States, or skating in a digital skateboarding exhibition with Eric Koston. It is unknown whether such interactive sport video games will actually replace or simply extend other forms of sports media consumption (Crawford, 2004). This and related issues are discussed in the box "Win at Any Cost."

Game players have choices, but those choices are not unlimited, nor are they ideologically neutral. The experiences of video game players are influenced by the ethos that underlies the programmed images and actions in the games. The games clearly highlight traditional masculinity and other values associated with most major media sports today. It is important that we increase our understanding of how people integrate video game experiences into their lives.

The idea of virtual sports is so new that it has not been discussed in the sociology of sport. As the technology of virtual reality evolves, people will become immersed in physical activities in new ways. Although we don't know exactly what this means, it is possible that many people in the future will prefer virtual sports to what we define as sports today. Instead of going to a gym or fitness center, people may go to virtual sports complexes where they can put on lightweight headsets that present images allowing them to physically experience sport challenges that transcend time and space. This futuristic arcade will allow cyclists in the year 2050 to race with Lance Armstrong's granddaughter as they pedal and sweat their way along the virtual roads of the Tour de France on bikes and in environments where they experience feelings of speed, wind and rain in their faces, and the excitement of developing and carrying out strategies with virtual teammates in the Tour de France. Other sports will merge virtual and real spaces in other ways, changing the meaning of reality when it comes to sports (Marriott, 2004).

In the meantime, it is important to understand the relationship between sports and the media in the early twenty-first century and to know how each has influenced the other.

SPORTS AND THE MEDIA: A TWO-WAY RELATIONSHIP

The media and commercialization are closely related topics in the sociology of sport. The media intensify and extend the process and consequences of commercialization. For this reason, much attention has been given to the interdependence between the media and commercialized forms of sports. Each of these spheres of life has influenced the other, and each depends on the other for part of its popularity and commercial success.

Sports Depend on the Media

People played sports long before the media covered and re-presented sport events. When sports exist just for the participants, there is no urgent need to advertise games, report the action, publish results, and interpret what happened. The players already know these things, and they are the only ones who matter. It is only when sports become forms of commercial entertainment that they depend on the media to re-present them.

Commercial sports are unique in that they require the media to provide a combination of coverage *and* news. For example, when a stage play is over, it's over—except for a review after opening night and the conversations of those who attended the play. When a sport event is over, many people wish to know about and discuss statistics; important plays, records, standings; the overall performances of the players and teams; upcoming games or matches; the importance of the outcome in terms of the season as a whole and the postseason and the next season; and so on. The media provide this knowledge and facilitate these discussions, which in turn generate interest that can be converted into revenues from the sale of tickets, luxury suites, club seats, concessions, parking, team logo merchandise, and licensing rights. After games or matches are played, the scores become news, and interpretations of the action become entertainment for fans, regardless of whether they saw an event or not. This is the case worldwide—for bullfights in Mexico, hockey games in Canada, soccer matches in Brazil, and sumo wrestling in Japan.

Sports promoters and team owners know the value of media coverage, and they often go out of their way to accommodate reporters, commentators, and photographers. Credentialed media personnel are given comfortable seats in press boxes, access to the playing field and locker rooms, and summaries of statistics and player information. Providing these services promotes supportive and sympathetic media coverage.

Although commercial spectator sports depend on the media, some have a special dependence on television because television companies pay fees for the rights to broadcast games and other events. Table 12.1 and figure 12.2 indicate that rights fees provide sports with predictable, significant, and increasing sources of income. Once "rights contracts" are signed, revenues are guaranteed regardless of bad weather, injuries to key players, and the other factors that interfere with ticket

sales and on-site revenue streams. Without television contracts, commercial success is limited or unlikely for spectator sports.

Television revenues also have greater growth potential than revenues from gate receipts. The number of seats in a stadium limits ticket sales, and ticket costs are limited by demand. But television audiences can include literally billions of viewers now that satellite technology transmits signals to most locations around the globe. For example, it is estimated that 3.7 billion people in 220 countries watched television coverage of the 2004 Olympic Games in Athens, Greece. The audience was attracted by more than 4000 hours of coverage supplied by 180 broadcasting organizations that paid about $1.5 billion in rights fees to the International Olympic Committee (IOC). These organizations covered 300 events with over 12,000 personnel, 1000 cameras, 450 videotape machines, and nearly 60 trailers of equipment.

The goal of the IOC and other sport mega-events is to turn the entire world into an audience

Table 12.1   Escalating annual media rights fees for major commercial sports in the United States (in millions of dollars)*

Sport	1986	1991	1996	2001	2006
NFL	400	900	1100	2200	3735
MLB[†]	183	365	420	417	560
NBA	30	219	275	660	767
NHL[‡]	22	38	77	120	70
NASCAR	3	NA	NA	412	560
NCAA Men's Basketball Tournament	31	143	216	216	550[§]
NCAA (all women's championships)	NA	NA	NA	NA	18.5
WNBA	NA	NA	NA	0	0[¶]

*These amounts are not inflation adjusted. Data come from multiple sources, and amounts change whenever new contracts are negotiated.

[†]Amounts for baseball do not include local television and radio rights fees negotiated by individual teams, national radio rights fees negotiated by the league, or Internet revenues received by the league from individual subscriptions paid to receive games on MLB.com; amount for 1996 includes national radio rights.

[‡]Includes U.S. rights only for 2001 and 2006; there also are Canadian rights and European rights; beginning in 2006, all games will be available on the Internet for a subscription fee paid to Comcast (cable).

[§]Will gradually increase to $764 million in 2013; these amounts include rights to broadcast on television, radio, and the Internet the men's basketball tournament and other championship events, excluding football.

[¶]Information on this could not be found.

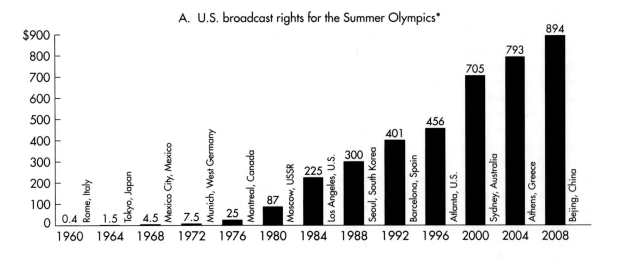

A. U.S. broadcast rights for the Summer Olympics*

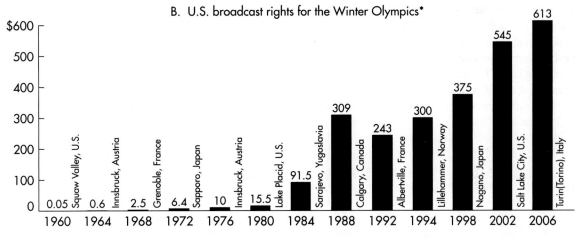

B. U.S. broadcast rights for the Winter Olympics*

*The IOC also receives rights fees from other television companies around the world. Europe, Japan, and continental Asia are paying increasingly higher fees. NBC paid about $250 million more for the Sydney Games than for the Atlanta Games because it televised 276 hours of coverage on its cable channels, CNBC and MSNBC. This was in addition to the 161 hours it televised on NBC. Its goal of using the Olympics to boost global legitimacy and viewer ratings for its cable stations was successful; plus, the network made a 50-million-dollar profit on the games themselves.

FIGURE 12.2   Escalating media rights fees for the Olympics (in millions of dollars).

that can be sold to sponsors. The size of the potential TV audience and the deregulation of the television industry are the reasons that television rights fees have increased at phenomenal rates since the early 1970s. For example, the IOC received $225 million from the U.S. company that televised the Summer Olympic Games in Los Angeles—the most commercialized Olympics in history at that time. In 2012 the IOC will receive $1.2 billion from NBC and $700 million from other television companies worldwide to broadcast the Olympic Games from London.

This growth in television rights fees makes commercial sports more profitable for promoters and team owners and increases the attractiveness of sports as sites for national and global advertising. This allows professional athletes to demand higher salaries and turns some of them into national and international celebrities, who then use their celebrity status to endorse products sold around the world. For example, the global celebrity and endorsement value of Tiger Woods is primarily due to the invention of satellite television.

As video streaming becomes more sophisticated and it becomes realistic to broadcast more sports events on the Internet, there will be interesting changes in how and with whom media rights are negotiated. The global reach of the web creates new possibilities for large corporations wanting to "teach the world" to consume. However, it also creates challenges because webcasts may compete with television—the medium that has traditionally paid rights fees to sport organizations. This challenge has, for example, prevented the IOC from selling Internet rights for Olympics coverage. Long-term broadcasting rights for the United States have already been sold to NBC, and NBC does not want people to have the choice of its coverage or InternetTV coverage. At the same time, this is why Rupert Murdoch and his global News Corporation is buying websites that attract people worldwide; he wants to combine the immediacy and interactivity of the web with the traditional allure of television, and he will use sports programming to attract InternetTV subscribers (Hansell, 2005). Eventually, television as we now think of it will become obsolete.

Have Commercial Sports Sold Out to the Media? Most commercial sports depend on television for revenues and publicity. For example, about 65-percent of NFL revenues come from television rights fees, up from 45-percent in 1979. However, television money comes with strings attached.

Accommodating the interests of commercial television has required many changes in the

ways that sports are organized, scheduled, and re-presented. Some of these changes include the following:

- The schedules and starting times for many sport events have been altered to fit television's programming needs.
- Halftime periods in certain sports have been shortened to keep television viewers tuned to events.
- Prearranged schedules of time-outs have been added to games and matches to make time for as many commercials as possible.
- Teams, leagues, and tournaments have been formed or realigned to take advantage of regional media markets and build national and international fan support for sports, leagues, and teams.

In other cases, the lure of television money has encouraged changes that eventually would have occurred in the course of commercializing sports. For example, college football teams added an eleventh and twelfth game to their season schedules, and professional teams extended their seasons by adding games and playoffs. But these changes probably would have occurred without the influence of television money. Commercial sports would have added games and extended seasons simply to increase gate receipts and venue revenues, but television money increased the stakes associated with these changes and hurried them along. The same is true for the additions of sudden death overtime periods in some sports, the tiebreaker-scoring method in tennis, the addition of medal play in golf, the 3-point shot in basketball, and the shootout in soccer and hockey. These changes are grounded in general commercial interests, but *television expands and intensifies* the financial stakes associated with producing more marketable entertainment for all spectators and a more attractive commercial package for sponsors and advertisers.

Most changes associated with television coverage have been made willingly by sport organizations. The trade-offs usually are attractive for both players and sponsors. In fact, many sports and athletes not currently receiving coverage gladly would make changes if they could gain the attention and/or money associated with television contracts. Are there limits to what they would change for television coverage? Yes, but limits are always negotiated around the issue of sharing control over the conditions of sports participation. For example, surfers have turned down television contracts because they would not allow television companies to dictate the conditions under which they would compete. The companies did not care if waves were too dangerous because they wanted to stay on schedule and provide live coverage. But surfers up until now have decided that selling control over their sport participation and being forced to risk their lives in competitions was not worth television coverage.

Have the Media Corrupted Sports? Some people complain that dependence on the media, especially television, corrupts the true nature of sports. However, these people fail to take into account two factors:

1. *Sports are not shaped primarily by the media in general or by television in particular.* The idea that television by itself has somehow transformed the essential nature of sports does not hold up under careful examination. Sports are social constructions, and commercial sports are created over time through interactions among athletes, facility directors, sport team owners, event promoters, media representatives, sponsors, advertisers, agents, and spectators—all of whom have diverse

The media enable some athletes to become global celebrities and benefit from windfall income related to their popularity. They know that their celebrity depends on using and maintaining close connections with the media. Seven-time Tour De France winner Lance Armstrong has become a master at dealing with the media in ways that work to his advantage. (*Source:* Christophe Ena; AP/Wide World)

interests. The dynamics of these interactions are grounded in power relations and shaped by the resources held by different people at different times. It is unrealistic to think that those who control the media determine sports to fit their interests alone, but it is equally unrealistic to ignore their power.

2. *The media, including television, do not operate in a political and economic vacuum.* People who control the media are influenced by the social, political, and economic contexts in which they do business. Government agencies, policies, and laws regulate the media in most countries. Although government regulations have been loosened or lifted in recent years, the media must negotiate contracts with teams and leagues under certain legal constraints. Economic factors also constrain the media by setting limits on the values of sponsorships and advertising time and by shaping the climate in which certain types of programming, such as pay-per-view sports and cable and satellite subscriptions, might be profitable. Finally, the media are constrained by social factors, which influence people's decisions to consume sports through the media.

Connections between the media and commercial sports are grounded in complex sets of social, economic, and political relationships, which change over time and vary from culture to culture. These relationships influence the media's impact on sports. In other words, the conclusion that the media corrupt sports is based on an incomplete understanding of how the social world works and how sports are connected with social relations in society.

With that said, it is also important to remember that nearly all of the most powerful people in sports around the world are CEOs or owners of major, global corporations. Nearly all of them are white men from English-speaking nations, and each wants to offer programming that people around the globe will watch and that corporations will sponsor and use as advertising vehicles. The sports selected for national and global coverage depend on the media for their commercial success, and the salaries and endorsement income of top athletes also depend on the media. However, there are two sides to this process.

The Media Depend on Sports

Most media do not depend on sports coverage. This is especially true for magazines, books, radio, movies, and the Internet, although it is less true for newspapers and television. The Internet does not depend on sports, but certain online services make money when sports fans use the Internet to get up-to-the-minute scores, obtain insider information about particular events, place bets with offshore bookies, or enter exclusive online discussions about athletes, teams, and events.

Neither book publishing nor the film industry depends on sports. Until recently, there were very few successful books or films about sports. The urgency and uncertainty that are so compelling in live sports are difficult to capture in these media. However, since the late 1980s, both publishers and film studios have produced projects with tragic, inspiring, or outrageous stories about sports figures.

Many radio stations give coverage to sports only in their news segments, although local football, baseball, and men's basketball games often are broadcast live on local radio stations. Some communities have talk radio stations that feature sports talk programs that attract listeners from a demographic that is attractive to certain advertisers—that is, young men with higher-than-average incomes. Most magazines devote little or no attention to sports coverage, although the number of general-and special-interest sport magazines and "fanzines" in the United States and other countries is significant. A visit to a local magazine rack shows that magazines are devoted to information

As more people go online for coverage of national sports, city newspapers promote their coverage of local high school and college sports. Editors have determined that this is an effective strategy to maintain circulation rates and the fees that newspapers charge to advertisers. (*Source:* Jay Coakley)

about skiing, skateboarding, snowboarding, biking, motocross, car racing, and dozens of other sports.

The media most dependent on sports for commercial success are newspapers and television. This is especially true in the United States.

Newspapers Newspapers at the beginning of the twentieth century had a sports page, which consisted of a few notices about upcoming activities, a short story or two about races or college games, and possibly some scores of local games.

Today, there are daily and weekly newspapers devoted exclusively to sports, and nearly all daily newspapers have sport sections often making up about 25-percent of their news content.

Major North American newspapers give more daily coverage to sports than any other single topic of interest, including business or politics. The sports section is the most widely read section of the paper. It accounts for at least one-third of the total circulation and a significant amount of the advertising revenues for big-city newspapers. It attracts advertisers who want to reach young to middle-aged males with ads for tires, automobile supplies, new cars, car leases, airline tickets for business travelers, alcoholic beverages, power tools, building supplies, sporting goods, hair-growth products, Viagra, testosterone, and hormone therapies. Additionally, there are ads for bars or clubs providing naked or near-naked female models and dancers, all-night massage parlors, and organizations offering gambling advice and opportunities (see a sample of major-city newspapers to confirm this). Ads for all these products and services are unique to the (men's) sport section, and they generate considerable revenues for most newspapers.

It is difficult to predict the future of newspapers' dependence on sports. As the Internet becomes a primary source of information about big-time sports nationally and worldwide, newspapers may focus mostly on local sports, including high school varsity teams, small college teams, and even youth sports. This has already occurred as more major-city newspapers publish weekly "prep sections" and regularly highlight local athletes.

Television Some television companies in North America also have developed a dependence on sports for programming content and advertising revenues. For example, sport events are a major part of the programming schedules of national network stations in the United States and many cable and satellite-based stations. Some television companies even sponsor events, which they then promote and televise, such as ESPN's ownership and presentation of the X Games.

Sports account for a growing proportion of income made on the sales of commercial time by television companies. Many cable and satellite companies have used sport programs to attract subscribers from particular segments of the viewing public and then sell the audiences to advertisers for a nice profit. For example, in 2005 ESPN's multiple networks showed over 5100 hours of live sports and 2300 live or taped sport events watched by about 95 million people each week.

Between ESPN, ESPN2, ESPNews, ESPN Classic, ESPN Deportes, ESPN HD, ESPN Today, ESPNU, and ESPN International, people in 192 countries received sport information and event broadcasts in twelve languages. These networks provide content for ESPN.com, ESPN Radio, ESPN Deportes Radio, ESPN broadband, ESPN Mobile, ESPNDeportes.com, ESPNRadio.com, ESPNSoccernet.com, EXPN.com, ESPN Radio, *ESPN The Magazine*, *Bassmaster Magazine*, BASS Times, ESPN Books, ESPN Interactive, ESPN On Demand, ESPN 360, ESPN HD, and ESPN2 HD. And all of these create consumer demand for products available at ESPN Zone, TeamStore@ ESPN, and Fishing Tackle and Retailer.

Both ESPN and Fox became major networks after they went out on a limb and spent massive amounts of money to buy the rights to cover NFL games in 1987 and 1993, respectively. The NFL put them on the map of major media companies. Today, Fox Sports and other Fox networks also televise a range of sports coverage around the world. Additionally, there are dozens of multimedia companies that broadcast sports, including CSTV, a twenty-four-hour college sports television network that combines with CSTV.com, college sports radio, and SIRIUS College Sports Radio. Others include the Sports Network, Turner Sports Network, OLN (Outdoor Life Network), the Tennis Channel, Blackbelt TV, MLB.com, NBA TV, and The Football Network.

An attractive feature of sport programs for the major U.S. networks (ABC, CBS, Fox, and NBC) is that events often are scheduled on Saturdays and Sundays—the slowest days of the week for general television viewing. Sport events are the most popular weekend programs, especially among male viewers who may not watch much television at other times. For example, in 2004 NFL games were five of the six most-watched TV programs among men aged eighteen to forty-nine years old (McCarthy, 2005). Therefore, networks can sell advertising time at relatively high rates during what normally would be dead time for programming.

Media corporations also use sport programs to attract commercial sponsors that might take their advertising dollars elsewhere if television stations did not cover certain sports. For example, games in major men's team sports are ideal for promoting the sales of beer, life insurance, trucks and cars, computers, investment services, credit cards, and air travel. The people in the advertising departments of major corporations realize that sports attract male viewers. They also realize that most business travelers are men and that many men make family decisions on the purchases of beer, cars, computers, investments, and life insurance. Finally, advertisers also may be interested in associating their product or service with the culturally positive image of sports. This is especially important for a product such as beer, which is a target for neoprohibitionists, or tobacco, which is a frequent target of health advocates, among others.

Golf and tennis are special cases for television programming. These sports attract few viewers, and the ratings are exceptionally low. However, the audience for these sports is attractive to certain advertisers. It is made up of people from the highest-income groups in the United States, including many professionals and business executives. This is why television coverage of golf and tennis is sponsored by companies selling luxury cars and high-priced sports cars, business and personal computers, imported beers, investment opportunities with brokers and consultants, and trips to exclusive vacation areas. This is also why the networks continue to carry these programs despite low ratings. Advertisers are willing to pay high fees to reach high-income consumers and corporate executives who make decisions to buy thousands of "company cars" and computers at the same time that they invest millions of dollars for employee pension plans or 401k plans. With such valued viewers, these programs don't need high ratings to stay on the air.

In the mid-1990s, television executives "discovered" women viewers and women's sports.

Data indicate that women have made up more than half the viewing audiences for both Winter and Summer Olympic Games since 1988. This led NBC to hype women's sports, appeal to female viewers during subsequent telecasts of the games, and emphasize gender equity in scripted studio commentary, although on-site coverage of events has always favored men (Eastman and Billings, 1999).

Other women's sports also attract television coverage although the coverage they receive pales in comparison with coverage of men's sports. Women's events don't receive more coverage partly because female viewers of women's games have not been identified as a target demographic by advertisers. Furthermore, men make up over half the viewing audience for most women's sports, and they also watch men's sports, so sponsors have already bought access to them when they advertise during men's events.

Highly specialized cable and satellite television companies attract advertising money by covering sports that appeal to clearly identified segments of consumers. For example, the X Games attract young males between twelve and thirty years old, and this attracts corporate sponsors that sell soft drinks, beer, telecommunications products, and sports equipment such as helmets, shoes, skateboards, and dozens of other sport-specific products.

Over the past two decades, television companies have paid rapidly increasing amounts of money for the rights to televise certain sports. This was shown in the data in table 12.1 and figure 12.2. The contracts for these rights are negotiated every few years. In the case of the major men's spectator sports, contracts involve hundreds of millions of dollars and more than a billion dollars for the Olympics, the NFL, the NBA, NASCAR, the NCAA Men's College Basketball Tournament, soccer's World Cup, and premier-level soccer in England.

Table 12.2 shows that in the United States nineteen of the top twenty-five television programs

Table 12.2   The top twenty-five U.S. network telecasts as ranked by average household ratings

Program	Date	Average Household Rating (in millions of households)*
1. *M*A*S*H** (special)	2/28/83	50.2
2. Winter Olympics	2/23/94[†]	45.7
3. Super Bowl XXX	1/28/96	44.2
4. Super Bowl XXXII	1/25/98	43.6
5. Super Bowl XXXIV	1/30/00	43.6
6. Super Bowl XXVIII	1/30/94	42.9
7. Super Bowl XXXVI	2/3/02	42.6
8. *Cheers*	1/20/93	42.4
9. Super Bowl XXXI	1/26/97	42.0
10. Super Bowl XXVII	1/31/93	42.0
11. Super Bowl XL	2/5/06	41.6
12. Winter Olympics	2/25/94[†]	41.5
13. Super Bowl XX	1/26/86	41.5
14. *Dallas*	11/21/80	41.5
15. Super Bowl XXXVIII	2/1/04	41.4
16. Super Bowl XXXV	1/28/01	41.3
17. Super Bowl XXXIX	2/6/05	41.1
18. Super Bowl XXXVII	1/26/03	40.7
19. *Seinfeld*	5/14/98	40.5
20. Super Bowl XVII	1/30/83	40.5
21. Super Bowl XXI	1/25/87	40.0
22. Super Bowl XVI	1/24/84	40.0
23. Super Bowl XXXIII	1/31/99	39.9
24. Super Bowl XXIX	1/29/95	39.4
25. Super Bowl XIX	1/20/85	39.4

Source: Based on cumulative data from A. C. Nielsen as of February 6, 2006.

*Numbers refer to the average number of households tuned in to the program from the start to the end of the telecast; average telecast for a Super Bowl game is about 210 minutes (although it contains less than 15 minutes of football action).

[†]Telecasts on these days featured women's figure skating—specifically, the programs skated by Nancy Kerrigan and Tonya Harding.

in U.S. history have been Super Bowls, that the cost of advertising on the *top* sport events is generally much higher than it is for other types of programs ($2.5 million for a thirty-second slot during the 2006 Super Bowl), that sports events involve minimal production costs, and that they have relatively predictable ratings. Even though there are cases when television companies lose money on sports, profits are generally good. Furthermore, regular sports programming is a platform to promote other programs and boost ratings during the rest of the week; and it enhances the image and legitimacy of television among people who watch little other than sports.

As choices for sports television viewing have increased, audiences have fragmented and ratings for many sports have declined, even as the total number of people watching television sports has remained relatively steady. This means that rights fees for the very large events will remain high, but fees for other events, including "special-interest" events (such as bowling, in-line skating championships, and international skiing races) will be limited. When interest in special events is especially strong among particular viewers, pay-per-view (PPV) sports programming pushes rights fees to high levels, as in the case of championship boxing bouts. PPV can generate massive revenues, but events must be chosen selectively because most people are not willing to pay upfront for a single event on television. In the meantime, pay TV has become part of people's lives in the form of subscription fees for cable and satellite connections and special sports channels and packages. Such subscription fees in the United States increased over 400 percent between 1985 and 2005, partly due to rights fees paid by cable and satellite companies to televise sports.

Finally, sports programming has been used as a centerpiece for the global expansion of emerging sport networks. For example, in 1994, Rupert Murdoch, owner of the Fox Television Network, successfully used the coverage of sports to leverage his acquisition of local television affiliates around the United States and thereby compete with ABC, CBS, and NBC. Murdoch also used sports coverage as part of a global expansion strategy. He has been successful, and his News Corp conglomerate is the most powerful media organization in the world. Other corporations have used their ownership of sports rights and programming as a key component of their mergers and acquisitions in the entertainment, news, sports, television, and Internet industries. This influences the sports programs that we see and *don't* see, what we hear and *don't* hear in commentary, the sites that we visit on the Internet, and the corporate messages presented in connection with athletes, teams, events, and sport places. More important, it has implications for the viability of democracy around the world because democracy depends on the free flow of information from diverse sources. When only only a few corporations control the media, the flow of ideas follows the channels constructed by corporate executives.

Sports and the Media: A Relationship Fueled by Economics and Ideology

Commercial spectator sports depend heavily on the media although noncommercial sports continue to exist and often thrive without media coverage. Similarly, some media companies that publish daily newspapers in the United States and produce television programs depend on sports to generate circulation and viewer ratings.

When large corporations control the media, the interdependence of sports and the media revolves around revenue streams and profits. Sports generate identifiable audiences that can be cold to capitalists seeking consumers for products and services. In turn, the media generate revenues for sport organizations and create sport-related images, which can be sold in connection with everything from coffee mugs and credit cards to shoes and soccer balls.

Since the 1970s, global economic factors have intensified the interdependence between commercial sports and the media. Major transnational corporations have needed vehicles to develop global name recognition, cultural legitimacy, and product familiarity. They also want to promote ideologies that support a way of life based on consumption, competition, and individual achievement. Media sports offer global corporations a means of meeting these needs: Certain sport events attract worldwide attention; satellite technology takes television signals around the world; sport images are associated with recognizable symbols and pleasurable experiences by billions of people; sports and athletes usually can be presented in politically safe ways by linking them with local identities and then using them to market products, values, and lifestyles related to local cultures or popular forms of global culture. Therefore, powerful transnational corporations now spend billions of dollars annually to sponsor the media coverage of sports, especially on television (it will be the Internet in the future). This in turn gives global media companies significant power over sports worldwide (see figure 12.3)

An important source of corporate sponsorship money for sports comes from the alcohol and tobacco industries. For them, the sports media are key vehicles for presenting and promoting their products in connection with activities defined as healthy by most people around the world. This enables them to present positive corporate and brand images, which they hope will counteract negative images about their products. We find these images most frequently in print media and stadium signage. They regularly appear in the prime advertising space of sports magazines and on the surfaces of stadiums and other facilities that host car, dog, and horse races. This is important to tobacco and alcohol companies because their advertising has been banned on major television networks in some nations. A side benefit for these companies is that when they pay large amounts of advertising money to sports magazines, such as *Sports Illustrated*, they know that there will be few, if any, critical articles published about tobacco and drinking in connection with sports.

Finally, many male executives of large media corporations are dedicated sports fans, and they

FIGURE 12.3 A few powerful global media companies control most of the media representations of sports worldwide. This has serious implications for what sports we see or don't see, especially in developing nations. Some people wonder what this will mean in the long run, whereas others don't give it much thought as they watch what the media re-present.

like to be associated with sports as sponsors. Masculine culture is deeply embedded in most of the corporations that they control, and they use their sponsorship money to receive VIP (very important person) treatment at sports events. Furthermore, they use sport events to entertain clients, fellow executives, and friends, and pay all the bills with company credit cards. This combination of masculine ideology and government-supported tax deductions for sport entertainment in the United States is a key factor in the media dependence on sports.

The long-time marriage of sports and the media is clearly held together and strengthened by vast amounts of money from corporations whose executives see sports as tools for promoting profits and ideologies consistent with their personal and corporate interests. Ideology is a key factor in the sport–media marriage. This is not a relationship based solely on money, but its goal is to produce many offspring who will embrace capitalist expansion and become obsessive consumers.

This enables the sport–media couple to maintain its power and wealth long into the future.

IMAGES AND NARRATIVES IN MEDIA SPORTS

To say that sports are "mediated" is to say that they are re-presented to audiences through selected images and/or narratives. A growing number of people who study sports in society do research that involves digging into these selected images and narratives to identify the ideas or themes on which they are based. As they do their digging, they assume that media sports are symbolic constructions, much like Hollywood action films, television soap operas, and Disney cartoons (Andrews and Jackson, 2001; Crawford, 2004; McCullagh, 2000; Rowe, 2004a, 2004b; Wenner, 1998; Whannel, 2002).

To say that a telecast of an American football game is a symbolic construction means that it re-presents the ideas that certain people have about football, values, social life, and their relationships with the viewing audience. Although each of us interprets media images and narratives in different ways, many people use mediated sports as reference points as they form, revise, and extend their ideas about sports, social life, and social relations.

Because media sports are part of everyday experience in today's societies, it is important to consider the following questions:

1. How are sports constructed in and through the media?
2. What ideological themes underlie the images and narratives re-presented in media sports?
3. Does consuming media sports have an effect on our choices and actions in our everyday lives?

How Do the Media Construct Sports?

When media are privately owned and organized to make financial profits, sports are selected for coverage on the basis of their entertainment value and revenue-generating potential. Media images and narratives are presented to provide as much of the event as possible and fit the perceived interests of the audience and sponsors. Sports that are difficult to cover profitably usually are ignored by the media or covered only with selected highlights, emphasizing spectacular and heroic injuries or achievements.

Sports magazines and the sports sections of newspapers provide scores, statistics, accounts of big plays and individual heroics, and behind-the-scenes stories; they use photos to depict action. Television coverage focuses on the ball (puck and so on) and individual athletes, especially those who are currently winning the game, match, meet, or race. Television announcers provide narratives designed to entertain a mass audience. The major differences between print and broadcast media are summarized in table 12.3.

Sports media generally present images and narratives that hype sports by exaggerating the spectacular, inventing and focusing on rivalries, and manufacturing reasons that events are important. Furthermore, they strive to create and maintain the celebrity status of athletes and teams. Cultural studies scholar Garry Crawford explains the strategy used in this process:

> The mass media construction of celebrity often lacks depth of character, as figures are frequently painted in one-dimensional terms. . . . Much of the language used to describe sport stars . . . draws on the narrative of melodrama. Heroes rise and fall, villains are defeated, and women play out their roles as supporting cast members to men's central dramatic roles. (2004, p. 133)

Even the villains can be redeemed when they demonstrate that they are heroic warriors and

Table 12.3 Differences between newspaper/magazine and radio/television coverage of sports

Newspaper/Magazine Coverage	Radio/Television Coverage
• Emphasizes information and interpretation	• Emphasizes entertainment
• Offers previews and summaries of events	• Offers play-by-play images and narratives
• Provides written representation of events	• Provides real-time representations of events
• Success depends on credibility	• Success depends on hype and visual action
• Highlights facts and dominant ideology	• Highlights heroic plays and dominant ideology
• Most likely to provide criticism of sports and sport personalities	• Most likely to provide support for sports and sport personalities

Source: Based on material in Koppett (1994).

Image and Narrative Barriers
From a Special Interest Story to a Sports Story

Athletes with a disability receive little or no media coverage. The Paralympics, for example, have seldom been televised or covered in newspapers in the United States. Some coverage occurs in Canada and Western Europe, but the Paralympics occurs only once every four years. World Championships and other major events receive no mainstream-media coverage. Most people who make decisions about media coverage don't take disability sports seriously because the events would receive low audience ratings and therefore, wouldn't attract sponsors. The traditional belief is that covering athletes with a disability is a poor commercial risk. Additionally, most media people have never interacted or played sports with people who have disabilities, so they lack the words and experiences that would enable them to provide the kind of coverage that might build a media audience.

Research shows that when coverage does occur in the mainstream media, athletes with a disability often are portrayed in one of two ways: as "poster people" deserving pity for their impairments or as "supercrips" who have heroically overcome disabilities (Brittain, 2004). A closer look at media images and narratives indicates that re-presentations often fall into one of the following categories:

Patronizing: *"Aren't they marvelous!"*
Curiosity: *"Do you think she can really do that?"*
Tragedy: *"On that fateful day, his life was changed forever."*
Inspiration: *"She's a true hero and a model for all of us."*
Mystification: *"I can't believe he just did that!"*

Pity: *"Give her a hand for trying so hard."*
Surprise: *"Stay tuned to see physical feats you've never imagined!"*

Images and narratives organized around these themes construct disability in terms of a medical model—focused on personal deficiencies that must be overcome by individuals (see Breaking Barriers, pp. 50–51, chapter 2). This ignores issues about why particular social meanings are given to disabilities and how those meanings cause many of the problems faced by people with particular impairments (Brittain, 2004; Smith and Thomas, 2005). Consequently, the coverage does little to challenge the widespread belief that disabilities are abnormalities and that people with disabilities have one-dimensional identities.

Despite misguided representations in the media, most athletes with a disability would choose distorted coverage rather than no coverage at all. They want to be acknowledged and reaffirmed for their athletic competence and hope that becoming visible through the media will weaken and break down stereotypes. Visibility gives them an opportunity to challenge traditional medical discourse about disability and make people aware of the need for maximizing access and inclusion in all spheres of society.

Developing a media audience, says Jil Gravink, begins at the local, recreational level. Gravink is the founder and director of Northeast Passage, an organization that develops community-based programs to increase the relevance of disability sports among people with disabilities and among the general population. The programs provide opportunities for people with a disability and able-bodied people to interact,

commentators reframe them as "loyal blue-collar players"—"willing to take figurative bullets for their teammates"—and "always being there when the chips are down."

The major media also emphasize elite sport competition (Crawford, 2004; Lowes, 1999). For

example, U.S. newspapers and television networks increased their coverage of professional sports through the twentieth century and decreased coverage of amateur sports, except for big-time college football and men's basketball. This shift was accompanied by a growing emphasis on the

This wheelchair basketball program is similar to many local sports programs for people with a disability. It brings together people with particular disabilities. This is important for developing skills, self-confidence, and establishing relationships with others. When programs also foster the full inclusion of people with disabilities into the general community, they break down stereotypes and disability sports "move from a special interest story to a sport story." (*Source:* Rodolfo Gonzalez, *Rocky Mountain News*)

play sports, and identify one another in terms of multiple characteristics and abilities.

Gravink explains that only when average people with disabilities play sports and become fully integrated into the community can disability sports "move from a special interest story to a sport story" (in Joukowsky and Rothstein, 2002a, p. 98). Then poster people and supercrips will be exposed for the myths they are.

importance of winning and heroic actions instead of other factors associated with sports and sport participation. The result is that media audiences consume carefully selected and edited versions of sports. Re-presentations are constructed to gain the support of corporate sponsors and people in a mass audience. It is important to study this "construction process" because popular ideas about sports are heavily informed by the images and narratives in media sports. Furthermore, the ideological themes underlying these images and messages influence popular ideas about social relations and social life in general. This is discussed below and in the Breaking Barriers box on pages 426–427.

What Ideological Themes Underlie Media Images and Narratives?

Reality is so complex that it cannot be represented in the media without selecting particular images and narratives from a vast array of possibilities (Knoppers and Elling, 2004). The traditional media are partly like windows through which we view what others choose to put in our range of sight and hear what others choose to say to us. Therefore, the only way we can avoid being duped is to be critical media consumers. In most cases, this means learning to identify the ideologies that guide others as they construct media representations for us. In the case of sports, the most central ideologies that influence what we see and hear are those related to success, gender, race and ethnicity, nationalism, individualism, teamwork, aggression, and consumption.

Success Ideology   Media coverage of sports in the United States emphasizes success through competition, hard work, assertiveness, domination over others, obedience to authority, and big plays such as home runs, long touchdown passes, and single-handed goals. The idea that success can be based on empathy, support for others, sharing resources, autonomy, intrinsic satisfaction, personal growth, compromise, incremental changes, or the achievement of equality is not incorporated into narratives or images selected for commentary.

Media representations exaggerate the importance of competitive rivalries as well as winning and losing in athletes' lives. For example, ESPN has organized its coverage of the X Games around the competitive quest for medals when, in fact, many of the athletes and the spectators at the events are not very concerned about competition or medals (Florey, 1998; Honea, 2005).

Athletes in the X Games and similar events enjoy the external rewards that come with winning, and they certainly want to demonstrate their competence, but they also emphasize expression and creativity as more important than scores and competitive outcomes. Furthermore, their friendships with other competitors are more important than media-hyped rivalries. However, media coverage highlights competitive success because it is valued in the culture as a whole and it is easy to use to attract sponsors and consumers.

The success ideology emphasized in U.S. media sports is less apparent in media coverage in other cultures. Narratives in the United States focus on winners, losers, and final scores. Even silver and bronze Olympic medals are inferred to be consolation prizes, and games for third place are seldom played anymore, much less covered by the media. The "We're number 1" ideology so common among Americans is seldom used as a media focus in other nations where tie scores are not seen as being like "kissing your sister."

Sportswriters and announcers in the United States focus on "shootouts," sudden death playoffs, dominating others, and big plays or big hits. Rare are references to learning, enjoyment, and competing *with* others, even when players see their participation in these terms, and many do. Thus, the media don't "tell it like it is" as much as they tell it like people interested in productivity in the form of competitive success want to see and hear it. This ideological bias does not mean that most people do not enjoy media sports. Enjoyment is central and it drives media sport consumption. However, there are many ways to enjoy sports, and the media highlight the ways that fit popular and corporate interests simultaneously. Discovering other ways to enjoy sports is left to individuals and groups, who are curious enough to seek alternatives to commercialized media sports.

Gender Ideology   Masculinity rules in media sports. Men's sports receive about 90 percent of the coverage in all the media, and images and narratives tend to reproduce traditional ideas and beliefs about gender (Duncan and Messner, 1998, 2005). For example, after buying rights to telecast National Hockey League games in 2005–2007, the vice president of programming for OLN (Outdoor Life Network) said that OLN was a "very male-oriented network" and they wanted to emphasize competition by showing sports that involved "man versus man, man versus nature, man versus beast" (in Bechtel and Cannella, 2005, p. 17).

Coverage of women's sports is not a priority in the media, except for the Olympics, figure skating events, major tennis and golf tournaments, and a few professional and college basketball games. Soccer received attention in 1999 when the U.S. Women's World Cup champions were described as the "(middle-class, white) girls next door" and "babe city" and as people wondered about the meaning of Brandi Chastain's spontaneous removal of her jersey after scoring the winning goal in the World Cup. But women's soccer has received little coverage since 2003.

Overall, the coverage of women's sports in major newspapers has increased since the mid-1990s, but it remains less than 15 percent of the sports section of U.S. newspapers and even less in most other countries. Sports magazines have been notoriously slow to cover female athletes and women's sports although they frequently have images of women as sex objects in ads for cigarettes, liquor, and other products (Bishop, 2003). This pattern of under-representation of women's sports in the media exists around the world (see Urquhart and Crossman, 1999). For example, in 2001 the British Women's Sport Foundation reported that women received less than 3 percent of sports coverage in the national tabloids; only 2 percent of the sport photos pictured female athletes, and on most days there was no coverage of women's sports (www.wsf.org.uk/informed/campaign_for_coverage.php).

Progress has occurred in some cases, but it is uneven and does not represent a pattern of consistent growth. For example, *USA Today* now publishes a multipage section on the NCAA basketball tournament, with nearly 25 percent of the space devoted to the women's tournament and female athletes and coaches. Men receive nearly 50 percent of the space, and the remaining 30 percent is devoted to advertising. However, this is an exception to everyday patterns. Everyday coverage of women's sports continues to make up about 5 to 15 percent of total sports coverage across all media. A longitudinal study of samples of the sport news on the ABC, CBS, and NBC stations in Los Angeles and on ESPN's *Sports Center* and Fox's *Southern California Sports Report* indicates that between 1989 and 2004 the coverage given to women's sports peaked in 1999 at 8.7 percent and fell to 6.3 percent in 2004. Women were featured in less than 3 percent of the highlights shown on the ESPN and Fox programs in 2004, the year of the Olympic Games in Athens (Duncan and Messner, 2005). Overall, the proportion of coverage given to women's sports in 2004 was about the same as it was in 1989, despite significant increases in women's sport participation over those years.

Women's sports are televised more than they were in the early 1990s, especially now that cable stations are dedicated to sports generally and college sports in particular. But the proportion of coverage given to women remains at about 15 percent of all television sports programming. The women's sports covered regularly are tennis, gymnastics, figure skating, and golf. These are traditionally seen as sports emphasizing grace, balance, coordination, and aesthetics, all of which are attributes consistent with traditional images of femininity. This pattern is not as clear as it has been in the past, but it remains. For example, tennis receives over 40 percent of all coverage given to women's sports on the major networks although this varies depending on the physical appearance of the high-profile players. When Maria Sharapova won the Wimbledon Championship in 2004, she received extensive coverage. A Fox announcer introduced one segment of a sport show by saying, "She's young, she's talented, and very beautiful, but can [she] stay focused tonight"; another sport news "teaser" before a commercial said, "They slapped her on a billboard that read 'the closer you get, the hotter it gets'" (in Duncan and Messner, 2005, p. 15). Despite some male announcers being unable to describe Sharapova as they describe Derek Jeter or other physically attractive male athletes, most television coverage of women's sports now takes female athletes and their events more seriously than they did in the 1980s. Sport talk shows still make women the butt of jokes, but this is accepted only among men who have trouble accepting women as athletes and like to pretend that they are still in the locker room having adolescent male fantasies about "girls."

Olympic media coverage in the United States highlights women gymnasts, swimmers, and divers in the Summer Games and women figure skaters and skiers in the Winter Games. Individual sports continue to be given priority over team sports in the coverage, and women's figure skating is the most frequently televised women's sport event. For example, during NBC's coverage of the 2004 Olympic Games in Athens, women's basketball, softball, and soccer received no prime-time coverage, despite record-setting teams and the last games of soccer legend Mia Hamm and her World Cup teammates. The exception to this is that the two-person bikini-clad beach volleyball teams were aired regularly in prime time (White, 2004).

The men's sports most often covered in the media emphasize physical strength, speed, size, and the use of physical force and intimidation to dominate opponents—all qualities consistent with traditional images of masculinity. For example, football is by far the most popular televised men's

Football is the most popular media sport in the United States. The coverage reproduces traditional gender ideology in the culture. (*Source:* University of Colorado Media Relations)

sport in the United States, and television coverage emphasizes traditional notions of masculinity (Mihoces, 2002; Weisman, 2000).

Coverage of women's sports through the 1980s and most of the 1990s contained commentaries that often highlighted the personal characteristics of the athletes such as their attractiveness, their spouses and children, their domestic interests and skills, and their vulnerabilities and weaknesses (Eastman and Billings, 1999; Weiler and Higgs, 1999). Television commentators for women's sports have in the past referred to female athletes by their first names and as "girls" or "ladies" although this pattern has changed as researchers have called attention to its sexist implications.

Commentators for men's sports seldom refer to male athletes by their first names, unless they are black, and almost never call them "boys" or "gentlemen." It is assumed that playing sports turns boys into men, and it is hoped that playing sports does not keep women from being ladies. Similarly, references to physical strength have been much more common in commentaries about male athletes although women clearly demonstrate strength and power, even in sports such as figure skating, golf, and tennis. A recent exception to this has been the coverage given to Venus and Serena Williams. After white media personnel were able to look beyond the beads in their hair and the fact that they did not present themselves as if they were raised in country club settings, they began to refer to their strength, power, and speed. Similar comments have been made about Jennifer Caprioti although the focus on the physical characteristics of the Williams sisters is unprecedented in women's tennis coverage.

Men's sport events often are promoted or described as if they had special historical importance, whereas women's sports events usually are promoted in a less dramatic manner. Men's events usually are unmarked by references to gender and represented as *the* events, whereas women's events almost always are referred to as *women's* events. For instance, there has always been "The

World Cup" and "The Women's World Cup" in soccer coverage. This terminology reflects the low priority given to women's sports in all media. For example, when *Sports Illustrated* published in 2002 a list of the best 100 sport books of all time, only three books about women's sports were on the list: one on a high school basketball team (number 65), one on figure skating (number 81), and one on figure skating and gymnastics (number 100) (McEntegart et al., 2002).

ERASING HOMOSEXUALITY Homosexuality is ignored in nearly all media coverage, whereas heterosexuality is regularly acknowledged directly and indirectly among men and women in sports. Heterosexual female athletes are constantly shown with husbands, children, fiancés, boyfriends, and dates; heterosexual men are featured with wives in the *Sports Illustrated* swimsuit edition although their heterosexuality is so widely taken for granted that it is mentioned only in passing. Gay athletes are not erased as much as they are assumed not to exist. Lesbian images, however, are carefully erased from coverage, even though the partners of players and coaches are known and visible to many spectators (Collins, 2004). Lesbian relationships are ignored for fear of offending media audiences.

Lesbian athletes in golf, tennis, and basketball are never profiled in ways that acknowledge partners or certain aspects of their lifestyles—those parts of their personal stories are not told. In media-constructed sport reality, lesbians and gay men in sports generally are invisible unless they publicly come "out" as gay. Even then, they are marginalized in coverage. As media studies scholar Pam Creedon notes, "Homosexuality doesn't sell" (1998, p. 96). Meanwhile, heterosexual athletes and their partners are discussed and pictured in everything from the *Sports Illustrated* swimsuit edition to the television coverage of postgame victory celebrations, and nobody accuses these heterosexual athletes of pushing their values and agendas on others. Living in a heterosexual-dominated culture is especially difficult for female coaches and players who would like to acknowledge the support that they have received from longtime partners. Their partners, instead of sharing the moment in public like heterosexual spouses often do, sit in the stands or at home wondering if their very existence could jeopardize their partners' careers. Completely unknown are the men who discreetly watch their male partners win Super Bowls and World Series titles.

MEDIA ORGANIZATIONS ARE GENDERED The patterns associated with gender have been slow to change partly because sports media organizations in all societies are "gendered institutions" (Creedon, 1998). They have been structured and scheduled around men's sports. The work routines and assignments of sport reporters have been established around the coverage of men's events to such an extent that covering of women's events often requires changes in institutionalized patterns of sports media work. Furthermore, the *vast* majority of sports media personnel are men, and the highest-status assignments in sports media are those that deal with men's sports.

Even female reporters and announcers know that their upward mobility in the sports media industry demands that they cover men's events in much the same ways that men cover them. If they insist on covering only women's events or if they are assigned only to women's events, they will not advance up the corporate ladder in media organizations (Coventry, 2004). Advancement also may be limited if they insist on covering men's sports in new ways that don't reaffirm the "correctness" of the coverage patterns and styles developed by men. Although women in the print media regularly cover men's sports, few women ever have done regular commentary for men's sports in the electronic media apart from occasional "sideline reports" when they are expected to look cute and talk to the guys as if they were at a "frat house," obtaining the inside story with no girls or women around (White, 2005). An exception to this pattern occurred in 2005 when

Suzyn Waldman was hired by a New York radio station and became the first women to be a full time "color commentator" in Major League Baseball (MLB). This occurred after nearly 20 years of being a radio beat reporter for the New York Yankees.

Female reporters who cover men's sports are more readily accepted in the locker rooms of men's teams than they were in the past although male athletes and coaches have been very protective of this masculinized space. Changes have occurred partly because men have discovered clever ways to maintain privacy, such as wearing a robe and having designated interview times— just as female athletes have always done when male reporters cover their events. However, it took the men nearly two decades to think of wearing a robe because deeply rooted gender ideology often impedes one's ability to think creatively.

When it comes to issues of masculinity, most sports coverage uses images and narratives that reproduce dominant ideas about manhood. The television broadcasts of the NFL, for instance, are presented as soap operas for men. The vocabularies and storylines construct a symbolic male community that draws meaning from the culture of big-time men's spectator sports and allows men to apply those meanings to themselves in ways that women spectators cannot do, even if they are dedicated fans.

The sports coverage most often consumed by boys in the United States depicts aggression and violence as normal and exciting, portrays athletes who play in pain as heroes, uses military metaphors and terminology, and highlights conflict between individuals and teams. Women are seldom seen except when portrayed as sex objects, cheerleaders, spectators, and supportive spouses and mothers on the sidelines.

Overall, gender ideology informs media representations of sports. This is highlighted in the box "Meet the Press." However, it is important to note that few of us accept media representations at face value. We make sense of representations in our own terms although we are heavily influenced by the cultures in which we have been socialized. When we have special knowledge or personal connections with a sport or the athletes involved, we often give our own meanings to media representations, even if we are not critical in our assessments of them (Bruce, 2007; van Sterkenburg and Knoppers, 2004).

Racial and Ethnic Ideology Just as gender ideology influences media coverage, so does racial and ethnic ideology and the stereotypes associated with it (Davis and Harris, 1998; van Sterkenburg and Knoppers, 2004). For example, Grantland Rice, often identified by white journalists as the best sportswriter of the early twentieth century, described black heavyweight boxing champion Joe Louis as the "brown cobra." Millions of people read his words during the 1930s when he wrote that Joe Louis brought into the boxing ring "the speed of the jungle, the instinctive speed of the wild" (in Mead, 1985, p. 91). Ideology and stereotypes changed during the second half of the twentieth century, and white announcers commonly described black athletes as having natural abilities, good instincts, unique physical attributes, and tendencies to be undisciplined players; references to "jungle" and "the wild" were replaced with "ghetto." At the same time, they described white athletes as hard working, intelligent, highly disciplined, and driven by character rather than instincts (Davis and Harris, 1998).

Research in the 1970s and 1980s discredited the assumed factual basis of racial and ethnic stereotypes at the same time that media studies identified the ways that ideology influenced sport stories and commentaries, particularly in reference to black athletes. This made journalists and commentators increasingly aware of the need to avoid words, phrases, and inferences based on stereotypical ideas and beliefs (Sabo et al., 1996). People in the print media chose their words more carefully, and broadcasters doing live commentary on talk radio and during games became sensitive to the racial implications of what they said. But making these changes was difficult for media

people who accepted dominant racial ideology and never viewed it critically or from the perspectives of blacks, Latinos, Asians, and Native Americans. Therefore, some made mistakes and a few were fired for them. For example, in mid-2005, a white sport talk-radio host was fired from KNBR in San Francisco when he complained that the Giants baseball team was losing games because its "brain-dead Caribbean hitters" lacked the discipline to avoid swinging at bad pitches and because Felipe Alou, the team's seventy-year-old Latino manager, had a mind that had "turned to Cream of Wheat." Thinking that these comments by a white radio host were provocative, the white station manager approved the idea of playing them repeatedly on the following day. The other white host on the show mocked Felipe Alou's response to his cohost's comments. Neither the hosts nor the program manager knew anything about the perspectives or experiences of Latino players or the Latino manager who had endured blatant racism as an all-star player on the Giants forty-five years earlier. Most white listeners were outraged by the firings, apparently thinking that stupidity and a lack of knowledge of the people being covered in sports were not sufficient reasons for job termination.

Avoiding stereotypes and covering racial and ethnic relations in an informed way are two different things. Sport coverage today pretends that race and ethnicity don't exist; it is assumed that everyone in sports faces the same challenges and odds for success. But in actuality, race and ethnicity influence experiences and perspectives to such an extent that people cannot talk about them without discovering real, meaningful, and socially important racial and ethnic differences in what they think and feel. Ignoring this story about real differences allows whites in the media and media audiences to be comfortably color blind and deny the legacy and continuing relevance of skin color and cultural heritage in American society and in sports. At the same time, blacks, Latinos, Asian Americans, and Native Americans are reminded that acceptance in the dominant

reflect on **SPORTS**	**Meet the Press** *It's Not Always Easy for Female Athletes*

Johnny Miller is a former pro golfer. In July 2002, he was the NBC analyst covering the U.S. Women's Open. Julie Inkster, a forty-two-year-old veteran of the women's tour and winner of many tournaments, had just won the Open, the most prestigious event of the season. Miller met her as she was declared the winner and said excitedly, "It's big stuff when you win at 42. You're supposed to be home cooking meals at 42—you'd think, for most women." Apparently, when Miller looked at this champion golfer, he saw a mother and wife, standing in the kitchen preparing meals for her two children and husband. His vision was blurred by an ideology that distracted him as he interviewed a long-time champion golfer who had just won the biggest tournament of the year.

Miller knew he'd made a mistake, but ideology is powerful, especially when you talk or act spontaneously. Inkster was gracious in her response, saying that she had achieved balance in her life by coordinating her career and family. She was tactful as she dealt with Miller's gendered view of her, and she focused on her excitement about playing better golf than any woman in the world during the previous three days.

A few months before Miller interviewed Inkster, Tiffany Milbrett, the best soccer player in the United States during the 2002 professional Women's United Soccer Association season was being photographed for a magazine story about her. During the photo shoot, the photographer asked her to remove her bra. Milbrett was shocked at the request. Without hesitating, she reminded those at the shoot that "I'm not a model. I'm an athlete. I only want to make money doing my trade. The rest I don't really care for. I don't give a rat's ass about being sexy" (in Adelson, 2002, p. 76).

Like Milbrett, many young female athletes face a dilemma when people in the media insist on sexualizing them. They must decide if they should just play sports and hope they will be rewarded as athletes or if

they should also present their bodies in sexualized terms to attract attention, sponsors, and media support. Milbrett decided against allowing her body to be sexualized, but other female athletes either conform to or exploit expectations based on traditional ideas and beliefs about what women should be.

When Anita Marks, the quarterback for the Miami Fury in the Independent Women's Football League, explained her appearance in *Playboy* magazine, she said, "Women in sport need to have two personas. What they believe is right is not going to make them money. It isn't going to make you famous" (in Adelson, 2002, p. 76). Marks let the photographers call the shots although she chose from a limited and highly gendered set of alternatives to do what she hoped would make her famous.

Brandi Chastain took a different approach when she posed nude in *Gear* magazine. She stressed that she had "worked her ass off" to get her body in shape and was proud to have her physical strength and beauty represented in the media. Some female athletes agree with Chastain, and others do not.

Many people find it difficult to analyze these issues. In the case of Miller's interview with Inkster, is it always a problem when people in the media view athletic achievements in connection with other important identities, relationships, and activities in an athlete's life? Are there ways to interview athletes and talk about their lives without letting questions and comments be shaped by ideologies that have disadvantaged entire categories of people in society?

In the case of Milbrett, Marks, Chastain, and other female athletes, such as racecar driver Danica Patrick and tennis player Maria Sharapova, what are the guidelines and limits for media representations of athletes' bodies? More to the point, who should determine those guidelines and limits, and what can be done to increase the chances that those determinations will be based on critically informed choices? Tiffany Milbrett

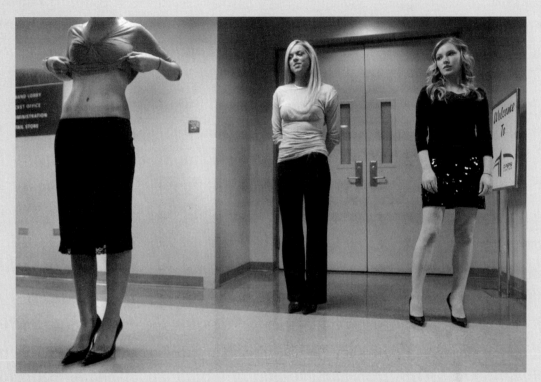

The gendered choices faced by athletes are also faced by women who apply for cheerleading and dance teams in men's professional sports. The bodies of these women are being assessed to see if they meet the criteria of the "judges" for an NBA team. If they do, they will be allowed to try out. In the process, the women view one another in objectified ways, as this photo illustrates. If these women had the power to choose how they are included and represented in sports, would they choose this? (Evan Semon; Rocky Mountain News/Polaris)

"doesn't give a rat's ass" about being sexy, at least in front of a camera under conditions that she had not chosen. But, if other athletes choose to be represented as sexy in the media, should they be targets of criticism and defined as sex objects instead of athletes?

These questions are best answered if we consider issues of power and ideology. If female athletes had the power to control how they are represented in the media and they critically understood the importance of media images in our culture, it would be much easier for them to meet the press. But that leaves the toughest question unanswered: How do women gain that power in sports and society? *What do you think?*

culture requires them to "be like whites" in how they think, talk, and act. They understand that to be embraced by the media and white fans they should smile in accommodating ways on camera and during interviews, just like Magic Johnson and Michael Jordan did so effectively for many years (Davis and Harris, 1998). But they also admire athletes who express their racial or ethnic identities and "don't forget where they came from." This creates tension for ethnic minority athletes and unique social dynamics in sports where players are racially and ethnically mixed. This is a newsworthy story, but it would make many people, especially white sports fans, uncomfortable, and it would be difficult for most journalists to tell. But as long as it remains untold, white privilege in sports will persist without being recognized, and anyone who does talk about it will be accused of "playing the race card."

IDEOLOGY AND OVERLOOKING WHITENESS
Media coverage unwittingly reaffirms dominant racial ideology when whiteness is overlooked. This is best illustrated with an example unrelated to sports: When two young men killed twelve students and a teacher at Colorado's Columbine High School in 1999, people in the media overlooked the whiteness of the killers, even though the shooters in the twelve preceding mass killings in U.S. schools during the 1990s were white males. Whiteness was never an issue in the coverage because it is overlooked in a white-centered culture to the point that people don't even "see" it. Therefore, people did not make generalizations about the problem of violence among white male teens, and nobody talked about crossing the street to avoid a white male teen on the sidewalk. However, if the two killers had been black, Latino, Asian, or Native American, the coverage and audience responses would have made race or ethnicity *the* issue, and all other factors would have been given lower priority. This is how ideology influences coverage and stifles critical questions about the accuracy of media representations of reality.

When the media ignore the dynamics of living in a white-dominated, white-identified, and white-centered culture, they unwittingly reproduce racial and ethnic stereotypes. For example, when black male athletes are represented as deviant, angry, and physically powerful and intimidating, some whites in society perceive them differently than they might perceive white male athletes represented in similar ways. Dominant racial ideology in the United States is deeply grounded in widespread (1) awe of the physical movements and "rhythm" of black male bodies and (2) fears of their imagined sexual prowess and physical power (see chapter 9, p. 296). This means that seeing a powerful and potentially violent black male athlete reaffirms, in the minds of some people, long-held ideas and beliefs about all black men. This is different from the ways that a powerful and potentially violent white male athlete is seen. Representations of white males are not given racial meanings, nor are the representations used to make generalizations about all white men. Social theorist Patricia Hill Collins (2004) suggests that these dynamics are in part related to the fact that black men are 7 percent of the U.S. population and 50 percent of the U.S. prison population.

Pretending to be color blind in a culture where a skin color–based racial ideology has existed for the last three centuries is a sure way to guarantee that white privilege is seamlessly incorporated into the media coverage of sports. It allows the sports media to avoid asking why nearly all sports at the high school, college, and professional level are exclusively white. It allows the editors at *Sports Illustrated* to not even think of featuring an article titled "What Ever Happened to the Black and Brown Athletes?" (see Price, 1997), even when they live in communities where hundreds of high school and college teams in swimming, volleyball, softball, tennis, golf, soccer, lacrosse, rowing, gymnastics, wrestling, and many other sports are *all* white. Therefore, they never ask questions about issues of residential segregation and issues of income and wealth inequality that deeply influence who plays what sports in the United States today. When they golf at their clubs they don't wonder why eight years after Tiger Woods won his first major tournament that there are fewer African American, Asian American, Native American, and Latino golfers than there were fifteen years before Woods played in his first PGA tournament. Whiteness is ignored because to acknowledge it would make too many people uncomfortable.

In 2005 the sports media that covered the NCAA's new rule about prohibiting the use of team names and mascots that were defined as "hostile and abusive" by many Native Americans seldom explored why and under what circumstances white male college students should be allowed to engage in ethnic cross-dressing as they represented their universities. Who are these white students who serve as "warriors" and "chiefs," what experiences do they have with Native American cultures, what books have they read and what courses have they taken about Native Americans, what reservations have they visited, what Native languages do they speak, what particular Native American culture do they represent, and what do they know of that culture and the people who live it today and incorporate it into their identities? A white-centered media does not ask such questions of fellow whites, and if they were asked, many would complain that "political correctness" is ruining a long accepted, morally unquestionable (white) way of life that they see in color-blind terms.

Ethnic studies scholars refer to this new insistence that we should ignore skin color as racism that is based on completely denying the existence of the history and relevance of skin color and ethnicity in societies where they influence everything from the distribution of income and wealth to where and how people live (Bonilla-Silva, 2001, 2003; Brown et al., 2005; Doane and Bonilla-Silva, 2003). Color-blind coverage in sports misses a significant dimension of sport reality and reproduces the racial and ethnic status quo. But it allows people to use sports as forms of social escapism, as whitewashed worlds devoid of the complex, messy issues that characterize real everyday life. In this way, the sports media don't "tell it like it is" as much as they tell it like many people want to hear it.

ETHNICITY AND NATIONALITY   Themes related to ethnicity and nationality also exist in sports media coverage. Although some sports reporters and broadcasters around the world are careful to avoid using ethnic and national stereotypes in their representations of athletes and teams, evidence suggests that subtle stereotypes regularly influence sports coverage (Mayeda, 1999; McCarthy et al., 2003; Sabo and Jensen, 1998; Sabo et al., 1996; van Sterkenburg and Knoppers, 2004). For example, some media coverage has portrayed Asian athletes as methodical, mechanical, machinelike, mysterious, industrious, self-disciplined, and intelligent. Their achievements are more often attributed to cognitive rather than physical abilities, and stereotypes about height and other physiological characteristics are sometimes used to explain success or failure in sports. Latinos, on the other hand, have been described as flamboyant, exotic, emotional, passionate, moody, and hot blooded (Blain et al., 1993).

The sports journalists most likely to avoid such stereotypes are those that understand the history, culture, and experiences of athletes. But this is a journalist's job, even if it is not taught in journalism courses or in professional development programs sponsored by newspapers and television companies. For example, when 26 percent of MLB players are Latino, it would be professionally responsible for media companies to hire bilingual sports reporters and broadcasters so that they could talk meaningfully with players whose lives on and off the field are not understood by most baseball fans. It would also be wise for a few journalists to learn Spanish or even Japanese so that they could access information and write or tell stories about players that no one else could.

MAKING CHANGES   The most effective way to reduce subtle forms of racial and ethnic bias in the media is to hire ethnic minority reporters, editors, photographers, writers, producers, directors, camerapersons, commentators, and statisticians (Rowe, 2004a, 2004b). Lip service is paid to this goal, and progress has been made in certain media, but members of racial and ethnic minorities are clearly underrepresented in most sports newsrooms, press boxes, broadcast booths, and media executive offices. This is unfortunate because ethnic diversity among people who represent sports through the media would enrich stories and provide multiple perspectives for understanding sports and the people who play and coach them. When ethnic diversity has existed, it has resulted in more accurate and insightful coverage (Thomas, 1996).

Many editors and producers are fond of saying that skin color is irrelevant to the quality of journalists, and most people agree with them. But if there are fewer than a half dozen Latino beat reporters in MLB and only a few black reporters covering the NBA with black players making up over 70 percent of the league, the *definition of quality* becomes an issue. Are experiences that enable a reporter to understand the backgrounds, orientations, and actions of players included in the definition of quality? It is important for a player to feel that a reporter understands who he is and how he views the world when he is interviewed? Is it important for the media to provide coverage from different vantage points, angles, and perspectives? If so, reporters and broadcasters defined as qualified should bring diverse ethnic perspectives to sports coverage.

In addition to critically examining the definition of quality used to hire people in sports media, current reporters and broadcasters must do their racial and ethnic homework if they wish to keep their jobs. This involves learning what it means to work in a white-dominated/identified/centered organization and cover sports organized around the values and experiences of white men. It involves learning to view the world through the eyes of the people whom you write and talk about. For whites, this means learning as much as possible about the history and heritage of everyone from athletes to owners and even reading classic books written by ethnic minority authors and recent research on race and ethnicity. Neither skin color nor gender precludes knowledge about sports or the people involved in them, but knowledge is based on a combination of experience and the richness of the perspectives one has to make sense of the ethnically and racially diverse social worlds that are covered by the media.

Other Ideological Themes in Media Sports Research using critical theories has identified other ideological themes around which images and narratives in media sports have been constructed. In addition to the three themes that we have already discussed (success, gender, and race and ethnicity), others include nationalism, individualism, teamwork, aggression, and consumption (Andrews and Jackson, 2001; Kinkema and Harris, 1998; Real, 1998; Rowe et al., 1998).

These themes should not surprise anyone who has consumed media sports in the United States. Images and narratives clearly emphasize *nationalism* and *national unity* grounded in traditional American loyalty and patriotism. In fact, the sports that were "invented" in the United States—football, basketball, and baseball—are the most widely televised sports in the country. Other sports are covered, but if they don't match traditional ideas about what it means to be an American, they don't receive priority coverage. When U.S. teams and athletes are competing against teams and athletes from other countries, events are usually framed in an us-versus-them format. When U.S. teams or athletes win, reporters and broadcasters declare proudly, "*We* won" (see chapter 13).

Media images and narratives also emphasize *individual efforts* to achieve competitive victories, even in the coverage of team sports. Games are promoted with announcements such as these: "Peyton Manning and his Colts are looking for revenge against Jim Brady and his Patriots," or "It's LeBron James against Carmelo Anthony as the Cavaliers meet the Nuggets." These promos emphasize the idea that individuals must take responsibility for what happens in their lives and that team failures can be traced to the failures and flaws of one or more individuals. This idea is central to the ideology of American individualism, which influences everything from the structure of our welfare system to the ways that employees are evaluated and rewarded in the economy: You are expected to make it on your own, and it is assumed that giving people support creates dependence and stifles initiative.

Images and narratives in sports coverage also stress *teamwork*, which usually means following a game plan developed by a coach/leader, being loyal to the team, and being willing to make sacrifices for the good of the team (Kinkema and Harris, 1998). Media coverage clearly identifies coaches as the organizers and controllers of teams. Commentators praise athletes as "team players" when they follow the game plan; similarly, they praise coaches for their ability to fit players into team roles that lead to victories. This ideological approach to teamwork matches the ideology underlying the American market economy and most American business organizations: Teamwork means loyalty to the organization and productivity under the direction of a leader-coach.

The importance of *mental* and *physical aggression* is another ideological theme around which images and narratives are constructed in media sports. Rough, aggressive play is assumed to be a sign of commitment and skill, and aggressive players are praised as "warriors" (Messner et al., 1999). The vocabulary stresses "bone-crushing hits" in football, "hard fouls" in basketball, and brushback pitches in baseball. These actions are represented as necessary parts of the game and as skills needed by players if they are to play the game well.

Scores during the nightly news are full of violent images: the Heat *annihilated* the Knicks, the Jets *destroyed* the Dolphins, the Blackhawks *scalped* the Bruins, Williams *crushed* Sharapova, and on and on. The scores sound like the results of military operations during a war. In fact, much of the language used in the media to represent sports in

"Yes, I KNOW you watch CSI *and* Alias, *but this hockey game contains real violence, so off to your room now!*"

....

FIGURE 12.4 This father distinguishes between fictional and real-life violence on television. If video games are rated for violent content, why isn't the same done for sport events in which the violence is real and has real consequences for players and their families?

the United States is taken from the realm of violence and warfare (see Figure 12.4). Aggression is celebrated, whereas kindness and sensitivity are seen as weakness.

This vocabulary clearly fits with the ideology that many Americans use to determine strategies in interpersonal, business, and international relations: "Kicking ass" is a celebrated goal, whereas failing to "take out" and "punish" the opposition is a sign of weakness. Presenting games as personal confrontations and mean-spirited turf wars has long been a theme in media sports. When this reaffirms dominant ideology in the culture as a whole, people accept this type of sports coverage.

Finally, the emphasis on *consumption* is clear in the media coverage of sports: About 20 percent of televised sports consists of commercial time, ads fill newspapers and magazines, and Internet sites use multiple strategies to present ads mixed with scores, commentary, and links. TV time-outs are a standard feature in football and basketball games, and announcers remind media spectators that, "This game is being brought to you by [fill in the corporate name]." Commercials are central in the telecast of the Super Bowl, and media audiences are polled to rate those commercials. The audiences for media sports are encouraged to express their connections to teams and athletes by purchasing thousands of branded objects. For example, Florida State proudly sells their mascot, Chief Osceola, on stadium seat cushions, bean bag chairs, kitchen cutting boards, car floor mats, and napkins so that fans can sit on, cut on, stand on, and wipe their mouths with images of their honored chief. This is clearly consistent with consumer ideology in American society. "You are what you buy" is one of the tenets of a market economy, and Florida State fans become Seminoles by consuming "their chief."

Media Impact on Sports-Related Behaviors

We know that media images and narratives influence people, but we don't know much about who is influenced or in what ways people are influenced. Media coverage is part of our experience, and experiences influence who we are and what we think, feel, and do. However, in this section, we focus only on the connections between consuming sport media and either playing sports or attending events.

Active Participation in Sports Do the media cause people to be more active sport participants or turn them into couch potatoes? This is an important issue, given the high rates of obesity, diabetes, and heart disease, especially in the United States. More people watch sports on television than ever before, and the rates of obesity and diabetes are the highest in U.S. history. This is not to say that watching sports on television causes obesity and the health problems associated with it, but it suggests issues that should be studied.

When children watch sports on television, some copy what they see if they have or can make opportunities to do so. Children are great imitators with active imaginations, so when they see and identify with athletes, they may create informal activities or seek to join youth sport programs to pursue television-inspired dreams. Participation grounded in these dreams does not last long, especially after children discover that it takes years of tedious, repetitive, and boring practice to compete successfully and make those glorious trips to the victory podium. However, other motives may develop in the process and inspire healthy sport participation patterns. But we don't know how many children decide to avoid or quit sports because they cannot meet performance expectations formed as they watch highly skilled athletes in the media.

Many adults who watch sports on television do not play anything that they watch, whereas others are active participants in one or more sports (Wenner and Gantz, 1998). Interestingly, there is little research on this issue. Therefore, the safest conclusion at this point is that consuming sports through the media is connected with each outcome in different situations and with different people.

Attendance at Sport Events Game attendance is related to many factors, and its relationship to the media is complex. On the one hand, the owners of many professional teams enforce a television blackout rule based on the belief that television coverage hurts game attendance and ticket sales. In support of this belief, many people say that they would rather watch certain sport events on television than attend them in person. On the other hand, the media publicize sports, promote interest, and provide the information that people need to identify with athletes and teams and become potential ticket buyers for events (Wann et al., 2001b; Weiss, 1996; Zhang et al., 1998).

The most logical conclusion is that people who watch more games on TV also attend more games in person (Zhang and Smith, 1997). However, this conclusion has two qualifications. First, as ticket prices increase and the number of elite, "live" games increase across various sports, people may limit attendance when there is the option of watching a local game on television. Second, because the media focus attention on elite sports, such as NBA basketball, they may undermine attendance at less elite events such as local high school games. Thus, the media may be positively related to attendance at the top levels of competition but negatively related to attendance at lower levels of competition (Zhang et al., 1997). Research is needed to explore this issue in more depth.

The media focus on elite sports, and they usually attract spectators to high-profile events such as this NBA playoff game in Seattle. Does this undermine attendance at less elite events such as minor league and high school games? (*Source:* Dennis Coakley)

AUDIENCE EXPERIENCES WITH MEDIA SPORTS

Media sports provide topics of conversation, sources of identity, feelings of success when favorite teams win, opportunities to express emotions, occasions for getting together with others, and a focus for those who are passing time alone (Wenner and Gantz, 1998). A summary of audience research done by media studies experts Lawrence Wenner and Walter Gantz (1998) indicates that U.S. adults integrate media sports into their lives in a variety of ways. Although studies have identified some adults, more men than women, who focus considerable attention on watching sports, overall patterns indicate that watching television sports is a major activity for relatively limited segment of the overall population in the United States. Furthermore, those studies do not tell us much about the ways that people include the consumption of media sports in their lives (Crawford, 2004; Wann et al., 2001b).

Research summarized by Wenner and Gantz shows that men and women who live together often watch televised sports together and that this usually is a positive activity in their relationships. In other words, "stay-at-home armchair quarterbacks" and "football widows" are not as common as many people believe. Men watch sports more than women do and are more likely to be committed fans. However, when women are highly committed fans, they watch and respond to sports on television in ways that are similar to patterns among men. Research suggests that being a fan is more important than gender or any other factor when it comes to people's viewing experiences. Some couples experience conflicts related to viewing sports, but most couples resolve them successfully. Partners usually learn to accommodate each other's viewing habits over time, and when differences are associated with problems, it usually is in relationships that have other problems unrelated to their patterns of watching sports on television.

Future studies will tell us more about the ways that media sport experiences are integrated into people's lives and when media sports become important sites at which social relationships occur. The use of the Internet and video games should be included in these studies.

THE PROFESSION OF SPORT JOURNALISM

Some people trivialize sport journalism by saying that it provides "entertaining material about people and events that don't *really* matter too much" (Koppett, 1994). However, sports *do matter*—not because they produce a tangible product or make essential contributions to our survival, but because they represent ideas about how the world works and what is important in life. Therefore, sport journalists do things that matter when it comes to ideology and public consciousness.

Sport Journalists on the Job: Relationships with Athletes

As televised sports have increased, sportswriters have had to create stories that go beyond the action and scores in sports. This leads them to seek information about the personal lives of the athletes, and this in turn has influenced relationships between journalists and athletes. For example, athletes today realize that they cannot trust writers to hold information in confidence, even if it was disclosed in the privacy of the locker room. Furthermore, the stakes associated with "bad press" are so great for athletes and teams that everyone in sports organizations is on guard when talking with journalists. Clinton Doaks, a long-time sportswriter explains that "today's sports world is so driven by public relations that there are very few stories to report. Every player, coach, and team is so image conscious . . . that they all offer the same homogenous quotes week in and week out, game after game" (Doaks, 2004).

As journalists seek stories that athletes don't want to tell, it creates tensions in their relationships with athletes. Tension is also caused by differences in the salaries and personal backgrounds of players and sportswriters. For example, wealthy black and Latino athletes without college degrees have little in common with middle-class, college-educated, Euro-American writers. As a result, writers feel less compelled to protect or empathize with athletes in their stories, and athletes feel that they must be wary of the motives of journalists.

Team owners and university athletic departments are so conscious of tensions between athletes and media personnel that they now provide players with training on how to handle interviews without saying things that sound bad or can be misinterpreted. However, tensions sometimes reach a point that players threaten people from the media, and sportswriters, in particular, quit their jobs to find less stressful occupations.

Tensions also call attention to ethical issues in sports journalism. Responsible journalists, including writers and announcers, are now sensitive to the fact that they should not jeopardize people's reputations simply for the sake of entertainment. This does not mean that they avoid criticism that might hurt someone, but they are less likely to hurt someone unintentionally or without good reason. Dan Le Batard, a regular columnist for *ESPN The Magazine*, explains that he tries to be "nonjudgmental" when he covers athletes because all people have flaws and exposing them because someone disappoints you with their actions smacks of self-righteousness and raises the ethical issue of invasion of privacy (2005b, p. 14). Unfortunately, journalists constantly face gray areas in which ethical guidelines are not clear, and the need to present attractive stories often encourages them to push ethical limits.

Sportswriters and Sports Announcers: A Comparison

Different media have slightly different goals and strategies. The print media focus on entertaining people with information and in-depth analysis, whereas radio and television entertain people with

Table 12.4   Sportswriters and sports announcers: a comparison of roles

Role Characteristics	Sportswriters*	Sports Announcers[†]
• Job security	High	Low
• Salary	Low	High
• Popularity/public recognition	Low	High
• Freedom of expression in job	Moderately restricted	Heavily restricted
• Purpose of role	Entertain and provide information	Entertain and "sell" sport events
• Role expectations	Be trustworthy investigators	Be knowledgeable entertainers
• Management expectations	Don't offend advertisers	Don't offend sponsors
• Opportunities to do investigative reporting	Occasionally	Rarely
• On-the-job contacts	Copy desk editors and subeditors	Broadcast executives, team management, sponsors/advertisers
• Relationships with players	Often tense and antagonistic	Often friendly and supportive
• Attachment with public	Based on style and writing skills	Based on credibility and personality

Source: Adapted from Koppett (1994).

*The primary focus here is on newspaper reporters. Magazine writers have similar jobs, but they are different in that they often cover issues and topics in greater depth.

[†]The primary focus here is on television announcers. Radio announcers have similar jobs, but they are different in that they must focus more on description in their commentary and less on interpretation.

images and commentary, which create on-the-spot urgency. The implications of these differences are summarized in table 12.4.

Although differences between sportswriters and announcers/commentators are often difficult to identify, the print media usually hire writers who can tell reliable and thorough stories, whereas broadcast companies hire announcers who can excite and entertain an audience with rapid commentary (see figure 12.5). This is why newspaper and magazine writers (especially the latter) usually do more thorough investigative reporting whereas announcers talk with a sense of urgency to entertain viewing or listening audiences. However, some writers go beyond information and analysis and write strictly to entertain, and some television and radio personalities work on investigative stories in which information and analysis are as important as entertainment.

The efforts of television companies to provide a combination of play-by-play commentary and entertainment lead them to hire popular retired athletes and coaches to be announcers. Media companies cover sports as "infotainment" rather than news, and those who announce the games must be entertainers. But they must be credible entertainers who can provide insider interpretations and stories. This is why announcers and commentators may be former athletes and coaches who fans perceive to be credible. However, all radio and television announcers are expected to self-censor their commentary so that they stay within limits set by teams and television companies. Popular radio and television announcer Chip Caray, who has worked on broadcasts for the Atlanta Braves, the Seattle Mariners, and the Chicago Cubs, explains, "Our bosses expect us to broadcast a certain way. No one has ever told me how to broadcast. But I draw my paycheck from the same place as the players" (in Russo, 1999, p. 7D). Consequently, announcers seldom stray from a fairly standard entertainment approach, and they provide no critical comments about sports as social phenomena as we watch them on television. For people who consume sports primarily through the popular media, critical discussions of sports, such as the ones in this book, may create defensiveness or discomfort.

"I used to do sports, so I know the rule at Fox: If it bleeds, it leads."

....

FIGURE 12.5   The media coverage of sports news is much like other news in that it contains representations of violence and drama. Such representations are not accurate indicators of what generally happens in sports or our communities.

summary

COULD SPORTS AND THE MEDIA SURVIVE WITHOUT EACH OTHER?

To understand social life today, we must give serious attention to the media and media experiences. This is why we study the relationship between sports and the media.

Media sports, like other parts of culture, are social constructions. They are created, organized, and controlled by human beings whose ideas are grounded in their social worlds, experiences, and ideologies. The media do not *reflect* reality as much as they provide *re-presentations* of selected versions of reality. Power relations in society influence these representations. Therefore, the images and narratives that comprise the media often reaffirm dominant ideologies and promote the interests of those who benefit most from them. The possible exception to this is the Internet, a medium that offers revolutionary potential for people to create their own media content.

Video games and virtual sports are important components of the new media. At this time, they complement existing media, but they will gradually provide sport-related experiences that are unique and unrelated to other media. As technology makes possible the exploration of virtual realities and participation in physical challenges with virtual teammates and opponents, sports will occur more frequently in virtual worlds.

Sports and the media have grown to depend on each other as both have become more important parts of cultures in many societies. They could survive without each other, but they would be different from what they are now. Commercial sports have grown and prospered because of media coverage and the rights fees paid to sport organizations by media companies. Without the publicity and money provided by the media, commercial sports would be local business operations with much less scope than they have today, and less emphasis would be given to elite forms of competitive sports. Without exposure to sports through the media, people would probably give lower priority to organized power and performance sports in their everyday lives, and they might give higher priority to pleasure and participation sports.

The media also could survive without sports. But they, too, especially newspapers and television, would be different if they did not have sports to make their programming attractive to young male audiences and the sponsors who wish to buy access to them. Without sports, newspaper circulation would decrease, and television programming on weekends and holidays would be different and less profitable for television companies.

The symbiotic relationship between sports and the media suggests that we will continue to see many commercialized sports covered by the media and the major media presenting regular coverage of sports. However, history also shows that this relationship has developed within a larger cultural context, one in which priority is given to commercial profits and the creation of megamedia events. Furthermore, the relationship between sports and the media has been created in connection with the ever-changing interactions among athletes, agents, coaches, administrators, sport team owners, sponsors, advertisers, media representatives, and a diverse collection of spectators. The power dynamics in these interactions have an important impact on the sports-media relationship.

Sports covered by the electronic media are represented to audiences with dramatic, exciting, and stylized images and narratives designed to be entertaining for audiences and attractive to sponsors. The influence of these media sports in our lives depends on how we integrate them into our relationships and routines. Direct experiences with sports influence how we interpret and use what we read, listen to, and view in the media. If we have little direct experience with and in sports, the media play a more central role in creating our sport realities and influencing how those realities are integrated into the rest of our lives.

Research suggests that dominant ideologies related to success, gender, race and ethnicity, nationalism, individualism, teamwork, violence, and consumption are perpetuated through the images and narratives represented in the media coverage of sports in the United States. These ideologies support the interests of corporate sponsors, males, and white people in the United States, and they are presented seamlessly in sports coverage so that the current distribution of power and privilege seems to be normal and natural. Future research will tell us more about how people use media content as they form ideas about sports, their social relationships, and the social world.

Especially important in the future will be research on how people use the Internet and video games as sites for constructing their experiences in and with sports. Some thirteen-year-olds would much rather play sport video games than watch games on television. In the future, some of them will do both at the same time. And some twenty-five-year-olds enjoy the sport-related interactive experiences that they have on the Internet more than the games themselves. Media sports and the experiences associated with them are changing rapidly, and it is important to study them in ways that promote critical media literacy rather than the uncritical celebration of media technology and culture (Kellner, 2003a, 2003b, 2004).

 See the OLC, www.mhhe.com/coakley9e, for an annotated list of readings related to this chapter. The OLC also contains a key concept list, a review test, and other helpful features.

WEBSITE RESOURCES

Note: Websites often change. The following URLs were current when this book was printed. Please check our website (www.mhhe.com/coakley9e) for updates and additions.

www.mhhe.com/coakley9e   Click on chapter 12 and check out the essays on the ideology underlying media sports, the interdependence of the Olympics and the media, and the impact of watching violent sports on behavior.

www.aafla.org   The Amateur Athletic Foundation site; go to "AAF Research Reports" for sports media studies on children and sports media, gender issues, race and ethnicity issues.

www.real-sports.com   The site for the magazine *Real SPORTS*, dedicated to the coverage of women in sports; no ads for beauty products, as in "fitness and sports" magazines for women.

www.nfl.com/fans/forher/index.html   This site was designed to recruit women to watch NFL games and become NFL fans.

chapter

13

(Victoria Arocho, AP/Wide World Photos)

SPORTS AND POLITICS

How Do Governments and Global
Processes Influence Sports?

NO PERSON SHALL play ball or any game of sport
with a ball or football or throw, cast, shoot or
discharge any stone, pellet, bullet, arrow or any
other missile, in, over, across, along or upon any
street or sidewalk or in any public park, except
on those portions of said park set apart for such
purposes.

—**Los Angeles Municipal Code,**
    sec. 56.16; 2005

Online Learning Center Resources

Visit *Sports in Society*'s Online Learning Center
(OLC) at **www.mhhe.com/coakley9e** for
additional information and study material
for this chapter, including

- Self-grading quizzes
- Learning objectives
- Related websites
- Additional readings

A complete outline is available online at
www.mhhe.com/coakley9e.

WE HAVE WAGED a lengthy and tireless battle
to create a [revolutionary] sports culture. . . .
This is what has allowed our country to reach
a place of honor in sports . . . recognized by
the entire world.

—**Fidel Castro, president of Cuba, 2001**

I AM PERSONALLY asking the U.S. World Cup
team . . . to insist that the next game they play,
they play with soccer balls that are certified
"not made with child labor."

—**Tom Harkin, U.S. senator from Iowa, 2002**

Organized competitive sports have long been connected with politics, governments, and global processes. **Politics** refers to *the processes and procedures of making decisions that affect collections of people, from small groups to societies and even multiple societies that are unified for certain purposes*, such as the European Union consisting of twenty-five nations with a common currency and shared policies. In a sociological sense, politics involves processes through which power is gained and used in social life. Therefore, people in the sociology of sport study politics in families, communities, local and national sport organizations, societies, and large nongovernment organizations (NGOs) such as the International Olympic Committee (IOC) or Fédération Internationale de Football Association (FIFA), the international governing body (NGB) for soccer.

Governments are *formal organizations with the power to make and enforce rules in a particular territory or collection of people*. Because governments make decisions affecting people's lives, they are political organizations by definition. Governments operate on various levels from local towns to nation-states, and they influence sports whether they occur in a local public park or privately owned stadiums that host international competitions.

Politics often involve the actions and interactions of governments but rule making in sports today often transcends the boundaries of nation-states and occurs in connection with global processes. For example, soccer became a global sport as British workers, students, and teachers brought the game to South America and British soldiers brought it to Africa, Asia, the West Indies, and other colonized areas of the nineteenth-century British Empire. Therefore, soccer was introduced to people around the world through the global processes of migration, capitalist expansion, British imperialism, and colonization. These processes clearly involve politics. Governments usually are involved, but the processes often transcend particular governments as people, products, ideas, technologies, and money move so rapidly across national borders that time and space become compressed.

This chapter deals with sports and politics. The goal is to explain the ways that sports are connected with politics, governments, and global processes. Chapter content focuses on four major questions:

1. Why are governments involved in sponsoring and controlling sports?
2. How are sports connected with global politics that involve nation-states, transnational corporations, and nongovernment organizations?
3. What is the role of the Olympic Games in global politics and processes?
4. What are the ways that political processes occur in sports and sport organizations?

When reading this chapter, remember that *power* is the key concept in politics. **Power** refers to *an ability to influence people and achieve goals, even in the face of opposition from others* (Weber, 1968/1922). **Authority** is *a form of power that comes with a recognized and legitimate status or office in a government, an organization, or an established set of relationships*. For example, a large corporation has *power* if it can influence how people think about and play sports and if it can use sports to achieve its goals. Sport organizations such as the IOC, FIFA, the NCAA, and a local parks and recreation department have *authority* over the sports that they administer as long as people associated with those sports accept the organizations as legitimate sources of control. This example alerts us to the fact that, in this chapter, *politics* refers to the power to make decisions that affect sports and sport participation at all levels of involvement.

THE SPORTS–GOVERNMENT CONNECTION

When sports become popular community activities, government involvement often increases. Many sports require sponsorship, organization, and facilities—all of which depend on resources that few individuals possess on their own. Sport facilities may be so expensive that regional and national governments are the only entities with the power and money to build and maintain them. Therefore, government involvement in sports often is a necessity. Government involvement also occurs when there is a need for a third party to regulate and control sports and sport organizations in ways that promote the overall good of people in a community or society.

The nature and extent of government involvement in sports is diverse, and it occurs for one or more of the following seven reasons (Houlihan, 2000):

1. To safeguard the public order
2. To maintain health and fitness among citizens
3. To promote the prestige and power of a group, community, or nation
4. To promote a sense of identity, belonging, and unity among citizens
5. To reproduce values consistent with dominant ideology in a community or society
6. To increase support for political leaders and government
7. To promote economic development in a community or society

Safeguarding the Public Order

Here are two sections from the Los Angeles Municipal Code, enforced by the city in an effort to safeguard citizens and the public order:

> No person shall ride, operate or use a bicycle, unicycle, skateboard, cart, wagon, wheelchair, roller skates, or any other device moved exclusively by human power, on a sidewalk, bikeway or boardwalk in a willful or wanton disregard for the safety of persons or property. (Section 56.15, Los Angeles Municipal Code)
>
> Within the limit of any park or portion thereof designated by the Board as a skateboard facility, whether the facility is supervised or unsupervised,
>
> 1. No person shall ride a skateboard unless that person is wearing a helmet, elbow pads and knee pads.
> 2. No person shall ride a bicycle or scooter in the skating area (Sec. 63.44, Los Angeles Municipal Code).

Governments often make rules determining the legality of sports, where they may and may not be played, the safety equipment that must be used, who must have opportunities to play, and who can use public sport facilities at certain times. Ideally, these rules promote safety and reduce conflict between multiple users of particular spaces. For example, a government might ban bullfighting, bare-fisted boxing, or bungee jumping off public bridges. In the case of commercial sports, governments may regulate the rights and duties of team owners, sponsors, promoters, and athletes. Local governments may regulate sport participation by requiring permits to use public facilities and playing fields. Likewise, local officials may close streets or parks to the general public so that sport events can be held under controlled and safe conditions. For example, marathons in New York City and London require the involvement of the government and government agencies such as the city police.

Governments may pass laws or establish policies that safeguard the public order by protecting the participation rights of citizens. Title IX in the United States and similar legislation in other countries are examples of government laws intended to promote gender equity in sports. Similarly, many national governments have enacted or are considering laws mandating the provision of sport participation opportunities for people with disabilities. The U.S. Congress passed the Amateur Sports Act in 1978 and created the USOC, the official NGO responsible for coordinating international amateur sports and protecting athletes from being exploited by multiple, unconnected, and self-interested sport-governing bodies that controlled amateur sports through much of the twentieth century. In 1998 the act was revised to require the USOC to support and fund Paralympic athletes because people with disabilities were systematically denied opportunities to play elite amateur sports. Unfortunately, people differ on how the act should be interpreted; as a result, athletes with disabilities have had to file lawsuits as they seek support and funding that they consider as fair.

AT YOUR *fingertips*   For more information on Title IX, see pages 238–243.

Safeguarding the public order also involves policing sport events. Local police or even military forces may be called on to control crowds and individuals who threaten the safety of others. During the Olympics, for example, the host city and nation provide thousands of military and law enforcement officials to safeguard the public order. In the face possible terrorist actions, the governments of Athens and Greece spent $1.5 billion on security at the 2004 Olympic Games (Waterford, 2004). They employed over 100,000 police, military personnel, firefighters, and private security contractors and used a high-tech surveillance system with 1000 cameras and links to ships, helicopters, fighter planes, the coast guard, minesweepers along the coast, bomb squads, and a NATO special forces battalion (fortunately, less than a dozen minor incidents occurred during the seventeen days of the Games).

Some governments attempt to safeguard the public order by sponsoring sport events and programs for at-risk youth. Sports, they believe, keep youth off the streets, thereby lowering crime rates, vandalism, loneliness, and alienation. However, these programs generally fail because they do not deal with the deprivation, racism, poverty, dislocation, unemployment, community disintegration, and political powerlessness that often create "at-risk youth" and social problems in communities and societies (Coakley, 2002; Hartmann, 2001, 2003).

Finally, sports are used in military and police training so that the soldiers and police will be more effective protectors of the public order

Local governments often regulate where and when certain sports can occur. This is true in Philadelphia's "Love Park," although "street skaters" do break the rules on weekends, holidays, and late at night. (*Source:* Jay Coakley)

(Mangan, 2003). Military academies in the United States and many nations traditionally sponsor sports for cadets, and the World Police and Fire Games are held every two years because people believe that sport participation keeps law enforcement officials and firefighters prepared to safeguard the public order.

Maintaining Health and Fitness

Governments also become involved in sports to promote health and fitness among citizens. Nations with government-funded health insurance programs promote and sponsor certain sports to improve physical health in the general population and thereby reduce the cost of health services.

Similar motives underlie government sponsorship and organization of fitness and sport programs in other nations. Many people believe that sport participation improves fitness, fitness improves health, and good health reduces medical costs. This belief persists in the face of the following factors (Waddington, 2000a, 2007):

- Many illnesses that increase health-care costs are caused by environmental factors and living conditions that cannot be changed through sport or fitness programs.
- Certain forms of sport participation do not produce physical fitness or identifiable health benefits.
- The win-at-all-cost orientation in certain competitive sports often contributes to injuries and increased health-care costs (for example, about 40,000 high school and college athletes in the United States have serious and costly knee injuries each year)
- The demand for health care often increases when people train for competitions because they seek specialized medical care to treat and rehabilitate sport injuries.

These factors lead governments to be cautious and selective when they sponsor sports for health purposes. Most governments now emphasize noncompetitive physical activities and exercise with clear aerobic benefits instead of competitive sports. The relationship between sport participation and overall health and fitness is a complex one. Although research clearly shows that physical exercise has health benefits, competitive sports involve more than mere exercise.

Competitive sports can promote overall health when athletes value physical well-being over performance and competitive success. Playing sports is beneficial when it helps us understand our bodies and maintain physical well-being; it is not beneficial when it involves overtraining, the use of bodies as weapons, and overconformity to the norms of the sport ethic (as explained in chapter 6). This is why health professionals sometimes disagree when it comes to recommending government involvement in sports to promote health and fitness.

Promoting the Prestige and Power of a Group, Community, or Nation

Government involvement in sports frequently is motivated by a quest for recognition and prestige (Allison, 2004; Bairner, 2005). This occurs on local, national, and even global levels. For example, the 1996 Olympic Games were used by Atlanta to present itself as a world-class city symbolizing the "new South," now open to all people regardless of race or national background. Sydney, host of the 2000 Summer Games, presented itself as a city with clean air in a country with a pleasant climate and vital business connections with emerging nations in Asia. Salt Lake City used the 2002 Winter Olympics to present itself as an economically progressive area and an attractive tourist destination. Athens used the 2004 Summer Games to show the world that Greece was part of the new Europe and that it was a nation that had more than monuments of a past era. China will spend over $10 billion to present itself during the 2008 Olympic Games in Beijing as a new world power and a dynamic nation that is ideal for business investments and tourism.

Quantifying and measuring the long-term social impact of sports is difficult. Will this girl's identity and her sense of Australia's place in the world be changed because Sydney hosted the 2000 Olympics? Sports provide immediate and temporary emotional experiences, but it takes careful planning to make those experiences the basis for real change in a city or nation. (*Source:* McGraw-Hill)

This quest for recognition and prestige also underlies government subsidies for national teams across a wide range of sports, usually those designated as Olympic sports. Government officials use international sports to establish their nation's legitimacy in the international sphere, and they often believe that winning medals enhances their image around the world.

Attempts to gain recognition and prestige also underlie local government involvement in sports. Cities may fund sport clubs and teams and then use them to promote themselves as good places to live, work, locate a business, or vacation. Many people in North America feel that, if their city does not have one or more major professional sport team franchises, it cannot claim world-class status (Delaney and Eckstein, 2003; Silk, 2004). Even small towns use road signs to announce the success of local high school teams to everyone driving into the town: "You are now entering the home

of the state champions" in this or that sport. State governments in the United States subsidize sport programs at colleges and universities for similar reasons: Competitive success is believed to bring prestige to the entire state as well as the school represented by winning athletes and teams; prestige, it is believed, attracts students, students pay tuition, and tuition pays for educational programs.

Promoting Identity and Unity

Groups, organizations, towns, cities, and nations use sports to express collective sentiments about themselves (Allison, 2000, 2004; Bairner, 2001, 2005; Jutel, 2002; Maguire, 1999, 2005; Maguire and Poulton, 1999; Poulton, 2004; Sam, 2003; Sato, 2005). An athlete or team representing a larger collection of people has the potential to bring individuals together and to create emotional unity among them.

When a nation's soccer team plays in the World Cup, citizens share a sense of "we-ness," regardless of their race, religion, language, education, occupation, or income. This emotional sense of "we-ness," or unity, is connected with their feelings of attachment to the nation's history and traditions and even about its destiny in the world order. However, this emotional unity seldom lasts long, and it often serves the interests of people with power and influence because they use sports as occasions to highlight the images, traditions, and memories around which national identities are expressed and then say that the status quo must be preserved lest we endanger the things that make us who "we" are as a nation.

When government involvement in sport is intended to promote identity and unity, it usually benefits some people more than others. For example, when men's sports are sponsored and women's sports are ignored, the sense of national identity and unity among men may be strong, but women may feel alienated. When sports involve participants from only one ethnic group or a particular social class, there are similar divisions in the "imagined community" and "invented traditions" constructed around sports. Identity is political in that it can be constructed around many different ideas of what is important in a group or society. Furthermore, neither the identity nor the emotional unity created by sports changes the social, political, and economic realities of life in a city or society. When games end, people go their separate ways. Old social distinctions become relevant again, and the people who were disadvantaged prior to the game remain disadvantaged after it (Smith and Ingham, 2003). However, they may feel less justified in making their disadvantage a political issue because, after all, everyone, even the rich and powerful, is part of the big "we" celebrated at the game. The emotional unity that sports create feels good to many people, and it may generate a sense of possibility and hope,

> Sport is an important tool for "imagining" nationhood. It is a perfect forum for constructing identity.
>
> —Annemarie Jutel, physical educator (2002)

but it often glosses over the need for social transformations that would make society more fair and just.

Local government involvement in sports is also motivated by concerns to promote and express particular forms of identity. Club soccer teams in Europe often receive support from local governments because the teams are major focal points for community attention and involvement. The teams reaffirm community identity among local citizens, and games often are social occasions at which people renew old acquaintances and maintain social networks. In this way, sports are *invented traditions* that people use to reaffirm social relationships.

When the population of a community or society is very diverse or when social change is rapid and widespread, governments are even more likely to intervene in sports for the purpose of promoting a sense of identity and unity (Maguire and Stead, 2005). For example, as national boundaries have become less and less visible and relevant in the lives of some people, national governments occasionally use sports to promote and reaffirm national identity (Houlihan, 1994; Maguire, 1999, 2005). The long-term effectiveness of this strategy is difficult to assess, but many government officials are convinced that sports create more than temporary good feelings of national "we-ness." Interestingly, nearly all these officials are men, and the sports that they support are tied to traditions that have privileged men in the past. This shows that there are several layers to the politics associated with sports.

Reproducing Values Consistent with Dominant Political Ideology

Governments also become involved in sports to promote certain political values and ideas among citizens. This is especially true when there is a need to maintain the idea that success is based on discipline, loyalty, determination, and hard work, even in the face of hardship and bad times. Sports are useful platforms to promote these values and foster a particular ideology that contains taken-for-granted assumptions about the way that social life is organized and how it does and should operate.

It is difficult to determine the extent to which people are influenced by sports presented in specific ideological terms, but we do know that in capitalist societies, such as the United States, sports provide people with a vocabulary and real-life examples that are consistent with dominant ideology. The images, narratives, and the often-repeated stories that accompany sports in market economies emphasize that competition is clearly the best and most natural way to achieve personal success and allocate rewards to people, whereas alternative approaches to success and allocating rewards (such as democratic socialism, socialism, communism, and the like) are ineffective, unnatural, and even immoral.

A classic example of a government's use of sport to promote its own political ideology occurred in Nazi Germany in 1936. Most countries hosting the Olympic Games use the occasion to present themselves favorably to their own citizens and the rest of the world. However, Adolf Hitler was especially interested in using the games to promote the Nazi ideology of "Nordic supremacy" through the "Berlin Games," which preceded World War II. The Nazi government devoted considerable resources to training German athletes, who won eighty-nine medals in Berlin: twenty-three more than U.S. athletes won and over four times as many as any other country won during the Games. This is why the performance of Jesse Owens, an African American, was so important to countries not aligned with Germany at that point in history. Owens's four gold medals and world records challenged Hitler's ideology of Nordic (white) supremacy, although it did not deter Nazi commitment to a destructive political and cultural ideology.

The cold war era following World War II was also a time when nations, especially the United States, the former Soviet Union, and East Germany, used the Olympics and other international sport competitions to make claims about the superiority of their political and economic ideologies. Today, such claims are less apt to be associated with international sports because the cold war is over. Furthermore, some corporations are now more powerful than many nations and use the Olympic Games and other major international events to make claims about the superiority of their products and services and the "naturalness" of capitalist, free-market principles and lifestyles based on consumption.

Increasing Support for Political Leaders and Government

Government authority rests ultimately in legitimacy. If people do not perceive political leaders and the government as legitimate, it is difficult to maintain social order. In the quest to maintain their legitimacy, political officials may use their connections with athletes, teams, and particular sports to boost their acceptance in the minds of citizens. They assume, as Antonio Gramsci (see At Your Fingertips, p. 373) predicted they would, that if they support the sports that people value and enjoy, they can increase their *legitimacy* as leaders. This is why so many political leaders present themselves as friends of sport, even as faithful fans. They attend highly publicized sport events and associate themselves with high-profile athletes or teams that win major competitions. U.S. presidents traditionally have associated themselves with successful athletes and teams and have invited champions to the White House for photo opportunities.

Some male former athletes and coaches in the United States have used their celebrity status from sports to gain popular support for their political candidacy. The most publicized example of this is Jesse Ventura, a former professional wrestler, who was elected governor of Minnesota in 1998 and flirted with the idea of running for president in 2000. Other former athletes and coaches have

President George W. Bush is frequently photographed with championship teams and successful athletes. As he campaigned in Ohio, a crucial swing state in the 2004 election, he visited the Cleveland Browns NFL team for a photo opportunity. As former partial owner of the Texas Rangers MLB team, he learned that being associated with elite sports serves a positive public relations function (*Source:* Charles Dharapak, AP/Wide World Photos)

been elected to state legislatures and to the U.S. Congress and Senate, using their status from sports and their sport personas to increase their legitimacy as "tough," "hard working," and "loyal" candidates who are "decisive under pressure" and "dedicated to being winners."

Promoting Economic Development

Since the early 1980s, government involvement in sports is based on the hope of promoting economic development (Delaney and Eckstein, 2003; Schimmel, 2000, 2002). Cities spend millions of dollars on their bids to host the Olympic Games, World Cup tournaments, world or national

championships, Super Bowls, College Bowl games, All-Star Games, high-profile auto races, golf tournaments, and track and field meets. Although some of these events create economic development, the pattern is that events often provide only a temporary boost to the economy and too often leave local citizens with public debt and facilities that require annual subsidies to keep the doors open.

Using sports for economic development is risky and controversial. Many cities have failed to meet any of the optimistic economic projections used to convince local voters and official to dedicate public money for events, facilities, and subsidies for sport team owners (Lenskyj, 2000,

2002; Schimmel, 2002). Recent evidence shows that the forms of economic development associated with sports often benefit relatively few people, usually those who are already wealthy and powerful (see chapters 10 and 11). For example, when Nagano, Japan, bid to host the 1998 Winter Olympics, Yoshiaki Tsutsumi, the richest man in the world at that time, heavily influenced the IOC selection committee. Tsutsumi owned many high-end ski areas, golf courses, and resort hotels in the Nagano region of northern Japan and would make hundreds of millions of dollars if the government would spend $16 billion to build a new 120-mile bullet train line from Tokyo to Nagano. The story of how Tsutsumi influenced Japan's government and the IOC so that Nagano was named the Olympic host city and the train line was built is a long one, but the story ends with overuse threatening the natural environment of the Nagano region and Tsutsumi's wealth increased (Jennings, 1996a; Jennings and Sambrook, 2000). This is neither a new story nor an old one—similar things occurred in Utah in connection with the 2002 Winter Olympics (Jennings and Sambrook, 2000). Sports can be used for economic development, but the critical question always is, Who benefits and who pays?

Critical Issues and Government Involvement in Sports

Government involvement in sports is justified because it serves the "public good." It would be ideal if governments promoted equally the interests of all citizens, but differences between individuals and groups make this impossible. Therefore, public investments in sports often benefit some people more than others. Those who benefit most are those capable of influencing policymakers. This does not mean that government policies reflect only the interests of wealthy and powerful people, but it does mean that policies are often contentious and create power struggles among various segments of the population in a city or society.

Government involvement in sports occurs in many ways, from funding local parks for recreation and sport participation to supporting elite athletes for national teams. When there are debates over policies and priorities, those who represent elite sports often are organized, generally have strong backing from other organized groups and can base their requests for support on visible accomplishments achieved in the name of the entire country, community, or school. Those who represent masses of recreational and general-ability sport participants are less likely to be politically organized and supported by powerful organizations, and they are less able to give precise statements of their goals and the political significance of their programs. This does not mean that government decision makers ignore mass participation, but it does mean that "sport for all" usually has lower priority for funding and support (Green, 2004; Green and Houlihan, 2004; Sam, 2003).

Those who believe the myth that there is no connection between sports and government are most likely to be ignored when government involvement does occur. Those who realize that sports have political implications and that governments are not politically neutral arbitrators of differences are most likely to benefit when government involvement occurs. Sports are connected with power relations in society as a whole; therefore, sports and politics cannot be separated.

SPORTS AND GLOBAL POLITICAL PROCESSES

Most people have lofty expectations about the impact of sports on global relations. It has long been hoped that sports would serve diplomatic functions contributing to cultural understanding and world peace. Unfortunately, the realities of sports have not matched the ideals. Nations and transnational corporations regularly use sports to promote ideologies favoring their special interests, and global political realities have changed so that now a few dozen corporations have assets and budgets surpassing those of most nations worldwide. Furthermore, sports themselves have become much more global with teams recruiting athletes outside their national borders and sports equipment being manufactured in developing nations where labor is often exploited. These are important issues to understand when studying sports in society.

International Sports: Ideals Versus Realities

Achieving peace and friendship among nations was emphasized by Baron Pierre de Coubertin, the founder of the modern Olympic Games in 1896. Through the twentieth century, many people have hoped that sports would do the following things:

- Create open communication lines between people and leaders from different nations.
- Highlight shared interests among people from different cultures and nations.
- Demonstrate that friendly international relationships are possible.
- Foster cultural understanding and eliminate the use of national stereotypes.
- Create a model for cultural, economic, and political relationships across national boundaries.
- Establish working relationships that develop leaders in emerging nations and close the resource gap between wealthy nations and poorer nations.

During the past century, it has become clear that sports can be useful in the realm of **public diplomacy** because it creates *public expressions of togetherness in the form of cultural exchanges and general communication among officials from various nations.* However, sports have no impact in the realm of **serious diplomacy,** which involves *discussions and decisions about political issues of vital national interest.* In other words, international sports provide political leaders from different nations with opportunities to meet and talk, but sports do not influence their discussions or decisions. Sports bring together athletes, who may learn from and about one another, but athletes make no political decisions, and their relationships with one another have no serious political significance. These points were illustrated clearly in 1999, when the Cuban National Baseball Team played the Baltimore Orioles in Cuba and then again in Baltimore. Media coverage and public conversations were affected temporarily, but the games had no impact on political relations between the United States and Cuba (Pettavino and Brenner, 1999).

Recent history shows that most nations use sports and sport events, especially the Olympic Games, to pursue self-interests rather than international understanding, friendship, and peace. Nationalist themes going beyond respectful expressions of patriotism have been clearly evident in many events, and most nations have used sport events regularly to promote their own military, economic, political, and cultural goals. This was particularly apparent during the cold war era following World War II and extending into the early 1990s. During these years, the Olympics were extensions of "superpower politics" between the United States and its allies and the former Soviet Union and its allies.

The connection between international sports and politics was so blatant in the early 1980s that Peter Ueberroth, president of the Los Angeles Olympic Organizing Committee, said that "we now have to face the reality that the Olympics constitute not only an athletic event but a political event" (*U.S. News & World Report,* 1983). Ueberroth was not being prophetic; he was simply summarizing his observations of events leading up to the 1984 Olympics in Los Angeles. He saw that nations were more interested in self-interest than global friendship and peace. The demonstration of national superiority through sports was a major focus of world powers.

Wealthy and powerful nations are not the only ones to use international sports to promote political self-interest. Many nations lacking international political and economic power have used sports in a quest for international recognition

The sports of wealthy and powerful nations in the Western Hemisphere form the foundation of the Olympic Games. This photo of the 1936 Olympic Games in Berlin shows the U.S. team saluting in contrast to straight-arm gesture of the Germans. The Nazi flag (far right) is prominently displayed by the host nation, and Adolf Hitler used the Olympics to promote Nazi ideology. (*Source:* USOC Archives)

and legitimacy. For them, the Olympics and other international sports have been stages for showing that their athletes and teams can stand up to and sometimes defeat athletes and teams from wealthy and powerful nations. For example, when the cricket teams from the West Indies or India play teams from England, the athletes and people from the West Indies and India see the matches as opportunities to show the world that they are now equals to the nation that once colonized their land and controlled their people. When their teams win, it is cause for political affirmation and great celebration.

National leaders know that hosting the Olympics is a special opportunity to generate international recognition, display national power and resources to a global audience, and invite investments into their economies. This is why bid committees from prospective host cities and nations have regularly used gifts, bribes, and financial incentives to encourage IOC members to vote for them in the bid selection process. Illegal and illicit strategies reached their peak during the bidding for the 2002 Winter Olympics when officials from Salt Lake City offered to IOC members and their families money, jobs, scholarships, lavish gifts, vacations, and the sexual services of "escorts" as they successfully secured the votes needed to host the games (Jennings, 1996a, 1996b; Jennings and Sambrook, 2000).

The political goals of the nations hosting major international events are especially clear when nations boycott the Olympics and other international sport events. For example, the 1980 Moscow Games were boycotted by the United States and its political allies to protest the Soviet Union's decision to unilaterally invade Afghanistan to eliminate Islamic rebels, including Osama bin Laden, who were subverting Soviet control of the region; the United States supported the autonomy of Afghanistan and armed the rebels. The U.S. boycott of the Olympic Games in Moscow was intended to show support for the rebels and demonstrate that the United States was clearly opposed to unilateral invasions. The Soviet Union and its allies then boycotted the 1984 Los Angeles Games to protest the commercialization of the games and avoid terrorist threats that they thought might be perpetrated by jingoistic American fans and citizens. However, each of these Olympic Games was held despite the boycotts, and each host nation unashamedly displayed its power and resources to the world. But neither the boycotts nor hosting the games had any major effects on American or Soviet political policies.

Increased global media coverage has intensified and added new dimensions to the connection between sports and politics. For example, television companies, especially the American networks, have attracted viewers to their Olympic coverage by stressing political controversies along with national interests and symbols. The theme of their coverage between 1960 and 1988 was less focused on international friendship than on "us versus them" and "this nation versus that nation." The networks justified this approach by claiming that U.S. viewers preferred to see an Olympics that extolled U.S. values and asserted the global superiority of American political and economic ideologies.

Although the coverage of the Olympics and other international sports by the U.S. media has traditionally encouraged ethnocentrism and nationalism, more recent coverage reflects the end of the cold war and the growth of global capitalism. Nationalist themes remain in the coverage, but they are now accompanied and sometimes obscured by images and narratives promoting capitalist expansion and the products and services of transnational corporations. These issues are discussed in the box "Olympism and the Olympic Games."

Nation-States, Sports, and Cultural Ideology

Sports often are used to promote ideas and orientations that foster the interests of powerful and wealthy nations. Participating in major international sport events often means that less powerful nations must look to powerful ones for guidance and resources. This encourages people in relatively poor nations to de-emphasize their traditional folk games and focus on sports developed around the values and experiences of powerful others. Furthermore, it leads them to be involved in events over which they have no control. If they wish to play, they must accept the conditions determined by people in powerful nations. When this occurs, people in poorer nations must buy, beg, or borrow everything from equipment to technical assistance from privileged others. To the extent that this promotes dependency on economically powerful nations, sports become vehicles for powerful nations to extend their control over important forms of popular culture around the world (Miller et al., 2001, 2003).

When people in traditional cultures want to preserve their native games, they resist the ideological influence associated with this form of "cultural imperialism," but resistance is difficult when popular international sports have rules and customs grounded in the ideologies of powerful nations (Ben-Porat and Ben-Porat, 2004; Mills and Dimeo, 2003). For example, when an American sport such as football is introduced to another country, it comes with an emphasis on ideas about individual achievement, competition, winning, hierarchical authority structures, physical power and domination, the body, and the use of technology to shape bodies into efficient machines. These ideas may not be completely accepted by those learning to play or watch football, but they do encourage orientations that privilege U.S. values and give low priority to the

reflect on SPORTS

Olympism and the Olympic Games
Are They Special?

Are the Olympics just another international sport event, or are they special? According to the Olympic Charter, the Olympic Games express and promote a special philosophy described in these words:

> Olympism is a philosophy of life, exalting and combining in a balanced whole the qualities of body, will and mind. Blending sport with culture and education, Olympism seeks to create a way of life based on the joy found in effort, the educational value of good example and respect for universal fundamental ethical principles.

The fundamental principles of the Olympic Charter are simple and straightforward. They emphasize that the Olympics should provide opportunities for people worldwide to learn about and connect with one another. This is important because our future and the future of the earth itself depends on global cooperation.

The goal of Olympism is to establish processes through which we learn to understand and appreciate our differences and work together to sustain healthy and safe lifestyles for people worldwide. If the Olympic Games can be organized and played to promote these goals, they are indeed special. However, at present, they fall short of meeting these ideals. Nationalism and commercialism exert so much influence on how the Olympic Games are planned, promoted, played, and represented by the media that the goal of global understanding and togetherness receives only token attention (Carrington, 2004). More important has been promoting national and corporate interests.

The current method of selling media broadcasting rights for the Olympic Games subverts Olympic ideals (Andrews, 2007; Real, 1996). Television companies buy the rights to take the video images they want from the Olympics and combine them with their own narratives to appeal to audiences in their countries. Thus, instead of bringing the world together around a single experience, the coverage presents heavily nationalized and commercialized versions of the Olympic Games. Viewers and readers may impose their own meanings on this coverage, but the coverage itself serves as a starting point for most people as they think about and make sense of the Olympics.

Audiences who wish to use the Olympics to visualize global community constructed around cultural differences and mutual understanding can do so, but current TV coverage provides little assistance in this quest. Most coverage highlights the association between human achievement, selected cultural values, and corporate sponsors. In the process, many people come to believe that corporations really do make the Olympics possible. As they watch the events, about 20 percent of television time presents messages from those corporations, the companies that, in the words of the announcers, "bring you the Olympics."

People don't accept media images and narratives in literal terms, but corporate sponsors bet hundreds of millions of dollars every two years that connecting their logos with the Olympic Rings discourages criticism of their products, encourages people to consume those products regularly, and fosters audience acceptance of consumption as a lifestyle.

The overt commercialism in the Olympics has led some people to question the meaning of the Olympics. As one multiple medal-winning Olympian says: "The Olympics is not about sports any more. It's about who can win the most money. It's like going to Disneyland" (in Reid, 1996, p. 4BB). A high-ranking Olympic official makes similar observations expressed in these words:

> I'm on the verge of joining those who think it's time for the Olympics, in their present context, to die. And they need to die for the same reason the ancient Olympic Games died—greed and corruption. (in Reid, 1996, p. 4BB)

Charles Barkley, an outspoken member of the U.S. men's basketball "Dream Team," noted in 1992 that the purpose of the games had little to do with Olympic ideals. He said,

> I know why we're here. We're here to spread basketball internationally and make more money for somebody. . . . We're going to win the gold medal, but there won't be any life changing decisions made because of it. . . . [P]oor people will still be poor and racism and sexism will still exist. (in DuPree, 1992, p. 7E)

Kevin Walmsley, director of the International Centre for Olympic Studies, supports these observations by saying that the Olympic Ideal "is an empty vessel filled up by the ideas of the day" (in Price, 2004).

These statements support the need to change the Olympic Games. The IOC issues regular press releases full of rhetoric about friendship and peace, but it has made no concerted effort to develop programs and processes making it clear to athletes and spectators that the games are about cultural understanding and working together in socially responsible ways. Bruce Kidd, a former Olympian who is now a physical and health educator at the University of Toronto, has made this point. Kidd (1996a) argues that if the Olympic Games are to be special, they must be used to highlight global injustice and promote social responsibility worldwide.

Kidd says that athletes should be selected to participate in the Olympics on the basis of their actions as global citizens as well as their athletic accomplishments. There also should be a curriculum enabling athletes to learn about fellow competitors and their cultures. The games should involve formal, televised opportunities for intercultural exchanges, and athletes should be ready to discuss their ideas about world peace and social responsibility during media interviews. The IOC should sponsor projects enabling citizen-athletes to build on their Olympic experiences through service to others around the world. A proportion of windfall profits coming from rapidly escalating TV rights fees could fund such projects, thereby giving IOC members opportunities to talk about real examples of social responsibility connected with the Olympics. The personal stories that television companies present during coverage of the games could then highlight the ways that athletes are socially responsible, rather than focusing on soap opera–like personal tragedies and triumphs. TV viewers may find such

Corporate sponsors pay millions of dollars to have their logos and products associated with the USOC. The USOC gives a prominent place to this display at its training center complex in Colorado Springs. One of the issues of concern in the sociology of sport is the extent to which the meanings and images associated with the Olympics are used to promote capitalist expansion rather than the goals of Olympism. (*Source:* Jay Coakley)

Continued

Olympism and the Olympic Games (*Continued*)

coverage more entertaining and hopeful than tabloid-like stories focusing on training and trauma.

Additionally, the IOC could control nationalism and commercialism more carefully as it organizes the games and sells broadcasting rights. I offer the following suggestions for consideration:

1. *Do away with national uniforms for athletes.* Let athletes choose from uniforms created by selected designers to express cultural themes from various regions of the world. This would minimize nationalism and inspire forms of expression that promote cultural understanding. Designs could be trademarked and sold with money going to projects to improve working conditions for people who make clothes for less than a living wage.

2. *Revise the opening ceremonies so that athletes enter the arena by event instead of by nation.* This would emphasize unity and fellowship rather than the political and economic systems into which the athletes were born through no choice of their own. Artists from around the world would be commissioned to design flags for various sports. National flags would be displayed collectively in the middle of the field to emphasize difference amid unity.

3. *Eliminate national anthems and flags during the award ceremonies.* Present medals in the stadium at the end of each day of competition in such a way that awards' ceremonies emphasize athletes first as representatives of all humanity and second as representatives of their nations. Most people are nationalistic enough without encouragement during an event that is declared to highlight global unity, not the superiority of some nations over others.

4. *Eliminate medal counts for nations.* National medal counts are contrary to the spirit and official principles of the Olympic movement. They foster chauvinism, intensify existing

political conflicts, and distract attention from the achievements of athletes as representatives of humankind.

5. *Eliminate or revise team sports.* Organizing team sports by nation encourages players and spectators to perceive games in we-versus-they terms. Therefore, eliminate all team sports or develop methods of choosing teams so that athletes from different countries play on the same teams and athletes from a particular nation play on different teams. Then "dream teams" would emphasize international unity rather than specific national and commercial interests. And athletes might make more friends worldwide and learn about other cultures.

6. *Add to each games "demonstration sports" native to the cultural regions where the games are held.* The IOC should specify that all media companies purchasing broadcasting rights and receiving press credentials must devote 5 percent of their coverage to these native games. Because the media influence the ways that people imagine, create, and play sports around the world, this would provide expanded images of physical activities, and facilitate creative approaches to sport participation worldwide. At present, many Olympic sports are simply a legacy of former colonial powers that had the power to export their games around the world (Bale and Christensen, 2004).

7. *Use multiple sites for each Olympic Games.* The cost of hosting the summer Olympic Games was $14.6 billion in Athens in 2004 and will be an estimated $30 billion in 2008 when Beijing (China) is the host (Waterford, 2004). Such costs privilege wealthy nations and prevent less wealthy nations from being hosts and having the opportunity to highlight their cultures and reap some of the profits now associated with

presenting the Games. If poorer nations could host a portion of the events, they would benefit culturally and economically, and media spectators would see a wider range of cultural settings as they viewed events over the eighteen days of coverage. At present, when nations host the entire games, they build massive and highly specialized facilities that may never be regularly used or filled to capacity in the future. This form of waste is ecologically irresponsible and often leaves citizens in cities or smaller nations smothered in massive debt created when public money has been used to build useless or underused facilities.

8. *Emphasize global responsibility in media coverage and commercials.* Television contracts should mandate an emphasis on global social responsibility. Athlete committees—working with committees from the Olympic Academy, which includes scholars committed to the spirit of Olympism—could develop expressions of this theme. This would link corporate sponsors to the special meaning of the Olympics and provide support for athletes as global citizens.

9. *Provide television time for public service announcements from nonprofit human rights groups that work with athletes and sport organizations to promote social justice and sustainable forms of development.* This would give viewers of the Olympics an opportunity to hear messages that are not created or censored by corporations and market forces. The commercial media may not like "donating" time for noncommercial purposes, but it should be a condition of receiving the rights to cover the games. The nonprofit groups receiving time would be identified and selected by athletes who are involved in human rights and social justice work.

10. *Integrate the Olympics and Paralympics.* Eli Wolff, director of Disability Sports at the Center for the Study of Sport in Society, says that just as the Olympic Movement has supported efforts to achieve gender equality and end racial apartheid in sports, it should "promote inclusion and equality of persons with disabilities within the Olympic Movement" (2005). This could be done by having common opening and closing ceremonies, awarding the same Olympic medals to athletes in both events, and referring to each as "Olympics." This would be in the spirit of Olympism, and it would be a powerful signal to the world that the full inclusion of people with disabilities is an achievable goal in all spheres of life.

Many people, especially from wealthy and powerful nations such as the United States, say that these suggestions are idealistic and do not match their view of the Olympics. However, the Olympic movement was founded on idealism and intended to inspire visions of what our world could and should be. Just because many of us have learned to define the Olympic Games in terms of national and corporate interests does not mean that we cannot think of changing them to achieve in more direct ways the ideals on which they were founded.

Because the Olympic Games capture the attention of 30 to 60 percent of the world's population every two years, it would be encouraging if they could be used as something other than global-marketing opportunities for transnational corporations and political platforms for wealthy nations that produce nearly all the medal-winning athletes. Now is a good time for the ideals of the Olympic Charter to shape the reality of the Olympics. Drop the motto *"Citius, Altius, Fortius"* ("Faster, Higher, Stronger") and replace it with "Achieving Excellence and Peace for Humanity." *What do you think?*

cooperative values more common in traditional cultures. As noted by an editor at *Newsweek*, "Sports may be America's most successful export to the world. . . . Our most visible symbol has evolved from the Stars and Stripes to Coke and the Nike Swoosh" (Starr, 1999, p. 44).

Ideally, sports facilitate cultural exchanges through which people from different nations *share* information and develop *mutual* cultural understanding. But true 50–50 sharing and mutual understanding are rare when nations have unequal power and resources. Therefore, sports often become cultural exports from wealthy nations incorporated into the everyday lives of people in other nations. These imported sports may be rejected, but they are usually revised and reinterpreted to fit with local values and lifestyles (Ben-Porat and Ben-Porat, 2004; Denham, 2004; Maguire, 2005). However, even when revisions occur, people in traditional cultures become increasingly open to the possibility of importing and consuming additional goods, services, and ideas from the wealthy nations (Jackson and Andrews, 2004). Unless political power and economic resources are developed in connection with this process, poorer nations become increasingly dependent on wealthy nations, and it becomes difficult not to adopt many of their values and ideologies. This is a complex process, involving many issues in addition to those related to sports.

New Political Realities in an Era of Transnational Corporations

Global politics have changed dramatically since the 1970s. Nation-states have been joined by powerful transnational organizations in global power relations. As noted in chapter 11, about half of the largest economies in the world are corporations, *not* nation-states. As nation-states promote capitalist expansion by lifting trade restrictions, lowering tariffs, and loosening regulations, major transnational corporations become increasingly powerful players in global politics; many of them are more economically and politically powerful than the nations in which their products are manufactured.

Therefore, the differences between national and corporate interests and identities are becoming increasingly blurred. This was highlighted by Phil Knight, the CEO of the U.S.–based Nike Corporation, as he explained his fan loyalties during the Men's World Cup in soccer:

> We see a natural evolution . . . dividing the world into their athletes and ours. And we glory ours. When the U.S. played Brazil in the World Cup, I rooted for Brazil because it was a Nike team. America was Adidas. (in Lipsyte, 1996a, p. 9)

Knight identified teams and athletes in terms of corporate logos, not nationalities. When Nike paid $200 million to sponsor Brazil's national team and used its popular players to market Nike products worldwide, Knight gave priority to his corporate logo and consumption as the most important global values. He sees international sports as sites for Nike and other corporate sponsors to deliver advertising messages promoting their products, the ideology of consumer culture, and the structural foundation for global capitalist expansion. Knight and other executives from powerful corporations see this as good for the world and everyone in it. For them, functionalist theory is their guide: Sport contributes to the operation of the global social system, and this is good for everyone in the world. Other theories explain global capitalist expansion in ways that view the world from vantage points other than the CEO's top-floor office window from which things down on the ground are difficult to see except in terms

> **Winning medals is a platform for us. It provides us the foundation, the basis, the significance to influence society. We influence society by winning medals and hearts and minds.**
> —Lloyd Ward, former CEO, U.S. Olympic Committee, 2002

of general patterns devoid subjective of human experiences (Lenskyj, 2004; Miller et al., 2001, 2003).

To the extent that corporate sponsors influence sport events and media coverage, international sports televised around the world present images and narratives directed at spectator-consumers, not spectator-citizens (see figure 13.1). Sports that don't enable corporations to deliver messages to consumers with purchasing power are not sponsored. If spectators and potential media audiences are not potential consumers, corporations see little reason to sponsor events, and commercial media have no reasons or resources to cover them.

The global power of transnational corporations is neither unlimited nor uncontested. There are documented cases where local populations have used their own cultural perspectives to make

sense of the images and narratives that come with global sports and global advertising and give them meanings that fit with their lives (Foer, 2004; Maguire, 1999, 2005). However, those who use critical theory note that global media sports and the commercial messages that accompany them often cleverly fuse the global and the local through thoughtfully and carefully edited images that combine local traditions, sport action, and consumer products in seamless and technically brilliant media representations (Andrews and Silk, 1999; Carrington and Sugden, 1999; Jackson and Andrews, 2004; Jackson and Hokowhitu, 2002; Jackson and Scherer, 2002; Miller et al., 2001, 2003; Silk, 1999; Tomlinson, 2004). They argue that these fused images tend to "detraditionalize" local cultures by representing local symbols and lifestyles in connection with consumer products.

"NBC Sports have worked hard to discourage nationalism during our coverage of the Olympics."

FIGURE 13.1 Nationalism is built into the very structure of the Olympics, and transnational corporations have been successful in combining global sport and national identities with an ideology that promotes individualism, competition, and consumption. Corporate logos now are as visible as national flags at most international sport events.

The observations of critical theories have not been explored sufficiently in research, but it is clear that, as corporations join or replace nation-states as sponsors of athletes and teams around the world, sports are framed in new political terms. According to John Horan, the publisher of *Sporting Goods Intelligence*, "It's not the Free World versus Communism anymore. Now you take sides with sneaker companies. Now everybody looks at the Olympics as Nike versus Reebok" (in Reid, 1996, p. 4BB). Horan's conclusion is distorted by his hope that global sports are perceived in this way, but it certainly captures the intent of transnational corporations as they spend billions of dollars to sponsor sports worldwide. Representatives from many major corporations see sports as vehicles for expanding markets and promoting an ideology that connects status and identity with consumption.

Coca-Cola may sponsor the Olympics because it wants to "teach the world to chill," but its real goal is to sell as many Cokes as possible to the world's 6.5 billion people. This is also why the MARS candy company pays millions to be the official snack food of the Olympics and why McDonald's does the same because they've been the Official Restaurant of the Olympic Games from 1996 through 2012. During the 2004 Games in Athens, McDonald's not only served 2 million meat patties (hamburgers) to the athletes and guests in their three venues in the Olympic Village, but they also used the nearly fat-free bodies of athletes to improve their corporate image so that they can more effectively sell hamburgers and fries worldwide and make everyone part of their McFamily (www.mcdonalds.com/usa/sports/olympic.html).

McDonald's and other corporations that sponsor global sports and use them as advertising platforms know that sooner or later the images and narratives associated with sources of pleasure and entertainment in people's lives will in some form enter the imaginations and conversations of those who see and hear them. Commercial images and messages do not dictate what people

think, but they certainly influence what people think about, and in this way, they become a part of the overall discourse that occurs in cultures around the globe.

This description of new global political realities does not mean that sports have fallen victim to a worldwide conspiracy hatched by transnational corporations. It means only that transnational organizations have joined nation-states in the global political context in which sports are defined, organized, promoted, played, presented, and given meaning around the world (Jackson and Scherer, 2002; Silk, 1999).

Other Global Political Issues

As sports become increasingly commercialized and national boundaries have become less relevant in sports, more athletes become global migrant workers. They go where their sports are played, where they can be supported or earn money while they play, or where they can have the cultural experiences they seek. This global migration of athletes has raised new political issues in connection with sports.

Another global political issue is related to the production of sporting goods. As the demand for sports equipment and clothing has increased in wealthy nations, transnational corporations cut costs for those products by manufacturing them in labor-intensive, poor countries where wages are extremely low. The result is a clear split between the world's haves and have-nots when it comes to sports. Those born into privilege in wealthy nations consume the products made by those born into disadvantaged circumstances in poor nations. This is not a new phenomenon, but it shows that sports are integrally linked with global processes and politics in yet another way.

Athletes as Global Migrant Workers   Human history is full of examples of labor migration, both forced and voluntary. Industrial societies, in particular, have depended on mobile labor forces responsive to the needs of production. Now that

In 2005 Steve Nash of Canada and Yao Ming of China were among the 20 percent of NBA players and 25 percent of NBA All-Star players from outside the United States. Over 300 million people in China watched the game—more than the entire U.S. population. Teams now recruit players from China in the hope of expanding marketing opportunities. (*Source:* Roy Dabner, AP/Wide World Photos)

economies are more global, the pervasiveness and diversity of labor migration patterns have increased. This is true in sports and many other occupational categories (Maguire, 2004, 2005; Maguire et al., 2002; Stead and Maguire, 2000).

Athletes frequently move from their hometowns when they are recruited to play elite sports, and then they may move many times after that as they are traded from team to team or seek continuing opportunities to play their sports. This migration occurs from state to state and region

to region within nations, as well as from nation to nation within and between continents (Bale and Maguire, 1994; Maguire, 2004; Maguire and Stead, 2005). Each of these moves raises issues related to (1) personal adjustments by migrating athletes, (2) the rights of athletes as workers, (3) the impact of talent migration on the nations from and to which athletes migrate, and (4) the impact of athlete migration on the identities of athletes and fans.

Some migration patterns are seasonal, involving temporary moves as athletes travel from one climate area to another to play their sports. Patterns may follow annual tour schedules as athletes travel from tournament to tournament around a region or the world, or they may involve long-term or permanent moves from one region or nation to another. For example, baseball players and snow skiers may travel alternately to the northern and southern hemispheres to play ball or ski year-round.

The range of personal experiences among migrating athletes is great. They vary from major forms of culture shock and chronic loneliness to minor homesickness and lifestyle adjustments. Some athletes are exploited by teams or clubs, whereas others make great amounts of money and receive a hero's welcome when they return home in the off-season. Some encounter prejudice against foreigners or various forms of racial and ethnic bigotry, whereas others are socially accepted and make good friends. Some cling to their national identities and socialize with fellow athletes from their homelands, whereas others develop more global identities unrelated to one national or cultural background. In some cases, teams and clubs expect foreign athletes to adjust on their own, whereas others provide support for those who need to learn a new language or become familiar with new cultural settings (Klein, 1991; Maguire, 2004, 2005).

Athletic talent migration also impacts the nations involved. For example, when the top baseball players in Latin American nations are recruited by Major League Baseball (MLB) teams in the United States and Toronto, it depletes the talent needed to maintain professional teams in Latin American nations and forces fans to depend on U.S.-based satellite television companies to watch players from their nations. As players from Japan and Korea sign contracts with MLB teams, some Japanese people worry that this trend could destroy professional baseball in their country. At the same time, they are proud that Japanese players excel on MLB teams (Cyphers, 2003). As they watch MLB games on satellite television, attendance and television ratings for Japanese baseball decline. Furthermore, as people in other countries and continents watch sports based in the United States and Canada, they often are exposed to images and messages consistent with the advertising interests of corporations headquartered in the United States.

Similar patterns exist in connection with European soccer teams that recruit players from around the world. In fact, soccer has higher rates of talent migration than other sports, although hockey, track and field, and basketball have high rates as well. The impact of this migration on national talent pools and the ability of local clubs and teams to maintain economically viable sport programs is complex. Talent migration usually benefits the nation to which athletes move more than it benefits the nation from which athletes come, but this is not always the case.

The global migration of athletes also may influence how people think about and identify themselves in connection with nation-states, but this topic has not been studied. Many people appreciate athletic talent regardless of the athlete's nationality (Cyphers, 2003), but they may also have special affections for athletes born and raised in their own nation. Does this make people more open minded and knowledgeable about other cultures, or does it make them more defensive and ethnocentric? This question becomes important because many teams and leagues recruit players from a wide range of national and cultural backgrounds. For example, prior to the 2006 season,

less than 20 percent of NHL players were U.S.-born; over half were from Canada, and about 30 percent were from European nations. Over one-fourth of the players on MLB teams and over 40 percent of the players at all levels of professional baseball in North America were born outside the United States. Among the 450 players in the NBA during the 2005–2006 season, there were 81 international players from thirty-five countries; 25 percent of the 2005 NBA All-Star selections were players born outside the United States.

These trends worry some people. This is why some leagues have quotas that limit the number of foreign-born or foreign-nationality players that teams may sign to contracts. For example, in the early 1990s, Japan banned U.S. female basketball players from its professional league. At the same time, professional leagues in Italy, Spain, and France allowed their teams to have up to two foreign players, many of whom were from the United States. In 1996 England lifted all quotas for both men's and women's pro basketball teams; during the same year, the new Major League Soccer (MLS) in the United States limited the number of non–U.S. players to four per team. Currently, some people in the United States want limits on the number of foreign athletes who can play on intercollegiate teams, but college coaches continue to recruit more athletes from outside the United States.

As commercial sport organizations expand their franchise locations across national borders and recruit athletes worldwide, talent migration will increase. The social implications of this trend are diverse and interesting to study.

Global Politics and the Production of Sports Equipment and Apparel Free-trade agreements allowing money and goods to flow back and forth across national borders without being taxed have created a new global economic environment. This makes it even more cost effective for large corporations selling products to people in wealthy nations to locate production facilities in labor-intensive, poor nations. Workers in these nations are desperate for jobs and will work for low wages under conditions that would be considered oppressive by everyone who buys the products.

Through the first few years of this century, many athletic shoes costing well over $100 a pair in the United States were cut and sewn by Chinese, Indonesian, and Thai workers, some of them children, making less than $2 per day (Sage, 1999). Children in Pakistan, India, and Bangladesh, where working conditions and pay were reprehensible, stitched soccer balls. Outrage among people who became aware of these situations in the late 1990s led to widespread social activism, much of which was fueled by the Internet. After years of confronting and struggling with companies such as Nike, Reebok, Adidas, and others, human rights activists forced some of these corporations to enact anti–child labor policies and to allow their factories to be monitored so that working conditions meet minimal standards of acceptance. But child labor and sweatshop conditions continue to exist, and a wide range of sporting goods and apparel consumed in wealthy nations is made by people living below local poverty levels and working under conditions that are difficult to endure.

A report in 2004 showed that MLB used balls stitched in Costa Rica by people who worked eleven hours a day, six days a week to earn about $2750 per year—compared to the $2.5 million average salary for MLB players. Starting at 6 A.M. and quitting at 5 P.M., unless they are forced to work overtime, the people in Costa Rican factories earn about 30 cents for sewing 108 perfect stitches on the seams of a ball. The work is hard says a thirty-seven-year-old man who sews baseballs in a factory where the temperature often is above 90 degrees. "Sometimes," he explains, "it messes up your hands, warps your fingers and hurts your shoulders" (Weiner, 2004). This man's 30 cents of labor produces a ball that Rawlings Sporting Goods sells for $15 at U.S. retail stores.

Workers' rights continue to be a significant global issue. Research shows that it is possible to improve working conditions among people who produce sporting goods and other products if enough people in wealthy nations participate in actions that make corporations accountable and provide exploited workers the resources they need to demand higher wages and better working conditions. Sport sociologist George Sage (1999) has documented the impact of the Nike Transnational Advocacy Network, an Internet-based form of political activism that mobilized people worldwide to force Nike to meet certain standards of social responsibility in the way they treated production workers. Sage's study is heartening because it shows that change is possible, even when dealing with multibillion-dollar corporations and the autocratic governments of nations that allow corporations to exploit their people. The study also is provocative because it indicates that unless consumers in wealthy nations are socially concerned about how their products are made, there is little to stop transnational corporations that operate in an underregulated global marketplace from pursuing profits in whatever ways they wish.

Such concerns among students at the University of North Carolina led them to make sure that the university's 2001 contract with Nike contained clauses guaranteeing that the apparel and equipment sold in the campus store and used in the athletic department were made in conformity with an antisweatshop code. Student leaders saw this as one step in dealing with the exploitation of labor in poor nations where few laws protect workers. Students at other universities have taken or considered taking similar steps (Sage, 1999). In the case of Nike, this type of action can be effective because it has contracts with hundreds of college and university athletic departments. But Nike is only one of many corporations seeking the cheapest labor they can find to manufacture products. Human rights and social justice groups have fought these battles for many years, but they need help.

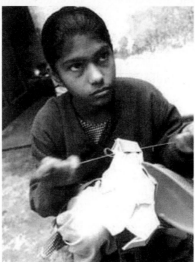

In the mid-1990s, many people became aware of the exploitive labor practices used to produce sports equipment and apparel. These photos, provided by the Global March Against Child Labour, show a twelve-year-old girl in India sewing a soccer ball. The ball is stamped with the claim that it is made with "Child Free Labour." Sweatshop labor is still used to produce sport products consumed by people in wealthy nations, but global social activism has stopped some companies from using child labor. (*Source:* Global March Against Child Labor)

Making Sense of Political Realities

Its not easy to explain all the changes discussed in this chapter. Are sports simply a part of general globalization processes through which various forms of sport come together in many combinations? Are we witnessing the modernization of sports? Are sports being Americanized? Europeanized? Asianized?

Do global processes involve the diffusion of sports throughout the world, with people in some countries emulating the sports played in other countries, or do they involve the use of sports in connection with capitalist expansion and new forms of cultural imperialism? Are sports used to make poorer nations dependent on wealthier ones, or do they provide emerging nations with opportunities to establish cultural and economic independence? As globalization occurs, will traditional sports and folk games around the world be replaced by the competitive sports favored by wealthy and powerful nations?

Those of us who study sports in society are increasingly concerned about these questions. The best work on these issues involves data collected at global *and* local levels (Bale and Christensen, 2004; Bale and Cronin, 2003; Ben-Porat and Ben Porat, 2004; Denham, 2004; Donnelly, 1996a; Foer, 2004; Harvey et al., 1996; Hastings et al., 2005; Maguire, 1999, 2004, 2005; Okubu, 2004). This work indicates that powerful people do not simply impose certain sport forms on less powerful people around the world. Even when sports from powerful nations are played in other parts of the world, the meanings given to them are grounded in the local cultures in which they are played. Global trends are important, but so are the local expressions of and responses to those trends. Power is a process, not a thing; it is always exercised through relationships and current forms of social organization, so our understanding of power must take into account the ways that societies are organized and the ways that people determine what is important as they live with one another. This is true in connection with sports and in all dimensions of social life.

POLITICS IN SPORTS

The term *politics* usually is associated with formal government entities in the public sphere. However, politics include all processes of governing people and administering policies, at all levels of organization, public and private. Therefore, politics are an integral part of sports, and many local, national, and international sport organizations are referred to as "governing bodies."

Most sport organizations provide and regulate sport participation opportunities, establish and enforce policies, control and standardize competitions, and acknowledge the accomplishments of athletes. This sounds like a straightforward set of tasks, but they seldom are accomplished without opposition, debate, and compromise. Members of sport organizations agree on many things, but conflicts often arise as decisions are made in connection with the following questions:

1. What qualifies as a sport?
2. What are the rules of a sport?
3. Who makes and enforces the rules in sports?
4. Who organizes and controls sport events?
5. Where do sport events take place?
6. Who is eligible to participate in a sport?
7. How are rewards distributed to athletes and others associated with sports?

These questions are inherently political because the answers affect different people in different ways. Most people understand this, but they complain about politics in sports only when the answers are not the ones they want to hear. This becomes clear in the following sections.

What Qualifies as a Sport?

As noted in chapter 1, there is no universal agreement on the definition of *sports*. What is considered a sport in a society or a particular event, such as the Olympics, is determined through political processes (Donnelly, 1996b). The criteria used to identify sports reflect the ideas and interests of some people more than others. In the Olympics, for example, a competitive activity or game for men must be played in at least seventy-five countries on four continents to be considered for inclusion in the Olympic Games; an activity or a game for women must be played in at least forty countries on three continents. It also must have an officially designated international governing body, a requisite number of national governing bodies, and a history of international championships before the IOC will consider recognizing it as an Olympic sport. However, IOC decisions about what qualifies as a sport can be changed, as seen in 2005 when baseball and softball were eliminated from the program for the 2012 Olympics in London.

In these days of multibillion-dollar media contracts, an activity or a game is more likely to be recognized as a sport if it is attractive to younger viewers, who will bring new advertisers and corporate sponsors to the Olympics and the television coverage of the Games. It also helps if women play the activity because more women than men watch the Olympics and the IOC knows it must highlight gender equity if it is to avoid bad publicity for the Olympics as a whole.

This method of determining what qualifies as a sport favors nations that historically have emphasized competitive games and had the resources to export their games around the world. Former colonial powers are especially favored because they used their national games to introduce their cultural values and traditions to people in the regions that they colonized. Wealthy and powerful nations today not only have their national sports broadcast on satellite channels around the world but also have the resources to subsidize the development of these sports worldwide. Therefore, when the IOC uses its method of recognition, the sports from wealthy nations are at the top of the list. When these sports are recognized as official Olympic sports, the cultural values and traditions of wealthy and powerful nations are reaffirmed. In this way, the sports in wealthy and powerful nations become part of an emerging global culture that favors their interests. This also is why native games in

traditional cultures are not a part of the Olympics. Games played only in limited regions of the world don't qualify for recognition as sports. Therefore, if people from nations with traditional cultures want to participate in the Olympics, they must learn to do sports as they are done in wealthy nations. If people in traditional cultures lack access to the equipment and facilities needed to train in their homelands, they must depend on support from people and organizations in wealthy nations to become athletes in recognized "international" sports. In this way, sports enable people and organizations in wealthy nations to gain a cultural foothold in other nations and use it to promote changes that foster their interests.

This type of political process also occurs in other contexts. For example, for well over a hundred years, the men who have controlled athletic departments in North American high schools and colleges have used a power and performance model to designate certain activities as varsity sports. They have organized these sports to emphasize competition and physical dominance, so they reaffirm male notions of character and excellence. This way of defining and organizing sports seldom has been questioned, but if power and performance sports attract fewer girls and women than boys and men, it may be time to ask critical questions about what qualifies as a varsity sport and why. When we ask these questions, we become sensitive to the politics that have long worked to the advantage of men in sports. Trying to change taken-for-granted political realities always creates resistance among those who have benefited from them. Ironically, many men say that people who challenge traditional realities are slaves to "political correctness." What they mean, however, is that they don't want to change the insensitive and self-interested ways of doing things that allow them to ignore the needs of others.

The development of criteria underlying the meaning and organization of sports also occurs on a global scale. Sociologist Peter Donnelly (1996b) illustrates this in his analysis of how the

Kato is an Asian game, played here at a Hmong Sports Event in St. Paul, Minnesota. The large Hmong population in the upper Midwest of the United States uses traditional sports to reaffirm their cultural heritage. However, it is unlikely that Kato or other traditional Asian or African games will be added to the list of Olympic sports. The definition of an Olympic sport favors sports developed and played in Western Europe and North America. (*Source:* Eric Miller; AP/Wide World Photos)

ideologies of "Olympism" and "professionalism" have been combined to form a global sport monoculture, which he calls "prolympism." Prolympism is now the model for determining what qualifies and is funded as "sport" in nations around the world. This occurs even in nations where prolympism is clearly inconsistent with traditional games. In this way, the politics of defining *sport* are both local and global in impact.

What Are the Rules of a Sport?

Sports are social constructions because people create them as they interact with one another within the constraints of culture and society. The rules that govern sports also are social constructions created through political processes. Why should first base be 90 feet from home plate in Major League Baseball? Why should a basketball rim be 10 feet above the ground? Why should

the top of a volleyball net be 88⅛ inches off the ground in international women's volleyball? Why can't pole vaulters use any type of pole they want? Why can't tournament golfers use any golf club or golf ball they want? Why is 6 centimeters the maximum height for the sides of bikini bottoms worn by women in beach volleyball when men wear long shorts? This list of questions could go on and on. The point is that the rules of sports can be based on many concerns, and this makes them political. Because sports have more rules than many human activities, they are especially political.

Who Makes and Enforces the Rules in Sports?

The rules of an "official" sport are determined by a recognized governing body that makes decisions affecting the sport and its participants. The process of becoming recognized as the *sole* governing body of a sport clearly involves politics. Governing bodies have power, status, and control over resources, so it is common for more than one organization to claim that it is the rightful rule-making body for a sport. The simultaneous existence of various governing bodies creates confusion for athletes and spectators. Professional boxing, for example, has at least four governing bodies (the WBO, the WBU, the WBF, and the IBO), each with its own weight categories and championships and each claiming to be the official rule-making body for boxing. "New" sports, such as skateboarding, snowboarding, in-line skating, and BMX (biking), each have had at least two organizations vying to be official governing bodies. As organizations seek power over sports and the athletes who participate in them, they battle one another to recruit dues-paying members and sponsor competitive events, especially national and international championships. In the process, their policies confuse athletes and limit participation opportunities. When this occurs, people clearly see politics in sports.

When rules exist, there is a need for rule enforcement. This adds another political dimension to sports. Anyone who has ever refereed or officiated a game or match will tell you that rule violations are seldom clear-cut. Identifying violations is difficult, and few people see violations the same way. Rule violations occur on a regular basis in many sports, but the best referees learn when to call fouls or penalties in connection with these violations. In fact, referees and officials discuss when they should or should not call fouls during games and matches. They realize that it is a political challenge to make sports appear to be fair to athletes and spectators.

Enforcing off-the-field rules is also a political challenge. The process of investigating rule violations, determining innocence or guilt, and punishing rule violators involves judgments based on ideas about fairness, moral principles, economic interests, personal reputations, organizational prestige, or other factors. How these factors are considered and which ones prevail in the rule enforcement process are political matters.

Who Organizes and Controls Sport Events?

Representatives of official governing bodies often organize and control sport events. Standards emerge when the governing body is stable, but standards don't exist once and for all time. For example, even though governing bodies devise formal standards for judging performances in figure skating, diving, and gymnastics, research shows that the votes of judges are influenced by political loyalties, personal connections, coercion, and bribes (Jennings, 1996a; Jennings and Sambrook, 2000; Seltzer and Glass, 1991). This has been a serious issue in many Olympic Games, but it became widely publicized in 2002 when a judge for the figure skating pairs competition allegedly favored a Russian couple over a Canadian couple. Her scores determined who received the gold and silver medals, respectively. After much debate, the International Skating Union (ISU) awarded the Canadian couple a gold medal without taking the gold medal away from the Russian couple. Then the ISU changed its rules to discourage unfair judging in the future, but the changes were widely criticized and have been revised at least twice between 2003 and 2006.

When international politics influence judges, it is disheartening to athletes, but it should be no more disheartening than the knowledge that "cuteness," "hairstyles," "body build," and "eye color" can also influence judges when it comes to female athletes in certain events. This is a form of cultural politics that force some athletes to spend thousands of dollars on everything from braces to straighten their teeth to plastic surgery if they wish to be successful. Politics come in many forms.

Now that sports are heavily commercialized, official governing bodies and a combination of corporate sponsors and media production people organize and control events. The location and

The size and wealth of the United States enables its athletes to win many Olympic medals. This makes American athletes and spectators happy. However, when New York City entered a bid to host the 2012 Games, it received little support because many IOC members were critical of U.S. hegemony in sports and in global affairs. Politics in sports often cannot be separated from politics outside sports. (*Source:* Jay Coakley)

timing of events, event schedules, the awarding of press credentials, and the choices of which television companies will broadcast the events and which corporate logos will be displayed are resolved through political processes. The participants in those processes and their interests change from one event to the next; this means that there is never an end to politics in sports.

Where Do Sport Events Take Place?

Site selection decisions have become increasingly political recently because more "places" now bid to host teams and events. The selection

of Olympic sites has always been political as clearly demonstrated by the site selection, vote-buying scandal involving the IOC and the Salt Lake Olympic Organizing Committee during the 1990s. As the stakes for hosting the Olympic Games have increased, bid committees have been willing to wine, dine, bribe, and pressure IOC members, whose votes determine which city hosts a particular Games (Jennings, 1996a; Jennings and Sambrook, 2000; Simson and Jennings, 1992). The politics of site selection also operate in other ways. For example, when Atlanta was selected to host the 1996 Games, it was clear to many people worldwide that the selection process was influenced by the television rights fees anticipated from NBC and the location of Coca-Cola's international headquarters in Atlanta. Coca-Cola had a sixty-seven-year history of paying hundreds of millions of dollars to support the IOC and sponsor the Olympics, and IOC members felt indebted to the corporation. During the Games, the red-and-white Coke logo was so evident in Atlanta and Olympic venues that many observers described them as the "Coca-Colympics."

The selection of Beijing, China, for the 2008 Summer Olympic Games involved political considerations and complex political processes. China was desperate to host the games because it wanted to showcase its culture, solicit tourism and business investments, and claim political legitimacy as a global power. The members of the IOC selection committee were influenced by many considerations: China was home to nearly 20 percent of the world's population, it had never hosted an Olympic Games, bringing Olympism to China would strengthen the Olympic movement, and the potential economic benefits of awarding the games to China were very high because corporate sponsors would see China as a prime site for capitalist expansion. NBC, the U.S. network with the rights to televise the 2008 Games, saw China as an attractive site for marketing its coverage. NBC knew that by 2008 many Americans would be very interested in China because of its size, power, culture, and economic growth potential. NBC also knew it could use that interest to boost ratings and sell high-priced advertising time to transnational corporations.

Site bids for events such as Super Bowls, All-Star games, NASCAR races, the NCAA men's and women's basketball tournaments, and large international events may not cost as much as bids to host the Olympics, but they are just as political. In many parts of the world, these politics reflect environmental issues. For example, the use of open space or agricultural land for golf courses is being contested in Europe, Japan, and even North America. As one researcher claims, "golf has

acquired the status of a four-letter word because of the havoc it has wrought across the globe" www.twnside.org.sg/title2/ttcd/TA-06.doc). The Global Anti-Golf Movement (www.antigolf.org/) is fueled by widespread objections to the use of chemical fertilizers and massive water resources to keep grass soft and green for golfers representing the economic elite in societies. It is a loosely organized collection of lobbying groups, often focused on environmental issues in densely populated regions of India and Southeast Asia.

Ski resort expansion in North America, Europe, and Japan also has been resisted for environmental reasons. The organizers of the 2000 Sydney Games faced severe criticism when they failed in important ways to live up to the environmental principles developed by the original bid committee (Lenskyj, 1998). Such examples highlight the fact that the politics of place in sports often involve local opposition to hosting events and building sport facilities.

Who Is Eligible to Participate in a Sport?

Yamilé Aldama was born in Cuba, she lives in London, and she is a citizen of Sudan; soon she will also be a British citizen (Price, 2004). To make things more interesting, let's imagine that she married a Jamaican and gave birth to a child in the United States. As an elite athlete, Ms. Aldama asks where her national team is because she wants to compete in the Olympics. Such questions are increasingly common today as athletes have parents from different nations and a birthplace that differs from the nations where they live, train, attend school, or get married (Layden, 2005; Wertheim, 2004a).

Who plays and who doesn't is a hotly contested issue in sports. As people in governing bodies make eligibility decisions, they use criteria such as gender, age, weight, height, ability (and disability), place of residence, citizenship, educational affiliation, grade in school, social status, income, or even race and ethnicity to determine

Political Barriers
I Think . . . This Opens Some Doors for People

When we talk about sports and people with a disability, we must talk politics; there's no way around it. Take Casey Martin as an example. In 1994 as a junior at Stanford, he was voted captain of the golf team. He responded by leading them to the collegiate championship. Tiger Woods joined the team in 1995, and Martin was his roommate when Stanford played tournaments away from Palo Alto. Martin won the U.S. Intercollegiate Golf Championship that year and led Stanford to the NCAA finals.

But all was not well with Martin. He was born with a congenital defect in his right leg. It prevented normal blood circulation and was gradually eroding his bone and causing him increasingly severe and chronic pain. There were times when he could barely walk, so his coach convinced him to use a golf cart, permissible under NCAA rules, given his medical condition. After graduating, Martin played professional golf and by 1997 found that there were times when he could not walk and needed a motorized cart to complete eighteen holes. But the PGA ruled that Martin had to walk or quit. Martin sued and won an injunction allowing him to use a cart. The PGA appealed and the case eventually went to the U.S. Supreme Court. In a split decision, the court ruled in 2001, that under the Americans with Disability Act of 1990, Martin must be allowed to use a cart because it did not force the PGA to make an unreasonable accommodation in his case.

Playing politics with the PGA for four years cost Martin well over $100,000. His pain and fatigue continued to increase and he played only nine tournaments between 2001 and late 2005. At thirty-three years old (in 2005), he knows that a leg amputation is a certainty.

In the meantime, Nike has established the Casey Martin Nike Award that honors an individual with a disability who has taken a public stand and engaged in political battles to inspire or expand sport participation rights for people with disabilities. Nike's position is that, "If you have a body, you are an athlete."

The Casey Martin story is not unique. People with disabilities have always fought political battles to avoid being invisible in the world of sport (DePauw, 1997). For example, even in 2005 as representatives of London, Madrid, Moscow, New York, and Paris gave detailed presentations in the hope of being chosen by the IOC to host the 2012 Olympics and Paralympics, only Madrid mentioned the Paralympics in their overall plan. Invisibility was in plain sight.

After the Supreme Court decision in 2001, Casey Martin said, "I"m thrilled . . . I think in the future this opens some doors for people." However, in the real world of sport where decisions are made about everything from eligibility and the rules of the game to where events are played and the distribution of rewards, people with disabilities know that if they don't play politics, eventually, they won't play at all.

Politics are related to sports for people with disabilities in many ways. War, land mines, and dangerous working conditions continue to be leading causes of disabilities worldwide. Elliot Mujaji of Zimbabwe lost his arm when he was electrocuted in an accident at work. He won gold medals in the 100-meter race in both Sydney and Athens. (*Source:* David Biene; photo courtesy of Ossur)

participation eligibility. Although eligibility policies often are presented as if they were based on unchanging truths about human beings and sports, they are grounded in political agreements. This is true in local youth sport programs and the Olympics.

People often debate the seeming arbitrariness of eligibility rules. For example, NCAA eligibility rules are so complex that the organization publishes brochures and supplements explaining who may and may not play under various conditions. Lawsuits are filed when people feel that they've been denied eligibility unfairly. High school students challenge eligibility rules when their families move from one school district to another and they are declared ineligible to play varsity sports. The "no pass, no play" rules in U.S. high school sports also are debated. Even in youth sports, there are frequent debates about the age and weight rules used to determine eligibility. These have increased as children of immigrants want to play youth sports and have none of the formal birth records that are routinely kept in the United States. Athletes with disabilities regularly challenge rules prohibiting their participation in certain sports. Within events such as the Paralympics there are frequent debates about disability classifications and eligibility. This is discussed in the Breaking Barriers box on page 477.

There are literally hundreds of other noteworthy cases of eligibility politics in amateur and professional sports. For example, eighteen-year-old basketball players may be denied an opportunity to make money playing in the NBA, but eighteen-year-old golfers can obtain their PGA or LPGA tour cards and win money in tournaments, and tennis players can earn prize money as young as fifteen years old. The meanings given to age vary from one context to another as eligibility is determined. As global mobility increases, there will be more questions about eligibility as it is related to citizenship, nationality, and place of residence. Amateur sports have long

been the scene for debates over the meaning of *amateur* and who qualifies as an amateur athlete. Because these meanings are socially determined, they change over time and from place to place. This is another reason why politics will always be a part of sports.

How Are Rewards Distributed to Athletes and Others?

The distribution of rewards is an issue at all levels of sport participation. Coaches, league administrators, sportswriters, judges, team owners, arbitrators, tournament committees, and parents decide who will receive special commendations, certificates of accomplishment, trophies, scholarships, contracts, pay increases, and so on. "Who gets what?" is a political question, and the answers are not always clear-cut. People discuss and sometimes argue about rewards. As the level of competition increases, so do the stakes associated with decisions. At the highest levels of competition, these decisions can involve massive amounts of money and status.

With the increased commercialization of sports, there are heated debates about the ways that revenues should be distributed among sport organizations, organization officials, owners and promoters, athletes, and others connected with sports. As noted in chapter 11, the political processes associated with the distribution of revenues in commercial sports are complex and never ending. These processes take various forms and come to different resolutions in different countries and sports.

An important "who gets what?" issue in U.S. sports concerns pay for intercollegiate athletes. Why should a talented intercollegiate football player who risks his health and endures pain and injury while generating millions of dollars for his university be limited to receiving an athletic grant-in-aid worth only a fraction of what NFL players are paid? Why is this player not allowed to make money selling his own image on shirts or coffee mugs, while the university uses his image to market everything from the school itself to merchandise with the university logo on it? Athletes in revenue-producing sports say this is unfair; university spokespeople say that there is no fair way to pay all athletes who play on varsity teams, and no way to determine the dollar value of the contributions made by athletes in revenue-producing sports. Regardless of current policy, the debate will continue, and athletes will continue to lose unless they organize and obtain more power.

Other debates revolve around questions such as these: Why should professional sport team owners make more money than the best players on their teams? What percentage should agents receive when they negotiate player contracts? Why should prize money in a NASCAR race reflect how many times a driver has raced during a season in addition to how the driver finishes a race? Why should Olympic athletes not be paid for their participation when they collectively generate over a billion dollars during the Games? Why should the IOC receive 33 percent of the revenues from every Olympics, and why should the USOC receive 12.8 percent of the money paid by U.S. television companies for the rights to broadcast the Olympics (about $114 million in 2008) when the United States already has more athlete-training money than any other nation? Should athletes receive compensation when their images and uniform numbers are used in video games? These and hundreds of similar questions show that the "politics of rewards" are an integral part of sports.

Sometimes rewards involve status or prestige rather than money, such as being selected to a Hall of Fame or an All-American team. Even youth league teams have "politics of status" awards for "the most improved player of the year," "the most valuable player," "the most dedicated player," and so on. When people agree on who should receive these awards, they forget that the selection process is political. It is only

when they don't agree that they complain about politics in sports.

summary

HOW DO GOVERNMENTS AND GLOBAL PROCESSES INFLUENCE SPORTS?

Sports and politics are inseparable. Government involvement in sports is generally related to the need for sponsorship, organization, and facilities. The fact that sports are important in people's lives and can be sites for social conflict often leads to government regulations. The forms of government involvement in sports vary by society, but they generally occur to (1) safeguard the public order, (2) maintain health and fitness among citizens, (3) promote the prestige and power of a group, community, or nation, (4) promote a sense of identity, belonging, and unity among citizens, (5) reproduce values consistent with dominant ideology, (6) increase support for political leaders and government structures, and (7) promote economic development.

The rules, policies, and funding priorities set by government officials and agencies reflect the political struggles among groups within any society. This does not mean that the same people always benefit when government involvement occurs, but involvement seldom results in equal benefits for everyone. For example, when funds are dedicated to the development and training of elite athletes, fewer funds are available to support general participation programs. Funding priorities could favor mass participation instead of elite sports, but the point is that the priorities themselves are subject to debate and negotiation. This political process is an inevitable part of sports.

History shows government intervention in sports usually favors groups with the greatest resources and organization, and with goals that support the ideological orientations of public officials. The groups least likely to be favored are those that fail to understand the connection between sports and politics or lack resources to effectively influence political decisions. When people believe the myth that sports and politics are unrelated, they are unlikely to be pleased when officials develop policies and allocate funds.

The connection between sports and global political processes is complex. Ideally, sports bring nations together in contexts supportive of peace and friendship. Although this occurs, the reality is that most nations use sports to foster their own interests. Displays of nationalism have been and continue to be common at international events. The Olympic Games are a good case in point. People who work with, promote, or follow the Olympics often focus on national medal counts and use them to support their claims for national status.

Powerful transnational corporations have joined nation-states as major participants in global political processes. As a result, sports are used increasingly for economic as well as political purposes. Nationalism and the promotion of national interests remain part of global sports, but consumerism and the promotion of capitalist expansion have become more important since 1991 and the end of the cold war. Within the context of global relations, athletes and teams now are associated with corporate logos as well as nation-states. Global sport events are now political *and* economic. They are sites for presenting numerous images and narratives associated with the interests of nation-states and corporate sponsors. The dominant discourses associated with sports are clearly consistent with the interests of corporate sponsors, and they promote an ideology infused with the capitalist values of individualism, competition, achievement, and consumption.

Global political processes also are associated with other aspects of sports such as the migration patterns of elite athletes and the production of sporting goods. Political issues are raised when athletes cross national borders to play their sports and when transnational corporations produce

sports equipment and clothing in labor-intensive, poor nations and then sell them in wealthy nations. These and other issues associated with global political processes are best understood when they are studied on both global and local levels. Data in these studies help determine when sports involve reciprocal cultural exchanges leading to mutual understanding among people and when they involve processes through which powerful nations and corporations exercise subtle influence over social life and political events in less powerful nations.

Politics are also part of the very structure and organization of sports. Political processes exist because people in sport organizations must answer questions about what qualifies as a sport, what the rules of a sport should be and how they should be enforced, who should organize and control sport events, where sport events should occur, who is eligible to participate, and how rewards will be distributed. This is why many sport organizations are described as governing bodies: They are responsible for making decisions that affect people connected with sports. This demonstrates that sports are inseparable from politics and political processes.

 See the OLC, www.mhhe.com/coakley9e, for an annotated list of readings related to this chapter. The OLC also contains a key concept list, a review test, and other helpful features.

WEBSITE RESOURCES

Note: Websites often change. The following URLs were current when this book was printed. Please check our website (www.mhhe.com/coakley8e) for updates and additions.

www.mhhe.com/coakley9e   Click on chapter 13 for information on sports and international relations, gift giving and the Olympic scandal, and politics and the Paralympic movement.

www.ucalgary.ca/library/ssportsite/   Scroll down to "National Sport Structures and Organizations" and find links to nearly every established organization in the world, including National Olympic Committees and government sport organizations around the world.

www.olympic.org   The site of the International Olympic Committee; has links to National Olympic committees around the world and information about the IOC and its programs.

http://europa.eu.int/comm/sport/index_en.html   The site of *Sport and European Union* covers issues related to the development of sport through the European Union; information about programs, government influence on sports, and the politics of coordinating national sport governing bodies with this international governing body.

www.usoc.org   The site of the United States Olympic Committee with links to thirty-five national governing bodies for Olympic sports, five governing bodies for Pan American sports, seven organizations for the disabled in sports, and other education-based and community-based multisport organizations.

www.iwg-gti.org   The site of the International Working Group on Women and Sport; contains information on programs, policy issues, and problems faced by girls and women in nearly one hundred countries; information reveals different patterns of government involvement as well as the cultural issues that influence programs, policies, and problems; key links to other international sport organizations.

www.un.org/sport2005/   This URL changes yearly from, for example, 2005 to 2006; the site contains up-to-date news related to sports and issues of development around the world; there are links to the latest reports and projects; also a link to a Sport for Development and Peace report entitled, "Sport as a Tool for Development and Peace: Towards Achieving the United Nations Millennium Development Goals" (33 pages).

www.un.org/Depts/dhl/resguide/r58.htm   This site has links to two U.N. resolutions: "Building a Peaceful and Better World Through Sport and the Olympic Ideal" (A/RES/58/6) and "Sport as a Means to Promote Education, Health, Development and Peace" (A/RES/58/5); to find them, start at the bottom of the list and move up.

http://olympicstudies.uab.es/eng/index.html   This is the site of the Olympic Studies Centre at the Universitat Autònoma de Barcelona; has many links to official information about the Olympics.

http://purl.access.gpo.gov/GPO/LPS28875 (PDF is at http://purl.access.gpo.gov/GPO/LPB28876)   The Beijing Olympics and human rights: roundtable before the United States Congressional–Executive Commission on China, 107th Congress, second session, November 18, 2002.

http://purl.access.gpo.gov/GPO/LPS31547 (PDF is at http://purl.access.gpo.gov/GPO/LPS31554)   Does the U.S. Olympic Committee's organizational structure impede its mission?: Hearing . . . United States. Congress. House. Subcommittee on Commerce, Trade and Consumer Protection, 180th Congress, first session, March 19, 2003. Sixty-one pages in PDF format

http://www.policyalternatives.ca/index.cfm?act=news&do=Article&call=163&pA=BB736455   Olympic costs and benefits: a cost–benefit analysis of the proposed Vancouver 2010 Winter Olympic and Paralympic Games, by Marvin Shaffer, Alan Greer and Celine Mauboules. Vancouver: Canadian Centre for Policy Alternatives, Feb. 2003.

www.aafla.com   This site of the Amateur Athletic Foundation in the United States has an outstanding collection of historical and political information about sports, especially international sports; go to "Sports Library."

www.globalmarch.org/campaigns/worldcupcampaign/Index.php   This is the site of the Global March Against Child Labour, an international movement based in India and focused on eliminating exploitive work that condemns millions of children to lives of servitude and suffering; this site takes you to its 2002 World Cup project.

www.educatingforjustice.org/   The site of Educating for Justice formed by former college students who began a grassroots campaign to end social injustice; its Nike Corporate Accountability Campaign is explained at this site.

(H. Armstrong Roberts)

SPORTS IN HIGH SCHOOL AND COLLEGE

Do Competitive Sports Contribute to Education?

IN AMERICA, ESPECIALLY in suburban communities, having a good football team or a basketball team is synonymous with being a good school.

—Gerald Tirozzi, executive director, National Association of High School Principals, 1999

Online Learning Center Resources

Visit *Sports in Society*'s Online Learning Center (OLC) at **www.mhhe.com/coakley9e** for additional information and study material for this chapter, including

• Self-grading quizzes
• Learning objectives
• Related websites
• Additional readings

A complete outline is available online at www.mhhe.com/coakley9e.

THE CURRENT COLLEGE sports landscape is meaner than ever, more overtly commercial, more winner-take-all. And just as in the rest of the economy, the gap between rich and poor is widening.

—**Michael Sokolove, journalist (2002)**

AMERICAN STUDENTS ENCOUNTER two distractions in high school that other nations minimize—part-time work and sports. . . . Part-time work may capture students' time. Sports captures their hearts.

—**Tom Loveless (2002)**

The emergence of modern organized sports is closely tied to education in England and North America. However, the United States is the only nation in the world where it is taken for granted that high schools and colleges sponsor and fund interschool varsity sport programs. In most countries, community-based athletic clubs funded by members or by a combination of public and private sources sponsor organized sports for school-aged young people. Only Canada and Japan have some schools that sponsor competitive teams, but they usually are no more important than other cocurricular activities. Interscholastic sports are an accepted and important part of U.S. high schools and colleges. When the emphasis on varsity sports dominates the cultures and public profiles of schools, many people become concerned about their impact on the quality of education.

This chapter is organized around four major questions related to interscholastic sport programs:

1. What are the arguments for and against the programs?
2. How are the programs related to the educational experiences of athletes and other students in high schools and colleges?
3. What effects do the programs have on the organization of schools and the quality of educational programs?
4. What are the major problems associated with the programs and how might the problems be solved?

ARGUMENTS FOR AND AGAINST INTERSCHOLASTIC SPORTS

Most people in the United States see interscholastic sports as an expected part of life in high schools and colleges. However, budget cutbacks and highly publicized problems in some programs have raised questions about the relationship between these sports, the development of young people, and the achievement of educational goals. Responses to these questions are varied and almost always based on strong emotions. Program supporters claim that interscholastic sports support the educational mission of schools and the development of young people, whereas critics claim that they interfere with that mission and distract students from the things that they should be learning to be responsible citizens. The main points made on both sides of this debate are summarized in table 14.1.

When people enter this debate, they often exaggerate the benefits or the problems associated with interscholastic sports. Supporters emphasize glowing success stories, and critics emphasize shocking cases of excess and abuse, but the most accurate descriptions probably lie somewhere in-between. Nonetheless, both the supporters and the critics call attention to important issues in the relationship between sports and education. This chapter focuses on those issues.

INTERSCHOLASTIC SPORTS AND THE EXPERIENCES OF HIGH SCHOOL STUDENTS

Do varsity sport programs affect the educational and developmental experiences of high school students? This question is difficult to answer. Education and development occur in connection with many activities and relationships. Even though interscholastic sports are important in most schools and the lives of many students, they constitute only one of many potentially influential experiences. Quantitative research on this issue, usually based on functionalist theory, has focused primarily on the characteristics of varsity athletes and how they compare with the characteristics of other students. Qualitative research, often guided by interactionist and critical theories, has focused on the ways that interscholastic sports are connected with school

Table 14.1 Popular arguments for and against interscholastic sports

Arguments For	Arguments Against
1. They involve students in school activities and increase interest in academic activities.	1. They distract students from academic activities and distort values in school culture.
2. They build the self-esteem, responsibility, achievement orientation, and teamwork skills required for occupational success today.	2. They perpetuate dependence, conformity, and a power and performance orientation that is no longer appropriate in postindustrial society.
3. They foster fitness and stimulate interest in physical activities among students.	3. They turn most students into passive spectators and cause too many serious injuries to athletes.
4. They generate the spirit and unity necessary to maintain the school as a viable organization.	4. They create a superficial, transitory spirit, that is unrelated to educational goals.
5. They promote parental, alumni, and community support for all school programs.	5. They deprive educational programs of resources, facilities, staff, and community support.
6. They give students opportunities to develop and display skills in activities valued in society and to be recognized for their athletic skills.	6. They create pressure on athletes and support a hierarchical status system in which athletes have excessive privilege and sometimes use it to assert dominance over other students.

culture and the everyday lives of high school students.

High School Athletes[1]

Studies have shown consistently that, when compared with students who do not play varsity sports, high school athletes, *as a group*, generally have better grade point averages, more positive attitudes toward school, lower rates of absenteeism, more interest in attending college, more years of college completed, more career success, and better health (see Barber et al., 2001; Broh, 2002; Carlson et al., 2005; Curtis et al., 2003; Eitle, 2005; Eitle and Eitle, 2002; Guest and Schneider, 2003; Hunt, 2005; Marsh and Kleitman, 2002; Miller et al., 2000, 2005; Miracle and Rees, 1994; Rees

and Miracle, 2000; Videon, 2002). These differences usually have been modest, and it has been difficult for researchers to separate the effects of sport participation from the effects of social class, family background, support from friends, identity issues, and other factors related to educational attitudes and achievement.

We do know that membership on a varsity team is a valued status in many U.S. schools, and it seems to go hand in hand with positive educational experiences for some students, reduced dropout rates, and increased identification with the school (Marsh, 1993; McNeal, 1995). However, research has not told us if sport participation actually *causes* these outcomes or why it affects students in certain ways (Carlson et al., 2005).

Why Are Athletes Different?   The most logical explanation for differences between varsity athletes and other students is that interscholastic sports, like other extracurricular activities, attract students who already have characteristics that lead to academic and social success in high school. Most studies have not been able to test this explanation because researchers don't actually follow students during their high school

---

[1]I do not use the term *student-athlete* because all members of school teams are students, just like band members and debaters. Using the term *student* is redundant. The NCAA has promoted the use of this term as a political strategy to deflect the criticism that big-time college athletic programs are overcommercialized, overprofessionalized, and generally unrelated to the academic mission of universities. I don't want to be co-opted by the NCAA's political agenda.

careers to keep track of how and why changes occur in their lives. Usually, people do studies in which they collect data at one point in time and simply compare students who play on sport teams with students who don't. These studies are not very helpful because they don't allow researchers to say whether playing varsity sports really changes young people in systematic ways or whether students who try out for teams, are selected by coaches, and choose to remain on teams are simply different from other students *before* they ever become varsity athletes.

The mere fact that young people grow and develop during the same years that they play interscholastic sports does not mean that sport participation *causes* the growth and development. Fourteen- to eighteen-year-olds grow and develop in many ways whether they play varsity sports or do other things. Most studies do not distinguish among all the different activities and experiences that might explain changes that occur in students' lives during high school. This is crucial because research shows that young people who play on varsity sport teams are more likely to come from *economically privileged* backgrounds and have *above-average* cognitive abilities, self-esteem, and past academic performance records, including grades and test scores (Child Trends, 2005; Carlson et al., 2005; Eitle, 2005; Fejgin, 1994; Hunt, 2005; Rees and Miracle, 2000; Spreitzer, 1995). This means that students who try out for, make, and stay on teams are different from other students *before* they become high school athletes.

This type of *selection-in process* is common in most extracurricular activities, not just varsity sports. Students who choose to participate in official, school-sponsored activities tend to be slightly different from other students. These differences are greatest in activities in which student self-selection is combined with formal

> **The U.S. permits sports a place in the life of high schools that other countries avoid. Team sports abroad are often organized by clubs outside the school.**
>
> —Tom Loveless, director,
> Brown Center on Education
> Policy (2002)

tryouts and eligibility requirements, whereby teachers or coaches select students for participation, *if* the students are academically eligible to be involved. In the case of varsity sports, this combination of self-selection, coach selection, and eligibility is especially powerful because it is an extension of a long-term selection-in process, which begins in youth sports and continues through junior high school. Gradually, students with lower grades and poor disciplinary records decide they don't want to be involved in school activities, including sports, or they are simply told that they are not eligible to participate.

Research also suggests that students who play varsity sports for three years during high school are different from those who are cut from or quit teams. Those who are cut or quit are more likely to come from less advantaged economic backgrounds and have lower cognitive abilities, lower self-esteem, and lower grade point averages than those who remain on teams (Spreitzer, 1995). Furthermore, athletes who receive failing grades, possibly due to an overemphasis on sports, are declared ineligible and become "nonathletes." This guarantees that nonathletes will have lower grades when researchers do studies in which their grades are compared with the grades of eligible athletes! Therefore, in addition to a selection-in process, there also is a *filtering-out process* that occurs in interscholastic sports. These processes combine to make athletes different from those who don't play on school teams. This means that if we want to determine if there are important educational or developmental consequences of playing sports, we must take into account that athletes are already a unique collection of students and then follow them over time so that we can measure and track changes in their lives that are primarily related to their participation in school sports.

Processes of self-selection and selection by coaches ensure that students who become high school athletes often have different characteristics than other students *before* they play on interscholastic teams. Athletes may learn positive and/or negative things in sports, but it is difficult to separate them from general learning and developmental processes that occur during adolescence. (*Source:* Marc Piscotty, *Rocky Mountain News*)

Studying Athletes in Context   Research over the past half century has produced confusing findings about the effects of playing interscholastic sports. This is because most researchers assume that playing on a school team has the same meaning in all contexts for all athletes in all sports and therefore must have the same consequences. But this is not true. Meanings vary widely depending on three factors:

1. The ways that athletes and sports are defined by people in particular contexts
2. The identities that young people develop in connection with sport participation
3. The ways that young people integrate an athlete identity into their lives

For example, playing on a junior varsity team or being a mediocre player on the varsity fencing team has different identity implications for a young man than being an all-state player and team captain on a successful high school football or basketball squad. Similarly, being a young woman ranked the number-one high school tennis player in the state would be given a different meaning and have different identity implications than being a young woman who sets state records on the weightlifting team or played on a junior varsity softball team.

When researchers at the University of Chicago used data collected over four years from two large samples of high school students, they found that interscholastic athletes at schools located in low-income areas were more likely to be identified as good students than were athletes playing at schools located in upper-middle-income and wealthy areas (Guest and Schneider, 2003). Additionally, having an athlete identity was positively associated with grades in schools located in lower-income areas but negatively associated with grades in wealthier areas where taking sports too seriously was seen as interfering with preparing for college and careers. Therefore, the academic implications of being an interscholastic athlete depended on the meaning given to playing sports and having an athlete identity in a particular social class context during the 1990s in American society.

Research by Kathleen Miller and her colleagues (1998, 1999) indicates that the meanings given to playing interscholastic sports also vary by gender. For example, young women on school teams had *lower* rates of sexual activity (fewer sex partners, lower frequency of intercourse, and later initiation of sexual activity) than their female counterparts who did not play sports, whereas young men on school teams had *higher* rates of sexual activity than other young men in the schools. The authors suggest that playing on interscholastic teams enhances the social status of young people and gives them more power to regulate sexual activity on their own terms. During the 1990s, many young women used this power to resist sexual relationships that they defined as inappropriate or exploitive, whereas young men used their power to gain sexual favors from young women (Risman and Schwartz, 2002).

In a more recent study, Miller and her colleagues (2005) suggest that identifying oneself as a "jock" in some schools connects an interscholastic athlete with other students who are socially gregarious and like to engage in risky actions such as heavy and binge drinking. This needs to be studied further, but it seems that playing on some interscholastic sport teams puts students in a position where they can choose how to align themselves with various cliques or social groups in their schools. The choices made by athletes are very likely to influence how others identify them and where they fit into the overall culture of the school. In some cases, this "positions" them so that they are likely to take their academic work more seriously, whereas in other cases, it positions them so that they focus on social activities with other jocks rather than academic work.

Tracking the influence of sport participation in a person's adult life and occupational career is more challenging than tracking it over a few years in high school. The meanings people give to participation change over time and vary with social and cultural forces related to gender, race and ethnicity, and social class. For example, when we hear that many CEOs of large corporations played one or more high school sports, it tells us nothing about the effects of sport participation. The occupational success of these people, most of whom are white men, is related strongly to their family backgrounds, social networks, and

> Athletes and jocks are not the same. . . . Together they represent the two faces of sport: one ascetic and disciplined, the other gregarious and risk-oriented. —Kathleen Miller et al., educational researchers (2005)

the gender and ethnic relations, which have existed in postindustrial societies during the past sixty years. This does not mean that these men have not worked hard or that sport participation is irrelevant to who they are and what they do, but the importance of playing varsity sports cannot be understood apart from other social factors related to occupational success.

Overall, we cannot make any conclusions about the effects of playing interscholastic sports without knowing about the context in which sport participation occurs. Playing basketball in a small, private, elite prep school where grades are all important means something very different than playing in a large, socially diverse public school where athletes often identify with a "jock subculture" that has a strong emphasis on creating memorable social occasions and little emphasis on excelling in the classroom.

Student Culture in High Schools

Sociologists long have recognized that interscholastic sports are among the most important *social* activities sponsored by high schools (Rees and Miracle, 2000). Being on a school team usually brings a student prestige among peers, formal rewards in the school, and recognition from teachers, administrators, and people in the local community. Athletes, especially boys in high-profile sports, often are accorded recognition that enhances their popularity in student culture. Pep rallies, homecomings, and other special sport events often are major social occasions on school calendars. Students value these events when they provide opportunities for social interaction outside the classroom. Furthermore, parents, even strict, controlling parents, usually define school-sponsored sport events as approved social activities for their sons and daughters. Parents permit their children to attend these events even when they forbid them from going other places.

From a sociological perspective, it is important to ask questions about the contributions that interscholastic sports make to student culture in high schools. Because sports and sport events are socially significant activities in the lives of many students, they have the potential to influence students' values, attitudes, and actions. For example, do sports influence how students evaluate one another or think about social life and social relations? The cultural and structural implications of school sports are discussed in the box, "Status and Privilege in Student Culture."

Sports and Popularity For many years, student culture was studied simply in terms of the factors that high school students used to determine popularity. Research usually found that male students wished they could be remembered as "athletic stars" in high school, whereas female students wished to be remembered as "brilliant students" or "the most popular." Although these priorities have changed during the last generation, the link between popularity and being an athlete has remained relatively strong for male students. At the same time, being an athlete does not by itself make a young woman popular unless it is combined with other characteristics, often related to physical appearance and social skills.

Most high school students today are concerned with academic achievement and attending college; furthermore, their parents regularly emphasize these priorities. But students also are concerned with four other things: (1) social acceptance, (2) personal autonomy, (3) sexual identity, and (4) becoming an adult. They want to be popular enough to fit in with peers and have friends they can depend on; they want opportunities to control their lives; they want a secure sense of their own sexual identity; and they want to show others that they are mature enough to be taken seriously as young adults.

This means that the *social* lives of adolescents revolve around a wide range of important factors. Because males and females in North America are still treated and evaluated in different ways, adolescents use different strategies for seeking acceptance, autonomy, sexual development, and recognition as young adults. As things are now, sport participation is an important basis for popularity for young men, as long as they don't completely neglect their academic lives (Miller et al., 2005). In fact, young men who don't act tough may be marginalized in student culture, so they put a premium on playing sports, especially contact sports (Messner, 2002; Miller et al., 2005). The dynamics are different for young women because physical attractiveness rather than toughness is tied to their popularity in student culture. Thus, it seems that the visibility and status gained by high school athletes have different implications for young men than for young

Sport participation often gives young women opportunities to establish personal and social identities based on skills respected by peers and people in the general community. However, playing sports usually does not bring as much status and popularity to girls as it does to boys in U.S. high schools. (*Source:* Tini Campbell)

---

reflect on SPORTS

Status and Privilege in Student Culture
Do Athletes Rule U.S. High Schools?

After the shootings that killed fourteen students and a teacher-coach at Columbine High School in Littleton, Colorado, in 1999, some people raised questions about interscholastic sports and the dynamics of status and privilege in student culture. Among other things, they wondered if some varsity athletes are given forms of privilege that other students perceive to be unfair and that some varsity athletes use to marginalize or bully others whom they identify as "deviant" or unworthy of respect as a person.

At the same time, a number of "antijock" webzines and websites emerged and served as vehicles for current and former students to express resentment of high school cultures in which people associated with sports were privileged whereas others were marginalized (Wilson, 2002; www.allnerdsandgeeks.com/index.AntiJock.html; http://internettrash.com/users/antijock/ ajlinks.html). This is a controversial issue, but it is important to study and understand how sports fit into the social organization and culture of schools. Most high schools have complex status systems and multiple popularity criteria.

Students identify and differentiate one another in many ways, depending on what they define as socially important in their social lives. These definitions vary from one school to another and group to group in the same school, but this process of identification and differentiation occurs in all social groups. However, when differences are used for ranking students as superior and inferior and identifying particular students as targets for harassment or intimidation, there is cause for concern. If students, teachers, and administrators ignore systematic and chronic harassment and intimidation, problems may become serious and volatile.

Data on the ways that varsity sport participation is connected with everyday student interaction are scarce. Interscholastic sports are associated with the status hierarchies in many U.S. high schools, but seldom have critical questions been asked about the ways that sport-related status might be connected with patterns of harassment and intimidation in student culture.

An ESPN survey done a month after the Columbine shootings indicated that one-third of the

---

women in high school student culture (Carlson et al., 2005).

Sports and Ideology   Interscholastic sport programs do more than simply affect the status structures of high school students. When Pulitzer Prize–winning author H. G. Bissinger wrote about a high school football team in Odessa, Texas, he observed that football "stood at the very core of what the town was about. . . . It had nothing to do with entertainment and everything to do with how people felt about themselves" (1990: 237).

Bissinger noted that football in Odessa and many other towns across the United States was important because it celebrated a male cult of toughness and sacrifice and a female cult of

nurturance and servitude. Team losses were blamed on coaches not being tough enough and players not being disciplined and aggressive. Women stayed on the sidelines and faithfully tried to support and please the men who battled on behalf of the school and town. Attending football games enabled students and townspeople to reaffirm their ideas about "natural differences" between men and women. Young men who did *not* hit hard, physically intimidate opponents, or play with pain were described as "ladies," and a player's willingness to sacrifice his body for the team was taken as a sign of commitment and character.

Bissinger also noted that high school sports were closely linked with a long history of racism in the town, and football itself was organized and played in ways that reaffirmed traditional racial high school students interviewed said that tension existed between athletes and nonathletes in their schools (ESPN, 1999). About half of the students knew of athletes who had physically mistreated nonathletes, and about 70 percent knew of athletes who verbally mistreated nonathletes. Seventy percent identified football players as the athletes who most often mistreated nonathletes, 10 percent identified male basketball players, 2 percent identified wrestlers, and 1 percent identified female basketball players. Nearly 80 percent said that athletes sometimes or often received special treatment from teachers or administrators. These data are sketchy, but they indicate that there is a need for research, that some athletes bully other students, and that these athletes are nearly always males and most often play high-profile sports in the school.

Systematic and chronic bullying is most likely in schools where there is little social, ethnic, and social-class diversity and where conformity to rigid norms related to clothes, hairstyles, music preferences, and general presentation of self is *the* basis for social acceptance. It is in these schools that some students in high-status groups define "difference" as "deviance." Problems are most likely if high-status students feel that they have (1) the physical power to enforce what they determine to be the norms for appearance, attitudes, and actions and (2) the social power to enforce these norms without being questioned or sanctioned by school authorities.

Students who assume the role of "policing student culture" on their own terms are *not* always jocks. Furthermore, being on a school sport team and being labeled as a "jock" in student culture are seldom one and the same thing. However, male athletes from certain sports are involved often enough in bullying behavior for us to examine critically (1) the impact of interscholastic sports on the lives of *all* students, (2) the forms of status and privilege enjoyed by athletes on different sport teams, and (3) the ways that athletes from various teams use their status and privilege in the social life of their schools. *What do you think?*

ideology among whites and produced racial resentment among African Americans. Many white townspeople in 1988 still referred to blacks as "niggers," and they blamed blacks and Mexicans for most of the town's problems. Furthermore, white people generally used physical explanations based on traditional racist ideology to explain the abilities or lack of abilities of black players: When these players succeeded, it was due to their "natural physical abilities," and, when they failed, it was due to a lack of character or intelligence.

Unfortunately, Bissinger did not write about the students who didn't play sports and often objected to the values celebrated by football. He provides only a partial picture of sports and student culture. However, a study by anthropologist Doug Foley (1990a, 1999b) provides a more complete description and analysis of student culture. Foley studied a small Texas town and focused much of his attention on the local high school. He paid special attention to the school's football team and how the team and its games were incorporated into the overall social life of the school and the community. He also studied the social and academic activities of a wide range of students, including those who ignored or avoided sports.

Foley's findings revealed that student culture "was varied, changing, and inherently full of contradictions" (1990a, p. 100). Football and other sports provided important social occasions and defused the anxiety associated with tests and overcontrolling teachers, but sports were only one part of the lives of the students. Athletes used

Ideology is learned in many ways through sports. When students from a school in Wisconsin built this mock grave containing "dead Indians" and put up a sign "11 little tiny INDIAN BOYS REST IN PEACE," they reaffirmed stereotypes and misperceptions about Native Americans. Some of the students who built this mock grave learned to count backwards by singing a song about "10 little, 9 little, 8 little Indians," and they integrated the vocabulary from the song into their sport-related rituals without thinking of the imagery of killing and burying "little Indians." (*Source:* Kristie Ebert)

their status as a basis for "identity performances" with other students and certain adults, but for most students, identity was grounded more deeply in gender, class, and ethnicity than in sport participation.

Foley concluded that sports were important to the extent that they presented students with a vocabulary they could use to identify important values and interpret their experiences. For example, most sports came with a vocabulary that extolled individualism, competition, and differences based on gender, skin color, ethnicity, and social class and then treated these values and differences as natural aspects of human life. As students adopted and used this vocabulary, they perpetuated the status quo at school and in their town. In this way, traditional ideologies related to gender, race, and class continued to influence social relations in the town's culture.

Research suggests that the most important social consequences of interscholastic sports may be their effects on ideas about social life and social relations in society as a whole, rather than their effects on athletes' grade point averages, attitudes toward school, and popularity.

Additional Effects of High School Sports

A few studies indicate that interscholastic sports may serve as contexts in which young people are noticed and rewarded for their skills outside the classroom where they can meet adults who become their advocates during a crucial developmental period in their lives and where they can have valuable learning experiences.

Being Noticed and Rewarded Research indicates that sports support educational goals when they are organized and played in certain ways. For example, when interscholastic sport programs are organized so that young people are taken seriously as human beings and valued by those who are important in their lives, sport participation can contribute to their educational development (Mahiri, 1998). However, if sport programs are organized in ways that lead young people to think that adults are controlling them for their own purposes, playing on a sport team often becomes a developmental dead end, and students become cynical about school and society.

Positive adolescent development is most likely when students (1) are active participants in their schools, (2) have a range of opportunities to develop and display competence in settings where they are noticed and rewarded, and (3) have chances to prove they are becoming valued adults in their communities. If interscholastic sports and other school activities are organized to do these things, they will contribute to education and to the development of students as citizens.

Attracting Adult Advocates Interscholastic sports are valuable when they provide young people with opportunities to meet adults who can be advocates in their lives. This is especially important when adolescents attend schools in areas where there are few adults who have the resources to help young people make important decisions and expand their awareness of the larger world in which they live. When adult advocates are scarce in the local neighborhood, sports can provide these young people with the "hook-ups" they need to gain access to opportunities that are simply taken for granted by young people in middle- and upper-class families and neighborhoods.

Providing Occasions for Learning Sports are valuable educationally if teachers and coaches take them seriously as learning experiences (Mahiri, 1998). For example, Jomills Braddock and his colleagues (1991) have studied the importance of sports to young black males and have argued that sports in middle schools could be used to spark a commitment to education among many young people ready to give up on classroom learning by the time they are seventh- or eighth-graders. They have suggested the following:

> Both players and non-players . . . could write or contribute to sport columns in school or local newspapers, thereby enhancing student writing and language skills. Students could collect and generate team and player statistics for a variety of school and local sport activities, utilizing . . . crucial . . . mathematical skills. . . . [Students] could organize the sport sections of school yearbooks, participate on a sports debate team, or perhaps start a sports enthusiast club. (Braddock et al. 1991, p. 129)

The point of these suggestions is to use sports as part of a larger process of giving students responsibility, including them in activities that will help them develop skills, rewarding them for their competence, and connecting them with adults who can exert positive influence in their lives.

This notion of deliberately designing sports to give students responsibility has been emphasized in applied research on moral and social development (Martinek and Hellison, 1997; Shields and Bredemeier, 1995). This research indicates that sport participation may take forms that actually subvert moral development and responsibility among young people, unless coaches and others make explicit attempts to prevent this. For example, some high school student-athletes may feel that playing sports is more important than anything they do and that they are entitled to special treatment, even if they fail to complete schoolwork or follow rules. When this occurs, interscholastic sports undermine student development and the academic goals of high schools.

INTERCOLLEGIATE SPORTS AND THE EXPERIENCES OF COLLEGE STUDENTS

Does varsity sport participation affect the educational and developmental experiences of college athletes?[2] This question is asked every time media stories tell about the academic failures of college athletes and the failures of colleges and universities to take the education of athletes seriously. Research on these issues is limited.

As we discuss intercollegiate sports in the United States, it is important to understand that college sport programs are very diverse. If we assume that all programs are like the ones we see or read about in the media, we are bound to have distorted views of athletes, coaches, and intercollegiate sports.

Intercollegiate Sports Are *Not* All the Same

The amount of money spent every year on intercollegiate sports varies from less than $200,000 at some small colleges to over $70 million at a few large universities. Large universities may sponsor ten to eighteen varsity sports for men and a similar number for women, whereas small colleges may have only a few varsity sports and many club sport teams. In small colleges, coaches may be responsible for two or more teams and teach courses as well. Larger universities may have ten or more coaches for football alone and multiple coaches for most sports. Few of these coaches teach courses, and most have no formal connection with academic programs at universities.

Schools with intercollegiate sports are generally affiliated with one of two national associations: the National Collegiate Athletic Association (NCAA) or the National Association of Intercollegiate Athletics (NAIA). With over a thousand member schools, the NCAA is the largest and most powerful association. Its member institutions are divided into five major divisions, reflecting program size, level of competition, and the rules that govern sport programs. *Division I* includes (in late 2005) 326 schools with "big-time" programs. This division contains three subdivisions: 119 schools with big-time football teams (I-A), 116 schools with smaller football programs based on stadium size and average paid attendance (I-AA), and 91 schools without football teams (I-AAA). *Division II* and *Division III* contain 281 and 421 schools, respectively. These schools have smaller programs and compete at less than a big-time level, although competition is often intense.

Schools with *big-time programs* usually emphasize either football or men's basketball because these sports have the best potential to generate revenue. Football has the greatest potential, and it brings large profits to about 60 to 70 of the largest universities, but it regularly loses money in the other 160 Division I universities (Fulks, 2002; Orszag and Orszag, 2005). Men's basketball seldom generates as much money as football, but it costs less and the risk of large losses is lower. Although hockey and women's basketball make money in a few schools, no other sports make enough money to pay their own expenses. "Big time" does not necessarily mean big profits or even big revenues.

The general level of athletic talent is higher in NCAA Division I schools than it is in Divisions II and III or in the NAIA. Athletes in Division I schools are more likely to have athletic grants-in-aid and access to academic support and tutoring programs funded by athletic departments.[3] In addition, the amount of team travel in Division I

---

[2]This chapter focuses on four-year institutions in the United States. Junior colleges and two-year community colleges are not discussed. Research is needed on similarities and differences between the sport programs in two- and four-year institutions.

[3]The amount of athletic aid given to students varies widely by sport. Less than 50 percent of the athletes at Division I universities receive full or partial scholarships, and a major proportion of these go to football players at major universities. About 65 percent of all athletes at NCAA schools receive no athletic aid. This is illustrated in Table 10.4, page 355.

schools is greater, the national and regional media coverage is more extensive, and the stakes associated with winning and losing are greater.

Some colleges and universities choose to affiliate with the NAIA rather than the NCAA. NAIA schools have teams in up to twelve sports for men and eleven for women. Athletic grants-in-aid may or may not be given, and most programs and teams are not considered big time. The NAIA listed 285 member schools in 2005, about 130 fewer than in 1993. The NAIA struggles to maintain members in the face of the power and influence of the NCAA, which has monopoly control over intercollegiate sports.

Christian colleges and Bible schools also have sport programs. Ninety-nine of these are affiliated with the National Christian College Athletic Association (NCCAA) although many have dual membership in the NCCAA and either the NAIA or NCAA Division III. Even though the vast majority of intercollegiate sport teams

are not big time, people use what they see and read in the media to make conclusions about all college sports. But this is a mistake because most sports at most schools do not resemble the sports covered by the mainstream media.

It is important to study big-time sports because they occupy a socially prominent place on major college campuses. However, when we focus only on those sports, we perpetuate distorted views of intercollegiate athletic programs and student-athletes.

Athletes in Big-Time Programs

Being an athlete in a big-time intercollegiate program is not always compatible with being a good student. This is especially true for those who play on *entertainment-oriented* sport teams—the teams that attempt to attract large audiences and revenues from media coverage. Athletes in big-time programs often have some form of

Most discussions of college sports focus on big-time Division I NCAA athletes and teams. Division II and Division III athletes and sports receive little attention. The everyday experiences of athletes in these programs are different from experiences in big-time programs, but we need more research about the educational implications of those differences. (*Source:* Hal Stoelzle, *Rocky Mountain News*)

scholarship aid, and they are expected to commit much time and energy to their sports. Not surprisingly, these commitments often interfere with coursework and academic progress.

Research done by sociologists Patricia and Peter Adler (1991, 1999) provides systematic information about the everyday lives of young men in a big-time intercollegiate program and how they make choices related to sports, school, and social life. After spending over five years observing, interviewing, traveling with, and hanging out with athletes and coaches, the Adlers concluded that playing in a big-time basketball program and being seriously involved in academic courses seldom go hand in hand. The young men who they studied usually began their first year of coursework with optimism and idealism because they expected their academic experiences to contribute to their future occupational success. However, after one or two semesters, the demands of playing basketball, the social isolation that goes along with being an athlete, and the powerful influence of the athletic subculture in a big-time program drew them away from academic life.

The men discovered that it was necessary to select easy courses and the least challenging majors if they were to meet the coaches' expectations on the basketball court. Fatigue, the pressures of games, and limited time kept them from becoming seriously involved in academic life. Furthermore, nobody ever asked these athletes about their academic lives. Attention always was focused on basketball, and few people really expected these young men to identify themselves as students or give priority to coursework. Racial ideology and stereotypes accentuated this social dynamic as many people assumed that young black men playing basketball had no interests or abilities other than running and jumping. This is one of the ways that racial ideology is part of the culture on many college campuses.

When these young men received positive feedback, it was for athletic, not academic, performances. Difficulties in their courses often led the athletes to view academic life with pragmatic detachment. Therefore, they learned to be practical when choosing classes and arranging course schedules. They knew what they had to do to stay eligible, and coaches would make sure their courses were scheduled so that the athletes could devote their time and energy to basketball. After taking a series of easy but uninteresting courses and having a tough time in other courses, the players gradually detached themselves from academic life on the campus.

This process of academic detachment was encouraged by the peer subculture that existed on the team. These young men were with one another constantly—in the dorms, at meals, during practices, on trips to away games, in the weight room, and on nights when there were no games. During these times, they seldom talked about academic or intellectual topics. If they did talk about the courses they were taking, it was in negative terms. They encouraged cutting classes rather than attending regularly, and they joked about one another's bad tests and failing papers. They provided one another with social support, but it was support for their athletic identities. Therefore, many came to see themselves as athletes registered for courses, not as *students*.

Not all the athletes who the Adlers studied experienced academic detachment. Some managed to strike a balance between their athletic and academic lives. This was most common among those who entered college with realistic ideas about academic demands and had parents and peers who actively supported academic achievement. However, striking this balance was never easy. It required solid high school preparation, combined with an ability to develop positive relationships with faculty and other students. These relationships with people outside of sports were important because they emphasized academic achievement and provided day-to-day support for academic identities.

The Adlers also found that the structure of big-time intercollegiate sports worked against maintaining a balance between athletics and academics. For example, as high-profile people on campus, these young men had many social opportunities, and it was difficult for them to focus on coursework instead of their social lives. Road trips to away games and tournaments took them away from classes for extended periods. They missed lectures, study groups, and tests. Their tight connections with fellow athletes isolated them from the general social and academic life of the university.

Unlike other students, these young men generated revenue and publicity for the university, the athletic program, and coaches. Academic detachment was not a problem for the school as long as the young men did not get caught doing something illegal or resist the control of their coach. Academic detachment was a problem only when it caused them to be ineligible and when they had completed their eligibility and had no degree and no opportunity to play at the professional level. From the university's perspective, there was always another collection of eager young men who could be recruited to attract fans and generate revenues with their exceptional basketball skills.

The Diversity of Athlete Experiences

Many entertainment-oriented intercollegiate sport teams are characterized by chronic problems, low graduation rates, and hypocrisy when it comes to education. However, many teams in nonrevenue sports are organized so that athletes can combine sport participation with academic and social development. This combination is most likely when athletes enter college with positive attitudes about school and the value of a college education and then receive support for academic involvement and the formation of academic identities (Meyer, 1988, 1990; Neinas, 2003; Shulman and Bowen, 2001).

Athletes on teams in which there is strong support for academic success may train hard and define athletic success as important, but most of

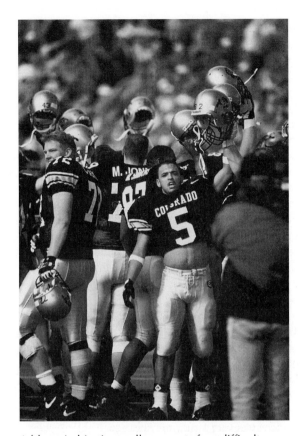

Athletes in big-time college sports face difficult choices when allocating time and energy to academic work, sport participation, and social activities. When academic work is given a low priority, the educational relevance of intercollegiate sports fades. (*Source:* Brian Lewis, University of Colorado Media Relations)

them take their education seriously. Those athletes who do best are the ones who have the following: (1) past experiences that consistently reaffirmed the importance of education, (2) social networks that support academic identities, (3) perceived access to career opportunities following graduation, and (4) social relationships and experiences that expand confidence and skills apart from sports.

Many coaches in programs that actively support academic success may schedule practices and games that do not interfere with coursework. Athletes may miss games and meets because they must study for or take tests, write papers, or give presentations. Team members may discuss academic issues and support one another when it comes to academic performance. In other words, there *are* sport programs and teams that do not subvert the educational mission of higher education. These programs generally include the following: (1) many teams in NCAA Division II and the NAIA; (2) many men's teams in sports in which the emphasis is not on providing entertainment, producing revenue, or becoming a professional athlete; (3) most women's teams; and (4) most teams in NCAA Division III.

Grades and Graduation Rates: Athletes in Big-Time College Sports

Unlike athletes in participation-oriented, lower-profile intercollegiate programs, many athletes in big-time university programs differ from other students on campuses. Although their characteristics vary from one sport to another, they often come from lower socioeconomic backgrounds than other students, and they often choose different courses and majors. This makes it difficult to compare their academic achievements with the achievements of other students. Comparisons are also difficult because grade point averages (GPAs) have different meanings from one university to another and from department to department within a single university. It is even difficult to use graduation rates as indicators of academic success across schools, because academic standards and requirements vary between universities and from one program to another within universities. For example, Gene Keady, the former longtime basketball coach at Purdue University has said, "There are some schools that academically you could be a slug and make it through" (in DiPrimio, 2005)—or at least stay eligible for a couple of years.

> The growing gap between college athletics and educational values is a major, unavoidable issue.
> —James Shulman and
> William Bowen (2001)

Research findings on grades are confusing. Some studies report that athletes earn higher grades than other students, and some report the exact opposite. Some studies show athletes attending graduate school more often than nonathletes, and others show athletes taking an abundance of courses requiring little or no intellectual effort. Any interpretation of information on grades must take into account the following possibilities:

1. Athletes in certain sports may be overrepresented in specific courses and majors. This phenomenon is known as *clustering*, and it occurs most often on teams emphasizing eligibility over learning and academic achievement (Lederman, 2003). Therefore, grades and graduation rates have different meanings in the context of different universities, athletic programs, and specific teams. Clustering does not occur among athletes in all sports, and some clustering occurs because athletes try to or must schedule courses so they do not interfere with practices and team meetings.

2. Athletes in certain sports, such as football and men's basketball, enter college with lower average high school GPAs and lower ACT and SAT scores than other students, including most other athletes, at their universities (Neinas, 2003). Sometimes their academic goals are quite different from the goals of other students, and this influences their academic choices and performance.

Prior to 1989, data on graduation rates were confusing because they were computed in many ways. However, because the rates for some highly visible teams were shamefully low, the federal government's Department of Education passed the Student Right-to-Know Act that forced universities to provide annual reports of graduation rates for athletes. Therefore, the NCAA began in 1992 to publish systematic records of "six-year graduation rates" for all member institutions and for each major division. This made public one dimension of the academic lives of athletes in all colleges and universities. The results of this law has been mixed. Progress has occurred but many problems remain. We no longer hear of college athletes who cannot read, as we did in the 1980s. But there are cases in which academic integrity is seriously compromised as coaches recruit athletes who have a low probability of succeeding academically. This is most likely to occur in universities where athletes help generate millions of dollars in revenues from TV rights money for bowl games and the men's NCAA postseason basketball tournament. According to 2004 data on graduation rates at NCAA Division I universities, we can draw the following conclusions about athletes who receive full or partial athletic scholarships (NCAA, 2005):

- Sixty percent of the athletes who entered Division I universities between 1993 and 1997 graduated within six years of taking their first courses, whereas 58 percent of the general student body entering the university at the same time graduated in six years. Therefore, athletes as a group have a slightly better graduation rate than other college students.
- The graduation rate for female athletes is 70 percent, and it is 54 percent for male athletes; graduation rates in the general student body are 61 percent for women and 56 percent for men. This supports the notion that women's sport teams have cultures that are much more supportive of academic achievement than is the case for men's teams.
- Graduation rates are lowest in revenue-producing sports, especially men's basketball (43 percent) and football (53 percent); these rates are below the rates for all athletes (60 percent) and the general student body (58 percent).

- Of the fifty-six football teams that played in bowl games at the end of the 2004 season, twenty-seven teams had graduation rates lower than 50 percent (Lapchick, 2005a). Of the sixty-five men's basketball teams that played in the 2005 NCAA tournament, forty-three of them had graduation rates lower than 50 percent (Lapchick, 2005b). This suggests that on average the football and basketball teams that win the most

Graduation rates for female athletes are higher than for men who play college sports. However, as women's teams have become entertainment oriented, graduation rates have declined slightly. This may be due to a shift in priorities or to the tendency of some athletes to leave school early or transfer to other schools when they see better sport opportunities. Research is needed on this issue in men's and women's sports. (*Source:* NCAA Photo)

games have lower graduation rates than other teams in those sports.

- The graduation rate for black male athletes (45 percent) is lower than the rate for male athletes generally (54 percent), but higher than the rate for black male students attending Division I universities (34 percent). The graduation rate for black female athletes (61 percent) is lower than the rate for female athletes generally (70 percent), but higher than the rate for black women students (45 percent). Graduation rates for black male athletes have increased since 1986 when minimum academic standards for scholarship athletes were established for Division I universities. However, the data on graduation rates among blacks continue to indicate that too many "predominantly white campuses are not welcoming places for students of color, whether or not they are athletes" (Lapchick, 2005b).

What do these patterns mean? With whom should we compare athletes when we assess the academic integrity of big-time sports? Should athletes be compared with regular full-time students who work thirty or more hours per week because athletes often devote that many hours to their sports? Should athletes be compared with other students who have scholarships, with those who enter college with similar ACT or SAT test scores and high school grades, or with those who enter college with similar academic goals and socioeconomic backgrounds? There is no single ideal comparison. Therefore, we must make many comparisons to reach a comprehensive and fair conclusion about the academic records of sport teams, athletic departments, and universities. Some teams clearly give higher priority to athletic success than to academic success. Such teams should not be used to make generalizations about all teams at all universities, but neither should we ignore them and their exploitive and hypocritical practices. Furthermore, we should not ignore all the "wannabe big-time"

teams in Division II in which athletes, coaches, and administrators aspire to be big time, even if it means compromising academic integrity.

Finally, even though graduation is an important educational goal, it should not be the only criterion used to judge academic success. College degrees are important, but they don't mean much unless sufficient learning has occurred. It is difficult to measure learning in a survey of athletes, but it is possible to hold athletic departments academically accountable.

The Challenge of Achieving Academic Goals

Since 1983 when the NCAA first set minimum standards for first-year students to be eligible to play on Division I college teams, there have been many attempts to make intercollegiate programs more educationally responsible. Graduation rates among athletes have increased as eligibility rules have become stricter. The most recent new rules for eligibility went into effect in 2003. Since then, athletes must complete 40 percent of their graduation requirements with a GPA of at least 1.8 by the end of their second year. Sixty percent of requirements must be completed with a GPA of 2.0 by the end of their third year, and 80 percent must be completed with a GPA of 2.0 by the end of their fourth year. Eligibility among first-year athletes requires completion of fourteen English, math, science, and other core high school courses (up from thirteen).

Additionally, first-year athletes must meet minimum requirements on a sliding scale that combines high school GPAs and ACT/SAT scores. This scale is now designed so that higher GPAs offset low standardized test scores. This approach was adopted because research shows that (a) standardized tests disadvantage students who do not come from middle-class, Euro-American backgrounds and (b) scores on such tests are poor predictors of academic success for particular students, especially those graduating from academically weak high schools.

Changes in NCAA eligibility rules have been designed to do three things: (1) Send messages to high schools and high school athletes that a commitment to academic achievement is required to play big-time college sports, (2) set new guidelines for schools that had ignored their academic mission in connection with their sport programs, and (3) encourage schools to provide college athletes the support they need to meet academic requirements and achieve academic goals.

Boosting eligibility standards has been somewhat successful, but many intercollegiate programs still fall short of meeting reasonable academic goals (Bowen and Levin, 2003; Knight Commission, 2001; Shulman and Bowen, 2001; Sperber, 2000). Experience clearly shows that it is difficult to reform big-time sport programs (see figure 14.1). Teams in those programs are tied to many interests having nothing to do with education. Some young people on those teams are in college only to receive the coaching that they need to stay competitive in amateur Olympic sports or to enter professional sports as soon as an opportunity presents itself. Coaches for those teams often view sports as businesses, and they

"I like your new recruit, coach; he's an excellent example of higher education!"

FIGURE 14.1 In big-time intercollegiate sports, coaches and university presidents have frequently distorted the meaning of higher education.

are hired and fired on the basis of win–loss records and the amount of revenue that they create for the athletic program. Even some academic administrators, including college presidents, use the programs for public relations and fund-raising tools instead of focusing on them as programs that directly serve educational purposes for athletes and the campus as a whole.

The corporations that sponsor teams and buy advertising on telecasts of college sports are not concerned about the education of athletes. When a shoe company pays a coach or school to put its shoes on the feet of intercollegiate athletes or when a soft-drink company buys an expensive scoreboard with its logo on it, company executives don't care about the athletes' GPAs as long as the athletes attract positive attention to the company's products. Similarly, the local businesses that make money when the home team attracts fans are not concerned about graduation rates as long as athletes fill the town with money-spending spectators for every home game.

Because of persisting problems, the NCAA in 2005 passed new rules that shifted more responsibility for academic reform to athletic departments in Division I universities. The rules, which apply to more than 5000 Division 1 teams, establish a minimum academic progress rate (APR) and a minimum graduation success rate (GSR). The APR is calculated at the beginning of each semester by awarding a team 1 point for each of its players who is academically eligible and 1 point for each player who has returned to school for that semester. There is a formula used to adjust the calculations for teams of different sizes, but the perfect score for all teams is 1000 points. A team that does not have a score of at least 925 points is subject to losing in the following year one or more of their allotted scholarships, depending on the difference between their score and the minimum 925 points. In 2005 and 2006, the APR is based on data from the past two and three academic years, respectively. In the fall of 2007, the APR is calculated by using data from the past four academic years (2003–2004 through

2006–2007). For each year after 2007, data from the most current academic year will be added, and data from the oldest year will be dropped. This creates a four-year rolling APR for each team.

The GSR also is calculated by using four years of rolling data. In 2005 it was based on the proportion of athletes who entered the university in 1995 through 1998 and graduated in no more than six years after they first registered for courses. The GSR is not reduced when athletes in good academic standing transfer to other universities or enter professional sports (Wieberg, 2005b). However, issues related to the meanings of the APR and GSR and the methods for calculating them are complex. The NCAA published a fifty-four-page document to provide universities with a basic explanation of these measures of academic success among scholarship athletes. As of early 2006, it appeared that the NCAA was serious about establishing a progressive set of penalties so that teams failing to meet standards in consecutive years will receive increasingly harsh sanctions. A first offense will probably evoke a public warning and a demand for an academic recovery plan; the second offense will be penalized with reductions in scholarships and/or limitations placed on recruiting; the third will lead the team to be banned from postseason competition, such as bowl games and NCAA championships; and the fourth may evoke a penalty for the entire university and all its teams.

These new rules are highly controversial, partly because over 30 percent of Division I football teams and 20 percent of basketball teams fell below the minimum standard in 2005 when the first APR scores were calculated. If the APR had been fully established and enforced in 2005, nearly half of the fifty-eight football teams playing in postseason bowls and half of the sixty-five men's basketball teams playing in the NCAA tournament would have been subject to penalties. Teams with consistently poor academic records could have been banned, in which case some individual universities would have lost up to $20 million of revenue in 2005 alone! For example, none of the four Bowl Championship Series games would have been played in 2005 if both teams in each bowl had been required to meet the minimum standard of a 50 percent graduation rate. But there were no sanctions in place, so the eight teams in these bowls received collectively $119.2 million for their schools and conferences. This means that the financial stakes associated with academic integrity in big-time intercollegiate sports may be boosted significantly if the NCAA follows through with a strong enforcement policy. NCAA President Myles Brand was clear about this when he introduced the new rules and wrote that "it is time to eliminate the notion that it is acceptable to matriculate prospective student-athletes without proper regard for their potential for educational success" (in Connolly, 2005).

Academic Support Programs   Starting in the late 1980s, athletic departments with big-time sport programs began to develop or expand their athlete academic support services. The stated goal was to assist athletes in the pursuit of educational achievement.

According to Jack Rivas, president of the National Association of Academic Advisors for Athletics, the counselors and staff in these centers help "student-athletes get the full college experience." He explains that their role is to help athletes "navigate the system" rather than checking eligibility and doing work for athletes (in Brady, 1999a, p. 3c). However, most academic support service programs are administered by and located in the athletic department. This separates athletes from academic life on their campuses and locates support in a setting where coursework is viewed differently than it would be viewed if academic support were located in a faculty-controlled program totally separate from the athletic department.

Research suggests that academic support services can be useful, but they don't necessarily boost graduation rates (Sellers and Keiper, 1998).

Furthermore, a series of highly publicized cases involving paid "tutors" who wrote papers and did other assignments for athletes raised questions about the real purpose of many "support centers." If the faculty controlled academic support services, things would be better, but problems would remain. Lynn Lashbrook, the former president of the National Association of Academic Advisors for Athletics, explains that even some university faculty are willing to bend academic principles when they deal with athletes in their classes. These are the "friendly faculty," and Lashbrook says, "every school has them, and every athletic department knows who they are" (in Wertheim and Yaeger, 1999, p. 92). Even faculty members who are not "friendly" with the athletic department sometimes feel pressure to give special consideration to athletes. What would happen to a professor or graduate teaching assistant who gives a failing grade that keeps a player out of the lineup and costs the university millions of dollars—and costs gamblers tens of millions of dollars when they lose their bets on the team? Lashbrook says, "If you're viewed as somebody against athletics, it could affect your career climb on that campus and even your job placement somewhere else because athletics is so powerful" (in Wertheim and Yaeger, 1999, p. 96). This has already happened often enough to make some faculty and teaching assistants nervous. Whether such pressures will affect APRs and GSRs remains to be seen.

Despite new rules for NCAA schools, some coaches expect certain junior colleges and private high schools to "create" academic records for athletes, enabling them to meet qualifying rules without much academic benefit. After two years in good standing at a community college, athletes often are accepted at major universities without meeting typical first-year admissions

> I'm a UCLA Prostitute. I sell my body to them. They pay me to perform for them. When my teammates and I perform well, the school makes lots of money . . . Regardless of how much money the school makes, we get the same, just our scholarship.
>
> —College football player (in Anderson, 2004)

standards. Coming from community colleges, athletes may be registered for relatively easy courses, which keep them eligible without giving them the credits they need to graduate in a timely manner. Rules are supposed to prevent this, but there are ways around those rules if academic integrity does not exist.

Prospects for Change The challenge of achieving academic goals remains difficult. Research shows that there is a growing separation between intercollegiate sports and the stated academic goals of universities (Bowen and Levine, 2003). This is fueled by powerful historical, commercial, and political factors that influence the culture of college sports. These factors will not disappear with new NCAA rules, nor will the NCAA enforce their rules without considering these factors. This dilemma has led The Drake Group (TDG), established by a national collection of college professors concerned with helping "faculty and staff defend academic integrity in the face of the burgeoning college sport industry" (www.thedrakegroup.org/) to develop and lobby for proposals to reform intercollegiate sports. TDG has even lobbied the U.S. Congress, asking that it intervene to mandate reforms. TDG has argued that all the tax-free income received by the NCAA and its members interferes with reform from the inside of intercollegiate sports. The problems have existed for so long and are so serious that externally mandated reforms are necessary to produce meaningful change.

The reforms recommended by The Drake Group are listed later in this chapter (p. 517), but the important point here is that members of the organization say there will be no significant change unless Congress establishes a policy whereby the NCAA and/or individual institutions risk losing their nonprofit status if they do not put academic goals ahead of making money. For example, if a football team reports profits of $5 million year after year while its athletes fail to meet academic standards, it should be treated as a business rather than a nonprofit educational organization to which boosters can donate money and claim tax deductions. TDG is not antisport, but it *is* dedicated to eliminating factors that have a corrupting influence on big-time intercollegiate teams and subvert the education of many athletes.

The events that occur between 2006 and 2010 will provide important information about the prospects for significant changes in intercollegiate sports. Some people are hopeful that changes will be made because there is now a critical spotlight shining on the NCAA and big-time teams; others are skeptical because there has been a century of studies and recommendations calling attention to problems in college sports, and many of the problems have become worse rather than being solved.

DO SCHOOLS BENEFIT FROM VARSITY SPORTS?

High school and college sports affect more than just athletes. In this section, we look at the influence of these programs on schools as organizations. In particular, we examine school spirit and budgets.

School Spirit

Anyone who has attended a well-staged student pep rally or watched the student cheering section at a well-attended high school or college game realizes that sports can generate impressive displays of energy and spirit. Of course, this does *not* happen with all sport teams in a school, nor does it happen in all schools. Teams in low-profile sports usually play games with few, if any, student spectators. Teams with long histories of losing records seldom create a spirited response

among more than a few students. Many students don't care about school teams, and some are hostile to varsity sports and the attention received by some teams and athletes. However, in some cases, sports provide spirited social occasions, and some students use those occasions to express feelings about their teams and schools.

Proponents of varsity sports say that displays of school spirit at sport events strengthen student identification with schools and create solidarity organized around the school. In making this case, a high school principal in Texas says, "Look, we don't get 10,000 people showing up to watch a math teacher solve X" (McCallum, 2003, p. 42). Critics say that the spirit created by sports is temporary, superficial, and unrelated to educational goals. A football coach in a Florida high school points out that "[students] all yell and scream at the pep rally and only a few hundred kids will show up at the game. On Monday morning 70% of them won't know whether we won or lost" (in Wahl, 1998, p. 100).

Being a part of any group or organization is more enjoyable when feelings of togetherness accompany the achievement of goals. In the United States, sports are one of the ways that these feelings of togetherness are created. However, there is nothing magical about sports. Schools in other countries have used many creative methods to bring students together and provide enjoyable, educational experiences revolving around recreation, student-controlled clubs, and community service.

People outside the United States often see varsity sports in U.S. schools as elitist activities that destine most students to be passive spectators, which produces little in the way of educational experiences. They note that the resources devoted to sports might be used to fund other integrative activities that would involve more than cheering for teams, while providing experiences that actually make young people feel that they are contributing members of their communities. In response to the belief that sports "keep kids off the streets," they say that, instead of varsity sports, there should be programs through which young people can make "the streets" into safe, vibrant public spaces in their communities.

The spirit associated with high-profile inter-collegiate sports is exciting for some students, but only a small proportion of the student body attends most big-time intercollegiate games. Either the students are not interested or the athletic department limits student tickets because they can sell seats at a higher price to fans who are not students. The games of big-time sport teams often are major social occasions that inspire displays of spirit on many university campuses, but does this spirit foster educational goals or simply allow students to drink, paint their faces, and yell for three hours? If it is the

latter, then many universities may be wasting their money if their goal is education.

If the spirit created by school sports is to have educational significance, it must be part of an overall program in which students are treated as valued participants and given a sense of ownership in the school and its activities. Unless students are actively involved in what happens every day at school, their cheering at weekly games is usually no more than a superficial display of youthful energy with little educational relevance.

School Budgets

High schools and colleges with big-time sport programs have different budget issues because

Division I basketball and football generate billions of dollars in revenue—for universities, the NCAA, and corporate sponsors and other businesses that depend on money and publicity related to games. This has made big-time college sports very difficult to change. Many people with political and economic power have a vested interest in maintaining them as they are. This is especially true of bowl games and the NCAA men's basketball tournament. (*Source:* NCAA Photos)

the financial stakes associated with big-time intercollegiate sports can be exceptionally high. For example, when a nineteen-year-old sophomore at the University of Notre Dame is sent onto the field to kick a field goal during the final minute of the last game of the season, his kick may mean the difference between his university receiving $16 million for an invitation to the Tostitos Fiesta Bowl (in January 2006) or receiving $2.5 million for an invitation to the AT&T Cotton Bowl. With over $13 million riding on the kick, the stakes are high for him, his coach, team, and school—and this does not include the $30 million that will be won or lost by gamblers who have bet on the game. This is not the case in high school sports. Therefore, high school and college budget issues are discussed separately.

High Schools Most interscholastic sport programs are funded through school district appropriations. In most cases, expenditures for these programs account for less than 1 percent of school budgets. When certain sports have large budgets, much of the money comes from gate receipts and booster clubs. This sometimes happens in towns where people are focused on a high-profile team that plays in a large stadium or arena (Brady and Sylwester, 2004b).

Interscholastic sports usually do not cut into the resources used for basic educational programs, but neither do they add to those resources. When educational funding is tight and classroom teachers try to do their jobs without adequate resources, they and others may call for cuts in athletic funding. In the face of recent budget shortfalls, this commonly occurs in schools around the United States. This leads to sport participation fees and/or a search for booster support and corporate sponsorships. Each alternative creates problems.

Participation fees make sport participation less accessible to many students and add to the elitist profile that high school sports already have (Carlson et al., 2005). In 2004 only sixteen states had no sport participation fees, and in other states, the fees ranged from $50 to over $600 per sport. Some families may pay as much as $3000 per year for their three children to play on high school teams (Brady and Glier, 2004) This creates real problems for coaches when parents who have just written a check for $500 make it known that they don't want their child sitting on the bench (Glier, 2004).

Booster support also creates problems because most boosters want to fund boys' football or basketball teams rather than the athletic program as a whole. This intensifies existing gender inequities and has led to Title IX lawsuits, none of which have been decided in favor of boosters who ignore girls' teams (Sanchez, 2003). Additionally, some boosters feel that they have the right to give advice to coaches and players, intervene in team decision making, and influence the process of hiring coaches. Seldom are these boosters concerned with anything but win–loss records and their bragging rights with their friends and business associates; education is not a high priority for them as long as the key players are eligible and can take the team to the finals of the state tournament.

Corporate sponsorships, on the other hand, connect the future of interscholastic sports to the advertising budgets and revenue streams of businesses. This means that schools can be left empty handed when advertising budgets are cut or sponsorships are not paying off enough to satisfy company owners, stockholders, and top executives. Other problems occur when the interests of corporate sponsors don't match the educational goals of high schools. For example, promoting candy, soft drinks, and fast-food consumption with ads and logos on gym walls, scoreboards, and team buses contradicts health and nutrition principles taught in high school courses. This subverts education and makes students cynical about the meaningfulness of their curriculum. If interscholastic sports are valuable educational experiences, they should be funded by taxes, including taxes paid by corporations, without noneducational strings attached.

Colleges and Universities The relationship between sports and school budgets at the college level is complex. Intercollegiate sports at small colleges are usually low-budget activities funded through student fees and money from the general fund controlled by the college president. The budgets at large Division I universities range from about $30 million to $91 million (at Ohio state for 2005). However, athletic department budgets are difficult to compare because universities use different accounting methods, athletic departments are organized in diverse ways, and athletic department administrators often report revenues and costs to serve the interests of intercollegiate sports and their programs. For instance, revenues might be hidden because teams and athletic departments are officially defined as nonprofit organizations that pay no taxes. To consistently report large profits would jeopardize their nonprofit status. On the other hand, costs might be hidden to prevent people from calling for budget cuts in the athletic department. This is done in many different ways. For example, a new weight-training facility for athletes might be built by using money from the campus health and fitness budget, a luxury club room at the stadium might be billed to the president's entertainment budget, or a new arena might house a few classrooms so that it is classified as an "educational building," and, therefore, funded by state tax dollars or student fees.

There are over 1400 intercollegiate sport programs in the United States, and fewer than 70 make more money than they spend (Sylwester and Witosky, 2004). With a few exceptions, the athletic programs that make money are associated with one of the six major college athletic conferences in the nation. At least one football team from each of these conferences is invited to play in one of the four major bowl games where payouts were as much as $17 million per team in 2005–2006. All teams in the conference share a large portion of bowl money, enabling them to break even or have a net profit for the year. At the same time, all but a very few of the athletic departments in other Division I universities lose money every year, and football teams regularly lose as much money as it takes to support all the women's teams at their universities. Ironically, in financial terms, men's sports do better than women's sports only in Division I-A schools with successful football teams and in Division I-AAA schools that have no football teams. In all other NCAA schools, including 116 Division I-AA schools (all with football teams) and 702 Division II and III schools (many with football teams), women's sport programs are less costly than men's programs—that is, they lose less money. This also is true at over 30 Division I-A universities where football teams spend more than they make.

Football teams are the biggest moneymakers *and* money losers. When a big-time sport team makes a profit, the money stays in the athletic department and is used to pay for other sports and additional compensation or perks for coaches and athletic department staff, including the athletic director. However, when an athletic department loses money, the losses are covered by the university through increased student fees, raising prices for game tickets, special fund-raising directed at boosters and corporations, and the general funds that come from tuition, state tax money, or endowments. At 326 Division I universities, about 20 percent of all athletic department funds come from student fees, and 60 percent of schools use student fees to support athletic teams (Sylwester and Witosky, 2004). This is not known by many students (or their parents) who often pay a significant portion of their annual student fees to support athletic teams that have little to do with their education. In Division II and III schools, virtually all sport teams depend on student fees to exist.

These are important points because many people believe that the revenue produced by men's teams pays for women's teams, but this is true in less than 100 of the 1400 colleges and universities with athletic programs. If money were the only factor used to determine the fate of men's and women's athletic programs, men's

In most NCAA schools, women's sport programs have smaller financial deficits than men's sports. This means that men's sports have a higher net cost than women's sports have in most schools. (*Source:* NCAA Photos)

programs would be dropped at 90 percent of all colleges and universities because they lose more money than women's programs. Additionally, because women outnumber men in the student body on most campuses, they pay more student fees than men pay and, therefore subsidize men's sports more than male students subsidize women's sports. This may be a violation of Title IX law although people concerned with gender equity have not raised the issue.

Recent research findings help us understand more fully the effects of intercollegiate sports at 326 Division I universities. An NCAA study that used the best data available has reported findings related to long-held beliefs about the benefits of big-time college sports (Orszag and Orszag, 2005). Here is a summary of those findings:

- Between 2001 and 2003, spending on intercollegiate athletics increased 20 percent, whereas spending in the rest of the university increased by less than 5 percent.
- The amount of money spent on big-time sports has no effect on academic quality or the academic qualifications of incoming students.
- Increasing the budget for sports does *not* increase alumni donations to the university.
- Increasing the budget for football and men's basketball does *not* produce more profits by those sport teams in a university, *nor* does it improve their win–loss records.
- Between 1993 and 2003, the "wealth gap" widened between financially successful Division I-A football and men's basketball teams and the teams that struggle financially.
- Increases in the budgets of athletic departments sometimes occur due to a desire to match athletic budgets at other institutions.

Other research shows that when universities decrease athletic spending they do *not* experience declines in alumni giving or the number and quality of student applicants (Frank, 2004). It is true that when universities have winning sport teams their athletic departments receive more donations, but when this occurs, there is less money donated to the universities' general funds (Stinson and Howard, 2004). In other words, many of the taken-for-granted benefits of big-time sports *do not exist*, despite frequently told stories about the good fortune of one university or another when its team wins a big bowl game or a high-profile NCAA game. These things may help coaches recruit athletes and provide college presidents with engaging stories to tell at alumni dinners, but they do little to change the quality of education on the campus as a whole.

Even though research shows that sports do not have the positive effects that many people think they have, most large universities could not drop intercollegiate sports without encountering serious problems. This is because campus culture and the public images of universities are tied to sport teams in the minds of many people. However, some outstanding universities have not depended on sports to create public images and have also been very successful in obtaining large research grants and major donations from foundations, corporations, and individuals. These universities emphasize quality academic and research programs rather than winning coaches and quarterbacks, and they still attract students and have interesting campus cultures. This raises the question: Sports are fun, entertaining, and great topics of conversation, but are they educationally necessary? If so, when and why? At this point, research has not supported the academic necessity of competitive interschool sports, but there is more research to be done.

Hidden Costs of Intercollegiate Sports Critics often argue that intercollegiate sports distort the image and mission of higher education, but they have not presented much reliable evidence to support their case. However, James Shulman and William Bowen (2001), respected experts on higher education, have identified hidden costs associated with college sports. They analyzed data from 1951 through the 1990s for thirty colleges and universities that have highly selective admissions policies and reported the following findings:

- Students recruited as athletes are given advantages in college admissions decisions. In the 1990s, athletes had a 50 percent better chance than other students of being admitted to selective colleges, whereas relatives of alumni had a 25 percent better chance, and minorities had only a 19 percent better chance. But the social, moral, or academic justifications for this "affirmative action program for athletes" have never been proven by systematic studies.

- The ACT/SAT differences between athletes and other students have grown consistently since the late 1980s. Athletes score significantly lower on these tests than other students admitted to the same schools, and this lowers the general academic qualifications of a student body.

- Since the late 1980s, the academic performance of athletes has been consistently lower than expected on the basis of test scores and other factors considered in the admissions process. This occurs most when athletes are immersed in a "culture of sport" in which academic excellence receives a lower priority than athletic excellence.

- The lives of athletes on college campuses have become increasingly different and separate from the lives of other students. Athletes now experience more pressure to focus on their sports, and they tend to socialize more exclusively with other athletes and form a separate culture that sometimes conflicts with general campus culture.

- The emphasis on sports and the money dedicated to intercollegiate teams has reduced other extracurricular activities to a secondary status on campuses. This includes publishing a school paper, staging plays, debating, and other activities that do not have paid coaches or budgets for recruiting, traveling, special meals, medical attention, tutoring programs, and other benefits. Per-student funding for sports is now two to three times higher than the *combined* funding for *all* other extracurricular activities on campus.

Shulman and Bowen's study focused on schools like Harvard and Yale, so their findings cannot be generalized to all colleges and universities. However, when their findings are combined with more recent evidence presented in follow-up studies (Bowen and Levine, 2003; Bowen et al., 2005), it appears that, even on campuses that don't have big-time sports programs, there is increasing tension between core educational values and decisions that favor intercollegiate sports in admissions and resource allocation in campus budgets. This tension has been building since the 1980s, and some faculty now believe that academic quality suffers when so many campus resources are dedicated to recruiting athletes, financially supporting teams that have ever-growing training and travel expenses, and building facilities for sports that are not organized or treated as educational. The belief that sports build character combined with media stories about former athletes who are successful help maintain the myth that winning sport teams are a sign of academic quality in universities (see figure 14.2).

This research on the hidden costs of intercollegiate sports has evoked widespread controversy. Those who support college sports call attention to the fact that women who play on teams in Division I universities graduate at far higher rates than other students and that many

men have played sports and excelled in a wide range of occupations. Bowen and his colleagues agree with these points, and they are careful to note that it is unfair to use their findings to make conclusions about individual athletes who may want to learn chemistry and English literature as much as classmates who play the saxophone or build computers for fun. They also point out that they are not antisport as much as they question the way that college sports are organized, funded, and connected with academic life on campus. They wonder if it is necessary to use valuable resources to enable coaches to recruit students with highly specialized sport skills when the head of the sociology department or the faculty advisor for the school newspaper does not have a similar budget. Sports, they say, can exist without recruiting because many students want to play sports for reasons other than athletic aid and media coverage.

As this debate continues, anecdotal statements about sports must be given a lower priority than systematic evidence about their consequences. Too often people make the functionalist assumption that if competitive interschool sports exist, they must serve a useful purpose in schools, communities, and society. However, research indicates that sports and sport experiences have a wide range of consequences depending on the meanings that people give to them and the ways they are integrated into people's lives in particular social and cultural contexts. Interestingly, we have only begun to study those meanings, contexts, and consequences in education, even though U.S. schools have sponsored competitive sport teams for well over a century.

"I told you we sent our daughter to a top-notch school—her basketball team just beat Stanford!"

FIGURE 14.2 Some people equate athletic success with academic quality, but research shows no relationship between these two factors. Spending money on sports does not enhance academic programs or learning in the classroom; and winning teams do not bring more money to academic programs.

VARSITY HIGH SCHOOL SPORTS: PROBLEMS AND RECOMMENDATIONS

High school sport programs are widely supported, and many people have vested interests in keeping them as they are. Some programs provide students opportunities to develop and display physical skills in ways that have educational relevance. Others have lost their connection with education and distracted some students from learning in their classrooms. Problems vary by schools, sports, and teams, but the most serious include (1) an overemphasis on "sports development," (2) limited participation access, and (3) school cultures in which certain athletes are privileged over other students.

Overemphasis on "Sports Development"

The Problem   Some high school administrators, athletic directors, and coaches think that high school sports should emulate big-time intercollegiate sports. This leads to excessive concerns with winning records and building high-profile programs that become the focus of attention in the school and community. These programs often center on football or boys' basketball, but other teams may be highlighted in certain regions. Building and maintaining high-profile programs often leads to administrative decisions that overlook the educational needs of all students in the school. Instead, decisions focus on maximizing wins, minimizing losses, and being "ranked" in the state.

> High school sports will continue to fester into shameful overemphasis in too many places, will continue to emulate the college sports model that is America's educational shame.
>
> —H. G. "Buzz" Bissinger (2004)

People who focus on sports development often give lip service to keeping sports in proper perspective as they fail to see that emphasizing sports in the school often marginalizes many students with no interest in sports. Additionally, the students who play sports often are encouraged to specialize in a single sport for twelve months a year, even though this may restrict overall social and educational development (Wolff, 2002). This turns off those students who want to play sports but do not want to make them the center of their lives. Other students become so dedicated to sports that they overconform to the sport ethic (see chapter 6) to the point that they jeopardize other important activities and relationships in their lives.

When people adhere to a sports development model, they hire and fire coaches on the basis of win–loss records rather than teaching abilities. They describe coaches as good teachers when teams win and as bad teachers when teams lose. Their goal is to build a winning tradition without critically examining how such a tradition fosters student learning. They assume that winning is educational.

The ultimate example of this approach is the IMG Academies in Bradenton, Florida. Students in these high schools train in a particular sport and schedule their classes around training (King, 2002, 2005; Latimer, 2005c; Sokolove, 2004a). Tuition ranges from about $25,000 for "day students" up to $80,000 for boarding students who buy private lessons in their sport (soccer, baseball, basketball, tennis, golf). Attending high-tech "education centers" for specialized physical or mental training costs extra. Students play their sports from September through May with the goal of earning a scholarship to college, becoming a professional athlete, or graduating with highly developed and specialized skills. These "sport schools" and high schools that maintain big-time sport programs often have organizational cultures in which many students mistakenly believe that playing sports is the best way to obtain financial support for college. However, aid based on academic records is far more common than aid based on athletic skills.

Recommendations for Change   Interscholastic sports should be critically assessed on a regular basis. Coaches need opportunities to learn how to organize sports as educational experiences. Coaching education programs should emphasize educational outcomes rather than simply giving lip service to such intent while teaching sport strategies and tactics focused on performance.

State education departments should conduct research on the educational value of state and national rankings and tournaments. Furthermore, if sport participation produces important educational outcomes, high school sport programs should be organized so that more students can play on teams and compete against similarly skilled students from other schools. If only 40 percent of all students play on teams and one-third of them never play in games, the educational benefits of sports are reserved for the few. If playing sports is educationally valuable, over half the student body should not be relegated to the sidelines.

Limited Participation Access

The Problem   Organizing interscholastic sports so that all students in the United States play the same sports ignores educational theory and the diversity of sport interests among high school students. Furthermore, when high schools emphasize power and performance sports, they discourage participation by some boys and many girls who prefer sports emphasizing pleasure and participation. This is one reason why schools don't meet gender equity goals, despite persistent attempts to provide "opportunities" for girls. Not surprisingly, many girls are not interested in playing sports that have been organized around the values and experiences of men. "Proving who the better woman is" through sports does not resonate with many high school girls.

The "adapted sports" of basketball, bowling, floor hockey, soccer, softball, and track are sanctioned by the National Federation of State High School Associations, but fewer than 60 schools out of over 17,000 U.S. high schools have teams in any one of these sports. There are over 6.9 million students who play on "standard" high school sport teams, and there are only 2359 students who play on teams in adapted sports (NFSHSA, 2005). Some athletes with disabilities play on standard teams, but apart from them, there is only 1 varsity athlete in adapted sports for every 5900 athletes on standard teams! This means that students with disabilities are overlooked in high school sports. Consequently, able-bodied students miss opportunities to see their peers with disabilities compete and to share sport experiences with them. This represents a missed educational opportunity for able-bodied students and students with disabilities.

Recommendations for Change   Many students are not interested in playing interscholastic sports, especially sports based on a power and performance model. Those who do not measure up to their bigger, faster, taller, and stronger classmates require alternatives to traditional power and performance sports or adaptations of those sports. For example, there could be three varsity boys' basketball teams organized by skill level and scheduled to play similarly skill-ranked teams from other schools. There could be an additional football league with players under 140 pounds, a basketball league with all players under 5 feet, 8 inches tall, and track meets with height and weight breakdowns for certain events. This would present organizational challenges that could be solved only if students became more involved in managing and coaching their own teams. This would add important educational experiences to sport participation.

Although sports like football and basketball receive much attention and many resources, there is a need for teams in Ultimate Frisbee, racquetball, flag football, softball, in-line skating, skateboarding, and other sports for which there is enough local interest to field teams. With guidance, the students themselves could administer and coach these teams and coordinate exhibitions or meets and games with teams from other schools. Students in other societies do this, and it cuts costs dramatically.

Girls' sports still lack the support that boys' sports enjoy. This problem has a history that goes far beyond high school, but the result is that girls still participate at lower rates than boys—in 2003–2004 there were about 1.17 million fewer girls who played high school sports than boys (see figure 14.3).

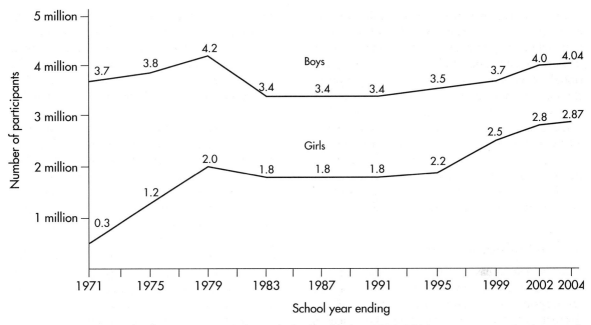

FIGURE 14.3   Boys and girls participating in interscholastic athletics, 1971–2004. (*Source:* National Federation of State High School Associations, 2005.)

One strategy for achieving gender equity is to have more gender-mixed (co-ed) sports such as long-distance running, doubles tennis and badminton, bowling, golf, cycling and tandem cycling, soccer, hacky sack, climbing, archery and shooting, volleyball, swimming, racquetball, and billiards. This would facilitate social development, interests in lifetime sports, and overall fitness. Why is football the centerpiece of many programs when few men and no women play football after they leave high school?

When participation fees limit access to sports among students from families that cannot afford extra expenses, school districts and state high school activities associations should provide automatic fee waivers for everyone who qualifies for federal lunch programs. Other strategies are needed as well so that "equality of educational opportunity" is more than a meaningless national slogan that allows students from wealthier households to feel that they are more special and

deserving than others. When financial status becomes a criterion for sport participation in public schools, it is time to raise public money or drop interscholastic sports.

Competitive sport participation by students with disabilities should occur through a combination of creatively designed programs. There are certain sports in which competitors with disabilities could be included in standard games, meets, and matches. When this is not possible and when individual schools cannot field teams in one or more adapted sports, there should be district teams or teams from combinations of schools. Furthermore, when students play on community-based teams sponsored by organizations for people with a disability, their participation should be publicized, supported, and formally rewarded as is done with other athletes in the schools. There are many ways to support athletes with disabilities. Strategies for doing this would vary from one school to another, but they

Inclusion Barriers
How Can I Wear Shoes if I Don't Have Feet?

Seventeen-year old Bobby Martin says, "I stand 3 foot 1 inch but I've got the soul of a 6-foot-4 person" (Grossfeld, 2005). Martin played backup noseguard and on special teams for Dayton's (Ohio) Colonel White High School football team in 2005. He was born without legs, but he wrestles, bowls, dances, and moves around school hallways and classrooms on a custom skateboard.

On the football field, Martin moves with his hands and hips. "I love the reaction people have when I make a tackle," he says. "People don't believe I can play, and I love to prove them wrong." But he was stopped from playing when a referee told his coach that the Ohio high school rules stated that all players had to wear shoes, knee pads, and thigh pads. Martin had all the necessary permissions to play, but the referees were not aware of them. As Martin pleaded his case, he asked, "How can I wear shoes if I don't have feet?" (in Reilly, 2005, p. 90) During subsequent games, Martin's coach presented referees with a letter in which the Dayton Public Schools declared his eligibility.

Bobby Martin's experiences received nationwide media coverage (Coffey, 2005; Grossfeld, 2005; Reilly, 2005; http://sportsillustrated.cnn.com/multi-media/photo_gallery/2005/09/27/gallery.martin/content.1.html), but none of the coverage mentioned that no U.S. high school has a varsity team in any sport for students with disabilities. Nor was it noted that only a handful of universities field even one "paravarsity team" or that the NCAA does not recognize any championships in sports for athletes with disabilities. The Universities of Illinois, Alabama, and Arizona are the only campuses that have women's wheelchair basketball teams, and disability services rather than athletic departments fund them. Paid coaches are rare for paravarsity teams, and the only scholarships for athletes with a disability are given by the president's office at the University of Alabama. All of this perpetuates the (in)visibility of (dis)ability and the resultant lack of opportunities in U.S. schools.

Bob Szyman teaches at the Chicago High School of Agricultural Sciences. He left his position as secretary general of the International Wheelchair Basketball Federation (IWBF) so that he could return to teaching special education and physical education. His goal is to establish a wheelchair basketball league in Chicago public schools, but his biggest challenge has been finding people who are excited about such a league. He explains that "there is no wheelchair sport culture" in the schools, so students with disabilities have no expectations and make no demands, especially in lower-income and ethnic minority communities; nor do administrators, teachers, and coaches ask why there are no paravarsity teams. When Szyman organizes wheelchair sports camps and competitions, the students who participate go out of their way to thank him, but they don't ask why their schools have no sports programs for them. They are accustomed to being ignored when it comes to sports.

The Americans with Disabilities Act (ADA) calls for access and equity in the classroom, but it doesn't mandate equal provision of extracurricular learning opportunities such as Title IX does for girls and women in public schools. Therefore, there is no clear legal mandate to provide or fund paravarsity sports or to encourage teachers, administrators, and coaches to think creatively about developing opportunities—such as organizing co-op teams representing two or more high schools as is done in rural areas when there aren't enough athletes in a school to field a particular team.

Few students are as assertive and determined as Bobby Martin, and this means that mainstreaming athletes with disabilities does not provide real access to the learning experiences available through high school and college sports. Some (dis)abilities require games, rules, and equipment adapted to physical characteristics. Public schools are traditionally where able-bodied young people develop and display their sports skills, but the myth that people with a disability are not interested in sports continues to subvert opportunities for them. Therefore, if Bobby Martin were speaking to educators about this issue, he might ask, "How can students with a disability play sports if we don't have teams?" This is a question begging for an answer.

can be developed only if people are willing to come together and be creatively inclusive in how they organize sports. This issue is discussed in the Breaking Barriers box, page 514.

Athletes Are Privileged Over Other Students

The Problem   This issue was raised in Reflect on Sports on page 490. I include it here because the growing emphasis on sports in North American culture will continue to carry over into high school culture. When this occurs, it often leads to the development of a status structure in which athletes are privileged over other students. This creates feelings of animosity among other students and patterns of harassment and exploitation perpetrated by some athletes who feel they have the power to do as they wish.

Leon Botstein, the long-time president of Bard College, has noted that today's high schools must be reformed because they "trap [adolescents] in a world of jock values and anti-intellectualism, like trying to cram a large person into a small, childish uniform" (1997; and in Applebome, 1999). These are harsh words, but they highlight the need for critical assessments of school cultures in which the most revered students are those who can "kick ass" on a football field or hit 20-foot jumpers at the buzzer. This subverts education.

Recommendations for Change   Administrators, teachers, and coaches are responsible for knowing about the ways that systems of privilege operate in schools. This is not easy because most adults are unfamiliar with the subtle ways that privilege is manifested through the actions of students in classrooms, hallways, cafeterias, parking lots, and other common spaces in and around the schools, even restrooms. The challenge is to become aware of this and develop methods to control it without using surveillance strategies that invade students' privacy and turn the schools into mini–police states.

An effective strategy is to bring diverse students together in policy-assessing and policymaking groups so that they can learn about one another and develop reasons for interacting in civil and respectful ways. Friendship groups are crucial factors in the development of adolescents, so it is important to accept the selective interaction patterns that young people find comfortable and reaffirming; at the same time, however, it is important to ensure that systems of privilege do not pit these friendship groups against one another in school-based status battles.

Another effective strategy is to give equal attention and recognition to students' accomplishments in activities other than sports. It is important to encourage local media to do the same. When high school athletes are exclusively privileged in the culture of their schools, some of them will exploit that privilege. If this goes unchecked, school cultures become distorted in ways that systematically disadvantage the educational and social development of many students, including athletes (Weiner, 2000, p. 50).

INTERCOLLEGIATE SPORTS: PROBLEMS AND RECOMMENDATIONS

Problems are not new to intercollegiate sports. Even in the late 1800s, college teams were accused of being too commercial and professional. In the mid-1920s, a Carnegie Corporation study found intercollegiate programs to have problems related to commercialism, professionalization, and the neglect of educational issues (Savage, 1929). These problems continued to grow along with the size, popularity, and scope of intercollegiate sports. Television created in the 1970s new sources of revenue, attracted new fans, and took sports further away from educational concerns. Then, in the light of the civil rights and women's movements, people realized that intercollegiate programs were discriminatory and unresponsive to the participation needs of minority and women students.

These and other issues, such as recruiting abuses and economic problems, led the American

Council on Education to sponsor another investigation in 1973. Not surprisingly, it reported the same problems found in past studies (Hanford, 1974, 1979). In 1991, 1992, 1993, and 2001 the Knight Foundation Commission on Intercollegiate Athletics issued influential reports calling for reforms that would eliminate the continuing excesses of college sports. These reports, combined with other research, indicate that at least four major problems confronting college sports today. (1) overcommercialization, (2) a lack of athletes' rights, (3) gender inequities, and (4) distorted racial and ethnic priorities.

Overcommercialization

The Problem   Big-time intercollegiate athletics is a major entertainment industry, with commercial goals and operating methods largely unrelated to the educational mission of U.S. universities. Evidence shows that financial concerns have overtaken educational concerns to the point that the academic progress of the college players is less important than television ratings and media company profits. Corporate sponsors are not concerned with educational issues because their well-being depends on profits, not the academic progress of athletes. Corporations provide significant revenues to *some* sports in *some* universities, but they also have intensified the emphasis on entertainment and marginalized sports that don't attract spectators.

Entertainment goals also intensify the hypocrisy underlying descriptions of programs as amateur sports that benefit the participants. ESPN's Tony Kornheiser notes that

> College basketball players watch the coach roaming the sidelines in his $1500 custom-made suit. They read about his $500,000 salary and $250,000 perk from some sneaker deal. They watch the schools sell jerseys [and T-shirts] with

the players' numbers on them. They see the athletic director . . . and NCAA officials getting rich and . . . you wonder why they might ask, "Hey where's my share? What am I, a pack mule?" (1999, p. 46)

This hypocrisy intensifies the expectation of privilege among many athletes. When athletes act on those expectations, they may do foolish or deviant things. If authorities catch them, they may be punished and condemned for a lack of personal character, especially if they are not valuable players. The people who benefit financially in "amateur" college sports blame problems on undisciplined athletes instead of a structure in which they use athletes for their own gain.

Commercialization now pervades intercollegiate sports at nearly all levels. This undermines most efforts to sponsor sports for athletes with disabilities. Commercialization is certainly not the only factor that has led people to ignore students with disabilities through the 130-year history of intercollegiate sports, but the existence of an entertainment model that emphasizes revenue-generating sports makes it more difficult to establish teams for athletes with disabilities.

> In a number of our major institutions with large athletic departments, expectations have become unsustainable.
>
> —Myles Brand, president, NCAA (in Roberts, 2005)

Recommendations for Change   There are many recommendations for eliminating or controlling problems in big-time college sports. However, the NCAA is a cartel with a great deal of power, and its officials resist changes that might jeopardize the income that they receive from media companies covering big-time football and men's basketball teams. According to The Drake Group, the only way to bring about real change is for the U.S. Congress to intervene and force the NCAA and universities to follow certain rules or lose their status as tax-exempt, nonprofit educational organizations—an outcome that would have serious financial consequences for the NCAA, universities, and the boosters who support big-time programs. The Drake Group's goal is to restore academic integrity to intercollegiate sports, and it proposes that Congress enforce the following rules:

1. Universities must disclose the courses taken by athletic teams, the average grades for all students in those courses, and the names of advisors and professors who teach those courses.
2. Restore the rule that makes first-year students ineligible to play on varsity teams and apply the rule to transfer students.[4]
3. Restore multiyear athletic scholarships by giving athletes five-year, need-based, grants-in-aid that can't be revoked because of injury or poor performance.[5]
4. Redefine athletic eligibility so that students on sport teams must maintain a 2.0 GPA, quarter–by–quarter or semester–by–semester, in accredited, degree-track courses.
5. Require all athletic departments to use the same system of financial accounting so that all income and expenses are clearly stated and open to public financial audits.
6. Reorganize academic counseling and support services so that they are the same for all athletes and relocate these services

> **Unlike professional teams, college sports programs do not pay taxes because their primary purpose is educational.**
> —Mark Alesia, journalist, *Indianapolis Star* (2004)

so that they are no longer controlled or influenced by athletic departments.
7. Reduce the number of athletic events and change game schedules so that students are not forced to miss classes or give higher priority to athletic participation than to class attendance.

None of these rules is radical; all are consistent with standard norms and processes in public universities. However, they are very controversial because they reduce the control that the NCAA and athletic departments have over athletes' lives and they prevent big-time sport programs from operating "under the radar" of normal academic and financial accountability.

Corporate support should also be regulated so that intercollegiate sport programs are not dependent on the advertising and profit needs of private companies. Requiring athletes to wear particular corporate logos is inconsistent with the notion that critical thinking is important in higher education. Classroom teachers and academic departments are not allowed to sell their students to corporations, and this policy should also apply to coaches and athletic departments. If corporate sponsorships do exist, they should be negotiated openly so that students may evaluate them in critical terms. For example, students may decide that no sweatshop labor be used to produce the apparel worn by athletes and sold in campus shops.

If these recommendations cannot be implemented, student-controlled club and intramural sports should replace intercollegiate sports. This is an extreme suggestion, but the chronic problems and glaring hypocrisy of existing entertainment–professional–commercial programs call for extreme measures. Furthermore, it makes democratic sense to use student fees and state money to benefit all students who wish to play competitive sports instead of the elite few.

---

[4]Until 1973 first-year college students were not eligible to play on intercollegiate teams. The purpose of this rule was to provide students one year to become acclimated to the academic demands of college before playing big-time sports. Through the 1960s, many athletic scholarships were four-year grants-in-aid, and they were guaranteed if the recipient did not play sports. Today, all athletic scholarships are one-year grants that are renewed each July only when a head coach decides that an athlete's scholarship should be renewed for another year.
[5]See note 4.

Lack of Athletes' Rights

The Problem Athletes in big-time intercollegiate programs may receive rewards in the form of prestige and athletic aid. However, much of their lives is controlled by others. If they have athletic scholarships, they are at the mercy of coaches who must tell them every July if scholarships will be renewed for another year. If athletes have a grievance with the coach or athletic department, they risk team membership and their scholarships if they speak out. There is no union or arbitration board to which they can go, and they are seldom represented on committees that make decisions about the conditions of their sport participation (Eitzen, 2003). In short, they have no institutionalized mechanism or process for challenging the system that controls them (Moye and Harrison, 2002).

Some athletes generate millions of dollars for coaches, athletic departments, and universities but are limited in what they can receive in return. They must make four-year commitments to schools, but schools make only year-to-year aid commitments to athletes. Coaches and athletic department officials may invade athletes' privacy, whereas athletes must accept all rules imposed by coaches, athletic departments, and the NCAA without any meaningful voice in the formation of those rules.

Intercollegiate sports are described as educational, even though athletes are not allowed to express critical thoughts about what happens to them in sports. Many athletes in big-time programs are aware that their sports are organized as capitalist enterprises that deny them opportunities to capitalize financially on their own names and reputations. However, if they ever said this in public, they risk being cut from teams.

Recommendations for Change Athletes should be represented as voting members on certain NCAA and all university athletic committees; they should have a formal means to register complaints and have them investigated without jeopardizing their status on teams; they should have regular opportunities, like students in courses, to evaluate coaches and team programs; and they should be in charge of athlete advisory/disciplinary committees that handle team issues. Furthermore, every university should provide an independent ombudsperson (an appointed official who investigates situations in which individuals' rights may have been violated) to whom athletes may go when they feel that their rights have been compromised.

Unless sport participation is part of an open and democratic educational experience, big-time sports should be treated as businesses, with employees who have a right to be paid and receive other workers' benefits. As they now exist, big-time college sports are the only major form of show business in society in which the entertainers earn less than the official minimum wage (Kornheiser, 1999). As revenues have increased dramatically since 1990, these sports are beginning to look much like gilded plantations where workers are fed and housed but have no opportunity to share in the fruits of their labor. If it is not practical to pay all athletes, there should be guidelines for allowing them to earn money and form economic relationships outside the university. This would eliminate the myth of amateurism and some of the hypocrisy in intercollegiate sports (Sack and Staurowsky, 1998).

Gender Inequities

The Problem Female students outnumber male students in most universities. All students pay student fees, and these fees are used to support intercollegiate sports. This was true long before there were women's teams at many universities. This means that for many years female students subsidized athletic programs that offered opportunities only to men. Men became accustomed to this sexist support system, and when Title IX became law in 1972, many of them resisted the mandate to share resources: They said sharing would hurt them because they had rightfully

FIGURE 14.4 After having all the "athletic toys" in high schools and colleges, rules mandating that boys share half of the "toys" with the girls were strongly resisted by boys. Many men who have administered school athletic programs over the past thirty years grew up when boys and men had all the athletic toys and learned that this was the right way to organize sports.

possessed nearly all athletic opportunities and resources for the previous eighty years (see figure 14.4). However, the law demanded that women and men have equal opportunities to play sports and fair shares of resources in any organization that receives money from the federal government (see chapter 8 for an explanation of this law).

Title IX was passed over three decades ago, but gender equity does not yet exist in most intercollegiate sport programs. Figure 14.5 presents NCAA data for the 2002–2003 academic year. The data show that in the very recent past women made up 53 percent of the student body and 44 percent of the athletes in 325 Division I universities; they received 45 percent of the scholarships, 33 percent of the recruiting budget, 34 percent of the total operating budget, and 34 percent of coaching salaries.

As of 2003, 42 percent of the athletes at all three NCAA Division levels were women (160,500), and 57 percent were men (214,500). At the same time, 55 percent of all undergraduate students at

those schools were women, and 45 percent were men. Although proportionality may not be the best way to measure equity, current patterns of opportunities and financial support strongly suggest that inequities continue to exist. For example, each year there are 54,000 more men than women who play intercollegiate sports. Of course, a large portion of these differences is due to the size of football teams and the expenses for football and men's basketball.

In the 73 universities in the top six intercollegiate conferences (the Atlantic Coast, Big East, Big Ten, Big 12, Pacific-10, and Southeastern), football and men's basketball often make enough money, due to massive increases in television rights fees, to boost the overall budgets for women's sports. However, at the same time, the expenses for football and men's basketball have increased dramatically. Therefore, women's programs at these universities have grown although they still operate on half the dollars spent on men's programs. The schools with the largest gender inequities are the approximately 170 universities

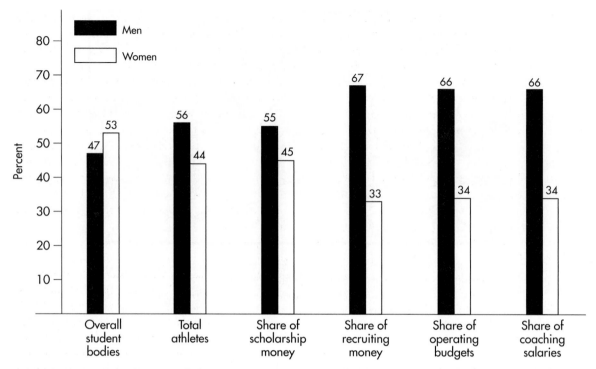

FIGURE 14.5   Gender equity in NCAA Division I universities, 2002–2003. (*Source:* Cory Bray, *2002–03 Gender Equity Report* [Indianapolis: National Collegiate Athletic Association, 2004])

in Division I-A and I-AA that maintain football programs but do not share the recent windfall television revenues enjoyed by the 73 universities in the wealthy conferences. The NCAA division that has the best gender equity record is I-AAA, which includes universities that have big-time sport programs but lack football teams (Bray, 2004). Overall, gender inequities are greatest at universities that have costly football programs that do not make profits.

In terms of gender equity, the supporters of intercollegiate football face a glaring contradiction. When they want to avoid issues such as paying athletes, paying taxes on profits, complying with antitrust regulations, raising money for stadiums and arenas without their tax-exempt bonding status, they say that football is part of education and must be treated as a nonprofit, tax-exempt educational activity. However, when others say that

universities must provide equal educational opportunities for women in sports, the football supporters change their argument and say that big-time football (and men's basketball) is a business and that market forces favor men in ways that cannot be controlled by universities. This is why Title IX remains controversial—it exposes the contradictions of big-time intercollegiate football, the sport in which so many people have a vested interest.

Recommendations for Change   Many people claim that *without* big-time intercollegiate football, there would be fewer resources to fund sport participation opportunities for women, but *with* big-time football, there will always be numerical forms of gender inequality related to budgets and the numbers of male and female athletes. The political position taken by the NCAA and most athletic departments is that there is no way to avoid this dilemma, so we should just learn to live with it. However, one way around the dilemma is to have universities cut football expenses through cost-containment measures established at each NCAA division level, cut the size of football teams, and build a few women's sports into revenue producers. If all men's football teams had similar budgets, we would see who the best coaches and teams are, rather than seeing the teams with fat budgets win year after year—at least during the years when they are not on probation for breaking NCAA rules. This would not compromise media revenues.

When revenue-production issues are discussed, it is also important to remember that it took about one hundred years to build intercollegiate football and men's basketball into sports that were attractive enough to make money for some universities. Women should be given the same amount of time to build their programs and make some women's sports important and visible parts of the culture on university campuses. This means that women's programs should have at least until 2078—one hundred years after Title IX was enforced—to build their programs with the full support of universities, including the use of student fees from male students. If not, we should abandon the idea that equal educational opportunity is an American value.

Distorted Racial and Ethnic Priorities

The Problem NCAA data in 2004 indicated that, although blacks made up about 10 percent of the student bodies at Division I universities, they accounted for 23 percent of the athletes, 53 percent of the football players, and 60 percent of the men's and 41 percent of the women's basketball players with athletic aid. About 82 percent of all black male athletes played in two sports—football or basketball—the only sports

that produce revenues and the sports with the lowest graduation rates (JBHE, 2005). For example, among the 328 Division I basketball teams in 2004, there were 45 that did not graduate one black male basketball player and 27 that did not graduate a black woman basketball player over the previous six years (Lapchick, 2005b). When combined with the fact that the graduation rate for all African American male students is only 34 percent, compared with a 59 percent rate for white male students, this means that many predominantly white campuses are not effectively supportive of black students, generally, and black men, in particular.

This also means that, in some big-time sport programs, black male athletes have consistently generated revenues that fund the programs, coaches, and scholarships of white athletes in other sports. Black athletes are keenly aware of this "white athletic welfare" and become frustrated when whites accuse them of being privileged on campus. Do black athletes feel that they should be accorded special privileges because of their contributions to their universities and the scholarships given to white students from families usually much wealthier than their families? Does this create tension on campus, and is it related to some of the actions of black male athletes? There are no systematic data to answer these questions, but if universities are serious about diversity issues, they should fund research to collect those data.

Overall, 17 percent of all black male students (1 in 6) in Division I universities are athletes. This is the case for 3.6 percent of white male students (1 in 29), 4 percent of black female students (1 in 25), and 3 percent of white female students (1 in 33). This creates in the minds of many people the impression that black males are superathletes who can use their physical skills to go to college. At the same time, it leads people to

> **Football is the S.U.V. of the college campus: aggressively big, resource-guzzling, lots and lots of fun and potentially destructive of everything around it.**
> —Michael Sokolove, journalist (2002)

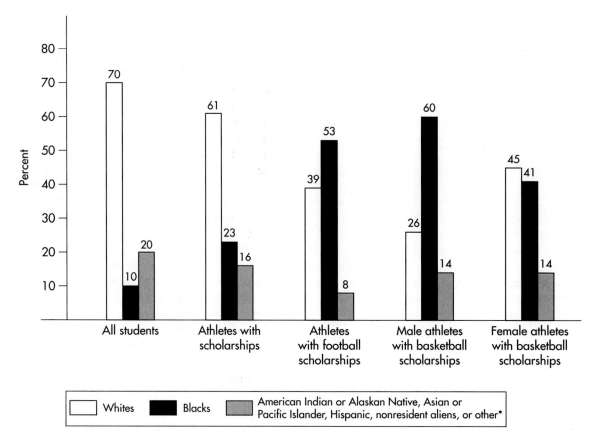

*Racial and ethnic classifications are based on self-identifications.

FIGURE 14.6   Percentages of students and athletes in NCAA Division I universities by skin color and ethnicity, 2004. (*Source:* 2004 NCAA Division I Graduation-Rates Report.)

overlook the fact that over 99.5 percent of all black American men between the ages of eighteen and twenty-three do not have athletic scholarships (Alesia, 2005).

Figure 14.6 highlights data on race, ethnicity, and big-time intercollegiate sports. The data suggest that if African Americans excel in revenue-producing sports, universities will actively identify and recruit them, but those same universities do a lousy job recruiting African American students who don't excel at scoring touchdowns or making jump shots. There is no denying that

a few African Americans benefit from athletic scholarships. But the problem is that universities have capitalized on the racist myth that blacks can use sports to improve their lives, while ignoring their responsibility to recruit black students and change the social climate on the campus so that they feel welcome, supported, and respected, even if they don't score touchdowns or score 20 points a game in basketball.

A related problem is that many black athletes feel isolated on campuses where there are few black students, faculty, and administrators

(Harrison and Lawrence, 2004; Lawrence, 2005). This isolation is intensified by many factors (Dempsey, 2004; Fudzie and Hayes, 1995; Hawkins, 2000):

1. Racial and athletic stereotypes that are dehumanizing and create barriers making it difficult for black athletes to be fully integrated into campus life and networked with other students in ways that support learning and success in classes
2. The time that athletes must devote to their sports often precludes involvement in other spheres of campus life
3. The lack of activities related to the interests and experiences of black students makes them feel like foreigners on campus
4. A lack of social self-confidence among black athletes who often find campus life so unrelated to their experiences that they withdraw from general activities through which they might initiate relationships with students who are not athletes
5. A lack of interracial academic and social experiences among most white students who have attended predominantly white schools and never had opportunities to interact with and befriend black students who come from backgrounds unlike their backgrounds
6. Feelings of jealousy among white students who mistakenly conclude that all black athletes are unfairly privileged and all black students are on campus only because of "racial preferences"

The isolation is especially intense when black athletes come from working-class or low-income backgrounds and white students come from upper-middle-income backgrounds. This provides a combination of ethnic and socioeconomic differences that create problems unless the administration, faculty, and professional staff make concerted and persistent efforts to promote understanding and connections between students from different backgrounds. Putting athletes in their own dorm wings, creating special academic support programs for them, and giving them athlete centers where they can go hang out with other athletes may make isolation more endurable, but it does little to foster overall learning and development (Hawkins, 2000).

Although most research has focused on black men, black women must deal with similar situations in predominantly white institutions (Bruening, 2004, 2005; Corbett and Johnson, 2000; Daniels, 2000; Smith, 1999; Stratta, 1995, 1998; Suggs, 2001; Winlock, 2000). However, black women also face gender inequities, so they have the dual challenge of coping with racism *and* sexism (Bruening et al., 2005). They see not only a lack of blacks in positions of power and authority within their schools and athletic departments but also a lack of women, especially women of color. Because black women face slightly different challenges than those faced by black men in U.S. society and because women's athletics often are defined differently than men's athletics, black female athletes have slightly different experiences than their black male peers have. These differences are poorly understood, and research is needed to identify them and explain what might be done by universities to make campuses more welcoming to students from backgrounds other than those experienced by white, middle-class students (Lucas and Lovaglia, 2002).

Another issue facing black women is that, apart from basketball and track, less than 3 percent of the women who receive scholarships in all other Division I women's sports are black; 73 percent of all black female athletes are in basketball or track.

As soccer, rowing, golf, and lacrosse have expanded with efforts to comply with Title IX, some black women have benefited, but few black girls have opportunities during their years in high school to develop high-level skills in these high-growth sports. When black women do play these sports, they may find their experiences to be socially isolating (Bruening et al., 2005). Tina Sloan Green of the Black Women in Sport Foundation has made the case that "Title IX was

African American women often face challenges when they play sports at predominantly white institutions. Apart from basketball and track, black women receive only 5 percent of the scholarships in NCAA sports. This means that many black women are on teams with only white teammates. In some cases, this creates social challenges for black female athletes. (*Source:* NCAA Photos)

for white women" and that black women have not been a priority when most whites think about expanding sport opportunities for girls and women (Suggs, 2001). This is a serious issue, which most people have ignored.

Recommendations for Change Universities must be more aggressive and creative in recruiting and supporting ethnic minority students who are not athletes, as well as in recruiting minority coaches and faculty. It is not fair to bring black or other ethnic minority athletes to campuses where they have little social support and little they can identify with. Furthermore, there needs

to be more opportunities for white students and faculty to learn more about the history, heritage, and experiences of African Americans and other ethnic minorities in the United States today (Perlmutter, 2003). If universities made more effective efforts to incorporate racial and cultural diversity into all spheres of campus life, recruiting black athletes would not be defined as part of a distorted set of priorities.

We need more visible models of campus cultures in which students, staff, faculty, and administration appreciate and represent cultural differences and use them to expand knowledge and understanding of the diverse world in which we all live. This should be one of the core organizing principles on all college campuses today. When universities present to the world an image of physically talented black athletes and intellectually talented white scientists, racism is perpetuated, intended or not. When campus cultures are organized around the beliefs that students from all racial and ethnic backgrounds are recruited and accepted primarily for their intellectual skills and that differences in identities and experiences foster learning, sports and the students who play them will be more integrally related to the process of education.

summary

DO COMPETITIVE SPORTS CONTRIBUTE TO EDUCATION?

Generalizing about high school and college sport programs is difficult. There are differences among and between them. However, varsity sports have no place in schools unless they are organized to achieve educational outcomes for athletes in particular and all students in general. At a minimum, if the programs do not benefit athletes educationally, they cannot be justified as school-sponsored activities.

There is no consistent evidence that high school sports produce negative consequences for those who participate in them. However, it is clear that there are some schools, coaches, parents, and athletes who lose sight of educational goals in their pursuit of competitive success. Sports can be seductive, and people connected with high school teams sometimes require guidance to keep their programs in balance with the academic curriculum. It is up to school superintendents, principals, athletic directors, teachers, and coaches to make sure that sport teams are organized to achieve legitimate and measurable educational goals. When many people assume that sport participation always is educational because "sports build character" automatically, it is likely

that little attention will be given to the need to carefully organize sport programs to foster education.

A main theme in this book is that sports are social constructions; that is, they are organized and played in many ways, and people give various meanings to sports and sport experiences and integrate them into their lives in many ways. However, most people associated with interscholastic sports simply have assumed that sports and sport participation *automatically* produce positive results regardless of how they are organized and the contexts in which they are played. This subverts the necessary process of critically examining sports in student culture as a whole.

The possibility that sport participation interferes with the education of athletes is greatest in big-time intercollegiate programs. The status and identity of athletes in big-time intercollegiate sports is so highly publicized and glorified that it can distract students from academic work. In some cases, it can make coursework nearly irrelevant in the lives of impressionable young people, especially young men who see their destinies being shaped by sport achievements, not academic achievements.

High school and college sport programs usually create school spirit among some students, faculty, and staff in schools. But it is not known if that spirit contributes to the achievement of educational goals or interferes with the development of a learning-oriented school culture. Although nonsport activities could be used to unite students and link them with community and society, sports often are used as the central activities that make schools more interesting places to be. Although sports are included in everyday discourse and covered by the media, we don't know much about their educational consequences because many studies of school sports have not taken into account the contexts in which they are played, given meaning, and integrated into people's lives. When there is a body of research that takes context into account, we will be able to say with more certainty when sports and sport participation are likely to have particular educational and developmental outcomes.

Most high school sport programs do not seriously cut into school budgets for academic programs. The money they require is well spent if they provide students with opportunities to learn about their physicality, develop physical and interpersonal skills, and display their skills in ways that lead them to be recognized and rewarded by others.

Funding issues are complex and often confusing in intercollegiate sports. However, it is clear that most programs are not self-supporting and that they do not generate revenues for their schools' general funds. What is not clear is the extent to which the athletic programs divert money from academic programs or undermine the development of other extracurricular activities that have more educational value at much less the cost.

High school programs subvert the achievement of educational goals when they (1) overemphasize sports development, (2) limit participation among certain segments of the student body, and (3) distort the status system and organizational culture that exists in a school. Similarly, intercollegiate programs are counterproductive to the reputation and mission of higher education when they (1) are overly commercialized, (2) contain no institutionalized mechanisms to protect athletes' rights, (3) have not achieved gender equity, and (4) are organized around distorted priorities related to race and ethnicity. If these problems are allowed to exist in high school and college sports, it is difficult to justify them as educational activities that are supported by valuable and scarce resources.

Competitive sport programs in high schools and colleges never will be perfect. There always will be a need for critical evaluation and change, just as there is in any part of the curriculum. This means that the educational relevance of these programs, like all academic programs and courses, depends on constant evaluation and assessment. A critical approach is the only approach that will

enable people to produce and reproduce sports as meaningful activities in the everyday lives of students and the social organization of the schools that sponsor them.

 See the OLC, www.mhhe.com/coakley9e, for an annotated list of readings related to this chapter. The OLC also contains a key concept list, a review test, and other helpful features.

WEBSITE RESOURCES

Note: Websites often change. The following URLs were current when this book was printed. Please check our website (www.mhhe.com/coakley9e) for updates and additions.

www.mhhe.com/coakley9e   Click on chapter 14 to find additional material on the sport participation–academic achievement relationship, discussions of school–community relations, and pay for intercollegiate athletes.

www.aahperd.org/nagws/template.cfm   The site of the National Association for Girls and Women in Sports, a member organization of AAHPERD; the site provides information on Title IX issues.

www.ncaa.org   The site of the National Collegiate Athletic Association; the site has information about intercollegiate sports and links to NCAA sport sciences programs and NCAA-sponsored studies, including graduation rate data. Two online publications (in PDF format) found on the NCAA website: (1) "Report on the Sportsmanship and Fan Behavior Summit, 2003," 17 pages and (2) "The Empirical Effects of Collegiate Athletics: An Interim Report," by Robert E. Litan; Jonathan M. Orszag and Peter R. Orszag (2003), 52 pages.

www.knightcommission.org   The site of the Knight Foundation; link to the Knight Foundation Commission on Intercollegiate Athletics where there are summaries of the 1991–1993 reports and a copy of the 2001 report "A Call to Action: Reconnecting College Sports and Higher

Education"; has a link to a 2004 study by Robert H. Frank titled "Challenging the Myth: A Review of the Links Among College Athletic Success, Student Quality, and Donations."

www.nfhs.org   The site of the National Federation of State High School Associations; has information about varsity high school sports in the United States and historical and recent data on participation total by sport and gender, rules, and other topics; click on link to "Survey Resources" to find these data.

www.naia.org   The site of the National Association of Intercollegiate Athletics; has information about this organization and its 285-member organizations.

www.njcaa.org   The site for the National Junior College Athletic Association; has information about intercollegiate sports at 511-member community/junior colleges in the United States.

www.thenccaa.org   The site of the National Christian College Athletic Association; has general information and news for its ninety-nine-member colleges.

www.sportinsociety.org   The site of the Center for the Study of Sport in Society; collects annual data on the ethnic and gender composition of athletic department employees at major colleges and universities; click on the "Racial and Gender Report Card" to find data on the affirmative action records of Division I institutions in the United States.

www.thedrakegroup.org/   The site of The Drake Group; assists faculty and staff maintain academic integrity as they deal with pressures from commercialized intercollegiate sports; has a network of college faculty that lobbies for academic standards. The site contains position papers and news related to sports and academic issues.

www.childtrendsdatabank.org/pdf/37%5FPDF.pdf   This site pulls together data on participation in school athletics; data comparing participation in 1991 and 2003 are presented in a PDF file, and they encompass variables not covered by data from the National High Schools Activity Association; the data are collected by Child Trends Data Bank, Washington, DC (2003).

www.disability.uiuc.edu/athletics/   The site of the University of Illinois Adapted Varsity Athletics Program; has complete information on the university's support of leadership and excellence in wheelchair sports.

www.insidehighered.com/views/why_the_u_s_should_intervene_in_college_sports   This site has an explanation of why the U.S. government should intervene in intercollegiate sports; presented by Frank Splitt (2/16/05), it focuses on issues related to the tax exemptions received by universities as they sponsor what is now considered to be an educational rather than a commercial activity.

www.ed.gov/about/offices/list/ocr/docs/title9guidanceadditional.html   The site of the U.S. Department of Education and the Office of Civil Rights provides a full explanation of new (2005) enforcement guidelines related to Title IX.

www.bus.ucf.edu/sport/cgi-bin/site/sitew.cgi?page=/ides/media.htx   This site contains news releases from the Institute for Diversity and Ethics in Sport and up-to-date data on graduation rates for university teams in postseason tournament and bowl games and on other diversity patterns in intercollegiate sports.

www.cstv.com   The home page of College Sports TV; provides schedules of television and online programming, highlights of games, scores and standings, and fan interaction platforms.

(Jay Coakley)

SPORTS AND RELIGIONS

Is It a Promising Combination?

I AM A MEMBER OF TEAM JESUS CHRIST

—**Sign posted in the locker room by Fisher DeBerry, head football coach, U.S. Air Force Academy, 2005**

WITH REGARD TO our participation in social and sport activities, we Muslim women have no intention whatsoever to resemble men.

—**Faezeh Hashemi, Iranian Parliament, founder, Islamic Countries Women Sports Games (in Good, 2002)**

OLC **Online Learning Center Resources**

Visit *Sports in Society*'s Online Learning Center (OLC) at **www.mhhe.com/coakley9e** for additional information and study material for this chapter, including

- Self-grading quizzes
- Learning objectives
- Related websites
- Additional readings

A complete outline is available online at www.mhhe.com/coakley9e.

THE GREATEST FEELING I get playing baseball right now is knowing that I can go out and be a warrior for the Lord. I can go out . . . and say my prayer and then be a very aggressive, warrior-like pitcher, glorifying Him.

—**Randy Johnson, Major League Baseball player (1996)**

WE SHOULD KEEP our daughters away from competitive sports and spend our time training them how to be Biblically feminine women, wives and mothers.

—**Scott Jonas, BeautifulWomanhood.org, 2005**

529

The relationship between sports and religions varies by time and place. As noted in chapter 3, physical activities and sports in many preindustrial societies were linked to religious rituals. This remains true today in traditional cultures where physical games and activities are included in cultural rituals that are linked to the supernatural. For example, the histories of many native cultures in North America contain long traditions of games and running races defined as having spiritual significance.

The histories of Jews and Christians in Europe and North America indicate that there have been times and places in which Judeo-Christian religious authorities approved or sponsored physical activities, games, and sports. In other cases, all or most physical activities were ignored or condemned as indulgent and sinful. During the last half of the twentieth century, religious organizations in North America and Europe were likely to approve sport activities as worthwhile pursuits and even sponsor them. Furthermore, individuals today combine sport participation and religious beliefs and publicly express the personal significance of this combination. This is an increasingly common practice, especially among Christian athletes in the United States.

The purpose of this chapter is to examine the ways that religion and religious beliefs are combined with sports and sport participation. As you read this chapter, remember that similar religious beliefs can be combined with sports in diverse ways, depending on the experiences, relationships, and interests of individuals and groups. The major questions we will discuss in this chapter are the following:

1. How is *religion* defined, and why do sociologists study it?
2. What are the similarities and differences between sports and religions?
3. Why have people combined sports and religions, and why are Christians more vocal about this combination than are Jews, Muslims, Hindus, Buddhists, Sikhs, and other people whose religious beliefs are not based on Christianity?
4. What are the challenges faced when combining sports with religion in general and Christianity in particular?

In discussing the last question, we will give special attention to whether the combination of religion and sports offers any promise for eliminating racism, sexism, deviance, violence, and other problems in sports and sport organizations.

HOW DO SOCIOLOGISTS DEFINE AND STUDY RELIGION?

Sociological discussions of religion often create controversy in sociology of sport classrooms. This occurs when students and teachers use only their own religious beliefs and practices as a point of reference. Therefore, they have strong feelings about what religion is and how it *should* be discussed.

Religion is powerful because it provides an organized set of beliefs and meanings that people use as they come to terms with ultimate issues and questions and conceptualize their relationships with God, gods, or the supernatural realm in general. These beliefs and meanings are a part of cultural ideology. They inform how people think about the world, and they affect social relationships and the organization of social life. They also inform ideas about the body, movement, physical activities, and even sports.

A sociological discussion of religion and sports requires that we view religion as a part of culture. Although there are many definitions of religion, the one used by many sociologists is that **religion** is *a socially shared set of beliefs and rituals that people use to transcend the material world and give meaning to important aspects of their lives.* Religious beliefs and rituals are unique because people connect them with a sacred and supernatural realm and accept this connection on *faith*, which is the foundation for all religions and religious beliefs.

When objects, symbols, and ceremonies are given meanings that connect them with the supernatural or with forces beyond the here-and-now world, people define them as **sacred.** Sacred things inspire awe, mystery, and reverence. Religious beliefs often distinguish between sacred and profane things. The realm of the **profane** *consists of everyday cultural objects and activities that are not connected with the supernatural or the divine.* For example, many Christians perceive churches as sacred places by connecting them with their God and spiritual Savior. The meaning of churches to Christians can be understood only in terms of their perceived connection with the supernatural.

On the other hand, the stadiums and arenas in which sports are played have no connection with the sacred or supernatural as defined by Christians. They may be important places for some people, but they are understandable in terms of everyday meanings and experiences, and they exist in the realm of the profane, not the sacred. Therefore, when large billboards advertising

In U.S. culture, there are usually clear distinctions between the sacred and the profane. However, in many cultures, it is difficult to make clear distinctions between these two spheres because they are merged almost seamlessly in everyday life. This is especially the case for many Muslims, who merge religion with all facets of everyday life. (*Source:* Marco Di Lauro, AP/Wide World Photos)

Pepsi, Budweiser, and McDonald's are mounted on scoreboards and stadium walls, few people object. However, if those billboards were mounted on or built into the altars, walls, or stained-glass windows of a church, synagogue, or mosque, most people would object. A Pepsi logo on an altar would be seen as degrading the sacred meaning given to the church and objects in it.

This explanation of religion requires qualification. For many peoples around the world, religion and religious beliefs are simply built into culture and cultural beliefs; they are one and the same (Fowler et al., 1997). Unlike Christianity and Judaism, some religions do not consist of identifiable dogma and are not organized under a central "Church Authority." Furthermore, drawing lines between the sacred and the profane is not always easy, but in most cultures, we can identify objects, beliefs, and rituals that people associate with a sacred and supernatural realm that transcends the everyday world.

The diversity of religions and religious beliefs around the world is extensive. Human beings have dealt with ultimate questions about life and death and coped with the inescapable problems of human existence in many ways (Lemert, 1999). In the process, they have developed thousands of rich and widely varied religions.

Sociologists are not concerned with the truth or falsity of particular religions or religious beliefs. Instead, they examine the ways that believers use religion to give meaning to their lives, their experiences, and the world in which they live. This makes religion important sociologically because it informs the ways that people think, act, and relate with each other. When religious beliefs connect power, authority, and wisdom with God, gods, or other supernatural forces[1] or when beliefs set some people apart from others, religion has significant social consequences.

These points help us understand that religions and religious beliefs can, under certain circumstances, lead to the following:

- Powerful forms of group unity and social integration *or* devastating forms of group conflict and violent warfare
- A spirit of love and acceptance *or* forms of moral judgment through which people are marginalized or condemned
- Commitment to prevailing social norms *or* rejection of those norms in the name of righteousness
- Policies and practices that produce inequalities between men and women, racial and ethnic groups, social classes, homosexuals and heterosexuals, able-bodied and disabled people, and other groups *or* opposition to those inequalities

None of these social consequences of religions is inevitable. All of them depend on the ways that religious people use their beliefs to give meaning to and make sense of the world in which they live.

SIMILARITIES AND DIFFERENCES BETWEEN SPORTS AND RELIGIONS

Discussions about sports and religions often are confusing and controversial. Some people argue that sports are a form of religion, or at least "religion-like," in important ways. Others argue that there are *essential* differences between what they define as the *true nature* of sport and the *true nature* of religion. Still others argue that sports and religions are simply two distinct sets of cultural practices, which sometimes overlap as people devise ways to live with one another and attempt to make their lives satisfying and meaningful. The purpose of this section is to explain and clarify each of these three positions.

Sports as Religion

When I've attended NFL games or World Cup soccer matches and watched 75,000 or more

---

[1]The word *God* refers to *the* Supreme Being or *the* Creator in monotheistic religions. The words *god(s)* and *godliness* refer to deities across all religions, including polytheistic religions, in which people believe in multiple deities, or gods.

people yelling, chanting, and moving in unison in the shadow of an altarlike scoreboard, I've wondered about the religious dimensions of sports. The most extreme position to take when discussing this issue is to say that sports are religion because they involve expressions of emotions and beliefs that are stronger and more relevant to people today than the emotions and beliefs associated with "Christianity, Judaism, or any of the traditional religions" (Prebish, 1993). Others stop short of this position and say that sports are simply religion-like because both sports and religions have similar characteristics and produce similar consequences (Hubbard, 1998; Mathisen, 1992; Novak, 1976). For example, comparisons of Judeo-Christian religions and sports have identified the following similarities:

- Both have places or buildings for communal gatherings and special events. Most sports have stadiums and arenas where fans attend regularly scheduled games or contests, and most religions have churches and temples where believers attend regularly scheduled services.
- Both emerge out of a similar quest for perfection in body, mind, and spirit. Sports emphasize physical training and discipline for physical development, and religions emphasize physical control and mental discipline for spiritual development.
- Both are controlled through structured organizations and hierarchical systems of authority. Sports have commissioners, athletic directors, and coaches, and religions have bishops, pastors, priests, and rabbis.
- Both have events that celebrate widely shared values. Sports have games and contests to celebrate competition, hard work, and achievement, and religions have ceremonies and rituals to celebrate commitment, community, and redemption.
- Both have rituals before, during, and after major events. Sports have initiations, national anthems, halftime pep talks, hand

slapping, band parades, and postgame hand shaking; and religions have baptisms, opening hymns, regular sermons, the joining of hands, and ceremonial processions.

- Both have heroes and legends about heroic accomplishments. Sport heroes are elected to "halls of fame," with their stories told repeatedly by sports journalists, coaches, and fans, and religious heroes are elevated to sainthood or sacred status, with their stories told repeatedly by religious writers, ministers, and believers.
- Both evoke intense emotions and give meaning to people's lives. Sports inspire players and fans to contemplate human potential, and religions inspire theologians and believers to contemplate the meaning of existence.
- Both can be used to distract attention from important social, political, and economic issues and thereby become "opiates" of the masses. Sports focus attention on athlete-celebrities, scores, and championships, and religions focus attention on a relationship with the supernatural, rather than here-and-now issues that affect the material conditions of people's lives.

This list highlights characteristics shared by sports and religions, and it helps us understand why some people see sports as religion or religion-like.

Sport and Religion Are Essentially Different

Some people argue that religion and sport each has a unique, separate truth, or "essence." The essence of religion, they believe, is grounded in divine inspiration, whereas the essence of sport is grounded in human nature.[2] They argue that religion and sport reveal different basic truths,

---

[2]These people refer to *sport* and *religion* in the singular because they assume that all sports and all religions express the same essence. I explain the problems associated with this approach in chapter 1, page 13.

People who use "essentialist" approaches to religion and sport might not like this statue and what it suggests. In sociological terms, the statue shows that both sports and religions are socially constructed cultural practices, which change over time in connection with larger social forces and contexts (see pp. 560–561). Few other religions would create a statue representing their prophet or "Savior" playing a heavy-contact sport that involves violence. (*Source:* Jay Coakley)

each of which transcends time and space. People "live out" those truths as they participate in religion or sport.

People who think this way are called *essentialists*. They are concerned with discovering the "truth" that they believe is inherent in "nature" and then presenting that truth in the form of laws about the universe. When they study religion and sport, they argue that the fundamental character of religion is essentially different from the fundamental character of sport. For example, they often identify the following differences:

- Religious beliefs, meanings, rituals, and events are fundamentally mystical and *sacred*, whereas sport beliefs, meanings, rituals, and events are fundamentally clear-cut and *profane*.

- The purpose of religion is to transcend the circumstances and conditions of the material world in the pursuit of spiritual goals and eternal life, whereas the purpose of sport is to focus on material issues, such as victories and the meanings that they have in this life.
- Religion is based on faith and cooperation between believers, whereas sport is based on concrete rules and competitive relationships between players and teams.
- Religion emphasizes humility and love, whereas sport emphasizes personal achievement and conquest.
- Religious services are expressive and process oriented, whereas sport events are goal driven and product oriented.

Essentialists argue that there are fundamental differences between Super Bowl Sunday and Easter Sunday, even though both are important days in different people's lives. Similarly, they would see fundamental differences between a hockey team's initiation ceremony and a baptism, a seventh-inning stretch and a scheduled prayer, a cathedral and a stadium.

Some essentialists are religious people who believe that religion and sport are fundamentally different because religion is divinely inspired and sport is not. They often claim that the essentially sacred character of religion becomes corrupted when combined with the essentially profane character of sport (Hoffman, 1992a, 1992c, 1992d, 1999; Ramsey, 2005). Nonreligious essentialists don't believe in divine inspiration but argue instead that the cultural meanings and social consequences of religion and sport are fundamentally different.

Religions and Sports as Cultural Practices

Most people who study sports in society see religions and sports as cultural practices created by collections of people as they struggle to live with each other in satisfying and meaningful ways. This is a *social constructionist* approach. It assumes that religions and sports have neither identical nor essential characters because people produce them as they interact with each other under particular social and cultural conditions. Therefore, they have social structures, dynamics, and consequences related to those conditions, and they change over time as conditions change.

Social constructionists generally use critical theories to guide their work. They focus on social relations and issues of power when they study religions and sports. Therefore, they study the meanings given to the body by people who have different religious beliefs and the ways that beliefs influence movement, physical activity, sport participation, and even the organization of sports. They ask why sports and religion are male-dominated spheres of life and then study gender ideology as it is related to religion, the body, and sports. They also are concerned with the ways that people combine religious beliefs with sport participation and the social consequences of those combinations in particular cultural and subcultural settings.

Social constructionists assume that the meanings and practices connected with sports and religions vary by time and place. For example, religious beliefs and rituals change with new revelations and visions, new prophets and prophecies, new interpretations of sacred writings, and new teachers and teachings. Usually, these changes reproduce the cultural contexts in which they occur, but there also are times when they inspire transformations in social relations and social life. Sports are viewed in similar terms—as changing cultural practices that usually reproduce existing meanings and social organization, but with the potential to challenge and transform them.

Studying Sports and Religions: An Assessment

The issue of whether sports and religions are essentially the same or different does not inspire critical sociological questions. More important

> **Jesus would be aghast at how we use his name to bless our sports contests.**
> —Col. F. R. Lewis, retired U.S. Army chaplain (1996)

are the ways that people participate in the formation and transformation of social and cultural life and how they use sports and religions in those processes. A constructionist approach guided by critical, feminist, and interactionist theories often leads directly to questions that deal directly with people's experiences and social relations. It also calls attention to the different meanings that religions and sports have for different people and to the importance of understanding those meanings in terms of the social and cultural contexts in which they are formed and changed.

Few people who study sports in society have done research on sports and religions. The scholars who study religions are seldom interested in studying sports, and the scholars who study sports are seldom inclined to study religions. Furthermore, published studies of sports and religion focus primarily on Christian belief systems, in North America in particular. Therefore, we know little about sports and religious beliefs other than those based on Christianity, even though it is important to understand the ways that different religious beliefs are related to conceptions of the body, expressions of human movement, the integration of physical activity into everyday life, and participation in sports. Such knowledge could be used to establish programs that improve health and reduce the cost of medical care around the world.

A few scholars in the sociology of sport have studied the influence of Islamic beliefs on the participation of Muslim women (Hargreaves, 2000; Nakamura, 2002; Pfister, 2001). Religious beliefs often define, in moral terms, expectations related to femininity and masculinity. These expectations then regulate bodies and have an impact on sport participation patterns in societies and between cultures. For those who study sports and gender, this makes religion a potentially important topic to include in their analyses (Chandler, 2002; Randels and Beal, 2002).

Despite the scarcity of information about sports and religions other than Christianity and Judaism, issues related to this topic are discussed in the section, "Sports and Religions Around the World." But first, we focus on why certain forms of Christianity have become closely associated with organized competitive sports.

MODERN SPORTS AND RELIGIOUS BELIEFS AND ORGANIZATIONS

Despite important differences between the organization and stated goals of modern sports and those of religions, many people have combined these two spheres of life in mutually supportive ways over the past 150 years (Ladd and Mathisen, 1999; Putney, 2003). In some cases, people with certain religious beliefs have used sports to achieve religious goals; in other cases, people in sports have used religion to achieve on-the-field performance goals.

The increasing tendency to combine religions and sports raises interesting questions. Why have Christian organizations and beliefs, in particular, been combined directly and explicitly with sports? Why have these combinations not occurred in connection with most other religions? How have Christian organizations used sports, and how have athletes and sport organizations used Christianity and Christian beliefs? What are the dynamics and social significance of these combinations? These are the major issues discussed in sections, "The Protestant Ethic and the Spirit of Sports" and "How Have Christians and Christian Organizations Used Sports?"

The Protestant Ethic and the Spirit of Sports

It is useful to have historical information when trying to understand the links between modern sports and contemporary Christian beliefs. In the late nineteenth century, German sociologist-economist Max Weber did a classic study titled *The Protestant Ethic and the Spirit of Capitalism* (1904/1958). His research focused on the connection between the ideas embodied in the Protestant Reformation and the values underlying the growth of capitalist economic systems. His conclusion was that Protestant religious beliefs, especially those promoted by the reformer John Calvin, helped create a social and cultural environment in which capitalism could develop and grow. For example, Weber explained that Protestantism promoted a "code of ethics" and a general value system that created in people deep moral suspicions about erotic pleasure, physical desire, and all forms of idleness. "Idle hands are the devil's workshop" was a popular Protestant slogan.

Weber also used historical data to show that this "Protestant ethic," as he referred to it, emphasized a rationally controlled lifestyle in which emotions and feelings were suppressed in a quest for worldly success and eternal salvation. This orientation, developed in Calvin's notion of predestination, led people to define their occupation as a "calling" from God and work as an activity through which one's spiritual worth could be proven and displayed for others to see. This was socially significant because it linked material success with spiritual goodness: Being rich was a sign of "being saved" as long as you didn't spend the money on yourself.

The Protestant ethic has been defined and integrated into different cultures in different ways since the nineteenth century. However, it always emphasizes values consistent with the spirit that underlies organized competitive sports as they have developed in Europe and North America since the middle of the nineteenth century. Sociologist Steven Overman explains this in his book, *The Influence of the Protestant Ethic on Sport and Recreation* (1997). Overman shows that the Protestant ethic has emphasized a combination of the following seven key values, or virtues:

1. *Worldly asceticism* refers to the idea that suffering and the endurance of pain has a spiritual purpose. Therefore, goodness

Organized competitive sports emphasize work and achievement. These values are compatible with traditional Protestant religious beliefs; they represent the core of the Protestant ethic as sociologists define it. Therefore, playing football on a church-sponsored team is consistent with secular and Protestant-Christian values. (*Source:* Kristie Ebert)

is tied to self-denial and a disdain for self-indulgence; and spiritual redemption is gained through self-control and self-discipline.

2. *Rationalization* refers to the idea that the world is rationally organized. Therefore, religious truth can be discovered through human reason, and virtue is expressed through efficiency and measured by concrete achievements.

3. *Goal directedness* refers to the importance of focusing on salvation. Therefore, the spiritual worth of human action is demonstrated through its results—if actions lead to measurable achievements and success, they are good; if they do not, they are spiritually worthless.

4. *Individualism* refers to the belief that salvation is a matter of individual responsibility, initiative, and choice. Therefore, people control their destiny by making the decision to have a personal relationship with God/Christ.

5. *Achieved status* refers to the idea that success is associated with goodness and salvation, whereas failure is associated with sin and damnation. Therefore, worldly success is a means of earning salvation.

6. The *work ethic* refers to the notion that work is a calling from God. Therefore, people honor God by working hard and developing their "God-given potential" as they work.

7. The *time ethic* refers to the idea that time has a moral quality. Therefore, it is not to be wasted; efficiency is valued and idleness is sinful.

Overman argues that these seven virtues are closely matched with the orientation and spirit that informs the meaning, purpose, and organization of modern sports, especially power and performance sports in the United States. This argument has some weaknesses in that expressions of the Protestant ethic have been integrated into people's lives in many different ways, depending on historical and cultural factors. Furthermore, some of these virtues are not exclusive to Protestantism. They also exist in forms of Catholicism and other religions, although no religion other than mainstream forms of Protestantism has a set of beliefs that are exactly the same as these seven.

The seven virtues outlined by Overman have important implications for the ways that people in Europe and North America view the body. Traditional Catholic beliefs, for example, emphasized that the body was a divine vessel—a "temple of the Holy Spirit" (I Corinthians 6:19). As a result, Catholics living in the nineteenth and early twentieth century were taught to keep the body pure rather than engaging in a self-indulgent pursuit of physical development. Most Protestant believers, on the other hand, emphasized that the body was a divine tool to be used in establishing mastery over the physical world and oneself (Genesis 1:28; I Corinthians 9:24–27; Philippians 4:13). The perfect body, therefore, was a mark of a righteous soul (Overman, 1997).

Protestant beliefs have also supported the idea that individual competition is a legitimate means of demonstrating individual achievement and moral worth. Overall, organized competitive sports, because they are oriented around work and achievement, are logical sites for the application of Protestant beliefs. Unlike free and expressive play, these sports are worklike and demand sacrifice and the endurance of pain. Therefore,

Protestant/Christian athletes can define sport participation as their calling (from God) and make the claim that God wants them to be the best they can be in sports, even if it involves the physical domination of others. Furthermore, Christian athletes can define sport participation as a valuable form of religious witness and link it to personal salvation. Past research has supported Overman's overall approach in that athletes from Protestant nations disproportionately outnumber athletes from nations where there are many Muslims, Hindus, or Buddhists (Lüschen, 1967; Overman, 1997, pp. 150–157). Even the international success of athletes from non-Protestant nations can be traced in some cases to the influence of cultures where Protestant beliefs are dominant. However, the global diffusion of work-related achievement values has muted the influence of particular religious beliefs to the point that athletes from non-Protestant nations often excel in sports and win many international competitions today.

Sports and Religions Around the World

Most of what is known about sports and religions focuses on various forms of Christianity, especially evangelical fundamentalism. Little has been written about sports and Buddhism, Confucianism, Hinduism, Islam, Judaism, Sikhism, Shinto, Taoism, or the hundreds of variations of these and other religions. The beliefs and meanings associated with each of these religions influence how people perceive their bodies, view physical activities, and relate to each other through human movement (see figure 15.1). However, few people other than Christians, especially evangelical fundamentalist Christians, use their religious beliefs to directly support and give spiritual meaning to their participation in competitive sports.

It appears that no religion has an equivalent of the self-proclaimed "Christian athlete," which is an increasingly visible character in competitive sports in North America, Australia, New Zealand, and parts of Western Europe. This may be due in part to the Christian notion of individual salvation

"Well, sports fans, let's hope you've placed your bet on the right competitor here!"

············

FIGURE 15.1 Scholars who study religions and sports are not concerned with the truth or falsity of religious beliefs as much as they are with the ways that religion influences the meaning, purpose, and organization of sports in society.

and how certain believers have applied it to everyday life. Additionally, religions other than Christianity and Islam often focus on the transcendence of self—meaning that the goal of believers is to merge the self with spiritual forces rather than promoting the self through a quest for personal growth and spiritual salvation through competitive sports. In fact, the idea of using competition against others to publicly establish the superiority of self over others violates the core beliefs of many religions.

Unfortunately, our knowledge of these sport and religion issues is very limited. We know more about the ways that some North American athletes and coaches have converted Zen Buddhist beliefs into strategies for improving golf scores and marathon times than we do about how Buddhism is related to sports and sport participation

among 400 million Buddhists around the world. This is an example of how our knowledge is grounded in a combination of Eurocentric science and limited personal experiences.

Buddhism and Hinduism: Transcending Self
Buddhism and philosophical Hinduism emphasize physical and spiritual discipline, but they do *not* inspire believers to strive for Olympic medals or physically outperform or dominate other human beings in organized competitive sports. Instead, most of the current expressions of Buddhism and Hinduism focus on transcending the self and the material world. This focus does *not* support a person's interest in becoming an elite athlete, signing endorsement contracts, and being inducted into a sport hall of fame. The major beliefs emphasized by many Hindus and Buddhists are incompatible with seeking competitive success in physical activities. The idea of expressing self-development through a quest for competitive victories would make little sense within most Hindu and Buddhist traditions as they are practiced today.

It is primarily elite athletes from Christian, capitalist countries who want to know how the meditation practices and rituals from these religions can be used to improve sport performances and give meaning to lives that revolve around competitive sports. However, a segment of a growing Hindu nationalist movement in India uses exercises, games, and sports combined with yoga and prayers to develop loyalty and affection for Hindu culture and the Hindu nationhood (McDonald, 1999). This is consistent with historical evidence showing that sports have long been used as sites for training minds and bodies for military service and "defending culture." However, when this training is tied to religion and religious practices, it takes on new meaning because the sacred and the profane (secular) are mixed together in ways that often have strong social relevance. For example, in some cases this mix turns conflicts into religious wars in which killing others is sanctified and making peace with

This youth league game in Japan is played with a massive statue of Buddha in the background. However, athletes in Japan do not connect sport participation with religion as do some athletes in North America where sport participation is linked regularly with Christian beliefs. (*Source:* Jay Coakley)

enemies is often defined as a moral failure because it involves compromising religious beliefs.

Traditional Hindu norms in India call for women to be secluded and veiled—that is, confined to private, family-based spaces and covered with robes and scarves. These cultural practices are linked with the legacy of the caste system in which religion was used to establish and maintain social inequalities in India. The caste system consisted of complex norms and beliefs that regulated activities and relationships throughout Indian society. Individuals were born into a particular caste, and their caste position marked their social status in society as a whole. Officially, the caste system is illegal today, but its cultural

legacy continues to exist. For example, women from previously middle and upper castes have considerable freedom, but women and many men from previously lower castes live with persistent poverty, unemployment, and illiteracy. Patterns of sport participation are influenced by these factors. Although the caste system was never grounded exclusively in Hindu religious beliefs, Hinduism was organized so that it reproduced the social importance of castes and caste membership. This has yet to be studied in terms of its connection with sports and other physical activities.

Islam: Submission to Allah's Will Studying Islam and sports is a challenge because Muslims, like many Buddhists and Hindus, make few distinctions between the religious (sacred) and the secular (profane). Every action is done to please Allah (God) and is therefore a form of worship. Religious beliefs and cultural norms are merged into a single ideology, with an emphasis on peace through submission to Allah's will.

Muslims have long participated in physical activities and sports, but participation is regulated by their beliefs about what pleases Allah. The connection between sports and the Islamic mandate to submit to Allah's will has not been studied. However, historical research has referred to a form of "muscular Islam" that existed in a region of South Africa during the apartheid era (Nauright, 1997; Nauright and Magdalinski, 2002). For example, Muslim rugby players between 1930 and 1970 used a highly aggressive style of play to symbolize their struggle against racial apartheid. But we don't know if the players, or the women and families who supported them, connected rugby or their use of intimidation and violence on the field to Allah's will.

There are noteworthy examples in the United States of black Muslims who have excelled at sports. Boxer Cassius Clay's conversion to Islam in the 1960s created global publicity. When he changed his name to Muhammad Ali and articulated his Muslim beliefs, most Americans did not understand Islam or why some African Americans embraced it. Since then, other black male athletes who have grown up as Muslims or converted to Islam have played elite sports. However, the traditions of sport participation and the quest for excellence in sports are not as strong in Muslim countries as they are in secularized, Christian-Protestant countries, partly because low per-capita income makes full time training nearly impossible for many Muslims.

Although Muslim nations in many parts of Central and Southeast Asia have no religious restrictions on girls and women playing sports, Islamic beliefs in other parts of the world legitimize patriarchal[3] structures and maintain definitions of male and female bodies that discourage girls and women from playing sports and restrict their everyday access to sport participation opportunities (Fatwa Bank, 2004; Good, 2002; Moore, 2004; Taheri, 2004). For example, physical activities in many Muslim nations are sex segregated. Men are not allowed to look at women in public settings, and women must cover their bodies with robes and head scarves, even when they exercise. These norms are especially strong among fundamentalist Muslims. This is why national Olympic teams from some Muslim nations have few or no women athletes. For example, in 1992 thirty-five nations, half of them Muslim, sent no women to the Olympic Games in Barcelona. In 2004 only four Muslim nations had no women on their teams, but the total number of women from Muslim nations was the lowest since the 1960 Olympics (Taheri, 2004). The nations with the tightest restrictions include Iran, Afghanistan, Oman, Kuwait, Pakistan, Qatar, Saudi Arabia, the United Arab Emirates, and Sudan. However, Iran regularly holds events exclusively for women, the latest being the Fourth Women Islamic Games in September

2005. But these games are not televised because the women are allowed to dress as they wish, and there is a fear that men may watch them. No men are allowed in or near the event, and armed women guards guarantee that men keep their distance. The connection between gender, sport, and Islam is discussed further in the box "Allah's Will."

The popularity of sports among men in Islamic countries is often tied to expressions of political and cultural nationalism rather than religious beliefs (Stokes, 1996). Similarly, when Muslims migrate from Islamic countries to Europe or North America, they participate in sports, but their participation is tied more to learning about life and gaining acceptance in their new cultures than expressing Muslim beliefs through sports. Muslim girls and women in non-Islamic countries have very low sport participation rates (Nakamura, 2002; Verma and Darby, 1994), and Muslim organizations are unlikely to sponsor sports for their members. However, some people, including scholars in the sociology of sport, have organized programs that enable Muslim women to train and play sports under conditions consistent with their modesty norms. So far, these programs have been successful in attracting and providing participation opportunities for girls and young women (Weaver, 2005).

Shinto: Sumo in Japan Sumo, or traditional Japanese wrestling, has strong historical ties to Shinto, a traditional Japanese religion (Light and Kinnaird, 2002). *Shinto* means "the way of the gods," and it consists of a system of rituals and ceremonies designed to worship nature rather than reaffirm an established theology. Modern sumo is a nonreligious activity although it remains steeped in Shinto ritual and ceremony. The dohyo (rings) in which the bouts take place are defined as sacred sites. Religious symbols are integrated into their design and construction, and the rings are consecrated through purification ceremonies, during which referees, dressed as priests, ask the gods to bless the scheduled

---

[3]Patriarchy is a form of gender relations in which men are officially privileged relative to women, especially in regard to legal status and access to political power and economic resources.

reflect on SPORTS

Allah's Will
Dilemmas for Islamic Women Athletes?

Imagine winning an Olympic gold medal, receiving death threats from people in your country who brand you as an immoral and corrupt woman, and then being forced to live in exile. At the same time, imagine that you are a heroine to many young women, who see you as inspirational in their quest for equal rights and opportunities to play sports.

These is the situation faced by Hassiba Boulmerka, the gold medalist in the 1500 meters at the 1992 Olympic Games in Barcelona, Spain. As an Algerian Muslim woman, Boulmerka believed that she could be an international athlete without abandoning her faith or her commitment to Islam. Under the social and political conditions in traditional Muslim nations, this made Boulmerka a radical feminist who was feared and rejected by some people and embraced and followed by others.

Those who fear and reject Boulmerka are primarily fundamentalist Muslims. It is permissible, they say, for women to participate in sports—but *not* in shorts or T-shirts, *not* while men are watching, *not* when men and women train together, *not* when facilities do not permit total privacy, and *not*, if you are married, unless your husband gives his permission (Beiruty, 2002).

To complicate matters, Boulmerka has also been rejected by some Islamic feminists, who see her as a woman co-opted and used by a sport system that is grounded in men's values and sponsored by powerful corporations that promote a soulless, worldwide consumer culture. To participate in such a system, they say, is to endorse global forces that are dangerously oppressive to all humankind.

Boulmerka supporters are primarily liberal feminists and others who want to revise the restrictive norms governing many Muslim women. They promote women's rights and the transformation of societies and communities in which women live without a voice, without public legitimacy, and without power (Hargreaves, 2000). However, Boulmerka has also been embraced by those who do not know or understand Islam and

reject Muslim ways of life because of their own ethnocentrism and religious beliefs.

This complicated, real-life scenario illustrates that the bodies of Muslim women are "contested terrain." They are at the center of deep political, cultural, and religious struggles about what is important, what is right and wrong, and how social life should be organized. Women athletes embody and personify these struggles. On the one hand, they are active subjects who assert new ideas about what it means to be a Muslim woman. On the other hand, they are passive objects that are the focus of debates about morality and social change in the world today.

Is there social and cultural space in Islamic nations for Hassiba Boulmerka and others like her? Is it possible to merge Islamic beliefs with ideas about equal rights and sport participation among women? Can the Qur'an (Koran) be interpreted in ways that give women the power to make choices in their lives? Can people live peacefully together as they interpret the Qur'an in different ways?

Sociologist Jennifer Hargreaves (2000) explains that intervening in the struggles to answer these questions is a major challenge and must be undertaken with sensitivity and cultural awareness. Efforts to promote change from outside Islam are risky because they are easily linked with ethnocentric beliefs about the superiority of Western values and the need to reform cultural practices that seem strange. This means that intervention must occur through and with Muslim organizations that can make changes in their ways and on their terms. Hargreaves notes that these changes may not take the forms envisioned by Western observers, but if they free women from oppressive forms of social control, they will represent progress.

Many Muslims, including Muslim women, continue to disagree with each other about such changes. Therefore, struggles over issues of religion and gender will continue into the future. Understanding and coming to terms with "Allah's will" is not easy and creates dilemmas for Islamic women athletes. *What do you think?*

> We cannot ask them to pay municipal taxes but be denied the same facilities as men simply because we fear that some men may go wild by seeing women doing sport.
>
> —Esfandiar Mashaie, deputy mayor for social affairs, Tehran (Iran) (in Taheri, 2004)

Sumo wrestling in Japan occurs in connection with centuries-old Shinto beliefs. "Purity and purification rituals are central to the practice of Shinto and many have been incorporated into the contemporary practice of sumo" (Light and Kinnaird, 2002, p. 142). However, sumo wrestlers never talk about their own religious beliefs in connection with their sport. (*Source:* Katsumi Kasullara, AP/Wide World Photos)

bouts. Only the wrestlers and recognized sumo officials are allowed in the dohyo. Shoes must not be worn, and women are never allowed to stand on or near the ring.

The wrestlers take great care to preserve the purity of the dohyo. Prior to their bouts, they ritualistically throw salt into the ring to symbolize their respect for its sacredness and purity; they even wipe the sweat off their bodies and rinse their mouths with water presented to them by fellow wrestlers. If a wrestler sheds blood during a bout, the stains are cleaned and purified before the bouts continue. Shinto motifs are included in the architecture and decorations on and around

the dohyo. However, wrestlers do not personally express their commitment to Shinto, nor do Shinto organizations sponsor or promote sumo or other sports.

Religion and Life Philosophies in China Anthropologist Susan Brownell (1995) discusses very briefly the connections between physical culture and various forms of Taoist, Confucian, and Buddhist ideas and practices in her comprehensive study of the body and sport in China. She notes that each of these life philosophies is actually a general theory of the nature and principles of the universe. As with Islam, this makes it difficult to separate "religious beliefs" from cultural ideology as a whole. Each of these life philosophies emphasizes the notion that all human beings should strive to live in line with the energy and forces of nature. The body and physical exercise are seen as important parts of nature, but the goal of movement is to seek harmony with nature rather than to overcome or dominate nature or other human beings.

Tai chi is a form of exercise based on this cultural approach to life and living. Some versions of the martial arts are practiced in this spirit, but others, including practices outside China, are grounded in secular traditions of self-defense and military training. China's success in many international competitions raises other questions about the possible connections between religious beliefs and sport participation. These questions have not been explored in studies of sports or religion, but the 2008 Olympics in Beijing may change this as people become more curious about China and its ways of life.

Native Americans: Merging the Spiritual and Physical Through history, Native Americans have often included physical games and running races in religious rituals (Nabokov, 1981). However, the purpose of these games and races is to reaffirm social connections within specific native cultural groups and gain skills needed for group survival. Outside these rituals, sport participation has had no specific religious meaning.

Making general statements about religions and sports among Native Americans is difficult because there are many variations in their religious beliefs. However, many native cultures have maintained animistic religious traditions. They emphasize that material things, such as the earth, wind, sun, moon, plants, and animals, contain elements directly linked to the sacred and supernatural. Many native games reflect these beliefs, and, when Native Americans participate in sports constructed by people from European or other backgrounds, they often use their beliefs to give participation a meaning that reaffirms their own

ways of viewing the world and their connection with the sacred.

Anthropologist Peter Navokov has studied running among Native Americans and notes that prior to their contact with Europeans the people native to North America ran for practical purposes such as hunting, communicating, and fighting; but they also ran to to reenact myths and legends and to reaffirm their connection with the forces of nature and the universe. More recently, Native American athletes whose identities are grounded in native cultures often define their sport participation in terms of their cultural traditions and beliefs. However, little is known about how they incorporate specific religious beliefs and traditions, which vary across native cultures, into sport participation that occurs outside of their native cultures or how young Native Americans who play sports connect their participation to religious beliefs.

Sports and Religions Around the World: Waiting for Research We need more information about the connections among various religious beliefs around the world, ideas about the body, and participation in physical activities and sports. Research could help us understand the lives of billions of people who participate in various forms of physical activities and sports but do not connect them directly with religious organizations or use them as sites for religious witness. This is different from the tendency of some Christians who attach their religion to institutionalized, competitive sports that already exist for nonreligious purposes.

How Have Christians and Christian Organizations Used Sports?

Unlike other religions, Christianity has inspired believers to use sports for many purposes. These include (a) promoting spiritual growth, (b) recruiting new members and promoting religious beliefs and organizations, and (c) promoting fundamentalist beliefs and evangelical orientations.

To Promote Spiritual Growth During the mid-1800s, influential Christian men, described as "muscular Christians" in England and New England, promoted the idea that the physical condition of one's body had religious significance. They believed that the body was an instrument of good works and that meeting the physical demands of godly behavior required good health and physical conditioning. Although most religious people at the time did not agree with this approach, the idea that there might be a connection between the physical and spiritual dimensions of human beings grew increasingly popular (Guttmann, 1978, 1988).

The idea that the body had moral significance and that moral character was associated with physical conditioning, encouraged many religious organizations to use sports in their recruitment activities and membership programs. For example, the YMCA and the YWCA grew rapidly between 1880 and 1920 as they built athletic facilities in many communities and sponsored sport teams. Canadian James Naismith invented basketball in 1891 while he was a student at the Springfield, Massachusetts, YMCA. William Morgan, the physical activities director at a YMCA in Holyoke, Massachusetts, invented volleyball in 1895.

Although mainline Protestants endorsed sports through the end of the nineteenth century, many of them came to wonder about the religious relevance of the highly competitive forms of sport that emerged during the first half of the twentieth century. The publicity given to scandals, violence, and other problems in sports caused evangelicals, in particular, to question the value of sports. They were also wary of women playing sports because it contradicted their belief that God created men and women to be different and that female athletes would subvert God's plan by playing like men played (see Jonas, 2005).

It was not until after World War II that evangelical Christians again used sports in connection with their religious beliefs (Ladd and Mathisen, 1999). It is important to note that the evangelicals were not alone in establishing ties to sports

in the postwar period. Protestant churches and congregations, Catholic dioceses and parishes, Mormon wards, the B'nai B'rith, and some Jewish synagogues also embraced sports as worthwhile activities, especially for young people, boys in particular. These organizations sponsored sports and sport programs because their members and leaders believed that sport participation developed moral character.

For example, as World War II was ending in 1945, Pope Pius XII gave a worldwide address in which he talked about the moral value of sports from a Catholic perspective:

> Those who accuse the Church of not caring for the body and physical culture . . . are far from the truth. . . . In the final analysis, what is sport if not a form of education for the body? This education is closely related to morality. . . . Sport is an effective antidote to softness and easy living. (in Feeney, 1995, pp. 27-29)

Other religious leaders of the twentieth century gave similar messages about sports. In 1971 evangelist Billy Graham, a long-time outspoken promoter of sports as a builder of moral character, summarized the spirit in which many religious organizations have viewed sports over the last century:

> The Bible says leisure and lying around are morally dangerous for us. Sports keep us busy; athletes, you notice, don't take drugs. There are probably more committed Christians in sports, both collegiate and professional, than in any other occupation in America. (in *Newsweek*, 1971, p. 51)

Part of Graham's statement sounds naïve today, but he accurately noted that many Christians use sports as activities that symbolize and promote moral development—especially among boys and young men. This commitment remains strong today.

To Recruit New Members and Promote Religious Beliefs and Organizations Using sports to attract and recruit boys and men to churches and

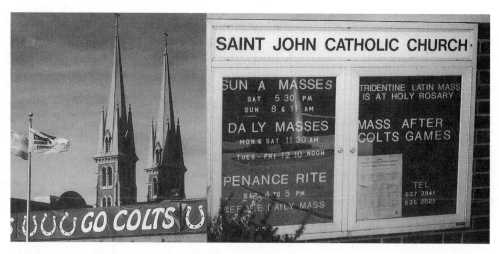

Stadiums and arenas now occupy a more prominent place than churches in urban areas, and sport teams attract more publicity than religious services. In this cultural context, religious services are scheduled around big games. This is true in Indianapolis where the local cathedral is dwarfed by the RCA Dome and Conseco Fieldhouse and where mass is scheduled after the Colts' NFL games. (*Source:* Jay Coakley)

religious organizations has occurred since the mid-1800s (Putney, 2003). This practice became so common after World War II that sociologist Charles Page referred to it as "the basketballization of American religion" (in Demerath and Hammond, 1969, p. 182).

In the early 1990s, for example, Bill McCartney, the former football coach at the University of Colorado, used sport images as he founded his religious organization, *The Promise Keepers* and recruited men to join. McCartney and others in the evangelical men's organization preached that a "manly man is a Godly man." Similarly, other Christian fundamentalist organizations have used images of tough athletes to represent ideal "Christian men." This strategy of presenting a "masculinized Christianity" is designed to attract men into churches so that they can "rescue the Bible from women and overly refined preachers" (Flake, 1992, p. 165).

Church-affiliated colleges and universities in the United States have also used sports as recruiting and public relations tools. Administrators from these schools know that seventeen-year-olds

today are more likely to listen to recruiting advertisements if they use terminology, images, and spokespeople from sports. For example, when the famous preacher Oral Roberts founded his university in Tulsa, Oklahoma, in 1965, he highlighted the importance of its sport programs in this way:

> Athletics is part of our Christian witness. . . . Nearly every man in America reads the sports pages, and a Christian school cannot ignore these people. . . . Sports are becoming the No. 1 interest of people in America. For us to be relevant, we had to gain the attention of millions of people in a way that they could understand. (in Boyle, 1970, p. 64)

Jerry Falwell, noted television evangelist, introduced intercollegiate athletics at his Liberty University in the 1970s with a similar explanation:

> To me, athletics are a way of making a statement. And I believe you have a better Christian witness to the youth of the world when you competitively, head-to-head, prove yourself their equal on the playing field. (in Capouya, 1986, p. 75)

Then, in his opening prayer, Falwell declared, "Father, we don't want to be mediocre, we don't want to fail. We want to honor You by winning" (in Capouya, 1986, p. 72).

Other church-affiliated colleges and universities have used sports in similar but less overt ways to attract students. Catholic schools—including the University of Notre Dame, Gonzaga, Georgetown, and Boston College—have used football and/or basketball programs to build their prestige as church-affiliated institutions. Brigham Young University, affiliated with the Church of Latter Day Saints (Mormons), also has done this. Smaller Christian colleges around the United States formed the National Christian Collegiate Athletic Association (NCCAA) in the mid-1960s to sponsor championships and recruit Christian student-athletes to their schools (Ladd and Mathisen, 1999).

Some religious organizations are developed around sports to attract people to Christian beliefs and provide support for athletes who hold Christian beliefs. Examples include Sports Ambassadors, the Fellowship of Christian Athletes (FCA), Athletes in Action (AIA), Pro Athletes Outreach (PAO), Sports Outreach America (SOA), and dozens of smaller groups associated with particular sports. There are Christian Surfers

The connections between sports and religions in general and Christian religious organizations in particular have changed throughout history. Today, for example, the public profiles of some universities are connected with both sports and religion. This is the football stadium at the University of Notre Dame. In the background is the library. The south wall of the library has a mural image of Christ. The image has come to be known affectionately among Notre Dame football fans as "Touchdown Jesus." (*Source:* Jay Coakley)

Australia, Cowboys for Christ, Golfers for Christ, Wheel Power Christian Cyclists, and the Christian Wrestling Federation, among hundreds of others (Asay, 2005). These organizations often have a strong evangelical emphasis, and members are usually eager to share their beliefs in the hope that others will embrace Christian fundamentalism as they do. For example, an athlete departing for Guatemala on a trip sponsored by the AIA said, "I am really looking forward to sharing God's word and introducing a personal relationship with Jesus Christ to others" (Lynch, 2005).

Many Christian organizations and groups also use sports as sites for evangelizing. For example, thousands of organized volunteers at recent Olympic Games have distributed Bibles, books, videos, audiotapes, CDs, magazines, pamphlets, pins, sport ministry kits, and sport-planning and clinic guides. Most of these feature athletes giving witness to the importance of Bible-based religious beliefs in their lives. Such efforts to evangelize are not new, but today they are highly organized and coordinated. For example, in 2005 the Jacksonville Baptist Association organized First Down First Coast (FDFC) to enable Christians to use the Super Bowl as an occasion for sharing the love and saving knowledge of Jesus Christ with thousands of people gathered for the game. FDFC provided training sessions for sharing the gospel, volunteers to organize churches and individuals, evangelistic gift bags for people coming to Jacksonville for the game, and game day materials (including football cards picturing NFL players and highlighting testimony about their Christian beliefs), videos, DVDs, and CDs with music by Christian bands and statements from visible Christian athletes and coaches.

Apart from major events, RBC Ministries and the FCA, both fundamentalist Christian organizations, publish *SportsSpectrum* and *Sharing the*

> Our youth basketball team is back in action Wednesday at 8 PM in the school recreation hall. Come out and watch us kill Christ the King.
>
> —Poster announcing an elementary school basketball game (2002)

Victory (*STV*), widely circulated magazines that use a biblically informed perspective to report on sports and athletes. Articles highlight Christian athletes and their religious testimony. Most athlete profiles emphasize that life "without a commitment to Christ" is superficial and meaningless, even if one wins in sports. This method of using athletes to evangelize is now a key strategy. As one FCA official explained, "If athletes can sell razor blades and soft drinks, why can't they sell the Gospel?"

In 2004 Pope John Paul II established a new Vatican office dedicated to "Church and Sport" (Glatz, 2004). Although its primary stated goal is to reform the culture of sport, it is also concerned with making Catholicism relevant in the lives of people, especially men, who are no longer involved in their parishes or using Catholic beliefs to guide their lives. The office now sponsors a talk radio sport program to attract Italian men who no longer see the Catholic Church as relevant to them; soccer is a central focus of the program on Vatican radio (Gladstone, 2005).

To Promote Fundamentalist Beliefs and Evangelical Orientations

Most of the religious groups and organizations previously mentioned promote a specific form of Christianity—one based on a loosely articulated conservative ideology and a fundamentalist orientation toward life.

Religious fundamentalism is based on the belief that the secular foundation of modern societies is inherently corrupt and there is a need for people to use the unerring and unchanging Truth contained in a sacred text as the basis for reorganizing personal lives and the entire social order (Hadden, 2000; Marty and Appleby, 1995; Pace, 2007). Religious fundamentalists emphasize that this reorganization requires that people be personally committed to the supernatural source of truth (God, Allah, Christ, Mohammed, "the universe," the spirit world), which is the source of clear answers to personal and social problems. These answers are revealed through sacred writings, the verbal teachings of divinely inspired leaders and prophets, and personal revelations.

Fundamentalist movements arise when people perceive moral threats to a way of life that was ideal in the past when it was based on religious principles. Therefore, fundamentalists emphasize the "moral decline of society" and the need to return to a time when religious truth was the foundation for culture and social organization. This belief may be so deeply held that it divides fundamentalists from other people in a society.

Ladd and Mathisen (1999) explain that fundamentalist Christians in the United States have used sports, in part, to reduce their separation from society and increase their legitimacy in it. The tendencies of Christian fundamentalist movements in other English-speaking, predominantly Protestant societies to use sports to promote their beliefs support this explanation, although there certainly are important variations between countries.

How Have Athletes and Coaches Used Religion?

Athletes and coaches use religion, religious beliefs, prayers, and rituals in many ways. Research on this topic is scarce, but there is much anecdotal information suggesting that athletes and coaches use religion for one or more of the following reasons:

1. To cope with uncertainty
2. To stay out of trouble
3. To give meaning to sport participation
4. To put sport participation into a "balanced perspective"
5. To establish team solidarity and unity
6. To reaffirm expectations, rules, and social control on teams
7. To assert autonomy in the face of power
8. To achieve personal and competitive success

To Cope with Uncertainty Through history, people have used prayers and rituals based in religion, magic, and/or superstition to cope with uncertainties in their lives (Ciborowski, 1997; Womack, 1992). Because sport competition involves uncertainty, it is not surprising that many athletes use rituals, some based in religion, to help them feel as if they have some control over what happens to them on the playing field.

Wrestler Kurt Angle, a gold medalist in the 1996 Olympic Games explained that, when he had a serious neck injury before his qualifying matches, he prayed to God for guidance. His doctor advised him not to wrestle because he would risk paralysis if he injured his neck again. However, in answer to his prayers, "God said to do it." Thus, before each match, his doctor shot novocaine into his neck so that he could endure the pain. After he won the gold medal, he said,

> I knew my neck was hurt . . . I knew when I was wrestling in the Olympic Games that He was watching over me. I knew when I won the gold medal that He intended me to win. He wanted someone like me to spread the Word and be a role model for kids. (in Hubbard, 1998, p. 147)

The use of prayers and rituals is not limited to Christian athletes. Former NBA player Hakeem Olajuwon engaged in a regular Islamic prayer ritual as he faced challenges in his life as a professional athlete. He explained that "my religion gives me direction, inner strength. I feel more comfortable. You can take life head on" (*USA Today*, 1994, p. 6C).

Not all religious athletes use prayer and religious rituals in this manner, but many call on their religion to help them face challenges and uncertainty. Therefore, many athletes who pray before or during games seldom pray before or during practices. For example, Catholic athletes who make the sign of the cross when they come up to bat or shoot a free throw during a game don't do the same thing when they bat or shoot

An increasing number of North American athletes use Christian beliefs to give special meaning to their sport participation. These young men use football as a form of Christian witness. (*Source:* Jay Coakley)

free throws at practices. It is the actual competition that produces the level of uncertainty that evokes the prayer or religious ritual.

Sometimes it is difficult to separate the use of religion from the use of magic and superstition among athletes. **Magic** consists of *recipe-like rituals designed to produce immediate and practical results in the material world*. **Superstitions** consist of *regularized, ritualistic actions performed to give a person or group a sense of control and predictability in the face of challenges*. Thus, when athletes pray, it may be a form of religion or magic and superstition, but in many cases, its primary goal is to control or deal with the uncertainty that exists in competitive sports.

To Stay out of Trouble   The late Reggie White was an ordained minister and a retired defensive lineman in the NFL (he was called the "minister of defense"). When he was asked about his religious beliefs during his years in the NFL, he said that "studying God's Word helped keep my life on track, even though there were bad influences like drugs and crime all around me" (IBS, 1996b, Section A). Other athletes say similar things about religion helping them to avoid the risky lifestyles

that often exist in the social worlds that develop around certain sports. NFL player Sean Gilbert has said, "Before I found the Lord, I drank! I whoremongered! I cussed! I cheated! I manipulated! I deceived!" (in Corsello, 1999, p. 435).

The fact that religious beliefs may separate athletes from risky off-the-field lifestyles and keep them focused on training in their sports has not been lost on coaches (Plotz, 2000). Journalist Andrew Corsello explains that "regardless of their own beliefs, coaches are attracted to the self-control that Christian convictions instill in a man" (1999, p. 435). Futhermore, team owners may see "born-again athletes" as better long-term investments because they believe that religious athletes "are less likely to get arrested" (Smith, 1997). Finally, religious beliefs also may keep athletes out of trouble by encouraging them to become involved in church-related and community-based service programs. This involvement can separate them from risky off-the-field lifestyles.

To Give Meaning to Sport Participation   Sport participation emphasizes personal achievement and self-promotion, and it involves playing games that produce no essential goods or services, even though people create social occasions around sport events. This makes sport participation a self-centered, self-indulgent activity. Although training often involves personal sacrifices and pain, it focuses on the development and use of personal physical skills, often to the exclusion of other activities and relationships. Realizing this can create a *crisis of meaning* for athletes who have dedicated their lives to personal achievements in sports.

Ironically, athletes who have money and fame are among those who experience this crisis of meaning. How do these athletes give meaning to the extreme self-centeredness that is required by their training and competition? How do they justify the expenditure of nearly all their time and energy on sports? How do they explain why they allow sport participation to disrupt their families or utilize a large portion of family resources? One way to answer these questions is to define sport participation as an act of worship, a platform for giving witness, or a manifestation of God's plan for their lives (Hoffman, 1992b, 1992c, 1992d, 1999). This enables athletes to "sanctify" their commitment to sport, thereby giving their participation ultimate meaning and making it their spiritual destiny. This answer also keeps athletes motivated. As volleyball player Kim Oden says, "Learning what Jesus knowingly went through for me gave me a lot of self-confidence. It also gave me a lot more reason to do what I do" (IBS, 1996b, Section D). Olympic swimmer Josh Davis, winner of four gold medals in the 1995 World University Games, explains that swimming is part of God's plan for him:

> I've been given a gift to swim fast, and I think God expects me to use that gift to the best of my ability to reach my potential. . . . What Christ did on the cross supplies me with an everlasting motivation. (in Robbins, 1996, p. 21)

Many Christian athletes and coaches like to quote Colossians 3:23 in the Bible: "Whatever you do, work at it with all your heart, working for the Lord, not for men." This enables them to shift their sport participation from the realm of the profane to the realm of the sacred. As a result, their doubts about the worthiness of what they do are eliminated because playing sports is now a calling from God.

To Put Sport Participation into a Balanced Perspective It's easy to lose perspective in sports, to let it define you and foreclose other parts of your life. In the face of this threat, some athletes feel that religious beliefs enable them to transcend sports and bring balance back to their lives. For example, former Olympic runner Elana Meyer explains that "running is a way God can use me for His glory. Athletics is not my life" (IBS, 1996c, Section G). Similarly, the legendary runner Jim Ryun, now a fourth term U.S. congressman from Kansas, confesses that when he was setting world records, "I would reach for that 'something more,' [and] I'd come up empty, because it was only sports and me" (Smale, 2005). With beliefs such as this, playing sports becomes part of God's plan in athletes' minds, and it becomes easier for them to face challenges and deal with the inevitable losses experienced in sports. In the process, they keep sports in perspective.

Tennis player Paradorn Srichaphan, a practicing Buddhist from Thailand, takes a different approach. After his matches, he performs a ritual in which he covers his face with his hands and bows in all directions, kneels, and touches his forehead to the earth as a show of reverence to the earth. He explains that the *wai* (the name of the ritual, pronounced WHY) "is a show of respect and a thank-you to the crowd and my opponent. It's like saying I am humbled to be here" (in Wertheim, 2003). He says that his Buddhism gives him an inner peace; on the ATP Tour, he was given the tour's sportsmanship award for how he treats the game, the crowd, and his opponents.

To Establish Team Solidarity and Unity Religious beliefs and rituals can be powerful tools in creating bonds between people. When they are combined with sport participation, they can link athletes together as spiritual teammates, building team solidarity and unity in the process (see figure 15.2). Many coaches know this, and some have used Christian beliefs as rallying points for their teams. For example, a former NFL coach once said that he supported religious worship and team prayers among his athletes because they "foster togetherness and mutual respect like nothing I have found in 21 years of coaching" (in Hoffman, 1982, p. 18). Similarly, Fisher DeBerry, a committed Christian and head football coach at the U.S. Air Force Academy, used religion to establish an esprit de corps on his team by hanging a sign in the locker room saying "I AM A MEMBER OF TEAM JESUS CHRIST"—a statement that is in the FCA Competitor's Creed (www.fca.org/TEAMFCA/CompetitorsCreed.lsp).

"She says this prayer is 'voluntary.' Who is she trying to fool?!?"

FIGURE 15.2 When coaches use religious beliefs and rituals on sport teams, they may create solidarity or dissent. Coaches say that team prayers are voluntary, but players may feel pressure to go along with the coaches' beliefs, even when they do not match their own.

Objections to such practices, especially when they involve pregame prayers in public schools, has led some U.S. students and their parents to file lawsuits to ban religious expression in connection with sport events. However, coaches and athletes continue to insist that prayers bring team members together in positive ways and serve a spiritual purpose in players' lives. Despite lawsuits, most people in the United States agree that it is appropriate for sporting events at public high schools to begin with a public prayer (Lieblich and Ostling, 2000). This controversial issue is discussed in the box "Public Prayers at Sport Events."

To Reaffirm Expectations, Rules, and Social Control on Teams Religion also can sanctify norms and rules by connecting them with the sacred and supernatural. Therefore, it can be used to connect the moral worth of athletes with the quality of their play and their conformity to team rules and the commands of coaches. Wes Neal, founder of the Institute for Athletic Perfection, a Christian sport organization, tells athletes the following:

> You may not agree with [your coach] on every point, but your role [as a Christian athlete] is to carry out his assignments. The attitude you have as you carry out each assignment will determine if you are a winner in God's sight. (1981, p. 193)

This means that following rules is a way for athletes to prove their moral worth.

This combination of religion and sport is very powerful: When the rules and assignments of coaches are tied to religious beliefs, the athletes are much more likely to obey coaches without question. In this way, coaches may use religion, either intentionally or unintentionally, as a means of controlling the behavior of athletes. From a sociological perspective, this connection between religion and social control is important because many coaches are very concerned with issues of authority and control on their teams.

reflect on SPORTS

Public Prayers at Sport Events
What's Legal and What's Not?

Prayers before sport events are common in the United States. They often are said silently by individuals, aloud by small groups of players or entire teams in pregame huddles, and over public address systems by students or local spokespeople.

Public prayers are allowed at private events, and *all people in the United States have the right to say silent, private prayers for any purpose at any time*. Some people have questioned the appropriateness of prayers said at events such as professional wrestling and extreme fighting, but as long as an event is sponsored by private organizations or as long as people pray privately and silently, prayers are legal.

According to a 1962 U.S. Supreme Court decision, which banned organized prayers in public schools, there *are* legal problems when prayers are said publicly and collectively at sport events sponsored by state organizations, such as public schools. The histories of these legal problems vary from state to state in the United States, but Texas has received much attention when it comes to this issue.

Controversy in Texas began in 1992, when two families near Houston filed a lawsuit requesting a ban on prayers in public schools. They appealed to the First Amendment of the U.S. Constitution, which says, "Congress shall make no law respecting an establishment of religion." After thinking about what "an establishment of religion" actually means, the federal district judge in the case ruled that public prayers are okay as long as they are nonsectarian and general in content, initiated by students, and not said in connection with attempts to convert anyone to a particular religion. This decision was qualified during an appeal when the appellate judges ruled that sport events are not serious enough occasions to require the solemnity of public prayer.

Despite this decision and two similar decisions in 1995 and 1999, people in many U.S. towns continue to say public prayers before public school sport events. Students often include references to "Jesus," "Lord," and "Heavenly Father" when they say prayers over the public address system and athletes do the same when they pray with their teams. These prayers often are "local traditions," and people object when federal government judges tell them that they are unconstitutional.

They argue that it violates their constitutional right to "freedom of speech."

What's the harm in public prayer? Those who have filed lawsuits usually argue that the prayers are grounded in Christian beliefs and create informal pressures to give priority to those beliefs over others. They also say that those who don't join in and pray are subject to ridicule, social rejection, or efforts to convert them to Christianity. The people who support public prayers say they don't pressure anyone and that Christianity is the dominant religion in their towns and in the United States. However, they also assume that the public prayers will *not* be Jewish, Islamic, Hindu, Buddhist, Baha'i, or Sikh prayers and *not* contradict their Christian beliefs about the sacred and supernatural. These assumptions ignore the possibility that prayers acknowledging "Jesus as the Son of God" contradicts the beliefs of Jews, Muslims, and Hindus and that prayers to a single "Lord" or "God," contradicts the beliefs of atheists, agnostics, and polytheists (those who believe in multiple gods).

When judges rule on these cases they usually consider what would occur in U.S. towns if public prayers at public school sports events represented beliefs that contradicted Christian beliefs. For example, would Christians object if public prayers praised Allah or the Goddess? Would there be religious conflict in public schools if Muslim students said their daily prayers over the public address system in conjunction with a basketball game, if teams were asked to pray to Allah or the Prophet Muhammad, or if all football games were rescheduled to accommodate Muslim customs during their three- to four-week observance of Ramadan in October? These are important questions because 4 billion people in the world do not hold Christian beliefs and nearly 1 in 4 Americans have beliefs that are not Christian.

In light of these issues, many judges have maintained the ban on public prayer at sport events sponsored by state organizations, such as public schools. The U.S. Supreme Court made the latest decision in July 2000. Therefore, *officially sanctioned public prayers* at sport events sponsored by public schools are illegal. *What do you think?*

They see obedience from players as necessary for team success, and religious beliefs can promote obedience and convert it into a divine mandate.

To Assert Autonomy in the Face of Power   This is a new reason that some athletes use religion. After interviewing NFL players about religion, journalist Andrew Corsello (1999) noted that "it should come as no surprise that the assertion of individuality through religious testimony in the NFL comes at a time when the game has never been more corporatized, more dehumanized" (p. 439). Corsello's point is that religion enables a player to establish an identity outside of the rigid, hierarchical structure of organized sports and therefore resist the power of coaches and team owners who control their lives. Corsello thinks that this is especially important for black athletes, who may have more reason to seek a way to assert their individuality and identity and feel personally empowered in the face of the white-dominated governance structures in sports, especially in college and professional football in the United States. This possibility has never been studied, but it is worth investigating.

To Achieve Personal and Competitive Success   People often debate whether it is appropriate to pray for victories or other forms of athletic success. Some people feel that using prayer in this way trivializes religion and turns it into just another training technique, such as weightlifting or the use of muscle-building substances. However, Howard Griffith, a former NFL running back, says, "It's not that we're trivializing anything. The question was posed to [the Christians on our team], 'Does He control wins and losses?' Yes, He does. . . . It is not anti-Christian to pray for wins" (in Nack, 1998, p. 47). Another player explains that he prays for victories "so I have even a bigger platform to use for [God]" (in Nack, 1998, p. 48).

Some athletes have believed that their God or gods actually intervene in the events that occur during sport contests. Isaac Bruce, a wide receiver in the NFL, said that prayers "work" for him: "Like when we played Minnesota last year. I had

a pretty good first half, but God really manifested in the third quarter—I had eighty-nine yards!" (in Corsello, 1999, p. 435). Other religious athletes dismiss this notion, saying that they pray to "play a good game and be able to walk off the field after the game. And that prayer also extends to your competitor—you want him to walk off the field, too" (in Cotton, 2004).

THE CHALLENGES OF COMBINING SPORTS AND RELIGIOUS BELIEFS

Organized competitive sports and religion are cultural practices with different histories, traditions, and goals. Each has been socially constructed in different ways, around different issues, and through different types of relationships. This means that combining religious beliefs with sport participation may require adjustments—either in a person's religious beliefs *or* in the way a person plays sports. Although a growing number of athletes around the world combine Islamic beliefs with their sport lives, this section focuses specifically on the challenges faced by Christian athletes.

Challenges for Christian Athletes

Physical educator Shirl Hoffman (1992a, 1992d, 1999) has made the case that there are built-in conflicts between some Christian religious beliefs and participation in elite power and performance sports. Christianity, he explains, is based on an ethic that emphasizes the importance of means over ends, process over product, quality over quantity, and caring for others over caring for self. Today's sports, however, especially those based on a power and performance model, emphasize an ethic focused on winning, final scores, season records, personal performance statistics, and self-display.

Do these differences present a challenge to Christian athletes? If so, how do they deal with it? For example, do Christian athletes wonder if their actions in highly competitive power and performance sports are proper spiritual offerings and acts of worship? Does a Christian boxer have any doubts about using performance in the ring as a spiritual offering, even though the goal is to punch another human being into senseless submission, possibly killing him in the process? (See figure 15.3.) Do Christian football players see any problems associated with using intimidation and "taking out" opponents with potentially injurious hits and then saying that such behaviors are "acts of worship"? Can athletes turn these actions into Christian acts simply by saying they are motivated by Christian love? Does this help heal the concussions and broken bones of those injured by "loving hits"?

What about Christian pitchers who throw high and inside as part of their pitching strategy? Does a strategy that deliberately risks hitting a batter's head with a ball thrown at 90 miles per hour qualify as an act of worship? Is it part of

"I just want to thank my Lord and Savior, who made this all possible."
....

FIGURE 15.3 This statement has become a standard part of postgame interviews with some athletes from victorious teams. This boxer assumes that violently attacking another human being in the ring is an acceptable way to express his Christian beliefs. How is this different from a prostitute in a legal brothel in Nevada thanking her Lord after a night of work?

God's plan for Christian base runners to slide into second base with spikes aimed at the opposing infielders in attempts to break up double plays? Do Christian athletes ask such questions, and if so, how do they answer them?

Research suggests that Christian athletes combine their religious beliefs with sport participation in many ways. A study by Betty Kelley and her colleagues (1990) found that, at small liberal arts colleges, Christian varsity athletes who valued religion as a tool for achieving secular goals tended to emphasize the importance of winning in sports. Those who valued religion for its own sake were more likely to emphasize personal goals and the enjoyment of competition. Overall, the Christian athletes asked no critical questions about the "fit" between their religious beliefs and their actions in sports. However, these were athletes in small colleges where a power and performance orientation was not heavily emphasized.

A study by Robert Dunn and Christopher Stevenson (1998) at the University of New Brunswick in Canada reported that the members of a local church-sponsored hockey league were successful in their attempt to play hockey in a way that reflected Christian values. Fair play was a stated goal in the league. Prohibited were body contact, fights, swearing on the ice, and drinking beer in the locker rooms. There was a public prayer before each game, and official league standings were not kept although scores were kept in the games. Interviews with twenty players indicated that the league generally was a success. Most players conformed to the spirit of the rules although some had difficulty applying Christian principles in all game situations, especially when they were emotionally caught up in the action. A few others seemed to be only nominally committed Christians, and they were more interested in being "good hockey players" than "Christian hockey players." The authors concluded that, *in a recreational league*, it is possible to have a reasonably good fit between Christian values and sport participation.

Chris Stevenson's (1991a, 1991b, 1997) research on elite athletes associated with Athletes in Action (AIA) indicated slightly different patterns. Some of the elite athletes avoided conflicts by clearly separating their religious beliefs from sport participation. They ignored the possibility that their Christian values did not fit with how they played sports. They asked no questions, and had no problems playing sports as everyone else did. However, most of the elite Christian athletes in Stevenson's sample were troubled by conflicts between their religious beliefs and what they did as athletes. They usually dealt with this situation through one or both of the following strategies: (1) They defined their sport participation, regardless of what they did on the field, as a means of giving glory to God, and/or (2) they defined sport, as it was organized and played, as a platform for spreading the Gospel. In other words, the athletes accepted that it was their Christian duty to perfect their skills and that their skills increased the effectiveness of their evangelizing. Without changing how they played, they redefined their actions as athletes to fit their beliefs about what a Christian is supposed to do. A few athletes were uncomfortable with this approach and eliminated conflict by dropping out of elite sports to do other things more consistent with their beliefs.

Stevenson's research focused on young men in the AIA, but there have been no studies of Christian athletes who are not members of such organizations. Anecdotal data in magazines and newspapers suggest that elite athletes who identify themselves as Christians do not play sports differently than others. Some even make the point that their religious beliefs make them more intense, if not more aggressive, on the playing field. For example, Mike Barrows, an NFL linebacker and a devout Christian, was fond of saying that his violent hits on the field were attempts to "knock the sin out of somebody," but he also said that he was "not trying to hurt anyone" (Saunders, 2001). Baseball pitcher Paul Byrd, a Christian who has a reputation for hitting players with a pitch and then telling them he is sorry, explains that because God didn't give him a stronger arm, he must throw inside pitches to keep batters off guard.

However, the batters who he has injured may wonder about God's approval of this strategy.

Other statements from Christian athletes and stories about their lives (as described in Christian publications) suggest that some of them combine their religious beliefs and sport participation by becoming especially dedicated to the ascetic aspects of sport. **Asceticism** *emphasizes discipline, self-denial, and avoiding bodily pleasures.* Focusing on the ascetic dimension of sport helps them give moral meaning to their actions as athletes. For Christian athletes who view sports in this way, "Jesus the teacher" becomes "Christ the competitor," and, "if Jesus were alive today, he would play sports like everyone else, only better." For example, the Competitor's Creed of the FCA highlights the importance of asceticism in these words:

> My sweat is an offering to my Master. My soreness is a sacrifice to my Savior. I give my all—all of the time. I do not give up. I do not give in. I do not give out. I am the Lord's warrior—a competitor by conviction and a disciple of determination. (www.fca.org/TEAMFCA/CompetitorsCreed.lsp)

Research and anecdotal information suggests that many Christian athletes do not see any conflict between their religious beliefs and what they do as athletes. However, there are some who doubt the suitability of their sport participation as an act of worshipping God. These athletes do one of three things to reduce their doubts:

1. They focus on the ascetic aspects of sports and see themselves as a "servant" enduring pain.
2. They play sports as usual, strive to be the best that they can be for God's sake, use sport as a platform for evangelizing, and/or focus on good works off the field.
3. They give priority to their religious beliefs, drop out of power and performance sports, and seek other sports and activities that fit with their beliefs.

A model that identifies the origin of doubts experienced by athletes and the strategies used to reduce doubts is depicted in figure 15.4.

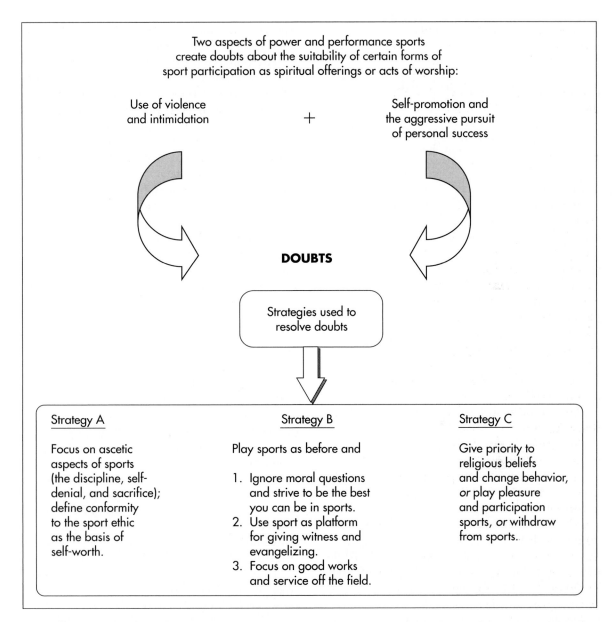

FIGURE 15.4 Christian religious beliefs and power and performance sports: a proposed model of conflict, doubt, and resolution.

Challenges for Christian Sport Organizations

Do Christian organizations for athletes focus on issues and problems in sports and develop strategies for reform? The record of these organizations clearly shows that they give primary emphasis to building faith one person at a time, not changing sports. Consequently, they have not identified problems, promoted changes in how sports are played, or sought to reform the meaning, purpose, and organization of sports.

This is surprising to people who think that religious beliefs should be connected with action and community involvement. For example, physical educator and evangelical Christian Shirl Hoffman says,

> The extent to which people are willing to overlook the moral crisis in sports to have a vehicle of mass evangelism is astounding. As soon as you apply the tenets of the [Christian] message to the medium [of sports, you would expect these organizations] to become staunch critics of sport. (in Blum, 1996, p. A36)

However, this has not happened. The policy position of nearly all Christian sport organizations is that sports will be reformed only when everyone in sports accepts Christ into their lives. Therefore, the racism, sexism, deviance, substance use, violence, recruiting violations, exploitation, greed, and other problems that exist in certain sports are ignored in favor of using those sports as platforms for evangelizing.

When journalist Frank Deford did a feature story on sports and Christianity in a 1976 issue of *Sports Illustrated*, he observed,

> No one in the movement—much less in any organization—speaks out against dirty play, no one attacks the evils of recruiting, racism or any of the many other well-known excesses and abuses. Sport owns Sunday now, and religion is content to lease a few minutes before the big games. (p. 100)

Although some Christian organizations have condemned drug use and commercial values in sports (Ladd and Mathisen, 1999), Deford's comments still describe, three decades later, the policy orientation of most Christian organizations with sport ministries. In recent years, a few representatives of these organizations have given lip service to reform from their pulpit but have taken no explicit action to change sports.

This orientation is troubling among people interested in more progressive goals, regardless of their religious beliefs. For example, there are people in Christian organizations who have recognized the need for changes in sports and who wish that the organizations would support and promote reforms in sports. However, they have had little influence on policies and programs in these organizations.

Others accuse Christian sport organizations of being hypocritical when they ignore ethical and social problems. This accusation often is grounded in a response to organizational philosophies and policies that are based on the "primacy of faith." This means that faith is given priority over action and that salvation is linked with accepting Christ into one's life rather than simply performing "good works" intended to transform social worlds and promote social justice. The critics claim that faith should be combined with good works and that good works should be done as ends in themselves rather than as means for recruiting souls. Evangelical organizations, however, rarely accept such an approach. For them, faith is primary and good works are the means for spreading the faith by which people are saved, regardless of their status in the material world.

Does this approach have an impact on issues related to sports for people with disabilities, and how is religion related to our ideas about disabilities and people who have disabilities? This question is examined in the Breaking Barriers box, page 559.

Adapting Religious Beliefs to Fit Sports

History shows that both religion and sports undergo changes as people's values and interests

Belief Barriers
I Was "One of God's Favorites"

Many people use religious beliefs as they give meaning to their bodies and embodied experiences, including experiences of disability. For instance, as a child, Margaret Orlinski contracted a virus that partially paralyzed her legs. She could walk, but everyone saw that it was a struggle. Margaret's family lived in a Catholic neighborhood and attended weekly mass at the local parish church. Margaret explains that everyone she knew used Catholic beliefs to explain her paralysis. She remembers in this way:

> I was called a saint. "God loves her so much to have given her this cross to bear." I heard that so many times. I felt an enormous amount of pressure to be perfect because I was "one of God's favorites." (in Phillips, 1988, p. 206)

This approach to disability is based on Paul's letter to the Hebrews (12:6–10) in which he explains that hardship is a gift from God and provides a unique opportunity to submit to his will and share in his holiness.

Do religious beliefs influence cultural definitions of disability? Do those definitions influence opportunities and interests to play sports? Existing research doesn't answer these questions, but sacred writings serve as a starting point for thinking critically about possible answers.

Other than the Bible, most sacred texts make only passing references to disabilities, if they mention them at all (see the Koran, 24.61 and 48.17). But the Bible speaks occasionally about disability. For instance, the Lord in the Old Testament told Moses to tell Aaron that people with disabilities were unworthy of bringing gifts to his altar. The words in Leviticus are clear:

> No man who . . . is blind or lame, disfigured or deformed . . . with a crippled foot or hand, or who is a hunchback or a dwarf . . . is to come near to present the food offerings to the LORD . . . or approach the altar, and so desecrate my sanctuary. (Leviticus 21:16–23)

In the New Testament, Jesus treated disabilities as defects to be healed, and he taught that people should care for and give charity to people with disabilities (for example, see Matthew 11:4–6; 15:29–31; 21:12–14).

Through history, religious organizations have been primary providers of care and services to people with disabilities. They have not given priority to providing opportunities to be active and play sports, but sacred texts in nearly all religions identify a norm for people to follow as they consider sports and people with disabilities. The words of Confucius, written around 500 B.C., highlight this norm:

> Tsze-kung asked . . . "Is there one word which may serve as a rule of practice for all of one's life?" The Master said, "Is not RECIPROCITY such a word? What you do not want done to yourself, do not do unto others." (The Confucian Analects, chapter 15)

Although research on religious beliefs about the body is scarce, sociologists have done many studies of the "norm of reciprocity" in human interaction. Whether we connect this norm with religious beliefs and humanistic approaches to social life, it can be used as a guide for thinking about sports and people with disabilities: If able-bodied people don't wish to be denied opportunities to play sports, they should not deny people with disabilities similar opportunities to play sports. However, as Margaret Orlinski would remind us: Don't provide them in ways that lead people with disabilities to feel that their moral worth depends on being perfect.

change and as power is gained or lost by various groups in communities and societies. However, when Christian religious beliefs are combined with the most visible forms of competitive sports in society, sports change little, if at all. Instead, it appears that religious beliefs and rituals are called into the service of sports or modified to fit the ways that sports are defined, organized, and played.

When religious beliefs are combined with power and performance sports, some people construct religious images and beliefs to fit their ideas about sports. This image of a muscular Christ on a T-shirt, found in a Christian gift shop, clearly shows how some athletes conceptualize their religion. Research clearly shows that images of deities in a culture or group tend to reflect idealized concepts of dominant values. Among Christians who value muscles, their image of Christ often is a muscular one.
(*Source:* Jay Coakley)

Robert Higgs makes this point in his book *God in the Stadium: Sports and Religion in America* (1995). He explains that the combination of sports and Christian beliefs has led religion to become "muscularized" so that it emphasizes a gospel of discipline, duty, and self-righteousness rather than a gospel of stewardship, social responsibility, and humility. Muscularized religion gives priority to the image of the knight with a sword over the image of the shepherd with a staff (Higgs, 1995). This approach, emphasizing a Christian's role as "the Lord's warrior," fits nicely with the power and performance sports that are popular today.

Similarly, Higgs points out that Christian religious beliefs have been used more often to transform winning, obedience to coaches, and commitment to improving sport skills into moral virtues than to identify problems in the social worlds created in connection with sports. Therefore, Christian beliefs have been used in ways that reproduce sports as they currently exist. The only exception to this appears to be in sports played in recreational settings where all the participants have the same religious beliefs.

IS IT A PROMISING COMBINATION?

Religion is focused on a connection with the sacred and supernatural. This makes the beliefs and meanings associated with religion a unique part of cultural life. Because religion influences how believers think about the world, themselves, and their connections with others, it has sociological significance.

Discussions about sports and religions often focus on how these two spheres of cultural life are similar or different. Certainly, they are socially similar because both create strong collective emotions and celebrate certain group values through rituals and public events. Furthermore, both have heroes, legends, special buildings for communal gatherings, and institutionalized organizational structures.

On the other hand, those who assume that sport and religion each have unique fundamental essences fixed in nature argue that the inherent differences between these spheres of life are more important than any similarities. Some have even argued that sports corrupt religious beliefs.

Most of those who study sports in society, however, recognize that sports and religions are socially constructed sets of cultural practices and meanings that may overlap or differ, depending on the social circumstances. This *constructionist approach* leads sociologists to see the beliefs and rituals of sports and religions as subject to change as people struggle over what is important in their lives and how to live together.

Little is known about the relationships between sports and major world religions other than particular forms of Christianity. It seems that certain dimensions of Christian beliefs and meanings can be constructed in ways that fit well with the beliefs and meanings underlying participation and success in organized competitive sports. Organized competitive sports seem to offer a combination of experiences and meanings that are uniquely compatible with the major characteristics of the Protestant ethic.

Sports and certain expressions of Christianity have been combined for a number of reasons. Some Christians promote sports because they believe that sport participation fosters spiritual growth and the development of strong character. Christian groups and organizations have used sports to promote their belief systems and attract new members, especially young males who wish to see themselves as having "manly virtues." They also have used visible athletes as spokespersons for their messages about fundamentalist beliefs.

Athletes and coaches have used religious beliefs and rituals for many reasons: to cope with the uncertainty of competition; to stay out of trouble; to give meaning to sport participation; to put sport participation into a balanced perspective; to establish team solidarity and unity; to reaffirm expectations, rules, and social control on teams; to assert autonomy in the face of power; and to achieve personal and competitive success.

Although the differences between the dominant ethos of Christianity and the dominant ethos of competitive sports would seem to create problems for Christian athletes and sport organizations, this has not occurred to a significant degree. With the exception of sports played at the recreational level and sponsored by Christian organizations, data suggest that many athletes define their religious beliefs in ways that generally reaffirm and intensify the orientations that lead to success in competitive sports.

Neither Christian athletes nor Christian organizations have paid much attention to what might be identified as moral and ethical problems in sports. Instead, they have focused their resources on spreading religious beliefs in connection with sport events and sport involvement. Their emphasis has been on playing as hard and as well as possible for the glory of God, using athletic performances as a platform for giving Christian witness, and working in worthwhile off-the-field church and community programs.

In conclusion, the combination of sports and religious beliefs offers little promise for changing dominant forms of sport, especially in the United States. Of course, individual athletes may alter their sport-related behaviors when they combine sports and religion in their own lives, but at this time such changes have had no observable effect on what occurs in elite, competitive sports.

OLC See the OLC, www.mhhe.com/coakley9e, for an annotated list of readings related to this chapter. The OLC also contains a key concept list, a review test, and other helpful features.

WEBSITE RESOURCES

Note: Websites often change. The following URLs were current when this book was printed. Please check our website (www.mhhe.com/coakley9e) for updates and additions.

www.mhhe.com/coakley9e   Click on chapter 15 for a list of Christian sport organizations; discussion of "Total Release Performance," a concept developed by a Christian sport

organization; discussion of the uses of rituals and magic in sports.

www.crosssearch.com/Recreation/Sports   This site has forty links to Christian sport groups and organizations, such as Anglers for Christ, Christian Surfers, Christian Skateboards and Skate Gear, Christian Deer Hunters, and Rodeoministries.

www.infinitysports.com   This is the site of an organization that mobilizes churches, sports ministries, campus ministries, and other Christian groups to use sports to evangelize around the world; the organization is committed to Christianizing every person in the world.

www.mauiinc.org   This is the site of an organization formed to inspire and support Muslims on all levels of sports from youth sports to professional sports around the world. The goal is to bring Muslim athletes together to promote Islam while following the rules and regulations of particular sports.

www.zawaj.com/articles/women_sports.html   This site has an article written in 1997 and published in *Nida'ul Islam* magazine; author Hikmat Beiruty outlines fundamentalist Islamic moral guidelines for girls and women in sports; this article is reprinted on dozens of sites, including http://womensissues.about.com/od/womensports/#more.

www.icwsf.org/English/INDEX.HTM   This is the site of Islamic Countries Women Sports Federation (ICWSF), an all-women's organization that promotes and organizes physical education and sports for girls and women so that they are consistent with Islamic values and norms.

www.traditioninaction.org/Cultural/B003cpWomenSports.htm   Author Marian T. Horvat, Ph.D., outlines fundamentalist Catholic moral guidelines for girls and women in sports; although ignored by nearly all Catholics today, these guidelines are based on statements from popes prior to the 1960s, and they influenced the sport participation of millions of girls and women worldwide through the first half of twentieth century.

www.christiancoaching.com   This is the site of Christian Coaching Network, an organization dedicated to training and supporting Christian coaches as they build their lives around the "foundational truths of the Bible."

www.thenccaa.org   This is the site of the 107-member National Christian College Athletic Association; provides general information and news.

www.fca.org   This is the site of the Fellowship of Christian Athletes; provides information about its mission, organization, and programs.

www.athletesinaction.org   This is the site of Athletes in Action; provides information about its mission, organization, and programs.

SPORTS IN THE FUTURE

What Can We Create?

THE PRIMARY GOAL of futurists is not to predict the future but to uncover images of possible, probable, and preferable futures that enable people to make informed decisions about their lives.

—Wendell Bell, futurist (1997)

 Online Learning Center Resources

Visit *Sports in Society*'s Online Learning Center (OLC) at **www.mhhe.com/coakley9e** for additional information and study material for this chapter, including

- Self-grading quizzes
- Learning objectives
- Related websites
- Additional readings

SPORT IS THE MOST DYNAMIC ACTIVITY in the world today, with the potential to contribute powerfully to a better world. . . . The power and influence of sport is only just being understood.

—Robert Davies, chief executive, International Business Leader Forum (2002a)

SPORT IS NOT SO MUCH a power on its own, more a movement, which has a pivotal role to play in improving the values of the society we live in.

—Jacques Rogge, IOC president, 2003

Discussions of the future often involve exaggerations. Predicting dramatic changes always is more exciting than declaring that tomorrow will look much like today. Therefore, people often describe the future in science-fiction terms revolving around extreme hopes or fears. This sparks our interest and sometimes leaves us temporarily awestruck, but such images of the future are rarely helpful.

For better or worse, the future seldom unfolds as rapidly or dramatically as some forecasters would have us believe. Instead, changes occur in combination with emerging social conditions and the efforts of people to create a future that fits their visions of what life should be like. Of course, some people have more power and resources to create the future than others. And they seldom want revolutionary changes because their privileged positions depend on stability and controlled change. This often slows the rate of progressive cultural and structural transformations and focuses attention on growth in the production and distribution of consumer goods.

As you read this chapter, it is important to remember two things:

1. Sports are social constructions, and many aspects of sports are contested as people integrate them into their lives.
2. People will create the future of sport; fate, computer forecasts, supernatural forces, or the predictions of sociologists will not determine the future.

The future of sports cannot be separated from general social and cultural factors, but neither can it be separated from the visions that we have for sport. It is those visions that influence the choices that we make about the kinds of physical games that we include in our lives and the conditions under which we play and/or watch them. Sports will take many forms in the future, and each will be produced through the collective actions of human beings. Therefore, the goal of this chapter is to describe and evaluate the various models of sports that we might use to

envision possibilities for the future and make informed choices as we participate in social worlds.

MAJOR SPORT FORMS IN THE FUTURE

Sports are social constructions. This means that dominant sports at any particular place and time are consistent with the values, ideas, interests, and experiences of those who have power in a group or society. However, dominant sports are not universally accepted in many social worlds. History shows that people often modify them or develop alternative sports that challenge current power relations and promote ideas that resist or oppose people with power.

Through much of history, dominant sports in societies have been grounded in the values and experiences of men concerned with military conquest, political control, and economic expansion. As noted in previous chapters and explained in chapter 4, these sports are based on a **power and performance model.**

Although many people use the power and performance model as the standard for determining the meaning, purpose, and organization of sports, not everyone accepts it. Some people have developed and maintained alternative sport forms grounded more directly in their unique values and experiences. As noted in chapter 4, many of these sports are based on a **pleasure and participation model.**

These two models do *not* encompass all the possibilities for defining and playing sports. But they represent two popular conceptions of sports in contemporary societies, so they are practical starting points for envisioning and thinking about what we'd like sports to be in the future.

Power and Performance Sports

Power and performance sports will continue to be highly visible and publicized sport forms in the near future. They are based on key aspects of dominant ideologies in many postindustrial

Club sports and intramurals may include elements from both power and performance sports and pleasure and participation sports. Ultimate Frisbee is a good example of this. (*Source:* Bob Byrne, Ultimate Players Association)

societies as demonstrated by their emphasis on strength, power, speed, and a competitive quest for victories and championships.

Although power and performance sports take many forms, they are based on the idea that excellence is proved through competitive success and achieved through dedication, hard work, and a willingness to take risks. They stress setting records, pushing human limits, using the body as a machine, and defining technology as a performance aid. According to many athletes in power and performance sports, the body is to be disciplined and monitored, preparing it to meet the demands of sports. Sports are defined as battles in which the goal is defeat opponents. Power and performance sports are exclusive in that participants are selected for their physical skills and abilities to achieve competitive success. Those

who lack these "qualities" are cut or relegated to "developmental" programs. Organizations and teams have hierarchical authority structures in which athletes are subordinate to coaches and coaches are subordinate to owners and administrators. It is widely accepted that coaches can humiliate, shame, and derogate athletes when motivating them to excel. Athletes are expected to endure these motivational tactics and show that they are willing to give all of themselves in the quest for excellence.

The sponsors of power and performance sports want to be associated with people and activities that stress competition, hard work, and the endurance of pain for the sake of productivity and progress (Hoberman, 1994). Being endorsed by winning athletes and teams is important when promoting and selling products. Sponsors assume that being connected with winning athletes and teams makes them special in the eyes of people in a society or even around the world. As long as sponsors reward those who excel in power and performance sports, the future of those sports are secure, and the athletes who play them will be cultural celebrities paid to endorse the values of sponsors. Power and performance sports will remain dominant for the foreseeable future in most societies, mostly because people who possess power and influence will use their resources to make it so.

Pleasure and Participation Sports

Although power and performance sports are highly visible, many people realize that there are other ways to organize and do sports that more closely match their values and experiences. Over the last century, this realization has led to the creation of sport forms that differ from the highly publicized, dominant sports covered in the media. This occurs today and will continue to occur in the future.

A sport form that often coexists with power and performance sports is organized around a combination of *pleasure and participation*. It involves physical activities in which participants value freedom, authenticity, challenges, and connections between each other, mind and body, and physical activity and the environment.

Although pleasure and participation sports take many forms, they generally emphasize an ethic of personal expression, enjoyment, growth, good health, support for others, including opponents, and respect for the environment. They focus on personal empowerment and the notion that the body is to be experienced and enjoyed rather than trained and used as a machine to dominate others. People who play pleasure and participation sports tend to see their bodies as inseparable from their experiences rather than tools or weapons to be used to achieve rewards and then repaired when they break down.

Pleasure and participation sports are inclusive. The process of involvement is valued over competitive success. Skill differences among participants often are accommodated by using handicaps so that players can enjoy together the challenges associated with an activity. Sport organizations and teams based on this model have democratic decision-making structures characterized by cooperation, power sharing, and give-and-take relationships between coaches and athletes. Humiliation, shame, and derogation are inconsistent with the spirit underlying these sports.

The sponsorship of pleasure and participation sports is based on the beliefs that it is socially useful to promote widespread participation in a wide range of sports and that it is important to emphasize health and enjoyment in sports. This is why public and nonprofit organizations rather than corporations sponsor many pleasure and participation sports. Corporations seek exposure to mass audiences that are inclined to consume their products when they identify with elite athletes or teams. However, some corporations sponsor pleasure and participation sports as part of an overall emphasis on

> In 1899, no one could foresee sports becoming such a national obsession.
> —Tom Weir, *USA Today* (1999)

social responsibility or because it will help them boost sales with a clearly identified collection of consumers.

TRENDS IN SPORTS

It's likely that power and performance sports will grow faster than pleasure and participation sports although social, economic, and demographic factors support growth in both sport forms. An emphasis on power and performance will pervade most sport spheres, but future developments in all sports will be influenced by technology, the media, a cultural emphasis on rationalization and consumerism, a continuing commitment to gender equity, and growing racial and ethnic diversity in most societies worldwide.

The following discussion of trends and the factors that will influence them is meant to be a guide for making informed choices about sports and what we want them to be over the next generation. As many futurists explain, "there are no future facts" and "the best way to predict the future is to create it" (in Bell and Mau, 1971).

The Growth of Power and Performance Sports

Power and performance sports will be the most visible and publicized sport forms in the foreseeable future. Vested interests in these sports are very strong, and those who benefit from them have considerable power and influence. For example, the popularity of these sports is tied to dominant forms of gender relations. When the goal is to push physical limits, men are the center of attention, especially when limits are tied to strength, power, and speed. This means that many sports reaffirm sex differences and the superiority of men over women. When cultures highlight sex in terms of *difference*, dominant sports are usually based on a power and performance model.

A continued emphasis on power and performance sports also rests on maintaining corporate sponsorships. American football, the classic embodiment of these sports, has become the most popular spectator sport in the United States because it attracts billions of dollars in television rights fees and other revenues. Athletes in the NFL and other power and performance sports are portrayed in the media as heroic figures and exemplars of corporate images emphasizing productivity, efficiency, and dedication to performance despite pain and injury. Spectators are encouraged to identify with these athletes and express their identification through the consumption of licensed merchandise and other products. As long as this dynamic persists, these sports will remain dominant in the future.

Because power and performance sports often involve pushing human and normative limits, they are exciting and seductive. This makes them relatively easy to market and sell if they are combined with storylines that resonate with the experience of consumers. This is why the media now emphasize the personal lives of athletes and their families. Dedicated, life-long fans may be satisfied with coverage focused on games, scores, and statistics, but attracting the attention of new and less knowledgeable fans depends on presenting tabloid-style information about players' lives. For instance, in 2005 the Tour de France set a new precedent by allowing Lance Armstrong to bring his three children to the victory podium after winning his seventh consecutive Tour. The television cameras focused on his six-year-old son and three-year-old twin daughters and then turned to Armstrong's girlfriend, rock star Sheryl Crow who traveled with him, the children, and their nanny for the duration of the three-week, 2250-mile race. Viewers asked, where was his ex-wife, the mother of his children? Does she get along with Sheryl Crow? Do Armstrong and Crow want children of their own? If so, did Armstrong freeze enough sperm cells before the testicular cancer treatment made him sterile? And what would happen to Crow's career if she had a child with Armstrong? Such are the questions of viewers who don't know much about cycling but are attracted to Armstrong because he is one of the most widely recognized athletes in the world, a cancer survivor, and living with a rock star (in 2005). Such coverage has become typical in nearly all other power and performances sports, and it serves to keep them popular.

The Growth of Pleasure and Participation Sports

Through history, many physical activities and sports have embodied characteristics of the pleasure and participation model. The primary reason for this is that sports have always been social occasions in people's lives, and people incorporate into them the things that give them pleasure or reaffirm their values. Pleasure and participation sports continue to be popular to the extent that people define them as attractive alternatives to the more culturally dominant power and performance sports. Factors that fuel this search for alternatives today are concerns about health and fitness, participation preferences among older people, values and experiences brought to sports by women, and groups seeking alternatives to highly structured, competitive sports that constrain the range of their experiences.

Concerns About Health and Fitness   As health-care policies and programs around the world emphasize prevention rather than expensive cures, people become more sensitive to health and fitness issues. In North America, for example, health-care and insurance companies now encourage strategies for staying well as they seek to cut costs and maximize profits. This encourages people to more actively seek alternatives to power and performance sports and increase

Young people seeking alternatives to organized competitive sports will increase the diversity of pleasure and participation sports in the future. Mountain boarding is a good example. (*Source:* Jason Lee, Mountain Board Sports)

participation in pleasure and participation sports for which health benefits are much higher (Waddington, 2000b, 2007).

In the United States where physical education classes have been eliminated in many schools, new concerns about health, fitness, and obesity are reviving interests in forms of physical education that focus on lifetime activities, noncompetitive challenges, inclusive participation philosophies, respect and support for other participants, and responsible attitudes toward the environment— all of which are characteristics of pleasure and participation sports. If these concerns continue

to grow, they will influence the sport preferences of people through the life course. If this happens, they will demand reasonable memberships to publicly funded local recreation complexes rather than season tickets to NFL games or expensive cable packages allowing them to sit on a couch and watch hundreds of hours of sports each year.

If people realize that healthy exercise can be organized to create family fun and a sense of community, there will be powerful incentives for them to give priority to a wide array of pleasure and participation sports in their lives. But this depends on how people choose to create the future.

Participation Preferences Among Older People

As the median age of the population in many societies increases, as people live longer, and as older people represent an increasingly larger proportion of the world's population, there will be more interest in sports that do not involve intimidation, the use of physical force, the domination of opponents, and the risk of serious injuries.

As people age, they're less likely to risk physical well-being to establish a reputation in sports. Older people are more likely to see sports as social activities and make them inclusive rather than exclusive. Older people also realize that they have but one body, and it can be enjoyed only if it they cultivate it as though it were a garden rather than driving it as though it were a racing machine or a bulldozer.

People such as baby boomers in the United States, who grew up playing competitive sports, are not likely to completely abandon their interest in those sports as they age, but they will avoid participation in power and performance sports that have high injury rates. Most will play modified versions of competitive activities in which rules emphasize the pleasure of movement, connections between people, and controlled challenges. Many older people also will engage in walking, hiking, strength training, yoga, tai chi, and similar activities, which will be taken seriously but done in settings where the focus is on health, fitness, and social connections rather than setting records, using the body to dominate opponents, or bragging about who sweats the most during their Bikran yoga sessions.

Pleasure and participation sports will be sites where older people will challenge dominant ideas about aging. Aging has often been seen as a process that involves increasing dependency and incapacity, but the sport participation of older people supports the idea that aging doesn't automatically mean becoming weak and incapacitated. "Seniors" and "masters" sport programs will increase as people demand them. As a result, images of older people who are fit, healthy, and accomplished athletes will become more visible and serve as models for others.

Values and Experiences Brought to Sports by Women As women gain more power and resources in sports, many will reject the culture that often accompanies traditional power and performance sports. In the process, they will challenge the very gender ideology on which such sports are organized. A possible outcome of this will be new norms and structures that emphasize dimensions of pleasure and participation sports. For instance, when women play sports such as rugby, soccer, and hockey, there are indications that they often emphasize inclusiveness and support for teammates and opponents in explicit ways that are seldom present in men's versions of these sports. The "in-your-face" power and performance orientation exhibited by some men is replaced by an orientation that is expressive of the joy and connections resulting from participation.

Women face difficulties when recruiting sponsors for sports that differ from men's power and performance sports. Without an emphasis on physical domination, women's sports are often seen as second-rate or not "real" enough to attract the attention that sponsors seek. However, if women choose such sports in greater numbers,

sponsors may respond if they see benefits for their bottom lines. If they do, pleasure and participation sports will receive increased support.

Groups Seeking Alternative Sports People who reject power and performance sports or certain dimensions of them also will contribute to the growth of sports organized more closely around the pleasure and participation model. There is evidence of this in the unique sport subcultures that have been developed around many alternative sports. Studies of skateboarders and snowboarders show that some young people resist attempts to turn their sports into commercialized, competitive forms (Beal, 1995; Honea, 2005). Even in official, formally sponsored contests, skaters have deliberately subverted the power and performance dimensions of events. Unregistered skaters have crashed the events. Registered skaters have pinned competition numbers on their shirts so that they were upside down or difficult to read. "Competitors" have focused on expressing themselves rather than outdoing opponents, and they have deviated from the prearranged patterns for warming up and competing. In some cases, mass protests have stopped events after nonconforming athletes were disqualified for their actions. Of course, none of this appears on television broadcasts that are edited to attract young viewers (Crissey, 1999). As illustrated in figure 16.1, the athletes often feel frustrated when they are pressured by sponsors to say things that don't represent their experiences.

People sometimes resist attempts to change the pleasure and participation emphasis in their activities. They don't want competition and the domination of opponents to replace the expression and support of fellow participants. For example, when a twelve-year-old snowboarder was asked about adding his sport to the Olympics, he said, "Don't kill the ride, dude. Let us be free." Even at age twelve, he knew that the ideology of power and performance would subvert desired elements

"I love the X Games . . . because they're all about . . . freedom and individual expression."

FIGURE 16.1   Some athletes in alternative sports are uneasy about what happens when their sports become commercialized and represented in terms that fit the interests of sponsors.

of pleasure and participation in his sport. After snowboarding was added to the Olympics in 1996, Terje Haakonsen, reputedly the best boarder in the world, refused to compete in Nagano, Japan. He said, "Snowboarding is about fresh tracks and carving powder and being yourself and not being judged by others; it's not about nationalism and politics and money" (in Perman, 1998, p. 61).

Male athletes in alternative-action sports are more likely than others to resist a traditional power and performance model, even though they have a reputation for taking risks and marginalizing girls and women. They know that losing control of their sports means that an emphasis on pleasure and participation will be given low priority. This led skateboarder Tony Hawk to declare that "it's about time the riders took the competitions into their own hands—the only

ones who truly know the sport are the ones who are actively doing it and pushing the limits along the way" (in Higgins, 2005). Hawk organized his Boom Boom Huck Jam tour to preserve the spirit of skateboarding and other action sports in a format that would generate revenues and media coverage. Similarly, Terje Haakonsen and other snowboarders created "Ticket To Ride" (TTR), a series of events designed to preserve the pleasure and participation ethos of their sports. They describe TTR events in this way:

> [It's] a movement connected to the core of snowboarding's identity. . . . The sense of fun and friendship, the appreciation of nature, the travel and the unique experiences, the freedom and creativity—this is snowboarding. This is what happens every time you strap in, stand up and drop in. (www.the-arctic-challenge.com/)

People with a physical or intellectual disability have developed alternative sports and adapted

Athletes with a disability will participate in sports in greater numbers. Creatively designed equipment will permit new forms of sports involvement for both the able-bodied and the disabled, as shown in this photo of trail riders. (*Source:* Rob Schoenbaum)

dominant sports to fit their interests and needs. Although some of these sports emphasize power and performance, others emphasize pleasure and participation. Concern and support for teammates and opponents, as well as inclusiveness related to physical abilities, characterize these latter sports.

When people with a disability participate with able-bodied people in sports organized around a power and performance model, it presents an opportunity for all athletes, regardless of age or ability, to deal with the reality that human relationships always involve accommodating difference and uniqueness. Dealing with this reality involves a choice: Maintain power and performance sports as they are and marginalize those with a disability or revise them with features from the pleasure and performance model to be inclusive. It is difficult to predict how people in different situations and at different points in their lives will handle this choice, but it is certain that their decisions will create at least part of sports' future.

The Gay Games and the EuroGames provide additional examples of alternative sport forms emphasizing participation, support, inclusiveness, and the enjoyment of physical movement (Pronger, 1999). The sixth quadrennial Gay Games in Sydney, Australia, in 2002 involved more than 11,000 competitors from eighty-two nations. Although the Gay Games resemble dominant sports in some ways, they explicitly challenge the gender ideology that underlies dominant sports, and they are free of the homophobia that permeates them. But they are not free of internal politics as demonstrated in 2004 when the Federation of Gay Games (FGG) had a dispute with the organizers planning the 2006 Games in Montreal. The FGG wanted to focus almost exclusively on sport events, whereas the Montreal organizers wanted to link the Games with other events for gay men, lesbians, bisexuals, and transsexuals (GLBTs). As I write this, it appears that there will two events in 2006: The Gay Games in Chicago and the OutGames in Montreal, both of which integrate inclusion and other aspects of the pleasure and participation model into their sports. At the community level, GLBTs organize sports to provide enjoyable experiences in their social lives. A gay man explains in this way:

> The nice thing about playing gay sports is . . . to interact with gay people . . . [so you] don't have to be on guard. You can joke around, you can play. That's a good feeling. It's also the sense of community that comes from it. . . . It's not that I didn't fit in [when I played volleyball at work, but it] is probably more relaxed in gay sports. (in Pronger, 1990, p. 238)

The range of sports that incorporate elements of the pleasure and participation model will grow if more people realize that sports are social constructions that can be created to fit even temporary interests and passing situations. This was illustrated recently in Syracuse, New York, where a local adult kickball league, organized in 2004, was so overwhelmed with registrations in 2005 that they expanded to 24 adult teams. At first, people said, "You're kidding me. That's not a real sport!" But the attitude of players now is, "It's an activity off the beaten path. It's fun. It's social. And you get some exercise" (Kates, 2005). Others must agree because in 2005 there were over 17,000 registered players on more than 700 teams in eighteen states (www.world-kickball.com/). They have already created a piece of the future.

Although it often is a challenge to find corporate sponsors, forms of pleasure and participation sports usually survive because people are creative enough to find the resources to maintain them. Furthermore, corporate or media sponsors are needed only when a sport hires administrators, focuses on national and international tournaments, and requires equipment and travel expenses. When a sport is done simply for pleasure and participation, the primary resource needed is people wishing to play it. This resource has existed through human history.

Trends in Sport Spheres

Predicting the future is less important than knowing about current trends and using that knowledge to participate in creating the future. For instance, some people study trends so that they can more effectively plan strategies to create sports that are humane, accessible, inclusive, and democratically organized. Others have different goals, but in any case, our knowledge of current trends in various sport spheres is useful. If the result is *multiple futures*, that's ideal.

Professional Sports   Current trends in professional sports involve the following:

- Profit-driven national and global expansion
- Staging expensive total entertainment events
- Dependence on public funds to build facilities designed as shopping malls
- Contentious negotiations between players and leagues/owners over working conditions

Although people think they have little control over these trends, most professional sports exist in democratic societies where citizens often vote on use of public funds to build sport stadiums and arenas. They also elect political representatives who determine the legal environment in which businesses, including professional sports, operate. This means that people could organize and pressure local legislators to impose ceilings on ticket prices in facilities built with pubic money. Legislators could also mandate that a lottery be used to sell tickets to major events rather than letting corporations buy all the good seats and run up prices. If people learn to act as citizens before professional leagues and team owners convert them into consumers, they will create futures more in line with their interests and resources.

Intercollegiate Sports   Current trends in intercollegiate sports in the United States involve the following:

- Escalating expenses for big-time spectator sports
- Struggles over gender equity

AT YOUR *fingertips*   See the OLC, chapter 16 Additional Readings, for more detailed forecasts about the future of sports.

- Athletes seeking rights and representation, especially in revenue-producing sports
- Students seeking opportunities to play sports that do not generate revenues

Knowing about and understanding these trends is important. Students, administrators, and state legislators make decisions about the use of student fees and campus sport facilities. Faculty and administrators should determine how to organize intercollegiate sports so that students experience educational benefits at a reasonable cost. The possibilities for students to create futures in connection with these trends are many. Students on large campuses are like citizens in small cities who can influence the use of local resources to support their sport interests—if they are organized and insist that community decisions are made democratically. If students don't do this, it will be administrators, athletic directors, and boosters who create the future for them.

High School Sports   Current trends in high school sports involve the following:

- Increasing stakes associated with competitive success
- Parents and athletes expecting that high school sports are vehicles for obtaining athletic scholarships and admission into the colleges of their choice
- Struggles over gender equity
- Increasing elitism favoring skilled and highly specialized athletes
- Continuing focus on playoffs, championships, state titles, and national rankings
- "Outsourcing" certain sport teams to private clubs

Gender equity in intercollegiate sports will continue to be an issue. Future issues will focus more on women gaining power and changing the culture of athletic departments. Men now make nearly all the important decisions, and the culture of athletic departments reflects their values and experiences. (*Source:* NCAA Photos)

Debates about the meaning, purpose, and organization of high school sports often are contentious. However, they provide opportunities for students, parents, teachers, and local citizens to present their visions of what school sports should be in the future. Historically, people who want high school sports to be like big-time college sports have dominated these debates. But they don't represent a majority of citizens in most communities. Therefore, the futures of high school sports depend on who participates in the debates and how prepared they are to argue their cases. School sports are funded with tax money and their stated goal is education. To allow boosters who covet state titles to create the future seems undemocratic and subversive to education.

Youth Sports Current trends in organized youth sports involve the following:

- Declining public programs due to federal and state tax cuts that create local budget crises
- Increased privatization favoring people who can pay club and facility fees
- Segregation of programs by socioeconomic status, race, and ethnicity
- Decreasing opportunities for children in low-income families and communities
- More children seeking alternatives to adult-controlled organized sports

These trends mimic trends in society as a whole. As ideology emphasizes individualism and a form of "family values" that calls for every family to provide for itself, those who have resources will use them to create playgrounds in their fenced backyards and to buy access to private programs and facilities for their sports. They don't need public parks or publicly funded programs and seldom vote to support them. As a result, public services, including sports and parks, are cut back or eliminated. The future of youth sports will involve escalating social-class divisions unless people decide they want something different. Decisions

breaking BARRIERS   **Vision Barriers**
I Have to Believe

In 1997 a youth baseball coach in Conyers, Georgia, noticed that one of his five-year-old players came to every practice and game with his seven-year-old brother. The seven-year-old loved baseball, but there were no teams for a child in a wheelchair. So the coach invited him to play.

This coach's action precipitated a series of events. The following season, Dean Alford and others organized the Conyers "Miracle League" for children with disabilities. It was the first baseball league of its kind, so creative rules were made: Every player on a team would bat each inning, all base runners were safe, and every player scored a run. Able-bodied young people and volunteers served as buddies, assisting players when the need arose.

During the first year there were thirty-five players on four teams. Watching them play inspired Alford, a former Georgia state representative and president of the local Rotary Club. He saw that a conventional ball field with grass, dirt, and elevated bases created barriers for players who were blind, in wheelchairs, or using walkers and crutches. Alford worked with two Rotary Clubs to raise the money needed to design and construct a rubberized turf playing field combined with restrooms, a concession stand, and picnic area—all accessible. Three grass fields were included and designed so that they could be converted to synthetic surfaces as the Miracle League grew.

The field, 25 miles east of Atlanta, opened in 2000. It attracted national media attention and interest among families of more than 75,000 children with disabilities in the Atlanta area.* By 2005 there were 123 Miracle League organizations in the United States, each in different stages of development. Rubberized turf playing surfaces had been built in twenty-six communities. Sixty-one new fields were under construction, and twenty-four communities broke ground in 2006 for Miracle League complexes. Nationwide participation was up to 10,000 in 2005, with the goal of reaching 500 fields and 1.3 million participants looking less idealistic than originally thought.

When people hear of the Miracle League, visit websites, and watch games, their idealism often pushes them to think further outside the box of traditional parks and playing fields. For example, some communities have built a universally accessible playground adjacent to the smooth-surface baseball fields. Playground designers eliminate barriers and create an

similar to this will determine many aspects of our collective futures, not just youth sports.

Sports for People with a Disability   Current trends in sports for people with a disability involve the following:

- Increasing numbers of people disabled by war, land mines, lack of medical care, and poverty
- Increasing recognition that people with a disability want to play sports and have a right to do so
- Continuing use of sport participation as therapy
- More visible examples of sports for elite athletes with a disability

- New technologies that facilitate sport participation
- Emerging ideas, vocabularies, and orientations that support people with a disability and their participation in sports

Disability is so multifaceted that there are many needs. In postindustrial societies, this is a crucial time for envisioning possibilities and working to create desired futures. In developing nations where poverty rates frequently surpass 50 percent, possibilities are limited unless people from wealthier nations provide assistance. Believing or hoping that new technologies will eliminate disabilities is unrealistic and subverts actions that could create futures in which people recognize environment that is attractive to children with varying physical (dis)abilities. This enables families and friends to play safely as they encounter physical challenges and have fun regardless of (dis)abilities.

Idealists in other communities have envisioned and organized similar play environments and sport programs for adults with disabilities. When people see a Miracle League baseball field combined with a universally accessible playground they often think, "This makes so much sense," and then they ask, "Why doesn't my community have one of these?" This is heartening to those who know one of the nearly 6 million children in the United States who, due to (dis)abilities, cannot play in existing youth baseball leagues and other sport programs.

It is also heartening to the thousands of veterans returning from Iraq and Afghanistan with amputated limbs, sight and hearing impairments, and injuries that impair walking. Making sports accessible to them would seem to be a no-brainer, even among those who lack idealism. As veterans return to communities, universities, gyms, parks, trails, and workplaces, idealism is essential if barriers are to be broken.

Jayne Craike, who competes on the New Zealand Equestrian Federation national dressage circuit and also represents her country in the Paralympics, encourages people to be idealistic as they envision and work to create the future. She says, "*I have to believe that there is still more to come in a world that is continually changing, and that we can make a difference*" (Joukowsky and Rothstein, 2002, p. 55, emphasis added; see also, http://www.lupus.org.nz/PersonalExperiences.htm). Craike knows that sports are more than therapeutic tools for people with (dis)abilities. In cultures where sport participation is highly valued, they are normalizing activities; they enable people to establish important identities; and they are sites for meeting others and forcing everyone who watches to acknowledge that (dis)abilities are a normal part of the human condition. It may be idealistic to envision and work for universal accessibility, but who wants to settle for the alternative?

---

*See and hear some of this media coverage at www.miracleleague.com/index.htm; www.moodymiracleleague.com/Articles.htm; www.gsml.org; www.npr.org/templates/story/story.php?storyId=4527882; www.npr.org/templates/story/story.php?storyId=1132318].

• •

the abilities rather than the (dis)abilities of others. To do this, we need a vocabulary to imagine a future in which ability exists on a continuum and cannot be classified in two boxes, one able and one disabled. When people think outside these two boxes, many futures become possible. This is illustrated in the Breaking Barriers box above.

Spectators and Spectator Sports   Current trends related to spectators and spectator sports involve the following:

• Continuing commitment to watching sports as a central leisure activity
• Increasing use of the Internet and other technologies that provide spectator experiences
• Defining spectators as consumers who are receptive to advertising messages

Spectator sports are deeply embedded in many cultures. However, people can decide how much they will pay in terms of money, time, and effort to be spectators; what meanings they will give to their experiences; and how they will integrate those experiences into their lives. They also can envision futures that deviate from those envisioned by corporate sponsors and media executives. For example, if people voted to bring free or low-cost wireless (Wi-Fi) Internet access to their communities, the future would involve incredibly diverse spectator experiences. But if people allow giant cable and telecom corporations to control the conditions of broadband access, their futures as spectators will be limited and expensive. Imagine futures in which broadband access is publicly provided like other essential services, such as roads and schools, and available to people around the world. Such futures would enable people to be interactive spectators with access to sports they would otherwise not see.

Factors Influencing Trends

When creating futures it's useful to know about factors that influence current trends. This enables us to anticipate possibilities, avoid resistance, and make more informed decisions as we participate in social worlds.

Many factors influence trends in sports, but the discussion here is limited to five: technology, telecommunications and electronic media, a widespread commitment to organization and rationalization, a cultural emphasis on commercialism and consumption, and the demographic characteristics of communities and societies.

> The use of drugs, and, perhaps more startling, the engineering of genes to enhance performance, raises questions about the notion of what an athlete is. —Richard Sandomir, journalist (2002)

Technology Technology is *the application of scientific or other organized knowledge to solve problems, expand experiences, or alter the conditions of reality.* It is used to make sports safer, detect and treat injuries more effectively, assess physical limits and potential, expand the experiences available in sports, train bodies to perform more efficiently, provide athletes with more control of their bodies, increase the speeds at which bodies move and the risks involved in sports, enhance the size and strength of bodies, alter bodies to match the demands of particular sports, identify rule infractions and enforce rules more accurately, measure and compare performances with precision, and improve the durability and functionality of equipment.

The major issue related to technology is when and how to use it and regulate it. The governing bodies of sports try to regulate the technologies used by coaches, officials, trainers, and athletes, but the number of new technologies has made this difficult. Assessing technology is not easy, as explained in the discussion of performance-enhancing substances in chapter 6. Technologies are a part of sports, and we can make consistent and sensible decisions about them only when we know what we want sports to be in the future. Consider genetic-enhancement technologies. They can be used to improve human performance, heal injured bodies, and correct certain physical impairments. If we want to create a future in which sports are organized around the power and performance model, the framework and criteria for assessing genetic enhancement would be different than if we want sports organized around a pleasure and participation model. This is why it is important to have a clear sense of the place of sports in society and the purpose we want sports to serve in our lives and the world as a whole.

Telecommunications and Electronic Media Television, computers, the Internet, wireless phones, and other devices are technologies, but they have special implications for sports. Television and the Internet, for instance, provide visual images and narratives that many people use to imagine future possibilities for sports. Some people even use them to make choices about participation and to formulate standards for assessing their sport experiences (see figure 16.2). Therefore, those who control electronic media around the world have considerable power to create the future. Media do *not* control what people *think*, but they certainly influence what people *think about* when it comes to sports. The events, athletes, and stories re-presented in the media provide topics and issues that people *think about* and discuss in their relationships. In this way, media content influences the everyday

"Oh, Mom! Why go outside to play when I can be on my own virtual World Cup Team right here."

....

FIGURE 16.2 The future of sports is difficult to predict. Will children prefer video games and virtual sports over the dominant sport forms of today? Will there ever be a video soccer game based on women players?

discourse out of which people form their ideas about what sports could and should be in the future.

To understand this process, imagine that football was the only sport you ever saw on television. Your sense of what sports are and could be would be limited. This is what occurs in our experience as media companies select for coverage only those sports that generate profits on commercial television. As a result, those are the sports we see and talk about. For example, when the media do not cover women's sports, people are less likely to talk about them, learn about the athletes and teams, and incorporate them into the experiences they use to envision the future.

The electronic media can expose us to new worlds, but when market forces shape media content, those worlds look much the same after a while. If we realize this, we can seek images and

narratives about sports that are not re-presented exclusively through commercial media. This expands our experience and enables us to think more creatively about the present and future. The more versions of sports we see and talk about, the more we can invent and modify sports to match our interests and circumstances today and tomorrow.

Organization and Rationalization   All sports contain the element of play. But sports today focus so much on purpose, planning, and productivity that play has been pushed to the sidelines. "Fun" in organized, purpose-driven sports is associated with achieving goals rather than emotional expression and joy. Process is now secondary to product, and the journey is secondary to the destination.

People in postindustrial cultures live with the legacy of industrialization. They emphasize organization according to rational principles based, whenever possible, on systematic research. Being organized and making plans to accomplish goals is so important that spontaneity, expression, creativity, and joy—the elements of play—are given low priority or may even be considered frivolous.

When this orientation is used in sports, it allows for standardization so that scores and performance data can be objectively and rationally compared from one event and year to the next. But it limits possibilities for play. For instance, legendary snowboarder Terje Haakonsen decided against participating in the Olympics because he felt that it was a form of sport in which organization and rationalization had subverted play. His thoughts about this are summarized in his description of snowboarding:

> That was a fun time . . . I was always learning new tricks, figuring out ways to get better. When I'm having fun snowboarding, it's like meditation. I'm not thinking about anything but what I'm doing right now. No past, no future. . . . [But today, too many] people get stuck and all they do the whole year is pipe, and that's too bad for them. They do the same routine over and over, get the moves

down. It becomes like this really precise, synchronized movement, like they're little ballerinas or something. It's no longer this spontaneous sport, like when you're a kid screwing around.
(in Greenfeld, 1999)

Haakonsen knows that fun, seriousness, effort, and discipline often go together. He explains that he would be exhausted after a day of fun and effort, and when he missed a trick, he would focus, get serious, and try it again and again. But he was doing it for himself on his terms rather than for judges on terms he did not control.

When creating sports, these are important things to keep in mind because there is a tendency in postindustrial cultures to organize them so that they make sense for the purposes of rationally assessing skills and performances. Wanting to improve physical skills so that you have more opportunities to engage in different forms of play is one thing, but spending years to improve a single skill to conform to someone else's idea of

technical perfection is another. Once we "feel" this distinction in our own sport participation, we become much more creative when thinking about and creating the future, not only for ourselves but also for our children and grandchildren.

Commercialism and Consumption   We have become so deeply embedded in commercial culture than many people think of themselves as customers instead of citizens. I even hear students say that they are customers at the university. Instead of learners and citizens of a college community, they see themselves as consumers who buy courses. When this form of commercialism pervades our lives, it changes the way we think about others, our experiences, and ourselves. We measure everything in terms of material criteria such as dollars, profits and losses, and bottom lines.

When commercial ideology pervades sports, play becomes secondary to playoffs and payoffs. As discussed in chapter 11, commercialization

Trying to improve skills on your own terms is different than doing a routine over and over to meet someone else's idea of technical perfection. Once we "feel" this distinction in our own sport participation, we become much more creative as we think of how to do sports and incorporate them into our lives. (*Source:* McGraw-Hill)

influences sports in the sense that games, athletes, and even experiences become commodities—things to be bought and sold for bottom-line purposes. Sports become "sportainment" created for profit and played for external rewards. Participation revolves around the consumption of equipment, lessons, clothing, nutritional supplements, gym and club memberships, and other things. Status becomes associated with where you do sports, the equipment that you use, and the clothing that you wear.

Some people are turned off by this approach, but unless they've experienced alternatives, they may struggle to think about sports devoid of commercialism and consumption. This is why it is important to have public spaces where people can play sports that do not require fees, permits, or memberships. Creativity thrives in such spaces. But when they are not widely available, people who can afford to do so play sports in commercial spaces. In this sense, public policies at all levels of government can create or subvert possibilities for noncommercial sport futures.

Demographic Characteristics of Communities and Societies   Sports are social constructions. This means that some of the richest sport environments are those in which people have diverse cultural backgrounds and sport experiences.

Even when people play the same sport, strategies and styles often vary with their cultural backgrounds. For example, Canadians created a secular and rationalized version of lacrosse that was different from the traditional, sacred game invented and played by Native Peoples in North America (King, 2007a). People in the United States took the sport of rugby as played in England and adapted it to fit their preferences; the result was American football, a game that is relatively unique in the world (Riesman and Denny, 1951). In 2004 the New York Mets hired a Latino general manager, signed notable Latino players, and developed a style of play that was fast, aggressive, and emotional. This style is now part of a larger cultural shift in Major League

Baseball, a shift that celebrates diversity by incorporating it into everything from baseball strategy to marketing the game to Latino fans in the United States and Latin America (Mahler, 2005).

Although demographic diversity presents challenges, it also presents possibilities for creating new forms and versions of sports. As geographical mobility, labor migration, and political turmoil push and pull together people from diverse backgrounds, there will be many opportunities to borrow and blend different sports, styles of play, and game strategies. If people take advantage of those opportunities without systematically privileging games from one culture and marginalizing games from other cultures, it will be possible to envision and create sports that fit a wide range of interests and abilities.

ENVISIONING POSSIBILITIES AND CREATING FUTURES

Robert Davies, chief executive of the International Business Leaders Forum, an organization dedicated to promoting global social responsibility, tells corporate leaders worldwide that the visibility and popularity of sports at the local and global levels provides opportunities to improve health, develop communities, boost education and literacy, and empower girls and women. He says that "the power and influence of sport is only just being understood" by people concerned with social responsibility (Davies, 2002a). He also told an international assembly of journalists and media representatives that "high profile global sporting events are seen as a frontier for raising issues of injustice and social responsibility" and that the media have a responsibility to explore that frontier (Davies, 2002b).

As Davies thinks about the future from the perspective of corporate social responsibility, he sees possibilities for changing sports and using them to facilitate changes beyond playing fields and locker rooms. Other perspectives alert us to even more possibilities. To assess them and work to convert selected possibilities into realities, there is a need to understand connections between sports and the rest of the world, This is why social theories are especially useful; they provide frameworks to identify and explain those connections. This, in turn, enables people to develop focused and consistent strategies for creating the future.

Using Social Theories to Create Futures

Each of the theories discussed in chapter 2 provides a different perspective for understanding connections between sports and social worlds, identifying problems, and selecting approaches to create sports in terms of their anticipated consequences in people's lives. The following sections provide only brief summaries of how those theories may be used for these purposes.

Major professional sport teams have their own foundations and community service organizations. Players, even those with radical ideas about change, are encouraged by agents to handle their community involvement through these team-controlled programs. These programs, such as the Pacers Academy in central Indianapolis, are valuable assets in communities, but they usually take a conservative approach to change. They emphasize supporting youth sports, educational programs and scholarships, disaster relief, and health-related charities. (*Source:* Jay Coakley)

Functionalist Theory   Functionalist theory continues to be used to envision sports in the future. For example, when Robert Davies talks to corporate leaders, he bases many of his ideas on a functionalist approach. This appeals to those leaders and to others with power and influence because such an approach takes the existing social system for granted and explains how sports help to preserve and improve that system. A functionalist approach to the future emphasizes that existing sport forms should be supported and maintained through the use of *conservative* and *reformist* strategies.

A **conservative strategy** is *based on the belief that sports reaffirm traditional values and established forms of social organization and therefore should be strengthened and expanded rather than transformed.* The focus is on management issues designed to make sports and sport organizations more efficient while maintaining the culture and structure of sports as they are. Conservative strategies are very common in sports because few people view sports in critical terms and because the people who control sports and have the resources to influence them in the future are advocates of growth, not social and cultural transformation.

A **reformist** *strategy* is based on *a similar belief about the merits of sports, but it focuses on eliminating problems, promoting fairness, controlling cheating and drug use, urging athletes to be positive role models, and making sport organizations more efficient.* In this way, more people will have access to sport participation and experience its benefits. In other words, eliminate problems but keep the culture and structure of sports as they are. For example, women, people with disabilities, and others who have lived on the margins of mainstream sports and wish to be included in existing structures, programs, and organizations frequently use reformist strategies. Reformers focus mostly on issues such as equality of opportunity and social justice.

The Women's Sports Foundation (WSF) in the United States is an example of an organization that often uses reformist strategies based on a functionalist approach. The WSF lobbies for gender equity so that girls and women have equal opportunities to participate in sports, and it calls attention to the need for more women in decision-making positions in existing sport organizations. Because the WSF depends on national fund-raising to survive, it is very careful when it uses more radical strategies based on critical and feminist theories. It does not want to alienate the majority of their donors who favor a functionalist approach and want sports to be maintained much the way they are today.

Conflict Theory   Conflict theory is seldom used when Americans think about sports and society. Although some intellectually oriented people today think that it is fashionable to discuss injustices related to race and gender, they avoid discussing injustices related to social class and class relations (hooks, 2000). Conflict theory with its explicit focus on social class makes them uncomfortable. It challenges the very ideologies on which their class privilege rests and forces them to think about problems inherent in a capitalist economy that survives on profits made by paying workers as little as possible.

Conflict theory focuses attention on class relations in sports and the ways that sports are used to preserve and disguise basic social-class divisions in society. People using conflict theory to create sports adopt a particular form of **radical strategy** *in which the goal is to transform the economic organization of society so that class differences fade away.* This would make possible forms of sport in which there are no constraints on freedom, creativity, and enjoyment. The profit motive would be gone, so there would be no reason to exploit or oppress people.

Nearly everyone who uses conflict theory in the United States understands that eliminating capitalism is unrealistic at this point in history. Therefore, they favor specific strategies through which citizens, athletes, and spectators organize themselves and challenge those who have used wealth and economic power to shape sports in

ways that maintain their privilege. Over the last half century, people using conflict theory have worked with like-minded reformers and people using other radical strategies to reduce racism, sexism, nationalism, and militarism in sports. Additionally, they have inspired athletes to form players' associations to bargain for their rights with leagues and team owners. In a few cases, people who used conflict theory during the 1960s and 1970s continue to work in and with those associations.

Outside the United States, conflict theory remains popular among many people. In cultures where people are less devoted to consumption as a form of status expression, class-related and economic ideologies are more open and widely discussed. This makes them more sensitive to the social and political implications of extreme gaps between the very wealthy and powerful and everyone else. It also makes them less resistant to using conflict theory to envision possibilities that do not depend on commercialism and the use of large amounts of capital.

Critical Theory   People who use critical theory are concerned with the processes through which culture is produced, reproduced, and changed. Therefore, they focus their attention on issues related to ideologies, representation, and power in society. They are especially interested in the ways that people use power to maintain cultural practices and social structures that represent their interests and the ways that people resist or oppose those practices and structures.

Critical theory helps people envision possibilities for sports that are free of exploitation and oppression; organized to be inclusive in connection with age, gender, race, ethnicity, religion, and (dis)ability; and used to empower people to participate actively in the social worlds in which they live. Reformist and radical strategies are used because the goal is to transform sports so that a diverse range of participation opportunities is available to all people. For example, radical strategies are used to disrupt and transform the

Motorized sports impact the environment and the experiences of hikers, cross-country skiers, and other wilderness users. As more people incorporate technology into their sports and leisure, critical theories provide a useful basis for asking questions and doing research on these issues. (*Source:* Jay Coakley)

structure and dynamics of social relations related to gender, race, class, sexuality, and (dis)ability so that previously marginalized or underrepresented categories of people have equal opportunities to create and participate in sports that fit their interests and needs.

The radical strategies favored by people using critical theory emphasize eliminating inequities, creating democratic forms of participation, and making ideological and structural changes in sports and society as a whole. These strategies usually involve efforts to redistribute power and give voice to previously disenfranchised segments of the population in social worlds.

People with power and wealth usually strongly oppose radical strategies because they are designed to transform the ideas, beliefs, and forms of social organization on which their power and wealth depend. Privileged people dislike radicals because privilege depends on preserving the ideologies that legitimize elitist lifestyles and maintain the structures through which power is exercised over others. Their success in opposing radical strategies depends primarily on convincing most other people in society that the current, dominant ways of thinking and doing things are natural, normal, and supportive of everyone's interests in society. This is a primary reason why radical strategies are seldom used in sports; they are very risky because those who use them become targets of those who have power and influence in society. Furthermore, most people who favor radical strategies dedicate all their attention and resources to issues of poverty, homelessness, universal health care, quality education for children, accessible public transportation, full employment, and guaranteed minimum standards of living. However, a few radicals who are concerned with ideological issues have used sports as sites for the following purposes: challenging dominant definitions of *masculinity* and *femininity*, raising questions about the meaning of race, highlighting the difficulties of preserving democracy in the face of a growing gap between the haves and have-nots in society, destroying long-held stereotypes about (dis)abilities, and encouraging people to think critically about the antidemocratic features of the exclusive and hierarchical structures that characterize most organized sports today.

Critical Feminist Theory   People who use critical feminist theory are concerned with gender, gender relations, and gender ideology. They see sports as sites where dominant forms of masculinity and femininity may be reproduced or transformed. Therefore, much of their attention is focused on struggles over gender equity and issues related to changing sports.

Critical feminist theory focuses on transforming sports and gender ideology so that women are not systematically disadvantaged. It helps people envision what sports could be if there were no sexism, misogyny, heterosexism, or homophobia. People guided by critical feminist theory use reformist and radical strategies—reformist strategies to promote equity and radical strategies to resist and transform the dominant gender ideology, which privileges men and gives high priority to all sports based on the values and experiences of men, especially those in positions of power. Both strategies are used to push the boundaries of gender and expand accepted ways of "doing gender" in sports and everyday life.

The International Working Group on Women and Sport (IWG) is grounded primarily in critical feminist theory. Its members around the world use many strategies, including radical strategies aimed at changing ideologies and institutions that systematically exclude women from sports and disadvantage women when they do play sports. Strategies vary from nation to nation because the problems faced by women are different in various societies (Hargreaves, 2000). The IWG uses reformist strategies to increase opportunities for girls and women to play sports and to advance women into positions of power in society and in sport organizations. Radical strategies are used to transform the gender ideologies on which male privilege is based and female disadvantage is guaranteed in many cultures around the world.

Interactionist Theory   When people use interactionist theory, they focus on social processes through which social worlds are created. They view those worlds, including the ones created around sports, through the eyes of the participants themselves. They assume that socialization occurs in and through sport experiences, that people give meaning to sports and sport participation as they interact with each other, and that people form identities as they integrate their experiences into their sense of who they are and how they are connected with the rest of the world.

Interactionists view the future in terms of the possibilities for social interaction associated with sports. They may use *conservative, reformist,* or *radical* strategies to facilitate the creation of sports in which participants have representative control over the meaning, purpose, and organization of the sports they play. For example, reformist or radical approaches have been used to create sports and sport organizations that are democratic and inclusive (Birrell, 2000; Donnelly, 1988; Donnelly and Coakley, 2003). As this has been done, ideas have often been borrowed from other theories, especially critical and critical feminist theories.

Vantage Points for Creating Futures

Creating futures is a never-ending process. Being an active agent in this process is always challenging, regularly frustrating, and sometimes rewarding. For those interested in creating futures related to sports and social life, strategies can be initiated from four vantage points (Hall et al., 1991):

1. *Work within the system of sports.* You can become involved in sports and sport organizations and then use your position or power to influence and initiate changes.

reflect on SPORTS   Athletes as Change Agents
Does It Happen?

Athletes are visible and popular. Some have the highest name and face recognition of any human beings in history. This puts them in good positions to be change agents in society—or does it?

The visibility and popularity of athletes depends heavily on media coverage and overall public image. Leagues, teams, and corporations use athletes' images to promote events and products, but this does not mean that athletes can readily convert their celebrity status into power related to serious social, political, or economic issues.

The "context of sport celebrity" limits the extent to which athletes can be effective agents of change. If their words and actions don't match the interests of those who control their images, they risk losing the coverage and support that sustains their visibility and popularity. Team owners and corporate sponsors shy away from players who speak out on social issues; owners do not want to anger fans, and corporations don't want to anger consumers.

A former basketball player at the University of North Carolina explained that he kept quiet during his years in college because "athletes are loved by everybody until their consciousness is raised and they start to speak out on social issues" (Hayes, 1993, p. 18). When Tiger Woods was selected by *Time* magazine as one of "the 25 most influential Americans" in 1997, he was widely condemned for saying that "Golf has shied away from [racism] for too long, [and] I hope . . . [to] change that" (*Time*, 1997). His influence, he discovered, was limited to selling clothes and golf balls, not changing golf clubs run by powerful white men. Since 1997 Woods has supported only conservative approaches to changes, if he talks about change at all.

NBA player Steve Nash had a similar experience when he was selected to play in the 2003 NBA All-Star game. He wore a T-shirt saying, "No War. Shoot for Peace," to media day interviews, and he was widely criticized by journalists, players, and coaches (Candaele and Dreier, 2004).

It is not surprising that athletes use conservative strategies based on a functionalist approach when they become involved in their communities. They focus on reaffirming dominant societal values and strengthening the status quo by building playgrounds, visiting children in hospitals, promoting literacy, and delivering antidrug messages in high schools. Even when retired athletes enter politics, they generally represent conservative political positions aligned with preserving the status quo. If athletes in the United States used reformist or radical strategies based on critical or feminist theories, the American media would discredit and marginalize them, and their careers would be in jeopardy.

The most effective way for athletes to be agents of change is to work in or through established organizations. For example, the Center for the Study of Sport in Society (CSSS) is a reformist organization in which current and former athletes can work to change social conditions. The center's Project Teamwork enlists former college and professional athletes to train high school students to think critically about social issues, form local Human Rights Squads, and become involved in community projects to reduce prejudice, violence, and other problems. This and other CSSS programs have been effective, and they demonstrate that athletes can be agents of change when they are part of and clearly supported by an established and respected organization that has resources to achieve goals.

NBA player Adonal Foyle (Golden State Warriors) realized this when he established his foundation, Democracy Matters (www.democracymatters.org) to provide him with legitimacy and support. He now speaks out on selected issues, and his foundation staff members use an array of strategies to promote change. He also serves in the players' union as the player representative for his team, because he believes that a "player's rights should not be violated by powerful owners." But Foyle is unique in that, when he came to the United States from St. Vincent and the Grenadines (in the West Indies), he lived in the home of a sociologist and economist who favored reformist and radical approaches to change.

Recent history shows that even suggesting the need for ideological or structural changes can create problems for athletes. When Cassius Clay (Muhammad Ali) spoke against racism during the 1960s and, as a

Muslim, refused induction in the military during the Vietnam War, he was stripped of his boxing title and sentenced to five years in prison. When 400-meter champions Tommy Smith and John Carlos protested racism and global poverty on the victory podium during the 1968 Olympics in Mexico City, they encountered over twenty years of contempt and rejection in the United States. Is this why athletes today choose to act as corporate shills instead of agents of change? *What do you think?*

Tommy Smith and John Carlos used this gesture to protest U.S. racism and global poverty during the 1968 Olympics. As soon as the anthem was over, they were expelled from the Olympic village, sent back to the United States in disgrace, and widely condemned and rejected for over two decades. Then, in 2005, they received honorary doctorates from San Jose State University where a 23-foot high statue is being built to commemorate what people now define as their courageous actions on the podium over a generation ago. (*Source:* AP/Wide World Photos)

Having an "insider" vantage point can be very effective; sometimes, you can even use it to promote changes in society as a whole. However, becoming an insider often involves adopting the existing values and culture of the organization where you work. This means that, even though you may favor certain reforms or transformations, your commitment to actively promoting change may decrease as you move up the organization into positions of power. Once you reach a position that enables you to make changes, you often develop an interest in keeping things as they are and using a conservative strategy to slowly make things bigger and more efficient. This is not inevitable, but it is customary. Although an insider vantage point can be a good place from which to create futures, it is important to be realistic about what insiders can do. This is highlighted when we consider athletes as change agents. This issue is discussed in the box "Athletes as Change Agents," pages 586–587.

2. *Join "opposition" groups.* You can become a change agent by forming or joining political groups that challenge unjust or exploitive sport policies and put pressure on sport organizations that have such policies and programs. For example, opposition groups would lobby for the building of a community sport center in a low-income neighborhood or lobby against using public funds to build a stadium that would serve primarily the interests of already privileged people in a community. Opposition groups would apply pressure so that there would be a mandate to build low cost housing and dedicate funds to economic development in low-income neighborhoods in connection

> I started Democracy Matters to help students fight for progressive change by standing up to big money interests corrupting our democracy. I hope you will join me.
>
> —Adonal Foyle, NBA player, www.democracymatters.org, 2005

with hosting a major sport event, such as the Olympics. The possibilities for opposition are many.

3. *Create alternative sports.* You can reject or ignore dominant power and performance sports, and the organizations that sponsor them, and develop new sports grounded in the values and experiences of a wide array of different groups of people. This is often difficult because resources are seldom available when you choose this vantage point for making change. However, working from this vantage point can be effective even when it doesn't lead to concrete institutionalized changes because it provides clear-cut examples of new ways to look at and play sports, as well as new ways to look at and interact with other people. These examples then may inspire others to envision how they can create alternative sports in their own lives and communities. Former Olympian and current health and physical educator Bruce Kidd reminds us, "The effort to create alternatives to the commercial sport culture will continue to be an uphill fight. But such alternatives do exist. They have a long, rich, and proud history" (1997, p. 270).

4. *Focus on transforming culture and social relations.* You can ignore sports and work directly on producing changes in the ideologies and social structures that support and legitimize the current organization of sports in society. For example, groups that work to lower sexual assault rates in the United States have pressured the NFL, the NCAA, and other sport organizations to support policies that increase awareness of the problem and encourage progressive changes in gender relations.

Regardless of the vantage point for creating futures, significant social transformation always requires a combination of the following three things:

1. Visions of what sports and social life *could* and *should* be like
2. Willingness to work hard on the strategies needed to turn visions into realities
3. Political abilities to rally the resources that will make strategies effective

The future of sports and the impact of sports in society will be created as people combine vision, hard work, and politically effective strategies. Doing this is seldom easy, but if we don't create the future, it will be created for us on terms that will continue to privilege some people over others.

summary

WHAT CAN WE CREATE?

Sports are social constructions; they change as ideas and relationships change in sports and society. Although the meaning, purpose, and organization of sports will become increasingly diverse in the future, power and performance sports will remain dominant. They will receive continued funding and sponsorship from those with resources and power in society. Pleasure and participation sports will grow in connection with demographic trends and ideological changes, but they will not receive the funding and support enjoyed by sports organized around the power and performance model.

Sports at all levels will be sites for struggles over who should play and how sports should be organized. Major trends at all levels of sports are influenced by many factors including technology, telecommunications and electronic media, values supportive of organization and rationalization, a cultural emphasis on commercialism and consumption, and the demographic characteristics of communities and societies.

Futures come to be as people envision possibilities for what sports could and should be. Social theories are important in this process because they explain the connections between sports and social worlds, identify problems, and help in the selection of strategies to turn visions of the future into realities.

Most people, especially those who are advantaged by the status quo, do not want to change sports as much as they want to expand and make them more efficient. This conservative strategy fits with the assumptions and goals of functionalist theory. Reformist and radical strategies are more apt to be inspired by conflict theory and combinations of interactionist, critical, and critical feminist theories.

Changes in sports can be made from any one of four vantage points: within sport itself, in connection with opposition groups, through efforts to create new and alternative sport forms, and by working to transform those aspects of culture and social structure that support current forms of sports.

Regardless of the vantage point, change and transformation depend on clear visions of what sports could and should be in the future, a willingness to work hard to turn visions into realities, and the political abilities to initiate and maintain strategies that produce results. Unless we work to create the sports we want in the future, sports will represent the interests of those who want us to play on their terms and for their purposes.

This leaves us with an interesting choice: we can be consumers who accept sports as they are, or we can be citizens who use sports as contexts for actively making the world a better place. The goal of this book has been to prepare you to be informed citizens.

OLC See the OLC, www.mhhe.com/coakley9e, for an annotated list of readings related to this chapter. The OLC also contains a key concept list, a review test, and other helpful features.

WEBSITE RESOURCES

Note: Websites often change. The following URLs were current when this book was printed. Please check our website (www.mhhe.com/coakley9e) for updates and additions.

www.mhhe.com/coakley9e   Click on chapter 16 to read the predictions on what happens to the control and organization of sports when more people play them; also has information on the impact of technology on sports and athletes.

www.sportinsociety.org   The official site of the Center for the Study of Sport in Society; click on all the center's programs—Athletes in Service to America, Disability in Sport, Mentors in Violence Prevention (MVP) Program, Project TEAMWORK, Urban Youth Sports—to see examples of how sports can be changed, how sports can be used to create changes in communities and society, and how athletes can have a positive impact on the social world.

www.un.org/sport2005/   The site of the UN International Year for Sport and Physical Education 2005; also a link to a Sport for Development and Peace report entitled, "Sport as a Tool for Development and Peace: Towards Achieving the United Nations Millennium Development Goals" (33 pages).

www.un.org/Depts/dhl/resguide/r58.htm   This site has links to two U.N. Resolutions: 'Building a Peaceful and Better World Through Sport and the Olympic Ideal" (A/RES/58/6) and "Sport as a Means to Promote Education, Health, Development and Peace" (A/RES/58/5).

www.educatingforjustice.org   This site was originally the home of the Olympic Living Wage Project, part of an international effort to make athletes in the 2000 Olympic Games in Sydney aware of labor abuses related to the production of their equipment and uniforms; today it is a nonprofit organization that presents justice-oriented programming and content for educational purposes and to raise awareness that sparks social change.

www.sportsphilanthropyproject.com/   This is the site of the Sports Philanthropy Project; provides services to professional sports teams to set up foundations in their communities to enhance social development and community programs.

www.paralympic.org   The official website of the International Paralympic Committee.

www.gaygames.com   The site of the Federation of Gay Games; links to the history of the games, what occurred in Sydney at the 2002 Gay Games, and what happened in Montreal at the 2006 Gay Games.

www.AforBW.org   The site of Athletes for a Better World, an organization that now focuses primarily on self-change and making sports more ethical rather than changing communities; there are no specific statements about the types of "difference" athletes can or should make, other than just making things better.

www.bmxweb.com/   This site contains links to hundreds of sites used by BMX bikers; illustrates that athletes in the future will be able to form networks with fellow athletes around the world.

www.hotrails.com/   The key site for aggressive in-line skaters; provides a "feel" for the sport, who participates, and the norms underlying participation; note gender, racial/ethnic, and social-class patterns among participants because they provide information about the social dynamics of certain alternative sports as they develop.

www.gravitygames.com; www.dewactionsportstour.com/   Sites such as this attract many more young people than do sites like nfl.com.

www.boomboomhuckjam.com/   The site for Tony Hawk's (and Mat Hoffman's) new tour that ideally provides skaters and BMX bikers the opportunities to display skills in a format of their own choosing rather than a competitive format established by media companies or outside organizations.

www.the-arctic-challenge.com/   The site for snowboarders who resist dominant sport forms; use the TTR link to see the pleasure and participation philosophy of this Norway-based group; the group works on environmental issues as well as organizing events that emphasize expression, spontaneity, and creativity.

REFERENCES

AAA. 1998. Statement on "Race." Washington, DC: American Anthropological Association. Online: www.aaanet.org/stmts/racepp.htm (retrieved June 2005).

Acosta, R. Vivien. 1999. Hispanic women in sport. *Journal of Physical Education, Recreation and Dance* 70, 4, 44–46.

Acosta, R. Vivien, and Linda Jean Carpenter. 2004. Women in Intercollegiate Sport: A Longitudinal, National Study Twenty-Seven Year Update, 1977–2004. http://webpages.charter.net/womeninsport/.

Adelson, Eric. 2002. Hot to trot. *ESPN The Magazine* 5.13 (June 24): 74–76.

Adelson, Eric. 2003. Driven. *ESPN The Magazine* 6, 26 (December 22): 70–71.

Adler, Patricia A., and Peter Adler. 1991. *Backboards and blackboards: College athletes and role engulfment.* New York: Columbia University Press.

Adler, Patricia A., and Peter Adler. 1998. *Peer power: Preadolescent culture and identity.* New Brunswick, NJ: Rutgers University Press.

Adler, Patricia A., and Peter Adler. 1999. College athletes in high-profile media sports: The consequences of glory. In J. Coakley and P. Donnelly, eds., *Inside Sports* (pp. 162–170). London: Routledge.

Albert, Edward. 2004. Normalizing risk in the sport of cycling. In Kevin Young, *Sporting bodies, damaged selves: Sociological studies of sports-related injury* (pp. 181–194). Amsterdam: Elsevier.

Alesia, Mark. 2004. Lawmaker to the NCAA: Get tougher or be taxed. *Indianapolis Star* (May 19). Online: www.indystar.com/articles/0/147733-6820-036.html.

Alesia, Mark. 2005. Off court, schools lacking color: Most players are black, but few male students are. *Indianapolis Star* (March 17): 1A.

Alfred University. 1999. *Initiation rites and athletics: A national survey of NCAA sports teams.* See www.alfred.edu/news/html/hazing_study.html.

Allison, Lincoln. 2000. Sport and nationalism. In J. Coakley and E. Dunning, eds., *Handbook of sports studies* (pp. 344–355). London: Sage.

Allison, Lincoln. 2004. *The global politics of sport: The role of global institutions in sport.* London/New York: Routledge.

American Academy of Pediatrics. 2000. Intensive training and sports specialization in young athletes. (RE9906). Pediatrics 106, 01: 154–157 (or http://www.aap.org/policy/RE9906.html).

Anderson, Eric. 2000. *Trailblazing: America's first openly gay track coach.* Hollywood, CA: Alyson.

Anderson, Eric. 2002. Gays in sport: Contesting hegemonic masculinity in a homophobic environment. *Gender and Society* 16, 6: 860–877.

Anderson, Eric. 2004. Exploitation of the scholarship athlete. Unpublished manuscript.

Anderson, Eric. 2005. *In the game: Gay athletes and the cult of masculinity.* Albany: State University of New York Press.

Anderson, Jason, 2005. Most dangerous game. Online: www.eye.net/eye/issue/issue_04.21.05/film/murderball.html (retrieved November 2005).

Anderson, Kristen L. 1999. Snowboarding: The construction of gender in an emerging sport. *Journal of Sport and Social Issues* 23, 1: 55–79.

Anderson, Sarah, and John Cavanagh. 2000. *The top 200.* Washington, DC: Institute for Policy Studies.

Andrews, David L. 1996a. The fact(s) of Michael Jordan's blackness: Excavating a floating racial signifier. *Sociology of Sport Journal* 13, 2: 125–158.

Andrews, David L., ed. 1996b. Deconstructing Michael Jordan: Reconstructing postindustrial America. *Sociology of Sport Journal* 13, 4. Special issue.

Andrews, David L. 2000. Posting up: French post-structuralism and the critical analysis of contemporary sporting culture. In J. Coakley and E. Dunning, eds., *Handbook of sport studies* (pp. 106–138). London: Sage.

Andrews, David L. 2001. Sport. In R. Maxwell, ed., *Culture works: The political economy of culture* (pp. 131–162). Minneapolis: University of Minnesota Press.

Andrews, David L. 2007. Sport as spectacle. In George Ritzer, ed., *Encyclopedia of sociology* (in press). London/New York: Blackwell.

Andrews, David L., and Steven J. Jackson. 2001. *Sport stars: The cultural politics of sporting celebrity*. London/New York: Routledge.

Andrews, David L., and Michael Silk. 1999. Football consumption communities, trans-national advertising, and spatial transformation. Paper presented at the annual conference of the North American Society for the Sociology of Sport, Cleveland, OH (November).

Anonymous. 1999. Confessions of a cheater. *ESPN The Magazine* (November 1): 80–82.

AP (Associated Press). 2000. Fox relishes his role as Lakers' enforcer. *Denver Post* (June 20): C10.

Applebome, Peter. 1999. Alma maters: Two words behind the massacre. Online: www.lieye.com/articles/littletonli/nytimes.shtml.

Araton, Harvey. 2002. Playing with pain has no gender. *New York Times* (December 22). Online: www.nytimes.com/2002/12/22/sports/soccer/22ARAT.html.

Armstrong, Gary. 1998. *Football hooligans: Knowing the score*. Oxford: Berg.

Armstrong, Gary. 2007. Football hooliganism. In George Ritzer, ed., *Encyclopedia of sociology* (in press). London/New York: Blackwell.

Armstrong, Jim. 2000. Coors Field is not the patient's place. *Denver Post* (April 24): 3D.

Asay, Paul. 2005. Opening church's doors first step to conversion. *Colorado Springs Gazette* (December 11). Online: www.gazette.com/display.php?id=1312798&secid=3.

Ashe, Arthur. 1993. A hard road to glory. 3 vols. New York: Amistad.

Assael, Shaun. 2003. Cut and run. *ESPN The Magazine* 6.14 (July 70): 40–49.

Assael, Shaun. 2005. Shape shifter. *ESPN The Magazine* 8.09 (May 90): 88–96.

Atkinson, Michael. 2002. Fifty-million viewers can't be wrong: Professional wrestling, sports-entertainment, and mimesis. *Sociology of Sport Journal* 19, 1: 47–66.

Atlanta Journal/Constitution. 1996. America's Olympic teams are increasingly marked by less diversity, more elitism (October 1): H7. Special report.

Axthelm, Pete. 1970. *The city game*. New York: Harper and Row.

Bacon, Victoria L., and Pamela J. Russell. 2004. Addiction and the college athlete: The Multiple Addictive Behaviors Questionnaire (MABQ) with college athletes. *The Sport Journal* 7, 2. Online: www.thesportjournal.org/2004Journal/Vol7-No2/.

Bairner, Alan. 2001. *Sport, nationalism, and globalization: European and North American perspectives*. Albany: State University of New York Press.

Bairner, Alan. 2004. Inclusive soccer—exclusive politics? Sports policy in Northern Ireland and the Good Friday agreement. *Sociology of Sport Journal* 21, 3: 270–286.

Bairner, Alan, ed. 2005. *Sport and the Irish. Histories, identities, issues*. Dublin: University College Dublin Press.

Baker, William J. 1988. *Sports in the Western world*. Urbana: University of Illinois Press.

Bale, John, and Mette Christensen, eds. 2004. *Post-Olympism: Questioning sport in the twenty-first century*. Oxford/New York: Berg.

Bale, John, and Mike Cronin, eds. 2003. *Sport and postcolonialism*. Oxford/New York: Berg.

Bale, John, and Joseph Maguire, eds. 1994. *The global sports arena: Athletic talent migration in an interdependent world*. London: Frank Cass.

Ballard, Chris. 2004. Fantasy world. *Sports Illustrated* 100, 25 (June 21): 80–89.

Ballard, Steve. 1996. Broken back doesn't stall Indy winner. *USA Today* (May 28): A1.

Bandow, Doug. 2003. *Surprise: Stadiums don't pay after all!* Cato Institute Report (October 19). Washington, DC: Cato Institute.

Banet-Weiser, Sarah. 1999. Hoop dreams: Professional basketball and the politics of race and gender. *Journal of Sport and Social Issues* 23, 4: 403–420.

Barber, Bonnie L., Jacquelynne S. Eccles, and M. R. Stone. 2001. Whatever happened to the jock, the brain, and the princess? Young adult pathways linked to adolescent activity involvement and social identity. *Journal of Adolescent Research* 16, 5: 429–455.

Bartimole, Roldo. 1999. The city and the stadia (panel). Presentation at the annual conference of the North American Society for the Sociology of Sport, Cleveland, OH (November).

Bast, Joseph L. 1998. *Sports stadium madness: Why it started, how to stop it.* Heartland Policy Study, No. 85. Chicago: Heartland Institute.

BBC Sport Academy. 2005. Rugby league—Disability. Online: http://news.bbc.co.uk/sportacademy/hi/sa/rugby_league/disability/newsid_4019000/4019549.stm (retrieved November 2005).

Beal, Becky. 1995. Disqualifying the official: An exploration of social resistance through the subculture of skateboarding. *Sociology of Sport Journal* 12, 3: 252–267.

Beal, Becky. 1999. Skateboarding: An alternative to mainstream sports. In J. Coakley and P. Donnelly, eds., *Inside Sports* (pp. 139–145). London: Routledge.

Beal, Becky, and Lisa Weidman. 2003. Authenticity in the skateboarding world. In Robert E. Rinehart Synthia Sydnor, eds., *To the extreme: Alternative sports, inside and out* (pp. 337–352). Albany: State University of New York Press.

Beal, Carol R. 1994. *Boys and girls: The development of gender roles.* New York: McGraw-Hill.

Beals, Katherine A. 2000. Subclinical eating disorders in female athletes. *Journal of Physical Education, Recreation and Dance* 71, 7: 3–29.

Beaton, Rob. 1993. Mexicans best-suited to pitch, scouts say. *USA Today Baseball Weekly* (February 24–March 2): 11.

Bechtel, Mark, and Stephen Cannella. 2005. Scorecard: Cable ready. *Sports Illustrated* 103, 8 (August 29): 16–17.

Becker, Debbie, 1996. Nothstein: "I enjoy the pain." *USA Today* (July 24): 14E, 17E.

Becker, Debbie. 1999. Leaping past the pain. *USA Today* (April 1): 1E, 4E.

Beiruty, Hikmat. 2002. Muslim women in sport. *Nida'ul Islam Magazine.* Online: www.islamzine.com/women/women-sports.html (retrieved, October 15, 2005).

Bell, Jack. 2005. M.L.S. has a wide range of salaries. *New York Times* (July 11). Online: www.nytimes.com/2005/07/11/sports/soccer/11mls.html (retrieved July 14, 2005).

Bell, Wendell. 1997. Foundations of futures studies. 2 vol. New Brunswick, NJ: Transaction.

Bell, Wendell, and James Mau. 1971. Images of the future: Theory and research. In W. Bell and J. Mau, eds., *The sociology of the future* (pp. 6–44). New York: Russell Sage Foundation.

Belson, Ken. 2003. The N.B.A. takes its style and attitude to Japan. *New York Times*, section D (October 30): 6

Belson, Matthew. 2002. Assistive technology and sports. In Artemis A. W. Joukowsky III and Larry Rothstein, eds., *Raising the bar* (pp. 124–129). New York: Umbrage Editions.

Benedict, Jeff. 1997. *Public heroes, private felons: Athletes and crimes against women.* Boston: Northeastern University Press.

Benedict, Jeff. 1998. *Athletes and acquaintance rape.* Thousand Oaks, CA: Sage.

Benedict, Jeff. 2004. *Out of bounds: Inside the NBA's culture of rape, violence, and crime.* New York: HarperCollins.

Benedict, Jeff, and Don Yaeger. 1998. *Pros and cons: The criminals who play in the NFL.* New York: Warner Books.

Ben-Porat, Guy, and Amir Ben-Porat. 2004. (Un)bounded soccer: Globalization and localization of the game in Israel. *International Review for the Sociology of Sport* 39, 4: 421–436.

Berger, Jody. 2002. Pain game. *Rocky Mountain News* (February 23): 6S.

Berger, Jody. 2004. Straight shooter. *Denver Post* (January 24): 1B.

Berghorn, Forrest J., Norman R. Yetman, and William E. Hanna. 1988. Racial participation and integration in men's and women's intercollegiate basketball: Continuity and change, 1958–1985. *Sociology of Sport Journal* 5, 2: 107–124.

Berkowitz, Leonard. 1969. Roots of aggression: A reexamination of the frustration-aggression hypothesis. New York: Atherton Press.

Berlant, Anthony. R. 1996. Building character or characters? What the research says about sport participation and moral development. *Research Quarterly for Exercise and Sport* (Supplement): A95.

Bernstein, Alina. 2002. Is it time for a victory lap?: Changes in the media coverage of women in sport. *International Review for the Sociology of Sport* 37, 3–4: 415–428.

Bernstein, Alina, and Neil Blain, eds. 2003. *Sport, media, culture: Global and local dimensions.* London: Frank Cass.

Berra, Lindsey. 2005. This is how they roll. *ESPN The Magazine* 8.24 (December 5): 104–111.

Bigelow, Bob, Tom Moroney, and Linda Hall. 2001. *Just let the kids play: How to stop other adults from ruining your child's fun and success in sports.* Deerfield Beach, FL: Health Communications.

Bilger, Burkhard. 2004. The height gap. *New Yorker* (April 5): 38–45.

Birrell, Susan. 2000. Feminist theories for sport. In J. Coakley and E. Dunning, eds., *Handbook of sport studies* (pp. 61–76). London: Sage.

Birrell, Susan., and Diana M. Richter. 1994. Is a diamond forever? Feminist transformations of sport. In S. Birrell and C. L. Cole, eds., *Women, sport, and culture* (pp. 221–244). Champaign, IL: Human Kinetics.

Bishop, Ronald. 2003. Missing in action: Feature coverage of women's sports in *Sports Illustrated. Journal of Sport and Social Issues* 27, 2: 184–194.

Bissinger, H. G. 1990. *Friday night lights.* Reading, MA: Addison-Wesley.

Bjerklie, David, and Alice Park. 2004. How doctors help the dopers. *Time* 164, 7 (August 16): 58–62.

Blades, Nicole. 2005. Lucia Rijker. *ESPN The Magazine* 8, 11 (June 6): 96–97.

Blain, Neil, Raymond Boyle, and Hugh O'Donnell. 1993. *Sport and national identity in the European media.* Leicester, England: Leicester University Press.

Blake, Andrew. 1996. *The body language: The meaning of modern sport.* London: Lawrence and Wisehart.

Blauvelt, Harry. 2003. Stephenson says Asian players hurt LPGA tour. *USA Today* (October 10): 13C.

Blinde, Elaine M., and Lisa R. McClung. 1997. Enhancing the physical and social self through recreational activity: Accounts of individuals with physical disabilities. *Adapted Physical Education Quarterly* 14, 3: 327–344.

Blinde, Elaine M., Diane E. Taub, and Lingling Han. 1994. Sport as a site for women's group and societal empowerment: Perspectives from the college athlete. *Sociology of Sport Journal* 11, 1: 51–59.

Block, Martin E. 1995. Americans with Disability Act: Its impact on youth sports. *Journal of Health, Physical Education, Recreation and Dance* 66, 1: 28–32.

Bloom, Gordon A., and Michael D. Smith. 1996. Hockey violence: A test of the cultural spillover theory. *Sociology of Sport Journal* 13, 1: 65–77.

Bloom, John. 2000. *To show what an Indian can do: Sports at Native American boarding schools.* Minneapolis: University of Minnesota Press.

Bloom, Marc. 1998. Slower times at American high schools. *New York Times* (January 29): C27.

Blum, Debra. E. 1996. Devout athletes. *Chronicle of Higher Education* 42 , 22 (February 9): A35–A36.

Blumenthal, Ralph. 2004. Texas tough, in lipstick, fishnet and skates. *New York Times*, section 1 (August 1): 14.

Blumstein, Alfred, and Jeff Benedict. 1999. Criminal violence of NFL players compared to the general population. *Chance* 12, 3: 12–15.

Bolin, Anne. 1998. Muscularity and femininity: Women bodybuilders and women's bodies in culturo-historical context. In K Volkwein, ed., *Fitness as cultural phenomenon* (pp. 187–212). Munster: Waxmann.

Bolin, Anne. 2003. Beauty or the beast: The subversive soma. In A. Bolin and J. Granskog, eds., *Athletic intruders: Ethnographic research on women, culture, and exercise* (pp. 107–130). Albany: State University of New York Press.

Bonilla-Silva, Eduardo. 2001. White supremacy and racism in the post-civil rights era. Boulder, CO: Lynne Rienner.

Bonilla-Silva, Eduardo. 2003. *Racism without racists: Color-blind racism and the persistence of racial inequality in the United States.* Lanham, MD: Rowman and Littlefield.

Booth, D., and J. Loy. 1999. Sport, status and style. *Sport History Review* 30: 1–26.

Botstein, Leon. 1997. *Jefferson's children: Education and the promise of American culture.* New York: Doubleday.

Bourdieu, Pierre. 1986. *Distinction: A social critique of the judgment of taste.* London: Routledge.

Bowen, William G., and Martin A. Kurzweil, Eugene M. Tobin, and Susanne C. Pichler. 2005. *Equity and excellence in American higher education.* Charlottesville: University Press of Virginia.

Bowen, William G., and Sarah Levine. 2003. *Reclaiming the game: College sports and educational values.* Princeton, NJ: Princeton University Press.

Boyle, Robert H. 1970. Oral Roberts: Small but OH MY. *Sports Illustrated* 33, 22 (November 30): 64–66.

Brackenridge, Celia. 2001. *Spoilsports: Understanding and preventing sexual exploitation in sport.* London: Routledge.

Brackenridge, Celia, and Kari Fasting, eds. 2003 *Sexual harassment and abuse in sport: International research and policy perspectives*. London: Whiting and Birch (see also *Journal of Sexual Aggression* 8, 2 [2002]).

Braddock, Jomills Henry, et al. 1991. Bouncing back: Sports and academic resilience among African-American males. *Education and Urban Society* 24, 1: 113–131.

Braddock, Jomills Henry, Jan Sokol-Katz, Anthony Greene, and Lorrine Basinger-Fleischman. 2005. Uneven playing fields: State variations in boys' and girls' access to and participation in high school interscholastic sports. *Sociological Spectrum* 25, 2: 231–250.

Brady, Erik. 1996. Some legislators say Baltimore's money misspent. *USA Today* (September 6): 19C.

Brady, Erik. 1999a. Term of non-endearment? *USA Today* (May 12): 1C, 2C.

Brady, Erik. 1999b. Colleges help to make the grade. *USA Today* (October 19): 3C.

Brady, Erik, and Ray Glier, 2004. No free ride: Many students pay to play sports. *USA Today* (July 30): 14C.

Brady, Erik, and D. Howlett. 1996. Ballpark construction booming. *USA Today* (September 6): 13C–21C.

Brady, Erik, and MaryJo Sylwester. 2004a. High schools in the money also are rich in sports titles: Least affluent teams win half as many trophies. *USA Today* (June 17): A1.

Brady, Erik, and MaryJo Sylwester. 2004b. Kentucky school maintains edge with fundraising booster groups. *USA Today* (June 17): A4.

Brady, Erik, and MaryJo Sylwester. 2004c. "Great athletes and great desire" produce titles for least wealthy schools. *USA Today* (June 17): A4.

Bray, Cory. 2004. *2002-03 gender equity report*. Indianapolis: National Collegiate Athletic Association.

Bredemeier, Brenda Jo Light, Ellen Brooke Carlton, Laura Ann Hills, and Carole Ann Oglesby. 1999. Changers and the changed: Moral aspects of coming out in physical education. *Quest* 51, 4: 418–431.

Brennan, Christine. 1996. *Inside edge: A revealing journey into the secret world of figure skating*. New York. Scribner.

Brennan, Christine. 2002. Augusta sticks with boyish act. *USA Today* (July 11): 3C.

Bretón, Marcos. 2000. Field of broken dreams: Latinos and baseball. *ColorLines* 3, 1: 13–17.

Bretón, Marcos, and José Luis Villegas. 1999. *Away games: The life and times of a Latin baseball player*. Albuquerque: University of New Mexico Press.

Bridges, Lee. 2003. Out of the gene pool and into the food chain. In Robert E. Rinehart Synthia Sydnor, eds., *To the extreme: Alternative sports, inside and out* (pp. 179–189). Albany: State University of New York Press.

Briggs, Bill. 2002. A heavy burden: Way of life leads to early death for many NFL linemen. *Denver Post* (October 20): 1J, 8J.

Briggs, Bill. 2004. Crowds gone wild. *Denver Post* (November 28): 1B.

Brittain, Ian. 2004. Perceptions of disability and their impact upon involvement in sport for people with disabilities at all levels. *Journal of Sport and Social Issues* 28, 4: 429–452.

Broh, Beckett A. 2002. Linking extracurricular programming to academic achievement: Who benefits and why? *Sociology of Education* 75, 1: 69–95.

Brooks, Dana, and Ronald Althouse. 2000. African American head coaches and administrators: Progress but . . .? In D. D. Brooks and R. C. Althouse, eds., *Racism in college athletics: The African-American athlete's experience* (pp. 85–118). Morgantown, WV: Fitness Information Technology.

Brookes, Rod. 2002. *Representing sport*. New York: Oxford University Press.

Brown, Adam, ed. 1998. *Fanatics! Power, identity and fandom in football*. London/New York: Routledge.

Brown, Bruce Eamon. 2003. *Teaching character through sport: Developing a positive coaching legacy*. Monterey, CA: Coaches Choice. Online: www.coacheschoice.com/.

Brown, Gary T. 2000. Beating the odds. *NCAA News*, extra section (December 18): A1, A4.

Brown, Matthew, Mark Nagell, Chad McEvoy, and Daniel Rascher. 2004. Revenue and wealth maximization in the National Football League: The impact of stadia. *Sport Marketing Quarterly* 13, 4: 227–236.

Brown, Michael F. 2003. *Who owns native culture?* Cambridge, MA: Harvard University Press.

Brown, Michael K., et al., eds. 2005. *Whitewashing race: The myth of a color-blind society*. Berkeley: University of California Press.

Brown, Tony N., James S. Jackson, Kendrick T. Brown, Robert M. Sellers, Shelley Keiper, and Warde J. Manuel. 2003. "There's no race on the playing field": Perceptions of racial discrimination among white and black athletes. *Journal of Sport and Social Issues* 27, 2: 162–183.

Brownell, Susan. 1995. *Training the body for China: Sports in the moral order of the People's Republic.* Chicago: University of Chicago Press.

Bruce, Toni. 2007. Media and sport. In George Ritzer, ed., *Encyclopedia of sociology* (in press). London/New York: Blackwell.

Bruening, Jennifer E. 2004. Coaching difference: A case study of four African American female student-athletes. *Journal of Strength and Conditioning Research* 18, 2: 242–251.

Bruening, Jennifer E. 2005. Gender and racial analysis in sport: Are all the women white and all the blacks men? *Quest* 57, 3: 330–349.

Bruening, Jennifer E., Ketra. L. Armstrong, and Donna L. Pastore. 2005. Listening to the voices: The experiences of African American female student-athletes. *Research Quarterly for Exercise and Sport* 76, 1: 82–100.

Bryant, Adam. 1999. Shock treatment. *Newsweek* 134, 18 (November 1): 58–59.

Bryshun, Jamie, and Kevin Young. 1999. Sport-related hazing: An inquiry into male and female involvement. In Philip White and Kevin Young, eds., *Sport and gender in Canada* (pp. 269–292). Don Mills, ON: Oxford University Press.

Buffington, Daniel. 2005. Contesting race on Sundays: Making meaning out of the rise in the number of black quarterbacks. *Sociology of Sport Journal* 22, 1: 19–37.

Bull, Chris. 2004. The healer. *ESPN The Magazine* 7, 04 (February 16): 90–95.

Burstyn, Varda. 1999. *The rites of men: Manhood, politics, and the culture of sport.* Toronto, ON: University of Toronto Press.

Butler, Judith. 2004. *Undoing gender.* New York: Routledge.

Butryn, Ted M., and Matthew A. Masucci. 2003. It's not about the book: A cyborg counternarrative of Lance Armstrong. *Journal of Sport and Social Issues* 27, 2: 124–144.

Buysse, Jo Ann M., and Melissa Sheridan Embser-Herbert. 2004. Constructions of gender in sport: An analysis of intercollegiate media guide cover photographs. *Gender and Society* 18, 1: 66–81.

Cagan, Joanna, and Neil deMause. 1998. *Field of schemes: How the great stadium swindle turns public money into private profit.* Monroe, ME: Common Courage Press.

Canavan, Tom. 2003. Mourning risked heart attack if he continued playing. *The Coloradoan* (November 26): C3.

Candaele, Kelly, and Peter Dreier. 2004. Where are the jocks for justice? *The Nation* 278, 25 (June 28). Online: www.thenation.com/doc.mhtml?i=20040628&s=candaele.

Capouya, John. 1986. Jerry Falwell's team. *Sport* 77, 9: 72–81.

Carlson, Deven, Leslie Scott, Michael Planty, and Jennifer Thompson. 2005. *Statistics in brief: What is the status of high school athletes 8 years after their senior year?* Washington, DC: U.S. Department of Education, Institute of Education Sciences, National Center for Educational Statistics (NCES 2005-303; http://nces.ed.gov/pubs2005/2005303.pdf).

Carlston, D. 1986. An environmental explanation for race differences in basketball performance. In R. Lapchick, ed., *Fractured focus.* Lexington, MA: Lexington Books.

Carpenter, Linda Jean, and R. Vivian Acosta. 2005. *Title IX.* Champaign, IL: Human Kinetics.

Carrington, Ben. 2004. Cosmopolitan Olympism, humanism and the spectacle of race. In John Bale and Mette Christensen, eds., *Post-Olympism: Questioning sport in the twenty-first century* (pp. 81–98). Oxford/New York: Berg.

Carrington, Ben, and John Sugden. 1999. Trans-national capitalism and the incorporation of world football. Paper presented at the annual conference of the North American Society for the Sociology of Sport, Cleveland, OH (November).

Cashmore, Ellis, 2007. Gambling and sports. In George Ritzer, ed., *Encyclopedia of sociology* (in press). London/New York: Blackwell.

Caudwell, Jayne. 2003. Sporting gender: Women's footballing bodies as sites/sights for the (re)articulation of sex, gender, and desire. *Sociology of Sport Journal* 20, 4: 371–386.

Cavallo, Dominick. 1981. *Muscles and morals.* Philadelphia: University of Pennsylvania Press.

Chafetz, Janet. S., and J. A. Kotarba. 1995. Son worshippers: The role of Little League mothers in recreating gender. *Studies in Symbolic Interaction* 18: 219–243.

Chafetz, Janet, and Joseph. Kotarba, 1999. Little League mothers and the reproduction of gender. In J. Coakley and P. Donnelly, eds., *Inside Sports* (pp. 46–54). London: Routledge.

Chalip, Laurence, and B. Christine Green. 1998. Establishing and maintaining a modified youth sport program: Lessons from Hotelling's location game. *Sociology of Sport Journal* 15, 4: 326–342.

Chandler, Timothy J. L. 2002. Manly Catholicism: Making men in Catholic public schools, 1945–80. In Tara Magdalinski and Timothy J. L. Chandler, eds., *With God on their Side: Sport in the service of religion* (pp. 99–119). London/New York: Routledge.

Chapin, Tim. 2002. *Identifying the real costs and benefits of sports facilities.* Cambridge, MA: Lincoln Institute of Land Policy. Online: (www.lincolninst.edu/pubs/dl/671_chapin-web.pdf).

Chastain, Brandi. 2004. *It's not about the bra.* New York: Harper Resource.

Chiba, Naoki. 2004. Pacific professional baseball leagues and migratory patterns and trends: 1995–1999. *Journal of Sport and Social Issues* 28, 2: 193–211.

Child Trends. 2005. Participation in school athletics. Child Trends Data Bank. Online: www.childtrendsdatabank.org (retrieved September 5, 2005).

Christenson, Marcus, and Paul Kelso. 2004. Soccer chief's plan to boost women's game? Hotpants. *The Guardian* (United Kingdom) (January 16): http://football.guardian.co.uk/News_Story/0,1124460,00.html (retrieved December 1, 2005).

Ciborowski, Tom. 1997. "Superstition" in the collegiate baseball player. *The Sport Psychologist* 11, 3: 305–317.

Clancy, F. 1999. Warriors. *USA Weekend* (February 12–14): 4–6.

Clark, John. 1978. Football and working class fans: Tradition and change. In R. Ingham, ed. *Football hooliganism: The wider context.* London: Inter-Action Imprint.

Cleveland, Robert W. 2005. Alternative income estimates in the United States: 2003. *Current Population Reports,* June (P60-228). Washington, DC: U.S. Census Bureau. Online: www.census.gov/prod/2005pubs/p60-228.pdf

Coakley, Jay. 1983a. Play, games and sports: Developmental implications for young people. In J. C. Harris and R. J. Park, eds., *Play, games and sports in cultural contexts* (pp. 431–450). Champaign, IL: Human Kinetics.

Coakley, Jay. 1983b. Leaving competitive sport: Retirement or rebirth? *Quest* 35, 1: 1–11.

Coakley, Jay. 1988–1989. Media coverage of sports and violent behavior: An elusive connection. *Current Psychology: Research and Reviews* 7, 4: 322–330.

Coakley, Jay. 1990. *Sport in society: Issues and controversies* (4th ed.). St. Louis: Times Mirror/Mosby.

Coakley, Jay. 1992. Burnout among adolescent athletes: A personal failure or social problem? *Sociology of Sport Journal* 9, 3: 271–285.

Coakley, Jay. 1993. Sport and socialization. *Exercise and Sport Science Reviews* 21: 169–200.

Coakley, Jay. 1994. Ethics in coaching: Child development or child abuse? *Coaching Volleyball* (December–January): 18–23.

Coakley, Jay. 1998. *Sport in society: Issues and controversies* (6th ed.). New York: McGraw-Hill.

Coakley, Jay. 2002. Using sports to control deviance and violence among youths: Let's be critical and cautious. In M. Gatz, M. A. Messner, and S. J. Ball-Rokeach, eds., *Paradoxes of Youth and Sport* (pp. 13–30). Albany: State University of New York Press.

Coakley, Jay. 2006. The good father: Parental expectations and youth sports. *Leisure Studies* 25, 2: forthcoming.

Coakley, Jay. 2007. Socialization and sports. In George Ritzer, ed., *Encyclopedia of sociology* (in press). London/New York: Blackwell.

Coakley, Jay, and Peter Donnelly, eds. 1999. *Inside sports.* London: Routledge.

Coakley, Jay, and Peter Donnelly. 2004. *Sports in society: Issues and controversies* (1st Canadian edition). Toronto: McGraw-Hill Ryerson.

Coakley, Jay, and Anita White. 1999. Making decisions: How young people become involved and stay involved in sports. In J. Coakley and P. Donnelly, eds., *Inside Sports* (pp. 77–85). London: Routledge.

Cochran, Johnnie L., and Cyrus Mehri. 2002. *Black coaches in the National Football League: Superior performance, inferior opportunities*. Report presented to the National Football League (October).

Coffey, Wayne. 2005. Player without legs shows the heart of a champion. *New York Daily News KRT* (October 12). Online: www.isubengal.com/media/paper275/news/2005/10/12/Sports/Player.Without.Legs.Shows.The.Heart.Of.A.Champion-1017369.shtml.

Cohen, Greta L. 1994. Media portrayal of the female athlete. In G. L. Cohen, ed. *Women in sport: Issues and controversies* (pp. 171–184). Newbury Park, CA: Sage.

Cohen, Leah Hager. 2005. *Without apology: Girls, women, and the desire to fight*. New York: Random House.

Cole, Cheryl L. 2000a. Body studies in the sociology of sport. In J. Coakley and E. Dunning, eds. *Handbook of sport studies* (pp. 439–460). London: Sage.

Cole, C. L. 2000b. The year that girls ruled. *Journal of Sport and Social Issues* 24, 1: 3–7.

Cole, C. L. 2002. The place of golf in U.S. imperialism. *Journal of Sport and Social Issues* 26, 4: 331–336.

Collins, Michael F., and James R. Buller. 2003. Social exclusion from high-performance sport: Are all talented young sports people being given an equal opportunity of reaching the Olympic podium? *Journal of Sport and Social Issues* 27, 4: 420–442.

Collins, Patricia Hill. 2004. *Black sexual politics: African Americans, gender, and the new racism*. New York/London: Routledge.

Connolly, Mike. 2005. The bad news lies in the big three. *Bristol Herald Courier*, sports section (March 2): 1

Conroy, Pat. 1986. *The prince of tides*. Boston: Houghton Mifflin.

Cooky, Cheryl. 2004. Raising the bar? Urban girls' negotiations of structural barriers in recreational sports. Paper presented at the annual conference of the American Sociological Society, San Francisco (August).

Corbett, Doris, and William Johnson. 2000. The African American female in collegiate sport: Sexism and racism. In D. Brooks and R. Althouse, eds. *Racism in college athletics: The African American athlete's experience* (pp. 199–226). Morgantown, WV: Fitness Information Technology.

Corsello, Andrew. 1999. Hallowed be thy game. *Gentlemen's Quarterly* (September): 432–440.

Cotton, Anthony. 2004. Breaking the code. *Denver Post* (November 15): 1D.

Cotton, Anthony. 2005a. Pain in the grass. *Denver Post* (October 16): 1J.

Cotton, Anthony. 2005b. NFL is making a big play for Mexican fan base. *Denver Post* (October 2): 1A.

Couser, G. Thomas. 2000. The empire of the "normal": A forum on disability and self-representation—introduction. *American Quarterly* 52, 2: 305–310.

Coventry, Barbara. 2004. On the sidelines: Sex and racial segregation in television sports broadcasting. *Sociology of Sport Journal* 21, 3: 322–341.

Cox, Barbara, and Shona Thompson. 2000. Multiple bodies: Sportswomen, soccer and sexuality. *International Review for the Sociology of Sport* 35, 1: 5–20.

Crawford, Garry. 2004. *Consuming sport: fans, sport, and culture*. London/New York: Routledge.

Creedon, Pamela J. 1998. Women, sport, and media institutions: Issues in sports journalism and marketing. In Lawrence A. Wenner, ed., *MediaSport* (pp. 88–99). London/New York: Routledge.

Crissey, Joy. 1999. *Corporate cooptation of sport: The case of snowboarding*. Ft. Collins, CO: Master's thesis, Colorado State University.

Crist, Steven. 1998. All bets are off. *Sports Illustrated* 88, 3 (January 26): 82–92.

Critcher, Charles. 1979. Football since the war. In J. Clark, ed., *Working class culture* (pp. 161–184). London: Hutchinson.

Crosset, Todd. 1995. *Outsiders in the clubhouse: The world of women's professional golf*. Albany: State University of New York Press.

Crosset, Todd. 1999. Male athletes' violence against women: A critical assessment of the athletic affiliation, violence against women debate. *Quest* 52, 3: 244–257.

Cunningham, George B., and Michael Sagas. 2005. Access discrimination in intercollegiate athletics. *Journal of Sport and Social Issues* 29, 2: 148–163.

Curry, Timothy. 1991. Fraternal bonding in the locker room: A profeminist analysis of talk about competition and women. *Sociology of Sport Journal* 8, 2: 119–135.

Curry, Timothy. 1993. A little pain never hurt anyone: Athletic career socialization and the normalization of sports injury. *Symbolic Interaction* 16, 3: 273–190.

Curry, Timothy. 1998. Beyond the locker room: Campus bars and college athletes. *Sociology of Sport Journal* 15, 3:, 205–215.

Curry, Timothy J., Kent P. Schwirian, and Rachael Woldoff. 2004. *High stakes: Big time sports and downtown redevelopment*. Columbus: Ohio State University Press.

Curry, Timothy, and R. H. Strauss. 1994. A little pain never hurt anybody: A photo-essay on the normalization of sport injuries. *Sociology of Sport Journal* 11, 2: 195–208.

Curtis, James, William McTeer, and Philip White. 2003. Do high school athletes earn more pay? Youth sport participation and earnings as an adult. *Sociology of Sport Journal* 20, 1: 60–76.

Cyphers, Luke. 2003. Next. *ESPN The Magazine* 6.26 (December 22): 58–66.

Dacyshyn, Anna. 1999. When the balance is gone: The sport and retirement experiences of elite female gymnasts. In J. Coakley and P. Donnelly, eds., *Inside sports* (pp. 214–222). London: Routledge.

Daniels, Donna. 2000. Gazing at the new black woman athlete. *ColorLines* 3, 1: 25–26.

Danielson, Michael N. 1997. Home team: Professional sports and the American metropolis. Princeton, NJ: Princeton University Press.

Dater, Adrian. 2005. Female boxer, 34, dies after Golden Gloves bout. *Denver Post* (April 5): 1D.

Davies. Robert. 2002a. Sports, citizenship and development: Challenges and opportunities for sport sponsors. Presentation at the World Sports Forum Lausanne (September). See www.iblf.org.

Davies, Robert. 2002b. Media power and responsibility in sport and globalisation. Presentation made to the Third International Conference for Media Professionals in a Globalised Sport World, Copenhagen (November). See www.iblf.org.

Davis, Caroline. 1999. Eating disorders, physical activity, and sport: Biological, psychological, and sociological factors. In Philip White and Kevin Young, eds., *Sport and gender in Canada* (pp. 85–106). Don Mills, ON: Oxford University Press.

Davis, F. James. 2001. *Who is black: One nation's definition*. University Park, PA: Penn State University Press.

Davis, Laurel, and Othello Harris. 1998. Race and ethnicity in U.S. sports media. In L. A. Wenner, ed., *Media Sport* (pp. 154–169). London/New York: Routledge.

Deford, Frank. 1976. Religion in sport. *Sports Illustrated* 44, 16: 88–100.

Deford, Frank. 1996. The new women of Atlanta. *Newsweek* (June 10): 62–71.

Deford, Frank. 2002. Black coaches still can't make headway in football (January 31). Online: http://www.sportsillustrated.cnn.com.

De Jonge, Peter. 2003. The leap of his life; a rookie and his burdens. *New York Times*, section 6 (June 22): 26–36.

Delaney, Kevin J., and Rick Eckstein. 2003a. The devil is in the details: Neutralizing critical studies of publicly subsidized stadiums. *Critical Sociology* 29, 2: 189–210.

Delaney, Kevin J., and Rick Eckstein. 2003b. *Public dollars, private stadiums: The battle over building sports stadiums*. Piscataway, NJ: Rutgers University Press.

Demerath, Nicholas J., and Philip Hammond. 1969. *Religion in social context: Tradition and transition*. New York: Random House.

Dempsey, Chris. 2004. Many blacks feel isolation at CU. *Denver Post* (June 27): 1A, 19A.

Denham, Bryan E. 2004. Hero or hypocrite?: United States and international media portrayals of Carl Lewis amid revelations of a positive drug test. *International Review for the Sociology of Sport* 39, 2: 167–185.

Denver Post. 2004. Toughen up. *Denver Post* (August 1): 2B.

DePauw, Karen. 1997. The (in)visibility of disability: Cultural contexts and "sporting bodies." *Quest* 49, 4: 416–430.

Dewhirst, Timothy, and Robert Sparks. 2003. Intertextuality, tobacco sponsorship of sports, and adolescent male smoking culture: A selective review of tobacco industry documents. *Journal of Sport and Social Issues* 27, 4: 372–398.

DiPasquale, Mauro G. 1992. Editorial: Why athletes use drugs. *Drugs in Sports* 1, 1: 2–3.

DiPrimio, Pete. 2005. Seeking tweaks—school officials say new NCAA academic rules should be adjusted. *Ft. Wayne* (Indiana) *News Sentinel* (August 17): 1S–3S.

Doaks, Clinton. 2004. We can handle the truth. *Mile High Sport Magazine* (November): 10.

Doane, Ashley W., and Eduardo Bonilla-Silva. 2003. *White out: The continuing significance of racism.* New York/London: Routledge.

Dobie, Michael. 1987. Facing a brave new world. *Newsday* (November 8): 13.

Dobie, Michael. 2000. Race and sports in high school. In C. Scanlon, ed., *Best newspaper writing 2000* (pp. 319–387). St. Petersburg, FL: Poynter Institute for Media Studies.

Dodd, Mike. 2002. Tiger: Membership up to Muirfield. *USA Today* (July 17): 1C.

Domhoff, G. William. 2002. *Who rules America?* New York: McGraw-Hill.

Domi, Tie. 1992. Tough tradition of hockey fights should be preserved. *USA Today* (October 27): C3.

Donegan, Lawrence. 1994. Clubs winning fight against racism. *Guardian*, Home News (May 11): 2.

Donnelly, Peter. 1988. Sport as a site for "popular" resistance. In R. Gruneau, ed., *Popular cultures and political practices* (pp. 69–82). Toronto: Garamond Press.

Donnelly, Peter. 1993. Problems associated with youth involvement in high-performance sports. In B. R. Cahill and A. J. Pearl, eds., *Intensive participation in children's sports* (pp. 95–126). Champaign, IL: Human Kinetics.

Donnelly, Peter. 1996a. Prolympism: Sport monoculture as crisis and opportunity. *Quest* 48, 1: 25–42.

Donnelly, Peter. 1996b. The local and the global: Globalization in the sociology of sport. *Journal of Sport and Social Issues* 20, 3: 239–257.

Donnelly, Peter. 1997. Child labour, sport labour: Applying child labor laws to sport. *International Review for the Sociology of Sport* 32, 4: 389–406.

Donnelly, Peter. 1999. Who's fair game? Sport, sexual harassment, and abuse. In P. White and K. Young, eds., *Sport and gender in Canada* (pp. 107–128). Don Mills, ON: Oxford University Press.

Donnelly, Peter. 2000. Interpretive approaches to the study of sports. In J. Coakley and E. Dunning, eds., *Handbook of sport and society* (pp. 77–91). London: Sage.

Donnelly, Peter, and Jay Coakley. 2003. *The role of recreation in promoting social inclusion.* Monograph in the Working Paper Series on Social Inclusion published by the Laidlaw Foundation, Toronto, Ontario.

Donnelly, Peter, and Jean Harvey. 1999. Class and gender: Intersections in sport and physical activity. In P. White and K. Young, eds., *Sport and gender in Canada* (pp. 40–64). Don Mills, ON: Oxford University Press.

Donnelly, Peter, and LeAnne Petherick. 2004. Workers' playtime?: Child labour at the extremes of the sporting spectrum. *Sport in Society* 7, 3: 301–321.

Donnelly, Peter, and Kevin Young. 1999. Rock climbers and rugby players: Identity construction and confirmation. In J. Coakley and P. Donnelly, eds., *Inside Sports* (pp. 67–76). London: Routledge.

Downward, Paul, and Alistair Dawson, 2000. *The economics of professional team sports.* London/New York: Routledge.

Drahota, Jo Ann T., and D. Stanley Eitzen. 1998. The role exit of professional athletes. *Sociology of Sport Journal* 15, 3: 263–278.

Draper, Electa. 2005. Trying to turn the game into more than a dead end. *Denver Post* (May 17): 1A, 10A

DuBois, William Edward Burghardt. 1935. *Black reconstruction in America.* New York: Harcourt, Brace.

Dukes, Richard L., and Jay Coakley. 2002. Parental commitment to competitive swimming. *Free Inquiry in Creative Sociology* 30, 2: 185–197.

Duncan, Margaret Carlisle, and Michael A. Messner. 1998. The media image of sport and gender. In L. A. Wenner, ed., *Media Sport* (pp. 170–185). London/New York: Routledge.

Duncan, Margaret Carlisle, and Michael A. Messner. 2005. *Gender in televised sports: News and highlights shows, 1989–2004.* Los Angeles: Amateur Athletic Foundation. Online: www.aafla.org/9arr/ResearchReports/tv2004.pdf.

Dunn, Katherine. 1994. Just as fierce. *Mother Jones* (November–December): 35–39.

Dunn, Robert, and Christopher Stevenson. 1998. The paradox of the Church Hockey League. *International Review for the Sociology of Sport* 33, 2: 131–141.

Dunning, Eric. 1999. *Sport matters: Sociological studies of sport, violence and civilization*. London: Routledge.

Dunning, Eric. 1986. Social bonding and violence in sport. In Norbert Elias and Eric Dunning, eds., *Quest for excitement: Sport and leisure in the civilizing process* (pp. 224–244). Oxford, England/Cambridge, MA: Blackwell.

Dunning, Eric, Patrick Murphy, Ivan Waddington, and Antonios E. Astrinakis, eds. 2002. *Fighting fans: Football hooliganism as a world phenomenon*. Dublin: University College Dublin Press.

Dunning, Eric, Patrick Murphy, and John Williams. 1988. *The foots of football hooliganism: An historical and sociological study*. London: Routledge and Kegan Paul.

Dunning, Eric, and Chris Rojek, eds. 1992. *Sport and leisure in the civilizing process: Critique and counter-critique*. Toronto: University of Toronto Press.

Dunning, Eric, and Kenneth Sheard. 1979. *Barbarians, gentlemen and players: A sociological study of the development of rugby football*. New York: University Press.

DuPree, David. 1992. Controversy wears down Dream Team. *USA Today* (August 5): 7E.

Duquin, Mary. 2000. Sport and emotions. In J. Coakley and E. Dunning, eds., *Handbook of sports studies* (pp. 477–489). London: Sage.

Dworkin, Shari L. 2001. "Holding back": Negotiating a glass ceiling on women's muscular strength. *Sociological Perspectives* 44, 3: 333–351.

Dworkin, Shari L. 2003. A woman's place is in the . . . cardiovascular room? Gender relations, the body, and the gym. In Anne Bolin and Jane Granskog, eds., *Athletic Intruders: Ethnographic research on women, culture, and exercise* (pp. 131–158). Albany: State University of New York Press.

Early, Gerald. 1991. Delusions of grandeur: Young blacks must be taught that sports are not the only avenue of opportunity. *Sports Illustrated* 75, 8 (August 19): 78.

Early, Gerald. 1998. Performance and reality: Race, sports and the modern world. *The Nation* 267, 5: 11–20.

Eastman, Susan Tyler, and Andrew C. Billings. 1999. Gender parity in the Olympics: Hyping women athletes, favoring men athletes. *Journal of Sport and Social Issues* 23, 2: 140–170.

Eccles, Jacquelynne S., and Bonnie L. Barber. 1999. Student council, volunteering, basketball, or marching band: What kind of extracurricular involvement matters? *Journal of Adolescent Research* 14, 1: 10–43.

Eckstein, Rick, and Kevin Delaney. 2002. New sports stadiums, community self-esteem, and community collective conscience. *Journal of Sport and Social Issues* 26, 3: 236–248.

Edwards, Harry. 1973. *Sociology of sport*. Homewood, IL: Dorsey Press.

Edwards, Harry. 1993. Succeeding against the odds. *Black Issues in Higher Education* 10, 20: 136.

Edwards, Harry. 2000. The decline of the black athlete (as interviewed by D. Leonard). *ColorLines* 3, 1: 29–24.

Eitle, Tamela McNulty. 2005. Do gender and race matter? Explaining the relationship between sports participation and achievement. *Sociological Spectrum* 25, 2 (March–April): 177–195.

Eitle, Tamela McNulty, and David J. Eitle. 2002. Just don't do it: High school sports participation and young female adult sexual behavior. *Sociology of Sport Journal* 19, 4: 403–418.

Eitzen, D. Stanley. 2003. *Fair and foul: Beyond the myths and paradoxes of sport*. Lanham, MA: Rowman and Littlefield.

Elias, Norbert. 1986. An essay on sport and violence. In N. Elias and E. Dunning, eds., *Quest for excitement* (pp. 150–174). New York: Basil Blackwell.

Elias, Norbert, and Eric Dunning. 1986. *Quest for excitement*. New York: Basil Blackwell.

Eliasoph, Nina. 1999. "Everyday racism" in a culture of political avoidance: Civil society, speech, and taboo. *Social Problems* 46, 4: 479–502.

Elkington, John. 2004. Praying for rain. *SustainAbility Radar* (sports issue, August–September): 4–5.

Elling, Agnes, Paul de Knop, and Annelies Knoppers. 2003. Gay/lesbian sport clubs and events: Places of homo-social bonding and cultural resistance? *International Review for the Sociology of Sport* 38, 4: 441–456.

Engh, Fred. 1999. *Why Johnny hates sports*. Garden City Park, NY: Avery.

Eskes, Tina. B., Margaret Carlisle Duncan, and Eleanor M. Miller. 1998. The discourse of empowerment: Foucault, Marcuse, and women's fitness texts. *Journal of Sport and Social Issues* 22, 3: 317–344.

ESPN. 1999. High school athletes: Do jocks rule the school? *Outside the Lines* (June 20–June 24) (edited by T. Farrey). Online: www.espn.com/gen/features/jocks.

ESPN The Magazine. 2005. Special report: Turning a blind eye to steroids—The inside story of baseball's open secret. *ESPN The Magazine* 8.23 (November 21): 69–84.

Ewald, Keith, and Robert M. Jiobu. 1985. Explaining positive deviance: Becker's model and the case of runners and bodybuilders. *Sociology of Sport Journal* 2, 2: 144–156.

Falk, William B. 1995. Bringing home the violence. *Newsday* (January 8): 12–13.

Farber, Michael. 2002. Clubhouse confidential. *Sports Illustrated* 96, 2 (January 14): 52–57.

Farber, Michael. 2004. Code red. *Sports Illustrated* 100, 12 (March 22): 56–60.

Farhood, Steve. 2000. Typical girls. *Boxing Monthly* 12, 1. Online: www.boxing-monthly.co.uk/content/0005/three.htm.

Farrey, Tom. 2005. Baby you're the greatest: Genetic testing for athletic traits. *ESPN The Magazine* 8.03 (February 14)**:** 80–87. Online: http://sports.espn.go.com/espn/news/story?id=2022781.

Fasting, Kari. 1996. 40,000 female runners: The Grete Waitz Run—Sport, culture, and counterculture. Paper presented at International Pre-Olympic Scientific Congress, Dallas (July).

Fasting, Kari, Celia Brackenridge, and Jorunn Sundgot-Borgen. 2004. Prevalence of sexual harassment among Norwegian female elite athletes in relation to sport type. *International Review for the Sociology of Sport* 39, 4: 373–386.

Fatsis, Stefan. 2002. On sports: The good fight. *Wall Street Journal* (May 24): W6.

Fatwa Bank. 2004. Islam's stance on women's practicing sport. Online: www.islamonline.net/fatwa/english/FatwaDisplay.asp?hFatwaID=48375 (retrieved July 5, 2005).

Fausto-Sterling, Anne. 2000. *Sexing the body: Gender politics and the construction of sexuality.* New York: Basic Books.

Feeney, Robert. 1995. *A Catholic perspective: Physical exercise and sports.* Allentown, PA: Aquinas Press.

Fejgin, Naomi. 1994. Participation in high school competitive sports: A subversion of school mission or contribution to academic goals? *Sociology of Sport Journal* 11, 3: 211–230.

Fenstermaker, Sarah, and Candace West, eds. 2002. *Doing gender, doing difference: Inequality, power, and institutional change.* New York: Routledge.

Ference, Ruth, and K. Denise Muth. 2004. Helping middle school females form a sense of self through team sports and exercise. *Women in Sport and Physical Activity* 13, 1: 28–35.

Ferguson, Andrew. 1999. Inside the crazy culture of kids sports. *Time* 154, 2 (July 12): 52–61.

Fine, Gary Alan. 1987. *With the boys: Little League baseball and preadolescent culture.* Chicago: University of Chicago Press.

Finger, Dave. 2004. Before they were next. *ESPN The Magazine* 7.12 (June 7): 83–86.

Fish, Mike. 1993. Steroids riskier than ever. *Atlanta Journal-Constitution* (September 26): A1, A12–A13 (part one of four parts).

Fish, Mike, and David. A. Milliron. 1999. The gender gap. *Atlanta Journal-Constitution* (December 13–21) (eight-day series). Online: http://www.ajc.com.

Flake, Carol. 1992. The spirit of winning: Sports and the total man. In S. Hoffman, ed., *Sport and religion* (pp. 161–76). Champaign, IL: Human Kinetics.

Fleming, David. Stunt Men. *ESPN The Magazine* 8.24 (December 5): 64–70.

Florey, Brennen. 1998. Snow job. *Independent –* (Colorado Springs) (January 28–February 4): 9–14.

Foer, Franklin. 2004. *How soccer explains the world: An unlikely theory of globalization.* New York: HarperCollins.

Foley, Douglas E. 1990a. *Learning capitalist culture.* Philadelphia: University of Pennsylvania Press.

Foley, Douglas E. 1990b. The great American football ritual: Reproducing race, class, and gender inequality. *Sociology of Sport Journal* 7, 2: 111–135.

Foley, Douglas E. 1999a. Jay White Hawk: Mesquaki athlete, AIM hellraiser, and anthropological informant. In J. Coakley and P. Donnelly, eds., *Inside Sports* (pp. 156–161). London: Routledge.

Foley, Douglas E. 1999b. High school football: Deep in the heart of south Tejas. In J. Coakley and

P. Donnelly, eds., *Inside Sports* (pp. 133–138). London: Routledge.

Foucalut, Michel. 1961/1967. *Madness and civilization*. London: Travistock.

Fowler, Jeaneane, Merv Fowler, David Norcliffe, Nora Hill, and Diane Wadkins, eds. 1997. *World religions*. Brighton, England: Sussex Academic Press.

Frank, Robert H. 2004. *Challenging the myth: a review of the links among college athletic success, student quality, and donations*. Miami: Knight Foundation Commission on Intercollegiate Athletics. Online: www.knightfdn.org/.

Franseen, L., and S. McCann. 1996. Causes of eating disorders in elite female athletes. *Olympic Coach* 6, 3 (Summer): 15–17.

Frazier, Deborah. 1999. Rogers calls for massacre reparations: Payment sought for Sand Creek "butchery." *Rocky Mountain News* (November 30): 7A, 10A.

Fredrickson, Barbara L., and Kristen Harrison. 2005. Throwing like a girl: Self-objectification predicts adolescent girls' motor performance. *Journal of Sport and Social Issues* 29, 1: 79–101.

Freedman, Jonah. 2005. The fortunate 50. *Sports Illustrated* 103, 1 (July 4): 65–70.

Freeman, Mike. 1998. A cycle of violence, on the field and off. *New York Times*, section 8 (September 6): 1.

Freeman, Mike. 2000. Daunting issue of off-field violence. *San Francisco Examiner* (January 9): D9.

Freeman, Mike. 2002. Painkillers a quiet fact of life in the NFL. *New York Times* (January 31): C17, C19.

Friedman, Vicki A., Linda G. Martin, and Robert F. Schoeni. 2004. An overview of disability in America. *Population Bulletin* 59, 3 (special issue, "Disability in America").

Fudzie, Vince, and Andre Hayes. 1995. *The sport of learning: A comprehensive survival guide for African-American student-athletes*. North Hollywood, CA: Doubleplay.

Fulks, Dan L. 2002. *Revenues and expenses of Division I and II intercollegiate athletics programs: Financial trends and relationships*. Indianapolis: National Collegiate Athletic Association.

Garrett, Robyne. 2004. Negotiating a physical identity: Girls, bodies and physical education. *Sport, Education and Society* 9, 2: 223–237.

Garrity, John. 1989. A clash of cultures on the Hopi reservation. *Sports Illustrated* 71, 21 (November 20): 16–20.

Gavora, Jessica. 2002. *Tilting the playing field: Schools, sports, sex and Title IX*. San Francisco: Encounter Books.

Geffner, David. 2002. Just one of z-boys. *America West Magazine*, May: 41–43.

George, John. 1994. The virtual disappearance of the white male sprinter in the United States: A specula-tive essay. *Sociology of Sport Journal* 11, 1: 70–78.

Gerdy, John R. 2000. *Sports in school: The future of an institution*. London/New York: Teachers College Press (Columbia University).

Giardina, Michael D., 2003. "Bending it like Beckham" in the global popular: Stylish hybridity, performativity, and the politics of representation. *Journal of Sport and Social Issues* 27, 1: 65–82.

Giles, Audrey. 2004. Kevlar®, Crisco®, and menstruation: "tradition" and Dene games. *Sociology of Sport Journal* 21, 1: 18–35

Giordano, Rita, and Kristen A Graham, 2004. An early leg up. *Philadelphia Inquirer* (February 24): D1, D3.

Giulianotti, Richard, and Gary Armstrong. 2002. Avenues of contestation: Football hooligans, running and ruling urban spaces. *Social Anthropology* 10, 2: 211–238.

Gladstone, Brooke. 2005. The passion of the pitch. PBS, WNYC Radio. Online: www.onthemedia.org/transcripts/transcripts_052705_pitch.html (retrieved July 10, 2005).

Glatz, Carol. 2004. New Vatican office to promote culture of sport. *BC Catholic* (Vancouver diocesan paper). Online: http://bcc.rcav.org/04-08-16/ (retrieved July 10, 2005).

Glier, Ray. 2004. Reserve finds $425 a high price to sit. *USA Today* (July 30): 14C.

Glock, Allison. 2005. The look of love. *ESPN The Magazine* 8.12 (June 20): 66–74.

Godley, Amanda. 1999a. The creation of the student/athlete dichotomy in urban high school culture. Paper presented at the annual conference of the North American Society for the Sociology of Sport, Cleveland (November).

Godley, Amanda. 1999b. Transforming softball: Using a competitive model of sport to foster non-competitive adolescent peer culture. Paper presented at the annual conference of the North American Society for the Sociology of Sport, Cleveland (November).

Goffman, Erving. 1963. *Stigma: Notes on the management of spoiled identities.* Englewood Cliffs, NJ: Prentice-Hall.

Good, Regan. 2002. Women's share at Olympic competitions drops. Online: www.womensenews.org/article.cfm/dyn/aid/824 (retrieved July 5, 2005).

Goode, Erich. 1992. *Drugs in American society.* New York: McGraw-Hill.

Goodman, Cary. 1979. *Choosing sides: Playground and street life on the lower east side.* New York: Schocken Books.

Gore, Charles. 2002. *The least developed countries report, 2002: Escaping the poverty trap.* New York: United Nations Publications.

Gore, Charles. 2004. *The least developed countries report, 2004: Linking international trade with poverty reduction.* New York: United Nations Publications. Online: www.unctad.org/en/docs/ldc2004_en.pdf (retrieved December 1, 2005).

Gorman, Christine. 2005. Why more kids are getting hurt. *Time* 165, 23 (June 6): 58.

Gorman, Jerry, and Kirk Calhoun (with Skip Rozin). 1994. *The name of the game: The business of sports.* New York: Wiley.

Gramsci, Antonio. 1971. *Selections from the prison notebook* (Q. Hoare and G. N. Smith, Trans). New York: International Publishers (original work published in 1947).

Gramsci, Antonio. 1988. Selected writings: 1918–1935 (D. Forgacs, ed.). New York: Shocken.

Grant, Alan. 2002a. Body shop. *ESPN The Magazine* 5.03 (February 4): 50–54.

Grant, Alan. 2002b. A painful reality. ESPN Mag.com (January 30). Online: http://espn.go.com/magazine/grant_20020130.html (retrieved June 2005).

Grant, Christine H. B., and Charles E. Darley. 1993. Equity: What price equality? In G. L. Cohen, ed. *Women in sport: Issues and controversies* (pp. 251–263). Newbury Park, CA: Sage.

Grasmuck, Sherri. 2003. Something about baseball: Gentrification, "race sponsorship," and neighborhood boys' baseball. *Sociology of Sport Journal* 20, 4: 307–330.

Grasmuck, Sherri. 2005. *Protecting home: Class, race, and masculinity in boys' baseball.* New Brunswick, NJ: Rutgers University Press.

Green, Mick. 2004. Power, policy, and political priorities: Elite sport development in Canada and the United Kingdom. *Sociology of Sport Journal* 21, 4: 376–396.

Green, Mick, and Barrie Houlihan. 2004. Advocacy coalitions and elite sport policy change in Canada and the United Kingdom. *International Review for the Sociology of Sport* 39, 4: 387–403.

Green, Tina Sloan. 2000. The future of African American female athletes. In D. Brooks and R. Althouse, eds., *Racism in college athletics: The African American athlete's experience* (pp. 227–243). Morgantown, WV: Fitness Information Technology.

Greenfeld, Karl Taro. 1999. Adjustment in mid-flight. *Outside* (February). Online: http://outside.away.com/magazine/0299/9902terje_2.html.

Grenfield, Christopher C., and Robert E. Rinehart. 2003. Skating on thin ice: Human rights in youth figure skating. *International Review for the Sociology of Sport* 38, 1: 79–97.

Grey, Mark. 1999. Playing sports and social acceptance: The experiences of immigrant and refugee students in Garden City, Kansas. In J. Coakley and P. Donnelly, eds., *Inside Sports* (pp. 28–36). London: Routledge.

Griffin, Pat. 1998. *Strong women, deep closets: Lesbians and homophobia in sport.* Champaign, IL: Human Kinetics.

Grossfeld, Stan. 2005. New spin on rugby: Quadriplegic athletes take sport to the extreme with wheelchair version. *Boston Globe* (May 31): D1

Gruneau, Richard. 1988. Modernization or hegemony: Two views of sports and social development. In J. Harvey and H. Cantelon, eds., *Not just a game* (pp. 9–32). Ottawa, Ontario: University of Ottawa Press.

Gruneau, Richard. 1999. *Class, sports, and social development.* Champaign, IL: Human Kinetics.

Gruneau, Richard, and David Whitson. 1993: *Hockey night in Canada: Sport, identities, and cultural politics.* Toronto: Garamond Press.

Guest, Andrew, and Barbara Schneider. 2003. Adolescents' extracurricular participation in context: The mediating effects of schools, communities, and identity. *Sociology of Education* 76, 2 (April): 89–09.

Guilbert, Sèbastien. Sport and violence: A typological analysis. *International Review for the Sociology of Sport* 39, 1: 45–55.

Gulick, Luther. 1906. Athletics do not test womanliness. *American Physical Education Review* 11, 3 (September): 158–159.

Guttmann, Allen. 1978. *From ritual to record: The nature of modern sports.* New York: Columbia University Press.

Guttmann, Allen. 1986. *Sport spectators.* New York: Columbia University Press.

Guttmann, Allen. 1988. *A whole new ball game: An interpretation of American sports.* Chapel Hill: University of North Carolina Press.

Guttmann, Allen. 1998. The appeal of violent sports. In J. Goldstein, ed., *Why we watch: The attractions of violent entertainment* (pp. 7–26). New York: Oxford University Press.

Guttmann, Allen. 2004. *Sports: the first five millennia.* Amherst: University of Massachusetts Press.

Hadden, Jeffrey. K. 2000. Religious movements. In E. F. Borgotta, and R. J. V. Montgomery, eds., *Encyclopedia of sociology* (pp. 2364–2376). New York: Macmillan Reference.

Hall, A., T. Slack, G. Smith, and D. Whitson. 1991. *Sport in Canadian society.* Toronto: McClelland and Stewart.

Hall, M. Ann. 2002. *The girl and the game: A history of women's sport in Canada.* Peterborough, Ontario: Broadview Press.

Haney, C. Allen, and Demetrius W. Pearson. 1999. Rodeo injuries: An examination of risk factors. *Journal of Sport Behavior* 22, 4: 443–467.

Hanford, George. 1974. *An inquiry into the need for and the feasibility of a national study of intercollegiate athletics.* Washington, DC: American Council on Education.

Hanford, George. 1979. Controversies in college sports. *Annals of the American Academy of Political Science* 445: 66–79.

Hansell, Saul. 2005. More people turn to the web to watch TV. *New York Times* (August 1): C1.

Hargreaves, Jennifer, 1994. *Sporting females: Critical issues in the history and sociology of women's sport.* London: Routledge.

Hargreaves, Jennifer. 2000. *Heroines of sport: The politics of difference and identity.* London: Routledge.

Harp, Joyce B., and Lindsay Hecht. 2005. Obesity in the National Football League. *Journal of the American Medical Association* 293, 9 (March 2): 1061–1062.

Harris, John. 2005. The image problem in women's football. *Journal of Sport and Social Issues* 29, 2: 184–197.

Harrison, C. Keith. 1995. Perceptions of African American male student-athletes in higher education. Unpublished dissertation, School of Education, University of Southern California.

Harrison, C. Keith. 1998. Themes that thread through society: Racism and athletic manifestation in the African-American community. *Race, Ethnicity and Education* 1, 1: 63–74.

Harrison, C. Keith, and Suzanne Malia Lawrence. 2004. College students' perceptions, myths, and stereotypes about African American athletes: A qualitative investigation. *Sport, Education and Society* 9, 1 (March): 33–52.

Harrison, Louis, Jr. 1995. African Americans: Race as a self-schema affecting physical activity choices. *Quest* 47, 1: 7–18.

Harrison, Louis, Jr., Laura Azzarito, and Joe Burden, Jr. 2004. Perceptions of athletic superiority: A view from the other side. *Race Ethnicity and Education* 7, 2: 149–166.

Harrison, Louis, Jr., Amelia M. Lee, and Don Belcher. 1999. Race and gender differences in sport participation as a function of self-schema. *Journal of Sport and Social Issues* 23, 3: 287–307.

Hart, M. Marie. 1981. On being female in sport. In M. M. Hart and S. Birrell, eds., *Sport in the socio-cultural process* (pp. 291–301). Dubuque, IA: Brown.

Hartmann, Douglas. 2001. Notes on midnight basketball and the cultural politics of recreation, race, and at-risk urban youth. *Journal of Sport and Social Issues* 25, 4: 339–371.

Hartmann, Douglas. 2003a. The sanctity of Sunday afternoon football: Why men love sports. *Contexts* 2, 4: 13–21.

Hartmann, Douglas. 2003b. Theorizing sport as social intervention: A view from the grassroots. *Quest* 55, 2: 118–140.

Hartmann, Douglas. 2004. *Race, culture, and the revolt of the black athlete : The 1968 Olympic protests and their aftermath.* Chicago: University of Chicago Press.

Harvey, Jean, Alan Law, and Michael Cantelon. 2001. North American professional team sport franchises ownership patterns and global entertainment conglomerates. *Sociology of Sport Journal* 18, 4: 435–457

Harvey, Jean, Geneviève Rail, and Lucie Thibault. 1996. Globalization and sport: Sketching a theoretical model for empirical analyses. *Journal of Sport and Social Issues* 20, 3: 258–277.

Hasbrook, Cynthia A. 1999. Young children's social constructions of physicality and gender. In J. Coakley and P. Donnelly, eds., *Inside Sports* (pp. 7–16). London: Routledge.

Hasbrook, Cynthia A., and Othello Harris. 1999. Wrestling with gender: Physicality and masculinities among inner-city first and second graders. *Men and Masculinities* 1, 3: 302–318.

Hastings, Donald W., Sherry Cable, and Sammy Zahran. 2005. The globalization of a minor sport: The diffusion and COM modification of masters swimming. *Sociological Spectrum* 25, 2: 133–154.

Hawes, Kay. 1999a. Weighing in. *NCAA News* 36, 24: 1, 24–25.

Hawes, Kay. 1999b. Dangerous games: Athletics initiation—team bonding, rite of passage or hazing? *NCAA News* 36, 19 (September 13): 1, 14–16.

Hawes, Kay. 2001. Mirror, mirror. *NCAA News*, special report (September 24): A1–4.

Hawkins, Billy. 2000. *The new plantation: The internal colonialization of black student athletes*. Winterville, GA: Sadiki.

Hayes, Dianne Williams. 1993. Sports images and realities. *Black Issues in Higher Education* 10, 20: 15–19.

Heath, Thomas. 2003. For the investor who has everything. *Washington Post* (October 14): A1. Online: www.washingtonpost.com/ac2/wp-dyn/A21700-2003Oct13 (retrieved July 20, 2005).

Heckert, Alex, and Druann Heckert. 2002. A new typology of deviance: Integrating normative and reactivist definitions of deviance. *Deviant Behavior* 23: 449–479.

Heckert, Alex, and Druann Heckert. 2004. Using a new typology to analyze ten common norms of the American middle class. *Sociological Quarterly* 45: 209–228.

Heckert, Alex, and Druann Heckert. 2007. Positive deviance. In George Ritzer, ed., *Encyclopedia of sociology* (in press). London/New York: Blackwell.

Heywood, Leslie. 1998. *Bodymakers: A cultural anatomy of women's bodybuilding*. New Brunswick, NJ: Rutgers University Press.

Heywood, Leslie, and Shari Dworkin. 2003. *Built to win: The female athlete as cultural icon*. Minneapolis: University of Minnesota Press.

Hiestand, Michael. 2002. Security tighter, more costly for teams, venues. *USA Today* (September 11): 3C.

Higgins, Matt. 2005. A sport so popular, they added a second boom. *New York Times* (July 25). Online: http://query.nytimes.com/mem/tnt.html?emc=tnt&tntget=2005/07/25/sports/othersports/25boom.html.

Higgins, Paul C. 1992. *Making disability: Exploring the transformation of human variation*. Springfield, IL: Thomas.

Higgs, Robert J. 1995. *God in the stadium: Sports and religion in America*. Lexington: University of Kentucky Press.

Hilliard, Dan C., and J. M. Hilliard. 1990. Positive deviance and participant sport. Paper presented at the annual conference of the North American Society for the Sociology of Sport, Las Vegas (April).

Hilliard, Dan C. 1994. Televised sport and the (anti)sociological imagination. *Journal of Sport and Social Issues* 18, 1: 88–99.

Hoberman, John M. 1992. *Mortal engines: The science of performance and the dehumanization of sport*. New York: Free Press.

Hoberman, John M. 1994. The sportive-dynamic body as a symbol of productivity. In T. Siebers, ed. *Heterotopia: Postmodern utopia and the body politic* (pp. 199–228). Ann Arbor: University of Michigan Press.

Hoberman, John M. 1995. Listening to steroids. *Wilson Quarterly* 19, 1 (Winter): 35–44.

Hoberman, John M. 1997. *Darwin's athletes: How sport has damaged black America and preserved the myth of race*. Boston: Houghton Mifflin.

Hoberman, John M. 2004. *Testosterone dreams: Rejuvenation, aphrodisia, doping*. Berkeley: University of California Press.

Hoffman, Mathew (with Alyssa Roenigk). 2005. Fall guy. *ESPN The Magazine* 8.15 (August 1): 62–70.

Hoffman, Shirl. 1982. God, guts and glory: Evangelicalism in American sports. Paper presented at the meetings of the American Alliance for Health, Physical Education, Recreation and Dance, Detroit.

Hoffman, S. 1992a. *Sport and religion*. Champaign, IL: Human Kinetics.

Hoffman, Shirl. 1992b. Evangelicalism and the revitalization of religious ritual in sport. In

S. Hoffman, ed., *Sport and religion* (pp. 111–125). Champaign, IL: Human Kinetics.

Hoffman, Shirl. 1992c. Recovering a sense of the sacred in sport. In S. Hoffman, ed., *Sport and religion* (pp. 153–160). Champaign, IL: Human Kinetics.

Hoffman, Shirl. 1992d. Nimrod, nephilim, and the athletae dei. In S. Hoffman, ed., *Sport and religion* (pp. 275–286). Champaign, IL: Human Kinetics.

Hoffman, Shirl. 1999. The decline of civility and the rise of religion in American sport. *Quest* 51, 1: 69–84.

Honea, Joy. 2005. *Youth cultures and consumerism: Sport subcultures and possibilities for resistance.* Ft. Collins: Ph.D. dissertation, Colorado State University.

Honea, Joy. 2007. Alternative sports. In George Ritzer, ed., *Encyclopedia of sociology* (in press). London/New York: Blackwell.

Hong, Fan. 2004. Innocence lost: Child athletes in China. *Sport in Society* 7, 3: 338–354.

hooks, bell. 1992. Theory as liberatory practice. *Yale Journal of Law and Feminism* 4, 1: 1–12.

hooks, bell. 2000. *Where we stand: Class matters.* New York/London: Routledge.

Houlihan, Barrie. 1994. *Sport and international politics.* Hemel Hempstead, England: Harvester-Wheatsheaf.

Houlihan, Barrie. 2000. Politics and sport. In J. Coakley and E. Dunning, eds., *Handbook of sport studies* (pp. 213–227). London: Sage.

Houlihan, Barrie, and A. White. 2002. *The politics of sports development: Development of sport or development through sport?* London/New York: Routledge.

Hovden, J. 2000. Gender and leadership selection processes in Norwegian sporting organizations. *International Review for the Sociology of Sport* 35, 1: 75–82.

Howe, P. David. 2003. Kicking stereotypes into touch: An ethnographic account of women's rugby. In Anne Bolin and Jane Granskog, eds., *Athletic intruders: Ethnographic research on women, culture, and exercise* (pp. 227–246). Albany: State University of New York Press.

Howe, P. David. 2004. *Sport, professionalism and pain: Ethnographies of injury and risk.* London/New York: Routledge.

Hubbard, Steve. 1998. *Faith in sports: Athletes and their religion on and off the field.* New York: Doubleday.

Hudson, Ian. 2001. The use and misuse of economic impact analysis: The case of professional sports. *Journal of Sport and Social Issues* 25, 1: 20–39.

Hughes, Glyn. 2004. Managing black guys: Representation, corporate culture, and the NBA. *Sociology of Sport Journal* 21, 2: 163–184.

Hughes, Robert, and Jay Coakley. 1991. Positive deviance among athletes: The implications of overconformity to the sport ethic. *Sociology of Sport Journal* 8, 4: 307–325.

Hughson, John. 2000. The boys are back in town: Soccer support and the social reproduction of masculinity. *Journal of Sport and Social Issues* 24, 1: 8–23.

Hui, Stephen. 2004. Transexual Olympiads. Online: www.alternet.org/rights/19525/ (retrieved December 1, 2005).

Hunt, H. David. 2005. The effect of extracurricular activities in the educational process: Influence on academic outcomes? *Sociological Spectrum* 25, 4: 417–445.

IBS (International Bible Society). 1996a. *Path to victory: A sports New Testament with testimonies of athletes who are winning in life.* Colorado Springs, CO: IBS.

IBS (International Bible Society). 1996b. *More than gold.* Colorado Springs, CO: IBS.

IBS (International Bible Society). 1996c. *Path to victory: A sports New Testament with the testimonies of athletes who are winning in life* (No. 1144). Colorado Springs CO: IBS.

Ingham, Alan G., B. J. Blissmer, and K. W. Davidson. 1999. The expendable prolympic self: Going beyond the boundaries of the sociology and psychology of sport. *Sociology of Sport Journal* 16, 3: 236–268.

Ingham, Alan G., Melissa A. Chase, and Joanne Butt. 2002. From the performance principle to the developmental principle: Every kid a winner? *Quest* 4, 4: 308–332.

Ingham, Alan, and Alison Dewar. 1999. Through the eyes of youth: "Deep play" in peewee ice hockey. In J. Coakley and P. Donnelly, eds. *Inside Sports* (pp. 7–16). London: Routledge.

Ingham, Alan, and Mary McDonald. 2003. Sport and community/communitas. In R. Wilcox,

D. L. Andrews, R. L. Irwin, and R. Pitter, eds., *Sporting dystopias: The making and meaning of urban sport cultures* (pp. 17–34). Albany: State University of New York Press.

Irwin, Katherine. 2003. Saints and sinners: Elite tattoo collectors and tattooists as positive and negative deviants. *Sociological Spectrum* 23, 1: 27–57.

Ives, Nat. 2004. Coming for gamers: Football unfettered. *New York Times* (December 20): C8.

Jackson, Susan A., and Mihaly Csikszentmihalyi. 1999. *Flow in sports*. Champaign, IL: Human Kinetics.

Jackson, Steven J., and David L. Andrews, eds. 2004. *Sport, culture and advertising: identities, commodities and the politics of representation*. London/New York: Routledge.

Jackson, Steven J., and Brendan Hokowhitu. 2002. Sport, tribes, and technology: The New Zealand All Blacks Haka and the politics of identity. *Journal of Sport and Social Issues* 26, 2: 125–139.

Jackson, Steven J., and Jay Scherer. 2002. Screening the nation's past: Adidas, advertising and corporate nationalism in New Zealand. Paper presented at the annual meetings of the North American Society for the Sociology of Sport, Indianapolis (November).

James, C. L. R. 1984. *Beyond a boundary* (American edition). New York: Pantheon Books.

Jamieson, Katherine. 1998. Navigating the system: The case of Latina student-athletes in women's collegiate sports. Paper presented at the annual conference of the American Alliance for Health, Physical Education, Recreation and Dance, Reno, NV (April).

Jamieson, Katherine. 2005. "All my hopes and dreams": Families, schools, and subjectivities in collegiate softball. *Journal of Sport and Social Issues* 29, 2: 133–147.

Jay, Kathryn. 2004. *More than just a game: Sports in American life since 1945*. New York: Columbia University Press.

Jayson, Sharon. 2004. On or off the field, it's a "civility" war out there. *USA Today* (November 30): 9D.

JBHE. 2005. Are the flagship state universities exploiting black athletes? *Journal of Blacks in Higher Education* 48. Online: www.jbhe.com/news_views/48_blacks_stateuniversities.html.

Jenkins, Chris. 2000. Caught in gambling's web. *USA Today* (March 13): 1C–2C.

Jenkins, Chris. 2002. The new face of NASCAR. *USA Today* (May 24): 1A–2A.

Jenkins, Chris. 2005. Steroid policy hits Latin Americans. *USA Today* (May 6): 7C.

Jenkins, H. 1997. "Never trust a snake": WWF wrestling as masculine melodrama. In A. Baker and T. Boyd, eds., *Out of bounds: Sports, media, and the politics of identity* (pp. 48–28). Bloomington: Indiana University Press.

Jennings, Andrew. 1996a. *The new lords of the rings*. London: Pocket Books.

Jennings, Andrew. 1996b. Power, corruption, and lies. *Esquire* (May): 99–104.

Jennings, Andrew., and Clare Sambrook. 2000. *The great Olympic swindle: When the world wanted its games back*. New York: Simon and Schuster.

Jinxia, Dong. 2003. *Women, sport, and society in modern China: Holding up more than half the sky*. London/Portland, OR: Frank Cass.

Johns, David. 1992. Starving for gold: A case study in overconformity in high performance sport. Paper presented at the annual conference of the North American Society for the Sociology of Sport, Toledo (November).

Johns, David. 1996. Positive deviance and the sport ethic: Examining weight loss strategies in rhythmic gymnastics. *Hong Kong Journal of Sports Medicine and Sport Science* 2 (May): 49–56.

Johns, David. 1997. Fasting and feasting: Paradoxes in the sport ethic. *Sociology of Sport Journal* 15, 1: 41–63.

Johns, David P., and Jennifer S. Johns. 2000. Surveillance, subjectivism and technologies of power. *International Review for the Sociology of Sport* 35, 2: 219–234.

Jonas, Scott. 2005. Should women play sports? Online: www.jesus-is-savior.com/Womens%20Page/christian_women_and_sports.htm (retrieved July 8, 2005).

Joravsky, Ben. 1995. Hoop dreams: A true story of hardship and triumph. New York: HarperCollins.

Joukowsky, Artemis A. W. III, and Larry Rothstein, eds. 2002a. *Raising the bar*. New York: Umbrage Editions.

Joukowsky, Artemis A. W. III, and Larry Rothstein. 2002b. New horizons in disability sport. In Artemis A. W. Joukowsky III and Larry Rothstein, eds.,

Raising the bar (pp. 8–17). New York: Umbrage Editions.

Jutel, Annemarie. 2002. Olympic road cycling and national identity: Where is Germany? *Journal of Sport and Social Issues* 26, 2: 195–208.

Kamiya, Gary. 2000. The black edge: Are athletes of African descent genetically superior? *Salon* 28. Online: (http://dir.salon.com/books/feature/2000/01/28/taboo/index.html).

Kaplan, David A. 2002. The end of baseball again. *Newsweek* 140, 9 (August 26): 46–47.

Kates, William. 2005. Newest kick for adults—that red rubber ball from grade school days. *North County Times* (July 24). Online: www.nctimes.com/ articles/2005/07/25/ sports/amateur/17_16_237_24_05.txt.

Katz, Jackson. 2003. When you're asked about the Kobe Bryant case. Online: www.jacksonkatz.com/bryant.html.

Kay, Joanne, and Suzanne Laberge. 2003. Oh say can you ski? In Robert E. Rinehart and Synthia Sydnor, eds., *To the extreme: Alternative sports, inside and out* (pp. 381–398). Albany: State University of New York Press.

Kearney, Jay. 1999. Creatine supplementation: Specifics for the trained athlete. *Olympic Coach* 9, 2: 3–5.

Keating, Peter. 2002a. Boys, don't cry. *ESPN The Magazine* 5.13 (June 24): 78.

Keating, Peter. 2002b. Artful dodging. *ESPN The Magazine* 5.01 (January 7): 93.

Keating, Peter. 2004a. The biz. *ESPN, The Magazine* 7.25 (December 6): 14.

Keating, Peter. 2004b. Insurance run. *ESPN The Magazine* 7.14 (July 5): 70–73.

Keating, Peter. 2005. Baseball has solved its steroid problem—at least that's what they want you to believe. *ESPN The Magazine* 8.24 (December 5): 16.

Keith, Susan. 1999. Native American women in sport. *Journal of Physical Education, Recreation and Dance* 70, 4: 47–49.

Kelley, Betty C., Shirl J. Hoffman, and Diane. L. Gill. 1990. The relationship between competitive orientation and religious orientation. *Journal of Sport Behavior* 13, 3: 145–156.

Kellner, Douglas. 2003a. Toward a critical theory of education. *Democracy and Nature* 9, 1 (March): 51–64. Online: www.gseis.ucla.edu/faculty/kelllner/.

Kellner, Douglas. 2003b. *Media spectacle*. London/New York: Routledge.

Kellner, Douglas. 2004. The sports spectacle, Michael Jordan, and Nike. In Patrick B. Miller and David K. Wiggins, eds., *Sport and the color line* (pp. 305–326). New York/London: Routledge.

Kensler, Tom. 2005. Wie playing PGA Tour event seems out of bounds to some. *Denver Post* (July 3): 1B, 10B.

Keown, Tim. 2004. World of hurt. *ESPN The Magazine* 7.16 (August 2): 57–77.

Kerr, John H. 2004. *Rethinking aggression and violence in sport*. London/New York: Routledge.

Kidd, Bruce. 1984. The myth of the ancient games. In A. Tomlinson and G. Whannel, eds., *Five-ring circus* (pp. 71–83). London: Pluto Press.

Kidd, Bruce. 1987. Sports and masculinity. In M. Kaufman, ed., *Beyond patriarchy: Essays by men on pleasure, power, and change* (pp. 250–265). New York: Oxford University Press.

Kidd, Bruce. 1995. Inequality in sport, the corporation, and the state: An agenda for social scientists. *Journal of Sport and Social Issues* 19, 3: 232–248.

Kidd, Bruce. 1996a. Worker sport in the New World: The Canadian story. In A. Kruger and J. Riordan, eds., *The story of worker sport* (pp. 143–156). Champaign, IL: Human Kinetics.

Kidd, Bruce. 1996b. Taking the rhetoric seriously: Proposals for Olympic education. *Quest* 48, 1: 82–92.

Kidd, Bruce. 1997. *The struggle for Canadian sport*. Toronto: University of Toronto Press.

Kidd, Bruce, and Peter Donnelly. 2000. Human rights in sports. *International Review for the Sociology of Sport* 35, 2: 131–148.

Kilvert, Gwen. 2002. Missing the X chromosome. *Sports Illustrated Women* 4, 4: 21–22.

King, Anthony. 1996. The fining of Vinnie Jones. *International Review for the Sociology of Sport* 31, 2: 119–138.

King, C. Richard, ed. 2004a. *Native Americans in sports*. Armonk, NY: Sharpe Reference.

King, C. Richard. 2004b. Re/claiming Indianness: Critical perspectives on Native American mascots. *Journal of Sport and Social Issues* 28, 1: (special issue).

King, C. Richard. 2007a. Sport and ethnicity. In George Ritzer, ed., *Encyclopedia of sociology* (in press). London/New York: Blackwell.

King, C. Richard. 2007b. Postcolonialism and sports. In George Ritzer, ed., *Encyclopedia of sociology* (in press). London/New York: Blackwell.

King, C. Richard, and Charles Fruehling Springwood, eds. 2001a. *Team spirits: The Native American mascots controversy.* Lincoln: Bison Books and University of Nebraska Press.

King, C. Richard, and Charles Fruehling Springwood. 2001b. *Beyond the cheers: Race as a spectacle in college sport.* Albany: State University of New York Press.

King, Kelley. 2002. The ultimate jock school. *Sports Illustrated* 97, 21 (November 25): 48–54.

King, Kelley. 2005. Little shred schoolhouse. *Sports Illustrated* 102, 12 (March 21): (in Scorecard section).

King, Peter. 1996. Bitter pill. *Sports Illustrated* 84, 21 (May 27): 24–30.

King, Peter. 2004. Painful reality. *Sports Illustrated* 101, 14 (October 11): 60–63.

Kinkema, Kathleen M., and Janet C. Harris. 1998. MediaSport studies: Key research and emerging issues. In L. A. Wenner, ed., *MediaSport* (pp. 27–54). London/New York: Routledge.

Kiszla, Mark. 2001. Denver "D" short for "dark side." *Denver Post* (March 20): 1D, 3D.

Kiszla, Mark. 2005. Hey—these girls are good. *Denver Post* (July 3): 1B, 12B.

Klein, Alan. 1991. *Sugarball: The American game, the Dominican dream.* New Haven, CT: Yale University Press.

Klein, Alan. 1993. *Little big men: Bodybuilding subculture and gender construction.* Albany: State University of New York Press.

Knight Commission. 2001. *A call to action: Reconnecting college sports and higher education.* Report of the Knight Foundation Commission on Intercollegiate Athletics. Miami. Online: Knight Foundation http://www.knightfdn.org/.

Knoppers, Annelies, ed. 2000. *The construction of meaning in sport organizations: Management of diversity.* Maastricht, Netherlands: Shaker.

Knoppers, Annelies, and Agnes Elling. 2004. "We do not engage in promotional journalism": Discursive strategies used by sport journalists to describe the selection process. *International Review for the Sociology of Sport* 39, 1: 57–73.

Knudson, Mark. 2005. The Mark: The whole IX yards. *Mile High Sports Magazine* 3, 9 (May): 21–23.

Kooistra, Paul, John S. Mahoney, and Lisha Bridges. 1993. The unequal opportunity for equal ability hypothesis: Racism in the National Football League. *Sociology of Sport Journal* 10, 3: 241–255.

Koppett, Leonard. 1994. *Sports illusion, sports reality.* Urbana: University of Illinois Press.

Kornheiser, Tony. 1999. Six billion? Where's mine? *ESPN The Magazine* (December 13): 46.

Koukouris, Konstantinos. 1994. Constructed case studies: Athletes' perspectives of disengaging from organized competitive sport. *Sociology of Sport Journal* 11, 2: 114–139.

Kozol, Jonathan. 1991. *Savage inequalities.* New York: Crown.

Kozol, Jonathan. 2002. Malign neglect. *The Nation* 274, 22: 20–23.

Krane, Vikki. 1996. Lesbians in sport: Toward acknowledgement, understanding, and theory. *Journal of Sport and Exercise Psychology* 18, 3: 237–246.

Krane, Vikki, Precilla Y. L. Choi, Shannon M. Baird, Christine M. Aimar, and Kerrie J. Kauer. 2004. Living the paradox: Female athletes negotiate femininity and muscularity. *Sex Roles* 50, 5/6: 315–329.

Krane, Vikki., Jennifer Waldron, Jennifer Michalenok, and Julie Stiles-Shipley. 2001. Body image concerns in female exercisers and athletes: A feminist cultural studies perspective. *Women in Sport and Physical Activity Journal* 10, 1: 17–54.

Kristal, Nicole. 2005. "Tutoring" rich kids cost me my dreams. *Newsweek* 145, 15 (April 11): 19.

Laberge, Suzanne, and Mathieu Albert. 1999. Conceptions of masculinity and of gender transgressions in sport among adolescent boys: Hegemony, contestation, and social class dynamic. *Men and Masculinities* 1, 3: 243–267.

Laberge, Suzanne, and David Sankoff. 1988. Physical activities, body *habitus*, and lifestyles. In J. Harvey and H. Cantelon, eds., *Not just a game* (pp. 267–286). Ottawa: University of Ottawa Press.

Ladd, Tony, and James A. Mathisen. 1999. *Muscular Christianity: Evangelical Protestants and the development of American sport.* Grand Rapids, MI: Baker Books.

Lafferty, Yvonne, and Jim McKay. 2004. "Suffragettes in satin shorts"? Gender and competitive boxing. *Qualitative Sociology* 27, 3: 249–276.

Lamb, L. 2000. Can women save sports? An interview with Mary Jo Kane. *Utne Reader* 97: 56–57.

Lance, Larry. M. 2005. Violence in sport: A theoretical note. *Sociological Spectrum* 25, 2: 213–214.

Lapchick, Richard. 1984. *Broken promises: Racism in American sports.* New York: St. Martin's Press/Marek.

Lapchick, Richard. 2004. *Racial and gender report card, 2003.* Orlando: Institute for Diversity and Ethics in Sports, University of Central Florida.

Lapchick, Richard. 2005a. *Keeping score when it counts: Assessing the graduation rates of the 2004-05 bowl-bound college football teams.* Orlando: Institute for Diversity and Ethics in Sport at the DeVos Sport Business Management Graduate Program, University of Central Florida.

Lapchick, Richard. 2005b. *Keeping score when it counts: Graduation rates for 2005 NCAA men's and women's Division I basketball tournament teams.* Orlando: Institute for Diversity and Ethics in Sport at the DeVos Sport Business Management Graduate Program, University of Central Florida.

Lapchick, Richard. 2005c. *2004 racial and gender report card.* Orlando: Institute for Diversity and Ethics in Sports, University of Central Florida.

Laqueur, Thomas. 1990. *Making sex.* Cambridge, MA: Harvard University Press.

Latimer, Clay. 1999. NBA springs from humble roots. *Rocky Mountain News* (October 24): 31C.

Latimer, Clay. 2005a. More than child's play: Giving the young a sporting chance. *Rocky Mountain News* (December 16): 1B, 12B–14B.

Latimer, Clay. 2005b. More than child's play: Under a nonstop watch. *Rocky Mountain News* (December 19): 1C, 8C.

Latimer, Clay. 2005c. More than child's play: Studies in determination. *Rocky Mountain News* (December 20): 1C, 11C–14C.

Latimer, Clay. 2005d. More than child's play: To market, to market. *Rocky Mountain News* (December 21): 1C, 11C–13C.

Latimer, Clay. 2005e. More than child's play: Change is in the heir. *Rocky Mountain News* (December 22): 1C, 12–13C.

Laurendeau, Jason. 2004. The "crack choir" and the "cock chorus": The intersection of gender and sexuality in skydiving texts. *Sociology of Sport Journal* 21, 4: 397–417.

Lavoie, Marc. 2000. Economics and sport. In J. Coakley and E. Dunning, eds., *Handbook of sports studies* (pp. 157–170). London: Sage.

Lavoie Marc, and Wib M. Leonard II. 1994. In search of an alternative explanation of stacking in baseball: The uncertainty hypothesis. *Sociology of Sport Journal* 11, 2: 140–154.

Lawler, Jennifer. 2002. *Punch: Why women participate in violent sports.* Terre Haute, IN: Wish Publishing.

Lawrence, Suzanne Malia. 2005. African American athletes' experiences of race in sport. *International Review for the Sociology of Sport* 40, 1: 99–110.

Layden, Tim. 1995a. Better education. *Sports Illustrated* 82, 13 (April 3): 68–90.

Layden, Tim. 1995b. Book smart. *Sports Illustrated* 82, 14 (April 10): 68–79.

Layden, Tim. 1995c. You bet your life. *Sports Illustrated* 82, 15 (April 17): 46–55.

Layden, Tim. 2001. Does anyone remember the Titans? *Sports Illustrated* 95, 15 (October 15): 72–83.

Layden, Tim. 2002. The loneliest losers. *Sports Illustrated* 97, 20 (November 18): 69–72.

Layden, Tim. 2005. I am an American. *Sports Illustrated* 103, 17 (October 31): 60–69.

LeBatard, Dan. 2002. ALT.Hoops. *ESPN The Magazine* 5.10 (May, 13): 78–86.

Le Batard, Dan. 2005a. Open look: Pat Riley may be about to stab a good friend in the back. *ESPN The Magazine* 8. 15 (August 1): 14.

Le Batard, Dan. 2005b. Open look: So you're tired of the Barry Bonds act? *ESPN The Magazine* 8.07 (April 11): 18.

Le Batard, Dan. 2005c. Open look: Is it cheating if you don't understand the rules? *Es posible. ESPN The Magazine* 8.10 (May 23): 14.

Le Batard, Dan. 2005d. Open look: The fight that tore the NBA apart? *ESPN The Magazine* (May 9): 14.

Lederman, Douglas. 2003. Major issue: Athletes' studies. *USA Today* (November 19): 1C.

Lefkowitz, Bernard. 1997. *Our guys: The Glen Ridge rape and the secret life of the perfect suburb.* Berkeley: University of California Press.

Lehrman, Sally. 1997. Forget *Men are from Mars, women are from Venus.* Stanford Today Online, www.stanford.edu/dept/news/stanfordtoday/ed/9705/9705fea401.shtml (retrieved December 1, 2005).

Leland, J. 2000. Why America's hooked on wrestling. *Newsweek* 135, 6 (February 7): 46–55.

Lemert, Charles. 1999. The might have been and the could be of religion in social theory. *Sociological Theory* 17, 3: 240–263.

Lenskyj, Helen J. 1986. *Out of bounds: Women, sport and sexuality*. Toronto: Women's Press.

Lenskyj, Helen J. 1998. Sport and corporate environmentalism. *International Review for the Sociology of Sport* 33, 4: 341–354.

Lenskyj, Helen J. 1999. Women, sport, and sexualities: Breaking the silences. In P. White and K. Young, eds., *Sport and gender in Canada* (pp. 170–181). Don Mills, ON: Oxford University Press.

Lenskyj, Helen J. 2000. *Inside the Olympics industry: Power, politics, and activism*. Albany: State University of New York Press.

Lenskyj, Helen J. 2002. *The best Olympics ever? The social impacts of Sydney 2000*. Albany: State University of New York Press.

Lenskyj, Helen. 2003. *Out in the field: gender, sport and sexualities*. Toronto: Women's Press. Online: http://www.womenspress.ca/.

Lenskyj, Helen J. 2004. Making the world safe for global capital: The Sydney 2000 Olympics and beyond. In John Bale and Mette Christensen, eds., *Post-Olympism: Questioning sport in the twenty-first century* (pp. 135–146.). Oxford, England/New York: Berg.

Leonard, David J. 2004. The next M. J. or the next O. J.? Kobe Bryant, race, and the absurdity of colorblind rhetoric. *Journal of Sport and Social Issues* 28, 3: 284–313.

Leonard, Wilbert Marcellus II. 1995. Economic discrimination in major league baseball: Marginal revenue products of majority and minority groups members. *Journal of Sport and Social Issues* 19, 2: 180–190.

Levy, Don. 2005. Fantasy sports and fanship habitus: Understanding the process of sport consumption. Paper presented at the annual conference of the American Sociological Society, Philadelphia (August).

Lewin, Tamar. 2002. Ruling fuels drug-test debate in schools. *Denver Post* (September 29): 12A.

Lewis, Amanda E. 2003. *Race in the schoolyard: Negotiating the color line in classrooms and communities*. New Brunswick, NJ: Rutgers University Press.

Liddle, Eric. 2003. Black is best. www.spectator.co.uk (retrieved June 2005).

Lieber, J. 2003. Playing dirty, playing mean. *USA Today* (January 3): 1C–2C.

Lieblich, Julia, and Richard N. Ostling. 2000. Little prayer of resolving church and state debate. *Rocky Mountain News* (January 16): 2A, 63A–64A.

Light, Richard, and Louise Kinnaird. 2002. Appeasing the Gods: Shinto, sumo and "true" Japanese spirit. In T. Magdalinski and T. J. L. Chandler, eds., *With God on their side: Sport in the service of religion* (pp. 139–159). London/New York: Routledge.

Ligutom-Kimura, Donna Ann. 1995. The invisible women. *Journal of Physical Education, Recreation and Dance* 66, 7: 34–41.

Lipsyte, Robert. 1996a. One fell swoosh: Can a logo conquer all? *New York Times*, section B (February 7): 9.

Lipsyte, Robert. 1996b. Little girls in a staged spectacle for big bucks? That's sportainment! *New York Times* (August 4): 28.

Lipsyte, Robert. 1998. A step in the healing process. *New York Times* (March 5): C22.

Lipsyte, Robert. 1999. The jock culture: Time to debate questions. *New York Times*, section 8 (May 9): 11.

Lipsyte, R. 2001a. In purest form, basketball is a playground game. *New York Times* (October 28): S13.

Lipsyte, Robert. 2001b. Questions line the road as NASCAR steers into a new year. *New York Times* (December 30): S9.

Lipsyte, Robert, 2005. Outraged over the steroids outrage. *New York Times* (March 22): 13A.

Long, Jonathan A., and Mike J. McNamee. 2004. On the moral economy of racism and racist rationalizations in sport. *International Review for the Sociology of Sport* 39, 4: 405–420.

Longman, Jere. 1996. Slow down, speed up. *New York Times* (May 1): B11.

Longman, Jere. 2001. Getting the athletic edge may mean altering genes. *New York Times* (May 11). Online: http://www.nytimes.com/2001/05/11/sports/11GENE.html.

Lopiano, Donna. 1991. Presentation at the Coaching America's Coaches Conference, United States Olympic Training Center, Colorado Springs, CO.

Lovaglia, Michael J., and Jeffrey W. Lucas. 2005. High-visibility athletic programs and the prestige of public universities. *Sport Journal* 8, 1. Online: www.thesportjournal.org/2005Journal/Vol8-No1/michael_lovaglia.asp.

Loveless, Tom. 2002. *The 2002 Brown Center report on American education: How well are American students learning?* Washington, DC: Brookings Institution.

Lowe, Maria R. 1998. *Women of steel: Female bodybuilders and the struggle for self-definition.* New York: New York University Press.

Lowes, Mark Douglas. 1999. *Inside the sports pages: Work routines, professional ideologies, and the manufacture of sport news.* Toronto: University of Toronto Press.

Lucas, Jeffrey W., and Michael J. Lovaglia. 2005. Can academic progress help collegiate football teams win? *Sport Journal* 48. Online: www.thesportjournal.org/2005Journal/Vol8-No3/jeffrey_lucas.asp.

Lupton, Deborah. 2000. The social construction of medicine and the body. In G. Albrecht, R. Fitzpatrick, and S. Scrimshaw, eds., *The handbook of social studies in health and medicine* (pp. 50–63). London: Sage.

Lüschen, Günther. 1967. The interdependence of sport and culture. *International Review of Sport Sociology* 2, 127–141.

Lynch, Andy. 2005. Three track teammates head to Guatemala. Online: www.athletesinaction.org/news.aspx?newsitem=41 (retrieved July 8, 2005).

Lyons, B. 2002. Fallen legends were beset by life's frailties. *Denver Post* (September 29): 4C.

MacNeill, Margaret. 1999. Social marketing, gender, and the science of fitness: A case-study of ParticiPACTION campaigns. In P. White and K. Young, eds., *Sport and gender in Canada* (pp. 215–231). Don Mills, ON: Oxford University Press.

Madison, James K., and Sarita L. Ruma. 2003. Exercise and athletic involvement as moderators of severity in adolescents with eating disorders. *Journal of Applied Sport Psychology* 15, 3: 213–222.

Maguire, Brendan. 2005. American professional wrestling: Evolution, content, and popular appeal. *Sociological Spectrum* 25, 2: 155–176.

Maguire, Joseph. 1988. Race and position assignment in English soccer: A preliminary analysis of ethnicity and sport in Britain. *Sociology of Sport Journal* 5, 3: 257–269.

Maguire, Joseph. 1999. *Global sport: Identities, societies, civilizations.* Cambridge, England: Polity Press.

Maguire, Joseph. 2004. Sport labor migration research revisited. *Journal of Sport and Social Issues* 28, 4: 477–482.

Maguire, Joseph. 2005, ed. *Power and global sport: Zones of prestige, emulation and resistance.* London/New York: Routledge.

Maguire, Joseph, Grant Jarvie, Louise Mansfield, and J. Bradley. 2002. *Sport worlds: A sociological perspective.* Champaign, IL: Human Kinetics.

Maguire, Joseph, and Robert Pearton. 2000a. Global sport and the migration patterns of France 1998 world cup finals players: Some preliminary observations. *Soccer and Society* 1: 175–189.

Maguire, Joseph, and Robert Pearton. 2000b. The impact of elite labour migration on the identification, selection and development of European soccer players. *Journal of Sports Sciences* 18: 759–769.

Maguire, Joseph, and David Stead. 2005. "Cricketers of the Empire": Cash crops, mercenaries and symbols of sporting emancipation? In Joseph Maguire, ed., *Power and global sport: Zones of prestige, emulation and resistance* (pp. 63–86). London/New York: Routledge.

Mahany, Barbara. 1999. Parents drive free time from lives of kids. *Chicago Tribune* (May 27): LIFE1.

Mahiri, Jabari. 1998. *Shooting for excellence: African American youth culture in new century schools.* New York/London: Teachers College Press (Columbia University).

Mahler, Jonathan. 2005. Building the béisbol brand. *New York Times*, section 6. Online: www.nytimes.com/2005/07/31/magazine/31METS.html?oref=login.

Majors, Richard. 1986. Cool pose: The proud signature of black survival. *Changing Men: Issues in Gender, Sex and Politics* 17 (Winter): 184–185.

Majors, Richard. 1998. Cool pose: Black masculinity and sports. In G. Sailes, ed., *African Americans in sport* (pp. 15–22). New Brunswick, NJ: Transaction.

Majors, Richard, and Janet Mancini Billson. 1992. *Cool pose: The dilemmas of black manhood in America.* New York: Simon and Schuster.

Malcomson, Robert. W. 1984. Sports in society: A historical perspective. *British Journal of Sport History* 1, 1: 60–72.

Malloy, D. C., and Dwight H. Zakus. 2002. Ethics of drug testing in sport—an invasion of privacy justified? *Sport, Education and Society* 7, 2 (October): 203–218.

Mandelbaum, Michael. 2004. *The meaning of sports: Why Americans watch baseball, football, and basketball and what they see when they do.* New York: Public Affairs.

Mangan, J. A., ed. 2003. Militarism, sport, Europe: War without weapons. London/New York: Routledge.

Mannon, James M. 1997. *Measuring up: The performance ethic in American culture.* Boulder, CO: Westview Press.

Markula, Pirkku. 1995. Firm but shapely, fit but sexy, strong but thin: The postmodern aerobicizing female bodies. *Sociology of Sport Journal* 12, 4: 424–453.

Marriott, Michel. 2004. Your shot, he said, distantly. *New York Times,* circuits (August 26): 1.

Marriott, Michael. 2005. Cyberbodies: Robo-legs. *New York Times* (June 20): F1.

Mars, John. M. 1996. The right of publicity: Untested marketing rights of college football celebrities. *Journal of Sport and Social Issues* 20, 2: 211–222.

Marsh, Herbert. W. 1993. The effect of participation in sport during the last two years of high school. *Sociology of Sport Journal* 10, 1: 18–43.

Marsh, Herbert W., and Sabina Kleitman. 2002. Extracurricular school activities: The good, the bad, and the nonlinear. *Harvard Educational Review* 72, 4: 464–511

Marsh, Herbert W., and Sabina Kleitman. 2003. School athletic participation: Mostly gain with little pain. *Journal of Sport and Exercise Psychology* 25, 2: 205–228.

Marsh, Peter. 1982. Social order on the British soccer terraces. *International Social Science Journal* 34, 2: 247–256.

Marsh, Peter., and A. Campbell, eds. 1982 *Aggression and violence.* Oxford, England: Basil Blackwell.

Martin, Randy, and Toby. Miller, eds. 1999. *SportCult.* Minneapolis: University of Minnesota Press.

Martinek, Thomas J., and Donald R. Hellison. 1997. Fostering resiliency in underserved youth through physical activity. *Quest* 49, 1: 34–49.

Marty, Martin E., and R. S. Appleby, eds. 1995. *Fundamentalisms comprehended* (vol. 5 of *The fundamentalism project*). Chicago: University of Chicago Press.

Martzke, Rudy, and Reid Cherner, 2004. Channeling how to view sports. *USA Today* (August 17): 1C–2C.

Marvez, Alex. 2002. Steroid abuse grips wrestling, too. *Rocky Mountain News* (July 19): C8.

Marx, Jeffrey. 2004. He turns boys into men. *Parade* (August 29): 4–6.

Mathisen, James. 1992. From civil religion to folk religion: The case of American sport. In S. Hoffman, ed., *Sport and religion* (pp. 17–34). Champaign IL: Human Kinetics.

Matson, Barbara. 2004. A growth sport is stunting female coaches. *Boston Globe* (Dec. 5): www.boston.com/sports/articles/2004/12/05/a_growth_sport_is_stunting_female_coaches/

Mayeda, David Tokiharu. 1999. From model minority to economic threat: Media portrayals of major league baseball pitchers Hideo Nomo and Hideki Irabu. *Journal of Sport and Social Issues* 23, 2: 203–217.

McCallum, Jack. 2002. Citizen Barkley. *Sports Illustrated* 96,11 (March 11): 38.

McCallum, Jack. 2003. Thank God it's Friday. *Sports Illustrated* 99, 12 (September 29): 40–42.

McCarthy, D., R. L. Jones, and P. Potrac. 2003. Constructing images and interpreting realities: The case of the black soccer ptelevision. *International Review for the Sociology of Sport* 38, 2: 217–238.

McCarthy, Michael. 2005. Athletes on the outs in ads: Hip-hop artists outscore jocks in endorsements. *USA Today* (July 5): 1C–2C.

McChesney, Robert W. 1999. The new global media: It's a small world of big conglomerates. *The Nation* 269, 18: 11–15.

McClung, Lisa R., and Elaine M. Blinde. 1998. Negotiation of the gendered ideology of sport: Experiences of women intercollegiate athletes. Paper presented at the annual conference of the North American Society for the Sociology of Sport, Las Vegas (November).

McComb, David G. 2004. *Sports in world history.* London/New York: Routledge.

McCormack, Jane B., and Laurence Chalip. 1988. Sport as socialization: A critique of methodological premises. *Social Science Journal* 25, 1: 83–92.

McCullagh, Ciaran. 2002. *Media power*. New York: Palgrave.

McDonald, Ian. 1999. "Physiological patriots"?: The politics of physical culture and Hindu nationalism in India. *International Review for the Sociology of Sport* 34, 4: 343–358.

McEntegart, Pete, et al. 2002. The top 100 sports books of all time. *Sports Illustrated* 97, 24 (December 16): 128–148.

McGarry, Karen. 2005. Mass media and gender identity in high performance Canadian figure skating. *The Sport Journal* 8, 1. Online: www.thesportjournal.org (retrieved July 14, 2005).

McHale, James P., Penelope G. Vindon, Loren Bush, Derek Richer, David Shaw, and Brienne Smith. 2005. Patterns of personal and social adjustment among sport-involved and noninvolved urban middle-school children. *Sociology of Sport Journal* 22, 2: 119–136.

McKay, Jim. 1997. *Managing gender: Affirmative action and organizational power in Australian, Canadian, and New Zealand sport*. Albany: State University of New York Press.

McKay, Jim. 1999. Gender and organizational power in Canadian sport. In P. White and K. Young, eds., *Sport and gender in Canada* (pp. 197–215). Don Mills, ON: Oxford University Press.

McKay, Jim. 2005. Americans with Disibilities Act: A job not done (yet). *Pittsburgh Post-Gazette* (July 15). Online: www.post-gazette.com/pg/05196/538181.stm (retrieved July 21, 2005).

McKenzie, Bette. 1999. Retiring from the sideline: Building new identities on new terms. In J. Coakley and P. Donnelly, eds., *Inside Sports* (pp. 232–236). London: Routledge.

McNeal, Ralf B., Jr. 1995. Extracurricular activities and high school dropouts. *Sociology of Education* 64, 1: 62–81.

McShane, Larry. 1999. Winner take all (Associated Press). *Colorado Springs Gazette* (July 4): LIFE4.

Mead, C. 1985. *Champion Joe Louis: Black hero in white America*. New York: Scribner.

Mendelsohn, Daniel. 2004. What Olympic ideal? *New York Times Magazine* (August 8). Online: www.nytimes.com/2004/08/08/magazine/WLN1 30551.html.

Merrill, Dave. 2002. Skateboarding grinds out urban revival. *USA Today* (July 30): 6C–7C.

Merron, Jeff. 1999. Running on empty. *SportsJones* 3 (June). Online: www.sportsjones.com/running.htm.

Messner, Michael A. 1991. Women in the men's locker room. *Changing Men: Issues in Gender, Sex and Politics* 23 (Fall/Winter): 56–58.

Messner, Michael A. 1992. *Power at play*. Boston: Beacon Press.

Messner, Michael A. 1996. Studying up on sex. *Sociology of Sport Journal* 13, 3: 221–237.

Messner, Michael A. 2002. *Taking the field: women, men, and sports*. Minneapolis: University of Minnesota Press.

Messner, Michael A., Darnell Hunt, and Michele Dunbar. 1999. *Boys to men: Sports media messages about masculinity*. Oakland, CA: Children Now.

Messner, Michael A., and Mark A. Stevens. 2002. Scoring without consent: Confronting male athletes' violence against women. In M. Gatz, M. A. Messner, and S. J. Ball-Rokeach, eds., *Paradoxes of youth and sport* (pp. 225–240). Albany: State University of New York Press.

Meyer, Barbara B. 1988. The college experience: Female athletes and nonathletes. Paper presented at the North American Society for the Sociology of Sport Conference, Cincinnati.

Meyer, Barbara B. 1990. From idealism to actualization: The academic performance of female collegiate athletes. *Sociology of Sport Journal* 7, 1: 44–57.

Meyer, Jeremy. 2002. Ward's fire within. *Denver Post* (July 14): 1C, 12C.

Miah, Andy. 2004. *Genetically modified athletes: the ethical implications of genetic technologies in sport*. London/New York: Routledge.

Midol, N., and G. Broyer. 1995. Toward an anthropological analysis of new sport cultures: The case of whiz sports in France. *Sociology of Sport Journal* 12, 2: 204–212.

Mihoces, Gary. 2002. Football is king—now more than ever. *USA Today* (August 30): 6A.

Mihoces, Gary. 2005. Injured skaters struggle in world championships. *USA Today* (March 15): 7C. Online: www.usatoday.com/sports/olympics/winter/2005-03-14-skating-worlds_x.htm.

Miller, Kathleen E., Grace M. Barnes, Donald F. Sabo, Merrill J. Melnick, and Michael P. Farrell. 2002. Anabolic-androgenic steroid use and other adolescent problem behaviors: Rethinking the male athlete assumption. *Sociological Perspectives* 45, 4: 467–490

Miller, Kathleen E., Merrill J. Melnick, Grace M. Barnes, Michael P. Farrell, and Don Sabo. 2005. Untangling the links among athletic involvement, gender, race, and adolescent academic outcomes. *Sociology of Sport Journal* 22, 2: 178–193.

Miller, Kathleen E., Don F. Sabo, Michael P. Farrell, Grace M. Barnes, and Merrill J. Melnick. 1998. Athletic participation and sexual behavior in adolescents: The different world of boys and girls. *Journal of Health and Social Behavior* 39, 108–123.

Miller, Kathleen E., Don F. Sabo, Michael P. Farrell, Grace M. Barnes, and Merrill J. Melnick. 1999. Sports, sexual behavior, contraceptive use, and pregnancy among female and male high school students: Testing cultural resource theory. *Sociology of Sport Journal* 16, 4: 366–387.

Miller, Kathleen E., Don F. Sabo, Merrill J. Melnick, Michael P. Farrell, and Grace M. Barnes. 2000. *The Women's Sports Foundation report: Health risks and the teen athlete*. East Meadow, NY: Women's Sports Foundation.

Miller, Patricia S., and Gretchen Kerr. 2003. The role experimentation of intercollegiate student athletes. *The Sport Psychologist* 17, 2: 196–219.

Miller, Patrick B., and David K. Wiggins, eds. 2003. *Sport and the color line: Black athletes and race relations in twentieth-century America*. London/New York: Routledge.

Miller, Toby, Geoffrey Lawrence, Jim McKay, and David Rowe. 2001. *Globalization and sport: Playing the world*. London: Sage.

Miller, Toby, David Rowe, Jim McKay, and Geoffrey Lawrence. 2003. The over-production of U.S. sports and the new international division of cultural labor. *International Review for the Sociology of Sport* 38, 4: 427–440.

Mills, James, and Paul Dimeo. 2003. "When gold is fired it shines": Sport, the imagination and the body in colonial and postcolonial India. In John Bale and Mike Cronin, eds., *Sport and postcolonialism* (pp. 107–122). Oxford, England/New York: Berg.

Miracle, Andrew W., and C. Roger Rees. 1994. *Lessons of the locker room: The myth of school sports*. Amherst, NY: Prometheus Books.

Montville, Leigh. 1999. Shall we dance? *Sports Illustrated* 91, 22 (December 6): 98–109.

Mooney, Chris. 2003. Teen herbicide. *Mother Jones* 28, 3 (May–June): 18–22.

Moore, David Leon. 2002. Parents pay dearly to coach kids for stardom. *USA Today* (July 26): 1A–2A. Online: www.usatoday.com/educate/college/firstyear/casestudies/20040106-coaching.pdf.

Moore, Kathleen. 2004. Olympics 2004: Muslim women athletes move ahead, but don't leave faith behind. Online: www.payvand.com/news/04/aug/1056.html (retrieved July 5, 2005).

Moran, Malcolm. 2002a. Success fails to open college doors for black football coaches. *USA Today* (October 11): 1A–2A.

Moran, Malcolm. 2002b. Numbers speak volumes about blacks as head coaches. *USA Today* (October 11): 6D.

Morris, G. S. D., and James Stiehl. 1989. *Changing kids' games*. Champaign, IL: Human Kinetics.

Morris, Jenny. 1996. Introduction. In J. Morris, ed., *Encounters with strangers: Feminism and disability* (pp. 1–12). London: Women's Free Press.

Moye, Jim, and C. Keith Harrison. 2002. Don't believe the hype: Do the automatic suspensions of student-athletes for alleged misconduct withstand constitutional scrutiny? *Texas Entertainment and Sports Law Journal* 11, 1: 5–15.

Mrozek, Donald J. 1983. Sport and American mentality, 1880–1920. Knoxville: University of Tennessee Press.

Murderball. 2004. A documentary film by Think Film Company, New York (www.thinkfilmcompany.com/).

Murphy, Geraldine. M., Al J. Petipas, and Britton W. Brewer. 1996. Identity foreclosure, athletic identity, and career maturity in intercollegiate athletics. *The Sport Psychologist* 10, 3: 239–246.

Murphy, Patrick, Ken Sheard, and Ivan Waddington. 2000. Figurational/process sociology. In J. Coakley and E. Dunning, eds. *Handbook of sports studies* (pp. 92–105). London: Sage.

Murphy, Patrick, John Williams, and Eric Dunning. 1990. *Football on trial: Spectator violence and development in the world of football*. London: Routledge.

Murphy, Shawn. 1999. *The cheers and the tears: A healthy alternative to the dark side of youth sports today*. San Francisco: Jossey-Bass.

Myers, J. 2000. *Afraid of the dark: What whites and blacks need to know about each other*. Chicago: Lawrence Hill Books.

Nabokov, Peter. 1981. *Indian running: Native American history and tradition*. Santa Fe, NM: Ancient City Press.

Nack, William. 1998. Does God care who wins the Super Bowl? *Sports Illustrated* 88, 3 (January 26): 47–48.

Nack, William, and Lester Munson. 1995. Sports' dirty secret. *Sports Illustrated* 83, 5 (July 31): 62–75.

Nack, William, and Lester Munson. 2000. Out of control. *Sports Illustrated* 93, 4 (July 24): 86–95.

Nack, William, and Don Yaeger. 1999. Every parent's nightmare. *Sports Illustrated* 91, 10 (September 13): 40–53.

Nakamura, Yuka. 2002. Beyond the hijab: Female Muslims and physical activity. *Women's Sport and Physical Activity Journal* 11, 2: 21–48.

Nash, Bruce, and Allan Zullo. 1989. *The baseball hall of shame(2)*. New York: Pocket Books.

Naughton, Jim. 1996. Alcohol abuse by athletes poses big problems for colleges. *Chronicle of Higher Education* 43, 4 (September 20): A47–A48.

Naughton, Jim. 1996d. A book on the economics of college sports says few programs are financially successful. *Chronicle of Higher Education* 43, 7 (October 11): A57–A58.

Nauright, John. 1997. Masculinity, muscular Islam and popular culture: "Colored" rugby's cultural symbolism in working class Cape Town c.1930–70. *International Journal of the History of Sport* 14, 1: 184–190.

Nauright, John, and Tara Magdalinski. 2002. Religion, race and rugby in "coloured" Cape Town. In T. Magdalinski and T. J. L. Chandler, eds., *With God on their side: Sport in the service of religion* (pp. 120–138). London/New York: Routledge.

NBC/USA Network. 2005. Homosexuality and sports. Full-survey results online at http://sportsillustrated.cnn.com/2005/magazine/04/12/survey.expanded/; discussion and partial results in Wertheim (2005) and Smith (2005).

NCAA. 2004. *A career in professional athletics: A guide for making the transition*. Indianapolis: National Collegiate Athletic Association. Online: www2.ncaa.org/media_and_events/ncaa_publications/general_interest/.

NCAA. 2005. 2004 Division I graduation rates report. Online: www.ncaa.org/grad_rates/2004/d1/DI.html.

Neal, Wes. 1981. *The handbook on athletic perfection*. Milford, MI: Mott Media.

Neinas, Chuck. 2003. *2003 AFCA player survey*. American Football Coaches Association. Online: www.afca.com/lev1.cfm/88) (retrieved September 10, 2005).

Nelson, Mariah Burton. 1994. *The stronger women get, the more men love football: Sexism and the American culture of sports*. New York: Harcourt Brace.

Nelson, Mariah Burton. 1998. *Embracing victory: Life lessons in competition and compassion*. New York: Morrow.

Newbery, Liz. 2004. Hegemonic gender identity and outward bound: resistance and re-inscription? *Women in Sport and Physical Activity Journal* 13, 1: 36–49.

Newfield, Jack. 2001. The shame of boxing. *The Nation* 273, 15: 13–22.

Newsweek, 1971. Are sports good for the soul? *Newsweek* 77, 2 (January 11): 51–52.

Newsweek. 2004. Perspectives: Entertainment. *Newsweek* 143, 1 (December 29–January 5): 122.

Neyer, Rob. 2000. A matter of size. *Scientific American* 11, 3: 14–15.

NFSHSA. 2005. *NFHS 2003–04 high school athletics participation survey*. Indianapolis: National Federation of State High School Associations. Online: www.nfhs.org.

NHANES—National Health and Nutrition Examination Survey. 2002. *Prevalence of overweight and obesity among adults: United States, 1999–2000*. Hyattsville, MD: National Center for Health Statistics.

Nichol, Jon P., Patricia Coleman, and B. T. Williams. 1993. *Injuries in sport and exercise: Main report*. London: Sports Council.

Niiya, Brian, ed. 2000. *More than a game: Sport in the Japanese American community*. Los Angeles: Japanese American National Museum.

Nixon, Howard L. II. 1993a. A social network analysis of influences on athletes to play with pain and injuries. *Journal of Sport and Social Issues* 16, 2: 127–135.

Nixon, Howard L. II. 1993b. Accepting the risks and pain of injury in sport: Mediated cultural influences on playing hurt. *Sociology of Sport Journal* 10, 2: 183–196.

Nixon, Howard L. II. 1994a. Coaches' views of risk, pain, and injury in sport, with special reference to gender differences. *Sociology of Sport Journal* 11, 1: 79–87.

Nixon, Howard L. II. 1994b. Social pressure, social support, and help seeking for pain and injuries in college sports networks. *Journal of Sport and Social Issues* 18, 4: 340–355.

Nixon, Howard L. II. 1996a. The relationship of friendship networks, sports experiences, and gender to expressed pain thresholds. *Sociology of Sport Journal* 13, 1: 78–86.

Nixon, Howard. L. II. 1996b. Explaining pain and injury attitudes and experiences in sport in terms of gender, race, and sports status factors. *Journal of Sport and Social Issues* 20, 1: 33–44.

Nixon, Howard L. II. 2000. Sport and disability. In J. Coakley and E. Dunning, eds., *Handbook of sport studies* (pp. 422–438). London: Sage.

Noll, R., and A. Zimbalist, eds. 1997. *Sports, jobs, and taxes*. Washington, DC: Brookings Institution.

Noonan, David. 2003. High on testosterone. *Newsweek* 142, 13 (September 29): 50–51.

Novak, Michael. 1976. *The joy of sports*. New York: Basic Books.

NPR. 1996. Morning edition. *National Public Radio* (August 1), report from Atlanta.

Nylund, David. 2003. Taking a slice at sexism: The controversy over the exclusionary membership practices of the Augusta National Golf Club. *Journal of Sport and Social Issues* 27, 2: 195–202.

Nylund, David. 2004. When in Rome: heterosexism, homophobia, and sports talk radio. *Journal of Sport and Social Issues* 28, 2: 136–168.

O'Brien, Richard. 1992. Lord gym. *Sports Illustrated* 77, 4, (July 27): 46–52.

Oglesby, Carole, and Diana Schrader. 2000. Where is the white in the Rainbow Coalition? In D. Brooks and R. Althouse, eds., *Racism in college athletics: The African-American athlete's experience* (pp. 279–293). Morgantown, WV: Fitness Information Technology.

Okubu, Hideaki. 2004. *Local identity and sport: Historical study of integration and differentiation*. Sankt Augustin, Germany: Academica Verlag.

Oliver, Michael. 1996. *Understanding disability: From theory to practice*. New York: St. Martin's Press.

Omi, Michael, and Howard Winant. 1994. *Racial formation in the United States*. New York/London: Routledge.

Orszag, Jonathan M., and Peter R. Orszag. 2005. *The empirical effects of collegiate athletics: An update*. Indianapolis: National Collegiate Athletic Association.

Osterland, Andrew. 1995. Field of nightmares. *Financial World* (February 14): 105–107.

Otto, Allison Ann. 2003. Scoring with Latinos. *Denver Post* (May 13): 1A.

Overman, Steven J. 1997. *The influence of the Protestant ethic on sport and recreation*. Brookfield, VT: Ashgate.

Oxendine, Joseph B. 1988. *American Indian sports heritage*. Champaign, IL: Human Kinetics.

Ozanian, Michael K. 1995. Following the money. *Financial World* 164, 4 (February 14): 27–31.

Pace, Enzo. 2007. Fundamentalism. In George Ritzer, ed., *Encyclopedia of sociology* (in press). London/New York: Blackwell.

Paraschak, Victoria. 1995. The native sport and recreation program, 1972–1981: Patterns of resistance, patterns of reproduction. *Canadian Journal of History of Sport* (December): 1–18.

Paraschak, Victoria. 1997. Variations in race relations: Sporting events for Native Peoples in Canada. *Sociology of Sport Journal* 14, 1: 1–21.

Paraschak, Victoria. 1999. Doing race, doing gender: First Nations, "sport," and gender relations. In P. White and K. Young, eds., *Sport and gender in Canada* (pp. 153–169). Don Mills, ON: Oxford University Press.

Parkhouse, Bonnie L., and Jean M. Williams 1986. Differential effects of sex and status on elevation of coaching ability. *Research Quarterly for Exercise and Sport* 57, 1: 53–59.

Parrish, Paula. 2002. The height of gaining an edge. *Rocky Mountain News* (September 21): 1B, 12B–13B.

Pastore, Donna L., Sue Inglis, and Karen E. Danylchuk. 1996. Retention factors in coaching and athletic management: Differences by gender, position, and geographic location. *Journal of Sport and Social Issues* 20, 4: 427–441.

Patrick, Dick. 2002. U.S. Anti-Doping Agency willing to administer testing for baseball. *USA Today* (June 14): 6C.

Patrick, Dick. 2005. USOC lobbies for anti-doping agency funds. *USA Today* (May 25): 7C.

Pelak, Cynthia Fabrizio . 2002. Women's collective identity formation in sports: A case study from women's ice hockey. *Gender and Society* 16, 1: 93–114.

Pelak, Cynthia Fabrizio . 2005a. Negotiating gender/race/class constraints in the new South Africa: A case study of women's soccer. *International Review for the Sociology of Sport* 40, 1: 53–70.

Pelak, Cynthia Fabrizio. 2005b. Athletes as agents of change: An examination of shifting race relations within women's netball in post-apartheid South Africa. *Sociology of Sport Journal* 22, 1: 59–77.

Pennington, Bill. 2004. Reading, writing and corporate sponsorships. *New York Times*, section A (October 18): 1.

Pennington, Bill. 2005. Doctors see a big rise in injuries for young athletes. *New York Times*, section A (February 22): 1.

Peretti-Watel, Patrick, Valérie Guagliardo, Pierre Verger, Patrick Mignon, Jacques Pruvost, and Yolande Obadia. 2004a. Attitudes toward doping and recreational drug use among French elite student-athletes. *Sociology of Sport Journal* 21, 1: 1–17.

Peretti-Watel, Patrick, Valérie Guagliardo, Pierre Verger, Jacques Pruvost, Patrick Mignon, and Yolande Obadia. 2004b. Risky behaviours among young elite-student-athletes: results from a pilot survey in South-Eastern France. *International Review for the Sociology of Sport* 39, 2: 233–244.

Perlmutter, David D. 2003. Black athletes and white professors: A twilight zone of uncertainty. *Chronicle of Higher Education* 50, 7. Online: http://chronicle.com/weekly/v50/i07/07b00701.htm.

Perman, Stacy. 1998. The master blasts the board. *Time* (January 19): 61.

Perrottet, Tone. 2004. *The naked Olympics: The true story of the ancient games*. New York: Random House.

Perrucci, Robert, and Earl Wysong. 2003. *The new class society*. Lanham, MD: Rowman and Littlefield.

Petrecca, Laura. 2005. Marketers tackle participants in fantasy football. *USA Today* (August 25): 3B.

Pettavino, P., and P. Brenner. 1999. More than just a game. *Peace Review* 11, 4: 523–530.

Pfister, G. 2001. Doing sport in a headscarf? German sport and Turkish females. *Journal of Sport History* 27: 401–428.

Phillips, M. J. 1988. Disability and ethnicity in conflict: A study in transformation. In M. Fine and A. Asch, eds., Women with disabilities: Essays in psychology, culture, and politics. Philadelphia: Temple University Press.

Pike, Elizabeth C. J. 2004. Risk, pain, and injury: "A natural thing in rowing"? In Kevin Young, ed., *Sporting bodies, damaged selves: Sociological studies of sports-related injury* (pp. 151–162). Amsterdam: Elsevier.

Pike, Elizabeth C. J., and Joseph A. Maguire. 2003.Injury in women's sport: Classifying key elements of "risk encounters." *Sociology of Sport Journal* 20, 3: 232–251.

Pilz, Gunther A. 1996. Social factors influencing sport and violence: On the "problem" of football hooliganism in Germany. *International Review for Sociology of Sport* 31, 1: 49–68.

Pipe, Andrew L. 1993. J. B. Wolffe Memorial Lecture. Sport, science, and society: ethics in sports medicine. *Med Science Sports Exercise* (MG8), 25, 8 (August): 888–900.

Pipe, Andrew. 1998. Reviving ethics in sports. *Physician and Sportsmedicine* 26, 6 (June): 39–40.

Platt, Larry. 2002. *New jack jocks: Rebels, race, and the American athlete*. Philadelphia: Temple University Press.

Plotz, David. 2000. Does God care who wins the Super Bowl? *Denver Post* (February 13): 6G.

Pluto, Terry. 1995. *Falling from grace: Can pro basketball be saved?* New York: Simon and Schuster.

Polsky, S. 1998. Winning medicine: professional sports team doctors' conflicts of interest. *Journal of Contemporary Health Law Policy* (IDD) 14, 2 (Spring): 503–529.

Poppen, Julie. 2004. Pro performance. *Rocky Mountain News* (March 31): 6B.

Porterfield, Kitty. 1999. Late to the line: Starting sport competition as an adult. In J. Coakley and P. Donnelly, eds., *Inside Sports* (pp. 37–45). London: Routledge.

Poulton, Emma. 2004. Mediated patriot games: The construction and representation of national identities in the British television production of Euro '96. *International Review for the Sociology of Sport* 39, 4: 437–455.

Powers-Beck, Jeffrey P. 2004. *The American Indian integration of baseball*. Lincoln: University of Nebraska Press.

Prebish, C. S. 1993. *Religion and sport: The meeting of sacred and profane.* Westport, CT: Greenwood.

President's Council on Physical Fitness and Sports. 1997. *Physical activity and sport in the lives of girls.* Minneapolis: Center for Research on Girls and Women in Sport, University of Minnesota.

Preves, Sharon E. 2005. *Intersex and identity: The contested self.* New Brunswick, NJ: Rutgers University Press.

Price. S. L. 1997. What ever happened to the white athlete? *Sports Illustrated* 87, 23 (December 8): 31–55.

Price, S. L. 2002a. Indian wars: The campaign against Indian nicknames and mascots presumes that they offend Native Americans—but do they? *Sports Illustrated* 96, 10 (March 4): 66–70.

Price, S. L. 2002b. The savior of South Bend. *Sports Illustrated* 97, 13 (September 30): 38–44.

Price, S. L. 2002c. The Ichiro paradox. *Sports Illustrated* 97, 2 (July 8): 50–56.

Price, S. L. 2004. Flag jumper. *Sports Illustrated* 101, 8 (August 30.): 54–56.

Price, S. L. 2005. The sprinter. *Sports Illustrated* 102, 21 (May 23): 52–61.

Pronger, Brian. 1990. *The arena of masculinity: Sports, homosexuality, and the meaning of sex.* New York: St. Martin's Press.

Pronger, Brian. 1999. Fear and trembling: Homophobia in men's sport. In P. White and K. Young, eds., *Sport and gender in Canada* (pp. 182–197). Don Mills, ON: Oxford University Press.

Pronger, Brian. 2002. *Body fascism: salvation in the technology of physical fitness.* Toronto/Buffalo, NY: University of Toronto Press.

Putney, Clifford. 2003. *Muscular Christianity: Manhood and sports in protestant America. 1880–1920.* Cambridge, MA: Harvard University Press.

Q and A. 2003. Alana Beard. *Sports Illustrated* 99, 21 (December 1): 28.

Raboin, Sharon. 1999. Bela is back on U.S. team. *USA Today* (November 16): 1A–2A.

Rail, Geneviève. 1998. *Sport and postmodern times.* Albany: State University of New York Press.

Ramsey, David. 2005. Why? *Colorado Springs Gazette* (December 11). Online: www.gazette.com/display.php?id=1312798&secid=3.

Randels Jr., George D., and Becky Beal. 2002. What makes a man?: Religion, sport, and negotiating masculine identity in the Promise Keepers. In T. Magdalinski and T. J. L. Chandler, eds., *With God on their side: Sport in the service of religion* (pp. 160–176). London/New York: Routledge.

Real, Michael. R. 1996. The postmodern Olympics: Technology and the commodification of the Olympic movement. *Quest* 48, 1: 9–24.

Real Michael. R. 1998. MediaSport: Technology and the commodification of postmodern sport. In L. A. Wenner, ed., *MediaSport* (pp. 14–26). London/New York: Routledge.

Rees, C. Roger, and Andrew W. Miracle. 2000. Sport and education. In J. Coakley and E. Dunning, eds., *Handbook of sports studies* (pp. 291–308). London: Sage.

Reid, E. 1997. My body, my weapon, my shame. *Gentlemen's Quarterly* (September), 361–367.

Reid, S. M. 1996. The selling of the Games. *Denver Post* (July 21) 4BB.

Reilly, Rick. 2004. The silent treatment. *Sports Illustrated* 101, 20 (November 22): 144.

Reilly, Rick. 2005. Half the size, twice the man. *Sports Illustrated* 103, 13 (October 3): 90.

Rice, Ron (with David Fleming). 2005. Moment of impact. *ESPN The Magazine* 8.11 (June 6): 82–83.

Richtel, Matt. 2005. A new reality in video games: Advertisements. *New York Times* (April 11): C1.

Riesman, David, and Reuel Denny. 1951. Football in America: A study of cultural diffusion. *American Quarterly* (Winter): 302–325.

Rigauer, Bero. 2000. Marxist theories. In J. Coakley and E. Dunning, eds., *Handbook of sports studies* (pp. 28–47). London: Sage.

Rimer, Edward. 1996. Discrimination in Major League Baseball: Hiring standards for Major League managers, 1975–1994. *Journal of Sport and Social Issues* 20, 2: 118–133.

Rinehart, Robert E. 1998. *Players all: Performances in contemporary sport.* Bloomington: Indiana University Press.

Rinehart, Robert E. 2000. Arriving sport: Alternatives to formal sports. In J. Coakley and E. Dunning, eds., *Handbook of Sports Studies* (pp. 504–519). London: Sage.

Rinehart, Robert. 2005. "Babes" and boards. *Journal of Sport and Social Issues* 29, 3: 232–255.

Rinehart, Robert, and Chris Grenfell, 1999. Icy relations: Parental involvement in youth figure skating. Paper presented at the annual conference of the North American Society for the Sociology of Sport, Cleveland (November).

Rinehart, Robert, and Chris Grenfell. 2002. BMX spaces: Children's grass roots' courses and corporate-sponsored tracks. *Sociology of Sport Journal* 19, 3: 302–314.

Rinehart, Robert E., and Synthia Syndor, eds. 2003. *To the extreme: Alternative sports inside and out.* Albany: State University of New York Press.

Rintala, Jan, and Judith Bischoff. 1997. Persistent resistance: Leadership positions for women in Olympic sport governing bodies. *OLYMPIKA: The International Journal of Olympic Studies* 6, 1–24.

Riordan, James. 1993. Soviet-style sport in Eastern Europe: The end of an era. In L. Allison, ed., *The changing politics of sport* (pp. 37–57). Manchester, England: Manchester University Press.

Riordan, James. 1996. Introduction. In Arnd Krüger and James Riordan, eds., *The story of worker sport* (pp. vii–x). Champaign, IL: Human Kinetics.

Risman, Barbara, and Pepper Schwartz. 2002. After the sexual revolution: Gender politics in teen dating. *Contexts* 1, 1: 16–24.

Ritzer, George. 2005. *Enchanting a disenchanted world: Revolutionizing the means of consumption.* Thousand Oaks, CA: Pine Forge Press.

Robbins, R. 1996. Josh Davis: Overcoming the trials. *Sports Spectrum* (June): 20–21.

Roberts, John J. 2004. Ready to rumble. *Coloradoan* (November 9): D3.

Roberts, Selena. 2004. Augusta can't shield corporate executives from Burk. *New York Times* (April 8): D1.

Roberts, Selena. 2005. Big boosters calling the shots on campus. *The New York Times*, section 8 (January 2): 1

Robinson, Laura. 1998. *Crossing the line: Violence and sexual assault in Canada's national sport.* Toronto: McClelland and Stewart.

Rosentraub, M. 1997. *Major League losers: The real cost of sports and who's paying for them.* New York: Basic Books.

Roth, Amanda, and Susan A. Basow. 2004. Femininity, sports, and feminism: Developing a theory of physical liberation. *Journal of Sport and Social Issues* 28, 3: 245–265.

Roversi, Antonio. 1994. The birth of the "ultras": The rise of football hooliganism in Italy. In R. Giulianotti and J. Williams, eds., *Game without frontiers: Football, identity and modernity* (pp. 359–381). Aldershot, England: Arena, Ashgate.

Rowe, David. 2004a. *Sport, culture and the media: the unruly trinity* (2nd ed.). Maidenhead, Berkshire: Open University Press.

Rowe, David, ed. 2004b. *Sport, culture and the media: Critical readings.* Maidenhead, Berkshire: Open University Press.

Rowe, David, Jim McKay, and Toby Miller. 1998. Come together: Sport, nationalism, and the media image. In L. A. Wenner, ed., *MediaSport* (pp. 119–133). London/New York: Routledge.

Ruck, Rob. 1987. *Sandlot seasons: Sport in black Pittsburgh.* Urbana: University of Illinois Press.

Russo, R. D. 1999. Root, root, root for the home team. *Denver Post* (June 14): D1, D7.

Ryan, Joan. 1995. *Little girls in pretty boxes: The making and breaking of elite gymnasts and figure skaters.* New York: Doubleday.

Sabo, Don., Sue Curry Jansen, Danny Tate, Margaret Carlisle Duncan, and Susan Leggett. 1996. Televising international sport: Race, ethnicity, and nationalistic bias. *Journal of Sport and Social Issues* 20, 1: 7–21.

Sabo, Don, Kathleen Miller, Michael Farrell, Grace Barnes, and Merrill Melnick. 1998. *The Women's Sports Foundation report: Sport and teen pregnancy.* East Meadows, NY: Women's Sport Foundation.

Sabo, Don, Kathleen E. Miller, Merrill J. Melnick, Michael P. Farrell, and Grace M. Barnes. 2005. High school athletic participation and adolescent suicide: A nationwide study. *International Review for the Sociology of Sport* 40, 1: 5–23.

Sabo, Don, Kathleen E. Miller, Merrill J. Melnick, and Leslie Heywood. 2004. *Her life depends on it: Sport, physical activity, and the health and well-being of American girls.* East Meadow, NY: Women's Sport Foundation.

Sachs, Carolyn J., and Lawrence D. Chu. 2000. The association between professional football games and domestic violence in Los Angeles County. *Journal of Interpersonal Violence* 15: 1192–1201.

Sack, Allen L., and Ellen J. Staurowsky. 1998. *College athletes for hire: The evolution and legacy of the NCAA's amateur myth.* Westport, CT: Praeger.

Sadowski, Rick. 2005. Moore strikes back. *Rocky Mountain News* (February 18): 1C, 7C.

Safai, Parissa. 2003. Healing the body in the "culture of risk": Examining the negotiation of treatment between sport medicine clinicians and injured athletes in Canadian intercollegiate sport. *Sociology of Sport Journal* 20, 2: 127–146.

Sage, George H. 1996. Patriotic images and capitalist profit: Contradictions of professional team sports licensed merchandise. *Sociology of Sport Journal* 13, 1: 1–11.

Sage, George H. 1998. *Power and ideology in American sport: A critical perspective*. Champaign, IL: Human Kinetics.

Sage, George H. 1999. Justice do it! The Nike transnational advocacy network: Organization, collective actions, and outcomes. *Sociology of Sport Journal* 16, 3: 206–235.

Sage, George H. 2000. Political economy and sport. In J. Coakley and E. Dunning, eds., *Handbook of sports studies* (pp. 260–276). London: Sage.

Sailer, Steve. 2003. Commentary: A unique aspect of Arnold. *United Press International Release* (August 15). Online: www.upi.com/view.cfm?StoryID=20030811-101222-8174r (retrieved June 2005).

Sailes, Gary. 1998. The African American athlete: Social myths and stereotypes. In G. Sailes, ed., *African Americans in sport* (pp. 183–198). New Brunswick, NJ: Transaction.

Sam, Michael P. 2003. What's the big idea? Reading the rhetoric of a national sport policy process. *Sociology of Sport Journal* 20, 3: 189–213.

SAMHSA (Substance Abuse and Mental Health Administration). 2002. *The 2000 national household survey on drug abuse: Team sports participation and substance use among youths*. Rockville, MD: SAMHSA. Online: http://www.DrugAbuse Statistics.samhsa.gov.

Sammond, Nicholas, ed. 2005. *Steel chair to the head: The pleasure and pain of professional wrestling*. Durham, NC: Duke University Press.

Sanchez, Robert. 2003. Holding back boosters. *Rocky Mountain News* (November 10): 20A–21A.

Sandomir, Richard. 2002. Athletes may next seek genetic enhancement. *New York Times* (March 21). Online: http://nytimes.com/2002/03/21/sports/othersports/21DRUG.html.

Sapolsky, Robert M. 2000. It's not all in the genes. *Newsweek* 135, 15 (April 10): 68.

Saporito, Bill. 2004. Why fans and players are playing so rough. *Time* 164, 23 (December 6): 30–34.

Saraceno, Jon. 2005. Native Americans aren't fair game for nicknames. *USA Today* (June 1): 10C.

Sato, Daisuke, 2005. Sport and identity in Tunisia. *International Journal of Sport and Health Science* 3: 27–34. Online: www.shobix.co.jp/ijshs/tempfiles/journal/3/20040072.pdf.

Saunders, Patrick. 2001. Nasty boys. *Denver Post* (January 28): 1I–2I.

Savage, Howard J., ed. 1929. *American college athletics*. Bulletin no. 23. New York: Carnegie Foundation.

Savage, Jeff. 1997. *A sure thing? Sports and gambling*. Minneapolis: Lerner Publications.

Schaller, Bob. 2005. Toni Davis. Online: www.blackathletesportsnetwork.net/artman/publish/article_0510.shtml (retrieved December 3, 2005).

Scheerder, Jeroen, Bart Vanreusel, Marijke Taks, and Roland Renson. 2002. Social sports stratification in Flanders, 1969–1999: Intergenerational reproduction of social inequalities? *International Review for the Sociology of Sport* 37, 2: 219–246.

Schefter, Adam. 2003. Working through the pain. *Denver Post* (December 7): 1J, 6J.

Scheinin, Richard. 1994. *Field of screams: The dark underside of America's national pastime*. New York: Norton.

Schell, "Beez" Lea Ann, and Stephanie Rodriguez. 2001. Subverting bodies/ambivalent representations: Media analysis of Paralympian, Hope Lewellen. *Sociology of Sport Journal* 18, 1: 127–135.

Schilling, Mary Lou. 1997. Socialization, retirement, and sports. Online essay and links: http://edweb6.educ.msu.edu/kin866/resschilling1.htm (retrieved June 2005).

Schimmel, Kimberly. S. 2000. Take me out to the ball game: The transformation of production-consumption relations in professional team sport. In C. L. Harrington and D. D. Bielby, eds., *Cultural production and consumption: Readings in popular culture* (pp. 36–52). Oxford, England: Blackwell.

Schimmel, Kimberly. S. 2002. The political economy of place: Urban and sport studies perspectives. In

J. Maguire and K. Young, eds., *Theory, sport and society* (pp. 335–353). Oxford, England: JAI (Elsevier Science).

Schimmel, Kimberly, Alan G. Ingham, and Jeremy W. Howell. 1993. Professional team sport and the American city: Urban politics and franchise relocations. In A. G. Ingham and J. W. Loy, eds., *Sport in social development* (pp. 211–244). Champaign, IL: Human Kinetics.

Schroeder, Janice Jones. 1995. Developing self-esteem and leadership skills in Native American women: The role sports and games play. *Journal of Physical Education, Recreation and Dance* 66, 7: 48–51.

Schultz, B. 1999. The disappearance of child-directed activities. *Journal of Physical Education, Recreation and Dance* 70, 5: 9–10.

Schultz, Jaime. 2004. Discipline and push-up: Female bodies, femininity, and sexuality in popular representations of sports bras. *Sociology of Sport Journal* 21, 2: 185–205.

Seattle Times. 2003. *Coaches who prey: The abuse of girls and the system that allows it* (multiarticle series). Online: http://seattletimes.nwsource.com/news/local/coaches/ (retrieved June 2005).

Seeley, Morgan, and Genevieve Rail. 2004. Youth with disabilities: Rethinking discourses of the "healthy" body. Paper presented at the annual meeting of the North American Society for the Sociology of Sport, Tucson, Arizona (November).

Sellers, Robert, and S. Keiper. 1998. Opportunity given or lost? Academic support services for NCAA Division I student-athletes. Paper presented at the annual conference of the North American Society for the Sociology of Sport, Las Vegas (November).

Seltzer, R., and W. Glass. 1991. International politics and judging in Olympic skating events: 1968–1988. *Journal of Sport Behavior* 14, 3: 189–200.

Sernau, Scott. 2005. *Worlds apart: Social inequalities in a global economy.* Thousand Oaks, CA: Pine Forge Press.

Sewart, James. 1987. The commodification of sport. *International Review for the Sociology of Sport* 22, 3: 171–192.

Shaffer, Marvin, Alan Greer, and Celine Mauboules. 2003. *Olympic costs and benefits: a cost-benefit analysis of the proposed Vancouver 2010 Winter Olympic and Paralympic Games.* Vancouver: Canadian Centre for Policy Alternatives; see also the report online: www.policyalternatives.ca/bc/olympics/olympics_summary.html.

Shakib, Sohaila. 2003. Female basketball participation: Negotiating the conflation of peer status and gender status from childhood through puberty. *American Behavioral Scientist* 46, 10: 1404–1422.

Shakib, Sohaila, and Michele D. Dunbar. 2002. The social construction of female and male high school basketball participation: Reproducing the gender order through a two-tiered sporting institution. *Sociological Perspectives* 45, 4: 353–378.

Shapin, Steven. 2005. Cleanup hitters: The steroid wars and the nature of what's natural. *New Yorker* (April, 18): 191–194.

Shaw, Mark. 2002. Board with sports. Paper written in Introductory Sociology, University of Colorado, Colorado Springs, spring semester.

Sheil, Pat. 2000. Shed a tear or two . . . or else! Online: www.abc.net.au/paralympics/features/s201108.htm.

Shields, David L. L., and Brenda J. L. Bredemeier. 1995. *Character development and physical activity.* Champaign, IL: Human Kinetics.

Shields, David L. L., Brenda J. L. Bredemeier, D. E. Gardner, and A. Bostrom. 1995. Leadership, cohesion, and team norms regarding cheating and aggression. *Sociology of Sport Journal* 12, 3: 324–336.

Shilling, Chris, 1994. *The body and social theory.* Thousand Oaks, CA: Sage.

Shilling, Chris. 2005. The rise of the body and the development of sociology. *Sociology* 39, 4: 761–768.

Shipnuck, Alan. 2005. Meanwhile: Michelle! *Sports Illustrated* 103, 3 (July 25): 46.

Shogan, Debra, and Maureen Ford. 2000. A new sport ethics. *International Review for the Sociology of Sport* 35, 1: 49–58.

Shropshire, Kenneth L. 1996. *In black and white: Race and sports in America.* New York: New York University Press.

Shulman, James L., and William G. Bowen. 2001. *The game of life: College sports and educational values.* Princeton, NJ: Princeton University Press.

Siklos, Richard. 2005. News Corp. to acquire owner of MySpace.com. *New York Times* (July 18). Online: http://www.nytimes.com/2005/07/18/business/18cnd-newscorp.html?.

Silk, Michael L. 1999. Local/global flows and altered production practices. *International Review for the Sociology of Sport* 34, 2: 113–123.

Silk, Michael L. 2004. A tale of two cities: The social production of sterile sporting space. *Journal of Sport and Social Issues* 28, 4: 349–378.

Simons, Herbert D. 2003. Race and penalized sports behaviors. *International Review for the Sociology of Sport* 38, 1: 5–22.

Simpson, Kevin, 1996. Sporting dreams die on the "rez." In D. S. Eitzen, ed., *Sport in contemporary society* (pp. 287–294). New York: St. Martin's Press.

Simson, Viv, and Andrew Jennings. 1992. *The lords of the rings: Power, money and drugs in the modern Olympics.* London: Simon and Schuster.

Singh, Parbudyal, Allen Sack, and Ronald Dick. 2003. Free agency and pay discrimination in Major League Baseball. *Sociology of Sport Journal* 20, 3: 275–286.

Smale, David. 2005. Running with new purpose. *Sharing the Victory.* Online: www.fca.org/vsItemDisplay.lsp&objectID=5D502C9E-2307-4FE5-8D917053FFACB575 &method=display (retrieved July 10, 2005).

Smedley, Audrey. 1997. Origin of the idea of race. *Anthropology Newsletter* (November). Online: www.pbs.org/race/000_About/002_04-background-02-09.htm (retrieved October 15, 2005).

Smedley, Audrey. 1999. Review of Theodore Allen, *The Invention of the White Race, vol. 2. Journal of World History* 10, 1 (Spring): 234–237.

Smedley, Audrey. 2003. PBS interview for the series, *Race—the power of an illusion.* Online: www.pbs.org/race/000_About/002_04-background-02-06.htm (retrieved June, 2005).

Smith, Amanda. 1999. Back-page bylines: Newspapers, women, and sport. In R. Martin and T. Miller, eds., *SportCult* (pp. 253–261). Minneapolis: University of Minnesota Press.

Smith, Andrew, and Nigel Thomas. 2005. The inclusion of elite athletes with disabilities in the 2002 Manchester Commonwealth Games: An exploratory analysis of British newspaper coverage. *Sports, Education and Society* 10, 1: 49–67.

Smith, Brett, and Andrew Sparkes. 2002. Men, sport spinal cord injury and the construction of coherence: Narrative practice in action. *Qualitative Research* 2, 2: 143–171.

Smith, C. 1997. God is an .800 hitter. *New York Times Magazine* (July 27): 26–29.

Smith, Gary. 2005a. What do we do now? *Sports Illustrated* 102, 13 (March 28): 40–50.

Smith, Gary. 2005b. The shadow boxer. *Sports Illustrated* 102, 16 (April 18): 58–68. Online: http://sportsillustrated.cnn.com/2005/magazine/04/12/griffith0418/ (retrieved July 2005).

Smith, Jason M., and Alan G. Ingham. 2003. On the waterfront: Retrospectives on the relationship between sport and communities. *Sociology of Sport Journal* 20, 3: 252–274.

Smith, Michael. 1983. *Violence and sport.* Toronto: Butterworths.

Smith, Ronald. E. 1986. Toward a cognitive-affective model of athletic burnout. *Journal of Sport Psychology* 8, 1: 36–50.

Smith, Yvonne. 2000. Sociohistorical influences on African American elite sportswomen. In D. Brooks and R. Althouse, eds., *Racism in college athletics: The African American athlete's experience* (pp. 173–198). Morgantown, WV: Fitness Information Technology.

Snyder, Eldon. E. 1994. Interpretations and explanations of deviance among college athletes: A case study. *Sociology of Sport Journal* 11, 3: 231–248.

Sokolove, Michael. 2002. Football is a sucker's game. *New York Times Magazine,* section 6 (December 22): 36–41, 64, 68–70.

Sokolove, Michael. 2004a. The thoroughly designed American childhood: Constructing a teen phenom. *New York Times,* section 6 (November 28): 80.

Sokolove, Michael. 2004b. In pursuit of doped excellence. *New York Times Magazine,* section 6 (January 18): 28–33, 48, 54, 58.

Sokolove, Michael. 2004c. Built to swim. *New York Times Magazine,* section 6 (August 8): 20–5.

Solomon, Alisa. 2000. Our bodies, ourselves: The mainstream embraces the athlete Amazon. *The Village Voice* (April 19–25). Online: www.villagevoice.com/issues/0016/solomon2.shtml (retrieved October 15, 2005).

Solomon, Norman. 2000. What happened to the "information superhighway"? *Z Magazine* 13, 2: 10–13.

Sparkes, Andrew, and Brett Smith. 2002. Sport, spinal cord injury, embodied masculinities, and the dilemmas of narrative identity. *Men and Masculinities* 4, 3: 258–285.

Sperber, Murray. 2000. *Beer and circus: How big-time college sports is crippling undergraduate education.* New York: Holt.

Spirou, Costas, and Larry Bennett. 2003. *It's hardly sporting: Stadiums, neighborhoods, and the new Chicago.* DeKalb: Northern Illinois University Press.

Spreitzer, Elmer A. 1995. Does participation in interscholastic athletics affect adult development: A longitudinal analysis of an 18–24 age cohort. *Youth and Society* 25, 3: 368–387.

Starr, M. 1999. Voices of the century: Blood, sweat, and cheers. *Newsweek* 134, 17 (October 25): 44–73.

Starr, M., and A. Samuels. 2000. A season of shame. *Newsweek* 135, 22 (May 29): 56–60.

Stead, David, and Joseph. Maguire. 2000. "Rite of passage" or passage to riches?: The motivation and objectives of Nordic/Scandanavian players in English Soccer League. *Journal of Sport and Social Issues* 24, 1: 36–60.

Stevenson, Christopher. 1991a. The Christian-athlete: An interactionist-developmental analysis. *Sociology of Sport Journal* 8, 4: 362–379.

Stevenson, Christopher. 1991b. Christianity as a hegemonic and counter-hegemonic device in elite sport. Paper presented at Conference of the North American Society for the Sociology of Sport, Milwaukee (November).

Stevenson, Christopher. 1997. Christian-athletes and the culture of elite sport: Dilemmas and solutions. *Sociology of Sport Journal* 14, 3: 241–262.

Stevenson, Christopher. 1999. Becoming an elite international athlete: Making decisions about identity. In J. Coakley and P. Donnelly, eds., *Inside Sports* (pp. 86–95). London: Routledge.

Stevenson, Christopher L. 2002. Seeking identities: Towards an understanding of the athletic careers of masters swimmers. *International Review for the Sociology of Sport* 37, 2: 131–146.

Stinson, Jeffrey L., and Dennis R. Howard. 2004. Scoreboards and mortarboards: Major donor behavior and intercollegiate athletics. *Sport Marketing Quarterly* 13, 3: 129–140.

Stoelting, Suzanne Marie. 2004. She's in control, she's free, she's an athlete: A qualitative analysis of sport empowerment and the lives of female athletes. Paper presented at the annual conference of the American Sociological Society, San Francisco (August).

Stokes, M. 1996. "Strong as a Turk": Power, performance and representation in Turkish wrestling. In J. MacClancy, ed., *Sport, identity and ethnicity* (pp. 21–42). Oxford, England: Berg.

Stoll, Sharon K., and Jennifer. M. Beller. 1998. Can character be measured? *Journal of Physical Education, Recreation, and Dance* 69, 1: 18–24.

Stoll, Sharon K., and Jennifer. M. Beller. 2000. Do sports build character? In J. R. Gerdy, ed., *Sports in school: The future of an institution* (pp. 18–30). New York: Teachers College Press (Columbia University).

Stone, Jeff, Christian I. Lynch, Mike Sjomeling, and John M. Darley. 1999. Stereotype threat effects on black and white athletic performance. *Journal of Personality and Social Psychology* 77, 6: 1213–227.

Stone, Jeff, Zachary W. Perry, and John M. Darley. 1997. "White men can't jump": Evidence for the perceptual confirmation of racial stereotypes following a basketball game. *Basic and Applied Social Psychology* 19, 3: 291–306.

Stratta, Theresa. 1995. Cultural inclusiveness in sport—Recommendations from African-American women college athletes. *Journal of Physical Education, Recreation and Dance* 66, 7: 52–56.

Stratta, Theresa. 1998. Barriers facing African-American women in college sports: A case study approach. *Melpomene*, 17, 1: 19–26.

Strug, Kerri. 1999. Life in Romania, Texas. *Newsweek* 134, 17 (October 25): 73.

Sugden, J., and A. Tomlinson. 1998. *FIFA and the contest for world football: Who rules the peoples' game?* Cambridge, England: Polity Press.

Sugden, J., and A. Tomlinson. 1999. *Great balls of fire: How big money is highjacking world football.* Edinburgh, Scotland: Mainstream.

Sugden, J., and A. Tomlinson. 2000.Theorizing sport, social class and status. In J. Coakley and E. Dunning, eds., *Handbook of sport studies* (pp. 309–321). London: Sage.

Suggs, Welch. 2001. Left behind. *Chronicle of Higher Education* 48, 14 (November 30): A35–A37.

Suggs, Welch. 2005. *A place on the team: The triumph and tragedy of Title IX*. Princeton, NJ: Princeton University Press.

Sundgot-Borgen, J. 2001. Eating disorders. In K. Christensen, A. Guttmann, and G. Pfister, eds., *International encyclopedia of women and sports* (pp. 352–358). New York: Macmillan Reference.

Svinth, Joseph R. 2004. Death under the spotlight: The Manuel Velazquez boxing fatality collection. *Journal of Combative Sport* (February). Online: http://epe.lac-bac.gc.ca/100/201/300/ ejmas/jcs/2004/04-01/ejmas.com/jcs/ jcsart_svinth_a_0700.htm.

Swain, Derek. 1999. Moving on: Leaving pro sports. In J. Coakley and P. Donnelly, eds., *Inside sports* (pp. 223–231). London: Routledge.

Sweeney, Emily. 2005. Cost of prosthetics stirs debate. *Boston Globe* (July 5): 2. Online: www.boston.com/business/globe/articles/2005/07/ 05/cost_of_prosthetics_stirs_debate/?page=2 (retrieved July 21, 2005).

Sweeney, H. Lee. 2004. Gene doping. *Scientific American* 291, 1 (July): 69.

Swift, E. M., and D. Yaeger. 2001. Unnatural selection. *Sports Illustrated* 94, 20 (May 14): 87–93.

Swoopes, Sheryl. 2005 Outside the arc (as told to L. Z. Granderson). *ESPN The Magazine* 8.22 (November 7): 120–125.

Sylwester, MaryJo. 2005a. Hispanic girls in sports held back by tradition. *USA Today* (March 29): 1A–2A.

Sylwester, MaryJo. 2005b. Sky's the limit for Hispanic teen. *USA Today* (March 29): 4C.

Sylwester, MaryJo. 2005c. Girls following in Ochoa's, Fernandez's sports cleats. *USA Today* (March 29): 4C.

Sylwester, MaryJo, and Tom Witosky, 2004. Athletic spending grows as academic funds dry up. *USA Today* (February 18). Online: www.usatoday.com/ sports/college/2004-02-18-athletic-spending-cover_x.htm (retrieved October 15, 2005).

Taheri, Amir. 2004. Muslim women play only an incidental part in the Olympics. Online www. benadorassociates.com/article/6651 (retrieved July 5, 2005).

Taub, Diane E., Elaine Blinde, and Kimberly R. Greer. 1999. Stigma management through participation in sport and physical activity: Experiences of male college students with physical disabilities. *Human Relations* 52, 11: 146–149.

Taub, Diane E., and Kimberly R. Greer. 2000. Physical activity as a normalizing experience for school-age children with physical disabilities: Implications for legitimating of social identity and enhancement of social ties. *Journal of Sport and Social Issues* 24, 4: 395–414.

Taylor, Ian. 1982a. On the sports violence question: soccer hooliganism revisited. In Jennifer Hargreaves, ed., *Sport, culture and ideology* (pp. 152–196). London: Routledge and Kegan Paul.

Taylor, Ian. 1982b. Class, violence and sport: The case of soccer hooliganism in Britain. In H. Cantelon and R. Gruneau, eds., *Sport, culture and the modern state* (pp. 39–97). Toronto: University of Toronto Press.

Taylor, Ian. 1987. Putting the boot into a working-class sport: British soccer after Bradford and Brussels. *Sociology of Sport Journal* 4, 2: 171–191.

Temple, Kerry. 1992. Brought to you by . . . *Notre Dame Magazine* 21, 2: 29.

Theberge, Nancy. 1999. Being physical: Sources of pleasure and satisfaction in women's ice hockey. In J. Coakley and P. Donnelly, eds., *Inside Sports* (pp. 146–155). London: Routledge.

Theberge, Nancy. 2000a. Gender and sport. In J. Coakley and E. Dunning, eds., *Handbook of sport studies* (pp. 322–333). London: Sage.

Theberge, Nancy. 2000b. *Higher goals: Women's ice hockey and the politics of gender*. Albany: State University of New York Press.

Thomas, Carol. 1999. Narrative identity and the disabled self. In M. Corker and S. French, eds. *Disability Discourse* (pp. 47–56). Milton Keynes, England: Open University Press.

Thomas, R. 1996. Black faces still rare in the press box. In R. Lapchick, ed., *Sport in society: Equal opportunity or business as usual?* (pp. 212–233). Thousand Oaks, CA: Sage.

Thompson, Carmen Renee. 2004. The hook-up: McKay and Shinoda. *ESPN The Magazine* 7, 26 (December 20): 40.

Thompson, R., and R. T. Sherman. 1999. Athletes, athletic performance, and eating disorders: Healthier alternatives. *Journal of Social Issues* 55, 2: 317–337.

Thompson, Shona. 1999a. *Mother's taxi: Sport and women's labor*. Albany: State University of New York Press.

Thompson, Shona. 1999b. The game begins at home: Women's labor in the service of sport. In

J. Coakley and P. Donnelly, eds., *Inside Sports* (pp. 111–120). London: Routledge.

Thomsen, Steven R., Danny W. Bower, and Michael D. Barnes. 2004. Photographic images in women's health, fitness, and sports magazines and the physical self-concept of a group of adolescent female volleyball players. *Journal of Sport and Social Issues* 28, 3: 266–283.

Thomson, Rosemarie Garland. 2000. Staring back: Self-representations of disabled performance artists. *American Quarterly* 52, 2 (June): 334–338.

Thomson, Rosemarie Garland. 2002. Integrating disability, transforming feminist theory. *National Women's Studies Association Journal* 14, 3: 1–32.

Time. 1997. *Time's* 25 most influential Americans. *Time* 149, 16: 40–62.

Todd, Terry. 1987. Anabolic steroids: The gremlins of sport. *Journal of Sport History* 14, 1: 87–107.

Tomlinson, Alan. 2007. Sport and social class. In George Ritzer, ed., *Encyclopedia of sociology* (in press). London/New York: Blackwell.

Tomlinson, Alan, and Christopher Young, eds. 2005. *National identity and global sports events: Culture, politics, and spectacle in the Olympics and the football world cup.* Albany: State University of New York Press.

Torbert, Marianne. 1980. *Follow me: A handbook of movement activities for children.* St. Paul, MN: Redleaf Press.

Torbert, Marianne. 2004. A games model for facilitating a constructivist approach. In R. L. Clements and L. Fiorentino, eds., *The child's right to play: A global approach* (pp. 133–135). Westport, CT/London: Praeger.

Torbert, Marianne. 2005. *Follow me: A handbook of movement activities for children.* Eagan, MN: P.L.A.Y. (also Temple University: Leonard Gordon Institute for Human Development Through Play.)

Tracy, Allison J., and Sumru Erkut. 2002. Gender and race patterns in the pathways from sports participation to self-esteem. *Sociological Perspectives* 45, 4: 445–467.

Tracey, Jill, and T. Elcombe. 2004. A lifetime of healthy meaningful movement: Have we forgotten the athletes? *Quest* 56, 2: 241–260.

Trivett, Steve. 1999. Rampart goes back to smash-mouth in win over Mitchell. *Rocky Mountain News* (October 31): 30C.

Troutman, Parke. 2004. A growth machine's plan B: Legitimating development when the value-free growth ideology is under fire. *Journal of Urban Affairs* 26, 5: 611–622.

Trulson, Michael E. 1986. Martial arts training: A novel "cure" for juvenile delinquency. *Human Relations* 39, 12: 1131–1140.

Tuaolo, Esera. 2002. Free and clear. *ESPN The Magazine* 5.23 (November 11): 72–77.

Turner, Bryan S. 1997. *The body and society.* London: Sage.

Upton, Jodi. 2005. Violence at games means trouble for all. *USA Today* (November 23): 11C.

Urquhart, Jim, and Jane Crossman. 1999. The *Globe and Mail* coverage of the Winter Olympic Games: A cold place for women athletes. *Journal of Sport and Social Issues* 23, 2: 193–202.

USADA (U.S. Anti-Doping Agency). 2001. *USADA guide to prohibited classes of substances and prohibited methods of doping.* Colorado Springs, CO: USADA.

USA Today. 1994. Daily prayers are ritual for Olajuwon. *USA Today* (10 June): 6C.

U.S. Department of Labor. 2005. *Statistics about people with disabilities and employment.* Washington, DC: Office of Disability Employment Policy; online at www.dol.gov/odep/pubs/ek01/stats.htm (retrieved July 21, 2005).

USDHHS (U.S. Department of Health and Human Services). 1996. *Physical activity and health: A report of the surgeon general.* Washington, DC: USDHHS.

U.S. News and World Report. 1983. A sport fan's guide to the 1984 Olympics. *U.S. News and World Report* (May 9): 124.

USOC (U.S. Olympic Committee). 1992. *USOC drug education and doping control program: Guide to banned medications.* Colorado Springs, CO: USOC.

U.S. Supreme Court, 1896. *Plessy v. Ferguson.* Online: http://caselaw.lp.findlaw.com/scripts/getcase.pl?navby=search&court=US&case=/us/163/537.html (retrieved December 1, 2005).

van Sterkenburg, Jacco, and Annelies Knoppers. 2004. Dominant discourses about race/ethnicity and gender in sport practice and performance. *International Review for the Sociology of Sport* 39, 3: 301–321.

Veblen, Thorsten. 1899. *The theory of the leisure class.* New York: Macmillan. (See also 1953 paperback edition, New York: A Mentor Book.)

Vélez, Beatriz. 2003. Gender equity in Columbia (trans. B. Hughes). Online: www.theglobalgame.com/velez.htm (retrieved December 4, 2005).

Verducci, Tom. 2002. Totally juiced. *Sports Illustrated* 96, 23 (June 3): 34–48.

Veri, Maria J. 1999. Homophobic discourse surrounding the female athlete. *Quest* 51, 4: 355–368.

Verma, Gajendra K., and Douglas S. Darby. 1994. *Winners and losers: Ethnic minorities in sport and recreation.* London: Falmer Press.

Vertinsky, Patricia A. 1987. Exercise, physical capability, and the eternally wounded woman in late nineteenth century North America. *Journal of Sport History* 14, 1: 7–27.

Vertinsky, Patricia A. 1994. Women, sport, and exercise in the 19th century. In D. M. Costa and S. R. Guthrie, eds., *Women and sport: Interdisciplinary perspectives* (pp. 63–82). Champaign, IL: Human Kinetics.

Videon, Tami M. 2002. Who plays and who benefits: Gender, interscholastic athletics, and academic outcomes. *Sociological Perspectives* 45, 4: 415–435.

Vincent, John. 2004. Game, sex, and match: The construction of gender in British newspaper coverage of the 2000 Wimbledon Championships. *Sociology of Sport Journal* 21, 4: 435–456.

Wacquant, Loïc J. D. 1992. The social logic of boxing in black Chicago: Toward a sociology of pugilism. *Sociology of Sport Journal* 9, 3: 221–254.

Wacquant, Loïc J. D. 1995a. The pugilistic point of view: How boxers think and feel about their trade. *Theory and Society* 24: 489–535.

Wacquant, Loïc J. D. 1995b. Why men desire muscles. *Body and Society* 1, 1: 163–179.

Wacquant, Loïc. 2004. *Body and soul: Notebooks of an apprentice boxer.* Oxford, England/New York: Oxford University Press.

Waddington, Ivan. 2000a. Sport and health: A sociological perspective. In J. Coakley and E. Dunning, eds., *Handbook of sports studies* (pp. 408–421). London: Sage.

Waddington, Ivan. 2000b. *Sport, health and drugs : A critical sociological perspective.* London: Routledge.

Waddington, Ivan. 2007. Health and sports. In George Ritzer, ed., *Encyclopedia of sociology* (in press). London: Blackwell.

Waldron, Jennifer, and Vikki Krane. 2005. Whatever it takes: Health compromising behaviors in female athletes. *Quest* 57, 3: 315–329.

Wahl, Grant. 1998. Unintentional grounding. *Sports Illustrated* 89, 20 (November 11): 92–108.

Wahl, Grant. 2004. On safari for 7-footers. *Sports Illustrated* 100, 26 (June 28): 68–78.

Walker, Rob. 2005. Extreme makeover: Home edition—entertainment poverty. *New York Times,* section 6 (December 4). Online: www.nytimes.com/2005/12/04/magazine/04wwin_consumed.html.

Walseth, Kristin, and Kari Fasting. 2003. Islam's view on physical activity and sport: Egyptian women interpreting Islam. *International Review for the Sociology of Sport* 38, 1: 45–60.

Wann, Daniel L., Gaye Haynes, B. McLean, and P. Pullen. 2003. Sport team identification and willingness to consider anonymous acts of hostile aggression. *Aggressive Behavior* 29: 406–413.

Wann, Daniel L., Jamie L. Hunter, Jacob A. Ryan, and Leigh Ann Wright. 2001a. The relationship between team identification and willingness of sport fans to consider illegally assisting their team. *Social Behavior and Personality: An International Journal* 29, 6: 531–537.

Wann, Daniel L., Merrill. J. Melnick, Gordon W. Russell, and Dale G. Pease. 2001b. *Sport fans: The psychology and social impact of spectators.* New York: Routledge.

Wann, Daniel L., Robin R. Peterson, Cindy Cothran, and Michael Dykes. 1999. Sport fan aggression and anonymity: the importance of team identification. *Social Behavior and Personality: An International Journal* 27, 6: 597–602.

Wann, Daniel L., Joel L. Royalty, and A. R. Rochelle. 2002. Using motivation and team identification to predict sport fans' emotional responses to team performance. *Journal of Sport Behavior* 25, 2: 207–216.

Wann, Daniel, Paula J. Waddill, and Mardis D. Dunham. 2004. Using sex and gender role orientation to predict level of sport fandom. *Journal of Sport Behavior* 27, 4: 367–377.

Wasielewski, Patricia. L. 1991 Not quite normal, but not really deviant: Some notes on the comparison of elite athletes and women political activists. *Deviant Behavior: An Interdisciplinary Journal* 12, 1: 81–95.

Waterford, Robin. 2004. Athens suffers old stereotypes. *USA Today* (August 5): 15A.

Wearden, Stanley T., and Pamela J. Creedon. 2002. "We got next": Images of women in television commercials during the inaugural WNBA season. *Sport in Society* 5, 3: 189–210.

Weaver, Paul. 2005. Alma mater of Coe and Radliffe brings sport to Muslim women. Online: www.buzzle.com/editorials/2-23-2005-66148.asp (retrieved July 8, 2005).

Weber, Max. 1904/1958. *The Protestant ethic and the spirit of capitalism* (trans. T. Parsons). New York: Scribner.

Weber, Max. 1968/1922. *Economy and society: An outline of interpretive sociology* (trans. G. Roth and G. Wittich). New York: Bedminster Press.

Wechsler, Henry, et al. 1997. Binge drinking, tobacco, and illicit drug use and involvement in college athletics. *Journal of American College Health* 45 (March): 195–200.

Wechsler, Henry, and Bernice Wuethrich. 2002. *Dying to drink : Confronting binge drinking on college campuses.* New York: Rodale and St. Martin's Press.

Wedgewood, Nikki. 2004. Kicking like a boy: Schoolgirl Australian rules football and bi-gendered female embodiment. *Sociology of Sport Journal* 21, 2: 140–162.

Weed, Mike. 2001. Ing-ger-land at Euro 2000: How "Handbags at 20 paces" was portrayed as a full-scale riot. *International Review for the Sociology of Sport* 36, 4: 407–424.

Weiler, Karen H., and Catriona T. Higgs. 1999. Television coverage of professional golf: A focus on gender. *Women in Sport and Physical Activity Journal* 8, 1: 83–100.

Weiner, Jay. 1999. What do we want from our sports heroes? *BusinessWeek* (February 5): 77.

Weiner, Jay. 2000. *Stadium games: Fifty years of big league greed and bush league boondoggles.* Minneapolis: University of Minnesota Press.

Weiner, Tim. 2004. Low-wage Costa Ricans make baseballs for millionaires. *New York Times* (International Sunday) (January 25): 3.

Weinstein, Marc D., Michael D. Smith, and David L. Wiesenthal. 1995. Masculinity and hockey violence. *Sex Roles* 33, 11/12: 831–847.

Weir, Tom. 1999. The next century: Sports. *USA Today* (December 31): 7C.

Weir, Tom. 2000. Americans fall farther behind. *USA Today* (May 3): 3C.

Weir, Tom, and Erik Brady. 2003. In sexual assault cases, athletes usually cleared. *USA Today* (December 22): A1, A2.

Weise, Elizabeth. 2003. Seniors seek vitality in growth hormone. *USA Today* (November 4): 1D.

Weisman, Larry. 2000. Why the NFL rules. *USA Today* (December 22): 1A–2A.

Weisman, Larry. 2004. Propelled to think past NFL. *USA Today* (June 16): 1C.

Weiss, Otmar. 1996. Media sports as a social substitution pseudosocial relations with sports figures. *International Review for the Sociology of Sport* 31, 1: 109–118.

Welch, William M. 1996. Federal taxpayers shut out of stadium payoff. *USA Today* (May 31): A1.

Wendel, Tim. 2004. How fantasy games have changed fans. *USA Today* (September 20): 23A.

Wendel, Tim. 2005. What about the fans? *USA Today* (June 28): 11A.

Wenner, Lawrence A. ed. 1998. *MediaSport.* London: Routledge.

Wenner, Lawrence A., and Walter Gantz. 1998. Watching sports on television: Audience experience, gender, fanship, and marriage. In L. A. Wenner, ed., *MediaSport* (pp. 233–251). London: Routledge.

Wertheim, Jon. 2003. Rising in the East. *Sports Illustrated* 99, 5 (August 11): Scorecard section.

Wertheim, Jon. 2004a. Globalization in sports: The whole world is watching (part 1 of 4). *Sports Illustrated* 100, 2 (June 14): 72–86.

Wertheim, Jon. 2004b. Hot prospects in cold places (part 2 of 4). *Sports Illustrated* 100, 25 (June 21): 62–66.

Wertheim, Jon. 2005. Gays in sports: A poll. *Sports Illustrated* 102, 16 (April 18): 64–65. Online: http://sportsillustrated.cnn.com/2005/magazine/04/12/griffith_poll0418/ (retrieved July 2005).

Wertheim, Jon, and D. Yaeger. 1999. The passing game. *Sports Illustrated* 90, 24 (June 14): 90–102.

West, Brad. 2003. Synergies in Deviance: Revisiting the Positive Deviance Debate. *Electronic Journal of Sociology* 7, 4. Online: www.sociology.org/content/vol7.4/west.html.

Whannel, Garry. 2002. *Media sport stars: Masculinities and moralities.* London/New York: Routledge.

Wheaton, Belinda, and Becky Beal. 2003. "Keeping it real": Subcultural media and the discourses of authenticity in alternative sport. *International Review for the Sociology of Sport* 38, 2: 155–176.

Wheeler, Garry David, et al. 1996. Retirement from disability sport: A pilot study. *Adapted Physical Activity Quarterly* 13, 4: 382–399.

Wheeler, Garry David, et al. 1999. Personal investment in disability sport careers: An international study. *Adapted Physical Activity Quarterly* 16, 3: 219–237.

White, Anita, et al. 1992. *Women and sport: A consultation document.* London: Sports Council.

White, Anita, and Ian Henry. 2004. *Women, leadership and the Olympic movement.* Loughborough, England: Institute of Sport and Policy Research,

Loughborough University. Online: http://multimedia.olympic.org/pdf/en_report_885.pdf.

White, Kelly. 2004. Discriminating airwaves. Online: www.womenssportsfoundation.org/cgi-bin/iowa/issues/article.html?record=999 (retrieved August 25, 2005).

White. Kerry. 2005. Breaking news, Breaking boundaries. Online: www. womens sportsfoundation.org/cgi-bin/iowa/career/article.html?record=35 (retrieved August 25, 2005).

White, Philip. 2004. The cost of injury from sport, exercise and physical activity: A review of the evidence. In Kevin Young, ed. *Sporting bodies, damaged selves: Sociological studies of sports-related injury* (pp. 309–332). Amsterdam: Elsevier.

White, Philip, and Kevin Young. 1997. Masculinity, sport, and the injury process: A review of Canadian and international evidence. *Avante* 3, 2: 1–30.

White, Philip, and Kevin Young. 1999. Is sport injury gendered? In P. White and K. Young, eds., *Sport and gender in Canada* (pp. 69–84). Don Mills, ON: Oxford University Press.

Wie, Michelle. 2005. (audible). *ESPN The Magazine* 8, 15 (August 1): 128–129.

Wieberg, Steve. 1994. Conley nears end of six-year career. *USA Today* (November 17): 8C.

Wieberg, Steve. 2000a. A judgment in Vermont. *USA Today* (February 3): 16C.

Wieberg, Steve. 2000b. A night of humiliation. *USA Today* (February 4): 1C–2C.

Wieberg, Steve. 2004a. Boosters can provide quite a lift. *USA Today* (October 6): 10C.

Wieberg, Steve. 2004b. $2 million: A star player's value. *USA Today* (March 17): 1A–2A.

Wieberg, Steve. 2005a. Pay increases for women's coaches lag. *USA Today* (February 9): 3C.

Wieberg, Steve. 2005b. Grad rates carry warning. *USA Today* (December 20): 12C.

Wiggins, David K. 1994. The notion of double-consciousness and the involvement of Black athletes in American sport. In G. Eisen and D. K. Wiggins, eds., *Ethnicity and sport in North American history and culture* (pp. 133–156). Westport, CT: Greenwood Press.

Wiggins, David K., ed. 2003. *African Americans in sports*. Armonk, NY: Sharpe Reference.

Wilkerson, Martha. 1996. Explaining the presence of men coaches in women's sports: The uncertainty hypothesis. *Journal of Sport and Social Issues* 20, 4: 411–426.

Williams, Patricia J. 2005. Genetically speaking. *The Nation* 280, 24: 10.

Williams, Ricky (with D. LeBatard). 1999. Everything hurts. *ESPN The Magazine* (December 12): 78–82.

Willmsen, Christine, and Maureen O'Hagan. 2003. Coaches continue working for schools and private teams after being caught for sexual misconduct. *Seattle Times* (December 14). Online: http://seattletimes.nwsource.com/news/local/coaches (retrieved June 2005).

Wilmore, Jack H. 1996. Eating disorders in the young athlete. In O. bar-Or, ed. *The child and adolescent athlete* (pp. 287–303). Vol. 6 of the *Encyclopaedia of sports medicine* (IOC Medical Commission). London: Blackwell Science.

Wilson, Brian. 1999. "Cool pose" incorporated: The marketing of black masculinity in Canadian NBA coverage. In P. White and K. Young, eds., *Sport and gender in Canada* (pp. 232–253). Don Mills, ON: Oxford University Press.

Wilson, Brian. 2002. The "anti-jock" movement: Reconsidering youth resistance, masculinity, and sport culture in the age of the Internet. *Sociology of Sport Journal* 19, 2: 206–233.

Wilson, John. 1994. *Playing by the rules: Sport, society and the state.* Detroit: Wayne State University Press.

Wilson. Thomas C. 2002. The paradox of social class and sports involvement: The roles of cultural and economic capital international. *Review for the Sociology of Sport* 37, 1: 5–16.

Winant, Howard. 2001. *The world is a ghetto: Race and democracy since World War II.* New York: Basic Books.

Winlock, Colette. 2000. Running the invisible race. *ColorLines* 3, 1: 27.

Wise, Mike. 2003. The squabbling Illini: Rallying cries lead to rift. *New York Times* (December 16): D1; www.nytimes.com/2003/12/16/sports/othersports/16MASC.html.

Wittebols, James H. 2004. *The soap opera paradigm: Television programming and corporate priorities.* Lanham, MD: Rowman and Littlefield.

Wolfe, Tom. 1979. *The right stuff.* New York: Farrar, Strauss, Giroux.

Wolff, Alexander. 2000. Crying foul. *Sports Illustrated* 93, 24 (December 11): 42–47.

Wolff, Alexander. 2002. The vanishing three-sport star. *Sports Illustrated* 97, 20 (November 18): 80–92.

Wolff, Alexander. 2003. The American athlete: Age 10. *Sports Illustrated* 99, 13 (October 6): 59–67.

Wolff, Eli A. 2005. The 2004 Athens Games and Olympians with disabilities: Triumphs, challenges, and future opportunities. Presentation at the Forty-Fifth International Session for Young Participants International Olympic Academy. Athens, Greece.

Womack, Mari. 1992. Why athletes need ritual: A study of magic among professional athletes. In S. Hoffman, ed., *Sport and religion* (pp. 191–202). Champaign, IL: Human Kinetics.

Wong, Joyce. 1999. Asian women in sport. *Journal of Physical Education, Recreation and Dance* 70, 4: 42–43.

Wood, Skip. 2004. Leftwich's job skills include pain tolerance. *USA Today* (October 22): 15C.

Woodward. J. R. 2004. Professional football scouts: An investigation of racial stacking. *Sociology of Sport Journal* 21, 4: 356–375.

Woog, Dan. 1998. *Jocks: True stories of America's gay male athletes*. Los Angeles: Alyson Books.

Wosport Weekly. 1999. Quotes of the week (June 28): online newsletter covering women in sports.

Wulf, Steve. 2004. Basketbrawl. *ESPN The Magazine* 7.26 (December 20): 82.

Young, Iris Marion. 1990. *Throwing like a girl and other essays in philosophy and social theory*. Bloomington and Indianapolis: Indiana University Press.

Young, Iris Marion. 1998. Situated bodies: Throwing like a girl. In D. Welton, ed., *Body and flesh: A philosophical reader* (pp. 259–273). Oxford, England: Blackwell.

Young, Iris Marion. 2005. *On female body experience: "throwing like a girl" and other essays*. New York: Oxford University Press.

Young, Kevin. 1993. Violence, risk, and liability in male sports culture. *Sociology of Sport Journal* 10, 4: 373–396.

Young, Kevin. 2000. Sport and violence. In J. Coakley and E. Dunning, eds., *Handbook of sport studies* (pp. 382–407). London: Sage.

Young, Kevin. 2002a. From "sports violence" to "sports crime": Aspects of violence, law, and gender in the sports process. In M. Gatz, M. A. Messner, and S. J. Ball-Rokeach, eds., *Paradoxes of youth and sport* (pp. 207–224). Albany: State University of New York Press.

Young, Kevin. 2002b. Standard deviations: An update on North American crowd disorder. *Sociology of Sport Journal* 19, 3: 237–275.

Young, Kevin, ed. 2004a. *Sporting bodies, damaged selves: Sociological studies of sports-related injury*. Amsterdam: Elsevier.

Young, Kevin. 2004b. The role of the courts in sports injury. In Kevin Young, ed. *Sporting bodies, damaged selves: Sociological studies of sports-related injury* (pp. 333–353). Amsterdam: Elsevier.

Young, Kevin. 2007a. Violence among athletes. In George Ritzer, ed., *Encyclopedia of sociology* (in press). London/New York: Blackwell.

Young, Kevin. 2007b. Violence among spectators. In George Ritzer, ed., *Encyclopedia of sociology* (in press). London/New York: Blackwell.

Young, Kevin, and Philip White 1995. Sport, physical danger, and injury: The experiences of elite women athletes. *Journal of Sport and Social Issues* 19, 1: 45–61.

Young, Kevin, Philip White, and William McTeer. 1994. Body talk: Male athletes reflect on sport, injury, and pain. *Sociology of Sport Journal* 11, 2: 175–195.

Zengerle, Jason. 2002. Driving the company car. *New York Times Magazine* (February 10): 40–43.

Zhang, James J., Dale G. Pease, and E. A. Jambor. 1997. Negative influence of market competitors on the attendance of professional sport games: The case of a minor league hockey team. *Sport Marketing Quarterly* 6, 3: 31, 34–40.

Zhang, James J., Dale G. Pease, and Dennis W. Smith. 1998. Relationship between broadcasting media and minor league hockey game attendance. *Sport Management Quarterly* 12, 2: 103–122.

Zhang, James J., and Dennis W. Smith. 1997. Impact of broadcasting on the attendance of professional basketball games. *Sport Marketing Quarterly* 6, 1: 23–29.

Zimbalist, A. 1999. *Unpaid professionals: Commercialism and conflict in big-time college sports*. Princeton, NJ: Princeton University Press.

Zimmer, Martha Hill, and Michael Zimmer. 2001. Athletes as entertainers. *Journal of Sport and Social Issues* 25, 2: 202–215.

Zirin, Dave. 2004. Selective outrage in Detroit. Online: www.counterpunch.com/zirin11222004.html (retrieved June 2005).

Zorpette, Glenn. 2000. The chemical games. *Scientific American* 11, 3: 16–23.

NAME INDEX

SUBJECT INDEX

Note: t indicates tables; f indicates figures; n indicates note